The Dark Continent?

The Dark Continent?

Images of Africa in European Narratives about the Congo

By Frits Andersen

Aarhus University Press

II H.M. STANLEY – MAGIC AND MARKET 143

The Congo's position in global media around the year 1900 can be compared to that of Iraq and Afghanistan today. The country's immense resources and its late and savage colonisation made it a battlefield where travel accounts, testimonies, reports and novels competed to shape the European reader's images of Africa.

Preface

In an account from 1907 of an automobile journey through Belgium, the Netherlands and Germany, the reader comes across a chapter titled “Red Caoutchouc”. The narrator has stopped over in the Belgian port of Antwerp and is looking in the window of a shop, where some product samples of unusual colour and shape are displayed. When he enters the shop, he is proved right in assuming that they are rubber samples from the Congo – the raw material from which his car tyres are made, thus facilitating the wonderful journey, its staggering speed and this new way of perceiving the world. Octave Mirbeau’s travel account is a futuristic celebration of the car, its speed and the new century. However, when the narrator takes a couple of steps into the shop, more disturbing films are played out on his inner screen: initially, a series of images that could be taken out of King Léopold’s propaganda magazines, showing the colony as an idyll and the natives as happy rabbits jumping about at the edge of the woods; subsequently, the narrator imagines a series of photographs that depict atrocities and terrors, massacres and mutilated bodies. These photographs give rise to both fascination and indignation, leading the narrator to condemn Léopold’s brutal rubber collection methods, while at the same time acknowledging that his own enthusiasm about cars and progress make him an accomplice – both a participant and bystander. After this, the narrator switches to an objective, documentary style, before the chapter fades out in a satirical passage that critically addresses all the presented images of Africa and ways of referring to the Congo; it all reflects back on himself.

A combination of experimental narrative and sophisticated, precise criticism, Octave Mirbeau’s *La 628-E8* became, perhaps surprisingly, a scandalous success, published in several languages and a luxury edition with illustrations by Pierre Bonnard. The author, critic and journalist Mirbeau employs a plethora of strategies in his travel account without letting the reader escape his grip. In the passage about “Red Caoutchouc”, Mir-

The many travel accounts and novels based on the experiences of Scandinavian contract workers in the Congo constitute a forgotten chapter in Danish literary history. The novels introduce and draw on reader expectations of the exotic, but the writer's own ideas and perspective are often affected, challenged, and shaken. Otto Lütken was a steamboat captain working in the Congo from 1907 who had to return prematurely in 1915, as he was suffering from malaria. His *Mozuri's God* (1928) was followed by other disturbing stories, including *Black Moral and Fataki* (1932). In 1930, Lütken published "Joseph Conrad in the Congo", an article about *Heart of Darkness* and his reaction to the novel.

beau's display of various images of Africa is unlabelled – he does not specify who he is attacking. He assumes that the reader can distinguish between – and recognise – them as widespread, typical ways in which people talk about the Congo. To use a contemporary term: the reader is expected to recognise them as 'discourses'.

The Congo's position in global media around 1900 can be compared to that of Iraq and Afghanistan today. Vast numbers of stories were competing to raise interest in Africa, and the continent was displayed in spectacular ways at the great World's Fairs and cultivated through the abolitionist movement's captivating travel accounts from "the dark continent". Towards the turn of the century, the Congo's immense natural resources and late colonisation turned it into a battlefield where travel accounts, testimonies, reports and novels were competing to shape European readers' images of Africa. One camp disseminated colonial propaganda about the need for missionary efforts to civilise the savages; another camp advocated for the Congo Reform Association – the first international human rights movement – with accounts of atrocities and terror that condensed and detailed the horror at which Joseph Conrad's *Heart of Darkness* (1902) had only hinted.

Mirbeau's travel book is one of many examples of the Congo's prominent position in European media a century ago. Today, the Congo is all but forgotten, except for the atrocity accounts which now and then remind us about the victims of the civil war – the greatest and most gravely overlooked human disaster since the Second World War. Mirbeau's travel book is critical towards reports, idyllic tales and atrocity tales. The book is an example of alternative narrative forms that help move Africa closer to Europe, but his example is unknown today, despite the great need for model examples to describe, e.g., the Congo as part of our world and history.

The same patterns and mechanisms that Mirbeau exposed in 1907 can be observed today – and with similar political consequences. It is a fair claim that our attitudes towards Africa – free trade, participation, emergency aid or intervention – are rooted in literary-historical conditions: narratives and narrative forms that emerged in the wake of the colonial powers' 'scramble for Africa', adapted for the new conditions of globalisation and modern media. These narratives are the topic of the present book; oblivion is its critical horizon.

The selected material represents a broad field of travel literature and travel accounts, including: Joseph Conrad's literary novel *Heart of Darkness*; Henry Stanley's voluminous accounts of his famous explorations in Central Africa, which were international bestsellers; lesser known Danish literature about the Congo from the beginning of the twentieth century; popular fiction from the 1930s, such as *Tintin au Congo* and *Tarzan and the Leopard Men*; and novels by authors of world literature, including V.S. Naipaul, Graham Greene and Urs Widmer.

The decision to link the present study specifically to the Congo is also based on factors in literary history. One important factor is the central role played in world literature

by Joseph Conrad's *Heart of Darkness* and his account of his own journey to the Congo, about which extensive, continuously relevant material has been and is being written. Conrad condenses central, much-discussed questions in the history of travel writing; in his writing, testimony and credibility are put into play in the interrelationship between travel experience, travel account and travel novel.

Another factor is the attention towards a hitherto overlooked chapter in Danish literary history: the broad field of travel accounts and travel novels about the experiences of Scandinavian contract employees in the Congo. In particular, this interest was spurred by the Danish reporter Peter Tygesen's travel book *The Congo – I Presume* (2001), which shares many similarities with the internationally recognised *Congo. A History* (2010) by David Reybrouck. Both books have been praised for their gripping historical accounts, which facilitate complex, balanced understandings of the Congo's history, from Stanley's discoveries to the arrival of the Chinese today. With their combination of testimonies and source-based history, both books have drawn attention to a chapter in history which Europe – to a large extent – has forgotten and repressed, even though Europe has been – and still is – very much involved. Contrary to Tygesen's and Reybrouck's historical expositions, the present perspective is one of *literary* history: its focus will be on how the history of the Congo has been told, and how European travel accounts have contributed to creating mechanisms of oblivion and problematic notions of the place that are still in effect today.

A third factor is the accounts of Stanley's two major Congo expeditions, which present crucial, extensive and challenging material that has not previously been investigated in a literary studies context. Questions of credibility, testimony and authority not only pertain to traditional literary studies issues such as realism and representation; they encompass a far broader and more problematic field. The travel writer's authority not only concerns the connection between the textual rhetoric and the represented world; it also comes into play in relation to readers, scientific and literary institutions (who may accept or refuse the account), market conditions and the author's choice of genre, public reputation, as it is created between biography and media reception, and so on. In this light, Stanley, "Africa's great explorer", becomes a central and fascinating focal figure. His life and journeys are linked to the colonisation of the Congo, and his travel accounts are therefore topographically related to Conrad's texts. This provides an opportunity to compare two very different types of text and observe surprising common characteristics, among other reasons because they hold key positions in the literary-historical transformational field around the end of the nineteenth century, which, in turn, have defined the terms for the travel literature of the twentieth century.

The present book uses Stanley and Conrad as focal points of the period in which the Congo was a free state under the rule of King Léopold; however, it also includes travel accounts and travel novels from the period in which the country was a Belgian colony – and all the way through to the present day. While the prose perspective makes it possible to broaden the field of comparable texts, the topographic limitation has other advantages – e.g. a shared foundation for pursuing similar, dominant motives across genres and time, which are of general relevance to travel literature and research in the field.

Each travel description contributes to a literary topography of the Congo – a description of the place, its people and geography, resulting in redefinitions of traditional topographies inherited from earlier texts and travellers through an active process, which often takes place in explicit, dynamic dialogue with the predecessor. Throughout these transformations and variations of the literary topography of the Congo, however, it is still possible to trace some consistent patterns from the earliest travel accounts to the present day. A central component in this pattern is Conrad's image of the continent's interior as a "heart of darkness". Another, equally central constant is the idea of what will be termed "the exception": a consistent figure in twentieth-century travel description from the Congo, which structures the place as a geographical, historical, legal and rhetorical exception from norms, laws and rules.

The reason that these literary topographies have gained particular strength in descriptions of the Congo is partly due to the fact that the country is not a delimited historical, legal or geographical reality in the traditional sense. The political geography, today referred to as the Democratic Republic of the Congo, is an extremely unstable concept whose borders with the neighbouring countries of Uganda and Rwanda can be perceived as purely theoretical constructs when viewed in light of the wave of civil wars that have ravaged the country since independence. Before colonisation at the end of the nineteenth century, Central Africa consisted of a vast number of chiefdoms and a few kingdoms, which – in changing alliances – defined zones of power and influence that, naturally, did not adhere to the same well-defined borders as national states. In the country's era as King Léopold's private colony, under the misleading term *L'État Independant du Congo*, and subsequently under Belgian rule, the region was not organised as an independent, modern state, but rather divided according to the colonial, administrative districts that had been defined in the initial phase of colonisation on the basis of mercantile interests. Obviously, the first travellers did not imagine the Congo as a separate geographical or ethnographic unity, but as a sphere of influence – a battlefield for competing topographies: on a day's march in the 1880s, it was possible to travel through two or three chiefdoms each with their own culture, language and attitude towards foreigners. For centuries, the population in the coastal parts of the Congo drainage basin had established flexible social systems, partly dependent on interaction with Europeans, while the societies farther east did not have much contact with Europeans; instead, they were under pressure from Arab slave traders, who were expanding from east to west. The Congo to which the Danish Lieutenant-colonel H. Jenssen-Tusch refers in his encyclopaedic work *Scandinavians in Congo* (1905) is actually not a demarcated territory, but a sum of overlapping, partly conflicting definitions of geological, meteorological/climatic, political and ethnographic nature – albeit with the Congo River as a staple point of reference.

This image of the country as overlapping zones – both in relation to political power spheres, biotopes and ethnic diversity – is consistent in twentieth-century literature about the Congo, which comprises travel accounts as well as literary fiction and scientific literature. The complicated and detailed division into provinces and sub-districts during colonial rule can be seen as an attempt to subject the immense area – the size of Europe minus Spain and Italy – to effective control and discipline. This plan, however, never proved entirely effective, not even in the relatively stable period of the 1940s and 1950s. The passing of a new constitution in 2005 entailed even more detailed sub-divisions and bureaucratic administration, which – in most of the territories – was a symptom of powerlessness rather than control. From the founding of the colony to independence in 1960, the relationship between state and society has been precarious – and much worse under the successive, corrupt presidents. In vast parts of the country, the state is only present in the form of outposts. Vice versa, the population is not represented in the state, whose exercise of power is usually built on preferential treatment to – and alliances with – a few clans that are played off against each other, in addition to support from foreign nations: first the USA, later Angola, Rwanda and Uganda, among others. The UN's massive presence in the Congo before and during the election in 2006 was a symptom of the imbalance between state and society, whose institutions only functioned because of the Belgians' bureaucratic apparatus and ceased to function as intended a long time ago. In spite of changing truces and interim peace negotiations, the society-devastating conflict continues, and the deployed UN troops, whose mandate is far too weak, are powerless. Despite the fact that deployment of forces with a mandate to engage in offensive operations in March 2013 resulted in many militias laying down their weapons, new conflicts have broken out. Between five and six million people are believed to have died because of the war and its consequences – hunger and disease. And as part of the militias' strategy, whose goal is to gain control of the area's natural resources, the spectacular violence is carried out as a meticulously calculated scare campaign with massacres and savage, ritual rapes on an estimated scale of 400,000 every year.

Blogs by aid volunteers in Amnesty International and troops from the UN operation are written in tropes and figures that repeat the first descriptions of the place. This applies, for instance, to Sahara Sarah's blog from 2006, "Breaking Hearts in the Heart of Darkness". Fiction novels also use these rhetorical effects. John le Carré's novel *The Mission Song* (2006), about political intrigues and an attempted coup d'état – which refers to real political dramas, especially in relation to the question of whether Rwanda's mercenaries and allies in the Congo's eastern Kivu Province would allow the democratic election in 2006 to be held – plays out a number of possible scenarios under a motto quoted from the character Marlow in *Heart of Darkness*.

A very diverse field of texts and forms of communication partake in creating and maintaining topographical images of the Congo. Stanley's epic narratives about the mighty river and the great forests and Conrad's novel about the dark heart and the

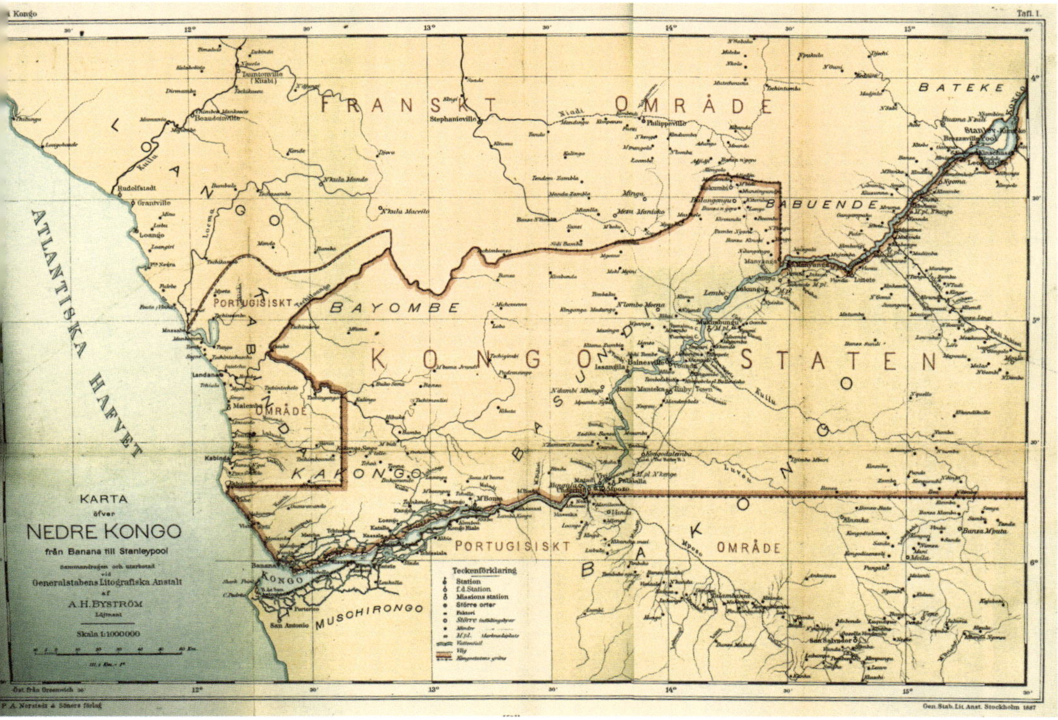

Maps played an important textual and visual role both in travel accounts like Rider Haggard's *King Solomon's Mines* (1886), and in travel reports like the great Scandinavian *Three Years in the Congo* (1887). Readers could orient themselves via the abstract overview of the map, while at the same time the strange place names and vast, unnamed expanses signified compellingly unfamiliar places.

terrifying images of violations against natives – which the first international human rights movement promoted in every accessible media to fight King Léopold's "Red Rubber" regime – are recycled in current accounts from the Congo. The bloody trail of Léopold's rubber collection methods leads all the way up to present day. Reports on mountain gorillas, who are threatened by the seemingly endless conflict in the border regions around the great lakes, contribute to the dehumanising perception of this part of the world by pathetically describing the animals as the reader's friends and objects of identification, while the human beings are beyond reach of both sense and solidarity. Similarly, human rights and relief aid organisations' campaigns, as well as global news, disseminate problematic images of "atrocities". Explicitly, they call for responsibility and solidarity with the millions of Congolese who are affected by the political, economical and ecological disaster; however, implicitly they promote a simplified, infantilising image of the population as passive victims – irrational beings of nature – who are at the mercy of the 'evil spirit' of the area. Current travel reports also contribute to the tendency, like the many examples of "tragic tourism" in which the reader is guided through the war-torn, brutalised Congo, including shocking accounts of cannibalism, exploitation

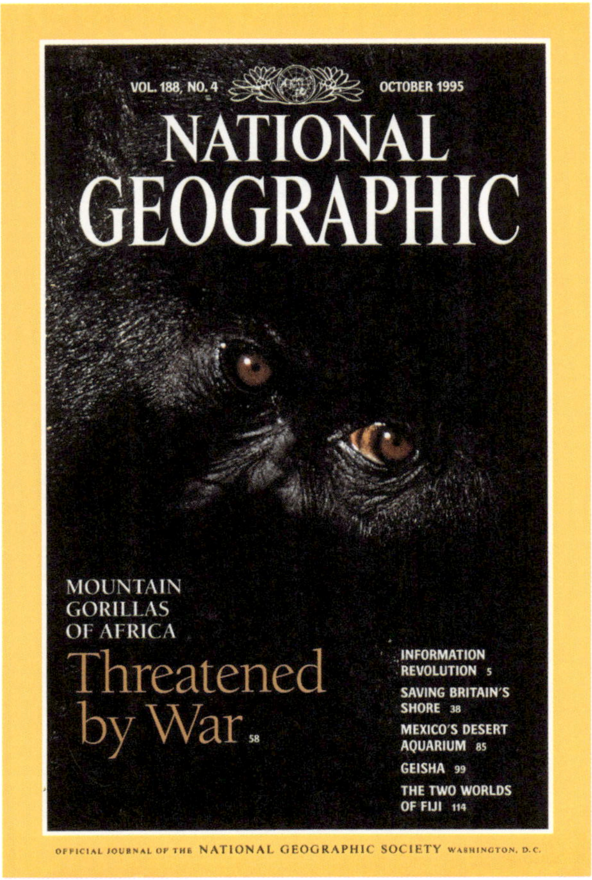

Contemporary reports about mountain gorillas, threatened by tourism or civil wars, represent the animals as the reader's friends and objects of identification, while the human players are located beyond reason and solidarity. Ever since Paul du Chaillu's description of the first encounter between a white man and his distant relative in the book *Explorations and Adventures in Equatorial Africa* (1859), the gorilla has been a staple element in images of Africa in popular culture. The 1903 July edition of *National Geographic* features an article about the recently deceased du Chaillu, his legendary travels – also including the first encounter with a Pygmy – and his amazing talk at the National Geographic Society. In the 1995 October edition, the point of view is with the gorilla; however, the structure of the atrocity account is the same.

and victimisation. Masked by the reporter's objectivity, once more the ghost stories are presented, which have – first and foremost – sealed the country off inside a world of evil imagery to which rationality has no access. This place is beyond our comprehension; it is the horrible and bestial site of meaningless violence – a dystopia whose images affect the European reader without bringing about any fundamental changes in our understanding, responsibility or solidarity.

The abolitionist movement and subsequent missionary tales, whose moral crusades addressed violations and oppression in Africa, were – ironically – main players in the colonisation of the Congo and the formation of the problematic discourse of 'the Dark Continent', which still characterises present-day human rights campaigns and the majority of political thinking regarding Africa. Humanitarianism's moral feelings and the media's compassion discourse are both superficial and fleeting, drawing our attention away from the structural inequality that can only be addressed through considered analysis and political pragmatism. In relation to the literary history of the present book, this entails that compassionate and indignant testimonies must be investigated in a historical and critical perspective and compared with *other* testimonies. At this principal level, the book can be said to present a literary-historical contribution to the current debate about liberal humanitarianism and human rights.

Like the travel accounts about the European discovery of Tahiti, which constitute a literary-historical transformational field in the eighteenth century, where various branches of travel literature converged and ramified into new tendencies, the accounts of the European discovery of the Congo constitute a similar transformational field around the end of the nineteenth century. The present study places Stanley and Conrad as central players in this field, comparing their descriptions of the same place within the defined art-historical era of *fin de siècle.* The late colonisation at the end of the nineteenth century, when European nation states were facing profound internal crises and external rivalry in Europe and Africa, in conjunction with the specific media and technology-related conditions for the discovery, make the Congo a crucial example for research into historical developments in a global sense of place. The Congo's status as a *not yet* fully formed national state makes twentieth-century travel accounts from the country relevant in relation to current redefinitions of places and frontiers in Europe – changes which are also subjects of travel descriptions and essay novels.[1] The Congo's status in the international public sphere as a non-place, or as a vaguely defined zone of crossing, overlapping topographies, makes it a relevant topic for literary-historical studies of mixed, overlapping prose perspectives and investigation into the relation between literature and globalisation. Bernard Piniau writes, from an international political relations perspective, in the introduction to his book *Congo-Zaïre. 1874-1981 La perception du lointain* (1992) that the global forgetting and political isolation of the Congo make it an apt topic for studying literary rhetoric's influence on global media and politics. Although Edward Said (and Erich Auerbach before him) has been a source of inspiration to the present book, the critical basis is not the postcolonial theoretical tradition, which has, for a long time, held a monopoly in the area of travel studies and "Africanism". On the contrary, this book is a contribution to the current development in the field of world literature, albeit in a new direction, where it is an important point that a very broad field of texts and testimonies are compared. Emphasis is not put on how the texts *represent* Congolese reality, but how they *create* European ideas of that reality. World literature is not used to describe a specific canon, but to characterise the dynamic creation of images of the world, which have powerful influence on the formation of 'real' world history and geography. This entails a different appraisal of Conrad's canonical story and results in Stanley's travel accounts being positioned differently in world literature, at the same time as access is created to a different understanding of Stanley's rhetoric than the one typically advocated by postcolonial criticism. Moreover, it is demonstrated that a vast number of forgotten texts played an important role in the creation of our conceptions of Africa, making them interesting objects of study and reappraisal. This entails their potential in regard to both complexity of experience and complexity of interpretation.

The present study of the history of this type of prose is an attempt to write literary

history on globalised conditions. It is rooted in a contemporary and local context, which limits the knowledge about the place the texts address. However, it does not hinder a critical approach to the texts as European narratives about a different place in the world, and – in an expanded sense – as dominant narratives about places in the world which – like the Congo – have been assigned positions in a distant, asynchronous, completely different world, far away from the global media reality. The texts investigated in this book not only describe the historical preconditions for the West's images of Africa today; they actively contribute to their creation. The present narrative aims to contribute to the understanding of this literary history – how the place has been forgotten and repressed. On the other hand, it also intends to demonstrate that from the earliest texts about the Congo, there have been opposing tendencies, e.g. represented by Octave Mirbeau, which today may serve as model examples for the much-needed revision of western images of Africa. A crucial motivational factor has been the opportunity to contribute a literary-historical understanding of the background to the recent twenty years of extremely violent conflicts in the Congo – the apparent unsolvable nature of which is intrinsically linked with the combination of demonisation, oblivion and non-participation that still pervades the media, despite declared intentions of the opposite. However, the goal is not to expose the myths in the belief that there once existed a state of innocence to which we can return; nor is it the intention to deny that the Congolese reality is so chaotic and terrifying that it is difficult to conceive rationally. However, part of this book's drive and horizon is to contribute to overcoming this obstacle, though it is beyond the scope and subject area of the book itself.

As suggested above, the selection of text types and genres is broad, ranging from

---

Many hundreds of maps, photographs, portraits, and sketches of people, landscapes, fauna, prospects, and colonial situations illustrate the pages of Jenssen-Tusch's encyclopaedic *Scandinavians in the Congo* (1905). Some were borrowed from the private collections of travellers, but most were copied from the plethora of travel books and magazines of the era, including *Voyage au Congo*, *Le Congo Illustré* and *Le Mouvement Antiesclavagiste*. "The Dance of the Fetish Man" illustrates the section of the book on religion and superstition. It is an exact copy of the original, "The Antics of the Charm-Doctor" in Herbert Ward's *Five Years with the Congo Cannibals* (1890), a typical travel account derived from Ward's service under Stanley during the first years of the colonisation, 1884-89. Based on a rough sketch by Ward, the picture was created by the professional illustrator W. B. Davis; however, many of the other illustrations in the book are the author's own. After his return from Stanley's final, failed expedition in 1890, Herbert Ward set up as a visual artist in Paris. Based on his sketches and huge collections, he created, among other works, the allegorical sculpture "Sleeping Africa" (1902), which depicts a naked native woman lounging on a map of the continent, and the sculpture "The Charm Doctor" (1902), which closely resembles the travel book's illustration.

1902.

unpublished diaries and letters to popular literature, canonised novels and completely forgotten travel accounts. This selection may seem rather eclectic, but will be substantiated in the introduction. Briefly explained, it is part of an attempt to encompass crucial aspects of the history of travel literature, which a narrower selection of material would lose sight of, as well as a more general attempt to describe tendencies in the history of prose – processes of differentiation that are seldom given specific attention.

Not including Congolese texts, the book deselects the issues pertaining to the reciprocity of cultural encounters, which today is a topic of much attention. It is a point in relation to many of the texts selected, most obviously the key examples by Stanley and Conrad, that they are read in a non-national perspective. This decision is based on the authors' positions as cultural 'mongrels' and in consideration to the globalisation processes that the readings aim to investigate. Furthermore, the trans-national perspective is connected to specific factors in the history of the Congo: during the colony's first period as Free State, the contractual employees, who contributed many of the travel accounts, were recruited in countries such as England, Switzerland, Italy, France, Norway, Sweden, Denmark and – obviously – Belgium, albeit Belgians did not receive preferential treatment. There were – and are – undoubtedly national differences in the backgrounds and receptions of the travel accounts, but they are not central to the focus of this book.[2]

This book is written in accordance with inductive exposition – both as a whole and in the individual parts and chapters. In order to provide the reader with a basis for following the argumentation through the material, which cannot be assumed to be known, detailed examples will be presented and subsequently expanded upon in analyses, followed by reflections that tie the observations together. Furthermore, it has been the ambition also to accommodate readers who are more interested, for instance, in the reappraisal of Stanley's expeditions or the Danish narratives about the Congo than in subject-specific, research discussions. For that reason, an attempt has been made to minimise subject-specific terminology and references, instead including presentations of, e.g., historical conditions that may benefit the reader's sense of orientation and the text's usefulness. The vast majority of illustrations have been selected from the books analysed. They are not intended as documentation, but rather to provide an impression of the often lavishly illustrated publications and visual narratives through which the texts were disseminated. The book consists of five sections.

In "The Congo in Prose – Introduction", Stanley is presented via a chapter that deals with the great explorer's closely linked biography and journeys on mundane, global and world literary terms. This is followed by a chapter about the prose perspective in which all the texts are read. It is not about genre discussion, but rather a specific way of reading, which is developed through so-called "model examples" in the history of travel literature. The chapter "Literary Topography of the Congo" presents basic topographical figures and the history of the European discovery of the Congo, while the last chapter in this part links the method to related subject positions.

The second section, "H.M. Stanley: Magic and Market", focuses on the author's two major texts, *Through the Dark Continent* and *In Darkest Africa*. The former is read with a focus on the work's opening rhetoric and equilibristic perspectives, arguing that they should not merely be seen as oppressive and dominant, but as transcending, critical and self-critical. The latter is read in a broader context, discussing the status of the testimony in relation to other, competing, accounts and to media and market forces. The last chapter, "The Space of Prose: Magic and Pragmatism", reads 'between' the texts, pointing towards a number of spaces and material characteristics that explain why Stanley has been forgotten, while at the same time being crucial factors in the magical and exemplary qualities of the travel books.

In the third section, "Red Rubber - Tales of Terror", Joseph Conrad's *Heart of Darkness* is at the centre. The text is investigated via changing constellations with other prose narratives about the same period, especially Conrad's own travel diaries. This facilitates a nuanced look at - and criticism of - widespread misinterpretations of the novel, especially historians' and literary scholars' use of the text as a testimony about atrocities. This section ends with readings of texts that serve to put Conrad's novel into perspective: C.J. Cutcliffe Hyne's "The Transfer", Dane Jürgen Jürgensen's Congo novels and Octave Mirbeau's transnational colonial criticism of the Red Rubber regime.

The fourth section, "The Twentieth Century", deals with the history of Congo literature in the twentieth century, and the influence of the legacy from Stanley's and Conrad's seminal texts on Europe's relationship with Africa. Though the prose perspective aims to avoid traditional genre divides, the material is divided into three main branches, all of which are present in Stanley's and Conrad's texts: the first chapter puts emphasis on Scandinavian accounts of journeys to the Congo and the rhetoric of oblivion which they instigated. The second chapter addresses Graham Greene's, V.S. Naipaul's and Urs Widmer's Congo novels as readings of *Heart of Darkness* - adaptations that pick up the thread of the exoticism and discourse critical characteristics of the original. The third chapter addresses a number of popular cultural films, comics and texts. The last chapter works across the divides in order to map essential characteristics in the field and highlight connecting lines and patterns in the extensive material. It all ends in one of the places where it began - with Peter Tygesen's *The Congo – I Presume*, the narrative in whose wake the others followed.

The fifth and last section, "The Congo in Prose", sums up the points about place, testimony, atrocity accounts, human rights, world literature and globalisation discussed in the book

Several of the Scandinavian works referred to in the book have not yet been translated into English. In order to improve readability, these titles and all citations from them appear in English translation. Please refer to the bibliography for the original titles.

The Stanley Archives at the Musée Royal de l'Afrique Centrale provided me with the opportunity to work with Stanley's manuscripts, letters and diaries.

I

Each travel account contributes to a literary topography of the Congo – a description of place, people and geography – while at the same time transforming inherited topographies. Nevertheless, despite all the transformations and variations, it is still possible to trace consistent patterns from the earliest travel accounts up to the present day.

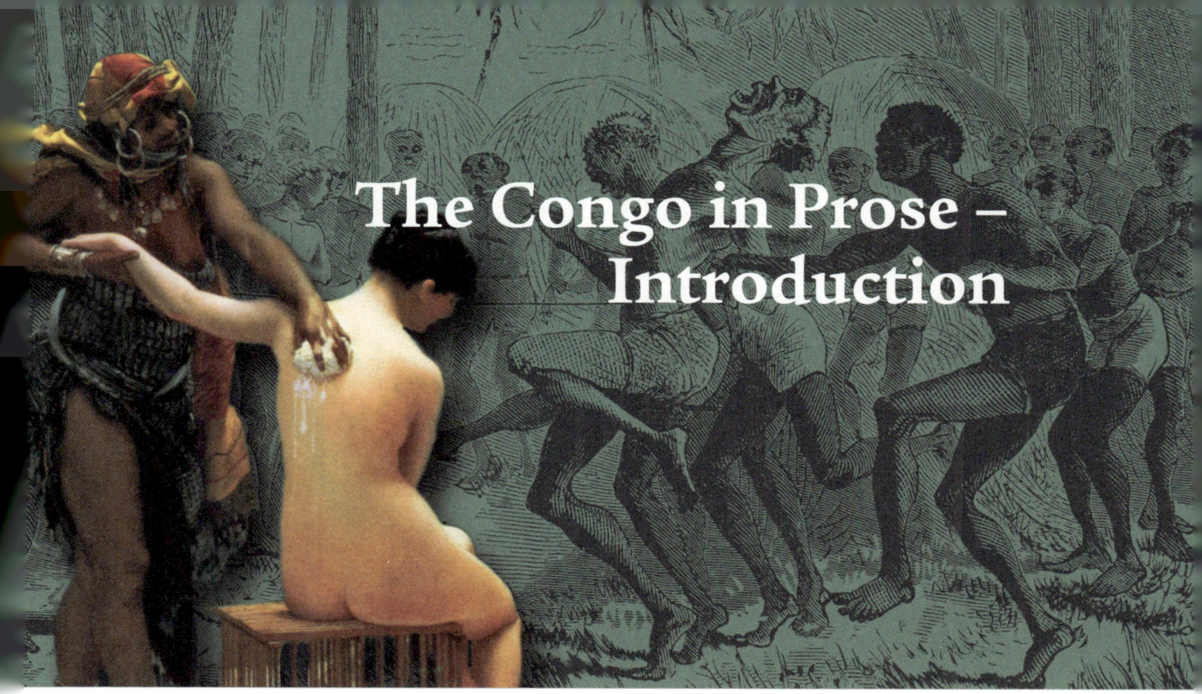

The Congo in Prose – Introduction

1 Life and Works: Reading Stanley

In his article “Lost and Found: Exploring the Legacy of Stanley and Livingstone” (*The New Yorker*, 2 June 2003), the American historian Adam Hochschild describes how explorers have been subjected to extremely conflicting appraisals in historical writing. Initially, they were seen as self-sacrificing front-runners for the spreading of civilisation; since then, historians have proven that both private and national motivations were far more ambiguous, leading to the current situation in which Native Americans, among others, are protesting about an American national holiday named after Columbus. In the thousands of books written about Livingstone and Stanley, a line can be drawn around 1968: before then, biographies on one or both of the explorers basically painted a picture of them as pioneers for progress and standard-bearers for the dissemination of morality and civilisation. However, this interpretation mainly concerned the great Livingstone’s saint-like achievements, while Stanley was assessed with more reservation. Livingstone was the first European to cross the African continent in 1852-56. He described the Victoria Falls in one of the earliest and most successful bestsellers in a long series of Victorian travel accounts, and he allegedly paved the way for Christianity and civilisation in Africa. Livingstone’s travels were accident-ridden and produced few results, which only helped to further the romanticised idea of him as a lonesome wanderer and pilgrim: a national icon. Stanley’s explorations and travel accounts were more

Stanley dressed up and photographed in a studio in 1885, as reproduced in the autobiography published in 1909, which was edited by his widow Dorothy Stanley. In the autobiography, Stanley mentions his discomfort at being portrayed in the notebooks of his fellow travellers. During the hardships of the journey, one is not dressed to be exposed, but exists rather in a state of "undress". In Herbert Ward's *My Life with Stanley's Rear Guard* (1891), Ward can only imagine that the irreconcilable anger Stanley directs against him after the scandalous Emin Pasha expedition must have been caused by Stanley's coming across one of Ward's "harmless" caricatures of the great expedition leader when he opened James Jameson's sealed crates. While Stanley was writing *In Darkest Africa* in Cairo after the expedition, an American tried to purchase his famous homemade tropical cap with air holes, wanting to exhibit it in a collection of curiosities. However, the cap ended up in the Royal Geographical Society museum, where it can be viewed with Stanley's boots.

modern and efficient; they also created a lot more conflict in Africa and in the British public sphere, where people found it difficult to come to terms with his very American approach. This goes for all Stanley's great travels in Africa: the meeting with Livingstone in 1871, described in *How I Found Livingstone* (1872); the trans-African expedition 1874-77, during which he mapped the source of the Nile river system and became the first European to follow the Congo River from its source at Lake Tanganyika to the Atlantic, described in *Through the Dark Continent* (1878); the 1879-84 colonisation expedition in King Léopold's service described in *The Congo and the Founding of Its Free State* (1885); and, finally, the most controversial of the expeditions, the rescuing of Emin Pasha in 1887-89, described in *In Darkest Africa* (1890).

After 1968, portraits of Livingstone and Stanley became increasingly negative. Due to their almost mythological positions as the foremost representatives of Victorianism, these heroes of yesteryear were the first to be dethroned when the African colonies achieved independence, and universities in Europe and the USA rewrote colonial history from a historical perspective focusing on oppression and racism. Hochschild's article offers a panorama of different texts in the critical tradition after Livingstone and Stanley with examples from biographies, various exhibitions and auctions selling all sorts of objects from the great expeditions. It also accounts for the way that Hollywood, within changing environments and ideologies, has fictionalised the legendary meeting. In the article, Hochschild lays claim to an objective view; he is, nevertheless, deeply involved. The author of *King Leopold's Ghost: A Story of Greed, Terror, and Heroism in Colonial Africa* (1999), Hochschild is responsible for the most biased of critical history's portraits of Stanley, who, without hesitation, is declared to be the model for Joseph Conrad's cannibalistic Kurtz in *Heart of Darkness*; moreover, Stanley is accused of having major responsibility in the extermination of millions of Congolese forced labourers in the 1890s.

Regardless of whether biographies are critical or lionising, their structures and appraisals unwittingly continue the discourse of personality cult and heroism that was associated with explorers in the nineteenth century. At that time, expedition leaders' achievements were seen as direct results of their determination, bravery, stamina and, most importantly, their outstanding morals, which became clear through rhetoric and decorum, as well as power of judgement – characteristics which, in the iconography of the time, were closely related to equivalent national qualities.

The race between competing explorers was also perceived as a trial of strength between nations, and the expedition leaders, e.g. de Brazza and Stanley, were sketched as Latin and Anglo-Saxon archetypes respectively. The value, authority and reliability of travel accounts whether by Livingstone, Burton or Stanley

Illustration from Stanley's first extensive travel account, *How I Found Livingstone* (1872). The caption reads: "Look out, you drop that box – I'll shoot you". This kind of image earned Stanley a reputation as the most brutal of all explorers and made him the favourite scapegoat of post-colonial criticism. Recent studies indicate that most of the situations were exaggerated and staged in order to accommodate the reader's expectations of excitement, determination and action.

were interpreted as aspects of the traveller's moral character. A book's reception by the *Royal Geographical Society*, and through constant media attention in the newspapers, could canonise a traveller and create a national icon, a condensed image of Victorian ideals, as happened with Livingstone's *Missionary Travels and Researches in South Africa* (1857). However, critics could also sow doubts about the reliability of the account by pointing out flaws in the author's morals, thereby creating national scandals. This often happened to Stanley.

In a similar way, retrospective biographies about Stanley have concentrated on conjuring up a psychological and moral image that is assumed to explain everything. Whether he is portrayed as a sadistic and ruthless criminal who initiated and lead innumerable genocides – often associated with sexual perversion – or as a disciplined and determined explorer who fought against slavery in deeply felt sympathy with the natives, the benchmark is basically the same type

Stanley with his field notebook, in which he recorded valuable observations during the marches, later to be organised in diaries, edited for telegrams, and finally compiled in tomes that would recreate Africa as a stage and Stanley as a celebrity, both of which became issues of contention in years to come. The picture shows Sean Lynch in the role of Stanley in the TV documentary *Henry Morton Stanley: Congo River, 1874* (1976). Spencer Tracy played Stanley in Henry King's *Stanley and Livingstone* (1939), and numerous films and computer games have rewritten the story. The lighting and lamp company *Stanley Electric Co.* is named after the explorer "who brought light to many places in the world, hitherto unknown to man".

of heroism. One would expect that the personality cult would be the target of criticism rather than the aim – at least in more recent biographies.[3] Given that biographies today carry almost the same authority as the scientific societies in the nineteenth century, it is of interest to refer to a recent and interesting example, Tim Jeal's *Stanley: The Impossible Life of Africa's Greatest Explorer* (2007).[4] Jeal argues for a moral re-evaluation of Stanley and a more positive appraisal of his role in Africa's history of colonisation. In a revisionist way, the book turns the negative appraisals in biographies by Richard Hall, Frank McLynn and John Bierman upside-down.

In the introduction, Tim Jeal explains the genesis of the book as a concurrence of different circumstances. First, during the writing of the biography *Livingstone* (1973), which is also revisionist but with the aim of downplaying predominantly positive appraisals, Jeal had already planned to continue with a

biography about Stanley. However, he had to give up the idea when he realised that Richard Hall had already gained access to parts of the Stanley family's enormous archive of unpublished material during his research for *Stanley: An Adventurer Explored* (1974). Secondly, while working on *Livingstone*, Jeal had come across correspondence that gave an impression of Stanley as self-effacing, generous and loyal towards his friends, which was in blatant contrast to his reputation as self-promoting, sadomasochistic and ruthless, as presented in, e.g., McLynn's *Stanley: The Making of an African Explorer* (1990) and John Bierman's *Dark Safari* (1992) – books that also presented Stanley as a willing accessory to King Léopold's brutal colonisation. Thirdly, Jeal, exceptionally, gained access to a plethora of archival materials on Stanley, which the Belgian colonial museum Musée Royal de l'Afrique Centrale had purchased at great expense in the meantime.

Jeal's book is presented as a tale of extraordinary discoveries, an exploration in the archive, unearthing an entirely different image of Stanley than that of the militant conqueror. The scoop is a detailed argument that Stanley's famous "Dr. Livingstone, I presume?" is to be understood as a literary invention without any basis in what was actually said. In reality, Stanley continued Livingstone's ideals, but he undermined his own reputation, initially by lying about his past in order to avoid it catching up with him and compromising his fame, and subsequently by lying about his lies. For instance, he exaggerated the idea of his travels as military operations in a misconceived and failed attempt to copy and fit in with the style and moral code of English officers.

Particularly in post-colonial criticism, there is a strong and problematic tendency towards the biased and undocumented use of Stanley as a scapegoat for colonial cruelty. Tim Jeal's criticism is, in that respect, completely justified. However, apart from a few isolated corrections of earlier biographies, the archival material does not contribute much to the book's reasoning. Most of his points had already been presented in earlier biographies, including the discussion of "Dr. Livingstone, I presume?"[5] Jeal's introductory claim of revolutionary finds in the Belgian Stanley archive cannot change the fact that he does *not* provide anything new about the main points; he merely adds more anecdotal layers, e.g. gossip about what Stanley's fiancée was doing in London, at the cost of actual accounts of the expeditions.

The positive re-evaluation of Stanley is practised within the aforementioned glorifying moral discourse. The attempt to save Stanley from criticism, and glorify his conduct when at all possible, builds upon often dubious assumptions and linked sentimentalised anecdotes about his compassionate and empathetic nature. Sources from Stanley's own hand that compromise his reputation are rebutted with reference to his tendency to exaggerate and lie. On the other

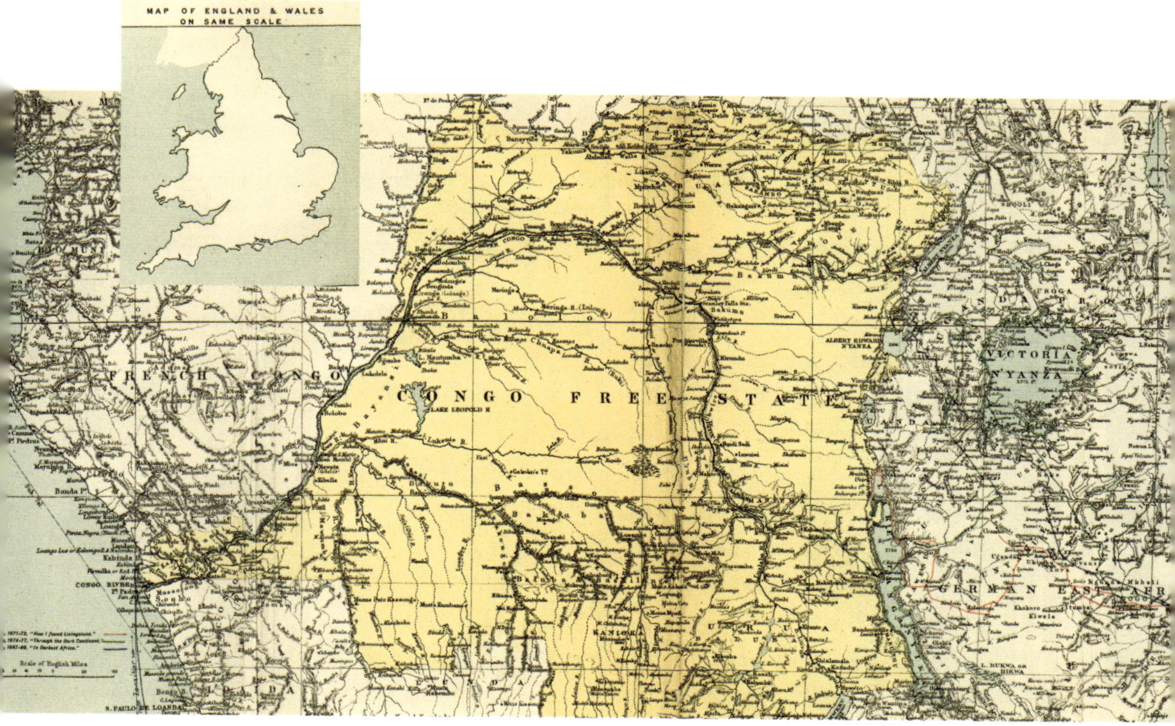

"Sir H. M. Stanley's Three African Journeys" and "Map of England & Wales on same scale", from *Autobiography of Sir Henry Morton Stanley, G.C.B., edited by his wife, Dorothy Stanley* (1909). The maps are part of the monumental tale of the autobiography.

hand, Jeal emphasises and over-interprets sources that support the heroic image, without ever doubting *their* credibility. Stanley's reservations towards King Léopold's excessive territorial expansion plans in the 1890s, for instance, are interpreted as a counterfactual point that cleanses him of any colonial guilt: if King Léopold had employed Stanley as governor of the Congo Free State, instead of leaving him out in the cold, the "Red Rubber" terror of the 1890s would have been avoided.

This goes to show that the most recent extensive biography about Stanley relies on the same problematic methods and revisionist bias as previous ones, which obstructs rather than facilitates a much-needed new understanding of the expeditions and the time. The biographers' continuation of the nineteenth-century preoccupation with heroism, which also characterises the structure of iconoclastic biographies, can in general be described as an internal paradox. By applying a moral and sentimental model for the portrayal and describing historic events as results of individual characteristics and morals, the idea of the sentimental traveller is inscribed as the hidden standard for the appraisal

of Victorian explorers who, in fact, distanced themselves from the paradigm of sensitivity. Biographies, including Tim Jeal's, never relate to the texts as anything other than sources for assessing the traveller's morals, resulting in their failure to acknowledge Stanley's unique position in the period as a modern though maladjusted outsider, who fits neither one nor the other typological category, and whose travel literature offers highly unusual descriptions of the world. In this way, the black and white polemic about Stanley as a person ends up overshadowing the texts and their exemplary traits.

In contexts where they are compared, Joseph Conrad's *Heart of Darkness* and Stanley's travel accounts are usually considered to be complete opposites.[6] There are valid reasons for this point of view, although it is somewhat simplified and obscures the understanding of conflicting *internal* traits in both writers' descriptions of experiences in Africa. In the same way that retrospective criticism of Conrad's *Heart of Darkness* represents a clear divide between those who distance themselves from the book, claiming that it is colonial and racist, and those who admire it for its literary qualities and emphasise its criticism of colonialism or universal traits, the reception of Stanley's Africa books has, from the very first reactions to the present day been equally biased – either condemning or glorifying – with only a very few exceptions.[7] In Conrad's case, the dispute has lead to an increased focus on the text, subjected to any number of imaginable, subtle textual analytic strategies, while Stanley's are rarely analysed within the area of comparative literature. It might seem like a paradox that Conrad's novella steals all the attention, considering the corpus and historical significance of Stanley's expeditions and texts.

One of the main claims in this chapter is that Stanley's texts played a crucial part in the development of a modern, global iconography of the Congo and Central Africa in the late nineteenth century, and that they to a great extent defined the conditions for subsequent literary and documentary interpretations. The expeditions and the texts about them became matrixes with consequences for the region's reality, economy and political attitude; however, they are not necessarily consistent with the very reductive ideas found in post-colonialism of the explorer as someone who was inevitably followed by a bloody wake of oppression and racism. Instead of allowing our knowledge of colonialism's oppression and violations to stand in the way of our reading, we need to approach and *read* Stanley in order to achieve an important basis for forming up-to-date images of the world in a time of global media.

The question is: what is required to read Stanley properly? "Stanley" in this context is being used both as a description of the texts published under his name, and to describe the author-persona that has been invented as an inseparable part of the texts. In literature about Stanley his explorations are usually recounted with the travel accounts as the main source, often chronologically and appropriately focusing on dramatic climaxes, echoing the epic structure in Stanley's own texts, projecting him through either critical or noncritical reflections that rarely take into account the orchestrated and performative nature of the texts.

Biographies after 1990 unsurprisingly focus on Stanley's fragmented life story, a clear contrast to his own and earlier biographers' attempts to create homogeneity.[8] Stanley was born John Rowlands in Wales in 1841, where he grew up in conditions similar to those of a poorhouse, practically an orphan. At eighteen he travelled to the USA, where he was adopted by Henry Hope Stanley, a wealthy businessman in New Orleans. The Stanley name replaced Rowlands, and during a hectic period in which he fought on both sides in the civil war and wrote his first reports of retributions against Native American rebels, he invented a new autobiography piece by piece erasing his Welsh past.

The obscured facts have gradually been disclosed through disputes about Stanley's credibility, which followed every new published version of his accounts of extraordinary deeds. The first time it happened was in connection with the 'discovery' of Livingstone. This expedition was funded by the *New York Herald*, an anti-British newspaper that did not mince its words in its derogatory articles about the British lack of will and determination. The fact that Stanley chose to present his account to the members of the Royal Geographical Society, with strikingly dramatic use of language and gestures, as well as his attempt to invent a fictitious identity, was bound to compromise the credibility of his accounts. Had Stanley even met Livingstone, or was the whole story pure fabrication?

The fundamental suspicion surrounding Stanley's personal and national identity is an important aspect of his activities as a traveller and writer. References to his shady past are continuously used to question his motives, and the texts' value as evidence is under constant attack. At the same time, the travel accounts, and the extraordinary endurance and determination they express, can be seen as Stanley's attempt to establish a post-national – Welsh, American, British, Belgian – identity as an entrepreneur for the Congo Free State. Stanley was imperturbable and hard as a rock, but he had an almost superhuman ability to force his way forward, which earned him the nickname Bula Matari, 'Breaker of Rocks'. Viewed in this light, the aim of the travels and accounts was first and foremost to create a sense of truth and authority, fatherhood and belonging that nobody could take away from him. Alongside his legendary sense for dramatisation and capturing the audience's imagination in the books that instantly became international bestsellers, we find a quest for the truth. Most obviously, it was about winning acknowledgement and prestige, but it was also a challenge for this explorer who had no scientific background and a

symptom of an identity project in which several competing backgrounds were addressed simultaneously.

The travel books were written and published as quick as lightning, in accordance with Stanley's reputation as a modern journalist who stuck at nothing to be the first to bring news. When covering the British Expedition to Abyssinia for the *New York Herald* he paid the telegrapher to send off his news telegrams before everyone else's. When, in 1868, he sent the final report on the British victory, one of many anecdotes claims that Stanley blocked the only telegraph line by sending one hundred pages of the Bible, which meant that the British government had to face the humiliation of receiving the news from New York. The *New York Herald* enjoyed a large circulation because of Stanley's telegrams from Central Africa, and continued its attacks against British apathy while at the same time not refraining from printing articles that questioned Stanley's credibility – anything to create what was then unprecedented media hype. The following expedition across the continent was financed by a far from harmonious collaboration between the British *Daily Telegraph* and the American *Herald*. The articles were rolled up in specially made secure containers and brought to Zanzibar by sprinters. Soon after, they stole the headlines and satisfied millions of readers' cravings for news.

Most of the articles begin with a brief summary that brings the reader up to date, followed by a description of the hot spot of conflict and the strategic considerations that Stanley finds himself in. They are brilliant, fluent and swift pieces of evidence considering the physical strain and time pressure that the expedition leader was subject to. Readers could identify with Stanley and find themselves on location in real time, plot the travel route into the unknown, and keep count of the casualties in pretend simultaneity with Stanley, as if it were thrilling fiction. The fact that the stories were real, despite being truly extraordinary, added to the thrill; every day's march was perceived as a new landmark in history. Stanley's journalistic style was a precursor of New Journalism, which gained ground at the end of the nineteenth century and featured new narratives that surpassed former conventions in regard to language and genre, as well as a candid will to penetrate global and private spheres alike.

The telegram articles subsequently became the nuclei of the travel books.[9] They were supplemented with letters or excerpts from letters from personal friends and business partners, which shed light on the events or provided a kind of day-to-day diary. Stanley's own notebooks were the main source in the editing process of the travel books, but excerpts from them were also quoted directly. In the course of a day, Stanley would take notes and draw sketches, which he elaborated on in his log book in the evenings. Furthermore, the travel books include material that is not directly related to the expeditions. There is

Stanley's travel accounts were highly popular and therefore subject to all kinds of piracy, the best countermeasure to which was rapid translation, sometimes simultaneous, into several languages and for several markets. Even when the 900-page travel account was split into cheap 55-page parts, it was clearly stated that this was an "Official Account" and the "Authorised Version for Norway and Denmark".

extensive statistic material with records of personnel, provisions and equipment; calculations of population density in the visited territories, including estimates of the inhabitants' capability and willingness to work on various colonial projects; and accounts of the territories' current production of wares and potential yield through colonial investments. We also find sudden changes of style in the accounts, when Stanley enters into dialogue with the reader about future civilisation projects, often in the context of imagined landscapes where tropical fertility, work, free trade and welfare replace the laziness and hopelessness that was part of the popular notion of African people and nature respectively in the nineteenth century. Some of these passages were clearly written after the travels, which becomes evident through quoted poems and literary references.

Finally, we find the illustrations, a good many of which are based on Stanley's own unsuccessful photographs. Some depict events from his travels; others play a more independent role as decoration or ornament, as drawings of weapons and hairstyles are designed to meet the reader's expectations of ethnographic curiosity and wild beauty, although Stanley's prose is not notable for these traditionally compulsory elements of travel writing.

Through the direct use of – sometimes fake – quotations from letters, diaries, notebooks and telegram articles in the travel books, Stanley achieves a powerful double effect of documentary objectivity and movement. In the quotations we find ourselves in the traveller's present, alternating between the ominous and promising indecisiveness of the moment. Here we are close to the conventions of letter and diary writing, both of which create an intimacy between the writing and the reading where there is, at least in principle, no room for lies, and where geographical and social distances are surpassed via pretended simultaneity. At the same time, these passages appear to be documented. Though they are, for the most part, written by Stanley, they create the sense of factual archival work and source criticism which was so important to him; unlike most explorers, he was unable to support his authority with natural history and ethnographical inventories.

The success of the travel books was, among other things, a result of the effective and reader-friendly homogeneity that Stanley managed to create from his multilayered compositions, along with his talent for addressing a variety of different recipients in the same text. The books were quickly translated and published on the international market. After the success of *How I Found Livingstone: Travels, Adventures and Discoveries in Central Africa, Including an Account of Four Months' Residence with Dr. Livingstone* (1872), Stanley's introductions indicate a clear knowledge of the political potential of the books in regard to international audiences. In *The Congo and the Founding of Its Free State* (1885) this becomes particularly evident when Stanley argues for the prospects of investments in the Congo, alternately addressing British, Belgian, Scandinavian, French, Spanish, and German interests while at the same time mentioning that the book is being published concurrently in eight languages.[10] Other important recipients were Europe's scientific societies; as institutions they could add to or take away from Stanley's authority as an explorer, traveller and writer. Further, there is no doubt that Stanley targeted knowledgeable readers – it is in this light we should read the occasional passages of nature romanticism and humanism. Naturally, the books also targeted the vast audiences of urban newspaper readers that grew towards the end of the nineteenth century, spanning class and educational backgrounds. The telegram articles had already established this audience for Stanley, but he continued his journalistic style in the travel books – often in the form of very effective prose in the specific type of report that gained ground from around the turn of the century. Finally, the author himself was a recipient of the text, aiming to create a self-image he could live with.

While all these recipients are addressed rhetorically with great success in the texts, and contribute considerably to the impact of Stanley's writing, the separate contexts they constitute are highly conflicting. It is obvious that industrial workers from Christiania or Copenhagen who bought Henry M. Stanley's account in separate numbers for kr. 1.50 apiece did not have the same credibility criteria as the *Royal Geographical Society* or committees who financed the expedition in the hope of establishing a flourishing business or gaining political ground. The many layers of the texts should therefore be seen as a wider, although still very entangled, web of economical and political interests that challenged Stanley's authority as a traveller, writer and person – and on a greater scale the legitimacy of explorers in the nineteenth century. Stanley's deeds and books signify both the culmination and the final collapse of a discourse on exploration as conquest that dates all the way back to the renaissance.

The chapter "H.M. Stanley: Magic and Market" focuses on Stanley's two main texts, *Through the Dark Continent* (1878) and *In Darkest Africa* (1890), not be to summarise in full the myth about the man and his actions, but rather to identify central points in the exhaustive material and to shed light on the evidence and authority of the travel accounts – that is, evidence and authority in the context of the globalisation of literature and media. A general picture of the complexity of Stanley's life, texts and activities as a traveller will be established.

The title of the following chapter, "Traveller on Global Terms", refers to the performative dimension, which will be a central theme of this book: the travel accounts constitute a profound correlation between the creation of Stanley's identity, the travels and the 'opening up' of Africa with its far-reaching consequences. This double inscription is created through the texts' superposition of traditionally isolated scenes and spaces. In the texts, a traveller's intimate autobiography is acted out on a worldwide stage, celebrated and anonymous at the same time. The quest for identity is communicated to the world through journalistic means, while being carried out as a process of the subject constantly going forward on an exploration through the landscape.

Stanley's travel accounts are central to literature about the Congo. It is the author's belief that the texts, due to their radical nature, demonstrate fundamental characteristics of literature in general and the formation of identity on global terms in particular. Their many shifts in genre, perspective and scene challenge our traditional assumptions and methods of reading literature. In the following two chapters, two frameworks for understanding this type of literature are presented: first, "Prose: A Framework and Reading Perspective" is

in this context not chiefly a genre discussion but rather a sketch of perspectives in travel literature that will help to explain the idea of the "Traveller on Global Terms" and explicate the starting point of this book. Second, a chapter about the country which all the texts mentioned in this book are about: "Literary Topography of the Congo". This chapter does not pretend to be a historical or geographical description, but rather introduces the Congo as a place in literary history, and as the object of competing and overlapping discursive interpretations. Topography and prose are the points of reference for this examination of Stanley and of Conrad's *Heart of Darkness* respectively, followed by a wide spectrum of texts about the Congo. This part encompasses the author's reading perspective and method, which will be summarised briefly at the end of the introductory chapter, "Anthropoetic Narrative and Method".

2 Traveller on Global Terms

Literature about Stanley often focuses on how he invented a new biography and identity for himself to replace his somewhat shady past, or alternatively recounts the outline of Stanley's travels with added critical footnotes. There are several reasons why the actual texts are seldom mentioned. First, many have probably found it intolerable to spend the required time with the author, whose works run to thousands of pages. In the same way that his insistence on camping away from the other travellers – in order not to be seen in a state of 'undress' that would no doubt be portrayed in their diaries – gave the European officers an impression of antagonism and reservation, Stanley's combination of discipline and smooth-running journalism can be tiring for the educated reader, who expects literature to be based on free, learned dialogue or intimacy.[11] Secondly, Stanley's immense global popularity has in itself contributed to disqualifying the works to a degree that has stood in the way of rediscovery, republishing or adoption into the academic branch of the literary establishment in the twentieth century. While considerable portions of older travel literature draw great attention, and are embraced by institutional renaissance for their aesthetic, scientific and not least cultural qualities, Stanley is excluded as a politically incorrect outsider who cannot be assimilated. Finally, if a literary scholar or publisher did decide to approach the texts, they are so monstrous in both size and content that they would not easily fit into any existing academic or publishing standard.

A combination of genres, styles and historical layers are found in Stanley's travel books that are peculiarly anachronistic and for that reason alone worth considering. These anachronisms are also closely related to an almost unprecedented presence in the period: the texts played an active role in the historical context and political agendas, the travels focused on challenging circumstances and goals, and the travel books and particularly the articles attempted to create simultaneity between the discoveries and the reader's re-discovery. As regards the consequences of all this, Stanley was on par with the greatest explorers, which commands respect. At the same time, it raises the question of how he, a reputed journalistic charlatan, within a very short span of time managed to solve all the problems that his predecessors had left unsolved or nebulous. This leads on to questions of Stanley's credibility, authority and authorship in the light of his biography and the institutions that chose either to uphold or discredit his authority.

Bula Matari, Breaker of Rocks

On the dark blue cover of *Autobiography of Henry M. Stanley* (1909), the title is stamped into the binding in gold letters. This is also the case for the logo found underneath the title, which depicts Africa in a golden circle with the words "Bula Matari" in the shape of a rainbow above the Sahara. A closer inspection reveals the Congo River drawn across Central Africa with the letters H.M.S. dancing on its winding line. The book's cover clearly conveys the intentions of Stanley and the publisher, who was his widow, Dorothy Stanley. It is a revised reprint of the inscription on Stanley's six-tonne headstone, which reads "Henry Morton Stanley", then "Bula Matari", and as the epitaph only the word "Africa". Dorothy writes, with the intention of creating an unchanging and eternal memorial for Stanley: "imperishable as the name, cut deep into its face" (p. 517). In these epitaphs, "Bula Matari", Stanley's African nickname as the breaker of rocks, commemorates a figural play on the explorer's habit of scratching his name into a rock as an incontestable sign that he had actually been at the place in question. It also brings the prosopopoeia to mind, the rhetorical trope for personification or animation of non-human phenomena, originally meaning "putting a human-looking mask on something non-human". The inscriptions appear to establish a solid, unbreakable connection between biography and mapping – a connection that will act as a common thread in the following. While Dorothy Stanley undoubtedly wanted to carve a lasting impression of the man and his deeds, the current author views the relationship between biography, inscription, mapping, travel books and epitaph as interplay. In this light, it appears that Dorothy Stanley was not in full control of her figurative language when the nickname 'Breaker of Rocks' was carved into resistant stone.

Without going into too much detail regarding the many questions about the editing of the *Autobiography*, it is obviously not the untouchable monument carved in stone that both Henry and Dorothy Stanley wanted. The first nine chapters contain Stanley's own childhood memories, the escape to America, and his 'discovery' of a new identity. The rest is Dorothy's orchestration, made up of letters, notes, fragments of manuscripts and her own summaries of the main works. The result is a narrative of Stanley's life which – with its many excuses and evasive explanations – makes an interesting read. The document is arranged with the survivor's excruciatingly sensible determination to avoid scandal, seal off suspicious lacunae and blur or reconcile the controversy that Stanley caused throughout his life. Because of this, the *Autobiography* – especially Dorothy's additions – comes off as an unresolved, dislocated and distorted version of a life story that, even while the main character was alive, lacked coherence and plot.

The greatest challenge posed to biographies about Stanley has been to separate the many editorial layers that surround his activities. In Frank McLynn's

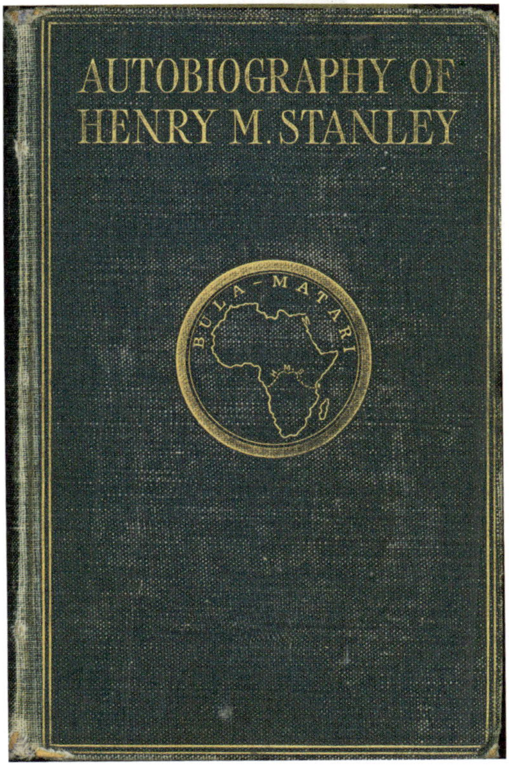

Dorothy Stanley's edition of the autobiography is a staunch attempt to create an unyielding image of the late explorer. In the preface, she links the inscription on Stanley's gravestone to the design on the cover, which looks like a stamp or a seal with Stanley's initials written on the route of his trans-African expedition. Dorothy Stanley was the illustrator of many great travel books of the era.

Stanley: The Making of an African Explorer, the *Autobiography* is a core text that is examined through cumbersome archival studies in order to achieve a corrected and purified authentic narrative about Stanley. One of McLynn's main points is that Stanley lied about or misrepresented even crucial events, especially in the time before he found Livingstone and became famous. Tim Jeal's biography is basically a continuation of McLynn's, though Jeal exalts the determining events to create a more positive portrait. Stanley's recounting of a childhood deprived of love or friends, deserted by his parents and left in the care of sadistic guardians in an orphanage, is more or less correct, although there are a striking number of omissions and fabricated additions. The same goes for the escape to America where Stanley, according to his own narrative, felt free and acknowledged for the first time, which is why he was able to open up to others'

compassion, especially that of his new 'father', the trader Henry Stanley who adopted the young Henry Rowlands. According to Jeal, this is probably also a romantic invention, but other biographies accept this part of the adventure as fact. In Stanley's version we are looking at a formative leap, in which the young man's broken faith in the world is healed through literature and edifying conversations with Stanley Sr. After McLynn's and Jeal's archival work, it is, however, hard to believe more than rudimentary facts in this tale of formation, which seems rather to be shaped on the basis of fictitious literary precursors. A very dramatic description of a bloody fight with a teacher at the insufferable "workhouse" and his subsequent escape, which would ultimately bring Stanley to Africa, is a fabricated imitation of Dickens' *Nicholas Nickleby*. Other stories from his first stay in America are extraordinarily risqué, for instance one in which the young Stanley discovers that the boy Dick, with whom he shares his bed, is in fact a girl called Alice. This story is, according to biographers, completely invented, taken from the Shakespeare paperbacks that the young Stanley readily devoured as bedtime reading.

In the *Autobiography*, Stanley maintains a depiction of Stanley Sr. as a gentle and forgiving man and provides a thorough account of his death, which once again threw the young man out on a roaming quest as a roustabout, adventurer and coincidentally a soldier enrolled on both sides in the civil war. Biographers have proved that this picaresque tale is also more fiction than fact, allowing Stanley to add meaning to several miserable years as an outlaw, deserter and fraud. Even in the versions about the final step from vagabonding to the initial step towards becoming a journalist – first by reporting from the civil war, and later as a war correspondent in the last of the American Indian Wars – Stanley remains inclined to add layers to the truth, as if he were only able to recognise himself through fiction.

Stanley puts great emphasis on the role that literature played in his formative years. Throughout his troubled childhood in Wales, books formed a shield against his hostile surroundings and a sanctuary where he became untouchable in his fantasy. The description of his early days in New Orleans is also closer to the world of fiction than the new American reality, which first and foremost required drive and initiative from the young man. Nevertheless, Stanley immersed himself in "cheap copies of standard books" (p. 97), and goes as far as to link his initial steps towards manhood with the discovery of an antiquarian bookshop where he, for very little money, bought Spenser's *Faerie Queen*, Tasso's *Jerusalem Delivered*, Pope's *Iliad*, Dryden's *Odyssey*, Milton's *Paradise Lost*, Plutarch's *Lives* and so on, until his recently acquired bookcase was bursting with a highly eclectic collection.

"My attic became my world now, and a very great expansible world, full of kings, emperors, knights, warriors, heroes, and angels. Without, it might have been better, less sordid: within, it was glorious for great deeds and splendid pageantry. It affected my dreams, for I dreamed of the things that I had read. I was transported into Trojan Fields, and Odyssean Isles, and Roman Palaces" (pp. 97-98).

Stanley describes his "little library" as a safeguard against all the amusing activities with which his colleagues tempted him: "a dip into a page soon effaced all desire for other pleasures" (p. 98). This is followed by a confession that is unusually frank for Stanley:

"What I am I owe to example, nature, school-education, reading, travel, observation, and reflection. An infinitesimal amount of mannerisms observed clung to me, no doubt. The housewifely orderliness of Aunt Mary, the serious propriety of Cousin Moses, - then, when I went to sea, the stern voice of the captain, the reckless abandon of the sailors, - after that, the conscientious yielding of myself to details of business, - all this left indelible impressions on me" (p. 98).

The model of formation that Stanley seems to base his narrative on, which Dorothy strongly supports, insists on depicting the bad years as a period of learning and the meeting with Mr. Stanley as a rebirth into cultivated circles by means of educated conversation. However, the narrative reveals an uncertainty about the power behind Stanley's personal formation. There is a striking link between his first steps from boy to man and the disappearance into a private, "very great expansible world", where he moves freely among Homeric heroes on Trojan fields, discovering a "pleasure" that protects him against more mundane and perhaps more natural temptations for a young man. The connections between inner imaginary worlds and outer reality are blurred - something that Stanley uses several times as a retrospective theme - and this blurring allows him to portray the important people around him as heroes and heroines like those in the romances that Mr Stanley advises him against reading. Mrs Stanley is seen as an icon and the image of an angel. The Dick/Alice comedy of errors is taken from Shakespeare, possibly mixed with real sexual experiences. Later on in the book, Stanley describes an embarrassing encounter with his still unsympathetic mother through imagery that shows how difficult he found it to talk about himself without taking refuge in paraphrases and fiction: "Like a bride arraying herself in her best for her lover, I had arranged my story to please one who would, at last, I hoped, prove an affectionate mother!" (p. 219).

Stanley's description of his own identity formation is similarly peculiar. Distinct from both the idea of organic growth in the formation model and the Dickensian model, we are looking at a process in which the completely isolated characteristics of a series of influential people impregnate Stanley with a considerable number of so-called "mannerisms", i.e. unexplainable but permanent habits, traits and tendencies: the fear of a captain on his illegal crossing to America, for instance, teaches him to speak in a harsh voice, a phenomenon we can actually trace in the later travel accounts as a sign of authority.

Although Stanley and Dorothy make a collaborative effort to create a plot in the biography and a motivating principle that sheds light on the childhood denials and adult triumphs, the main points are profoundly conflicting. This conflict becomes most obvious in Stanley's extensive shaping of the material relating to experience; here, many contradictory cultural systems of reference are at play. It is, however, also deeply rooted in the autobiographical project *per se*. As Stanley points out in the book's introduction, he has always been "in the habit of confining myself to myself" (p. xv). The motivating principle in the narrative is his "reserve". Dorothy admits in her introduction that Stanley's childhood story is pathetic, but she uses it to excuse his notorious stringency, discipline and self control – characteristics that helped him through the expeditions. She also points to the sensitivity behind the mask of reserve. In his introduction, Stanley describes his reservation as a longing for friendship and love, which throughout his life has remained unrequited – a rather harsh and uncompromising beginning to an autobiography. However, the indifference achieved in old age was what allowed him to be completely frank, because no malevolent gossip could harm him anymore and he was not in the way of anyone. Stanley's wish is to reveal everything about himself, and yet he admits: "No doubt there will be much self-betrayal in these pages, and he who can read between the lines, as a physiognomist would read character, will not find it difficult to read me" (p. xvi).

When Stanley assures us that "Indeed, I wish to appear without disguise", this may be so, but in reality it is impossible to distinguish between facts and disguise. Furthermore, it is hard to believe that his principle in life – never to reveal himself, which according to him builds a bridge from childhood to adulthood – is suddenly to be abandoned in the quest to reveal all. Stanley's own reflections on the autobiography rather indicate that the portrait is created between the lines; that is, through the performative aspects of the text.

The discrepancy between the affectionate description of Mr Stanley in the chapter "I Found a Father" and the fictitious and hazardously disparate tale about how the young Stanley lost both him and the privileges he ensured – the chance to be someone altogether – is an example of the extensive editing process. According to McLynn, the break between the two was a result of them increasingly getting on each others' nerves. When Stanley was finally kicked out, a period followed during which he led a shady life under a number of aliases. What he describes as a rebirth and a newly-found identity was rather a hollow and directionless existence, as every identity he tried out was immediately rejected, and every sought-after human relationship immediately destroyed.

Despite this, there are still bits and pieces to be found between the lines that may help one to understand how Stanley suddenly, years later, happened to be in the right place at the right time. Mr Stanley's masterful attempt to put some knowledge into the young man's head is described as the ideal dialogue between people. On the sailing trips up and down the Mississippi they had their "portmanteau packed with choice literature", which they renewed in all the big cities on the way. However, "novels and romances were rigidly excluded" (p. 127). Stanley learned that books needed to be read out loud in order to be understood, and Stanley Jr. and Sr. read vast numbers of "essays, memoirs, biographies, and general literature". The river trips were, according to the biography, intense and disciplined studies of prose that excluded novels and romances. When they were not reading, Mr Stanley educated the young man by pointing out remarkable phenomena on the shore from the deck in order "to impress on me some useful, or moral lesson".

We see here the initial steps towards the genre of prose called travel literature; many of Stanley's thousands of pages of travel accounts consist of observations from a boat floating down a river. Moreover, when Stanley talks about the Congo River in his travel books, he often compares it to the Mississippi, though he seems unable to keep the romances and novels out of the text: knights, emperors and Homeric heroes are, as was the case in his room in the attic, key parts of his prose. They are embedded in the travel books' observational and essayistic "general literature", inviting readers to leave the real journey's often paranoid space and transporting them into the world of fiction, a "very great expansible world".

Similarly, Stanley's chaotic days as an outlaw, shabby soldier and deserter can be understood – regardless of the perspective we see him from – as the perfect preparation for his travels in Africa: apart from practical skills, he learned to survive in a mean and absolutely meaningless war by wearing disguises, inventing new identities and travelling through enemy territory by means of scams and false papers. Maybe even more importantly with regard to the expeditions, he learned that common law and rules did not apply on military journeys – and he thought of the expeditions as military journeys.

Stanley's gravestone with the inscription: "Henry Morton Stanley. Bula Matari 1841-1904. Africa". From *Autobiography of Henry M. Stanley.*

"I had to learn that that which was unlawful to a civilian was lawful to the soldier. The 'Thou shalt not' of the Decalogue, was now translated 'Thou shalt'. 'Thou shalt kill, lie, steal, blaspheme, covet, and hate'; for, by whatever fine names they were disguised, everyone practised these acts, from the President down to the private in the rear rank. The prohibition to do these things was removed, and indulgence in license and excess was permissible" (p. 168).

To all appearances, Stanley had already learnt to bend the Ten Commandments to his own advantage before he was discovered among "the Dixie Greys", but his descriptions of six years of terror in confusing, cruel and meaningless battles and confrontations resemble Stendahl's shaky ditch perspective of Waterloo. Stanley's opinion on the American Civil War, however, is pacifistic, which we can choose to interpret as a retrospective justification of his choice to desert repeatedly. It makes more sense, though, to interpret the narrative as a critical description of what Stanley refers to as the "curious 'volte-face' in morality": something he later on had reaffirmed by British officers' double moral standards, especially during the Emin Pasha Relief Expedition. Furthermore, Stanley's chilling and critical descriptions of the meaninglessness of the civil war point towards something else that would become important for his unique travels and travel accounts: he was by no means patriotic. In fact, there was a period at the end of the nineteenth century when he was often explicitly antinationalist. This period saw increasing tension between European countries, and in their relationships with the USA. This situation made nationalism the natural attitude for any text that wanted to appeal to a large audience. Among several factors that can help explain the controversy surrounding Stanley is his equivocal, inadequate or explicitly polemical representation of nationalism. This puts him in a central position for reappraisals of the history of colonisation and travel literature in a globalised perspective.

Stanley's reports from the American Indian Wars are practical introductions to the scenic-dramatic style of the travel books, which during his employment with the *New York Herald* developed towards New Journalism, the hallmark of this early international newspaper; at the same time they give indications of Stanley's methods of negotiating with the native Africans. Stanley's eyewitness reports from spectacular battles towards the end of the civil war attracted much attention due to their new visual and energetic narrative style. In the year that followed the war, 1865, his diary only briefly mentions a few towns spread out in the Wild West. Stanley was apparently, as Dorothy writes, filled with an "overflowing youthful energy, and an innate love of novelty and adventure" (p. 221), showing much interest in "the sights and novelties, the many-coloured life of the West". He was probably broke and roaming around without any sense of direction, and it was very lucky for him that he was chosen as a sort of press officer for General Hancock's quest against the Kiowa and Comanche Indians, and later on for General Sherman on "the Peace Commission to the Indians". These experiences as a press officer lead directly to his livelihood as a correspondent for *The Missouri Democrat*, and later as a freelancer for, among others, *The Times* and the *New York Herald* – of which the latter would become his employer on the African expeditions. Stanley managed to save up one thousand dollars, which made it possible for him to sign a contract with the *New York Herald* regarding his covering the British Expedition to Abyssinia (now Ethiopia). He had to meet the costs himself but was paid well for telegrams of "exclusive intelligence" – the telegrams that would come to result in his sensational breakthrough with a new type of hard-hitting report that had the entire world as stage and audience.

During the American Indian Wars Stanley developed a formula for dealing with native peoples. Under the colonisation of "the great prairies of the West" in the years that followed the civil war, he closely followed the establishment of the Union Pacific Railroad and military stations along the Powder River, and the conflicts between Native Americans and settlers. These articles were collected in two volumes in *My Early Travels and Adventures* (1885). In all its simplicity, Stanley's formula assumed that although the native populations' apprehensiveness towards the white colonists was understandable, it was also

an inevitable side-effect of progress and civilisation. The military intervention, and the allocation of reservations, must be understood as an attempt to save the natives from the consequences of their own savagery. The tactics mainly consisted of giving gifts and drawing up treaties through exclusive negotiations with individual chiefs, who had no other choice than to agree to peace and relinquish their land. In this way, strong tribes such as the Sioux and Cheyenne were isolated and could be defeated separately, for instance by burning down their villages. According to an addition by Dorothy, Stanley simply transferred this form of 'diplomacy' to Africa: "The tone in which Sherman, Henderson, and Commissioner Taylor spoke to the Indians, now as to warriors, now as to children, gave hints, which, later, Stanley put to good use. And the experience of the Indians suggests a parallel with that of the Congo natives as each met the whites" (p. 227). From a postcolonial perspective it makes sense that Stanley's operations in Africa be seen as genocide, in line with the white settlers' persecution of the Native Americans. However, Stanley's reports on the American Indian Wars also show a double position. On the one hand he agitates in dramatic detail against the horrifying customs of the natives, such as scalping, and clearly takes the white people's side; on the other hand he tries to moderate the readers' racist view of the 'savages'.

As Stanley suggests in the introduction to his autobiography, his character is created between the lines, partly through the foibles – "mannerisms" – that his behaviour to a large extent was built around. Internal forces in the narrative, however, cause this formative model to collapse, which becomes clear when we compare the autobiography with the archival evidence that tells a completely different story. This ghostly existence, while he could not and would not be Rowlands but was not allowed to be Stanley, was also when he learned to survive without being himself. Reading fiction filled his inner world with forbidden novels and romances whose heroic, sentimental and nostalgic models were to be transferred later to his spectacular reports. He was still a fatherless nobody, but in principle he could be anywhere and become *present* in the moments when he wrote about the world's hot spots: the opening of the Suez Canal, the war on Crete, the planned coup in Spain etc.

In this sense, he was the incarnation of the perfect traveller towards the turn of the century, when history seemed to stand still while the world was opening up beyond its frontiers. Stanley was in the right place at the right time, because he was in effect a man without a past or a history. He was but "a football to Chance", as he writes in the introduction to his autobiography. The autobiography was intended to be undisguised, but if we read between the lines, we see it sticks to presenting only loose fragments, entangled and twisted, about how Stanley was still only "confining myself to myself". This self was exclusively created in the writing moment, which – when it comes to Stanley – is always located somewhere on the map. In other words: Stanley is to be found *where* he is. This is made clear in Dorothy Stanley's use of the epitaph on the cover of the autobiography: the drawing of the map of Africa, and the travel books' descriptions of routes, places, landscapes and people are also attempts to create a stable identity, a signature, carved in map and stone alike.

Mr Stanley, I Presume?: New Journalism

John Rowlands became an American and found a new name for himself, which, for a long time, he used to cover up his past. However, he was not reborn in a formative sense, or in the sense of having been re-shaped or finding a new, stable identity. His appetite for news and adventure, so subtly described by Dorothy Stanley to indicate Stanley's drifting after Mr Stanley's death, lasted for many years and implicated an entire catalogue of possible fates with which he experimented – often under violent circumstances, falling foul of the law and desperately risking everything, his life included.

When Gordon Bennett, the infamous editor at *New York Herald*, sent him out to 'find' Livingstone and make an even greater scoop than the coverage of the British Expedition to Abyssinia, it appeared to be nothing more than a repetition of earlier times' restless adventures. At Zanzibar, Stanley was informed that Livingstone was not even interested in being found and that apart from that, he was unpredictable and hostile towards Europeans and reportedly living in promiscuous relationships with native women. Other rumours reported Livingstone long dead, devoured by the Dark Continent.

This picture of Livingstone was very different from that of him as an icon of pilgrimage and Victorianism, and it was this – according to Stanley's own version of the events – hat caused the distant, tentative and nervous greeting "Dr Livingstone, I presume?", which caused a lot of hullabaloo on both sides of the Atlantic and thus became an important factor in the canonisation of Livingstone's and Stanley's fame.

In *Dr. Livingstone, I Presume? Missionaries, Journalists, Explorers, and Empire* (2007), Clare Pettitt points out that the phrase was received very differently in Britain from in the USA, which contributed to the sensationalisation of the event. Both sides found Stanley's greeting amusing, because it indicated a lack of formality – the assumption was that the meeting took place as an unlikely coincidence in the middle of the African wilderness. While the British interpreted it as a comical display of Stanley's typical American awkwardness in regard to etiquette, the Americans understood it as an ironic and satirical joke about British imperialism. Whether inadvertently witty or misunderstood,

the phrase caught on in both Europe and the USA, creating an unprecedented publicity effect for the tale of the two explorers' far from coincidental meeting in Africa. This inherent misalignment in reception also enhanced the scepticism towards the story, which other parties, the Royal Geographical Society in particular, promoted for alternative reasons. The joke helped the story spread, while at the same time sowing doubt about the credibility of the entire affair, and both these factors contributed to the canonisation of the incident in popular culture.[12]

The Livingstone expedition established a pattern, refined during the following expeditions, of peace agreements with the natives with whom Stanley could speak as "children" and declarations of war against those he felt forced to address as "warriors". In his autobiography he describes it as the effect of a conscious decision to focus on the essential goal: "All I had to do was to free my mind from all else, and relieve it of every earthly desire but the finding of the man whom I was sent to seek. (...) Intense application to my task assisted me to forget all I had left behind, and all that might lie ahead in the future" (p. 255).

When the two men actually met, the somewhat worn-down Livingstone gave Stanley a friendly reception and offered him a meal in return for new supplies and news from the big world. Stanley, on his part, rewards the reader's perseverance with a narrative about the great explorer who willingly takes on the role as Stanley's long lost father. During their joint expedition on Lake Tanganyika, Livingstone teaches Stanley things he needs to know as an explorer, and while Stanley's description expresses only respect and admiration, it takes into consideration the worldwide audience who are led to believe that the object of the expedition is a valuable and slightly mysterious item. Stanley's iconicising portrait of Livingstone betrays several interrelated motives. First, it appears that at this point, when the rest of the world was shut out and past and present did not exist, Stanley could be reborn once again in a shape which linked him inextricably to the exploration of Africa. Secondly, the appreciation of this father figure, who Stanley would later come to defend doggedly in his first lecture for the Royal Geographical Society, also became an appreciation of his legacy as Livingstone's successor, accompanied by the hope that he had at long last invented an identity that was invaluably prestigious and highly durable. In his very first telegram to the *New York Herald*, Stanley introduced this legacy with quite detailed accounts of all of Livingstone's dramatic discoveries, before Livingstone himself had the chance to do so. He thereby claimed some sort of copyright on the story of Livingstone's achievements since *Missionary Travels* – under the pretence of defending him against various accusations. In this way, Stanley basically claimed Livingstone's discoveries as his own and later on published an extended version of them in *How I Found Livingstone*, as well as

Stanley on adventures in Somalia, 1869, dressed in the Oriental style, probably inspired by the most extravagant Africa explorer of the era, Richard Francis Burton, who published *Lake Regions of Equatorial Africa* in 1860. The image stems from one of Stanley's early trips, which were more hazardous than grand, yet proved his striking determination to become an explorer, or act like one, before he actually became one. Twenty years later, Stanley had solved the big question that Burton and others had been forced to leave unsolved, regarding the Nile and the great African lakes.

taking over his predecessor's patent on solving the geographical mysteries of Central Africa. In Stanley's telegrams to the *New York Herald*, the conversation between the two men after their first meeting is described in his usual staggering and captivating style:

"Then began conversation; I forget what about; (...) I know the Doctor was talking, and I was answering mechanically. (...) Every hair of his head and beard, every line and wrinkle of his face, the wan face, the fatigued form, were all imparting the intelligence to me, which so many men so much desired. It was deeply interesting intelligence and unvarnished truths these mute but certain witnesses gave. They told me of the real nature of the work in which he was engaged. Then his lips began to give me details – lips that cannot lie. I cannot repeat what he said. (...) The man's heart was gushing out, not in hurried sentences, in rapid utterances, in quick relation – but in still and deep words. (...) Upon my first introduction to him Livingstone was to me like a huge tome, with a most unpretending binding. Within, the book might contain much valuable lore and wisdom, but its exterior gave no promise of what was within. Thus, outside, Livingstone gave no token – except being rudely dealt with by the wilderness – of what element of power and talent lay within" (*Despatches*, pp. 94-95).

From Stanley's *My Early Travels and Adventures in America and Asia* (1895). Stanley's telegrams from the Indian Wars in America and other subsequent hot spots tell of a world that changed at a staggering pace and could only be captured in a new, direct, and gripping style by a writer who was moving at the same pace. Stanley developed from an adventurer to a reporter.

Stanley is reading Livingstone like a book, with peculiar emphasis on the fact that what he is saying cannot be repeated – just like the conversation itself, which is described as a hypnotic transference of profound truths between mute witnesses. As a matter of fact, the reader is hypnotised, which enables Stanley to take over the entire subsequent narrative without letting on that he is stealing the story from Livingstone. On closer inspection, we are looking at an extensive dissection or "study" of Livingstone, one that is in many ways more rude and transgressive than the vicious rumours Stanley's narrative keeps returning to and consequentially keeps alive. Stanley's presentation forms a double text: for the first time in his life he encounters the prospect of a caring relationship between father and son, while his exuberant expressions of admiration function as an illusion from within which Livingstone himself is not allowed to speak.

In this sense, Stanley's discourse is similar when he scrutinises Livingstone 'the book' and when he describes the exploration; in his attitudes to both Livingstone and Africa we are dealing with an appropriation of the same basic type. Stanley's discovery of Livingstone as a father figure, and his subjugation as a son and inheritor of Livingstone's project, are performed through complex rhetorical agendas designed to strip Livingstone of his authority while ascribing the father role to him. For Stanley, this meant that his identity was linked entirely to the discovery of Africa and his next expedition was in fact presented as the completion of his filial obligations that he had taken on in return for Livingstone's fatherly recognition. It also meant that the identity Stanley had conjured up through his reading of Livingstone must be recognised as a

"The American Traveller

HENRY STANLEY,

who was cruelly robbed by the Turks on September 18, 1866, and stripped, by overwhelming numbers, of his arms, passports, letter of credit, and over $ 4000 in cash, will lecture on his

TRAVELS AND ADVENTURES IN TURKEY
AND
LIFE IN THE ORIENT!!!!

Doors open at 7 o'clock. Lecture commences at 7½ o'clock.

Mr. Stanley served in the American Navy from January 1862, till the fall of Wilmington, at which he was present, in January 1865.

He then took a grand tour through the interior of Asia Minor, from which he has just returned.

During his lecture he will appear in the costume of a Turkish naval officer.

He will also show to the audience a Saracen coat of mail, needlework by a Turkish maiden, a Turkish Fez and the elegant cap of a Greek pirate, a Turkish Chibouque, a piece of skull from the tomb of Sultan Bajozet, commonly called "Lightning" or "Thunderer", a whetstone from Mount Olympus, near the ancient city of Troy, of which Homer and Virgil sang about 2,000 years ago.

There will also be on exhibition a Firman, signed by the present Sultan of Turkey, Abdul Azziz. Also, a passport signed by our Secretary of State, William H. Seward.

Mr. Stanley will repeat the Moslem call to prayer after the manner of the Muezzin, in the sacred Arabic language used by 140,000,000 people.

The lecturer will close the exercise of the evening by singing a Turkish song à la Turque ...." (Despatches, p. 420).

(*Stanley's Despatches*, p. 420).

legitimate version of the truth. Based on his unpleasant experience with his deceitful parents, but also as a tactical afterthought, Stanley made sure that Livingstone wrote letters to various people, including Gordon Bennett, to document that the historical meeting actually took place in the real world, not just in fiction.

However, in the very moment Stanley believed he had not only conquered the world but also found himself, the ingenious construction showed threatening signs of collapse. Some doubted that Stanley had even been to Africa, and many regarded the story to be a fake. The sensational and hypnotising style of a lecture he gave at the Royal Geographical Society placed him in a suspicious

light, exacerbated by numerous rumours claiming that his American identity was a fabrication with spectacular fragments of his real biography appearing in the newspapers, often outrageously misrepresented. In America, former disreputable acquaintances were interviewed to reveal wild stories about risky expeditions during the American Civil War, when Stanley deserted to Asia Minor together with a couple of comrades in the hope of making a fortune and experiencing Oriental adventures.

Lewis Noe's interview in *The Sun* on 29 August 1872 (printed in full in *Stanley's Despatches to the New York Herald*) leaves that very impression, and it is difficult to repudiate with its many details, photos and other documentation. Noe recounts how Stanley, on arrival in Istanbul, earned money for the penniless party by forging references from a fictitious father in New York. Then he had made for him an American naval officer's uniform – but it sported Turkish buttons, which the reporter was able to spot in a photograph. The photo was part of a series of portraits in Noe's possession showing Stanley assuming very diverse identities, including in Oriental costume as Khan Bahadoor, Burburra, Soumalé, with a turban, Turkish trousers and a meerschaum cigar holder, a small black boy standing in front of him and a big black woman behind him. "The group makes a decidedly novel picture", the reporter adds to Noe's story about Stanley in fact being Welsh, not English or American. He relates how they deserted together from the navy ship the Minnesota in Portsmouth, then moves on to the main story of their hazardous travels in Turkey.

The group had no money, but Stanley turned out to know a vast number of scams to help them along the way; he admitted early on to Noe that he was planning a robbery that would enable him to take out a big loan on the basis of false documents and then escape to Persia before the scam was discovered. The opportunity arose when they met a lone Turk with two horses. Stanley improvised, offering Noe as a sex toy to the Turk. While he was distracted, Stanley tried to kill the Turk with his sword. However, the man managed to escape, though Stanley fired several shots after him. Later on, the victim caught up with the Americans; during their captivity they were threatened and beaten, and Noe was raped several times.

At that point Stanley launched the initial plan, inventing a version of the incident in which it was the Americans who had been assaulted. He managed to bring so much doubt to the factual circumstances that the local authorities did not dare reject a court case. The eloquent Stanley successfully convinced them that his version was true, and this, in combination with the international political implications, got them off the hook. Stanley claimed to have lost cash and bonds worth about $1,500 and, with reference to his wealthy father in Liberty Street, New York, he managed to get a loan of £150 from the American consul,

Stanley as sentimental explorer. Photograph insert in *How I Found Livingstone* (1872).

which enabled him to visit his mother in Wales – where the naval uniform failed to have the desired effect.

When Stanley returned to America, he once again tried to make money from his Oriental failure. Lewis Noe handed a printed poster about a planned tour of talks across the USA to the reporter. The tour was not a success, but the poster displays important characteristics of Stanley's earliest ideas of "travel", his fluid concept of identity, credibility and testimony, as well as his talent for the spectacular and almost exhibitionistic, which was perhaps his most prominent quality throughout his life:

Although Stanley after these exposés mobilised anyone he could convince to speak out for him, Noe's tale is still convincing, not least because it exposes him personally. It does not appear spiteful or cunning, but rather as a confession of his role in the evidently chaotic circumstances during the civil war and what Stanley in his autobiography calls the U-turn – the "volte face" – in regard to law and morals. Furthermore, Noe produced a number of letters that demonstrated Stanley's many changes of name and identity and his formidable talent for imitating other people's handwriting. On that basis, Noe did not think that it necessarily substantiated Stanley's credibility when Livingstone's family, shortly before, had confirmed the authenticity of the letters and diaries brought home by Stanley; he believed that Stanley could easily have invented Livingstone's texts and imitated his handwriting.

In London, Stanley was under fire. He was still accused of forging Livingstone's letters; it was said, for instance, that Livingstone did not have any knowledge of the American literature mentioned in them, that the style was not his and that if the two had met at all, Livingstone must have found Stanley and not the other way around. The press portrayed Stanley as a charlatan, and the Royal Geographical Society sowed doubt about the validity of both Livingstone's and Stanley's discoveries. Meanwhile, Gordon Bennett from the *New York Herald* arranged the entire course of events after Stanley's return so that the newspaper would profit as much as possible from the commotion. He waited months, until the general opinion in Britain was that Stanley's discovery was a fictitious invention, before publishing the letters from Livingstone that irrefutably conjured away any doubts about the expedition. Subsequently, Bennett launched an attack against the Royal Geographical Society, accusing them of being jealous, conspiratorial and scientifically unreliable. This shocked the hallowed institution who, in its own understanding, was anything but that. A further aspect of Bennett's spin on Stanley's authority was the clever exploitation of the mutual negative feelings between the British and the Americans. It was almost unbearable for the Royal Geographical Society and the British government to have to accept the fact that Americans were behind the rescue operation that they themselves had been unable or unwilling to carry out. It did not help that the British national icon, Livingstone, praised Stanley and the *New York Herald* while sharply criticising the British consul at Zanzibar and others for inaction and ignorance. This turned the situation upside-down, causing the British press to launch an offensive against the Royal Geographical Society, whose attack on Stanley now backfired and undermined the society's own authority. Stanley was safe, he was granted an audience with Queen Victoria, his enemies had to apologise and the Royal Geographical Society reluctantly gave him a gold medal.

However, stories that brought into doubt Stanley's identity kept resurfac-

Taken by the same 'Stereophonic Company' as the previous photograph. From *Autobiography*.

ing, mentioning John Rawlings, John Rollins and other names he had used in his chaotic past. So when he was lecturing in America, with the ambition of earning $50,000 from the Livingstone affair, he was still on shaky ground. Initially, he was welcomed by an enormous crowd, who showed up to celebrate the humiliation of the Royal Geographical Society rather than out of any interest in geographical discoveries from a distant continent. Having learnt from his mistake of talking in an overly popular style with excessive use of gesture at the lecture for the Royal Geographical Society, Stanley chose to stick to dry, scientifically detailed lectures for the American audiences who – expecting great entertainment, provocative attacks and daring anecdotes – were surprised at Stanley's awkward performances. Once more he was ridiculed in the newspapers, his former employer the *New York Herald* launching the attack on his awful

"Dr. Livingstone, I presume", from *How I Found Livingstone*. Stanley bitterly regretted the silly remark, which spread as a joke in both Europe and America, albeit for different reasons. The handshake could be seen as the symbol of a new world order in which England and America would unite to promote freedom and democracy in the rest of the world. Aside from being a contributing factor to Stanley's fame, it can be seen as the first global media event in history, and the launch of a new Anglo-American public.

performance, his way of speaking, his tone of voice, pace, pronunciation, gestures, etc. Consequentially, his much promoted tour of the USA was cancelled.

These public confrontations and misinterpretations on one hand expose Stanley's vulnerable position as a bastard and a parvenu in high society and on the other hand illustrate fundamental changes in the understanding of science, society, written and oral dissemination and high and popular culture. They are also symptomatic of the national characteristics of the American and British public cultures.

With his authority being questioned at every turn, Stanley continued his struggle to create a lasting role for himself as an explorer and an identity that would not be undermined by the tales about the life he had in fact lived. The journey in Turkey was retold as a travesty – a highly theatrical grotesque comedy full of disguises and curious events. However, to Stanley it was a deadly serious performative staging of the character he never managed to become on the actual journey. The very peculiar repertoire of scenes and curiosities announced on the poster can, of course, be interpreted as a coolly calculated attempt to meet the expectations of popular culture about the Orient as the cradle of civilisation, but its disorganised, erratic and fragmented nature also reflects Stanley's no less fragmented self image. Fact and fiction are mixed in an attempt to create the image of a 'real' explorer who retrospectively – through the audience's approval – turns the scattered fragments of his own identity into a journey of true exploration.

Similarly, we find in the description of the meeting with Livingstone a peculiar theme: Stanley assumes a hypnotised state in which the Livingstone book opens up to him and transfers mute testimonies to the son and heir, who absorbs the father-predecessor's authority without confronting compromising questions about his rightful claim or merits. In *How I Found Livingstone* this construction, simultaneously related to authority, testimony and identity, is performed as a court case in which Stanley defends Livingstone against an endless series of hypothetical attacks. What he actually does is take over Livingstone's authority which, compared with the journalist's perseverance, appears old and frail. At the same time, the book's 'courtroom' is a written version, exclusively edited by Stanley, of the highly critical debate after his lecture at the Royal Geographical Society, where he was asked to account for his nationality and past, and where the entire exchange to a vast extent concerned the contrasts between America and Britain, between classes and between the academic geographers' formal criteria for scientific authority and Stanley's field study observations. While Stanley ought to have presented the scientific account to the Royal Geographical Society and saved the entertaining version for his American audiences, the spin continued on the other side of the Atlantic, where his talks were once again rendered fraudulent and his authority was shaken. In the time immediately after the discovery of Livingstone, it was extremely difficult for Stanley to claim authority, but his travel book *How I Found Livingstone* changed things.

Stanley's narrative about Livingstone's campaigns against slavery is in many ways an exaggeration, given that the pilgrim had long ago ceased his missionary activities to concentrate on the Nile. Still, the tale of the handshake between the two men symbolised a new world order, in which Britain and America incarnated a common aspiration to promote freedom and democracy in the rest of the world. The handshake could be seen both as a reconciliation after the British support for the Southern States during the American Civil War, and as an establishment of a new, common Anglo-American public sphere. As Claire Pettitt points out in *Dr. Livingstone, I Presume?*, this was the first global media event in history, motivated by two factors: firstly, by a beneficial political turn

in the relationship between Britain and America, as the joint effort towards abolitionism found iconic expression in the image of the handshake between the Briton and the – assumed – American; secondly, the development of technology that allowed the press to operate on a worldwide scale, thus creating the conditions for a new political, global British-American public order as well as a "celebrity culture".

Gordon Bennett already used the modern term 'world press' and sent his reporters to the world's hot spots. Putting his faith in New Journalism's vivid and scenic descriptions of the political through the "human interest" perspective, the shortened interval between event and editors facilitated by the telegraph, and the shortened production time and bigger circulations made possible by the rotary press, Gordon Bennett had already acted as a pioneer in globalised media. His well-planned global news report followed closely in the wake of a transatlantic copper cable laid between Britain and America in 1866, making it the first major story to be communicated to both continents simultaneously.

The media hype surrounding the discovery of Livingstone had both negative and positive influences on Stanley's performative biography. Within the textual universe of the travel books, he was able to employ a broad range of rhetorical techniques and figures of transition in hypothetical experiments with vast numbers of identities; however, the publication of telegram articles and travel books confronted him with new contexts and conditions for global communication, challenging his private self-images. Stanley's texts became part of a public sphere in which, towards the end of the nineteenth century, new mass media increased their influence on the political opinions of the press and popular literature, putting old institutions such as the Royal Geographical Society under pressure. Stanley's use of a wide range of stylistic traits from New Journalism exposed a historical change in the relation between private and public spheres.

As was the case when it was relaunched in the 1960s, the first wave of New Journalism was characterised by a far more personalised style and approach than existed in "old journalism". Stanley signed his articles from the Indian Wars, and he used interviews and chats with Wild Bill Hickok and others. He also relied heavily on"showing" rather than "telling" and cut out summaries in favour of action-packed present-tense accounts of events. In the telegram articles and travel books we find the same very personal perspective, putting Stanley at the centre of events that are described in a pretended temporal and spatial present.

"Showing", as a formal element, is his staple form of presentation. As textual analyses will show in later chapters, there are often a plethora of points of view, which not only create close and effective visualisation and simulation of intimacy and immediacy, but also personalise the presentation in regard to both narrator and reader. Unlike the many travellers before him – 'mobile libraries' who lectured learnedly about different cultures – Stanley positions himself as a peer who appeals to the reader's senses. At the same time, the increasing tendency to personalisation is, in New Journalism as well as in Stanley's travel books, filtered through mass culture's tendency to anonymise: the newspapers become fetishised commodities and intimacy is paraded about in a trivialising way. This is done, for instance, via pseudo-interviews with celebrities that purport intimacy, orality and authenticity, but in reality follow a rigidly codified practice. This duality is inherent in the massive expansion of the media's sphere of influence and the thematic space, which is also apparent in Stanley's first conversation with Livingstone. The interviews are described through a kind of anonymising hypnosis and highly visual metaphors concerning the transferral of the "mute" testimony via the reading of a sacred book in a worn binding.

In the article "Journalistic Discourses and Constructions of Modern Knowledge", Kate Campbell suggests – with reference to cultural theorists such as Anthony Giddens and Andreas Huyssen – that New Journalism should be viewed not in contrast but in parallel to the development of the artistic and intellectual avant-garde at the end of the nineteenth century, and as one of several modernism*s*.[13] Campbell provides examples of "high art" authors such as Flaubert and Henry James, who make extensive use of themes and techniques similar to the ones used in New Journalism: great variation in point of view and "showing" techniques, and exposure and expropriation of hitherto private and intimate areas, in order to disclose and make public hidden and often sensational stories about real life. In addition to this comes a fascination with the mundane, which is depicted through visualised facets of trivial details of "human interest" and scepticism towards metaphysical explanations. Similarly, New Journalism creates a world which, like Émile Zola's novels, fascinates and tantalises us with its fragmented and often scandalising "graphic scraps" and its "seeing observation" which, according to Campbell, resulted in much more sign-attentive, semiotic and sceptical newspaper readers than before. This last aspect is underpinned by encouraging readers to challenge authorities that had until then been safe – conservative institutions such as the Royal Geographical Society, or ones which were automatically granted with privileges, something we will return to in connection with the scandal surrounding the British officers' conduct in the Congo. A shared characteristic of "high art" and "low journalism" is that their respective modernisms challenged Victorian ideological ideas about a homogeneous, unified national culture, instead displaying a shattered, multi-perspectival image of several concurrent, competing and non-commensurable realities. This reading perspective will be examined further in the chapter "Prose: A Framework and Reading Perspective".

World Literature

The fact that Stanley continued New Journalism in his travel accounts opens up a new understanding of both his impact on readers and the opposition to the texts among contemporary conservative institutions as well as in more recent interpretations. New Journalism and Modernist art – though they often claim to be each other's worst enemies – both present a fragmented and modern image of a world in motion, in which contemporary mundane *faits divers* reveal wider perspectives on the imminent future than what the modern authors called the "inherited lies".

It follows that there is also a critical dimension to Stanley's stylistic balance: the role play, theatricality and personalised narratives indicate that the perspective changes as the journey progresses, creeps along the ground or surveys everything. Although the texts are invaded by romances and Homeric epic, the style and method snap up everyday "graphic scraps", which appear curious and contingent at the same time.

One of the consequences, however, is that New Journalism relinquishes control of the message, medium and reception in return for critically combining the traditional travel account with "low journalism", high culture with mass culture and traditional patriotism with declared post-nationalism. Whereas a newspaper could previously have acted as a mouthpiece for a political party, an editorial line or well-defined national interests, New Journalism created a platform that facilitated fast profiling of opinions and established authorship but also a "celebrity culture" in which a person could be famous one day and forgotten the next.[14] The destabilised, and reflective consciousness that characterises modernity in both "high art" and "New Journalism" also affected writers who attempted to achieve author identities. In Henry James, as well as Stanley, we find these endless mirror rooms that indicate the same fundamental doubt about whether the readers and the market will ultimately bestow any authority upon writers and their narratives. Readers and the market are ungrateful, and the radical doubt about systems of opinion and authors' authority in which New Journalism revelled contributed to Stanley's abysmal identity crisis. This theme will be thoroughly examined in the *fin de siècle* motives of Stanley's *In Darkest Africa.*

When Stanley describes his first journey to Africa as a rebirth, it is in a more definitive sense than when he invented Henry Morton Stanley in New Orleans. In Africa, Stanley's theatricality – i.e. his extrovert performance in the role of writer, explorer and world conqueror – was in accordance with a performative creation of self that was simultaneously a performative creation of the landscape and continent. In autobiographical retrospect, Stanley's African rebirth is described through striking comparisons with the Bible on one side and the

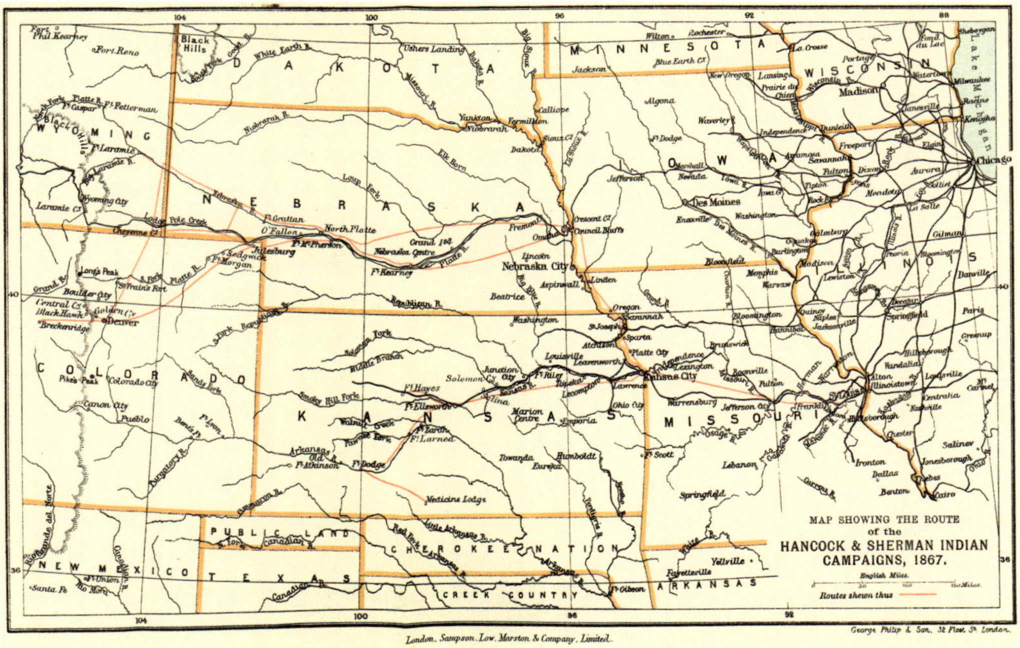

With his descriptions of battles and peace negotiations with the Indians in 1867, and interviews with celebrities in the Wild West, Stanley developed his new writing style, known as New Journalism. From volume one of Stanley's *My Early Travels in America and Asia* (1895).

newspapers on the other: "The one reminded me that, apart from God, my life was but a bubble of air, and it bade me remember my Creator; the other fostered arrogance and worldliness" (*Autobiography*, p. 254). The newspapers restrained him in a world where everything was replaceable; they represented everything he had been and wished to leave behind on his arrival in Africa. Loneliness taught him that newspapers are a waste of time, while he considered the Bible to be an inseparable part of "the deep melancholy of African scenery" that allowed him to feel at home in the strange surroundings and begin to know himself. The description of religious feelings, however, is closely related to "ghosts of bygone yearnings, haunting every cranny of the brain with numbers of baffled hopes and unfulfilled aspirations" (p. 253). Being in Africa distanced him from the world of newspapers and "worldliness", whose capriciousness had controlled his earlier life, while the Bible and the landscape might help him forget the ghosts of his past. The hypnosis that reaffirmed the father-son relationship with Livingstone corresponded to Stanley's religious experience of ablution and

After the success of the Indian letters, Gordon Bennett of the *New York Herald* dispatched Stanley as a correspondent to cover the British Expedition to Abyssinia in 1868. Having triumphed by making the British victory known before anyone else, Stanley was sent to Egypt, Crete, Spain, the opening of the Suez Canal, and through Persia and India to Caucasus, until he eventually arrived in Paris, where Bennett allegedly uttered: "Find Livingstone!" The letters in the second volume of *My Early Travels in America and Asia* (1895) "are the result of that long journey which was a kind of apprenticeship to the longer and more difficult one I was to continue into Unknown Africa", writes Stanley in the preface.

oblivion as different aspects of the same experience, and feed into his alternating descriptions of uncanny and blissful "self-forgetfulness".

Stanley's 'African' rebirth was related to a cutting back of everything that was antiquated and mundane, while he attempted to create a stable biography in a forward movement through the landscape. The landscape would subsequently be represented in the drawing of maps with routes, rivers and names - equivalent to Dorothy's signs on Bula Matari's headstone and the cover of *Autobiography*. The mundane, however, would return in the shape of New Journalism's textual style and methods, just as the past would return in the shape of romances and Homer's poetry.

While the newspapers belonged in the sphere of the short-lived, mundane and trivial, the Bible functioned as a catalyst for Stanley's African rebirth by resetting his biography and emptying his consciousness of everything except the journey's goal. From there, the mapping of Africa became linked to Stanley's creation of a new identity, which at the same time meant that he would take on a new role as traveller. Before he came to Africa, he had been a vagabond of a world whose routes and destinations switched and changed in a random, chaotic course. His escape to America, and the coordinates of his destinations during the civil war, were on one hand a traversing of several conflicting identities and nationalities - perhaps most evident in his 'expedition' to Turkey - but on the other hand, the routes he followed as a roustabout, sailor and freelance journalist created a narrative without direction or goals.

According to Dorothy Stanley, the diary consisted of mere brief cues about places and dates with unintelligible comments. In 1862 Stanley visited his mother in Wales; harvested in Maryland; worked on an oyster boat; and served as a sailor on ships to the West Indies, Italy and Spain, where a shipwreck is condensed in the comment "Wrecked off Barcelona. Crew lost, in the night. Stripped naked, and swam to shore. Barrack of Carabineers ... demanded my papers". In Brooklyn, New York: "Boarding with Judge X--. Judge drunk; tried to kill his wife with hatchet; attempted three times. - I held him down all night. Next morning, exhausted; lighted cigar in parlour: wife came down - insulted and raved at me for smoking in her house!" (*Autobiography*, p. 220). In 1864 he was back in the navy, where he had his debut as a journalist reporting on the bombardment of Fort Fisher. Over the course of a few months in 1865: "St. Joseph, Missouri - across the Plains, - Indians, Salt Lake City, - Denver, - Black Hawk, - Omaha" (p. 221). In 1866 Stanley threw himself into a potentially fatal raft expedition on the Missouri and other rivers in the hope of getting through the Indian districts, all the way to Asia; he actually succeeded in doing so. In 1867 the Indian Wars broke out in the west, and then the big cities in the east. In 1868 Stanley

got his first real job as a reporter, covering the British Expedition to Abyssinia, followed by a brief love affair on Crete; he then travelled to Smyrna, Marseille, Barcelona, London – and Paris, where he was summoned by Gordon Bennett for the expedition to find Livingstone under the circumstances that would become emblematic for New Journalism. Bennett's *New York Herald* was – as mentioned above – the first newspaper to promote the so-called New Journalism or 'yellow press', which mixed bold reports with "celebrity interviews, lavish illustrations, society gossip, salacious news" and "a guide to every prostitute in New York able to publicise her wares".[15]

Stanley's rushed zigzag movements across the globe did not stop when he was given the task of finding Livingstone. According to Bennett's cool calculation, the 'discovery' of Livingstone must be timed perfectly. Most importantly, a subtle balance was required to create the appropriate hype around Livingstone, who only a few people at the time were really interested in, and to set up a race between rival expeditions, which Stanley would obviously win. It was cool business, and Stanley was sent on yet another tour of the world's political hot spots in order to cover up the planned Livingstone scoop. Bennett's famous "Find Livingstone!" was accompanied by an equally important order to wait a year before commencing the search. Therefore, Stanley had to leave to cover the opening of the Suez Canal, then continue to Jerusalem, Odessa, Istanbul, the Crimean Peninsula, Caucasus, Teheran, Isfahan, Persepolis, Bombay – and finally Zanzibar, where he would prepare the Livingstone expedition. According to rumours, Livingstone had married an African princess and did not in any circumstances wish to be 'found'. The way Stanley writes about his rebirth in Africa, and his insistence on creating a picture of Livingstone as a father who welcomes a son, seem pathetic. Nevertheless, the creation of a constant figure appears logical in the light of the speed with which Stanley had been visiting places that ceased to be places because they only existed for the brief moment they were exposed in the newspapers' spotlight. On his arrival in Africa, Stanley's experience was that the world was permanently disappearing, which made all places and events equal and equally valid, while the Bible on the other hand set the counter to zero and created a definitive forwards path for a double inscription in biography and landscape.

In the same way that Stanley's biography was in front of him and created through his performative self-discovery and discovery of Africa – while his former self was left in oblivion and forgetful lies – the success of the travels and travel books was due to his persevering attempts to reject the world as a mundane place. He only partly succeeded in doing this, as the mundane and the modern returned in the mixed prose and New Journalism he never abandoned stylistically in his travel accounts.

The books *Through the Dark Continent* and *In Darkest Africa*, among others, became world literature due to a number of factors. First, the travel accounts are what can be termed 'creators of worlds'; not only did they change the map of the continent, they also played an important role in what has been called "the shape of Africa". Stanley rejected "worldliness", understood as the mundane, modern and fragmented requirements of life and identity; however, the worldly returned in the travel books' attempts to draw maps and create worlds. Secondly, Stanley tried to reject the unholy newspaper prose from his travel accounts, but New Journalism shines through on all textual levels in his visualising and essayistic style that merges effortlessly with that of his literary idol Homer, who also favoured vision, immediacy and the present moment.

Stanley was interested in international copyrights and insisted on simultaneous, transnational publications. This, of course, shows he was trying to maximise the earnings on the books, which – as noted by Dorothy in her introduction to the biography – was the only profit Stanley made in Africa. However, the transnational distribution was also important because it enabled him to convey one of his main principles: that the civilisation of Africa must not be subject to any national interests but rather a united American-European project. His civilisation discourse in the travel books is rooted in this 'world opinion' and underpinned by his ideas – typical of the period – that free trade and "human rights" were two sides of the same coin. Hence, Stanley's own transnational identity is mirrored in both the global literary launch of the travel accounts and their role as creators of worlds. Later on, Stanley would be engaged in King Léopold's service, in principle closely connected with the ideals behind État Indépendant du Congo, which he and many others naïvely thought of as a philanthropic organisation. The Emin Pasha Relief Expedition also took place early in the race for Africa, while national states did not have or desire the same colonial influence as the missionary movements and the trading companies. Stanley's performative "opening up" of Africa – which apart from his work as coloniser was the books' main effect as inscription and world creation – was not intended as an invitation to individual states; the partition of Africa was a post-Stanley phenomenon.

Compared to the learned cosmopolitans of the eighteenth century or authors such as Goethe, who promoted the concept of world literature in 1827, Stanley was a citizen of the world in a much more concrete sense. His transnational travels took place in a world that was itself in motion, yet to be completely mapped. In the same way that the prosaic turn towards the essay in the renaissance was linked to the discovery of the new world, Stanley's prose was very much world-renowned and directed towards the new world. He created a transnational literary genre through his modernist transformation of travel literature

as a genre, both as a revolt against conservative and national institutions and as a result of the newly globalised conditions for production and distribution.

These conditions, in combination with Stanley's unique personal situation, formed the basis of literature that defied a number of criteria in regard to art and good taste but on the other hand met other criteria, e.g. pertaining to innovation, perfection and complexity. From this perspective it is interesting that the contemporary exclusion of Stanley from 'literature' is typically justified by the same criteria that were used by the conservative British institutions he provoked in the nineteenth century. Claims of Stanley's political incorrectness and his trivialising of the travel literature genre – claims that often follow hand in hand – were and are still based on the ideal of the sentimental traveller who brings his own culture and nationality with him as a conciliatory and totalising medium that facilitates a friendly, sensible dialogue. Stanley's travel literature, on the other hand, is a modernised genre, updated with regard to the globalisation of the media and consequent changes in the perception of the world, the world market and the formation of identities. Stanley's modernism is far from trivial, although it encompasses and integrates exciting and innovative aspects of high and low culture that had previously been separated: mundane like New Journalism, magical like art.

Compared to other travellers, Stanley was far more flexible: he did not carry with him a colonial library of tailor-made imperialistic opinions, nor was he an out-and-out representative of Victorian culture. Rather, he was anti-literary, modern, transnational and incredibly inventive in how he pieced together the scraps at his disposal. He did not write for the educated upper classes, a fact that caused him many problems, but put on plays in his travel books, often allowing for improvised linguistic situations – something that was seldom seen in the travel literature of the nineteenth century. Stanley's alleged ruthlessness also deserves to be judged with less bias than the usual idea of him being the quintessence of all colonial terror. His companions, Jameson, Barttelot and Jephson etc., were far more brutal than Stanley, who spoke native languages and knew and respected his subordinates; due to their ideas about class privilege and their ingrained conceptions of spiritual superiority, these new arrivals conducted their journeys in Africa on the basis of racism and imperialistic ideology. Stanley insisted that the globalisation of the market was a liberating and equality-creating power, thus contributing to accelerating capitalist imperialism towards the turn of the century. Compared with fundamental conservative ideas about national and racial hegemony, the globalisation of the market also had an emancipatory effect.

The more general accusation often made against Stanley in relation to the development in the Congo is also misleading. It is true that the construction of the first posts and infrastructures took place under harsh conditions, where any opposition was crushed with force as described in *The Congo and the founding of its Free State: a story of work and exploration* (1885). As a ground rule, however, Stanley tried to inspire discipline in his men, and he was a highly accomplished negotiator with local authorities, pragmatically looking to avoid costly and tiring conflicts. He criticised most of his subordinate officers for being incompetent and morally tarnished, and for getting into unnecessary conflicts with the natives. On his way up the Congo River on the Emin Pasha Relief Expedition, he saw his old posts, now derelict and demoralised, and was grateful that he was no longer responsible for colonial administration. In the introduction to *In Darkest Africa* Stanley warns against the slave-like oppression of the natives, of which he had seen many examples, especially in Sudan, claiming that it was the main obstacle to the civilisation process. Only when Europeans were ready to respect the natives as equals and respect their right to own property, he wrote, would there be a basis for free trade, civilisation and Christianity (p. 9). It is fair to assume that Stanley's plans for philanthropic civilisation and free trade were not at this early stage in the history of the Free State counteracted by de facto trade embargos and worsened conditions for the natives. Trade at this early stage was – as the British Consul Roger Casement wrote some years later in a critical report – flourishing, and natives as well as Europeans seemed to be profiting.

Today, there are many simplifications in the history of travel writing in the nineteenth century that are based on a romanticised view, continuing a legacy from orientalism in which sentimentalism was central and pragmatics such as Stanley were ostracised. This perception has favoured Livingstone because he fits in with the literary and aesthetic standards of literary history, while Stanley's big break as a writer for the masses was connected to his position as a mundane reporter in 'low journalism'. Before returning to Stanley, the following chapters will draw up some of the basic conditions for Stanley's prose and for the reading perspective that will be employed both to re-evaluate him and to read Congo's literary history of the twentieth century.

3 Prose: A Framework and Reading Perspective

Stanley's travel books are examples of prose in a world of prose. In the introduction to this study, the texts' multiplicity of strategies and discourses was presented. The plurality of meaning-creating and aesthetic strategies in Stanley's texts will be examined further in textual analyses which will also elaborate on the prose perspective. This perspective points two ways, so to speak: on the one hand paving the way for literary-historical interrelations between descriptions of the Congo by Stanley, Conrad, Mirbeau and Naipaul; on the other, drawing up characteristics of the history of prose that have rarely been given specific attention in literary studies. While this study of European-American travel accounts from the Congo is intended as a contribution to the understanding of other mechanisms in the western perception of non-western regions on global terms, it is also – due to its text examples – an appraisal of the characteristics and mechanisms of the contemporary history of prose.

Only a few, tentative attempts have been made to historicise prose, which is telling of the way we perceive prose today as the natural state of written language – the raw material from which genres have emerged historically – instead of a norm that gained ground over a long, differentiated historical process and should be understood as a specific discursive practice. Wlad Godzich and Jeffrey Kittay's *The Emergence of Prose: An essay in Prosaics* (1987) was the first attempt to interpret prose as a domain for creating meaning that – contrary to our traditional understanding – comes *before* rather than *after* versified texts.

Godzich and Kittay date the emergence of European prose to late medieval times, substantiating this with detailed textual analyses of texts from the thirteenth century – particularly French examples – which explicitly turn away from the predominant versified form that was used by singers and so-called "jugglers". This prose was presented as a more truthful representation of historic events, while the rhyming, versified texts were characterised as distorted and untruthful, because the jugglers focused more on the situation, themselves and the effect of the rhyme on the audience than on the event described. The author quotes from the introduction to a prose chronicle from 1226: "For there never can be rhymed / A story where there has not been added / A lie to get a rhyme".[16] The fact that this defence of prose was written in verse illustrates the obstacles the emergent genre needed to overcome. The juggler's performative creation of meaning, in which truth was contingent, was gradually replaced as prose developed a number of mechanisms that enabled it – within its internal

Paul Gauguin's travel book *NoaNoa*, written during his stay in Tahiti around 1900, is a collage of images, travel account, creation myth, and poetics. Gauguin's journey and travel book aimed to establish a new beginning for the art of painting, but it is the prose that recreates what is European on new terms.

system of references – to substantiate the truth about an event outside the text. The spreading of written culture due to French translations, the increase in Latin texts, transcriptions of versified texts and the new bureaucracy's need for documentation helped prose spread as a form that apparently did not rely on interpretation, making it unbiased. According to Godzich and Kittay, a particularly important characteristic of prose in its initial phase was its attempt to avoid association with a single performing subject, genre or discourse, instead appearing as a generalised, often anonymised linguistic technique that was open to a plethora of discourses and cross-forms. This demanded something new of readers – an ability to read actively, assuming different, fleeting positions and leaping from one discourse to the next.

Prose is para-discursive and dialogic; Godzich and Kittay refer to Bakhtin's studies of the novel as an anti-genre which, in its responsibility towards the unfinished, continuously adopts and overwrites other genres and invents new dynamic narrative positions. While Bakhtin has his eye on prose and the history of prose, he also has a tendency to remain inside the genre perspective that his investigation of the novel as a genre intends to overturn. Bakhtin approaches prose though the novel, while Godzich, Kittay and Nylander approach the novel through prose: the novel has had an historical impact on the possibilities and qualities of prose, so when Bakhtin mentions the "novelisation" of other genres, it would make more sense to talk about a "prosofication".[17] Others have stressed the danger of monopolising the study of prose as a study of the novel as a genre, e.g. by perceiving the eighteenth-century novel as a finished genre that can be explained as the end product of genealogical predecessors in epic and romance. A transversal study of mixed forms, made up of elements from epistolary fiction, historical writing, travel accounts, romances, satire etc., raises doubt as to whether the rather limited functions we associate with novels today are the result of a retrospective understanding of genre.[18] Bakhtin suggests that the novel itself has been codified and caught up in a classic prose form that is different from prose itself, which still undergoes changes and new differentiations.

There is thus a world of difference between reading Conrad's *Heart of Darkness*, for example, as a novel and as a piece of prose. The most common approach, created by the text's canonisation in the twentieth century, perceives it as a novel and reads it under those conditions. An academic understanding of *Heart of Darkness*, however, entails an examination of its unique position as a piece of prose that points towards other, broader contexts. The same principle applies to all the examples in this book, e.g. Mirbeau's travel account, *Tintin au Congo* and *Tarzan and the Leopard Men*: they are variations of prose differentiations that did not die out in the eighteenth century but continued into the nineteenth and twentieth centuries, among other things as strategic approaches to new forms

of media and new technologies. The focus of this book is the transformation of prose, and its ramifications, in the period around 1900. This focus ensures that the development of prose in the twentieth century can be described in positive terms instead of negative – the deviation from a given norm, the "disintegration of the novel", etc. The Danish writer Jürgen Jürgensen's Congo narratives, for example, can be read as experiments with styles of writing and narration freed from the novel as a norm.

Along the same lines, Stanley's perspectival balancing act can be understood as utilising manifold dynamic positions – which Godzich and Kittay name as a key characteristic of prose, and which was enhanced by the new global opportunities in communication, the market and media – instead of being perceived negatively as a documentary, aesthetically substandard mix of New Journalism and novel. As J. Paul Hunter has pointed out, before the novel became 'novel' it resembled journalism: both forms of prose "shared the public taste for contemporaneity and novelty and quickly discovered how to blend it into a substantial and complex web of narrative and discursive prose, creating in effect a portable coffee-house of elongated conversation in print".[19]

According to several analyses of contemporary literary culture, recent years have witnessed a sweeping transformation of the basic perceptions of what literature is and should be.[20] The romantic idea of a well-defined and recognisably valuable literature is being challenged by experiments that blur the traditional dividing lines between fiction and documentarism, autobiography and novel and high and low literature. This new field, 'the prose', is not seen as a fall, but as a new opportunity for literature to rediscover its authority as testimony about the world. Literature as an academic field of study is encouraged to break free of its formalistic limitations for the benefit of "literary field studies", i.e. a way of dealing with literature that ascribes to the object the same status as the unknown, changeable, unclassified culture in anthropological studies. It is an important point that this turn does not only concern new literature: models and preferences that have restrained our readings and appraisals of older literature and literary history also need to be broadened.

In the following this approach will be used to read Stanley and a number of other texts about the Congo, from Naipaul to E. R. Burroughs' *Tarzan*. In the context of prose, these works about the Congo are comparable, and when viewed in relation to the Congo the *place*, it is possible to assess them critically within this framework. Whereas Stanley's reports, Conrad's novel and Burroughs' popular fiction have until now belonged to isolated literary areas, separated by impassable borders, the prose perspective facilitates literary history that encompasses the internal dialogue between the works and sees them as different representations of the same place and historical process.

The idea of a 'prosaic turn' makes it possible to define a renaissance in contemporary travel literature, which comes in numerous genre and media mixes, and overlaps a variety of different institutions. The prose perspective may also help to clarify how literature can maintain its influence on globalised market and media conditions. It is a fair assumption that literature as prose can wield significant power; it holds a prominent place in society when it manages to grasp the complexity of the world we live in – and make readers participate in and relate to that world – in a qualified and competitive way when compared with the news media's hurried, superficial information.

Furthermore, this perspective encompasses the knowledge that literature in such a prominent role must give up some of the privileges that come with being literature, in the narrower and more protected meaning. In return, a much broader field of application will be discovered for literature, much like the one that existed in the eighteenth century. This world-orientated literature came into being with the new *weltanschauung*, favouring the realistic and mundane, sensory and experimental: at times carnevalesque, at times essayistic and rationalistic. It used the entire range of genres: autobiography, novel, essay, treaty, pamphlet, etc., often in mixed and masked disguises, as the new world was exposed to new views and shifting perspectives alongside curious discoveries that did not necessarily fit into contemporary ideas of taste, and could not qualify as literature in the elevated and limited sense.

This situation was often linked to a certain perception of the curious, or "wonders". Until the end of the eighteenth century, when they were brushed aside by ideas of the "aesthetically sublime", curiosities were central to natural history, philosophy and literature. These phenomena were surprising and novel, yet they could be described in realistic, empirical terms. They therefore held a prestigious position in science as well as entertainment. Curiosities were described through the new prose we know from Montaigne's essays – i.e. in a sensory and natural style comprising a vast number of points of view, giving the reader a clear impression of the unusual and surprising proportions of discoveries like the hippopotamus, the rhinoceros, the sunflower and so on.

Collections of curiosities, and descriptions of them, were later criticised for indicating a perverted fascination with disparate objects and places, which were persecuted by exoticism, popular culture and world fairs. They were later restored to glory as "everyday wonders" studied by the Surrealists. In recent years, curiosities have been rediscovered and reassessed by anthropologists and literary historians, who once again have chosen to focus on the curious as the basis of all philosophy and art and an everyday, phenomenological, non-academic point of access to the world.

In this book, the prose perspective does not involve a genre discussion – i.e.

how to draw the line between prose and non-prose. Rather, it implicates comparative and critical literary history, operating with a broad range of text forms and facilitating other questions in relation to historical and aesthetic processes. This study is not about defining prose but about illustrating the reading perspective. For that purpose, examples from literary history have been chosen that do not refer to the geographical and historical delimitations of the book in general. These examples illustrate the reading method and what is at play in texts such as Stanley's. At the same time they provide points of reference and are constitutive of the patterns and connections between place and literature that are the focus of the rest of the book's analyses, which will be anchored in the Congo in the next chapter. It is important to note that the literary models for cultural encounters and travel accounts, which were formed during the eighteenth-century European expeditions to the Orient and Tahiti, were still used throughout the nineteenth and into the twentieth century.

Prosaic Model Examples

In the wake of the European 'discovery' of Tahiti in 1767, philosophical treaties and political pamphlets were published containing a rich and abundant literature about the first encounters with Polynesian culture, especially stories about a different kind of sexuality. These writings even caused some London brothels to arrange orgies after the Tahitian model. The discovery gave rise to a wide range of textual responses in European culture, including popular culture.[21] In a different context, this book's author has suggested a distinction between two separate directions in the extensive material, marking two very different tendencies in the history of travel literature. One direction in the eighteenth-century discovery of Tahiti is represented by Samuel Wallis' and James Cook's diaries, which were rewritten by the ghostwriter John Hawkesworth as one complete narrative;[22] the other direction is found in Bougainville's and Diderot's texts about Tahiti. Louis Bougainville arrived at and 'discovered' Tahiti the year after Wallis and wrote a classicistic, hesitant, incoherent narrative, *Voyage autour du Monde*.[23] Denis Diderot subsequently expanded on the doubt in Bougainville's original travel account with a fictitious addition, although not in a relativistic style. The first direction leads towards the nineteenth century's specialised sciences, cultural relativism and aestheticisation, often summed up as 'orientalism'; the latter leads towards the "anthropoetic narratives" of globalisation, to which we will soon return, and towards the prose perspective that is the main theme here. The distinction is important for this book's examination of images of Africa in travel literature from the end of the nineteenth century up to the present day. Although we are not talking about specific literary traditions, it

William Hodges' illustrations, represented here by *Tahiti Revisited* (1776), are more closely related to Bougainville's classicism than Cook's simple diary narrative. Tahiti is a utopia become real, a concrete version of Virgil's pastoral poetry. Sexuality is ascribed to the Venus cult; the native women are draped like the Venuses of Antiquity and their tattoos barely discernible.

still makes sense to describe some of the more problematic European narratives about the Congo as continuations of the former direction; it similarly makes sense to view the exemplary narratives, including Stanley's, Octave Mirbeau's, Jürgen Jürgensen's and Peter Tygesen's, as continuations of Bougainville's and Diderot's open, changeable prose.

While Wallis' and Cook's diaries are written in simple, unassuming prose, Hawkesworth's additions are the so-called "sentiments" and "observations". An everyday event on Tahiti in which a young girl is instructed in sex by older, more experienced women becomes in Hawkesworth's almost gothic rewriting a "ritual of Venus". Customs described by Cook in unassuming prose become the objects of literary and philosophical "embellishment". Hawkesworth's rewriting aestheticises and scandalises the original description, placing the experience of the unknown in the well-known discourse of pornography. The reader is titillated by the striptease, which in an aestheticised and sentimental version

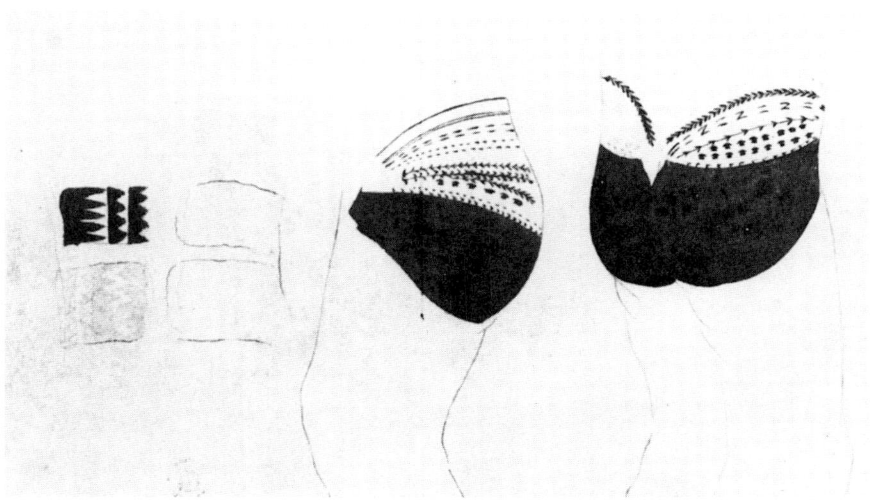

Sydney Parkinson, *Tahitian Tattoo Designs* (1769). In the mid-eighteenth century, the fascination with tattoos expressed not only an interest in wonders and the budding, specialised observations of details that were the precursors of ethnography as a scientific discipline; a closer look at this peculiar writing on the body reveals a completely different story, which cannot be understood within the framework of the utopian tales of beautiful marble bodies that dominates the Venus tradition. In *Observations Made during a Voyage round the World* (1778), J. R. Forster is fascinated with these "curious marks"; he describes them in detail but refrains from explaining them, as "collecting and recording the fact" is enough for him.

simultaneously emphasises and erases the differences between 'them' and 'us', thus pointing towards orientalism and the problematic culture-relativistic distinction between self-reliant, essentially different cultures.

Bougainville's descriptions of Tahiti are very different. He was fascinated by the Polynesian women, who were every bit as beautiful as European women. On his arrival, a young girl lets her clothes drop, "so she appeared before our eyes like Venus before the Phrygian shepherds". Bougainville continues the description of Arcadian pastures, where Odysseus' spellbound heroes were met by an irresistible Venus cult. "Everything oozes lust" he writes. In the following chapter, however, Bougainville interviews a Tahitian man and the text develops an ethnographic quality: in fact, the natives are constantly at war, thieves are hanged, etc. That which in classical rhetoric appeared whole is disclosed as disparate in the ethnographic account. The interview leads Bougainville to the conclusion that the population is not a homogeneous group but rather "compounded of two very different races of people", one of perfect beauty, the other rather like people of mixed race, stocky and with unattractive, woolly hair.

Diderot was so tempted by the unresolved doubt he found in Bougainville's description of the relation between pastoral harmony and ethnographic conflict that he wrote a fictitious addition in the form of a dialogue between two amateur philosophers, A and B: *Supplement au voyage de Bougainville*. When foggy weather keeps them from going on a walk, A and B start reading and commenting on Bougainville's text: "What is it I see there, added in the book's margin?" asks one. "Why, it is a note about the difference between the fertile and natural Venus on Tahiti and the coy, flirtatious, and gallant Venus we meet in the Parisian salons", answers the other.[24] A and B develop juxtapositions of the natural Tahitian Venus and the coy, European Venus. However, they reach a possible reconciliation between the two types when B says: "When I see how we plant trees round our palaces, or how a woman's bodice at once hides and exposes her breast, I seem to detect a secret wish to return to the forest, a recollected longing for the freedom of our first habitat" (p. 504). In all her coyness and flirtation, the Parisian Venus shows the promise of a possible return to her original nature.

Bougainville's text is unique in that it contains both a classicistic, utopian description of Tahiti as a harmonious love cult and an ethnographic description of the internal conflicts and differences in the society – and, what is more, without any mediation between the two descriptions. Diderot's fictitious addition is unique because it reworks the original text in a form that allows for rational criticism of customs in Europe and Tahiti without juxtaposing the two cultures as if they were essentially different. Diderot's method manages to maintain the differences between them and us, which are ever-changeable in the fictitious addition, while at the same time negotiating them from an open-ended dialogical perspective. This perspective includes not only A and B but also the relationships between the men and their wives; their homes and the wide world; philosophy and salon culture; Tahiti and Europe; and Diderot and the reader.

In Paul Gauguin's travel book *NoaNoa*,[25] which he wrote during his stay on Tahiti around 1900, the text and the artistic project are presented as a new beginning and a complete liberation from everything European. Closer inspection, however, reveals that it consists of a vast number of additions. The description of Gauguin's conversion to Maori is a precise repetition of Bougainville's and Diderot's play on the natural Venus versus the gallant and coy Venus, and the "secret path through the forest" that A and B discover in the margin. Likewise, Gauguin's newly found direction for nude painting, free of guilt, shame, kitsch and pornography, did not emerge purely from the innocent models: he had brought with him a rich collection of copies of European art,

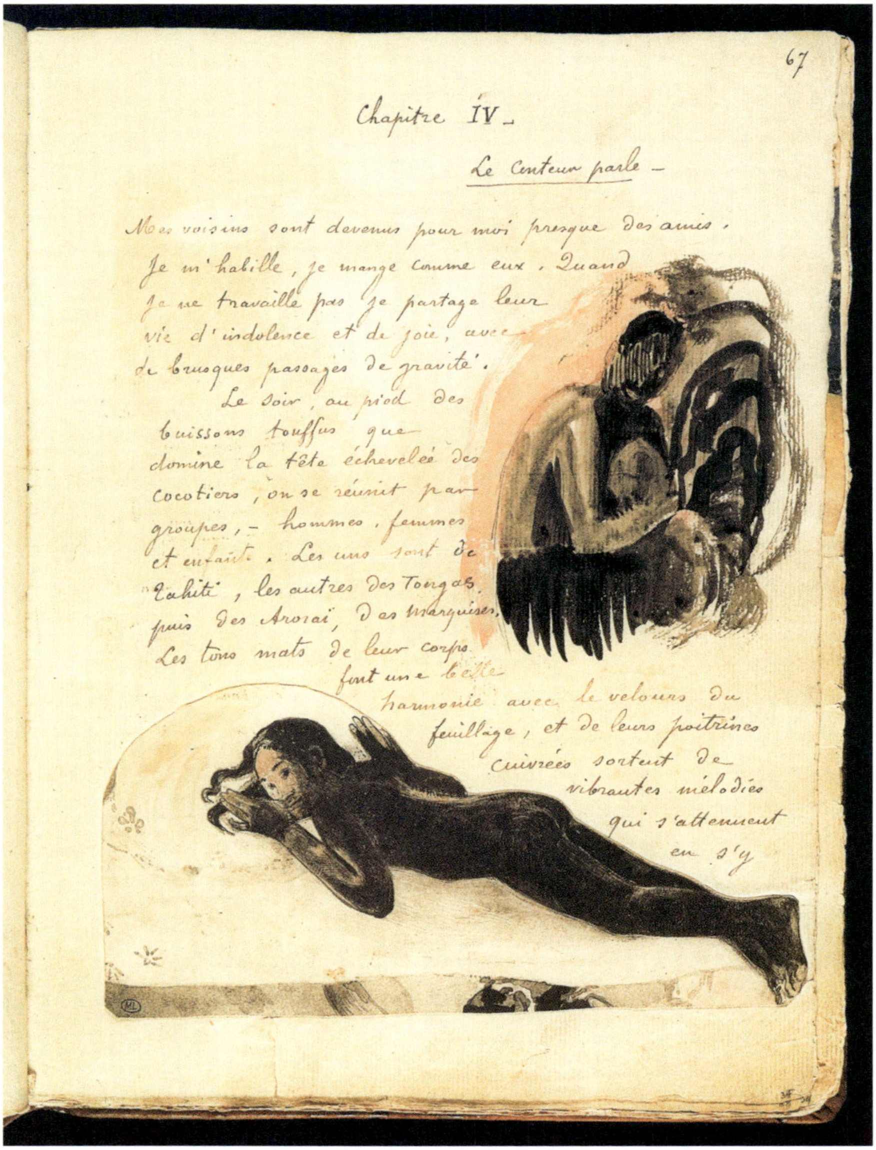

In the margin of his collage, Gauguin brings attention to his sources of inspiration, e.g. Manet's *Olympia*. Using the native woman as his model, Gauguin navigates between the natural and the coy Venus, thus repeating the main patterns in Bougainville's and Diderot's earliest travel accounts.

including Manet's *Olympia*, which he developed further in his tropical studio. The diary is a collage of images and text, which in its materiality – as well as in the margins – indicates the influence of earlier works. *NoaNoa*'s cosmology accordingly consists of conflicting amalgamations of highly disparate myths, but it also creates the basis for dissolving the dualism which Gauguin identified as the cause of European culture's decline: in *NoaNoa*'s Tahiti, the power of creation is fruit, movement and objects in motion – spirit and matter are one. The liberation from European dualism is to be found by renouncing the Christian idea of resurrection. Tahiti must perish some day, the same way that mankind must die in order *not* to rise from the dead; the idea of eternal matter should be celebrated here and now.

Although *NoaNoa* brims with internal contradictions, its changeable palimpsest implicates a recreation of the body as sexy and natural – created to be displayed without shame, a gift to the eye returned to canvas by the painter.[26] This fantastic and admirable new beginning somewhere outside Europe emanates not only from repetitions and copies of European art, but also from repetitions of tropes from the earliest travel accounts about Tahiti. The fertile Venus and the gallant Venus are found in Gauguin's text, where they continue a complex dynamic between closeness and distance, drawing the reader into a prose perspective that can be understood as a descriptive model both for the place and for reading the text.

This motif in the text material from Tahiti expanded on the dialogical and process-orientated strategy that Bougainville suggested and Diderot developed further. Victor Segalen arrived on Tahiti three months after Gauguin's death and took it upon himself to continue the painter's project through his literary experiments, e.g. the peculiar Tahiti novel *Les Immémoriaux* (1907), and in his work on a theory of "exoticism" that can be understood as a continuation, as well as a radicalisation and transformation, of orientalism's stereotypical models to describe the other.[27] Segalen himself saw *Les Immémoriaux* as an anthropological book that tried to describe the culture from within through a fictitious native narrator, who does not use western terms for time and space, but instead slips back and forth between mythic past and modern present. The narrator is at the same time inside and outside, a stranger to himself, and in that capacity the voice for experiences of the exotic which do not belong exclusively to one culture or the other. While Segalen in his age was mythologised to a degree that led to his actual work being forgotten, today his texts are headed towards canonisation as both world literature and anthropological science.[28] Segalen's dynamic understanding of discontinuity and reversibility in the relationship between European/western and native culture is commended as a contrast to the one-sidedness of postcolonial models, while his experiments balance science

and literature, autobiography and novel, thus constituting a striking example of the "anthropoetic narrative", which the literary historian Wlad Godzich coined to describe the role of literature in globalised conditions.[29]

The process of globalisation is a challenge both to anthropological theory – which according to James Clifford is redirected into travel accounts – and to basic assumptions regarding national identity in the writing of literary history. Wlad Godzich's term "anthropoetic speech" characterises personal, stylised, anecdotic and global narratives that encompass unresolved disputes about phenomena such as borders or cultural identities. They are profound narratives – positioned between literature and science – about what mankind is from a global perspective and where the individual belongs. Some of the travel accounts in what is here collectively referred to as the Congo literature can be said to express this anthropoetic horizon, while others counteract the very asking of these questions.

John Hawkesworth's rewriting of Wallis' and Cook's diaries as a first person narrative with modifying additions – the so-called "sentiments" and "observations" – obviously also belongs to prose, which became widespread and highly influential during the eighteenth century partly due to travel accounts. However, Hawkesworth's aestheticising and culturally relativistic additions create a problematic matrix for the textual characteristics and descriptions of place – something that can be traced later in sentimental travel accounts and orientalism's worship of the other. The grandiose subject is of paramount interest in the texts, while landscape and surroundings are reduced to a picturesque backdrop for internal emotions and sentimentality. The text's appeal is first and foremost directed at the reader's pathetic response: our compassion may increase, but at the same time the distance between 'us' and 'them' is cemented, resulting in the cultures appearing autonomous and isolated.

In Bougainville, Diderot, Gauguin and Segalen, on the other hand, we find models for describing encounters between cultures which we can still use today when we analyse literature in globalised conditions.[30] Diderot's and Segalen's additions bridge the gap between what today we call cultural and textual

Despite the contradictions and changeable prose, the myth of creation and travel account in *NoaNoa* allows for the recreation of the body as both sexy and natural – created to be displayed without shame as a gift, which the painter returns with the painted canvas. *Deux Tahitiennes* (1899).

"The South Pacific Venus" is the title of Aage Krarup Nielsen's image, which is part of a series of semi-nude "young girls" in Tahiti. The exotic travel account *Aloha. A Journey to the South Pacific* (1939) continues this classicist style, adding an orientalist twist and a characteristic mix of guilt and voyeurism. Carsten Jensen's description of a stay in Tahiti also emulates Diderot's play on the coy and the natural in a subtle manner; however, in his book *I Have Heard a Shooting Star* (1997), Venus born from the sea is a transvestite.

analysis. We are dealing with rationally based criticism, and a development of the possibilities in the original text, in which different societies' customs and rhetorical figures enter into open-ended dialogue. The precursors all constitute "multidirectional" reading strategies and perceive differences in societies as "processes rather than essences".[31] They are capable of combining intimacy with distance, so that the world they describe becomes both sensory and intelligible. In that capacity, they also constitute models for combining "close reading" with "distant reading", which has been discussed in relation to "world literature".[32]

The prose perspective, introduced here through the Tahiti material, creates access to alternative critical tendencies in literary history, compared to the ones that appear through the established genre system and its distinction between fiction, novel, autobiography, high culture and mass culture. Through this perspective, Stanley's works take centre stage in literary investigations, and they can be read as prose with an immense performative impact – in the same way that *Tintin au Congo*, for instance, can be read as a text that requires "multidirectional" reading strategies, which defuse the usual postcolonial criticism of crude descriptions of wild animals and the native population.

There was obviously a significant context and history behind Arne Melberg's suggestion to leave behind the formalistic tradition in comparative literature, which dominated the field for long periods in the twentieth century, in favour of experimental literary field work in the "country of prose". Melberg presents part of the history in his collection of essays, *In the centre of literature*, 2002. In the chapter "Critical CV", his route into academia's institutions and the intense theoretical turn in the subject, which accelerated during the 1980s, is described in retrospect. The theoretical turn is described as an unholy alliance between vain fundamentalism and globalisation of the subject areas, and as a threat to the very basis of literary criticism: the ability to remain "listening". After having critically re-read six of his own previous contributions to academia, Arne Melberg suggests a new perspective, which he launches in both a self-critical and an institutional-political dimension. The concluding chapter, "In the centre of prose", takes as its starting point the fact that the map of comparative literature corresponds poorly to the literary landscape:

"Once again, the starting point is the suspicion that the map corresponds poorly to the terrain. The map: the institutional definitions of the phenomenon of literature, which I will characterise with these two words: negation and fiction. Expressed in more detail: what is required of a piece of writing in order for us (that is, the academic institution of comparative literature) to accept it as literature is that it distances itself from (more) normal linguistic communication and creates the imaginary kingdom

that is fiction. The model for linguistic distancing is poetry; the model for fiction is the novel. Both can be perceived as variants of negation; both aim at autonomy. (...) The question now is whether or not this 'literature' corresponds with literature as it is being written today. I have already several times expressed a dwindling faith in negation and searched for (more) positive categories: listening; availability; encounter" (p. 145).

This is followed by suggestions for alternative readings of Montaigne and Nietzsche, among others, whose texts Melberg has previously read within changing literary frameworks. If categories such as travelling or life – which are neither fictitious nor negative – are given centre stage in the literary process of listening, the basic delimitations of comparative literature – for instance with regard to the closed, autonomous artwork or genres – will be shifted. Because of this, and because the criticism of comparative literature was presented as a self-criticism, Melberg's ideas were met with extreme disapproval in Norway. However, they were followed by similar self-critical writings, e.g. by Tzvetan Todorov – one of the leading international figures in the formalistic tradition – who received much positive attention for warning against letting literature become self-sufficient as an academic subject and burst into theoretical self-oscillation.[33] To Melberg, Montaigne and Nietzsche are mentors in the art of reading and understanding life and the journey; correspondingly, Diderot, Gauguin and Segalen are this book's role models for reading travel accounts about the Congo.

Travel Literature

While the prose perspective of *In the centre of literature* relies principally on dialogue with great essayists, only towards the end mentioning travels and travel accounts, this particular type of literature is the main focus of the article "Beyond fiction. Sebald, Solstad and other travellers in the country of prose". With a stronger basis in textual analysis, the cartographic metaphors are continued and developed in a discussion of the line between fictional and factual prose – travel literature functioning as a useful example. Contemporary texts by writers such as W. G. Sebald and Dag Solstad are used to clarify the frailty of established, dogmatic delimitations. Solstad's novel *16.07.41* (2002) is a novel and an autobiography, a poetics and a scientifically angled investigation, as well as a work of criticism including numerous footnotes on the concepts of novel and autobiography. It makes use of both conventional novel techniques and breaches of the established contracts of fictional writing in a collage of highly diverse types of text, in some respects reminiscent of Gauguin's *NoaNoa*. Travelling as a motive is a focal point in the novel – for the fictitious narrator as well as for the author, who travels back and forth between Norway and Berlin on walks between city zones and neighbourhoods. Furthermore, travelling plays a compositional role as the marker of changes between places and utterances in the text; these changes raise doubts as to who is narrating – and where – and ultimately they break down the wall between narrator and author, probably the most fundamental dogma in comparative literature. In the writings of Solstad and Sebald, travelling becomes an occasion to "search for new paths in the literary field" (p. 108) that belong neither to fictional or factual prose, but are part of a "reality work" or "recherche".

Despite this general definition of prose, it is important that we are not talking about a genre, and definitely not defining a term for a new and unknown literary phenomenon. The article provides examples of similar prose experiments, including Cervantes' *Don Quixote*, Defoe's *Robinson Crusoe*, as well as works by Fielding and Flaubert.[34]

Prose should instead be understood as a "strategic tendency", "field work in full flow in the field of literature", or, as written somewhere with reference to Roland Barthes: "a methodological field". The reality work carried out in prose is not reserved for fiction, but also applies to documentary travel accounts that use fictionalising techniques to create credibility. The dividing line is not drawn between fiction and documentarism but between the different perspectives and uses of rhetorical strategies.

> "Fiction is not viewed in opposition to truth, which, instead, is dependent on fictionalising techniques. Thus, it is the use of literary terms, strategies and perspectives that creates the difference: the literary field work installs fiction, as well as truth and credibility. Truth is not (only) a question of the presentation's referential correspondence with historic reality; truth also needs to be produced" (p. 102).

The weighting of *perspective* is important to this book's readings of literature about the Congo, especially with regard to Stanley, and it will be among the main arguments for a reappraisal of his contribution to travel literature; along the same lines, reservations about other texts will concentrate on limited perspectives and negative rhetorical consequences regarding reality work. As a consequence of this point of view, analyses will make little reference to the dominating tendencies in travel literature research: the epistemological tendency, which aims at defining the relation between fact and fiction, and the genre theoretical tendency, which reads travel literature with a focus on its delimitations.

In travel literature, two discourses that we have come to perceive as separate merge: a critical, analytical and philosophical discourse and an essayistic, literary

discourse. Travel literature can convey knowledge and science about another world to readers and thereby criticise the domestic. It can entertain and fascinate with the enchantment that is always ascribed to the unknown, and it can create a span between the universal and the particular because the exposure of the self, situated under the celestial sphere yet with its feet firmly on the ground, can wriggle free of prejudices and keep the mind in philosophical movement. It also tells tales of maturation, learning and insight, which may have some relevance but are not true in the strict sense of the word. Travel literature, perceived as reality work from the prose perspective, does not represent or process a fixed, well-defined reality; it creates a discursive space where a plurality of texts and places are articulated.

A travel account is not, as we will experience in a dramatic form with Stanley, only a textual representation of, for instance, a locality in Africa; first and foremost it is a description of self, and in a sense a description of 'locations' in other texts. Bougainville's incorporation of Virgil's pastoral landscape in the description of Tahiti and James Cook's observation of the planet Venus from Tahiti actualise the eighteenth century's discursive approach to aesthetics, sensitivity, science and sociability as a dialogue between skin pathology and empirical planet observations; Venus as a classical ideal beauty and the social significance of skin made to look smooth with cosmetics. The prose refers both to the locations of rhetoric – so-called topoi, well-known from language and literature – which the speaker can always reach back to, and to concrete locations in the world. Travel accounts include dynamic, rhetorical mechanisms of spatialisation and temporalisation, providing a heterogeneous space in which the same 'location' takes on different, changeable positions; in our example, Venus conjures up classicistic, harmonious pastoral idyll as well as modern, discursive conflict. It thus makes no sense to distinguish between fact and fiction in, for example, Cyrano de Bergerac's *Histoire comique des Etats et Empires de la Lune* from the mid-seventeenth century, because more than anything else the text is a discursive experiment which, in a model version, presents a methodological foundation for empirical analysis in the natural sciences.[35] Its fiction is not untrue but hypothetical – a first-person narrative that strategically uses a specific scope, established on and expanded around the travel account.

In the renaissance, the knowledge acquired about strange worlds through studies of books by Aristotle or Marco Polo was not fundamentally different from the knowledge acquired from personal experience or first-hand accounts.[36] The classical educational texts merged with accounts of the unknown, and comments would be added, as Montaigne's essay shows. When Columbus set out for America at the end of the fifteenth century, he based his journey on Marco Polo's text, as well as taking his own travel library: various Medieval 'mappae mundi' depicting biblical journeys and pilgrimages; John Mandeville's fictitious, yet at the time authoritative, travel account; Augustin's confessions, which provided instructions for life as a spiritual journey and doubt as an element in charting the course; and the Bible, in which the prophet Ezra's claim that there is relatively more land than water on the planet led Columbus to make fatal mistakes in his calculations of distances. None of these texts are random or irrelevant. They represent the age's text-based beliefs about the structuring of the world.[37] Navigating the world meant navigating the texts, whose authority was not dependent on their connection with the empiric but on their author's position, reputation and authority. The rhetorical art of Columbus' own texts consisted in achieving two things at the same time: first, they dismantled and corrected readers' superstitions and prejudices by offering empiric evidence and rendering probable the descriptions of a new, grander and richer world; secondly, they established credibility, reaffirming and proving the traditional, textual knowledge and myths. The travel account's conventional repertoire of, e.g., people with dog's heads and the specific location of the biblical Adam's house, was part of the reaffirmation of the textual function, while the empiric discourse, gradually established and developed in the renaissance, performed the corrective textual function.

The explorations functioned as forerunners for Europe's increasing power and influence, but also as shocking experiences. The world expanded and shrank at the same time. Territories grew vaster, but the perspective that governed description and understanding was shattered by becoming relative. From then on, the world could no longer be understood in one single perspective; one world had become several worlds. The phenomenon termed as "deterritorialization" by modern philosophers such as Michel de Certeau and Gilles Deleuze began with Marco Polo and Columbus. And as demonstrated by Timothy Reiss in *The Discourse of Modernism* (1982), doctrines about space as coherent and absolute are contradicted by experiences such as those communicated through travel accounts, where space is relative and split up; this idea is echoed in the perception of space that Michel Foucault has termed "heterotopia".[38]

The modern history of travel accounts began on these complex, prosaic terms. Text-based knowledge was challenged by convincing facts that resulted in relativism - an unstable world - because they paved the way for comparative, competitive studies of e.g. nudity and cannibalism; in Montaigne's case these studies led to basic questions about what it is to be human and how to distinguish empirical knowledge from fantasy. The temporal and spatial dynamics in the eighteenth-century narratives about the discovery of Tahiti rely on this superposition of discovery, expansion and relativisation in a new world and new prose. The narratives, like Diderot's supplement, position absolute space as a

"Prospect der Stadt Kamalia", from a German edition of Mungo Park's famous and rapidly distributed travel account *Travels in the Interior Districts of Africa: Performed in the Years 1795, 1796, and 1797* (1799).

hypothesis, but they are – like the greatest prose work of the period, Diderot and d'Alembert's *Encyclopédie* – not an implementation of total knowledge, but rather a series of tentative attempts at it, references to other entries and other 'places'.

Prose was created from and within this space, whose heterotopical characteristics constitute both travel account and essay. Soon, techniques were being developed to present familiar, extraordinary or unlikely events in a convincing fashion – something that would later come to be the foundation for the modern novel, with Defoe's *Robinson Crusoe* (1720) as a prominent example. Defoe drew on the vast numbers of travel accounts that filled the libraries with entertaining reading but also with material that could be used in a philosophical and scientific critique of modern society.[39] At the same time, *Robinson Crusoe* became a generic model for documentary travel accounts, many of which were heavily influenced by Defoe's realistic style, even emphasising – as Defoe does in the novel's preface – that they were not "fiction" or "invention". The novel's background is the breakdown of the classical world and classical aesthetics. The world can no longer be said to constitute a coherent cosmos; individual experiences and particular trajectories are described as unique. The foundation of the aesthetics of rules – one single, general idea as the organising principle of art – is disrupted by the revolution of detail. Deprived of the experience-based community with the reader, the narrator aims at building a rhetorical sense of community, established through intimacy and recognisability. The exhaustively detailed descriptions are generalised and made obvious by the narrator, thus turning the unusual and particular into something acceptable, while all the trivialities of everyday life are sensationalised.

The example of Defoe shows how the realistic novel and the travel account interacted in complex ways at the beginning of the eighteenth century. They borrowed from one another in order to convince readers that the surprisingly plain confessions of everyday life, as well as the surprisingly strange ones of travellers in far-off lands, were both probable phenomena in a multifarious world that was rapidly changing. In realistic narratives, such as Samuel Wallis' account of the first European discovery of Tahiti, the narrator may not conceal his disgust at certain customs; however, this dissociation is not systematised as an essential difference between the Europeans and the strange culture. The traveller's approach is dialogical and determined by the practical objectives of the exploration. Travellers saw themselves as naturally superior, which nevertheless did not prevent them seeing strangers as anthropological beings in their own right. In the mid-eighteenth century, some travel writers – such as Bougainville and James Cook – began to perceive their own texts as anti-colonial, neutral and innocent; according to Mary Louise Pratt, this was achieved by borrowing the writing style of the popular natural history of the period. Towards the end of the eighteenth century, the travel account became more sentimental. Mungo Park's famous *Travels in the Interior of Africa* (1799) does not pretend to be objectively descriptive. Park narrates in the same down-to-earth style as Cook, but the focus is shifted from the discovery of the new world to the discovery of new, surprising aspects of his own individuality. The text is sensory and subjective, although not introverted or enclosed, as is the case in later romantic and orientalist travel accounts. Mungo Park is a transitional figure; he may be a sentimental hero, but he learns from his encounter with a world that he chooses to understand in social and human terms.

The trend changed from realistic travel accounts, which were critically received and assessed as hypotheses about the organisation of the empiric world, to sentimental travel accounts, which were assessed on aesthetic terms. Towards the end of the eighteenth century, the exhaustive and accumulated facts of ear-

lier accounts were perceived as a flaw, while rhetorical inventiveness and stylistic embellishment, ornamentation and not least the affective function were emphasised as positive features of the new style.[40] Orientalism's veiled descriptions of the other, which became dominant in the first half of the nineteenth century, were a sophisticated interpretation of the linkage between sentimental rhetoric and romantic aesthetics that characterises travel literature even today. Earlier essayistic, world-orientated and hypothetical prose was replaced by a view of travel accounts as autonomous literary works. Both high literature and popular travel accounts in the first half of the nineteenth century incorporate the changeability of perspectives and the heterotopical diversity in world and text that characterised renaissance prose. Camels and minarets, palms, fir trees, lions and noble savages appear in the same moonlit scene, albeit only as colourful backdrops, as described with irony in Flaubert's *Madame Bovary*. Livingstone's and Stanley's travel accounts may have had James Cook's prose as a distant ideal, but their texts and world spaces reflect orientalism.

In the context of this book, orientalism serves as the final example of a strategic prose perspective in the history of travel writing. While the first edition of Edward Said's famous and infamous classic *Orientalism* described the dichotomy between Europe and the Orient as if it were an ideological construction that could be unveiled, later epilogues admitted that such dichotomies are anthropological constants found in all cultures.[41] Said's focus is on the staging of the Orient as a scientific object. Firstly, orientalist discourse does not, in Said's opinion, describe a specific, geographically localised culture, but rather produces the Orient as a common idea. Secondly, the discourse is expressed through an all-encompassing dichotomisation, which both essentialises and musealises the Orient – thus denying the term any history or life – regardless of the writer's opinion and potentially good intentions. Said does not mince his words, for instance when he quotes Stendhal's criticism of Chateaubriand's travel book as "stinking egotism". Chateaubriand's romantic orientalism is, ac-

---

Jean-Léon Gérôme's *Moorish Bath* (c. 1880-85) is a famous, late example of nineteenth-century orientalism. The Orient had already become fashionable early in the century as an object of scientific study, art, and popular culture. Travel accounts often provided the material and types, which – in the European art industry – were reshaped into easily recognisable, exotic stereotypes. As early as 1850-51, when travelling in Egypt, Gustave Flaubert complained that everyone had been there before, carving their names into the pyramids – including Jenny Lind, known as 'The Swedish Nightingale', with whom H. C. Andersen was unhappily in love.

cording Said, an example of how the Orient was perceived as a ruined canvas waiting to be restored by the poet who could rediscover the creative forces in the stillness of the desert and make it speak again, although in a version that was completely detached from the actual geographical place; the desert was but a topos in the literary work. Even Gustave Flaubert, who in his travel book *Voyage en Égypte* was very critical of the orientalist romanticism of his predecessors, is not spared Said's criticism.[42]

The critical reception of Said's book could fill entire libraries. In this context the relevant points were made by the anthropologist James Clifford in *The Predicament of Culture* (1988).[43] Clifford wrote that *Orientalism* should not be understood primarily as a criticism of imperialism or colonialism. On the contrary, the book's extensive geopolitical scope is an early example of a critical perspective made possible by globalisation. However, Clifford does not agree with Said's analysis: in fact, Said is intrinsically dichotomous, totalising and essentialising and – despite his alleged constructivism – naïve, when he refers to "the real Orient". Ultimately, Said's perception of literature is based on a notion of the book as an enclosed, organic entity rather than a discourse. Furthermore, given that Said has a tendency to apply his organic, autonomous idea about works of art to entire cultures, he is guilty of a culturally relativistic juxtaposition of Europe and the Orient as two enclosed worlds, and thus unable to understand dialogue and change. This book will try to take these points of criticism into account in its inclusive approach to prose, although it is clear that the criticism of European images of Africa is related to Said's criticism of orientalism.

Said's writings opened up a perspective from which orientalism could be reassessed; however, Clifford's criticism is legitimate. When compared, the two positions illuminate some exemplary characteristics of one of the recently rediscovered travellers in the Orient, the German-Danish surveyor and cartographer Carsten Niebuhr. This supports the hypothesis of a prosaic turn in the culture at the time which permits new readings of literary history, some of which retrospectively alter the entire field of study.

Carsten Niebuhr's *Reisebeschreibung nach Arabien und andern umliegenden Ländern* 1-2 (1774-78) and 3 (1837, posthumous) is a detailed account of the Danish expedition to Yemen, or Arabia Felix, Happy Arabia.[44] Niebuhr, the expedition's cartographer and only survivor, avoided European arrogance and vanity; he met the people and landscape with a straightforward, balanced sensibility. However, he also mentions situations in which this approach was challenged by overwhelming sensory impressions:

"And even though from the very beginning we did not find much pleasure in that sort of play, because the instrumental and vocal music was very poor, and because

Illustration from Niebuhr's chapter "Levantine Exercises and Pastime in Idle Hours". It is typical of Niebuhr that the perspective is flexible: he points out that just as the Europeans do not immediately like the music of the Arabs, the Arabs describe the concerts performed by himself and the expedition painter, Baurenfeind, as "wild, unpleasant screaming".

the women assumed all kinds of positions that were obscene to the virtuous eye; even though from the beginning we found them all hideous because their yellow hands, blood-red nails, the black or blue decorations on their faces, arms and chests, the large rings around their ankles and in their ears and noses, the amount of pomade in their hair which we could smell from far away, etc., were not to our liking at all, and hardly any of them had a nice voice; still, we did not believe to have heard or seen anything better, thinking one or the other sang very beautifully, that she was even beautiful, and eventually we enjoyed watching them as much as the best singers and dancers in Europe" (p. 21).

As is the case in Stephen Greenblatt's description of the Europeans' encounters in the renaissance with, for instance, the Tupinamba Indians, which we will return to in chapter five, we are looking at a curiosity – a "wonder". The belly dancers are in Niebuhr's eyes initially hideous only to become beautiful: the

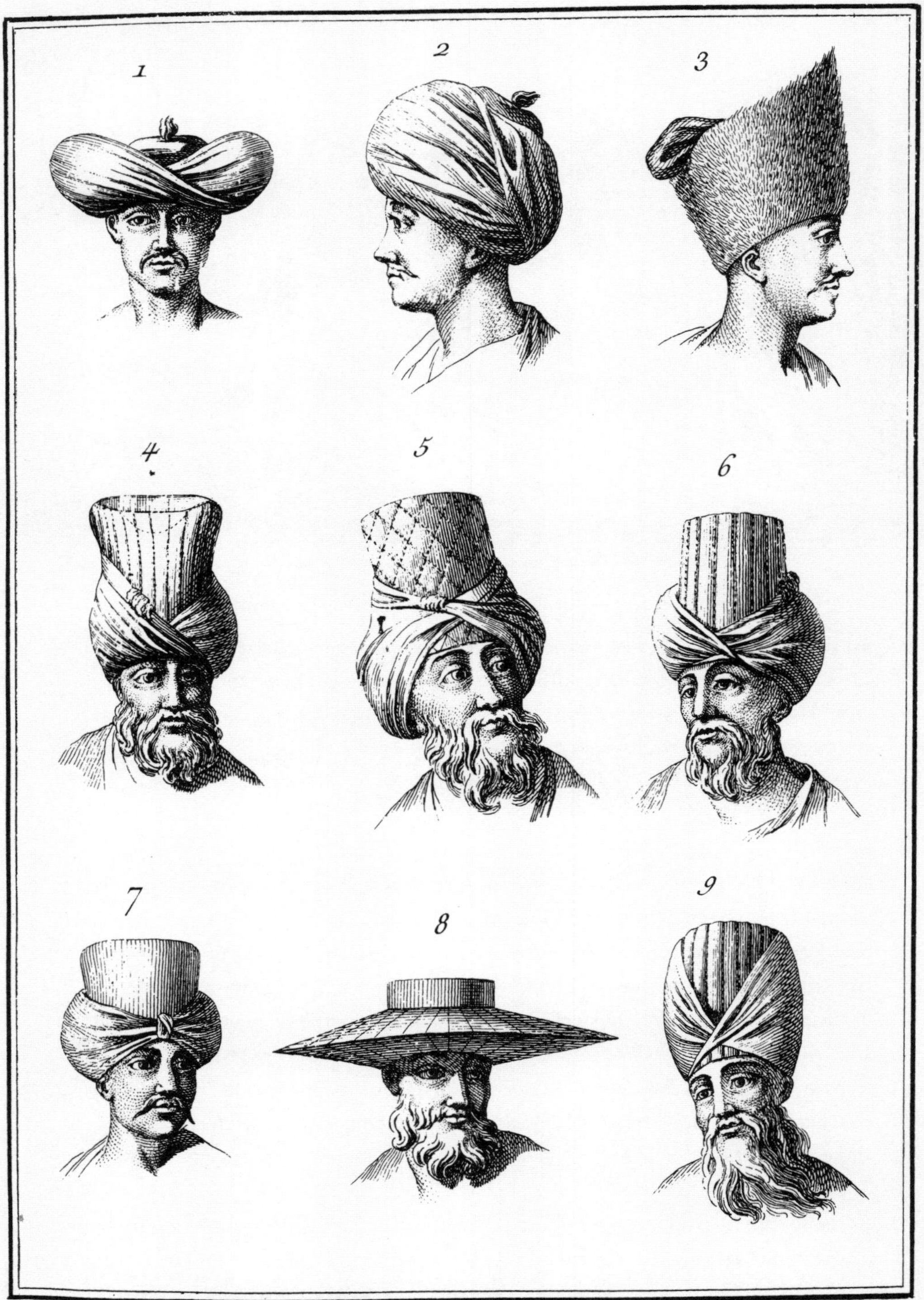
1
2
3
4
5
6
7
8
9
Defehrt Sc

opposite of his concepts of beauty and at the same time paradoxically the same. Yet he does not generalise his experience to juxtapose, for example, the female ideals of two cultures. We are dealing with a decontextualisation of the singular phenomenon, but also with a curious hesitation, which in a phenomenological sense overcomes distance and reservations and thereby ensures that the event is remembered in memory as well as text.

The comparisons between European and Arabic customs are exemplary, firstly because Niebuhr does not refrain from expressing his opinion, including criticising, for instance, the prophet Muhammad for not being very knowledgeable about nature; however, he expresses neither admiration nor disdain for the culture in general. Secondly, his comparisons appear unfinished and changeable, open to continued differentiation but at the same time – like Diderot's additions to Bougainville – presented in a rational and fully intelligible text. Commenting on "the Arabs' pastime", he mentions puppet theatres and shadow plays: "In the puppet theatres one will always see a comical character who is, without exception, a European". In addition to his precise surveys, plotted on the map, and the meticulous, multiperspectival descriptions of customs, Niebuhr has an awareness of his own comical mirror image.

Niebuhr was not a "man of letters" in the same sense as Bougainville; neither was he yet a specialist. His perspective is not classicistic but rather down-to-earth. Niebuhr was similar to Bougainville in his belief that unprejudiced and open dialogue was reason's most important tool. However, he had an advantage over the classically educated man: he did not perceive the relativity of the journey as a threat to a homogenous and harmonically formed worldview with educated Europeans at its centre. Niebuhr never saw his interaction with the Arabs as

---

From the chapter "The Dress of the Levantines". Niebuhr's presentation is thorough and systematic, but modern readers will often miss the prioritisation and selection that is characteristic of later, specialised sciences. In that respect, Niebuhr's work shares similarities with the major European work of the era, Diderot's great French *Encyclopédie* (1751-80) with its hyper-realistic illustrations of, e.g., different stages in the production of playing cards. Everything must be included, and in both the encyclopaedia and the travel account, scientific method has not yet been separated from the interest in the unique and curious. The tables show 48 different types of headdress, all described in detail in the text. Niebuhr apologises for the fact that the list is not comprehensive. A modern anthropologist and philosopher, such as Bruno Latour, would call Niebuhr's topics 'quasi things' – i.e. objects that have yet not been categorised by specialised sciences, but are rather described through a multitude of approaches and perspectives.

an encounter between two perceptions of the world or cultures that were set in stone, but as a logical exchange of information similar to exchanges about travel routes, food and transportation. Daily life was the same for him as for any other traveller in a caravan: he drank the same coffee, smoked the same pipe, saw the same night sky, yet he was a German-Danish parvenu – clever but not sly, knowledgeable but not learned. He was neither shocked nor allured by the tempting riddles that would draw other travellers into paranoid hermeneutics.

Carsten Niebuhr's achievement was not least that he kept both feet on the ground in his tenacious attempts to record things around him – even when faced with phenomena that did not fit into the defined fields of cartography and maths. His mapping of places and of customs followed the same multiperspectival method: "what is seen depends on one's position and point of view"; this method is "position-relativising", writes Michael Harbsmeier.[45] Though Niebuhr did not therefore penetrate deeply into Arabic culture, his superficial and positive method is the reason his descriptions are models today. Clifford's recommended "multidirectional" approach and focus on "processes rather than essences" is realised in Niebuhr's writing, not through theoretical speculation but through the accomplishment of a practical prose perspective for reading and describing the world. For most people his perspective is inextricably linked with the culture of the eighteenth century. Later, however, it will be argued that some of the method's characteristics are also to be found in Stanley's, Octave Mirbeau's and Peter Tygesen's multiperspectival, pragmatic prose.

Wonder

The renaissance saw both an expansion and relativisation of space and a correlated dialogical prose. Central to these tendencies is the mode of observing the world and its peculiarities as a phenomenon. In travel accounts from the sixteenth to the end of the eighteenth century, the discourse on the peculiar played a decisive role, until it was replaced by the discourse on the sublime. However, the development of the kind of prose we find in Montaigne's essays, and which still influences the realistic travel account today, did not take place as an internal, isolated event in literature, but in relation to changes in the field of natural history. Natural history prepared the ground for the style of the travel account, which was later adopted by the realistic novel; natural science also prepared the ground for sensibility towards the end of the eighteenth century, which would turn into an orientalist fever in the romantic period.

The collective work *Cultures of Natural History* (1996) outlines the discursive tradition of natural history after it had its breakthrough as an academic discipline in the renaissance. Natural history had been codified as a genre by

Curiosi pointing to, looking at and discussing wonders in Ferrante Imperato's collection in Napoli 1599. Based on illustrations in his Museum Wormianum seu Historia Rerum Rariorum (1665), Ole Worm's cabinet of curiosities was recreated and reinterpreted by the American artist Rosamund Purcell in 2003 and exhibited in several museums, including the Steno Museum in Aarhus, Denmark, as well as via different media, including the Internet. Printed from *Cultures of natural history*.

Aristotle and Pliny, but its status as a discipline is a recent invention. Before 1500, there were no natural historians employed at the universities, no botanical gardens existed, and although Aristotle and Pliny were translated into Latin around 1470, natural history was still seen as a frivolous sub-genre, a medieval mess disseminated through an impenetrable web of anecdotes and allegories.

The development of natural history is connected to the humanities' re-reading of antique texts, and naturalists came to act as links between the academics in the humanities and the increasing interest of royal families in collections, explorations and expeditions. In this capacity, naturalists became key figures who liaised between international circles of professional academics and the rich

Curiosities. From James Petiver's *Gazophylacium naturae et artis* (1702-06).

>

From Nehemiah Grew *Museum Regalis Societas* (1681)
Printed from Cultures of natural history.

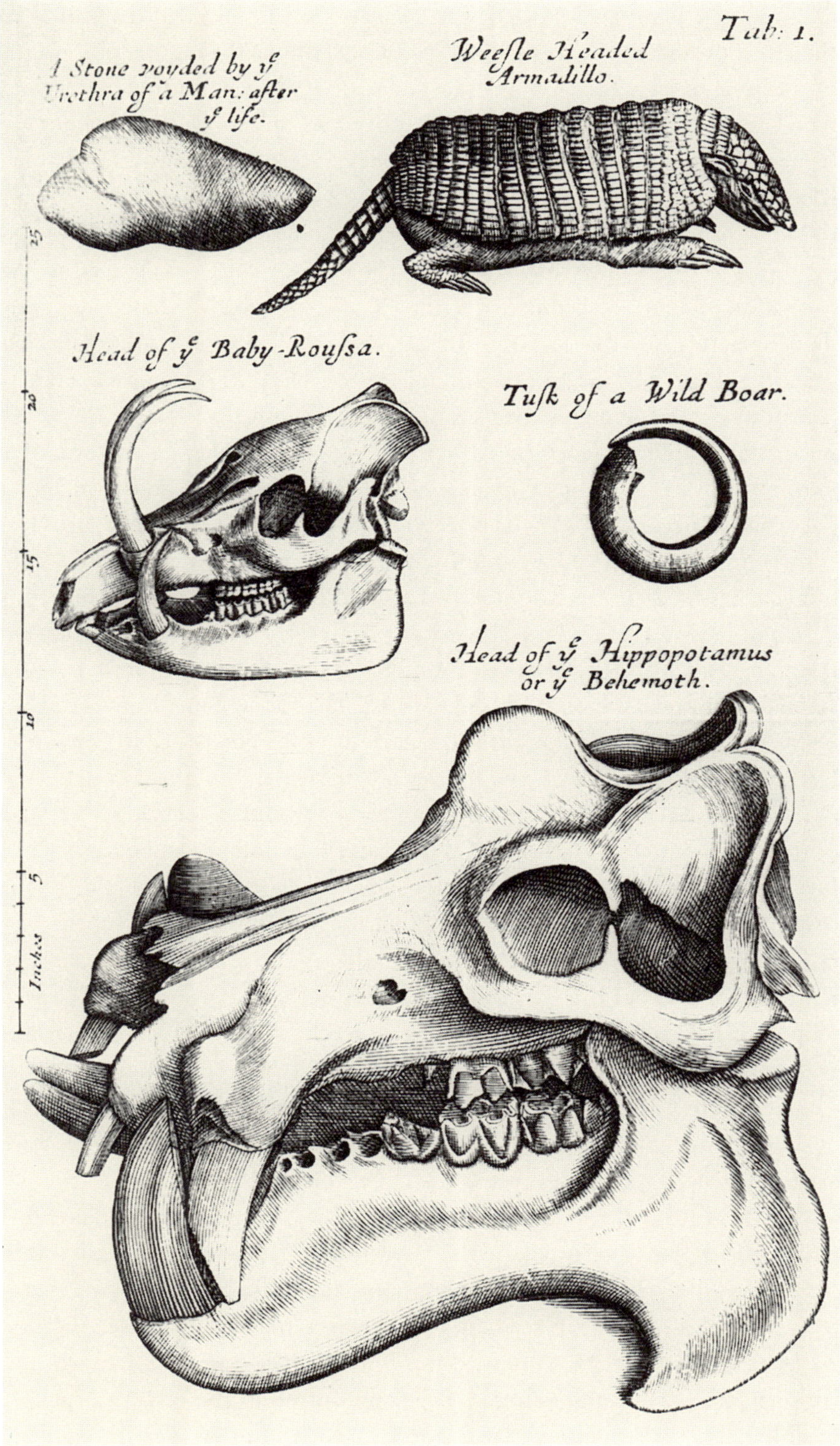
Tab: 1.
A Stone voyded by ye Urethra of a Man: after ye life.
Weesle Headed Armadillo.
Head of ye Baby-Roussa.
Tusk of a Wild Boar.
Head of ye Hippopotamus or ye Behemoth.
Inches
5
10
15
20
25

and powerful who saw knowledge as a leisure pursuit and had the money to finance coordinated efforts such as expeditions. Unlike the natural philosophy of medieval times, which was abstract and textual, the new natural history was tactile and visual, because it was descriptive and object-orientated. The new menageries, botanical gardens and museums exhibited collections that formed frameworks for a new scientific practice as well as allowing non-professionals to participate. Professional natural historians and amateurs would go on expeditions to the countryside together and botanise, which was crucial to the formation of a new perception of nature. Whilst enjoying the landscape, thus drawing nature into the field of aesthetics, they would refine the dissemination of natural history by means of art and literature. Nature became part of a new consumer culture, and prestigious collections became attractions for European scientists, including the so-called "curiosi" – young noblemen on formative journeys. The most exotic items were also the most precious, and exotic obviously meant from as far away as possible. A fascination with the rare, new and surprising was considered an important character trait, and guidebooks were published for the curiosi who travelled around Europe with their tutors.

According to Katie Whitaker, curiosity played the same role in the seventeenth century as the sublime did towards the end of the eighteenth: it was a standard for understanding art and nature.[46] The sublime involved "astonishment" and "terror" regarding the spectacular, infinite, powerful and grandiose. Curiosity, on the other hand, was an admiration for everything that was unusual in size, shape or craftsmanship. Hippopotamuses would raise curiosity because of their size, butterflies because of their marvellous colours and patterns and flies because of their strange lifecycles. The wonder of curiosity is different from the moving sublime, which Edmund Burke writes cannot be perceived rationally: this is why the sublime can only seldom, and always inadequately, be represented. To a curiosi, the curious could be described precisely and clearly, pinpointing exactly what it was about the object that was curious – for instance, the overwhelming impression of power attributed to the hippopotamus' muzzle. The curious must not become exaggerated or enter into the realms of occultism or superstition, and descriptions in travel books and exhibition catalogues were expected to be extraordinary, yet at the same time believable.

For this purpose, a style was developed that was unique in its detailed meticulousness. Plates with potsherds, taxidermic mice, teeth and plants were reproduced in hyper-realistic representations, and in the accompanying literature, meticulous detail replaced allegorical representation. The basic rhetoric was that of the essay, which in its down-to-earth style was apt for suggesting curiosity, knowledge and surprise. The composition is guided by a principle of differences and contrasts that is not systematic but develops through the texts according to the demand for new objects and points of view. This style of writing dominated natural history in the beginning of the eighteenth century, after which it underwent radical changes, specifically due to the principle of classification that Linnaeus introduced halfway through the century, which not only revolutionised botanical science but also made it exceptionally popular and sentimental.

The curiosities of natural history called for the same prose perspective as travel accounts in the effort to recount unexpected and unusual phenomena in a convincing way. Furthermore, natural history and travel accounts overlapped on the actual expeditions, where both aspects were narrated within the same text by a single narrator and discourses on phenomena such as landscape were motivated by similar interests, with a basis in early natural history's revolt against its own textual tradition at the expense of visually descriptive techniques.[47] Stanley's New Journalism is a modern variety of this discursive mode.

An important point of view in this book's literary-historical narrative about travel accounts from the Congo is that early characteristics of the discourse of wonder continued to appear in travel accounts long after the discourse had been rejected by science and philosophy. Nigel Leask mentions in *Curiosity and the Aesthetics of Travel Writing, 1770-1840* (2004) that though the discourse of wonder was subject to increasing criticism from scientific quarters towards the end of the eighteenth century, it still makes up a fundamental component in the early romantic travel accounts from the beginning of the nineteenth century and in the exhibition culture of the nineteenth century, bringing him to suggest that the boundary between eighteenth- and nineteenth-century travel literature should be drawn in 1820. Leask focuses on the transition between the two paradigms and the changing role of curiosity, offering a more nuanced view of the basic shift that constitutes an important background for the transformational field of travel literature around 1900 and Stanley's and Conrad's positions in it.

Nigel Leask quotes Lord Kames' *Elements of Criticism* (1762) as an example that uses the internal double nature of the curiosity concept and indicates the future historical development of the discourse. It illustrates the interconnection between the basic components of curiosity:

"Men tear themselves from their native country in search of things rare and new; and curiosity converts into a pleasure, the fatigues, and even perils of travelling. To what cause shall we ascribe these singular appearances? The plain account of the matter follows. Curiosity is implanted in human nature, for a purpose extremely beneficial, that of acquiring knowledge. New and strange objects, above all others, excite our curiosity; and its gratification is the emotion above described, known by the name of *wonder*" (p. 320).[48]

The discourse on the curious links singularity, novelty, pleasure and knowledge, and in Kames it is also opposed to the sublime. Kames emphasises that the effect of the curious is dependent on its novelty and uniqueness, both of these qualities being enhanced if the object is transported from places far removed in time and space; this is the case, for instance, with antique objects brought home from journeys to the Orient. However, this idea of "foreign curiosity" is in Kames' writings linked to "foreign luxuries", underpinning the strong link between curiosity and the market. The discourse of wonder's obsession with "novelty" links it to a market for fashion and luxury, in which circles of collectors contributed to the creation of a network that today we call the 'leisure economy': enjoyment, novelty, luxury, rare objects, etc. become central to lifestyles and identities.

At the same time, it is possible to trace an opposite tendency in Lord Kames' reflections. The curiosity culture had to maintain a certain distance from the market. The collector values and symbolic values were definitely higher if the object's link to the unique and exotic was not compromised by obvious signs of financial interests – e.g. travel funding or sales of both curiosities and travel accounts. In Kames' opinion, the desire for the novel and exotic furthermore put the collector at risk of becoming self-infatuated. If the desire was connected to knowledge and science, it was a path to insight, but if it was connected to vanity and the urge to possess, it was a sign of poor taste.

In his treatise, Lord Kames made an attempt to save a rational and philosophical concept of curiosity, because at the time it was perceived as vulgar. It became important to him to distinguish between curiosity as an infantile desire to possess and take pleasure in decontextualised objects, and the noble practice of collecting in order to gain knowledge – knowledge that might lead to an increased awareness of each object, and the similarities and differences between objects, enabling an encyclopaedic examination of nature.

Despite Kames' attempted rescue, the discourse of wonder was rejected from the fields of science and philosophy because of its emphasis on the singular, which was fundamentally at odds with the systematic and transcendent principles that became dominant both in natural science's classifications and in art philosophy's rules of criticism and appraisal. Nigel Leask mentions Georg Forster and Alexander Humboldt's travel accounts as transitional phenomena that attacked curiosity as vulgar, searching for a subjective objectivism – a holistic combination of systematic and transcendent principles for observing and communicating the observer's affective response. However, the wonder discourse prevailed at the world fairs and in the popular culture of the nineteenth century, as well as playing a discrete but important role in the history of travel writing. From here, it was brought to the fore once again by surreal-

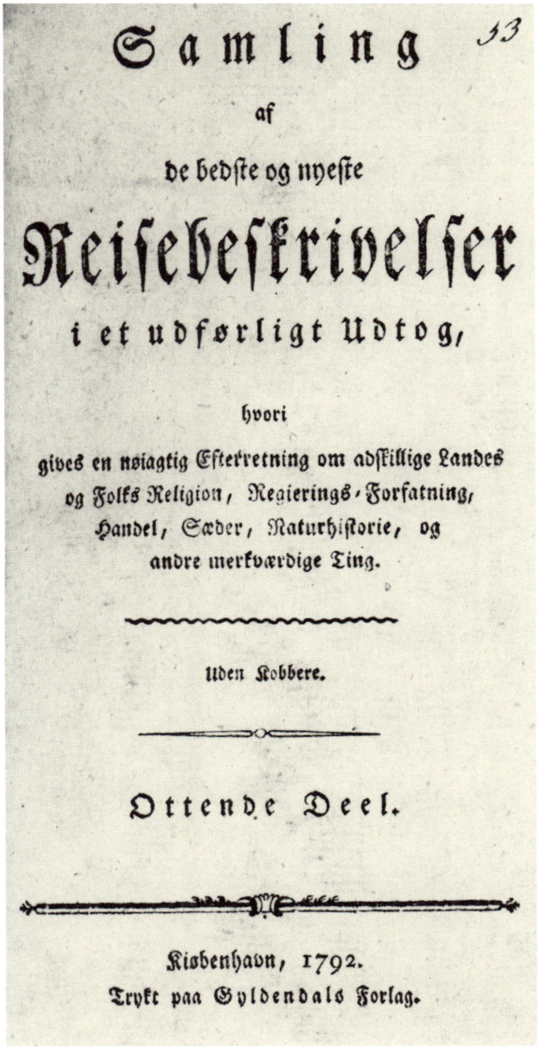
Samling 33
af
de bedste og nyeste
Reisebeskrivelser
i et udførligt Udtog,
hvori
gives en nøiagtig Efterretning om adskillige Landes
og Folks Religion, Regierings-Forfatning,
Handel, Sæder, Naturhistorie, og
andre merkværdige Ting.

Uden Kobbere.

Ottende Deel.

Kiøbenhavn, 1792.
Trykt paa Gyldendals Forlag.

Collection of the best and most recent travel accounts in an extensive selection, in which precise report is provided on several countries' and peoples' religion, government, trade, customs, natural history and other curious things. The collection has been translated from various languages; without engravings (1792). Søren Gyldendal partly founded his publishing company on this series in 16 volumes, launched in 1789. The series made Danish readers familiar with the very popular European accounts of travels in Tahiti and other places.

ism's interest in everyday wonders; it has since inspired a significant trend in twentieth-century sociology and anthropology led by figures such as Henri Lefebvre and Michel de Certeau.

As a category for experiencing the unexpected and unique, the discourse of wonder has had a great impact on travel literature throughout the twentieth century, sometimes in ironic disguises as is the case in Bruce Chatwin's *In Patagonia* (1977). It has not enjoyed the same prominent position in science, aesthetics and philosophy, where it has been associated with exoticism and orientalism, although these ideas ought to be seen as its opposites. The discourse of wonder is based on realism and it is scientific in its aim, which becomes clear when we

look at the detailed hyperrealism of both surrealism and the renaissance. While exoticism and orientalism tended to be fascinated with the obscure, dark and unrepresentable, the discourse of wonder is visualising and essayistic, minutely striving to map the proportions of the curious object. Seen in a long historical perspective, Stanley's travel accounts can therefore be understood as a continuation of the realism inherent in the discourse of wonder under the conditions of mass media and globalisation. The perspectival style of New Journalism and "graphic scraps", and the reporter's uneducated, non-specialised, uncultured yet curious approach to unique and unexpected events in a mundane world, shares common characteristics with the blend of entertainment and knowledge that attracted the curiosi in the renaissance. The discourse of wonder also plays a part in Conrad's *Heart of Darkness*, though it is soon flooded by the text's counteractive and far stronger discourse for describing the unknown: that of the sublime.

The prose perspective described above constitutes a basis for the interpretation suggested in the chapter "Traveller on Global Terms", which will be elaborated in the "H.M. Stanley: Magic and Market", foregrounding other literary-historical connections. The discourse of wonder as a category for sensory experience and phenomenological description of the unusual, unexpected and unique also played a central role in the subsequent definitions of prose genres and disciplines. The curious was more than an aesthetic spectre: it was shared by and formed a link between natural history, philosophy, aesthetics, drama, entertainment and the market in the nascent leisure economy. The discourse of wonder was not reserved for a single literary genre or even for 'literature' itself, but functioned across genres and outside the canon of 'major works'. The rewriting of the literary history of the renaissance, based on principles from New Historicism, proposed that the poetic was articulated anywhere *but* in poetry – i.e. in explorations, diaries and anecdotes forgotten by literary history that focused on major works.

A prose perspective on the literary history of the eighteenth and nineteenth centuries will lead to a reappraisal of the 'major works' style of literary history. In several groundbreaking books, Robert Darnton has warned against the widespread but simplified understanding of eighteenth-century literature that orbits around Voltaire, Rousseau and Diderot, explaining the French Revolution with the motto "c'est la faute de Voltaire, c'est la faute de Rousseau".[49] If, on the contrary, we take into consideration the literary-sociological knowledge available about the circulation of books and specific types of literature in eighteenth-century culture, the texts that we have come to see as crucial to the Age of Enlightenment play a minor role compared to the immense, entangled body of pamphlets, pornography, religious texts, satire, travel accounts and scandalous chronicles that were sold and read in vast numbers in the period.

According to Darnton's thesis, the French Revolution was not forestalled by the great philosophers but by forbidden bestsellers operating within a very widely defined field of prose, disseminating a performative rhetoric of disclosure that would come to subvert the legitimacy of the old regime.

Wlad Godzich and Jeffrey Kittay's *The Emergence of Prose* of 1987 put prose on the agenda of comparative literature, but few have followed their example, perhaps because the book was tied down by the formalism it aims to break with. Godzich and Kittay's "essay in prosaics" can be seen as an attempt to correct *Poétique de la prose* (1971) and Todorov's poetological and formalistic narrowness, using a method inspired by Michel Foucault's *Les mots et les choses* (1966), among others. Their analyses are rich in perspective; the attempt to write a theory and history of prose, however, is incredibly abstract, as is the case with Foucault, and therefore difficult to criticise or to continue. Arne Melberg's theory of prose, in contrast, does not base itself on a critique of poetics, but on readings of concrete works that challenge established genre definitions as well as the formalism that characterised literary studies throughout the twentieth century. His draft concerns a phenomenology of prose, most recently formulated in the book *Aesthetics of Prose* (2008), in which readings of "travel writing" and "life writing" are included together with new forms of prose in the media, e.g. blogs.

From a contemporary viewpoint the situation prose finds itself in looks different from when Godzich and Kittay published their book in 1987. In the last pages they explained that they had written the book because the object had become more visible due to its gradual disappearance: prose as an individual domain was dissolving, outmatched by the new media technologies. Melberg, on the other hand, sees the new media, especially the internet, as contributors to a new development in prose, the so-called "prosaic turn". This echoes Godzich and Kittay's emphasis on prose being ready for change and flexible in relation to print technologies, making e.g. the printing revolution in the fifteenth century or letter-writing and its communication structure in the eighteenth century favourable periods for prose.

Bakhtin has pointed towards a connection between the appearance of a polylingual trading culture and narrative prose.[50] Until approx 500 B.C. prose was mostly used in law documents, and the hexameter was dominant in epic poetry, but this changed with Greek trading culture and its increasing contact with Arabic and other cultures. It began in geographical and ethnographic texts about these foreign cultures and later spread to historical accounts – Herodotus being the most prominent example – through a narrative prose that opposed the epic tendency to stylise. Hellenism's cultural heterogeneity, with centres scattered around the Mediterranean Sea – the form of culture characterised as globalisation by modern archaeologists – is treated thematically in ancient

Greek travel accounts, but according to Bakhtin it also provided the linguistic conditions for the Greek fairytale novel and its playful self-consciousness.

In their book *The Project of Prose in Early Modern Europe and The New World* (1997), Elizabeth Fowler and Roland Greene refer to Godzich and Kittay, in emphasising the similarities between the renaissance discovery of the new world and new colonial markets on the one hand and the growth and proliferation of prose types on the other. Instead of seeing these diverse texts as, for instance, source texts for "Shakespeare studies", the authors suggest that we bring prose to the fore and study "early English fiction" and its complex links to law texts and travel accounts, without any literary sorting of the material. One of the hypotheses is that the prose texts of the sixteenth and seventeenth centuries are more flexible in their links to other kinds of prose because they can simultaneously uphold several opposing positions – cf. Bakhtin's "dialogism". Another hypothesis, in line with Stephen Greenblatt's, is that the shock of encountering the New World resulted in a boom in experiments with enunciative positions and narrative forms in prose.

All these various attempts to bring prose to the fore of literary studies come with a more or less explicit assumption about a close link between the emergence of prose and financial prosperity, or between the emergence of prose and explorations, colonisation and globalisation – cultural encounters that overthrew established perspectives and resulted in differentiated prose narratives. The scope and credibility of this speculative assumption are not the main concerns of this book; the focus here is close textual analysis. However, it is tempting to suggest a link between the relatively late colonisation of the Congo and the globalisation of media and literary markets on the one hand and the plethora of prose forms found in the *fin de siècle* culture on the other. Should we, at this very general explanatory level, understand the innovative experiments with prose as symptoms of colonisation's revolutionary effect on the conditions of globalised media?

4 Literary Topography of the Congo

The central question for this book's adoption of the prose perspective is how travel accounts constitute understandings of place. Its judgements are founded on a distinction between travel accounts that either invite or exclude rational, critical dialogue with the European reader about the place in question and its position in the world.

In the examples of Bougainville, Diderot and Gauguin, Tahiti is basically a utopia, but the texts reveal the place's internal contradictions and invite the reader to join the dialogue's or supplement's criticism of the place, while Hawkesworth's additions have the opposite effect. Tahiti's prominent role in the philosophy and literature of the eighteenth century, within a wide range of prose forms, political pamphlets and poems, as well as its role in popular culture's exploitation of pornographic opportunities in particular, was the result of the travel accounts' shaky and yet realistic perspective.

There were other factors in play: the technological circumstances surrounding explorations; their role in the history of sea voyages; the different forms of dissemination, e.g. the way the Royal Society distinguished between scientific reports and travel accounts, compiling the latter in novel-like narratives that were more widely read than Sterne's *Tristram Shandy*; and, finally, the physical-geographical circumstances, political structures and ethnography. Tahiti's location, far away from the mainland, made it the prototypical island – the classical utopian topos. The island's accessibility and specific characteristics of Maori culture, such as navigational skill and different sexual mores, became components in the construction of ideas about political and cultural equality, while at the same time, together with other curious phenomena and objects, contributing to the marketing first of Tahiti and second of the nation and science that discovered it.[51] Towards the end of the eighteenth century, Tahiti held a prominent position in Europe, albeit in a heterotopia in which the Venus figure's play on archaic and modern 'places' was especially active in creating a field of competing discourses.

Something similar, yet also very different, applied to the discovery of the Congo. The narratives from the Congo came to achieve an even more dominant role than the discovery of Tahiti a hundred years earlier – as we have seen in the first chapter on Stanley as a modern traveller – due to crucial changes in technology and the media. The Congo's geophysical conditions and ethnographic reality had made it impenetrable for Europeans, the opposite of Tahiti, and

therefore the object of a completely different kind of projection from the fuzzy assumptions about a paradisiacal Terra Australis that attracted the earliest European expeditions to the Pacific Ocean.[52] This part of the study will present the Congo as a place that established specific requirements for travel accounts. It is still maintained, however, that despite its unique conditions the Congo is an exemplar of a general complex problem regarding our understanding of places in a globalised world.

The River "That Swallows All Rivers"

In all texts about the Congo, the great river that runs through the country plays an important role; in the present selection it should be described as the dominant role. In scientific literature as well as in travel reports and diaries, the description of the river is the narrative outline that not only introduces the overall theme of the work, but also facilitates the structure of the ensuing narrative, which is often laid out as a journey on the river. This structure is in principle open to boundless variations, corresponding to the river's numerous tributaries, and the tributaries' tributaries. The vast area covered by the river – from its source south of Lake Tanganyika, north-west of the mountains that include the legendary Mountains of the Moon, arching westward towards the river mouth at the Atlantic Ocean – is a dramatic narrative in its own right, featuring obstacles, delays, triumphant charges and calm spells. Stanley's *Through the Dark Continent*, which describes the first complete journey on and mapping of the Congo River, tells the story from source to mouth, while *The Congo and the Founding of its Free State* (1885) tells the story in the opposite direction. The former, epic and dramatic narrative follows the stream, orchestrated as an exploration that is powered by the invincible forces of nature; the latter is a narrative about colonisation, to a large extent shaped rhetorically by the attempts to conquer and control the river through a tiresome upstream movement.

The narratives about the Congo River, often a metonymy for the country, form parts of a complex rhetorical figure which has influenced later topographies with far-reaching political consequences. On the one hand, the narratives are predetermined by geophysical circumstances: Africa's great watershed between the Nile and the Congo, metaphorically forming a dividing line between civilisation and barbarism, light and darkness. Furthermore, Livingstone Falls at the Crystal Mountains and Stanley Falls close to Kisangani, former Stanleyville – which Conrad termed the "inner station" and "heart of darkness" – create an effective closing mechanism. Viewed from within, it is a protection against invasion, and through the colossal drainage basin it offers a fantastic transport and communication system. Viewed from the outside, the closing

"A Map of the Congo Basin and Adjoining Territories Showing the Extent of the Congo Free State". The map is an appendix to the Danish version of *The Congo and the Foundation of its Free State* (1885), inserted in a separate cassette. It measures 110 x 93 cm and is made from durable canvas that can stand being unfolded on the dining table time after time. The book is a fascinating account of the discovery and colonisation of the Congo and the foundation of passable roads and posts along the river – the immense effort that earned Stanley the nickname 'Bula Matari', Breaker of Rocks. In the preface, Stanley mentions the accusations that he was a "'Quixotic journalist' or a mere 'penny-a-liner'" brought against him by "merchants in Manchester", when in 1878 he gave a talk about opportunities in the Congo. In 1885, Stanley could exclaim triumphantly: "I told you so!" However, the map also tells a different story to Danish readers who imagine themselves in the field with Stanley: the ease with which the eye can follow the great arc of the Congo River through Central Africa is in sharp contrast to Stanley's real 1874-77 journey, as described in *Through the Dark Continent*. The map also reveals that, apart from the areas surrounding the river, vast areas are still unmapped.

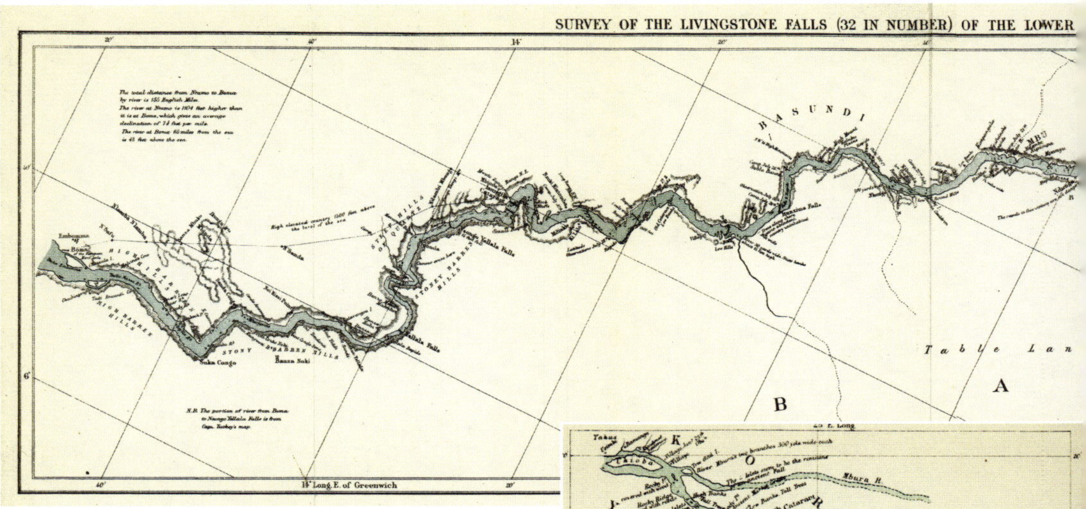

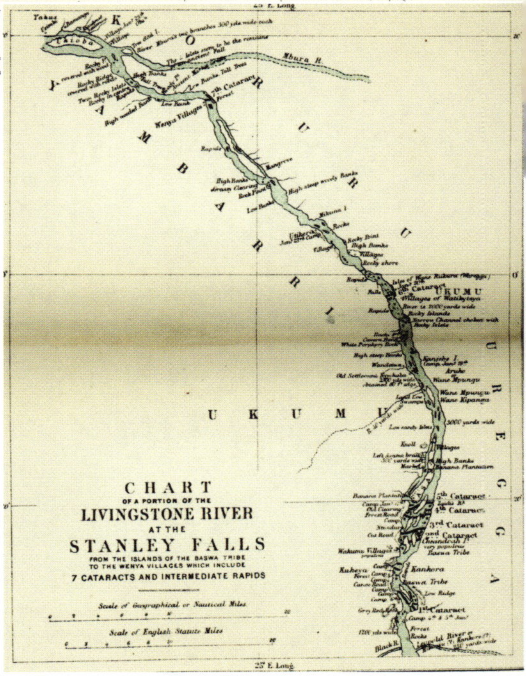

This map from *Through the Dark Continent* (1878) shows the part of the river by Stanley Falls where Stanley's trans-African expedition faced the greatest opposition, from a people he describes as "terrible cannibals". When he returned to Stanley Falls some years later, it was in order to sign contracts and cooperation agreements in relation to trade, labour, and relinquishment of government – the theme of *The Congo* (1885). Contrary to his reputation for ruthlessness established in the former book, Stanley proved to be a skilful and diplomatic negotiator in the latter. In subsequent topographies, Stanley Falls would once again become the heart of darkness.

mechanism creates an image of the country's heart, condensed in the expression "the dark continent". In addition to this geophysical predisposition of textual structures, the travel accounts, reports and literature actively contribute to maintaining, reinforcing and enhancing images of geographical inaccessibility, which subsequently have ideas of ethnic, legal and evolutionary exclusiveness attributed to them. These are descriptions of a permanent state of emergency: at once a fertile greenhouse for the creation of unique biological diversity and an inhumane laboratory in which man is unrestrained by law.

From 1879, Stanley and his men spent two years establishing a pathway through the Crystal Mountains. Among other things, they brought a disassembled paddle steamer to Stanley Pool and created a passable connection

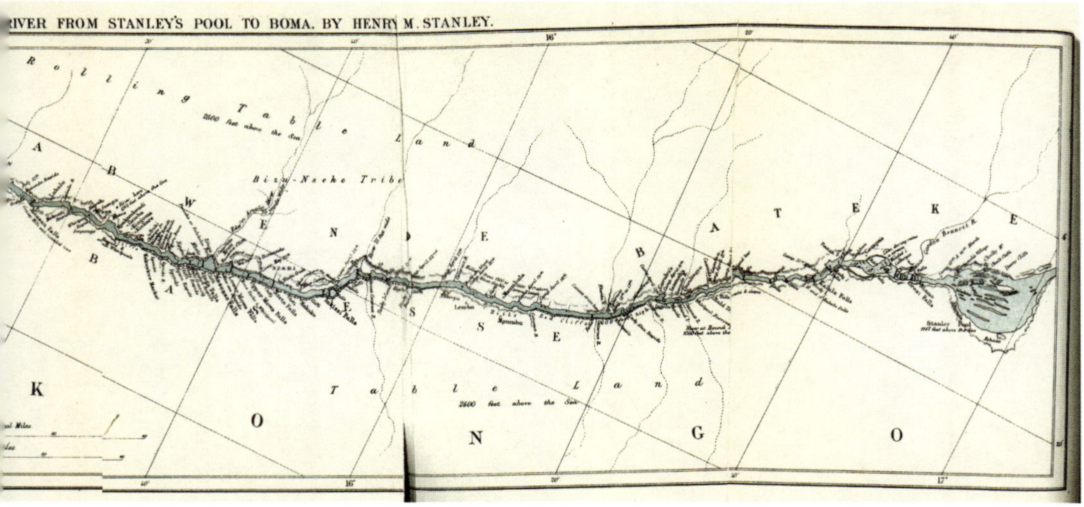

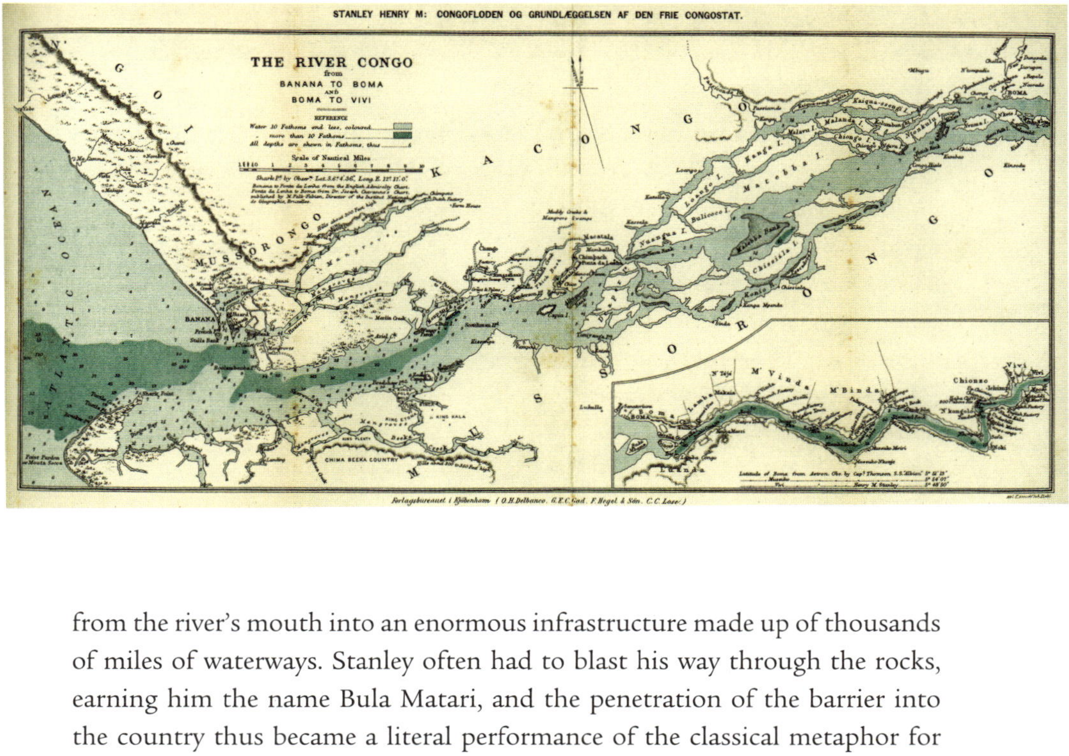

from the river's mouth into an enormous infrastructure made up of thousands of miles of waterways. Stanley often had to blast his way through the rocks, earning him the name Bula Matari, and the penetration of the barrier into the country thus became a literal performance of the classical metaphor for its colonisation: the *opening* of Africa. While *Through the Dark Continent* is an account of the unpredictable and perilous journey down the river, Stanley's *The Congo* is narrated in the style of a grandiose epos about the conquering of the country's centre, named in the classic style and fortified with stations and outposts. Stanley, however, also penetrated another barrier.

The period up until the 1870s was relatively stable for the communities along the coast of the Atlantic Ocean and for the princelings that protected and taxed

"Transportation of the steam boat 'Stanley'". The shore at Vivi, illustration from *The Congo* (1885). The river system had always been the main network for trade and communication in the Congo, but after colonisation it also became an extensive network through which the Europeans gained access and secured control. Due to the waterfalls and cataracts, the Congo River could not be navigated between Vivi by the mouth of the river and Stanley Pool. The post at Vivi was set up in September 1879; the steam boat 'Stanley' was launched in the waters near Léopoldville in December 1881. All contract workers, including Joseph Conrad, had to use the old caravan roads around the cataracts. It was a 350 km trek on foot – or, if the fever hit, in a carried hammock.

transport links and the transportation of wares to and from the coast. The trading posts by the coast wanted to bypass these intermediaries and establish direct trade with the producers, but apart from physical obstacles, such as mountains and waterfalls, the intermediaries attempted to secure their positions and income by telling stories about nameless terrors along the transportation links.

The opening of the river system and traffic was also therefore an opening for the light to penetrate the darkness. *The Congo* is written as a coherent break with the paranoid ideas of cannibalism and spectacular violence that were propagated by the native intermediaries – the so-called "linguists" – and had helped reinforce the nineteenth-century Victorian myth of the Dark Continent. Stanley's style is a mix of detailed realism and romantic lyricism, encompassing sudden stylistic shifts between, for example, letters to his employer criticising useless, brutal trade post managers, and informative, even touristic passages that describe the river as a panorama seen from an imagined vantage point and compared to the Rhine or the Mississippi. Stanley imagines that, if he could break free of the immense fatigue of the actual journey and instead travel along it on a steamboat with luxurious salons and modern facilities, he would be able to view the river in a "more grateful and a cheerier mood":

"But supposing that a steamer similar to those we have on the Mississippi bore you up the Congo, rushing up stream at the rate of twelve knots an hour against the current, while you could travel up and down a long, broad deck protected by a sun-proof awning, with luxurious board and lodging at your command, your view of the Congo would be very different. I do believe you would express a preference for it to any river known to you. You would naturally think of comparisons. The Rhine? Why the Rhine, even including its most picturesque parts, is only a microscopic miniature of the Lower Congo; but we must have the Rhine steamer, and its wine and food and accommodations to be able to see it properly. The Mississippi? The Congo is one and a half times larger than the Mississippi, and certainly from eight to ten times broader. You may take your choice of nearly a dozen channels, and you will see more beautiful vegetation on the Congo than on the American river. The latter lacks the palm and the *calamus*, while the former has a dozen varieties of the palm. Besides, it possesses herds of hippopotami, crocodiles innumerable; monkeys are gleefully romping on the islands and the mainland; elephants are standing sentry-like in the twilight of the dark forests by the river side; buffaloes red and black are grazing on the rich grass plains; there are flocks of ibis, black and white parrots, perroquets, and guinea fowl. The Mississippi is a decent greyish-coloured stream, confined between two low banks, with here and there a town of frame houses and brick. The Congo is of a tea-colour on its left half, and on its right half it is nearly chalky white. You take your choice, tea or milk, red or Rhine wine. And as for the towns, why, I hope the all-gracious Providence will bless our labour, and they will come by-and-by; meantime there is room enough, and to spare, to stow the half of Europe comfortably on its spacious borders. The Nile? Ask any of those gallant English soldiers who have tugged their way among the Nile cataracts, what they think of the Nile to spend a holiday upon. The Danube? Ah, it is not to be mentioned with the Congo for scenery! The Volga? Still worse. The Amazon? By no means. You will have to ascend very far up the Amazon before you will see anything approaching Congo scenery. Well, you must admit then that if the Congo could be seen from the deck of a commodious steamer, this feeling of weariness which we have to contend against now while ascending at this snail's pace against the current, because we have no room to move about, would be replaced by a more grateful and a cheerier mood" (*The Congo and the Founding of its Free State vol. II*, p. 8-9).

"Market scene at Stanley Falls". From Ward's *Five Years with the Congo Cannibals* (1890), which – compared to Stanley's *The Congo* – was less weighed down by political considerations, but equally well-written, with its changing perspectives and anecdotes about life, types, and landscapes in the colony: in this image, peaceful traffic on the river. Ward's sketches were developed by W. B. Davis.

This passage stems from the experience of very little variation on the thousands of miles travelled on the river, which over long stretches offered the same monotonous and limited view. This all-encompassing *tristesse* is only exacerbated by physical fatigue, a lack of commodities and extended periods of inactivity. However, Stanley turns this experience upside down, so that in comparison with other great rivers the Congo River becomes not only the most wonderful, but also the most promising. The imagined luxury of a tourist trip on the Rhine pales in comparison with the description of the river and the landscape as sating all appetites: there is red or white wine, tea or milk. There are countless examples in the text of these rhetorical markets for all kinds of amazing wares in a place where there is - in reality - only forest. Furthermore, by comparing the Congo River with other rivers its unattractive appearance is turned on its head, both promising and inviting future prosperity. The most important point is that, to Stanley, the river becomes a demystified, geographical fact instead of a legendary source of terror and curiosities, in contrast to the earlier *Through the Dark Continent* which is propelled by the stream of old tales about the river.

The Congo works its way upstream in a mapping discourse that stages a drama in which the curtain is drawn back to reveal hitherto unseen riches and opportunities, while also demystifying with its realistic descriptions, playing down hardship and normalising the relationship with the natives, who are portrayed as political negotiating partners rather than cannibalistic primitives. Both aspects of the rhetoric contribute to the opening and inviting gesture that the book performs. The central part of the country is thus made accessible for transport, trade, colonisation and a prose that addresses the world.

In literature about the Congo, Stanley's *The Congo* holds a central position together with a few other select texts that will be examined later. These texts stand out because they are not subject to the dominant rule that the Congo should be perceived as a place where anything can happen and everything is allowed. Stanley blasted the barrier that sealed off the central part of the country from Europeans, which had given rise to wild ideas of the region as a medieval bestiary. Later travel accounts and fictions, the most famous and influential being Joseph Conrad's *Heart of Darkness*, contributed in rhetorical and literary terms to the reconstruction of the barrier broken down by Stanley. To Conrad the journey up the river and into Africa is a journey into another world, and the destination shortly before the second great obstacle – Stanley Falls by present-day Kisangani – becomes the origin of nameless terror. The journey into the country was, in Conrad's version, a journey back in time, which facilitated events and narratives that contemporary civilisation on the other side of the barrier had repressed or held at bay.

The barrier in question is both concrete – even after Stanley's breakthrough there was still a long river journey from the river mouth to Stanley Pool, during which many travellers succumbed to fevers – and literary: it is a rhetorical predisposition in the texts, rooted in the geophysical and climatic conditions as well as in the preceding texts, some of which, such as Conrad's, were particularly influential. The topographical sluice function characterises the literary images and ideas of the Congo, but it has also had a profound effect on the country's recent political history; it has been common practice among local and international authorities to renounce any political responsibility for the Congo with vague references to the perceived idea of the country as a place in a permanent state of emergency.

This book's section on "The Twentieth Century" will investigate further the sluice mechanism's effect on a number of colonial travel accounts and literary novels. It will also examine texts that counteract and avoid this reductive exclusivity. Importantly, it is the critical and postcolonial texts in particular that propagate and continue to simplify the damning rhetoric it traces as a pattern in colonial times. This is the case, for instance, in highly polemic texts such as Adam Hochschild's *King Leopold's Ghost* (1999) and Sven Lindqvist's *Exterminate All the Brutes* (1992), but also in Michela Wrong's well-researched

King Léopold's *Musée du Congo* launched a series of pamphlets in 1903-5, documenting the progress in the colony by juxtaposing photographs from before and after the establishment of the Free State in 1885. In February 1904, the pamphlet "Roads and means of communication" was published, and in April of the same year "On the protection and heightened morals of the native". The explanatory text is very sparse, but the editing and arrangement of images, in the period fashion with winding art nouveau ornamentation, experiments with the possibilities presented by the relatively new medium. The photographic documentation was intended to speak for itself: it was well known to the Belgian reader that the journey on foot between the coast and Léopoldville had cost many lives, but on the following pages they could marvel at straight "European road systems" for automobiles, viaducts, telegraph systems, and the railway, which Stanley had invited the Manchester merchants to build in 1885 as a replacement for the old caravan roads. Reprinted from *Naissance du Congo Belge*, edited by Dirk Thys van den Audenaerde (1989).

and influential political report on the Mobutu era, *In the Footsteps of Mr. Kurtz* (2001).

Peter Forbath's *The River Congo: The Discovery, Exploration and Exploitation of the World's Most Dramatic River* (1978) can be seen as a prototype for the approach taken in most contemporary books about the Congo. The point of departure is an often very personal impression of a contemporary violent event. In Forbath's case this is the crushing of the rebellion in Stanleyville in 1964, when drugged jungle warriors, the so-called Simbas, dressed in monkey skins and lead by a witchdoctor, massacred thousands of people including hundreds of whites. Forbath relates in the introduction how he watched the great river in the ghostly atmosphere of the town and decided to write a book about its history, nature and myths in the style of Alan Moorehead's books about the Nile.

Forbath's genealogical method takes him in two directions. In the long chapter "The River That Swallows All Rivers", he follows the river from source to mouth, describing the climate and history of different parts of the country. Subsequent chapters tell the country's history, covering the first encounter with Portuguese colonists in 1482, the barbarising effect of the slave trade on the country's institutions, the explorations in the nineteenth century, King Leopold's reign of terror and Mobutu, who seemed only to repeat all the terrors. For both genealogies, the mythologising material is crucial: the legend about Prester John and the forgotten Christian kingdom in the middle of Africa, for instance, is mentioned as a strong motivational factor for the Portuguese endeavours on the Atlantic coast, while similar ideas of previous migrations from Egyptian civilisations are said to have stimulated the journeys into Central Africa from Zanzibar.

Although *The River Congo* was promoted as an exposition, illumination and explanation of the myths behind the Congo's closed world, the author is more interested in maintaining these myths in the present. He concludes his narrative by repeating his consternation with the massacre in Stanleyville, returning to a quotation from Conrad in which the river is described with the figure of the 'living dead', the classic oxymoron: "this stillness of life did not in the least resemble a peace. It was a stillness of an implacable force brooding over an inscrutable intention. It looked at you with a vengeful aspect" (*The River Congo*, p. 8). Forbath thus completes the circle of myths by reaffirming them: the river and the country remain obsessed by the demonic power that devours everything and explains nothing.

Forbath's starting point is critical and analytical, and his narratives about the branching network of stories and myths related to the river are both captivating and informative. Nevertheless, ultimately his project is a nostalgic romance – a longing to keep the Congo as a splendid adventure, a magic, dark

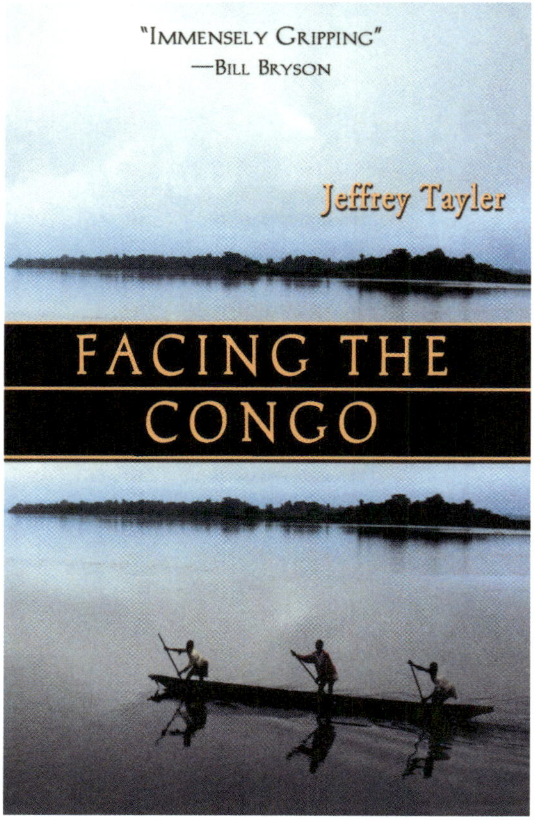

The cover of J. Tayler's *Facing the Congo* (2000). The author describes himself as a tragic Don Quixote who misreads the travel accounts of others and is compelled to repeat his predecessors' tribulations in order to feel alive. The most suitable locations for Tayler's travel accounts are places that are haunted by disasters and suffering, he claims. The journey behind *Facing the Congo* is an attempt to overcome a personal crisis by repeating Stanley's 1874-77 trans-African expedition in a canoe, whereas the *account* of the journey is an attempt to repeat Conrad's *Heart of Darkness*.

enclave exempt from modern disenchantment. This taste for gothic romance also appears in the titles of critical texts such as Hochschild's polemic *King Leopold's Ghost* and contemporary continuations of the adventure genre such as Jeffrey Tayle's *Facing the Congo: A Modern-Day Journey into The Heart of Darkness* (2000) and Tim Butcher's *Blood River: A Journey into Africa's Broken Heart* (2007), but also in factual accounts such as Michela Wrong's *In the Footsteps of Mr Kurtz* and Robert W. Harms' *River of Wealth, River of Sorrow* (1981). Although Wrong's book tries to maintain a critical distance from the subsequent, trite and twisted literary exploration of Conrad's *Heart of Darkness*, and the media's use of its metaphor as a means of demonising the country, Wrong does not manage to steer clear of the temptation of Conrad's suggestive gothic style. After the river was opened up for exploration and colonisation, it appears that the texts (except Stanley's *The Congo*) create new rhetorical barriers, once again shrouding the country as a ghostly backdrop for decadent fantasies.

This basic, almost compulsory mechanism in literature and the media's approach to the Congo replaced the original geophysical obstacles constituted by the river and the central country with new, equally durable rhetorical barriers. Moreover, these barriers often feed on the mistaken, though effective, use of *Heart of Darkness*. The background, historical course and consequences of this mechanism will be examined in the following. One example among thousands is an illustrated article by Simon Robinson from *Time Magazine*, "Inside Congo", about the photographer Marcus Bleasdale's book *100 Years of Darkness* (2002), which contains contemporary photos of atrocities and terrors in the period leading up to the first free election in 2006 alongside some of the gloomiest passages of *Heart of Darkness* as a continuous, poeticising and mystifying accompanying text:

"The forest and backwaters of the Congo, and the world they hide within them, have long fascinated those with a passion for the unknown. In *Heart of Darkness*, Joseph Conrad's 1902 classic novella of the horrors of colonialism, Congo's intricate geography acts as a metaphor for the recesses of the human kind – as if in the folds and bends of Africa's landscape we can find a meaning behind our hidden desires and nightmares. In such a vast and foreign place, though, even the most plainspoken facts – 4 million people dead since 1998; more than 1000 people dying of war-related disease and malnutrition a day – can remain beyond comprehension" (*Time* 29 January 2007).

This type of rhetoric is common in relation to the Congo, and to most people it appears at first sight to be harmless, just and politically correct. However, the linking of the "horrors" of the concrete place to human kind's universal, existential blackening – as well as the double appeal to both compassion and sublime incomprehensibility – constitutes a far more insurmountable obstacle for understanding the Congo than the obvious colonial stereotypes that postcolonial literary criticism aims to disclose.

How has travel literature contributed to the formation of this common ground? Which historical literary tendencies have contributed to maintaining the rhetorical cementation of the river and the country as dark and gothic, and which lead away from this dystopic simplification?

The Discovery

In a canon of explorations, Columbus, Marco Polo and Jean de Léry would be associated with the opening of the New World in the renaissance, La Pérouse, Bougainville and James Cook would be associated with the journeys around the world in the eighteenth century, while Alexander Humboldt holds a unique position as a transitional figure between the Enlightenment in the eighteenth century and the romanticism of the nineteenth. Burton and Speke, Cameron, Livingstone and Stanley are the great names of the nineteenth century, inextricably linked with Victorian culture and imperialistic ideology. Together

with German and French pioneer travellers in Central Africa, they provided the connections and maps that paved the way for missionaries and societies with scientific as well as mercantile ambitions. Their travel accounts often contain strong direct and indirect appeals to the readers, asking for support for the propagation of what Livingstone summed up as the three Cs in Africa: "Christianity", "civilisation" and "commerce".

Because the expeditions were land based, the explorers met far stronger resistance from the natives than the great fleet expeditions, of which the sea and the elements were the primary adversaries. The land expeditions were therefore subject to far more critical opinions, both in the travel accounts and in their general reception. James Cook could be a hero in the eyes of Joseph Conrad – an uncompromised character – because he was only interested in facts, and because his heroism, determination and courage were not associated with subjugation, victims and conquest. The Victorians' journeys, on the other hand, could not be defended as cosmopolitan trips but were obviously antagonistic and often resulted in war-like encounters.

Across the board, the Victorian era has retrospectively been subject to one of two fundamental interpretations. In the first, the expeditions' extraordinarily insurmountable obstacles result in the leaders being portrayed as Napoleonic commanders whose heroic fighting spirits, strategic understanding and culture overcame even the most fatiguing and – just as importantly – humiliating, circumstances. Even today, the basic formula for the majority of books about the great explorations is a blend of an arduous medieval quest for truth and the Victorian moral ideals of chastity, honour and dignity. In the second interpretation, the same virtues become the object of harsh postcolonial criticism that sees the travel accounts as particularly terrible examples of imperialistic ideology and the nineteenth century's racist doctrines: the explorations are all colonising campaigns. In the scope of this dominant and influential form of criticism, Burton, Speke, Livingstone and Stanley are accorded the main responsibility for subsequent colonial suppression. In Livingstone's words, by "opening up a path to the heart of Africa" they simultaneously paved the way for a global discriminatory practice that has kept Africa in wretchedness until the present day.

Although it is beyond doubt that we are dealing with unusual and impressive achievements, postcolonial criticism is right in claiming that the first explorers' descriptions created dominating and problematic images of Africa. Both models, however, are reductive and weighed down by a nostalgic and backward-looking use of present-day ideology and aesthetics. For instance, both ignore the travels' and travel accounts' dependency and influence on market and institutional conditions, as well as other internal and external contexts. We are usually dealing with assumptions about uniquely admirable or outrageous actions that are uncritically transferred to the criticism of travel accounts as a whole.

What many fail to notice is that the unique design of the explorations and the travel account genre were the result of a conjunction of several factors. These very risky projects were often fuelled by complicated feedback mechanisms. The Royal Geographical Society provided the funding for the expensive expeditions, and therefore contributed actively to their branding. It was of crucial importance that the travel accounts were widely distributed in order to gain an impact on public opinion and subsequently the government, thus securing the funding for science and other humanitarian and economic interests. In this way, the adventurous nature of the journeys, often directed towards blank spots on the map, was legitimised by the scientific institution itself. Burton's first major expedition in East Africa in 1856 followed the pattern of expeditions like James Cook's by publishing in two very different editions: one long, scientific article exclusively directed at the Royal Geographical Society, and the two-volume book *Lake Regions* (1860), which offered a captivating account of the eccentric traveller's romantic adventures. New printing technologies also ensured that the travel accounts could be printed and distributed in staggering numbers – often directly competing with other publications about the same blank spots on the map, or publishing new finds that other expeditions would subsequently question or correct.

The Royal Geographical Society contributed to the spectacular stagings and rituals surrounding the expeditions with the purpose of promoting their leaders as great icons of popular culture, thereby winning political support for the institution. It could, however, cause problems if the travel accounts became *too* popular. The Royal Geographical Society's role in the public controversies that made up a substantial part of the media's depiction of the great explorers was in principle that of an institution that could confirm or disqualify given travel accounts, for instance by arranging lectures and hearings among its members, awarding medals etc. However, the reputation and authority of the society could also be seriously questioned, since when a travel account became a bestseller it gained its own supporters in the new mass audience, who would bring pressure to bear through newspapers and parliament. The accounts of the expeditions to the Nile became part of such a process in which authority, credibility, adventure and science contributed to – and were highly affected by – profound changes in the scientific, literary and political public spheres. One of the most challenging and interesting aspects of Stanley's travel accounts is their place in this patchwork of different interests.

The unique status and popularity of the expeditions to Central Africa was also due to the region's geographical and ethnographical distinctiveness. As

previously mentioned, central Congo was inaccessible until Stanley's transatlantic expedition opened it up from east to west, and his colonising march from west to east created a passageway. Both the Portuguese and the British had several times attempted in vain to venture beyond the Crystal Mountains. From the Atlantic side, farther north, expeditions had aimed for the promised land of Timbuktu, which was assumed to offer fabulous riches. These expeditions, however, happened on the Niger River, known from the Arab traveller Leo Africanus' descriptions of travels in North Africa in the first half of the sixteenth century and made famous through Mungo Park's romantic descriptions from around 1800. Similarly, the centre of equatorial Africa was inaccessible for Europeans who wanted to gain access from the east and the Indian Ocean. The Arabs and the Chinese had sailed the coast since the fourteenth century, and the Portuguese had had some posts scattered there since the sixteenth century, but nobody had been in contact with the central part of the area.

Trade was dominated by the Arabs on Zanzibar, although the nineteenth century witnessed increasing competition from the growing settlements of Indian merchants on the east coast of Africa. The economic growth in the area led to a situation in which natives from the central parts of Africa brought ivory and slaves to the coast, while the Arabs followed them back in order to take control of this traffic. The British, who had initially decided to stay out of Central Africa, convinced that the expenses would not cover the profits, were reluctantly drawn into the control of Zanzibar – partly as an authority in relation to the Indian Diaspora, partly because the island became a global market place in which French and American ships were also involved. After Zanzibar became a British protectorate, the official foreign policy was – until the final negotiations about Africa in the 1880's – that Britain did not wish to interfere with the affairs of the mainland. This was the case even though it was the official opinion that the increasing slave trade on the east coast of Africa in the nineteenth century should be prevented. The trade was a result of the British having limited traffic on Zanzibar as a part of their protection agreement with the Arabs. The accounts of the first inland journeys from the east coast form part of a complex field of conflict, partly due to the region's ethnic and geographical conditions, partly due to Britain's ambiguous attitude towards the slave trade.

The game of politics between the Royal Geographical Society, British foreign policy, public opinion and the travel accounts was on a general level rooted in the balance between rivalry and pragmatic political considerations. The British government was torn between the desire to remain neutral and the ideological demands to end the slave trade, which were deeply rooted in the British collective identity. Livingstone's bestseller *Missionary Travels*, which in the two years after it was published in 1857 sold 70,000 copies, and his iconic status as a pilgrim, saint and national symbol, was linked to his position as a go-between in this conflict between Britain's pragmatic 'non-interfering' policy and the generally accepted ideological foundation in "Christianity, civilisation and commerce", the most important and legitimate agenda of which was abolition. The boom in expeditions aiming to penetrate Central Africa were an important basis for Livingstone's tempting pragmatic and religious programme, which basically aimed to protect good, innocent natives from Arab slave traders and native mediators. And although the slave trade in the rest of the world, including the African west coast, ceased towards the middle of the nineteenth century, the hunt for slaves from the east coast grew increasingly savage and intense, in particular due to the demand from markets in the Islamic world, which were not restricted by the British regulations of world trade. In other words, Livingstone and his successors had a just cause, critical towards the government's *laissez faire* attitude towards Africa, and affirmative of their readers' basic humanitarian and national feelings and morals.

Both these factors added to the travel account's popularity, but there was always the risk of backfire. Livingstone's romanticised account in *Missionary Travels* – about his 1852-56 expedition from Cape Town to Angola and along the Zambezi River to Mozambique, featuring the spectacular view of Victoria Falls as a highlight – resulted in an inflated confidence in the opportunities offered by settlements along the Zambezi. After a tour of lectures and propaganda, Livingstone became the leader of an expedition in 1858 that was funded by the Royal Geographical Society, the government and the missionary societies, aiming at realising these opportunities. Instead, the expedition ended after six years of disease, fatalities and miserable management. They also failed to find the archaic pastures that *Missionary Travels* hinted at and which Livingstone, in his account of the Zambesi expedition, stubbornly maintained existed in *Narrative of an Expedition to the Zambesi and Its Tributaries, and of the Discovery of the Lakes Shirwa and Nyassa* (1865). Livingstone's popularised and propagandic accounts, with their descriptions of disease-ridden swamps as inviting pastoral landscapes, thus resulted in unrealistic expectations and subsequently in criticism and scepticism. However, the criticism did not weaken his archaic style, in fact quite the opposite happened.

Livingstone's reputation as a pilgrim and peaceful wanderer who intervened in the slave traders' cruel violations was exploited in the retrospective reception that characterised Stanley as militant and insensitive. However, this characterisation is based on interpretations and extensive editing of the expeditions' actual, chaotic events, including the fact that Livingstone, in order to achieve his more egoistic goals, had to enter into agreements with the same people he

Thomas Baines: *Town of Tete from the north shore of the Zambesi*. Baines took part in Livingstone's expedition and created an enormous number of images of Africa – around 4000 paintings and sketches.

exposed as villains in the texts.[53] Livingstone's travel accounts established and popularised a rhetorical formula that would come to permeate subsequent travel accounts and humanitarian campaigns. The stylised balance between, on the one hand, the description of landscapes and customs as an inviting, pastoral idyll that facilitated a vision of a Europeans presence, and, on the other hand, the horrifying examples of the intruders' violations and destruction in an ethical and sometimes humanitarian spirit of intervention, is far from unproblematic.

Another determining factor in the enormous popularity of the Victorian travel accounts from the middle of the nineteenth century was the battle for the Nile. That, however, is beyond the scope of this book, although the accounts of the explorations to the great river definitely deserve literary investigation.

Livingstone's first journeys had their point of departure in the South African colony, but during his last, disastrous expedition from 1866 in the area north of Lake Malawi and Tanganyika, he was obsessed with the idea of answering the questions about the source of the Nile, at the expense of pilgrimage and ideology. And when Stanley met the fatigued, deserted and ruined explorer in 1871 at Ujiji close to Lake Tanganyika, Livingstone was ready to risk everything on a joint expedition with the American journalist if it would increase his chances of finding the ultimate answers.

In the end it was Stanley, not Livingstone, who with great efficiency and considerably more skill managed to solve all the remaining riddles. However, Stanley struggled to gain recognition for his results, which would allow him to step out of Livingstone's shadow – something that became even more difficult after the national hero's funeral at Westminster Abbey in 1873. Stanley's position as Livingstone's successor became a point of public interest in the popular conflict with the Royal Geographical Society. The furore and ruthless attacks on Stanley's person and credibility were rooted in the reluctance that the scientific society as well as the majority of the public showed in recognising his reports about the Nile, although they were in fact far more precise than his predecessor's. Despite Stanley's declared admiration for Livingstone, his corrections could only be perceived as depreciations of Livingstone's significance as a national icon.

With the discovery of the Nile's sources, the answers to many other questions came into focus, reaching far back in history and containing a fascinating mix of myth and adventure. The Nile's flooding in Egypt had created the basis of our own civilisation, although plausible explanations for this phenomenon had yet to be found. In *Histories,* Herodotus treated the source of the Nile as a riddle and let the answer be found in a barbaric region where the natives had no heads, eyes on their chests, and screamed like bats. Six hundred years later, Ptolemy situated the riddle and myth that surrounded it in the so-called Lunae Montes from which the meltwater allegedly provided the enormous amounts of water for the Nile's lakes. If Speke and Burton in 1856-58, or Grant and Speke in 1860-63, had drawn a map of the Nile's sources and the great Central African lakes, they would not only have been able to erase the hodgepodge of canards and legends that had corrupted Ptolemy's rather precise knowledge since medieval times; they would also have filled one of modern science's most significant blanks. Explorations with this aim, however, were in themselves mythological quests for profound truth and meaning: by delivering the *coup de grace* to the riddle's magical ability to generate new fables and tales, as well as localising the source of civilised man and the cradle of culture, the explorations in Central

Africa mythologised both modern science and the travellers' grandiose and god-like self-assertion, interspersed with paranoia and self-loathing. Richard Burton, in particular, was a highly complex, almost schizoid character, an apt representative of the conflicting impulses behind his expedition, which also formed a part of the readers' fascination with it. Discoveries relating to the Nile can be perceived as an important prerequisite for the discovery and description of the Congo among readers and explorers alike. It constituted a profound resonance for the mythological aspects of the Congo explorations, sometimes in comparison with e.g. the Nile's fertility and potential for art and culture, but first and foremost as a contrast: if the Nile was the origin of civilisation, the Congo represented the unfathomable depths of barbarism.

In the mid-nineteenth century, Central Africa was the last large, populated part of the world that had not been mapped by Europeans. Tales from Arab slave and ivory traders who reached it from the east coast or from Sudan in the north were still only loose and contradictory rumours. Obviously, the fact that the extensive encyclopaedia of natural science had not managed to create these maps contributed – along with economic and civilisation motives – to the eager interest in the region: an interest which, towards the end of the century, resulted in the final race for colonisation, the so-called 'scramble for Africa'.

The most significant reason for the worldwide focus on this apparently unwelcoming part of the world was the asynchronicity manifest in the themes, production and reception of the travel accounts. The inland expeditions in this climate and under circumstances that demanded day-to-day negotiations with new authorities about passage and road taxes were obviously different from the journeys around the world in the eighteenth century. It was necessary to bring large consignments of products, e.g. cloth and metal, which could be used as currency in the constant negotiations for free passage, and to acquire food, as supplies could not be brought from home. This meant that the expeditions brought a considerable and tempting stock that must be protected by armed men. At the same time, illnesses made it impossible to use pack animals such as horses, donkeys or mules, meaning that everything – scientific equipment,

"The steel boat 'Advance' (from a photograph)", from *In Darkest Africa* (1890). In the introduction to the book, Stanley provides the expedition list of purchases, specifying the companies that delivered the items, with special thanks to Hiram Maxim, the inventor of "The Maxim Automatic Gun", who donated all his "wonderful weapons" to the expedition.

weapons, ammunition and other often heavy and advanced equipment – had to be carried by native carriers. The need for protection and transportation was the main reason why the Central African expeditions required such a vast number of men; some of them made up of several hundred people, and the biggest up to a thousand. Most of these men were natives from other parts of Africa, such as Zanzibar, and they were followed by women and children. To the small African principalities these expeditions must have looked like veritable campaigns, and naturally that is how they were greeted. The retrospective collective term "militant geography", however, overemphasises the military element of the expeditions. They may have been equipped with modern weapons, but they were also vulnerable, exposed organisms – slow, often starved and fatigued by illness, weakened by desertion and theft and finding themselves in chaotic situations in which everyone had to fend for themselves, left to their own devices in the struggle to survive.

A key theme of the travel accounts, therefore, is the narrator's leadership, negotiating tactics, self-control, bodily control, disciplining of employees, problem solving under stress, and – of course – dramatisations and detailed, often masochistic, descriptions of the obstacles that must be overcome. In this sense, the texts can be understood as simplified projections of the rationalised versions of work and city life that had followed in the wake of industrialisation. The travels and travel accounts constitute a kind of "frontier romanticism" or Baden-Powell fantasy in which boy scouts can act out fantasies of power, otherwise only accessible in fiction, within the confines of nature reservations. The paradox – and what is truly appealing about this nostalgic project of men being forced to shed both cultural symbols and technological aids in order to test their resourcefulness and physical prowess – is that the travel accounts are at the same time closely related to the technology from which they are trying to distance themselves.

Technology was vital to the expeditions firstly, because they brought equipment and weapons that demonstratively displayed their superiority as a civilisation and secondly because the travels and travel accounts were highly dependent on steamships, the telegraph and the printing press that, in conjunction, created a network of effective and hyper-modern communication both before and after the expeditions. Until an expedition reached the coast, the accounts emphasised this network of global dimensions which, when the expeditions ventured into the interior, were abruptly forgotten as the writer focused on the enclosed sphere of the diary. Once contact with the global network was re-established, the diary could be edited and transformed into mass-produced travel literature for the international market. These shifts between high technology and low technology were prioritised by narrators, and readers were fascinated by the opportunity to alternate between shedding and wearing a number of civilisation's attributes, in the style of Robinson Crusoe. This style particularly applies to Stanley, who was noted for his inventions both in the production and distribution of travel literature – e.g. by using custom-made equipment and by sending telegrams not only before and after, but also *during* his expeditions. Among his famous inventions are the assembly kit boat and the legendary cap with ventilation holes – the latter becoming one of the eccentric components of the media hype

"The Kinshasa Post at Stanley Pool", from *The Congo*. In the book, Stanley criticises the state of disrepair and demoralisation that has befallen the posts, which is the impression he gets when he revisits them after having travelled to found new posts along the river. The ideal is well-organised vegetable plots and straight streets and avenues. Contemporary guide books warn travellers against even stopping in the capital of DR Congo, Kinshasa – the former Léopoldville.

about the expeditions to Africa at the time, and still attracting great attention today at the National Geographic Society's exhibition of curiosities.

The chapter about prose defined the space in which the expeditions unfolded, and to which travel accounts have contributed since the renaissance, as a *heterotopia*. In other words, the travel accounts contain several coexisting, competing formations of space and temporality. This becomes most apparent in the partly conflicting aspects of the accounts regarding the discovery of Tahiti, but it is also a fascinating element in the discourse of wonder, as phenomena from destinations distant in time and space are brought close to the reader, who, in return, becomes part of the heterogeneous space of the collection of curiosities.

The above sketch of the Congo as a place is not directed at the recipient's perception of place, but at the travel account's rhetorical effect on the perception

of the place described. It is obvious that such a distinction is a stylised representation that consciously ignores some important points (cf. the comments on heterotopia). In Stanley's case, the overlapping of traditionally separate spaces is simultaneously the accounts' strength and weakness. This applies to *In Darkest Africa* more than any of his other texts, because we are dealing with superposed spaces from the traveller's most intimate core, from the metropolis and from the *fin de siècle* culture. Despite this challenge, the travel accounts from the Congo will be examined with a focus on the topographies – or rather the *model topographies* – suggested via rhetorical and performative means to the reader. On a basic level, the idea is on par with Bertrand Westphal's emphasis on the double conditions of the discursive significance of places: first, the texts' rhetorical shaping of our conceptions and second, the actual geo-physical characteristics of the place.[54]

Another difficulty that has been mentioned in passing is that the material offers many competing detailed topographies – often within a single text – that are then organised in a unified topography or a generalised image of the Congo. In Stanley's case, the unified description of the Congo opens up to different partial topographies, each one containing individual fields, which we will soon come to analyse more thoroughly. The highlands around the lakes, the river and the great Ituri Forests, for instance, signified to Stanley important differences in travelling conditions and encounters with the local residents; this results in corresponding differences in the accounts' rhetoric and narratives.

In Conrad's case we find a distinction between the coastal areas, signified by an immediate accessibility through observations from a distance, and the geographical heart, which is incomprehensible. It is the latter that becomes all-encompassing in the text as a whole. In other texts, the region around Stanley Falls, and the significance endowed upon the place, actually becomes identical with the country of the Congo, and in turn identical with Central Africa. Others sketch topographical limits that actualise the limits between humans and animals, with Pygmies as the evolutionary transitional stage. One key example is the Ituri Forest, a reservation for a diversity of crypto-zoological beings such as the brontosaurus-like Mokele Mbeme. Topographies of this type can be localised in European travel accounts, but they have little or no connection to the local Congolese so-called "mental maps", i.e. the ideas of limits and places in relation to which the Congolese defined their identities. This immense subject area lies beyond the scope of this book but makes up a significant part of John le Carré's *The Mission Song* (2006).

5 Anthropoetic Narrative and Method

A common characteristic of many of the expeditions and travel accounts is their contributions to the colonisation of the Congo. The theme is the Europeans' description of the Congolese, not the opposite. For many years, this type of text has been examined via the theoretical approaches that fall under the umbrella term 'postcolonialism'. This book's criticism of dominant images of Africa in the media and literature is indebted to Edward Said's *Orientalism*, the central work in postcolonial theory. However, the starting point in this book is the close reading of the texts, without prior definition of their imperialist ideology or degree of political correctness. The reading perspective also differentiates from e.g. James Clifford's and Stephen Greenblatt's in focusing on the significance of place, which establishes a critical frame of reference for the comparison of different texts.

Stephen Greenblatt's *Marvellous Possessions. The Wonder of the New World* (1988) examines the discourse of wonder through close analyses of European renaissance accounts of the discoveries of the New World, while his *Learning to Curse: Essays in Early Modern Culture* (1992) transfers the results of these textual analyses to a method for writing literary history: a central contribution to New Historicism. With its methodical investigation of discursive points, coincidences and changes that focus social energy and contain both literary and historical "power", without necessarily being localised in canonised works, Greenblatt's strategy is related to the prose perspective identified in this part of the book. In the introduction to *Marvellous Possessions*, Greenblatt also localises his method in a context that is both personal and anthropological: he read "books of marvels" as a child and later went to Bali, where he was involved in a number of situations that challenged his acquired concepts of representation and culture. Moreover, Greenblatt's method shares common characteristics with the proposed literary history that aims at examining prose in a broad, interlinked spectrum as a kind of literary field work.

Consequentially, Greenblatt's method favours *anecdotes* or "petites histoires" at the expense of history's "grand récit". The anecdote contains, according to Greenblatt, compact information about unstable and unresolved moments in the historical process, which are usually disregarded in the writing of history from a retrospective and resolved position. While the explorers of the renaissance did not doubt Christianity's and Europe's clear advantages, the anecdotes, diaries and travel accounts nevertheless tell of instability and vulnerability – the "shock of the unfamiliar" (p. 2) – in the encounter with the New World. Here,

the curious consists in a unique, radical otherness, and the anecdote is the little tale that reports it without knowing what to do with it or how to contextualise it. Greenblatt's focus and method are clearly different from the postcolonial approach, which had dominated the area until the publication of his book. Stephen Greenblatt's starting point, as well as Bruno Latour's and Nigel Leask's, is that in most situations the Europeans were fundamentally vulnerable and that the changes of perspective on the New World, as well as on themselves, constituted shocking experiences.

Today, the classic example is Jean de Léry's anecdote from his *Histoire d'un voyage au Brézil* (1578) about witnessing the Tupinamba Indians' trance singing on a journey in 1557. Léry's anecdote describes the abhorrence he initially feels at the uncanny behaviour and the horrible singing, which must be the result of the Indians being possessed by the devil – lost in eternal damnation. In Greenblatt's dramatic orchestration of Léry's short narrative, a sudden shift in Léry's attitude is emphasised: from complete condemnation, it changes to a testimony about total ecstasy – a feeling that made Léry claim years after that he could still hear the singing voices.

On the one hand, Léry decontextualises the peculiar phenomenon and even divorces it from his own strong, ideological systems; on the other, he becomes completely absorbed in it, and his every heartbeat reminds him of it. Léry decontextualises the curious not to distance himself from it, but to keep it present in his memory. According to Michel de Certeau, who has also examined the passage, this creates a gash in time since neither Léry nor the historian, who follows in his trail to reconstruct the event, has access to a useful context, which is a prerequisite for our usual method of historicising events in the past. Just as Léry did twenty years later, we can only relate and repeat the initial curiosity as precisely as possible, which Léry in his text does by accompanying the narrative with a representation of the Tupinamba song in written notes. This approach is duly repeated by Greenblatt is *his* representation, which uses the form of prose characteristic of renaissance descriptions of wonder.

Greenblatt's method is to a large degree an attempt to present us with curiosities, making them present through stylistic variations, surprising points of view and dramatic visualisations, as if the readers themselves were curiosi visiting a cabinet of curiosities. Greenblatt concludes his introduction to *Marvellous Possessions* by returning to his own anecdote about his journey to Bali. By doing so, he underpins the concrete localisation and situation of the writing of literary history, as well as emphasising that the curious and peculiar phenomena that fascinate us in travel accounts from long ago, are not far away in a sealed past but present in the work of literary history here and now.

This book's interest in Greenblatt's investigation of Léry's approach to the

The size and beauty of the sunflower caused great excitement in Bologna in 1554, when it was first seen in Europe. Just a few years later it was seen as vulgar. Reprinted from *Cultures of Natural History*.

curious is his use of a prose perspective, both in the continuation of rhetorical characteristics of the discourse of wonder and in the adaptation of methods from anthropological field work in the writing of literary history. As Greenblatt writes in the essay "Resonance and Wonder" in *Learning to Curse: Essays in Early Modern Culture* (1992), the point of view and mode of communication found in the renaissance approach to curiosities is not a thing of the past, but rather fundamental for the wonderment that has always been at the root of philosophical and aesthetic reasoning. This wonderment at phenomena in their unique appearances is a basic characteristic of travel accounts about the unknown; the phenomena are attributed with meaning through contextualisation or what Greenblatt calls "resonance". The criticism that Lord Kames made in the eighteenth century of the vulgarisation of the discourse of wonder, as it threatened to become nothing but entertainment, vanity or commercialism, is also relevant in relation to New Historicism, which has been accused of reducing literary history to a spectacular freak show.

It is no coincidence that James Clifford introduces his famous book *The Predicament of Culture* (1988) with a reading of a passage from William Carlos

Williams' poetry collection *Spring & All* (1923). It indicates the interplay between anthropology and literature that runs through Clifford's entire authorship, and will be discussed as a conclusive aspect of this book's prose perspective. The poem from which the passage is taken describes a maid called Elsie, who is suddenly viewed in a special light: it is as if her figure epitomises the direction of everything. The poem's perspective is ethnographic, because Williams is positioned off-centre, surrounded by scattered traditions. The outlook is the modern conditions of life, where a state of rootlessness and constant mobility has become an increasingly common fate, for the Native Indian girl as well. Things fall apart; "there is no one to drive the car"; and the poem's associations are driven forward as a kind of cultural incest. The ancient idea that change is chaos is given a new twist in the beginning of the twentieth century. According to Clifford, it is now associated with a new way of connecting the local with the global, which, in William Carlos Williams' case, does not lead to nostalgia or essences dissolved in past or tradition, nor to an escape into art.

In the process of globalisation, which allows the "the pure products" to "go crazy", something emerges that Williams calls "isolate flecks"; they are not necessarily "dying sparks", and might even be "new beginnings". The answers to the poem's questions are more than aesthetic in nature, being expressed also its anthropological implications: what reality are we dealing with? What possible futures is man faced with? The poem's Elsie is a "something" that raises anthropological questions, which Clifford tries to answer by analysing, among other things, a court case from 1977 about the Wampanoag Indians' origin and rights to own land. The court case involved many different testimonies and very heterogeneous materials, which raised further questions about race, authority, place, nation, etc. – questions that cannot be solved with a court decision or through anthropological field studies. They can only be contained in the narrative itself, which approaches the answers by articulating and making visible the contradictions in the case, corresponding to Wlad Godzich's concept of the anthropoetic narrative.

The term 'anthropoetic narrative' alludes to the globalised conditions for the identity of a specific place, actualised, for instance, by a plane crash in a Sudanese desert region whose demarcations are unclear in regard to geographical, political, ethnic and discursive definitions. Anthropoetic narrative creates equivalent conditions for the literary historian who chooses to examine narratives that deal with ambiguous zones of overlapping topologies, as mentioned in the sketch of the Congo. The narratives contain knowledge about the globalised conditions for the place, which according to Godzich the literary historian can *recount* without, however, being able to escape these basic conditions and is therefore forced to navigate unstable zones between anthropological *bricolage* and field work on the one hand and recounting and criticising narratives on the other.

In the mind of Clifford, William Carlos Williams is a "doctor-poet-field-worker", an example of an anthropological perception of modernity and globalisation. Williams forestalls the themes of Clifford's essay on ethnographic surrealism and ethnography, in which he lists a number of common characteristics of artistic and anthropological field work, specifically an interest in cultural contamination and re-classifications. In the interview book *On the Edges of Anthropology* (2003), Clifford describes field work as a type of "travel writing". This becomes an explicit method in *Routes: Travel and Translation in the Late Twentieth Century* (1997), where the aim is not to create an overview of the culture of globalisation, but to simultaneously situate and set the project in motion: a collecting of narratives that are worth mentioning at home, exposed to the coincidences of travel, but also forced onto routes that are defined by dominating institutions, power relations and economic systems. In this sense, Clifford's travel account and prose are very similar to the kind of anthropoetic narrative this book will read into Octave Mirbeau's account of an automobile journey in the beginning of the twentieth century. The anthropoetic narrative in Mirbeau's text involves highly diverse materials, and challenges the reader with its conflicting, changeable perspectives on the pressing questions of the day – national and colonial identity – while at the same time challenging the limits for understanding questions of literary and humane nature.

With examples of the prose perspective found in the history of travel literature, anthropology and literature, and with reference to Roland Barthes, this book suggests that we perceive prose not as a genre but as "a methodological field". Travel accounts such as Bougainville's, Niebuhr's and Diderot's contain models for both their own reading and for the 'reading' of the cultural encounter. These models are on a par with 'neoclassical' contributions such as Greenblatt's, Godzich's and Clifford's. The explorers' texts serve as models for a method that deals with analysing travel accounts and writing literary history in a prose perspective: that is, not as a genre or in relation to an imagined divide between fiction and documentarism, but as performative creations of images of the world, corresponding to what was mentioned earlier as a turn from negative to positive categories or a focus on the texts' reality work.

The terms 'literary field work' and 'methodological field' additionally refer to the idea of literature and literary history as a *field* that is influenced by authors, readers, critics and researchers, who can change the limits, coordinates and forces of the domain. Solstad's and Sebald's autobiographical travel novels form part of a general turn in literary culture which not only supplies the field with new experiments but changes it to such an extent that it requires a new description that cannot fall back on, for instance, the formalist dogma of a clear separation between author and narrator.

This book's examples of travel accounts about Congo contribute to the literary historical background for examining questions in relation to the increasing overlap between the news media and the circulation of literature. Wlad Godzich's distinction between "emerging" and "emergent" literature in "Emergent Literature and the Field of Comparative Literature" is a general phrasing of this particular problem. While emerging literature might expand and challenge the field but remain within existing conceptual frameworks, emergent literature will change the field and consequentially the conditions for writing literary history.[55] Godzich emphasises the *field* constituted by emergent literature in order to stress its new, fundamentally different methodical challenge. This field is dynamic, and its methodology cannot be predetermined – the way texts are read determines the field. A genre theoretical conceptual framework would have maintained an idea of the travel accounts as emerging: well-defined and with a marginal status. However, the challenge for literary history of this type is to provide arguments to prove that the prose perspective – supported by the prosaic turn in contemporary literature – not only relocates the coordinates of central works, such as Stanley's and Conrad's, and leads to a re-evaluation of the determining forces behind e.g. the relationship between Europe and the colonies; first and foremost it defines a *field*. It will become clear that we are dealing with a shift from an epistemological or aesthetic terminology to a pragmatic and performative one – although obviously not as the result of applying existing theory. The reading strategy is being 'taught' by the texts.

The anthropologist Claude Lévi-Strauss pointed out that historical events, in exactly the same way as texts, are subject to readings and interpretations. The main interest in this context, however, is Lévi-Strauss' suggestion that historical science should leave behind the demand to reconstruct the past in the absurd hope of achieving a complete representation of history; this, according to Lévi-Strauss, would end in chaos. The alternative is a historiographic position that strives to avoid chaos by organising the material selectively and through a *perspective*. Transferring the field work method to the writing of literary history recognises that the schism in literary studies between internal and external approaches is irrelevant, which in turn reopens a perspective that corresponds with the prose perspective. Literary texts are not perceived as unique, hermetic works – they are in themselves stories: anecdotal, biographical and mythological, organised in different ways and with a different density of information from historical scientific narratives. Lévi-Strauss writes:

"Biographical and anecdotal history is the least explanatory; but it is the richest in point of information, for it considers individuals in their particularity and details for each of them the shades of character, the twists and turns of their motives, the phases of their deliberations. This information is schematised, put into the background and finally done away with as one passes to histories of progressively greater 'power'".[56]

Lévi-Strauss suggests a very simple model that makes it possible to eliminate the schism involved in writing literary history – between formalism and historism – and approach texts from within an inclusive, continuous field without sharply drawn borders between e.g. autonomous literature and subject-specific prose.

Claude Lévi-Strauss' recommendations, which were without doubt provocative at the time, arose from polemics with Jean-Paul Sartre. In a contemporary examination of the same question – although this time on the basis of intervening crises in the writing of history that have resulted in further doubts about its objectivity – Paul Ricœur points in the same direction as Lévi-Strauss. In "Humanities Between Science and Arts", Ricœur discusses historiography as a paradigmatic example of the humanities' position between science and art. At one end of the spectrum, the writing of history is based on documents and archives surrounded by a vast number of procedures for validity and acceptance; at the other end, history always disseminates its knowledge in the form of a narrative, which cannot strictly speaking be said to reconstruct or represent an event in the past but rather obeys its own rhetorical and narrative standards. Paradoxes that are inherent to the phenomenology of remembrance, however, affect all the phases of history writing, including the documentary, where they are brought into play through changing rhetorical devices. Ricœur emphasises that documents – the basis of history writing as well as the historical narratives that are the result – are written in a type of prose that necessitates a selection of testimonies and rhetorical editing regarding the recipients' acceptance. This basic rhetorical condition ultimately refers to historiography's questions of legitimacy in regard to the credibility of testimonies found in the archive:

"You have to regress from representation to explanation and comprehension, and from explanation to documentary evidence, and beyond documentary evidence to the testimonies provided in the archive. Then, by chance, you will hear the voice of the witnesses who said *I was there – believe me or not – and if you don't believe me, ask somebody else.* The reliability of witnesses is our ultimate resource. The confidence put in the word of somebody saying *I was there* is our only help. We have nothing better than testimony and the critique of testimony."[57]

A reappraisal of the limits between fiction and documentarism, fiction and non-fiction, travel novel and travel account does not necessarily result in a state of chaos for the writing of literary history; on the contrary, it facilitates new conditions, especially in relation to the perspectivism exemplified by Lévi-Strauss and

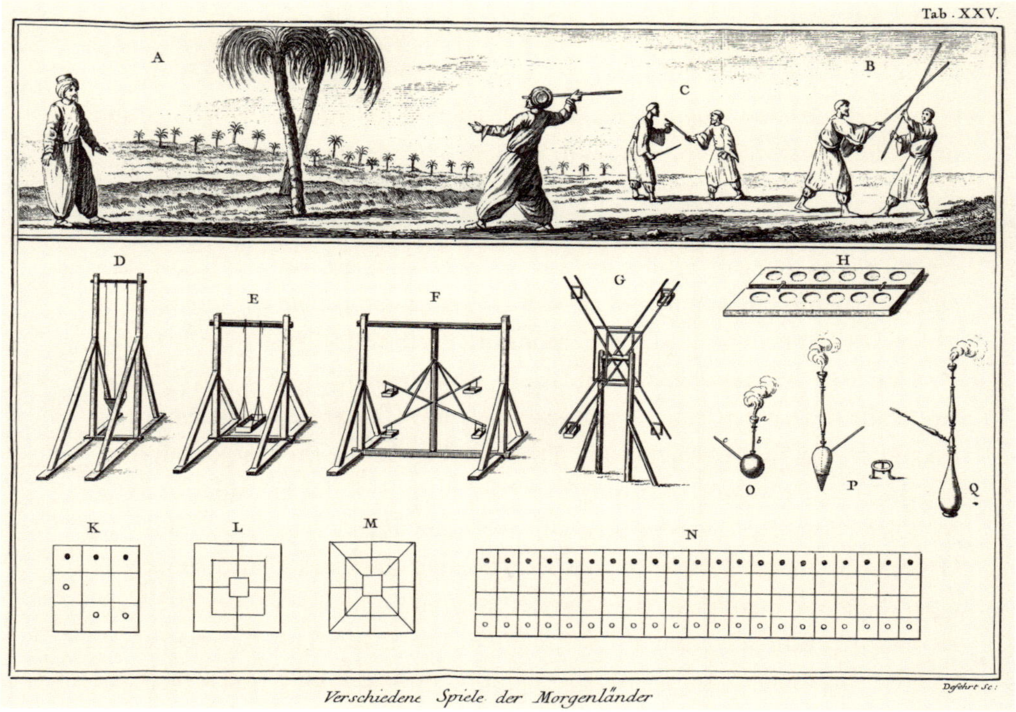

From the Danish version of Carsten Niebuhr's *Travels in Arabia and Other Countries in the East* (2003).

Ricœur. In relation to travel accounts, perspectivism as an organising, critical and terminological concept implicates two basic things in this book's selection of material: first, an obligation towards the current cultural situation at which the readings are directed, which will be the subject of the concluding part of the book; and second, an appraisal of the texts' description of place, which was the subject of the introductory chapter above.

The distinction between testimonies and criticism of testimonies is basically founded on the distinction between good and bad examples, and in that respect no history can avoid hagiographic tendencies. The first chapter dissociated itself from heroising biographies of Stanley, meaning the ones that portray him either as hero or villain. Immediately after, Bula Matari was presented as a *model* in a prose perspective that, in the introductory part of the book, was substantiated with other examples and models. This may seem contradictory; nevertheless, it differentiates heroising history based on assumptions about a person's character and morals from one in which the appraisal is based on the texts. In accordance with Godzich's understanding of work, field and method, the essential momentum of this book is the search for *historical* models, such as Bougainville and Niebuhr, which facilitate reading methods and cultural models that qualify its approach to prose and globalisation respectively. Historical models are the second aspect of perspectivism, presumably the underlying condition for any writing of history. While it often remains unseen, in this book this condition will come to the fore as a simple, basic and urgent reminder of the need to learn from history.

The assumption here is that further theoretical polemic against different theoretical positions is not the best way to develop apt cultural and interpretative models; we ought rather to seek out historical models and criticise the testimonies. Many of the problems discussed here are peripheral and have not been studied thoroughly in earlier research, which naturally sets a limit for the implications of this work. As mentioned, its analyses are orientated towards the effect of the travel accounts and the interactive processes of which they form a part, rather than towards uncovering their hidden, universal meanings. In this sense, the method is inspired by studies of performativity, with particular focus on the interplay between Stanley's cartographic and autobiographic projects. This leads to alternative interpretations of the testimonies, which also play central roles in the other sections of the book: if, rather than understanding them as finished works, we see the texts as events and open-ended processes that form parts of several systems and institutions at the same time – e.g. as performed court cases – we are then forced to distinguish between different 'positions' that a testimony can assume as a function of a travel account in the network of recipient institutions and performative situations. However, with the exception of specific elements in Stanley's texts, the more inclusive concept "reality work" will be used at the expense of "performativity". One of the most obvious advantages of this is that it does not lose sight of the texts' representations of reality, instead allowing us to look at them in several simultaneous dimensions of effect.

As emphasised in the introduction, there is no one specific theoretical frame of reference, since this could easily lead to the same limitations that the most biased branches of postcolonial theory and formalist genre theory suffer under. This is not to indicate a rejection of postcolonial criticism and genre studies *en bloc*, as they form the basis of the present perspective and furthermore take the same direction.[58] But instead of fighting through negative criticism, the ambition has been to point towards the potential of positive models such as Melberg's, as well as positive methodological models such as Bougainville's, Niebuhr's and Diderot's. The use of models does not necessarily preclude criticism, as exemplified by James Clifford's reservations about *Orientalism*. Rather, it denotes a learning perspective: like a student who – in a different situation and on different terms – follows a respected professor, determined to continue the predecessor's best achievements, just as Edward Said saw a model in Erich Auerbach's *Mimesis* (1946) – the great narrative about European literature written in exile and permeated by the destruction of the Second World War.

II

Stanley's prose carries out 'reality work' in different, albeit simultaneous, spaces in Africa, London and Cairo, investigating the question of authority in relation to courts of law as well as the marketplace. It has an almost magical ability to make things happen in the real world, which Stanley perceives as pragmatic – a place for trade and trading.

H.M. Stanley – Magic and Market

This section is a reading of Stanley's major works: first, *Through the Dark Continent*, focusing on the text's internal, rhetorical organisation; and second, *In Darkest Africa*, focusing on patterns in its reception, including links to competing narratives from the same expedition. Its conclusions about space and fetish in Stanley's travel books will return to the concepts from "Traveller on Global Terms" and Stanley's position in what has been established as a prose perspective. The subsequent section focuses on Joseph Conrad's *Heart of Darkness*, which has often been read incorrectly as an antipode to and critique of Stanley, before turning its attention on the reform movement's campaign against King Léopold's "Red Rubber". Stanley's documentary travel narrative and Conrad's literary one form the basis of the book's last section, which investigates how twentieth-century narratives about the Congo branched into travel accounts, novels and popular culture.

First, though, a detailed reading of Stanley's *In Darkest Africa* (1890) – the book about his final major, unsuccessful expedition – will attempt to demonstrate how politics, media and the literary market have had a determining influence on the perceptions of the travel accounts' authority and credibility. It is argued that these disputes are not only about the empirical validity of discoveries, or the literary rhetoric of the narrative as isolated phenomena, but are related to a dense network of determining contextual factors.

This analysis draws on Tim Youngs' *Travellers in Africa: British Travelogues 1850-1900* (1994), while other aspects of Stanley's reception and institutional circulation will refer to Felix Driver's *Geography Militant: Cultures of Exploration and Empire* (2001) and Annie Coombe's *Reinventing Africa: Museums, Material Culture and*

Popular Imagination in Late Victorian and Edwardian England (1994), among others. Mary Louise Pratt's influential *Imperial Eyes: Travel Writing and Transculturation* (1995) deals with African travel accounts, focusing on the texts' rhetorical organisation of gaze and power. Although Pratt's book can be seen as a substantial contribution to the understanding of colonial relations as dynamic and interactive processes, and has played an important role in filling out one of the major blanks in postcolonial criticism, the discourse's analytical perspective entails certain simplifications and fallacies: Pratt's criticism of Victorian explorers for using the trope "monarch-of-all-I-survey", thus paving the way for imperialistic rule, is in itself a dominant trope. With a panoptic and totalising aim, Pratt subjects a massive and highly heterogeneous series of texts to a single, unifying metaphor, which on closer inspection and through 'close readings' prove to be far more flexible and refined – in the contexts, too, of the staging of imperialism and scopophilic fantasies.[59] The main background source on the Emin Pasha Relief Expedition is Iain Smith's *The Emin Pasha Relief Expedition 1886-1890* (1972).

Considering the thousands of pages of material that present themselves for analysis, 'close reading' is probably a misleading term. In this case, however, we will be dealing with two main texts, the first being *Through the Dark Continent, or, The Sources of the Nile around the Great Lakes of Equatorial Africa, and Down the Livingstone River to the Atlantic Ocean*, I–II (1878), a 1100-page epic that immediately became an international bestseller. It also cemented Stanley's reputation as the greatest explorer of all time, since he managed in one expedition to solve several big questions about Africa's geography in a manner so energetic and categorical that even the critics of the sensational Livingstone expedition had to yield to the unquestionable facts. The second is *In Darkest Africa, or, The Quest, Rescue and Retreat of Emin, Governor of Equatoria*, I–II (1890). References to these two titles will be abbreviated as *TDC* and *IDA*. References to unpublished travel diaries and correspondences will refer to *The Stanley Archives*, abbreviated *SA*, and will include the numbers of the archival register, which is available via Musée Royal de l'Afrique Centrale's homepage.[60] References will be made to Stanley's description of his work for King Léopold in *The Congo and the Founding of its Free State* (1885), but the book will not be examined specifically.

In the chapter "Traveller on Global Terms", Henry M. Stanley's biography was presented, along with his travels, travel accounts and their contemporary and subsequent reception. These were not close readings, but accounts of a number of conflicting and interrelated areas that allowed for a description across four dimensions. First, it was argued that Stanley the phenomenon should be understood through the interplay between his creation of his own identity, his travels, his accounts and his mapping of Africa. Stanley's travels and travel accounts were more than representations of a different culture; they were events and actions that simultaneously affected various overlapping areas. If we look at the texts not as finished works of representation, but as events and open-ended processes that contribute to other processes, including court cases, we must distinguish between the different spaces that testimonies draw into the network of performative situations. Second, the institutional aspects of Stanley's performative prose were emphasised, especially his reception by scientific societies, and the conflicts about authority and credibility instigated by his travels and travel accounts. Contemporary and subsequently huge opposition – which almost became a smear campaign against Stanley – reveals cracks and blindspots both in the scientific societies of the time and in modern postcolonial biographies. Thirdly, Stanley's central role in the development of modern global media was examined. The boom in exploration around the middle of the nineteenth century was related to the development of new print techniques and communication technologies, e.g. the establishment of a transatlantic copper cable. Stanley's journeys were launched in close collaboration with the newspapers' conquering of a new world market, and his style – New Journalism – expressed this mundane and modernistic understanding of the world as unlimited, superficial and fragmented. Finally, the performative, institutional and media-related threads were gathered into a general definition of Stanley as an author of world literature, who worked on and contributed to the globalised conditions that are prevalent today.

The following section will be a closer examination of Stanley's development of prose under globalised conditions. The next chapter about *Through the Dark Continent* focuses particularly on his shifts between hyperbolic and paranoid constructions of space and place, concluding with an identification of the travel accounts' 'anthropology', which is claimed to contain access points and flexible models for the description of cultural encounters – models that nuance the meaning of the rhetoric of dominance that is also present. In Stanley's prose we will find a mobility and sense of inclusion regarding many more or less opposing positions. In the next chapter, about *In Darkest Africa*, the analytical perspective is broadened: Stanley's prose is perceived as a reality work in several different, although simultaneous, spaces in Africa, London, Cairo, etc. This aims to investigate the question of authority in relation to both the court of law and the market place. The Emin Pasha Relief Expedition disintegrated and resulted in a crisis of legitimacy for the classical exploration discourse. The dispute about the responsibility for this collapse was a moral-legal theme at the time, expressed through various discourses found in the participants' diaries, letters, threats and travel accounts. In the concluding chapter of the section, these readings of the two major expeditions and accounts are brought

together in two discussions. The first, "The Book as Fetish", looks at the book as a material phenomenon – its many layers of text, the map as a magical prop, illustrations, etc. – with the intention of clarifying the mechanisms that contributed to the travel books' almost magical effect, i.e. their incredible ability to make things happen in the real world. The second discussion, "Closed and Open Rooms: Stanley's Oblivion", points out aspects of the texts that helped prepare Stanley's subsequent oblivion and scapegoating in the twentieth century, as well as identifying good reasons to re-read and reassess the travel accounts today: their pragmatic prose and non-metaphysical descriptions of place contribute to a definition of the Congo as a real and synchronous place in the world, in contrast with the dominant tendencies in twentieth-century literature about the country.

1 Moving Perspective: *Through the Dark Continent* (1878)

In the introduction to *Through the Dark Continent*, Stanley explains the motive behind his second major expedition by referring to Livingstone's unfinished mission: Livingstone died "on the threshold of the dark region he wished to explore". The news reached Stanley in April 1874, and he decided to become the next martyr to geographical science, or – if he managed to survive – to solve all the riddles about the source of the Nile and the great lakes, which Livingstone, Burton and Speke and Speke and Grant had left unsolved. The mouth of Lake Tanganyika was still to be found, and knowledge of Lake Victoria was based on Speke's guesswork. Furthermore, the entire western part of the African continent was still "a white blank". Livingstone's burial, and a dispute with one of the *Daily Telegraph*'s editors, who in classic Jules Verne spirit challenged Stanley, are linked to a narrative about Stanley's intensive reading of more than 130 books about Africa, the first being the short *How to Observe.* With his sense for combining the randomly anecdotal with the historically ominous, Stanley staged the expedition as a joint venture between the USA and Britain with the *Daily Telegraph* and the *New York Herald* as sponsors and employers.

Before the introduction are five neatly drawn and coloured maps of Equatorial Africa, accounting for the cartographic knowledge in 1679, 1849-56, 1856-1863, 1866-75 and 1874-77. This makes it immediately clear that Stanley's expedition aimed to complete what his predecessors had only guessed at, and allow scientific certainty to replace geographic fantasy.

From the very beginning, Stanley showed that he had backbone – alternately as an expedition leader with specific practical, educational and scientific tasks and as a peacemaker in conflicts that, without his intervention, would ultimately have lead to savage massacres.

Towards the end of the second volume, Stanley wearily notes that he has fought 45 battles, some against up to 2000-3000 natives, although that, as mentioned earlier, it is an exaggeration. Throughout extended periods, the expedition was in an almost permanent state of crisis, having on a daily basis to enter into new agreements and pay levies according to complicated negotiations with the ruling chieftains, or fight their way forwards by means of wile or firepower. In addition, the expedition crew was constantly on the verge of mutiny owing to starvation and doubts about the entire project, which on a general level seemed

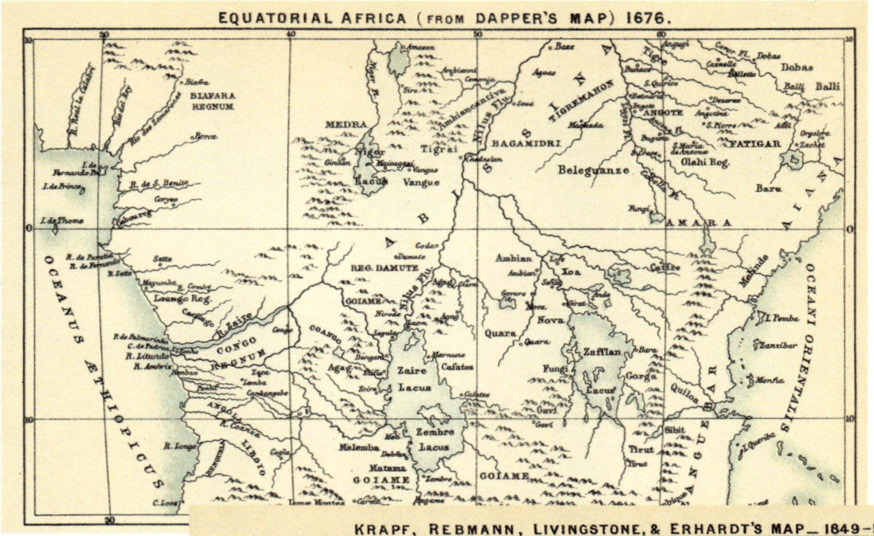
EQUATORIAL AFRICA (FROM DAPPER'S MAP) 1676.

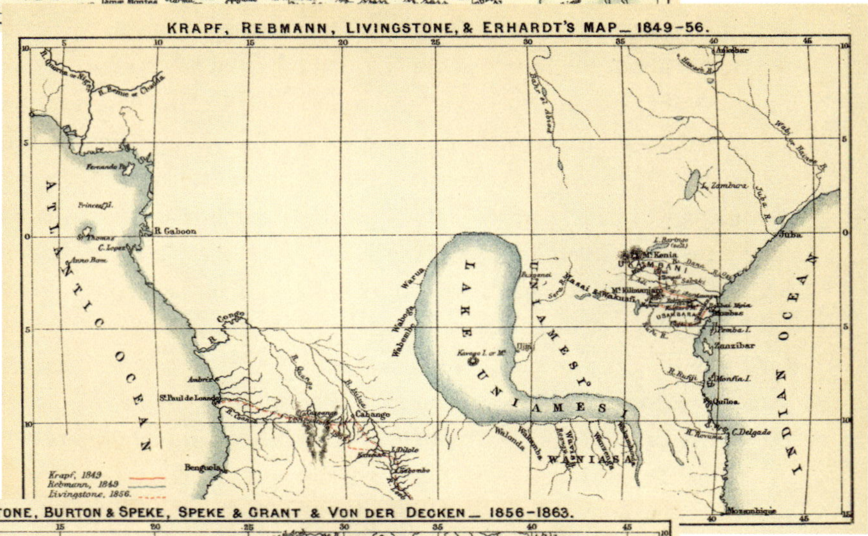
KRAPF, REBMANN, LIVINGSTONE, & ERHARDT'S MAP_ 1849-56.
Krapf, 1849
Rebmann, 1849
Livingstone, 1856.

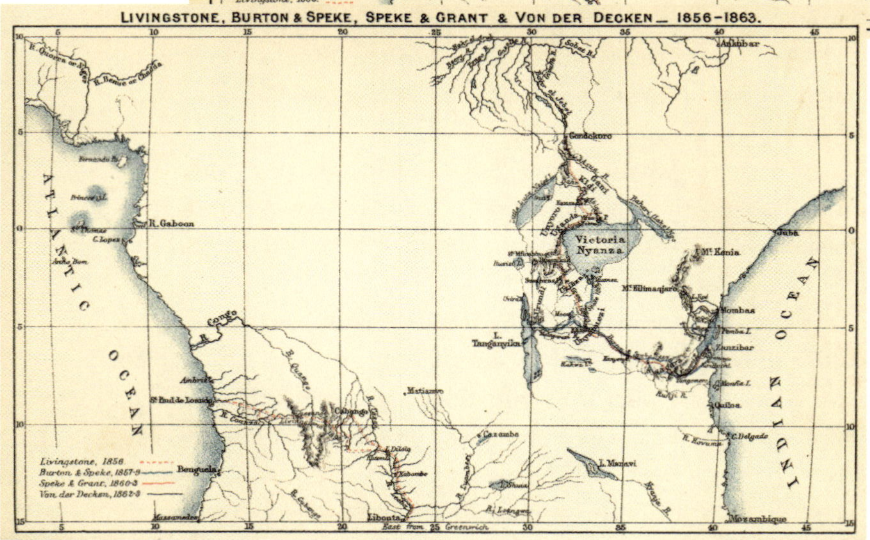
LIVINGSTONE, BURTON & SPEKE, SPEKE & GRANT & VON DER DECKEN_ 1856-1863.
Livingstone, 1856.
Burton & Speke, 1857-9
Speke & Grant, 1860-3
Von der Decken, 1862-3
East from Greenwich

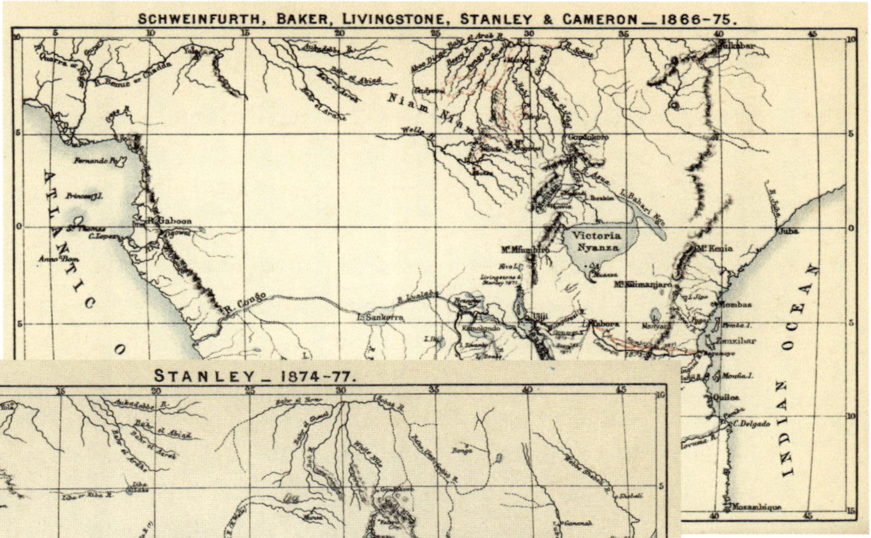

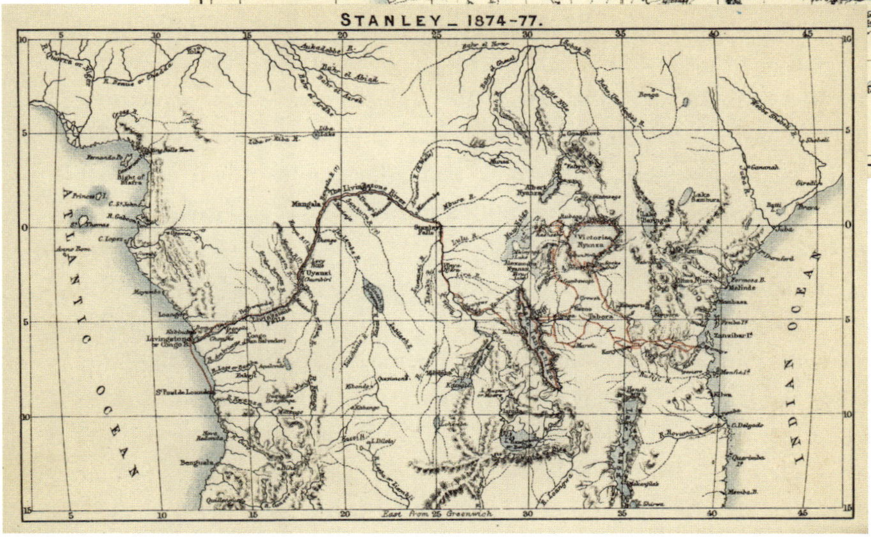

The first thing that meets the eye of the reader of the first volume of *Through the Dark Continent* is a portrait of Stanley, which was based on a photograph taken weeks before the expedition left England in 1874. This is juxtaposed with a photograph taken immediately after he arrived at the west coast of Africa in 1877, almost starved to death. The two images tell the story of a man hardened, but not crushed, by the journey. The dedication brings attention to the two newspapers the *New York Herald* and *Daily Telegraph*, which sponsored the expedition. In the preface, Stanley thanks providence for his survival and expresses his sorrow for the many who did not survive; he also explains that in order to avoid slowing down the narrative, he has left out much material. He has had great use of the camera that he "carried across the continent". From his photographs, Mr Weller and Mr Stanford have skilfully drawn and engraved the illustrations, which are listed in a separate section of 10 maps and 150 woodcarvings. Before the reader comes to the classical introduction of the travel account, which accounts for the launch of the expedition and earlier expeditions, five fine, coloured, and precious maps of the region are inserted, drawn in 1676, 1856, 1863, 1875, and 1877. They tell the story that is unfolded to the reader over the following 1100 pages. As a parallel to Stanley's retrospective organisation of the travel account, the reader knows the route, direction, and result of the journey beforehand. Yet, at the same time, Stanley's narrative style aims to grip the reader's attention in the drama and doubt of the moment regarding what comes next.

absurd to everyone except Stanley. As a traveller, Stanley was preoccupied with carrying out position surveys, taking "ethnological notes", negotiating with chieftains, administering medication to the ill and looking for solutions to desperate situations. As a narrator, he attempts to communicate the experience of stress while leaving space for extended reflections on the landscapes and people encountered. However, these registrations are rarely more than superficial notes of customs such as clothing and hair styles, architecture and crops. Clearly, Stanley's main interest was in the statistical information that was relevant to current power relations and appraisals of a strategic nature, with regard to potential trading connections in the area. In this way, his chapters are structured according to a unique pulse in which almost stagnant, harmonious, gentle passages interrupt the dominant, staggeringly and either exuberantly triumphant or paranoid gloomy style. Let us begin by looking briefly at a couple of examples of these quiet textual moments first.

The quiet situations are more frequent in the first parts, in which conflicts are generally solved through the usual gift-giving and brotherhood rituals, levies and agreements. Small populations ruled by chieftains as well as the kingdoms around the great lakes had already been in contact with, or received information about, the white explorers, and they were used to forming alliances with the Arab slave traders, who from their base on the east coast were travelling farther and farther west to find their 'goods'. Stanley's expedition was often greeted, therefore, with signs of interest in trade and recognition.

"Monarch-of-all I-survey"

The land of Mutesa, "Emperor of Uganda", is described as a sanctuary for Stanley and his men, who even after this relatively short distance had been decimated by dysentery, malaria, typhoid, trypanosomiasis and desertion. Uganda was fertile and well-organised, and the landscape lies open like an English estate. The expedition was washed and clothed for an audience with Mutesa, who Stanley does not hesitate to grant the title "Emperor": "The Foremost Man of Equatorial Africa". The city's straight and clean streets, the streamlined architecture of the palaces and the refined etiquette allowed Stanley to relax after having spent months in confusing cities and landscapes populated by a noisy rabble. The hierarchy of the court appealed to Stanley, and his position as Mutesa's equal allowed him to adopt the despot's disciplining perspective. Stanley was fascinated with Mutesa's power over the masses, and he saw in the Ugandan a perfect tool for the civilisation of Central Africa.

To substantiate this impression, direct quotations are used from the diary, in which Stanley corrects Speke's description of Mutesa as a murderer and tyrant with a preference for fat women. Instead, Stanley sees an intelligent ruler who, by means of his authority and with help from philanthropists, has the potential to become "the light that shall lighten the darkness of this benighted region" (*TDC* I, p. 193). Mutesa's physical appearance is described in admiring detail. His features remind Stanley of the large rock sculptures at Thebes, or statues at the museum in Cairo: "the general expression of amiability blended with dignity that pervades his face, and the large, lustrous, lambent eyes that lend it a strange beauty (...). His colour is of a dark red brown, of a wonderfully smooth surface" (p. 195).

Stanley enjoyed the stay in the villa he had at his disposal; he practised his shooting skills with Mutesa and visited his palace, which was situated high above sea level and offered a brilliant view in all directions for the "imperial eyes of the African monarch".

"On all sides rolled in grand waves a voluptuous land of sunshine, and plenty, and early summer verdure, cooled by soft breezes from the great equatorial fresh-water sea. Isolated hill-cones, similar to that of Rubaga, or square tabular masses, rose up from the beautiful landscape to attract, like mysteries, the curious stranger's observation. Villages and banana groves of still fresher green, far removed on the crest of distant swelling ridges, announced that Mutesa owned a land worth loving. Dark sinuous lines traced the winding courses of deep ravines filled with trees, and grassy extents of gently undulating ground marked the pastures; broader depressions suggested the cultivated gardens and the grain fields, while on the verge of the horizon we saw the beauty and the charm of the land melting in the blues of distance.

There is a singular fascination about this country. The land would be loved for its glorious diversified prospects even though it were a howling wilderness; but it owes a great deal of the power which it exercises over the imagination, to the consciousness that in it dwells a people peculiarly fascinating also. "How comes it," one asks, "that this barbarous, uneducated and superstitious monarch builds upon this height? Not for protection, surely, for he has smoothed the uneven ground and formed broad avenues to approach it, and a single torch would suffice to level all his fences? Does he, then, care for the charms of the prospect? Has he also an eye for the beauties of nature?"(pp. 200-201).

As Mary-Louise Pratt has pointed out in other travel accounts from Africa, we are clearly dealing with the discourse she calls "the-monarch-of-all-I-survey", i.e. a presentation in which the landscape is staged and made accessible for imperial rule in one single rhetorical trope. The traveller sees and conquers the landscape through panoramic vistas in which people who might put up a fight, as well as geophysical obstacles, are edited out of the picture. We are

"Rubaga, the New Capital of the Emperor Mutesa", from *Through the Dark Continent*. According to Stanley, Mutesa was the perfect tool for civilising the natives; he was hospitable and open towards other mindsets, both Arabic and European, and he was willing to negotiate about conversion to Christianity. If the Europeans succeeded, his subjects – and, in turn, all peoples of the continent – would allegedly do the same, given that they imitated everything in their ruler. As the illustration shows, this idea is based on a specific descriptive strategy termed "monarch-of-all-I-survey".

looking at a prospect where lines and colouring add variation and depth to the image. Isolated, mysterious details attract the gaze, but only subtly, because the dominating features are the lush, pastoral meadows and the total image toning out into the "blues of distance".

Assessed, isolated from the textual context, we are dealing with a particularly pure and refined version of this trope. First, because Stanley adds a mirroring and connecting link, allowing the native monarch to be the bearer of the imperialistic gaze. Stanley writes that Mutesa loved to imitate anything European, and that all his subjects imitated everything he did. This is one of the reasons why Stanley saw him as the perfect tool for colonising Africa. Secondly, Mutesa is also a mirror image – initially of Stanley, who desired this double gaze of Olympian order and youthful, fertile potential, and subsequently of the European fantasy of returning to a world of antique transparency – Stanley even refers to Homer's Hector – while at the same time making tremendous profits.

At the royal court Stanley also met the Frenchman Linant de Bellefonds. Together the two men enjoyed instructing Mutesa in the "wonders" of Christianity and French cuisine, with biscuits from Marseille, olive oil, sausage from Bologna and Parisian pâté de foie gras. Ultimately, Stanley had to leave to continue his planned journey on Lake Victoria with *Lady Alice* – the boat that he had designed as an assembly kit and named after his girlfriend. Before leaving, he posted letters written together with Bellefonds to the *Daily Telegraph* and the *New York Herald*, in which he recommended that future missionary efforts in Africa set their sights specifically on Mutesa. For the right missionary, who ought not to represent one nation but the entire white race, there were prospects that far exceeded those of the traditional, greedy missionary movements.

Elastic Composition

The stay with Mutesa was by far the most pleasant of his journey, and the part that gave rise to the most extravagant speculations. Shortly after the expedition left, the troublesome negotiations and disputes recommenced, and Stanley had to change his modus; he was no longer a resting Roman patrician or a missionary shepherd but an explorer in action. A few passages stand out: "Alone with Nature" and immediately after, "A Dream of the Future", because they both rhetorically and physically seem to be influenced by the time spent with Mutesa. After the expedition's arrival at Musira, a desert island where the crew were preoccupied for a while with a peaceful meal, with no external or internal threats, Stanley set out on a trek that was different from what we usually find in the travel books. It is described as a rare state of complete peacefulness and security, allowing Stanley to go on a "solitary exploration" (p. 219) with the boldness of a young boy. Who was there to keep him from standing on his head or rolling around in leaves and pieces of twigs and bark, "or laugh[ing] or sing[ing]"? Stanley describes it as if through renouncing his leadership and self-control he becomes his own superior: "Being thus absolute monarch and supreme arbiter over myself, I should enjoy for a brief period perfect felicity" (p. 219).

Freed of all the constraints and "conventionalisms" and the "sobriety and steadiness" he was usually subject to while affirming his role as a leader, Stanley manages to discover his "natural elasticity of body". The stiffness of both his personality and his body is loosened up, and for a moment he is transformed

into an elastic "serpent" that slides under fallen trees, squeezes through seemingly impassable passages and thrusts himself through densely entangled vines and creepers "with frantic energy". Through this snake-like perspective he observes a "miniature world" full of "eccentricities of creation", populated by ants of all colours – red, black, yellow, grey, white – alongside completely unknown "races". He observes the caste system among the ants: soldiers, workers, armies of destroyers.

"They swarmed among the foliage in columns of foraging and plundering marauders and countless hordes of ruthless destroyers. (...) Here the relentless antlions prepare their pitfalls, and there the ghostly mantis, green or grey, stood waiting for unwary insects. Diamond beetles abounded, and many other species, uncouth and horrid, scrambled away from before my feet. Nor are these a thousandth part of the insect nations that I disturbed; the secluded island was a world of infinite activities" (pp. 220-21).

It is noteworthy that Stanley uses the same style of writing here as he does in his 'anthropology'. Clearly, this is a world he cannot know or understand in any other context than the well-known image of the ants' caste system. The races are like the native tribes he encounters on his way, not characterised by their way of life or appearance, but by their specific colours – in the same way that unknown and surprising phenomena in the micro world, in accordance with the macro world, are categorised as deformed, terrifying and ghostly in all their glory. As the passage ends with a change in the snake-like perspective – so that the readers find themselves at the explorer's feet, as he is scares away the native "insect nations" with his footsteps – the picture is complete: this is a parable of Africa as a world populated by glorious, noisy, intimidating insects, a parable that becomes even more extraordinary given that the explorer himself is portrayed as a disturbing and destructive influence.

We also find another change of perspective in Stanley's fantasising walk: his elastic body, no longer a snake but Tarzan-like, carries him further via jasmines, lianas and mimosas, up a steep hill to the top of the island, from where he can take in "the grand encircling prospect" in one panoramic "gaze". This passage duplicates the aforementioned passage about the view from Mutesa's palace, now devoted completely to Stanley's undisturbed perspective; the placid Lake Victoria lies stretched out beneath him "until the clear sky and stainless water met, the clear bounds of both veiled by a gauzy vapour, suggesting infinity" (p. 221). Just as the horizon in the earlier description was blurred by "lines of hazy blue mountains", the area taken in by the gaze is both demarcated by Stanley's happy island and at the same time boundless. From this place, this topos in landscape and text, "undisturbed, the eye may rove over one of the strangest yet fairest portions of Africa".

In this orchestration, Stanley is "secure" and able from his "lofty throne" to observe cattle and huts from which smoke rises peacefully, and he can see the silhouettes of the natives as "thin dark figures". With this masked demarcation, the passage stretches the landscape out, so that it becomes a synecdoche for the entire Africa; but the panoramic gaze also creates a metonymic relation between Stanley's terrestrial and God's celestial thrones, making Stanley's gaze divine. The mechanism works both ways: rhetorically it is Stanley's "monarch-of-all-I-survey" trope that leads to the analogy with God's power and will; simultaneously it endows the author with a god-like power. The concluding apostrophe raises the question of how long these people will remain oblivious about "Him who created the gorgeous sunlit world they look upon each day" (p. 222), and how long they will remain "unvisited by the Teacher". Rhetorically, however, it is Stanley who is already in the position to see and write this, holding the higher power, spreading light in the darkness and acting as the teacher imparting the message.

In the following part, the image of creation – not God's but Stanley's – is unfurled still further: "What a land they possess! And what an inland sea! How steamers afloat on the lake might cause Usuri to shake hands with Usungoro, and Uganda with Usukuma" (p. 222). In this prophecy, steamers will soon come to reconcile cities and tribes in the area around Victoria Nyanza. All the region's produce will be exchanged for goods brought up from the coast; the country will be rid of its wilderness; the slave trade will cease – and it will all happen "permeated with the nobler ethics of a higher humanity". While at the time, the region was plagued by hatred and death, the passage expresses the hope that "a band of philanthropic capitalists shall vow to rescue these beautiful islands" (p. 222).

Within a short span of time, and without leaving the area, the narrator himself undergoes many changes that are closely linked to the text's changes of perspective. The last change evokes Moses on the mountain, who with God's help releases the slaves; these slaves are not led through the desert but rather into the utopia of the steam engine, with philanthropic capitalists relieving the earth of its riches of ivory, myrrh and coffee, in return for generous funding to pave the way for the gospel. This is where the text arrives, from the first change that saw Stanley go from boy to serpent, and Africa as an insect world whose nations the explorer tramples through.

Throughout the transformations and changes of perspective that begin with the description of Mutesa's palace, however, the pyramidal structure remains constant. The position of the gaze is fixed at the top of the pyramid, although

Stanley's description insists on a sudden, extremely physical elasticity. The most obvious effect of Stanley's intermezzo is the overlapping of several parallel narratives, including Rousseauian, romantic ideas about nature, Christian ideas of redemption and civilisation's progress models. From this rhetorical perspective, the description is an example of an extraordinary elasticity, which nevertheless only situates the meaning even more firmly in an unwavering hierarchical structure. Inherent in the elasticity is a comparison of Africa with insect states in which the European's journey interferes on the horizontal level, while on the vertical level he can only see himself as a teacher and saviour. This is far from the end of Stanley's elastic play with textual composition; we will return to these changes later on.

A dominant characteristic in the entire section dedicated to Victoria Nyanza and the stay at Mutesa's palace is the panoptic gaze and pyramidal perspective, in which society is perceived from above as a transparent and illuminated structure. The order and rest that Stanley found after the often chaotic conditions of the first stretches becomes the origin of a utopian figure that dominates the remainder of the first part of *Through the Dark Continent*. Light and hope briefly appears to conquer the powers of darkness.

Rhetoric and Violence

When the expedition arrived on Bumbireh Island – its members all close to death owing to starvation, according to Stanley – they encountered one of the sudden, dramatic changes of scene found throughout the book. While Stanley and his men discuss whether or not the natives of Bumbireh, who are crowding around the boat in vast numbers, are open to negotiation, *Lady Alice* is lifted up on to land in a jiffy. The expedition find themselves in the middle of the crowd – or ants' nest – deprived of the elevated perspective that gave them a feeling of supremacy, and their reaction is one of panic, even from their usually calm and collected leader. Compositionally the scene functions as the antithesis of Musira's wondrous "the monarch-of-all-I-survey", where the natives were viewed from a safe distance as "thin dark figures" or ants; in this scene they are very close, blocking the view and thus resisting domination. The change is accentuated by the rhetoric; everything is frantic confusion with two hundred "screaming black demons" and "a forest of spears". The expedition is absorbed in chaos. There are loud, long war cries of "Hehu-a-hehu-u-u-u!", and the situation is described in terms such as "riot and noise", "smouldering fury", and "violent, vituperative" (p. 229).

As a contrast, Safeni, who negotiates on Stanley's behalf, is "a born diplomat" – "a cordial frankness sat naturally on his face"; these characteristics

"Reception at Bumbireh Island, Victoria Nyanza", from *Through the Dark Continent*. The composition is highly antithetic, moving between light and darkness, and between commanding overview and paranoid, enclosed, and noisy spaces. In an attempt to accommodate the reader's expectation of action, Stanley's descriptions in his telegrams and travel book were far more violent and bloody than was the reality.

are summarised in the words "the man was an orator, pleading for mercy and justice" (p. 232). In Stanley's description, Safeni stands out, both as an individual and as a representative of civilisation and classical oration; his honesty is expressed as part of his physical appearance, and his good intentions are manifested through the rhetoric of his hand gestures.

This classical orator is contrasted to the bestial, hellish noise and yelling of the natives. Safeni assumes that he has solved the problem through his educated diplomacy, but soon the natives' seemingly good intentions turn out to be covering their preparations for war. Either the chieftain, Shekka, has no control over his subjects, or he is unreliable, insusceptible to political rhetoric and not prone to recognising the common principles of negotiation. In this manner, Stanley rhetorically prepares the reader for the violent actions that follow when he manages to avert the enemy's attention long enough for *Lady Alice* to be returned to the lake. The natives' spears and bows are no match for

Stanley's far heavier weapons: "the bullet ploughed through him and through the second"; "I sent two charges of duck-shot into their midst with terrible effect". When the natives give pursuit, Stanley grabs his elephant rifle, kills five men and sinks two canoes, while the natives' arrows fail to reach their targets. Then follows a gentle breeze that carries them into a dreadful storm, later to an island brimming with food and finally to the expedition camp, where Stanley is welcomed as a returned Homeric hero with a party and wild dancing that ironically resembles the noise and chaos from which the expedition had fled not long before: fifty men "danced me round the camp on their shoulders, amid much laughter, and clapping of hands, grotesque wriggling of forms, and real Saxon hurrahing" (p. 241).

This odyssey *en miniature* is an interruption of the sunlit visit to Mutesa, repeating the work's entire epic structure and in its individual subdivisions dealing with the same antitheses between light and darkness, control and loss of control, individuality and mass, rhetorical speech and bestial noise. The Bumbireh passage is structured in accordance with a formula that is repeated several times throughout *Through the Dark Continent* – a specific discursive compilation of political rhetoric and hyperbolic descriptions of violence. The boat journey paraphrased above only lasted a few days, and it is thus difficult to believe that it comprised so many dramatic shifts, fatal moments and visions. It seems more reasonable to assume that the description is composed on the basis of a complex and effective rhetorical strategy in which antitheses and repetitions underpin the text's theatrical, literary, aesthetic and entertainment requirements, as well as its performative effect in the role of provider of a certain 'readiness' – that which Stanley refers to with the metaphor of "the opening" of Africa.

Stanley's description of the episode on Bumbireh is repeated when he is forced to travel through the same waters on the way back. In a combination of punishment and self-defence he attacks and subjugates the hostile population of the island. These two passages were to become decisive for Stanley's reputation as a ruthless colonialist and his subsequent stagnant figure in literary history and postcolonialism. However, on closer inspection the text is rather ambiguous. The paraphrase above is based on the travel book *Through the Dark Continent*, which is similar to the telegram article published in the *New York Herald* and the *Daily Telegraph* on 29 July.

The telegram articles caused massive debate about Stanley's methods – a debate which he, on his return home, would have ample opportunity to take on board in his revised travel account. At the same time, however, he could not change the telegram version without being stigmatised as a liar, and he was thus trapped in a similar situation to when he was a reporter during the American

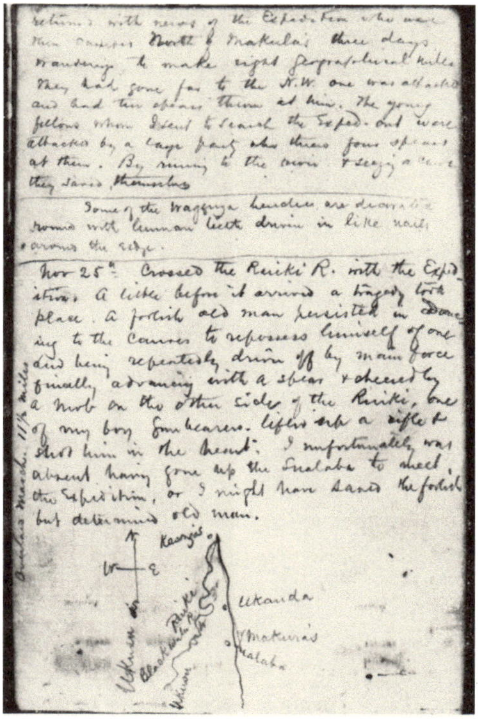
Nov 25th Crossed the Ruiki R. with the Expedition. A little before it arrived a tragedy took place. A foolish old man persisted in advancing to the canoes to repossess himself of one and being repeatedly driven off by main force finally advancing with a spear & cheered by a mob on the other side of the Ruiki, one of my boy gunbearers lifted a rifle & shot him in the heart. I unfortunately was absent having gone up the Lualaba to meet the Expedition, or I might have saved the foolish but determined old man.

Stanley's field notebook (SA No. 18). 25 November 1876: "Crossed the Ruiki River with the expedition. A little before it arrived a tragedy took place. A foolish old man persisted in advancing to the canoes to repossess himself of one and being repeatedly driven off by man force finally advancing with a spear. Cheered by a mob on the other side of the Ruiki, one of my boy gunbearers lifted a rifle and shot him in the heart. I unfortunately was absent having gone up the Lualaba to meet the Expedition, or I might have saved the foolish but determined old man". The episode is mentioned in *Through the Dark Continent*, but without Stanley expressing any regret.

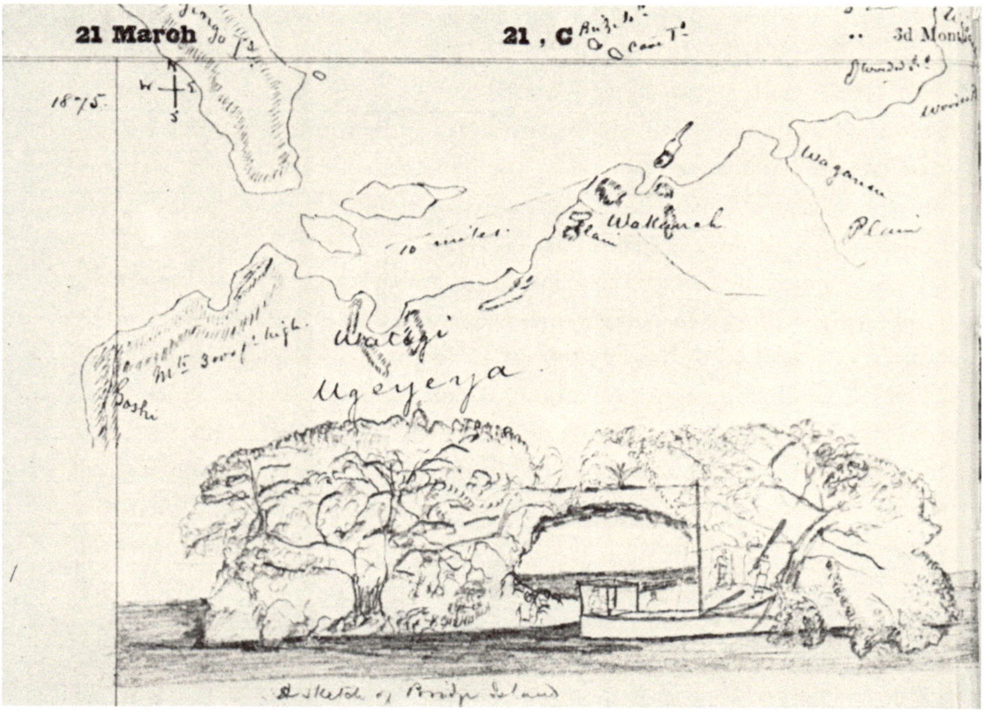

Indian Wars, facing readers' and editors' expectations of action and punishment. The notebook's description of the event mentions that the first engagement resulted in just one death, not nine, and that Stanley's situation was far more humiliating and exposed than was suggested by both the telegram article and the travel book.[61] Read from this perspective, the whole course of events, including the second encounter (the "punishment"), Stanley clearly indicates in *Through the Dark Continent* that he used all kinds of rhetorical means and arguments to talk his bloodthirsty crew out of the reprisal against Bumbireh, and when he did not succeed, he tried to avoid the veritable massacre that his native crew wanted. This, according to Tim Jeal, is reaffirmed by Frank Pocock's records of the episode.[62] The travel diary itself also indicates that Stanley was conscious of the moral dilemmas, e.g. when he writes that the aim was "to punish Bumbireh, with the power of a father punishing a stubborn & disobedient son" (Stanley Archives, No. 16).

In Britain, these tales caused a commotion, incited among others by John Kirk, the consul of Zanzibar and Stanley's archenemy from the time of the Livingstone expedition. Taking advantage of the fact that Stanley would not be in a position to respond for some time, Kirk and other rivals of Stanley discredited his name and honour on the basis of the Bumbireh scandal, which stuck in the public memory. Tim Jeal has pointed out that all Stanley did was unveil the circumstances of any inland expedition, which were usually left out. In this light, the shock caused by the Bumbireh telegram was not as much a reaction to Stanley's ruthless behaviour in Africa as it was a reaction to his lack of tact with British readers: they had been used to Livingstone and other explorers' pastoral descriptions, in which the extremely violent conflicts between the natives were toned down considerably. Stanley's text confronted them with the novel, candid style of New Journalism, and educated readers saw these strongly visualised descriptions of conflicts as obscene.

There are many different elements at play in these passages of *Through the Dark Continent*: they incorporate notebooks, travel diaries and telegram articles written during the expedition, attempting to avoid the scandal's destructive effect on Stanley's reputation without sacrificing the hyperbolic violence of the descriptions. It is remarkable, for instance, how Stanley's native ship's mate and interpreter, Safeni, is placed in the role of negotiator and classical rhetor, while the narrator himself for once is tongue-tied. The violence, a precondition of the exposed and fragile expedition, was a permanent threat both to their own lives and to the natives, resulting in a situation that is at the same time always both negotiation and conflict. If we read the textual patterns in this light, what is remarkable is not so much its revelations as its secrecy and its exaggerations. The violence is presented in the texts as rhetorical dramas which, as Laura Franey points out in *Victorian Travel Writing and Imperial Violence*,[63] can be perceived as imperialistic dreams about the real mutilation of natives; however, they also function as exposures and disclosures of contradictions and non-disclosures in the sentimental and orientalist travel accounts that dominated the end of the eighteenth and the first half of the nineteenth century. Stanley's conduct, and the description of it, was not more ruthless or insensitive than his precursors', but its editing in accordance with the standards of New Journalism did not pay the same regard to the codified sentimental aesthetics of readers.

Stanley's Real and Invented Discoveries

Stanley's description of the stay with Mutesa after the sail on Victoria Nyanza adds more pieces to the overall pattern. It contributes to a more critical and nuanced attitude towards Mutesa, which we can only perceive as a retrospective correction of the telegram articles' overly enthusiastic account, which attracted scepticism in Britain. This scepticism was partly due to Stanley's use of his rhetorical talents in presenting Buganda as paradise on Earth and partly due to the account's overwhelmingly positive contents which clashed with the established, sentimental ideas of the natives as either barbarians or children.

In Stanley's absence, Mutesa had initiated a war against the Wavuma, an event Stanley covered in detail in his capacity as war correspondent, but in a style with new epic and historical variations. The rhetoric is still scenic and theatrical, with war councils as Greek choruses in which messengers give their news in the high style of tragedy. Stanley's archaic model of Mutesa as a Roman emperor is orchestrated with the soldiers' march, the camps and the battles in which the two parties' navies collide in highly disciplined formations with thousands of spectators arranged on the mountain sides, enjoying the spectacle as sheer entertainment. Through Stanley's writing, the war becomes a scene where the crowds – which, including combatants and spectators, approached a million in number – are regulated by the same rituals and rules that applied to the arenas of antiquity. Stanley assumes the position in this epos as Mutesa's military advisor, passing time in the pauses between battles with "encyclopaedic talk" (p. 320), translating the Bible into Swahili – "the white man's book" – and completing Mutesa's conversion to Christianity, who had rejected Islam as an alternative by referring to the Arabs' slave trade.

Stanley promises to make the Wavuma surrender if Mutesa will act as a true Christian and turn the other cheek. He does this is by building a floating fort surrounded by tall palisades that appear to be made by "spirits" which, "well calculated to strike terror into the mind of the ignorant savage", are summoned

"One of the great naval battles between the Waganda and the Wavuma, in the channel between Ingira Island and Cape Nakaranga", from *Through the Dark Continent*. The description is scenic and theatricalised: up to a million warriors and spectators, a classical arena and Homeric heroes – and a reporter who not only describes it all for the benefit of the new newspaper mass audiences, but also influences and takes part in the course of events.

against the Wavuma, who finally see no other way than to enter into a peace treaty after the display of such magical powers. Peace was necessary for Stanley to be able to continue his journey.

The incident is so extraordinary that it appears fabricated, fictitious: the idea of a floating fort sounds like something out of a Jules Verne novel. While Hector and Achilles fight in the arena, Stanley acts as a resourceful Odysseus who, in order to continue his journey, and by means of his technological know-how and knowledge of the world, "devised a plan" (p. 334). The Trojan horse turns the natives' magic against themselves; from the floating fort sounds a mysterious voice, "a stentorian voice amid the deathly silence within" (p. 340), which conjures peace.

In the notebook, the floating fort is described in detail, but to Stanley's regret it was no help in practice. Perhaps inspired by a quotation in the notebook from Milton, Stanley expanded the fort's significance to give it the decisive and magical role it plays in *Through the Dark Continent* (SA, No. 15, 16.9). In the diary, the notes from the field notebook are reproduced, selectively transcribed and supplemented with finished maps to indicate a halfway point in the development of the invention: "the floating fort was paddled by the sailors who were seated in the central canoe, and not a soul could be seen by us. The Wavumas from Ingira could not make out what strange monster this thing was which moved as if by invisible means up and down the lake" (SA, No. 16, 6.10).

"The floating fortress moving towards to Ingira Island". From *Through the Dark Continent*. An example of Stanley's inventiveness in the roles of both Homer and Odysseus. As in Jules Verne's fantastic vessel, the power source is hidden; from within the strange phenomenon sounds a harsh and mysterious voice, which causes the enemy to capitulate, allowing Stanley to continue his journey.

In the diary, the fort is drawn in great detail, but the situation is dramatised and fetishised further with the addition of magic elements such as "what strange monster" and "invisible means". The final edition of the travel account completes this rhetorical trajectory, partly by linking the invention to Homeric references, and partly by adding a mysterious voice inside the fort, which suggests an obscure relationship between the situation of the textual statement and the author's biography. As mentioned in the introduction, the presence of the "stern voice" was one of those moments in which Stanley at the same time recognised himself and saw himself as a stranger.

Once again, we can trace the combination of several traditionally conflicting discourses. At one stage there is a battle between Islam and Christianity – Muhammad's and Moses' books, or two different scriptures. In another scene, or arena, it is not the scripture but an inarticulate, hypnotic "voice" that performs a curiosity, fabricated for the occasion, and ends the fighting. This battle between logos and phoneme would become the staple structure of the journey across the continent in the second volume of the work. However, this structure is already notable in the concluding passage about Mutesa, in the form of a juxtaposition of oral and written narratives.

After the description of the peace agreement and Mutesa's journey home to Buganda, Stanley asks the reader for forgiveness as he leaves the direct narrative behind for a while at the expense of a general presentation of Buganda's history and "manners". If the learned critic were to discover something "incredible or marvellous" through this, the author could take no credit, for he only passes on

the Bugandan's own legends of Kintu, Buganda's first king. Stanley's detailed and dramatic account is both a genealogical chronicle – a list of kings from Kintu to Mutesa, who introduced Europe to Central Africa – and an archive of Buganda's myths and historic battles. Once again, the style is Homeric, perceived by Stanley himself as an *Iliad*, presented to European readers here for the first time. Before that, Central Africa had been "like a closed oyster", but the legend opens up to "glimpses" of the place's origin, customs and history: "An epic poem might be written upon the legend of the search for the lost patriarch, or a prose romance" (p. 379).

Not only is this narrative a great work of art; it might also contain a deeper meaning, philosophises Stanley. Under the heading "A legendary Parallel" he suggests that the stories about Adam, Noah and David can be compared to the story about Kintu, which will reveal similar proto-types and lead to the discovery that we are perhaps dealing with the same origin. Stanley apologises that he has to condense his account; we are not looking at a shorthand version of an oral legend, as he claims by way of introduction, but an edited, written account in which we must assume that his expectation of parallels between European and African myths has had an impact. Nevertheless, the version in the travel account is more or less identical with the one in the field notes.

The striking parallels we find in the account draw in other parallels and juxtapositions from the text's many changes of scene. As mentioned earlier, Stanley had targeted Mutesa as the only person who in God's name would be able to lead the Africans out of slavery and through the desert to freedom in "a land of butter and wine and fullness, milk and honey, fat meadows and valleys" (p. 381). The legend of Kintu rhetorically underpins Mutesa's appointed role, recounting the immigration into Buganda as arrival in a country without a native population. The parallels to the Jewish exodus and settlement are clear. Mutesa is a Moses who assumes a god-like status in the same way as Stanley: together, they have been chosen to lead a cause that is bigger than either of them. This exodus-trace is present throughout the entire text and enhanced by the pyramidal perspectives on the country. Stanley repeats that Mutesa is the chosen one – the only one who can complete the mission. At the same time, he utilises the legend to illustrate Mutesa's old savage and bloodthirsty ways, documented by Speke, which, according to Stanley, he is not yet completely cured of, and which may therefore suddenly break through his vain and dissembled "polite" surface.

Therefore, it is necessary for Stanley to make Mutesa convert no less than three times, which in his conclusive reflection leaves him puzzled by Mutesa's "peculiar, wayward, petulant, inconsistent nature". Stanley is disappointed because he has realised that he has been "observed and noted" (p. 406) for his usefulness, knowledge and gifts rather than as a friend. Nevertheless he maintains that Mutesa in the hands of a missionary could "become moulded anew, or be re-born" (p. 407).

It is interesting that Stanley feels uncomfortable at the thought of having been subject to the same gaze that he uses on Mutesa – given that his interest in the emperor is to a large extent in his capacity as a tool for European colonisation. However, we need to read the passage in relation to the editing of the travel book, which took into account Stanley's initial overly enthusiastic expectations of Mutesa as Africa's saviour – the rash prophecy he expressed in his letters to the *New York Herald* and the *Daily Telegraph*. Here, the image of Mutesa is more nuanced; he is still worthy of support and understanding, but there is a dark side to him that requires a missionary's "moulding".

Mutesa's conversion is repeated, played out on different stages and rhetorically doubled in legends and stories. Homer's *Iliad* and the Old Testament are embedded as narratives that prepare and create the rhetorical basis for Mutesa's rebirth, while simultaneously opening up the oyster to European penetration on a concrete, literal level – but also figuratively and figurally, with wide-ranging consequences. Buganda's history is expropriated by Stanley, who combines it with his own rhetorical "moulding" of Mutesa as the perfect tool for the dissemination of "Christianity", "commerce" and "civilisation": we encounter the image of the emperor whose slightest gesture is uncritically duplicated by his subjects, as well as the image of the saviour in the shape of a converted, reborn Kintu. Through textual manipulation, the latter is transformed into a Christian ancestor who, as a secret prophecy, prefigures Stanley's intervention.

The exodus figure is repeated on many levels in the text, obviously linked to the myths about a remote Christian kingdom in Central Africa ruled by the legendary Prester John.[64] In the text's micro-narratives, such as Stanley's prophetic vision on the mountain, we also find the figure of Moses who will lead the slaves to freedom. Simultaneously, the rhetorical formation of the text is part of another paraphrase in which landscape and events are traced back to the archaic pastures where Hector and Achilles fought in transparent conflicts, the results of which were weighed meticulously on the scales of justice. The tendency towards the archaic can be interpreted as a nostalgic longing for a place and time when events could be interpreted unambiguously, while to Stanley the reality is obscure and absurd; it can also be seen as an attempt to attribute to Uganda a history of civilisation that would prepare it for a European invasion. However, Stanley's many shifts in perspective, and his uncontrollable admiration for Mutesa, establish a complexity that resists simplified explanatory models based on colonial criticism.

Stanley's presentations of this country in the guise of the Jewish exodus or Homer's "epic poems" are examples of the strategy that François Hartog termed "inversion" in a critical reading of Herodotus. The other is reduced to a mirror-image of the familiar, usually a reverse image of one's own culture, or is defined as an effective combination of analogous and reverse elements. The other is made transparent, albeit in a misleading way, as the truly other is discarded.[65] Stanley's descriptions nevertheless contain several layers that make them interesting representations of the other.

In the same way as Mutesa's subjects imitate everything about their ruler, Stanley also appears to fall into the role of admirer and imitator. It is striking that Stanley cannot be said to apply an unambiguously hostile European discourse to the other culture, as postcolonial criticism would typically claim. It is indeterminable whether the pyramidal and panoptical way of describing Mutesa is due to his *existing* imperial representational status, or whether Stanley projects his own preconceived models on to the African reality. Therefore, this entire part of *Through the Dark Continent* remains ambiguous in relation to who has priority - Mutesa observing Stanley or vice versa.

Stanley operates with a rhetorical distinction between logos, light and writing on one side and noise, darkness and voice on the other. However, his readiness to admit that Mutesa and his trusted men can read and write introduces an uncertainty: who is in fact learning what? Mutesa, writes Stanley, owns several "books of wisdom", described by Mutesa himself as "the results of his interviews with European travellers" (p. 411). And perhaps, Stanley wonders as he is getting ready to leave, some curious traveller will find it worth the trouble of translating these negotiations and conversations. In the same way that Stanley told the story of his adventures and of life and customs in Uganda, including an account of the country's history as both *Iliad* and Old Testament in the travel book *Through the Dark Continent*, Mutesa has also included *his* version of Stanley and the visitor's foibles in *his* "books of wisdom". Mutesa's books, however, remained inaccessible, and therefore disquieting, to the great explorer.

In the introduction to *Marvelous Possessions: The Wonder of the New World* (1988), Stephen Greenblatt discusses Tzvetan Todorov's hypothesis that European written culture provided a crucial technological advantage in the conflict with the Aztecs. The idea that writing enabled Columbus to represent and thereby manipulate his opponent is refuted by Greenblatt, with reference to various descriptions of the cultural encounter. According to Greenblatt, they may reflect an attitude of cultural superiority based among other things on written culture, but the dominant role of writing is not supported in the actual encounters. Both parties misinterpreted each other, but there was not

"Mtesa, the Emperor of Uganda, Prime Minister, and Chiefs" (from a photograph). From *Through the Dark Continent*. Mutesa and his court and 'ministers' are posing for the first photographs, which are among the best from Stanley's African journey. When he ran out of photographic plates, he used the camera lens and mirror system as an aid to draw portraits and landscapes by hand. The use of the camera was encouraged by both humanitarian and scientific societies, as well as readers. Publishers, like Stanley's publisher Edward Marston, invested their energy and money in being at the forefront of using the new medium in the travel books. Portraits of natives are arranged either on the basis of an anthropological interest in mapping types or, as in this case, through Stanley's classicistic filter. He was later criticised for his tendency to turn African villages and chieftains into palaces with kings and princesses. This tendency can be seen as a nostalgic move from the industrialised society of the turn of the century towards the imagined transparency of classicism, and entertaining displays of regal power.

necessarily a wide epistemological gap between them. Their primary interest was not in representing each other adequately, but in entering into practical negotiations and forming relations that were based on imagination rather than rationality.[66]

Stanley's travel account is obviously much more recent than the renaissance material Greenblatt examines, but the example serves to present a similar scepticism towards rash conclusions about power and discourse in the travel

accounts of the nineteenth century. The passages in *Through the Dark Continent* on the stay with Mutesa and the Homeric journey on Lake Victoria are not first and foremost dominating representations aiming at exhaustively describing the other; they are texts that, alongside representational characteristics, also include theatrical and performative functions.

The travel book incorporates a number of corrective elements addressing critical objections that arose after the stay with Mutesa but before the final editing. This temporal shift involves the opening of spaces other than the landscapes originally encountered, and new dialogical movements are incorporated in the text – most importantly the Homeric and Biblical mirror axes. And similarly to Bougainville's and Diderot's texts about Tahiti, the result is a multi-perspectival and changeable prose, in which the other culture is not fixed in relativistic or essentialist models. Instead of reading Stanley's use of basic figural structures – especially the Homeric transparency and the Biblical genealogy (equivalent to the Tahiti texts' use of Venus) – as distortions of the original otherness, the strategy might suggest something more ambiguously multi-directional.

Mutesa's regime is, in a literal sense, a model image for Stanley. In lengthy digressions he presents it as an ideal that appears more attractive than anything the philanthropic capitalists can envision. Furthermore, Stanley's account is unique in presenting Buganda as a civilisation with its own history – not only as a cluster of narratives mimetically entangled in our own, but with a written culture that challenges the European traveller. This creates a point of reversibility in the cultural encounter and vulnerability in the text, despite its strongly theatrical aspects. It seems reasonable to perceive the many imagined prospects and changes in perspective as suggestions and hypotheses seeking meaning *in* and *through* the text, rather than as, for example, anthropological representations of a strange culture. Viewed in this light, Stanley's description of the floating fort, used Homerically against the Wavumas, is not only a theatrical demonstration of technological and literary supremacy, but also a daring textual experiment in which the narrator's voice is concealed and exposed simultaneously; it is staged and explicated as a hypnotic fetish without identity or language, which magically causes things to happen. We will return to this question of performativity later.

Shibboleth

The description of the stay with Mutesa and the journey on Victoria Nyanza is by far the longest coherent narrative in *Through the Dark Continent*; it is also the most complex. Compared to the next section about the journey along the system of rivers that Stanley would later come to know with certainty was the River Congo, it appears as if the free view of the landscape also allowed a freer use of textual expansions. There is a remarkable correlation between the changes in the physical references in the travel description and the expedition's westward movement into unknown territory. Just as the expedition stayed at the centre of the river from fear of being attacked, Stanley's descriptions become much more strict – limited to a chronological account of events and close to the form of the travel diary, which is cited frequently. A long, dramatic chain of events – in which the expedition gets into conflicts with every tribe they encounter, are forced to manoeuvre canoes around dangerous waterfalls and cannot prevent the death of the only other white man, Francis Pocock – is, according to Stanley, cited entirely from the notebook. This can be confirmed by comparing the two texts: "The above, faithfully transcribed from my notebook, convey, more truly than any amount of after-written descriptions, the full sense of the miserable scenes we endured during the fatal month of June 1877" (p. 422).

On this final stretch of the expedition, Stanley did not conduct any ethnographic studies or abide by any goals other than mapping the river and staying alive. Everything is veiled in darkness; darkness is the all-dominant rhetorical figure that represents impenetrable and inconceivable nature, blocking his vision in all directions. Stanley had no time for romantic dreaming of the kind he had on the small island in Victoria Nyanza: partly because he must float with the current, partly because he more often had to defend himself against attacks. As a result of the increased speed of travel and the function of the river as a transit corridor, but also because the expedition's corps of interpreters was no longer able to communicate in the local languages, it was much more difficult for Stanley to carry out the often laborious, ritualised and vital negotiations for provisional peace treaties, safe-conduct, tolls, taxes and food trade. This often led to hostility, usually because of unprovoked attacks due to poor communication and deliberate use of force, for instance in the form of theft or hostage taking rather than negotiation with gifts or taxes in order to secure free passage.

The gentle darkness on the islands in the middle of the river is therefore only a brief sanctuary from the furious pace that the narrative gains in the second volume of *Through the Dark Continent*. Early in the course of events, when Stanley travels to areas beyond the reach of the Arabs, a completely different, alarming darkness is introduced. Here, Stanley receives numerous reports of Arab slave traders based in Nyangwé who are raiding the areas west and northwest of the Lualaba River in search of new districts where they can secure their supply of slaves and ivory. Occasionally, the Arab gangs formed alliances with tribes that

were at war with other tribes, but more often their manhunts were carried out independently. However, Stanley's reports on them – which were among the most important goals of the expedition – are ambiguous.

When Stanley writes about massacres and infamous gang leaders such as Muini Dugumbi, he expresses something resembling admiration for their callousness, and when he is forced to give evidence of the Arabs' cruelty he adds modifying reflections on the natives' own contribution to the slave trade. With few scruples, therefore, Stanley hires the slave traders Tippu Tib and Dugumbi and their mercenaries as an escort on the expedition into "the dark unknown" – a decision that had disastrous consequences: on every step the expedition from then on, the natives are perceived negatively, and all attempts to negotiate are seen as trickery. The rumour of a vast army of Arab soldiers results in a state of panic, leaving villages either completely empty or prepared for war. The mercenaries are beyond Stanley' control and act as aggressors whenever they are in the line for profit. However, Stanley does not refrain from participating in bloody confrontations in which the expedition, with their modern weapons, time after time manages to crush their opponents who, although they sometimes appear in thousands, are only equipped with primitive guns or bows and arrows.

However, the question in this case is, as in the Bumbireh event discussed above, how we should assess Stanley's descriptions of violent conflicts today. In the biography *Stanley* (2007), Tim Jeal focuses on character in his attempt at a full rehabilitation of Stanley's moral reputation. In this book, the focus is on the texts. Jeal is correct when, with reference to diaries and other new archival material, he claims that Stanley exaggerated the scope and outcomes of the conflicts with the natives, mainly in an attempt to satisfy readers' expectations of excitement and action. These exaggerations would later catch up with him, because his credibility as an explorer could not be put at stake by his admitting that he had taken the role of entertainer too far.

It is significant that the notebooks and notes in the archive only *modify* the dramatic form found in the travel account, something that in fact substantiates the tales of violent, fatiguing conflicts. The impression of stress and isolation, troubled communication and orientation and the pressure to feed the expedition's many participants is enhanced in the light of the diaries. The travel account's dramatised versions might in fact downplay a situation that was, in reality, far worse. The images of the violent river and the conflicts with the natives have a figurative and conciliatory function in the description of a gloomy and meaningless journey during which starvation, illnesses and paranoia were the actual antagonists. Furthermore, the fact that Stanley describes the exploration as a fundamentally violent action can be perceived as a strength

"The fight below the confluence of the Aruwimi and the Livingstone Rivers". From *Through the Dark Continent*. The text describes the "monster" canoes of the immense army with both interest and fear: "when, looking up stream, we see a sight that sends the blood tingling through every nerve and fibre of the body, arouses not only our most lively interest, but also our most lively apprehensions – a flotilla of gigantic canoes bearing down upon us, which both in size and numbers eclipse anything encountered hitherto".

rather than a weakness, compared with earlier explorations that concealed their violent circumstances. Finally, the account is inclusive, e.g. when it presents detailed knowledge about the natives' own contribution to the slave trade – a truth that the abolitionists did not care to read about and which did not fit discursively with the stereotypes of the slave trade in Africa.

Taking this into account, it would be inaccurate to describe the relation between the notebooks and the finished travel book as one of exaggeration and dramatisation. Dramatisation rather works as understatement of and diversion from the real uncertainty and danger that is evident in the notebooks. What is striking about the field notebook is the density of information: sketches of the course of the river are blended in with drafts for the travel book, side by side with hasty notes on the events of the day's march or unsorted, detailed and realistic descriptions of the practical reality of the slave trade, which are continued in

the broad spectrum of knowledge and opinions on the topic found in *Through the Dark Continent.* The relation between field notes and the edited travel account is therefore better thought of as the latter's interpretation of a complex pattern of information – both weeding out old information and adding new, in a way that corresponds to Lévi-Strauss' distinction between different levels of explanation in historical material.

The notes are not more realistic or less dramatised than the travel book, which, in turn, is not a more distant or derived version. Both texts were crucial for the expedition, not only as data records but also as activities undertaken during and after the journey – a fact that is often highlighted in *Through the Dark Continent.* When, for instance, the expedition struggle their way through a particularly impassable stretch in the forests, the march is described as a trek in "a feeble solemn twilight", where the border between the travel text and reality is cancelled out. On the verge of a breakdown and disease-ridden, the expedition crawl across the rotting forest floor while Stanley cites from his notebook: "It was so dark sometimes that I could not see the words, recording the notes of the track, which I pencilled in my notebook" (p. 133); in this way he indicates a link between the increasing darkness and the difficulty of "keeping track" in both notes and language.

When the expedition finally left the forest for the river, communication with the native population had become very difficult. The native interpreters in Stanley's crew were now dependent on gestures and the repetition of a few potentially helpful phrases the effect of which they can never be sure of. Meanwhile, Stanley completely abandoned his studies of the differences between tribes, now – with reference to Swift – only characterising them by their different battle cries: "the Ooh-hu-hus", "the Bo-bo-bos" and "the Yaha-ha-has" (p. 295). The whole situation is in this way complicated by a complete lack of rational language, and the interpreters must strain every nerve to ensure that the word for "friend" is perceived in a friendly spirit:

"The "Open Sesame" – "Sen-nen-neh!" – was loudly uttered by Katembo with his usual pathetic, bleating accent, and to our joy the word was repeated by over hundred voices. (...). For half an hour we glided down in this manner, keeping up a constant fire of smiling compliments and pathetic Sennennehs. Indeed, we were discovering that there was much virtue in a protracted and sentimental pronunciation of Sen-nen-neh! The men of the Expedition, who had previously ridiculed with mocking Ba-a-a-a-as, the absurd moan and plaintive accents of Sen-nen-neh, which Katembo had employed, now admired him for his tact. The good natives with whom we were now exchanging these suave, bleating courtesies proved to us that the true shibboleth of peace was to prolong each word with a quavering moan and melancholic plaint.

(...) A chorus of Sen-nen-nehs, longdrawn, loud, and harmonious, quickly following the notes of the last syllable, burst from the large assembly, until both banks of the great river re-echoed it with all its indescribable and ludicrous pathos" (pp. 213-14).

The river landscape in this area features lots of islands separated by narrow canals, which the expedition had to pass through. Likewise, the discourse only leaves narrow passages in which the pronunciation and tone of a single syllable determines whether the password will work as a shibboleth or result in hostility and attacks. It is all about being able to decode "the subtle differences of passion (...) the nicest shades of feeling which wild humanity is capable of expressing" (p. 215).

Parallel to this fascination with wordless gestures, which can only establish understanding and friendship by pathetic modulations of the voice, writing and written language function as magical powers in several remarkable passages. There are many variations on the theme of how the natives looked on Stanley's notebook as a fetish with either fear or envy, requesting that he either burn or sell it. The "note-book contained a vast number of valuable notes; plans of falls, creeks, villages, sketches of localities, ethnological and philosophical details, sufficient to fill two octavo volumes - everything was of general interest to the public" (*TDC*, p. 386, p. 306, SA, No. 18, 18 February 1877). In principal, the notebook already contained the path-breaking work, and obviously it was out of the question to sacrifice it to the whims of the savages. According to Stanley's dramatised account, which includes dialogue and theatrical effects, he therefore replaces the notebook with a worn copy of Shakespeare, which, to the natives' great relief, is tossed into the fire and burnt with ceremonial sobriety, while Stanley reminisces about the many nights on which the great playwright's words have driven away the countless hardships of the expedition. The anecdote is a condensation of *Through the Dark Continent* in its entirety. Stanley's dream of the travel book facilitating a real encounter with a vast audience is conveyed in the small mirror of the anecdote. The European recipients are addressed as informed and inquisitive readers who welcome the scientific descriptions with open hands, while the natives' 'reading' is characterised as "superstitious madness". This implicitly legitimises the exploration's civilising mission, while at the same time justifying its scientific aspects and the need to disseminate the acquired knowledge to European readers and natives alike. Although the *auto-da-fé* is presented as a sketch or dilettante comedy, it is very significant when it comes to the fundamental nature of travel accounts.

However, in the very last line of *Through the Dark Continent*, the two octavo volumes containing tables of the travel routes, crew and fatalities, leave a dif-

ferent impression of the expedition's project. In a farewell salute to the crew, Stanley looks back one last time on the incredible journey and adventurous tale:

"And in a flood of sudden recollection all the stormy period here ended rushed in upon my mind; the whole panorama of danger and tempest through which these gallant fellows had so staunchly stood by me – these gallant fellows now parting from me. Rapidly in some apocalyptic vision, every scene of strife with Man and Nature through which these poor men and women had borne me company, and solaced me by the simple sympathy of common suffering, came hurrying across my memory; (...). What a wild, weird retrospect it was, that mind's flash over the troubled past! So like a troublous dream!" (pp. 482-83)

Although the aim of the journey was to bring light and civilisation to the area, and the travel book's aim was to pass this light on to European readers, the conclusive vision is dark and apocalyptic, more nightmare than dream, backward-looking rather than forward-looking. The contrast with the dream of spreading light in the darkness is striking. Stanley recounts a conversation with Frank the night before they set out on the final leg of the journey into the unknown – according to *Through the Dark Continent*, without knowing if the river they travelled on was the Congo, the Niger or the Nile:

"Believe? Yes, I do believe that we shall all emerge into light again some time. (...) Now look at this, the latest chart which Europeans have drawn of this region. It is blank, perfectly white. (...) I assure you, Frank, this enormous void is about to be filled up. Blank as it is, it has a singular fascination for me. Never has white paper possessed such a charm for me as this has, and I have already mentally peopled it with most wonderful pictures of towns, rivers, countries, and tribes – all in the imagination – and I am burning to see whether I am correct or not. *Believe?* I see us gliding down by tower and town, and my mind will not permit a shadow of doubt" (pp. 194-95).

If we compare these three passages, in which Stanley characterises and summarises the exploration in conflicting ways, with the contents of the travel notebook, a distinct pattern appears. The notebook forestalled one important aspect of Stanley's orchestration of the journey: the discovery as a grandiose gesture and a force that is both concrete and rhetorical, and which simultaneously continues the sweeping stream of the river and trumps its singular endeavour to push through. This force fills a blank in the Europeans' knowledge, while at the same time adding new blanks – new pieces to the puzzle of ignorance: the force itself is a magical and irrational entity, expressed via an act of pure, blind determination, paraphrased in the play on the word "believe" in the passage.

The concluding retrospect in the book perceives the journey removed from the idea of conquest, enlightenment and discovery. Instead, we are dealing with the apocalypse: not a beacon in the dark but an experience of doom. The darkness is not only in the jungle and the river but also inside the travellers. As we will see later, this vision at the end of the trans-Atlantic expedition can be seen as an omen for the Emin Pasha Relief Expedition and the gothic qualities that would come to characterise all the texts about it.

Finally, viewed in the light of Stanley's forward- and backward-looking incantations, the anecdote about the notebook's "tara-tara" assumes a completely different meaning from the arrogant joke about the natives' superstition of European science: it expresses an insecurity in Stanley's self-assured burning of Shakespeare, and a suspicion that science is not the foundation of the journey, but nothing more than an opportunistic excuse. This pattern reveals a hidden knowledge in Stanley's visions and anecdotes: that the writing of notes and the travel book is at the end of the day a powerful phenomenon, like ancient runes, that makes things happen; it is a magic fetish, "tara-tara".

"An African Museum"

Stanley mentions several times that he is taking ethnographic notes, and he pretends that like explorers before him, he is gathering information about geography, languages, life and customs. This highly eclectic collection of knowledge plays an important role in the collective project of the travel books, both as ornamentation or *divertissement* from the dominant discourse dictated by the unrelenting forward movement of the march, and as a component of the text's realistic prose. Stanley did not have the patience to stay in one place longer than necessary. The stay with Mutesa was an exception, which therefore also contains the books' only attempt at exhaustive, ethnographic description. It is not written within the discourse of science or cultural anthropology, however, but in prose that constantly interrupts the recording of customs with changes of perspective.

On 19 June 1876 at Kiwesa, Stanley and his vanguard discovered a village that had just been attacked and burnt down, presumably by an Arab gang. At first they were taken aback by the incredible silence, but as they came closer they found a speared man and three or four other dead bodies, "a sight which froze the blood", and then various items that had been left behind and lay displayed in the ashes of the fire: "all the articles that constitute the furniture of African families lay scattered in such numbers around us that an Africa museum might

"A native of Rua, who was a visitor at Ujiji", from *Through the Dark Continent*. The portraits of natives place more emphasis on curious hairstyles than ethnic types. They stand out in the book as ornaments without further explanation. Based on Stanley's four hastily drawn sketches of the hairstyle fashions in the Kasangé region, 28 September 1877 (SA No. 18), the illustrator created a whole collection.

have been completely stocked. Stools, mats, spears, drinking-vessels, cooking-pots of all sizes, walking-staffs, war-clubs, baskets, trenchers, wooden basins, scoops, & etc." (II, p. 26). Stanley also notes how the village chieftain had decorated his house with thirty pale skulls and that the destruction of the village was probably self-induced: "It is the same story throughout Africa" (*TDC* II, p. 27).

The passage illustrates some key aspects of Stanley's 'ethnography'. Firstly, everything he sees and has access to is conditional on the war-like advance of the expedition. With the exception of the stay with Mutesa, the phenomena he records are often either influenced by escape or panic, which leads to an image of the natives as flocks of animals without individuality, or frozen in *nature mortes*, so that in the absence of people only lifeless objects can say anything about their way of life. The passage expresses the random order in which Stanley's ethnographica appear: interspersed throughout the commotion and endeavours of the march, we find observations such as "Hairdressing ad Absurdum" – a typical title for that type of diversion – often accompanied by illustrations, the hyper-realistic styles of which point backwards in time to the catalogues of curiosities from the renaissance. In the same way that pots and pans, furniture and battle axes lay spread all over the village after the attack, the ethnographic passages appear as unmotivated and isolated digressions that slow the reader's pulse and lead the mind in a more innocent and pleasant direction after descriptions of violent, often bloody events. After "Fabulous Terrors", for instance, we find this typical *divertissement*:

“the natives of Rua, Uguha, and Ubujwé appear to be the *élite* of the hairdressed fashionables of Africa. Hair-dressing is indeed carried to an absurd perfection throughout all this region, and among the various styles I have seen, some are surpassing in taste and neatness, and almost pathetic from the carefulness with which poor wild nature has done its best to decorate itself” (*TDC* II, p. 69).

The description is accompanied by illustrations of the splendid hairstyles that apparently kept attracting Stanley's attention, since both volumes include numerous illustrations of this kind. We find something similar in Carsten Niebuhr's travel accounts from a century earlier, interrupting the text for no specific reason. Much of Stanley's text is characterised by this early paradigm for describing nature and culture, which, in this book's introduction, is mentioned as a prominent discourse on the curious, closely related to the essay and to early travel accounts' visualising, perspectival prose. The lack of taxonomy and contextualisation in Stanley's ethnographic notes points in several different directions: the curious objects, phenomena or events act as entertainment, providing distraction and variation in the otherwise monotonous description of often monotonous terrain. However, they are also the remains of the discourse of wonder that was dominant in the renaissance and until the end of the eighteenth century, and in that capacity they have a number of traits that lost their prestige towards the end of the nineteenth century. Furthermore, Stanley's varied, visualising detail-orientated realism is related to New Journalism and the essayistic prose with which the discourse of wonder is associated.

Stanley's anthropological contemplations are usually rudimentary and primitive, limited to reflections on the evolutionary stage of the tribe in question regarding intelligence, beauty and taste. Generally, he seems to be of the opinion that if their physical appearance does not fit in with his norms it is the native who has no taste. Several times he throws himself into reflections on female beauty, which he has never really encountered in Africa; in one passage he believes he has found the most “unlovable” humans in existence:

"There was no one feature about them that even extravagant charity could indicate as elevating them into the category of noble savages. I do not think I was prejudiced; I examined their faces with eyes that up to that time had gazed into eyes of over five hundred thousand black men. They were intolerably ugly" (II, p. 212).

Whether Stanley placed natives – individually or as entire tribes – high or low on the evolutionary ladder depended very much on how close he came to them, and in what perspective he perceived them. From a distance, he saw them as ugly, savage and primitive, but if he was engaged in negotiations or stayed for some time, they usually rose in his esteem. We have looked at the regime of vision through which the text's fantasies of control are most often expressed, and here we are confronted with it once again in Stanley's reassurance that his assumptions are not based on prejudice but on having seen the people with his own eyes. Vision, however, is not always reliable – something Stanley ponders concerning his observations of another example of ultimate primitiveness. And like the description of the stay with Mutesa, in which changes of perspective interrupted the panoramic view, Stanley's ethnographic observations are exceptionally elastic, thus indirectly characterising his own observing anthropology and status as someone who is also being watched.

In "My primitive brothers and sisters", about a village in the district of Uhombo, Stanley describes what he calls a common procedure when someone arrives in a village; we can perceive it as a model for how Stanley wrote his ethnographic records. Although his business is to create a treaty of friendship with the chieftain and study the Uhombos, he is welcomed with such curiosity that the effect is the opposite – as if he has arrived only "to make a free exhibition of myself as some natural monstrosity". The anthropological model follows several separate courses: initially, Stanley writes how he regards the natives as "the most degraded, unpresentable type

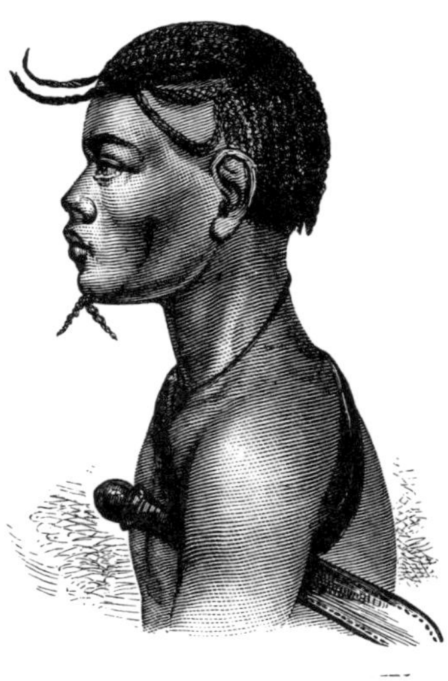

it is possible to conceive, and though I knew quite well that some thousands of years ago the beginning of this wretched humanity and myself were one and the same, a sneaking disinclination to believe it possessed me strongly" (*TDC* II, p. 73).

Later, Stanley admits that these "debased specimens of humanity" cannot be assessed on the basis of their hideousness alone. If one talks to them and takes into account their skills in farming and building, they appear intelligent, and one will discover that their senses and bodies are as developed as the Europeans'. Consequently, it is only "in taste and judgement, based upon larger experience, in the power of expression, in morals and intellectual culture" (II, p. 73), that the Europeans are superior.

In continuation of this comes the performance of a comical scene in which Stanley, apparently in accordance with good ethnographic method, conducts an unorthodox interview with the village chieftain, asking why his nose is so exceptionally flat. The chieftain's face is described as "an ugly and extravagant mask, clumsily manufactured from some strange, dark brown coarse material"; the mouth is weak, the hair follows "the capricious fashion of the country", in some strange manner imitating the typical landscape in Uhombo with its protrusions, ridges, flutes and canyons. The feet are "monstrous abortions", and when Stanley looks around at the other inhabitants he can only say "ugly – uglier – ugliest".

The chieftain, however, retorts with a joke and "a sly laugh": "it is the fault of my mother, who, when I was young, bound me too tight to her back" (II, p. 74). And while noting the chieftain's humorous and friendly attitude, Stanley also notes the physical signs of back-breaking work, poor hygiene and a rancid smell. Once again, he is distancing himself from his brothers and sisters in disgust and fear, when he is interrupted by the group's protracted cries of the word for men, "Waa-a-a-antu!" This makes him realise that they are also wondering if this stranger is indeed a human being: "Now imagine this! While we whites are loftily disputing among ourselves as to whether the beings before us are humans, here were these creatures actually exposing strong doubts as to whether we whites are men!" (p. 75). When he discovers shortly after that they are capable of laughing, which enables him to observe their shiny white teeth, and showing compassion and hospitality, Stanley must admit that his initial descriptions were unfair: "Under the new light which had dawned on me, I reflected that I had done some wrong to my dusky relatives, and that they might have been described less harshly, and introduced to the world with less disdain" (p. 77).

The passage is obviously stylised and arranged for the European reader, and yet it is still an apparently honest attempt to illustrate the course of a typical

ethnographic observation in a manner that is unusual when compared with earlier romantic and orientalist travellers, as well as with contemporary Victorians. Stanley shows how observation is dependent on a number of changes of perspective, which allow for conflicting perceptions of the natives and also of the viewer's perception of self.

Furthermore, the passage is parodic and self-parodic, in part due to the comical inversion of perspective and in part due to the style which obviously imitates and exaggerates different prejudiced procedures that are both admitted and exhibited as rudeness – for example the idea that it is possible on the basis of physical features alone to infer mental capacities, and consequently to place the culture in question on the evolutionary ladder. While the passage ultimately displays Stanley's combination of envy and contempt for the educated and scientific explorer, it also attempts to provide an insight into the actual conditions under which he set foot in an unknown village in order both to negotiate and to conduct ethnographical studies: it expresses his own fear and contempt, his ever-changing feelings of fascination and distance. In this way, his own discomfort behind the scientific or jovial surface is exposed as an inevitable influence on his observations. Finally, Stanley's critical model anthropology is also deeply rooted in the discourse of wonder and its tendency to place sentiment and curiosity in the foreground; it holds a position as the actual source of knowledge in the reversible and dialogical course of the encounter, expressed through the diary's note on the episode: "But it matters not much whether they make a wonder of me or I make a wonder of them" (SA, No. 17, 10.03.1876).

Other anthropological reflections take their starting point in another classical figure which is fundamental to the anthropology of the Victorian age: the image of the relationship between Europeans and natives as a family relationship,[67] as in the example of the brothers and sisters to whom Stanley balks at being related, or the children who he so paternally and affectionately must raise. "Primitive man" is positioned in a natural state, supported by countless analogies between the 'visage' of nature and the visages of the natives; in Stanley's descriptions, they seem to imitate each other, and both are uncultured and unfinished sketches. Similarly, the individual tribes' distinctive characteristics are often described in the language of zoology, as distinctiveness is defined through anatomy, habitats and eating habits, including whether they appreciate monkey or human flesh.

As an example, Stanley rather overdoes an incident in which he buys from a chieftain a couple of skulls that are adorning the village's main road. According to the chieftain, they came from some annoying chimpanzees, so-called *sokos*; however in a footnote Stanley writes about a Professor Huxley, whose examination of the skulls back in England clearly proved that the victims were not chimpanzees but humans. After this passage, Stanley provides some reflections on the natural explanation for the area's reports of men with tails; they are caused by some natives wearing loincloths made from monkey skins.

In various ways Stanley indicates the difference in species between monkeys and natives, yet still manages rhetorically to indicate similarities through that very distinction – which are further supported by the curious but frequent observation that the natives eat both monkeys and humans. The rhetoric suggests that the difference between the two species – from the long evolutionary perspective – is only a question of nuances. The kinship is further rhetorically supported by Stanley's many remarks about the natives as imitators. Like monkeys – and ants, as we saw in Buganda – they do not learn through cognition but through imitation. Drawing on a number of typical figures from Victorian anthropology, Stanley meets the expectations of a "dark continent" handed down to readers through hundreds of years of mythology.

However, Stanley also tells other tales which work against stereotypical images and mythological representations of the natives either as dormant in an innocent, paradisiacal state or as wild animals. As mentioned earlier, he attempted to endow Africa with the history that Hegel, among others, had denied the continent; later, we will see how his negotiation-orientated and pragmatic approach kept the travel accounts from becoming – as his predecessors' did – closed and self-sufficient texts based on problematic, culturally relativistic philosophy.

Compared with postcolonial studies' claims that Victorian travel accounts, in particular Stanley's, are pure rhetoric of conquest and colonial oppression of 'the other', a more detailed reading reveals complex texts with fluid, internally contested and contesting value systems. This also applies to the display discourse that characterises vast passages of *Through the Dark Continent.* We may choose to interpret the book as a crystal clear expression of the form of colonialism that makes museum displays of objects and people by placing them as decontextualised objects in the travel book's display cases. From this perspective, examples of weapons, utensils and hairstyles rank alongside examples of natives, tribes and races, creating a clear textual anthropology that expresses "An African Museum", in which both people and objects are ripped out of their contexts, history and culture, only to be admired or despised as isolated artefacts.

The travel account's exhibition of ethnographica removed from any context of consumption and life is particularly striking in the passages in which it seems to clash with the contents and tone of the narrative. Scattered through-

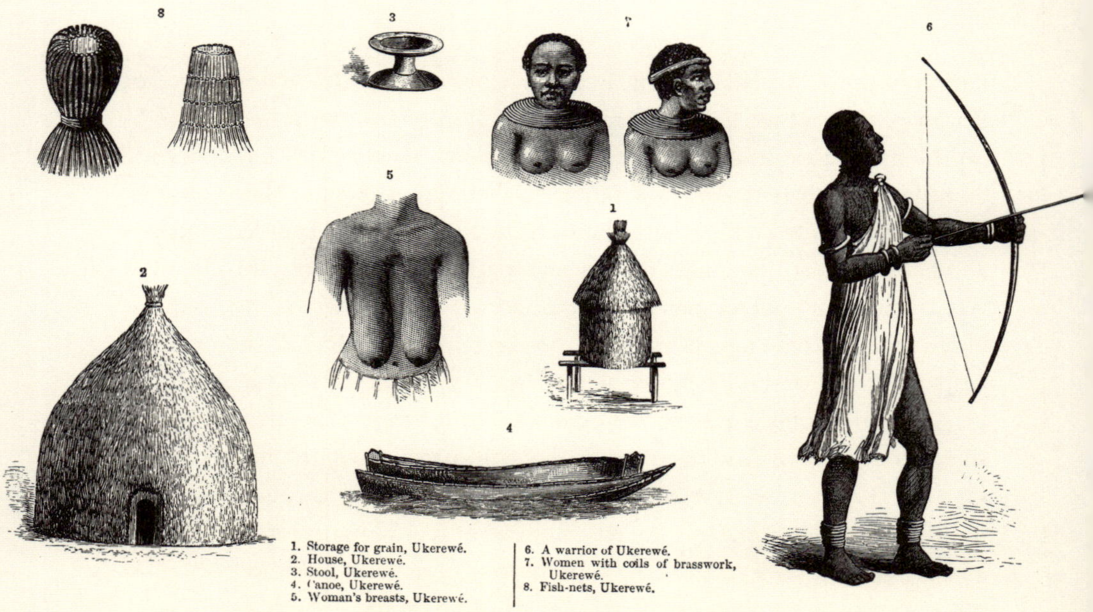

From *Through the Dark Continent*, the chapter "An educated Crocodile". Stanley's studies of the Wakerewé people in Ukerewé provide a mix of the anecdotes he heard from the natives and loose, curious observations of their dress and customs. For example, "Matrons who have fallen into the sere of life are peculiar for their unnatural length of breasts, which, depending like pouches down to the navel, are bound to their body with cords".

Musical instruments of Uganda, from *Through the Dark Continent*.

out the description of the hardship of the terrible walk through the great forests – deserted or only inhabited by very few, almost invisible, primitive forest people – are illustrations and disconnected descriptions of highly refined objects of art. Similarly, the description of the exploration's most dramatic course of events at Stanley Falls includes neat drawings of fish and signalling drums. It is as if the epic, heroic narrative requires an antithesis to balance the moral, aesthetic score between, on the one hand, starvation, suffering and violence and, on the other, the pleasure of beautiful objects that are linked to the journey as well as the reading. It is a reminder of the journey's fascination and beauty that the narrative could not encompass. Obviously, the museal aspects also have a colonising effect; however, if read without predetermined heroic or postcolonial measures, the 1,200 pages of *Through*

the Dark Continent are far from representative of a discourse of domination. On the contrary, the text proves to be dense and detailed: *not* controlled by pre-established, paradigmatic categories which, according to the standard criticism of nineteenth-century travellers, must be referenced in order to reaffirm European ethnocentric ideology.

Throughout long passages, the text's anthropological elements are almost impenetrable because they lack overview and typology. In return, their effect is one of suggestiveness: the lists of the strange names of native tribes, for instance, leave a purely phonetic resonance of unintelligible syllables with the reader, while also providing a dense and realistic impression of the journey's phenomenology and the Congo's changing topography. These qualities have been highlighted in recent studies of Stanley's narratives and maps based on source criticism and geographical history.[68] In the chapters about the stay with Mutesa, there is perspective, a pause that allows for an overview, but the transparency is far from simple and definitely not unambiguously dominant.

In the chapter "Life and manners in Uganda", Stanley makes use of a variation of the well-known nineteenth-century "scenes from life in the provinces", in which an omniscient, implied author has unhindered access to rural life, presenting it as an open book of scenes or images. The introduction portrays a native peasant with reference to the theatre: "Roll the curtain up and regard him and his surroundings" (*TDC* I, p. 383). After this, there is a number of changing scenes describing the different layers of society, all in the present

tense and with exacting information about the scene framing, lighting, foreground and background, as well as indications of the reader's point of view and "observations". In one passage, the narrator invites the reader to imagine a hut cut in half, a theatrical effect allowing the spectator to observe, and perhaps participate in, the intimate family scene. The chapter's performance ends with Stanley inviting the reader on an imagined train journey through the highlands that surround the great lakes, from Victoria Nyanza to Beatrice Gulf: "Let us imagine a railway constructed to run from one lake to the other – what scenes unrivalled for soft beauty, luxuriance, fertility, and sublimity would be traversed!" (I, p. 403).

Offhand, we might say that this museal discourse empties the landscape of life, allowing the conqueror's imagination to populate it with actors and manipulate its scenes. However, it would be wrong to perceive Stanley's hyperbolic expansions of perspective as mere domination; a train journey around the Ugandan highlands was – and still is – unimaginable in any way. It makes more sense to read the suggestion as an attempt to offer the reader comfort and luxury – a kind of funhouse in the middle of the strange surroundings – from which they can bypass the exertions of actually traversing the landscape, gliding effortlessly through a familiar prospect that is very similar to the Lake District in England. In this way, Stanley's imaginary elevated train journey appears as a direct parallel to the displays of exotic cultures at the world's fairs, which were laid out as if they were in a department store. The pleasure in this need not be derived from a sadistic tendency to oppress and dominate; it can also be perceived as a game involving utopian scenarios that allow the narrator and the reader to engage in a moment's free play with the unfamiliar and sometimes frightening prospects they encounter. This utopian space encompasses a multitude of incongruent sketches and is not strictly codified as imperialist rhetoric. However, the idea of a magnificent and unlimited space for such activity would later, from around the turn of the twentieth century, become a colonialist figure of oppression, linked to the idea of the Congo as a place beyond the law and constantly in a state of emergency.

Stanley's "singular fascination with white paper"

The expedition's task of revising existing geographical knowledge about Central Africa was closer to Stanley's own field of expertise, though he was not a professional in this field either. His revisions are visible in the maps that introduce the book – lines drawn to document the result of what Stanley called his "singular fascination with white paper". The discourse of natural science is apparent in a few notes inserted on altitude and positions; however, most of the surveying work is disseminated across various appendices. Generally, the book's geography – understood both as the lines drawn on the maps and the chosen routes – is subject to chance, both in regard to Stanley's mood and the unpredictable obstacles of the land itself. The most poignant example is when Stanley and Frank in a critical situation flip a coin to decide whether to continue across the continent or return home. Apart from the 'riddles' about the Nile system, which constituted a set mission that could be completed very effectively, the expedition was usually dependent on local political circumstances. The expedition to the Muta Nzigé Lake depended solely on whether the expedition could convince Mutesa to lend them an army, given that Stanley was fully aware that he was not welcome in the district. And as mentioned above, this obstacle resulted in a lengthy Homeric episode in which Stanley, a resourceful Odysseus, told tales, unravelled diplomatic situations and displayed practical ingenuity.

Similarly, the expedition's most eminent geographical achievement, the daunting journey to unknown Central Africa, was based on loose hypotheses about Lualaba and the Livingstone River joining the Congo, the Niger or the Nile, and seemed altogether to be more strongly motivated by mystical, fantastic visions than by scientific research. It was thus a decisive event when Stanley received a prophecy while peacefully watching the river and its "unspeakable majesty of silence" (*TDC* II, p. 148). The expedition had come to a halt and Stanley was at his wits end when he suddenly received a divine message telling him to follow the waterway to reach the Atlantic Ocean. The river was a "watery avenue cleaving the Unknown"; a messenger in its own right, "like a path of light" flowing through the "night-black clouds of mystery and fable", where legendary kingdoms were waiting to be discovered: "Something strange must surely lie in the vast space occupied by total blankness on our maps". From here on, the expedition's objective is the completion of this divinely inspired mission, connecting the point where Stanley had the vision of the river as guide and messenger and the point where the river met the sea. The expedition's original cartographic goal was no longer the most important, and Stanley's ideas about how the contact between whites and blacks through trade would lead to civilisation were not significant anymore. Instead, the motivating factors were ancient myths about the heart of Africa and its curiosities, as well as the purely formalistic objective of drawing a line between two points which, even before the last long stretch, was anticipated in the shape of the long graph representing the Congo River.

Although the travel books' presentation of Stanley's mapping appears to be profoundly influenced by medieval ideas of geography, there are also accounts of his dialogue with native knowledge about local geography. Many passages

stage situations in which Stanley interviews a local authority on local geography in order to take a bearing of names, places and, in particular, the many tributaries that form complicated networks only visible from above. These sources provided Stanley with highly differentiated and useful knowledge that would become crucial both for his own results in regard to the Nile system and for the hypotheses about the great river that runs northwards "for ever". Towards the end of the first volume, Stanley directs the reader's attention to the fact that Speke's correct assumptions about the sources of the Nile were to a great extent based on local knowledge. However, once again Stanley's descriptions of the exchange between local and global knowledge stand out for their sensitivity towards the reversible nature of this exchange.

During the description of his stay with Rumanika, "the gentle king", Stanley relates a number of testimonies from natives who had travelled or heard about travels far and wide. These testimonies express a diverse knowledge about their world and demarcate the boundaries of the unknown: the places where no-one has been, or which only exist in the form of rumours about terrifying savages. This kind of geographical knowledge, characterised by a dense, entangled web of narratives, is very similar to Stanley's own – in which, however, the distant areas on the map are entirely blank. For that very reason, the natives' knowledge was vital for his bearings and goals.

Stanley makes use of Swiftian satire, apparently assuming an attitude of superiority towards the natives' knowledge and its dependency on oral narratives; however, it is also a miniature reversal of his own "low journalism" and often uncomfortable relationship with scientific institutions and amateur geographers. Initially described as chatty and harmless – a club founded on exchange of gossip and adventures – the native institution whose advice he seeks is named "The Royal Geographical Society of Karagwé" (I, p. 470). However, in line with Stanley's anthropological field studies that demonstrate both self-awareness and parody, the superior perspective is deconstructed by the introduction of a joke. Stanley writes that a young man shatters his illusion that black people are incapable of philosophising, when he asks "Stamlee, how is it, will you tell me, that all white men have long noses, while all their dogs have very short noses, while almost all black men have short noses, but their dogs have very long noses?" (I, p. 472).

Subsequently, "the young philosopher" provides a detailed description of Muta Nzigé and Kagera, exceeding the knowledge Stanley is capable of establishing with his own 'discoveries', which are merely more lines on a map. The anecdote about the black and white noses, which at first sight appears to be a witty exposition of the native's faulty syllogism, becomes – through the comparison of the two geographical societies – a reference to similarly syllogistic chains of reasoning in the Royal Geographical Society, which, after Stanley's bitter experience during the dispute over his credibility following the rescue of Livingstone, had become even further removed from his reality. In other words, these daring anecdotes establish symmetries between local and global knowledge – symmetries that belie Stanley's absolute, ultimate and hegemonic status on which his authority as a writer and explorer was ultimately dependent.

The suggested symmetries between local and global knowledge, however, are controversial and subtly concealed in the boisterous sketch. In other passages we find a more traditional formula for the acquisition of cartographic knowledge, as links to the local tales that nurture the discoveries appear and then evaporate the moment they are inscribed on the expedition map. This form of logic is expressed in the attitude towards the trope of the unknown, dark Africa, which in the map's representation is depicted as completely white. First it is filled with imagined worlds, then emptied of concrete life, and finally the explorer is summoned, rhetorically, as the one who can draw the map and repopulate the landscape with people, life and worlds, although this time in the form of European projections.

The description of how Stanley climbs the mountain and in one, grand gesture takes in the entire African panorama plays out and varies the tropes that Mary-Louise Pratt sums up as "the monarch-of-all-I-survey". It has been demonstrated how this fantasy contains a multitude of perspectives and rhetorical figures, some of which support the idea of colonial dominance while others counteract and challenge it. The cartographic dream of the nineteenth century is expressed in the compass, which is superimposed on the panoramic prospect, connecting the exploration with dream and myth. The compass helps structure the prospect as a map that represents Africa from a pyramidal perspective. This perspective would determine the organisation of future travels, travel accounts, political opinions and conceptions, which makes it an important discursive factor in the colonisation of the Congo, the race for Africa and, in a wider context, the African conflicts as consequences of the drawing of colonial state lines in accordance with arbitrary bee-lines.

This perspective is not the only one present, and if we are aiming to understand *Through the Dark Continent* as a unique performative act, we need to consider more historical and rhetorical aspects than has so far been possible in this introduction to Stanley's method. Such aspects include his exceptional elasticity and the relationship between his perceptions of the text as magic and as performance.

While this chapter has focused on a number of rhetorical mechanisms in the internal organisation of the travel account, the following chapter on Stanley's

last major expedition and *In Darkest Africa* will place accounts in a wider context, including their use of mass media and marketing. Before we leave *Through the Dark Continent* it seems appropriate to emphasise the connection mentioned in the introduction between the journeys' geophysical circumstances and the form and composition of the travel accounts.

We have seen how the rhetorical illumination of sunny Uganda and the dark journey along the Congo River both have far-reaching aesthetic and political implications, while at the same time resulting from concrete experiences determined by the physical layout of the landscape: around the lakes, the space allows for freely moving aesthetic and political considerations; along the river, we are at the mercy of the direction and course of the river, through landscapes that remain invisible, shrouding the text in gloom and apocalypse. Stanley often mentions this predetermined structure of the journey and the travel account, for instance when he imagines that the river is the actual expedition leader. The river lies before him, and the journey is but a reaffirmation of its existence, subsequently to be represented on the map. Another link between the physical conditions and the textual composition is the great watershed between East and West Africa, described at the end of the first volume. It becomes a theme, marking the boundary between the known and the unknown worlds, as well as between the two volumes: a historical, geographical and literary divide between different sources.

There is one discourse, about the Nile and the highlands, that is related both to the tradition of the Enlightenment and to classicism's idea of the world as a transparent, harmonious and rational place. Classicism is expressed in form and style through the numerous references to antiquity's ideals, while the spirit of Enlightenment is visible in Stanley's insistence on Africa as a marketplace for goods and ideologies, a place under negotiation. This conveys an image of Africa as a habitable place, at the same time historic and part of the modern world. The other discourse, belonging to the Congo River and the forests, is linked to romanticism and the abolitionist movement's rhetorically constructed idea of Africa as 'a dark continent', filled with pathetic, gloomy, apocalyptic figures. Stanley thus brings characteristics from Bougainville and the sentimental travel account into different conditions, the globalised market and New Journalism being the most significant. In Stanley's most important piece of writing about the colonisation of the Congo, *The Congo and the Founding of its Free State* (1885), the discourses of classicism and the Enlightenment take precedence in the text's rhetoric of civilisation. The tension between light and reason on the one side and darkness and pathos on the other is further dramatised in *In Darkest Africa*, both because the travel account is not capable of expressing the chaotic journey as a textual whole, and because it is contradicted by other accounts. Reason and sentimentality not only struggle *within* the travel account; they are also publically exposed as conflicts *between* competing testimonies whose authority was being tried in imagined court cases and real marketplaces.

2 Conflicting Testimonies: *In Darkest Africa* (1890)

Stanley's last major expedition, the so-called "Emin Pasha Relief Expedition", occupies a unique position in the history of exploration in Africa. It started out as the most spectacular – and well-documented – expedition of the Victorian era; however, it was also chaotic and disastrous, and the consequences were grave. Before Stanley had even returned home, a host of conflicting accusations and rumours of betrayal and absurd events were threatening the expedition's ideological self-understanding. The fate of the expedition and the textual testimonies, as well as the subsequent scandal and increasingly sensational stories of the expedition's atrocities, resulted in a sudden decline in the prestige of exploration in general, and contributed to increasing reservations among the population towards the civilising mission in Africa. It was also one among several factors creating fertile soil for the formation, ten years later, of the Congo Reform Association, one of the world's first human rights movements.

Stanley's account of the expedition, *In Darkest Africa* (1890), will not be analysed in detail as *Through the Dark Continent* has been. Emphasis will be put on two principal issues: the credibility of the accounts, and the commodity value of *In Darkest Africa* – which was produced and sold in hitherto unprecedented editions. The course of events surrounding the expedition reveals a close connection between literary credibility and literary market value. Furthermore, the polemical conflict between different travel accounts from the same expedition will expose the brutality behind the rhetorical innocence of the traditional 'sentimental journey', which puts Stanley in a more favourable light than is usual and helps establish the expedition as a turning point in a long history of travel literature.

At the centre of the chapter is an event that shocked Stanley's contemporaries and put texts, genres and discourses to the test. One of the travellers, the expedition's natural historian James Jameson, incited a cannibalistic killing of a young native woman and drew sketches of the act, ranking it alongside his collection of insects and stuffed birds. Jameson's naïve account gave rise to both vehement and uneasy reactions among the British public, and Stanley's *In Darkest Africa* is very much marked by the notoriety of the event, which he simultaneously displays and tries to cover up. He does so, among other things, by attempting to seize control of other testimonies and accounts that will be traced here through a number of diaries and letters; they define a close relationship between, on the one hand, the formulation of a legal-moral discourse

From the publication *How Stanley Found Emin Pasha. Letters from the Finished Journey by H. M. Stanley. With Stanley's Facsimile and a Colour Print Map of his Travel Route* (1890). New Danish Publishing Consortium was the publisher; it is unclear, however, whether it is an authorised version. It is a small publication of 78 pages, consisting of a letter to Barttelot that did not reach the addressee while he was alive; a letter to the committee behind the expedition, posted 28 August 1888, in which Stanley takes stock halfway and prepares for the controversy by explaining himself; and a letter to Stanley's publisher Edward Marston, sent 3 September 1889, in which Stanley looks back upon the finished expedition, writing: "I could fill entire books with a list of the accidents, cases of illness, disputes, quarrels and minor incidents that have taken place since I set out on this expedition two years ago. You know that the route has gone through a land that has hitherto been unknown. The blank, white space on the maps must now be changed to a dense, black darkness. It is definitely the darkest area on Earth I have trekked through – this stretch between the 25th and 30th degree of longitude – full of thick, dense, night-black forest, where immense hordes of vicious, man-eating savages tirelessly plagued us with attacks". While the public was waiting for the proper travel accounts, vast numbers of unauthorised prints of letters gave rise to new 'disputes' and 'quarrels' about copyrights and the right to tell the stories.

of leadership, responsibility, authority and credibility, and, on the other, the creation of opportunities and the effects of the travel accounts on the literary market, particularly in relation to questions of copyright in the globalised world. In this chapter the prose perspective will be broadened to encompass more texts, genres and institutional circuits, while maintaining the focus on the texts' effect as descriptions of place. Continuing to address performativity, it is an important point that the travel accounts deal with several different places, spaces and times 'at the same time': the marketplace, in which the text is played out, and to which it contributes; Stanley's autobiographical space; the implicit court cases happening in the public sphere as well as in diaries before, during and after the expedition; and, naturally, the expedition's actual places and movements. The sections "The Forest" and "The Marketplace" aim to create an overall picture of this complexity, which will be elaborated in the ensuing summary chapter. This summary will also expand on Stanley's magical rhetoric, his New Journalism and the world literary configurations of place and space. It is split into two parts: the first presents the expedition's background, motives, course of events and consequences; the second presents and analyses the expedition accounts and diaries.

A Province in the Back of Beyond

The official background for the expedition was a rumour that Emin Pasha, the German-born governor of the South Sudanese Equatoria Province, had been cut off from the surrounding world owing to the Muslim Sudanese revolt against their Egyptian rulers.

Stanley was appointed leader of a costly and well-equipped expedition, which also included ten European officers. Instead of using the obvious and far easier route from the east coast, the expedition sailed up the Congo River to the Aruwimi River and continued north-east on foot through the Ituri Forest. They had to fight their way past hostile tribes, and on the treks through the impenetrable forest they suffered many casualties. The expedition was followed by unseen Pygmies shooting poisoned arrows at the group, who were already demoralised owing to illness and starvation. When the survivors finally left the forest, it was Stanley who was found by Emin Pasha, not the other way around, and it turned out that Emin – unlike his 'saviours' – was doing splendidly and by no means wanted to be 'saved'.

Of the 703 original expedition participants that set out from Zanzibar in February 1887, only 246 were there at the end in December 1889. There was also extensive loss of human lives and resources among the native populations. Furthermore, the expedition had cost double the amount of money and taken double the time calculated, and even then it was doubtful whether it had met any of the expectations that were placed upon it. When Stanley, bringing Emin Pasha with him as a reluctant trophy, reached the harbour and trade city of Bagamoyo in modern day Tanzania on the African east coast, it became clear to the key figures, as well as the public, that the expedition was in every aspect founded on an illusion – in retrospect, more like a nightmare.

The proclaimed aim of the expedition was to rescue the Equatorian governor, Emin Pasha, who was believed to be holding an isolated and threatened position in the politically vulnerable province in what is today South Sudan, including the cities of Lado, Gondoro, Dufile and Wadelai; the latter two were later annexed into Uganda due to the layout of colonial borders. In 1820, Egypt had annexed a very large Sudanese area, but without investing many resources or engaging politically in the administrative and military structure. There were, however, an increasing number of private expeditions travelling south from Khartoum with the specific aim of gathering huge quantities of ivory. Between 1840 and 1870, the price of ivory more than doubled, and the demand for ivory combs, piano keys and snooker balls increased considerably, causing the so-called 'Khartoumers' to become more violent on their raids. Because the native population's all-important resource was cattle, the ivory traders organised raids to capture cattle to trade with, and slaves to carry their goods. The Khartoumers, who were mainly North Sudanese, Egyptians, Syrians and Turks, gradually settled in regulated, heavily armed bases in South Sudan's primitively organised cattle-breeding societies, resulting in conflicts and other negative effects that still have an influence in the area. After 1862, Egypt tried to take better control of the area by organising a colonial administration modelled after the British colonisation of India; for they thus inaugurated a number of European governors.

The task, however, proved impossible, owing to the existing conditions. All the affected population groups opposed every administrative initiative, and the lines of communication were the worst imaginable – even in an African context. The new military bases, which were supposed to secure the governors' safety and a basis for Egyptian rule, proved to be nothing more than a continuation of the type of presence the natives associated with the notorious Khartoumers. The situation in Equatoria under the Governors Samuel Baker, Charles Gordon and Emin Pasha was even more chaotic than before – not unlike the effect on infrastructure and communication that the demand for slaves, ivory and, later, rubber had in the Congo. The resettled or stationed Egyptians were living in constant fear, trapped in their enclaves in fear of retribution for their massive oppression of the native population. There was no system of justice, the slave trade continued uninterrupted and the province became a merely

formal, administrative unit populated mainly by convicts and rebels who had been banished from Egypt.

The governors in the province were seen as technical experts stationed from Khartoum or Cairo, while they themselves felt isolated and far removed both from their superiors and from the information and supplies on which they depended. The route up the Nile to Khartoum was often impossible to navigate, as it involved sailing through a vast swampy area, the so-called 'sudd', and there were no roads leading to the African east coast. Despite these unfavourable conditions, Emin Pasha succeeded in his first term as governor – Gordon appointed him in 1878 – in maintaining the illusion of a well-organised province. He even travelled the area, which had never been explored scientifically, in the capacity of botanist.

The years 1883-84 saw grave changes, initially in the form of uprisings among local Dinka and Nuer peoples, followed by the Mahdists who forced the Egyptians to withdraw from the whole of Sudan, conquered Khartoum and killed Gordon in 1885. In 1881, Mohammed Ahmed Ibn el-Seyyid Abdullah, a boat-builder living by the Nile south of Khartoum, had declared himself a Mahdi – i.e. a reincarnation of the prophet Muhammad – and started a jihad to force the Egyptians out of Sudan. As a result, Emin Pasha had been completely cut off from his Egyptian employers, causing him to pull his headquarters away from the war zone. He had set his camp farther south in Wadelai, from where he sent the letters to Europe that resulted in Stanley's last major expedition. In these letters, Emin Pasha never pleaded for a rescue mission but rather requested supplies, in particular ammunition, to reinforce his military position.

At that time, however, only a few people were concerned with Emin Pasha or indeed that part of the world. The Egyptian government had more or less given up on Sudan though it did acknowledge responsibility for the subjects who were trapped there. Neither the British nor the German governments were interested in becoming involved in new, risky projects in central East Africa; until then they had kept to the coastal areas. In the kingdom of Buganda – which Stanley had named the African pearl in *Through the Dark Continent*, and identified as the central point of departure for the civilisation of Africa – several missionary movements who had been welcomed by Mutesa fell out of favour with his successor, his son Mwanga. Mwanga is also portrayed as a villain in Uganda's own history, completely lacking his father's talent for the arts of negotiation, politics and diplomacy. The possibility of rescuing both the missionaries in Buganda and Emin Pasha in Equatoria on the same expedition from the east coast was briefly considered. However, the British Foreign Ministry opposed it, arguing that it mixed very different affairs.

Iain Smith has pointed to the fact that the crucial decisions were first and foremost motivated by the relevant parties' increasing economic interest in the area.[69] While changing governments were still hesitating, many private companies were less hesitant in what was developing into a race for the most profitable concessions. Business was the main aim, but it could be combined advantageously with political ambitions to define administrative provinces or spheres of interest. The trading posts required protection, and it was thus the presence of missions and traders that justified the annexation and implementation of administrative institutions and instruments of power. In tune with the nineteenth century's ideological convergence of "civilisation", "Christianity" and "commerce", the political and mercantile aspects of colonisation were inseparable for pragmatic reasons. The power struggle for the Congo was more or less settled; in the period 1886-89, Equatoria became the focus area in East Africa, and once again Buganda became the goal of a spectacular and furious race between Britain and Germany.

Dubious Motives

The two main initiators of the Emin Pasha Relief Expedition were William Mackinnon – who would later come to found the *British East Africa Company* – and Mackinnon's good friend and Stanley's employer, King Léopold, who was still not satisfied with what he owned. After 1886 he shifted his attention to East Africa, though he had no success in purchasing profitable concessions. King Léopold's interests in the expedition were of a more complex nature: for a long time, he had nurtured a fantastic dream about connecting the Congo River with the Nile, expanding his possessions towards the north-east through Sudan and Equatoria and thus creating a trans-African communication and transportation line that could keep the French at bay and expand the potential earnings of his puppet agencies. Furthermore, it was important for him to re-establish the post at Stanley Falls, which had been conquered by the Arabs, and come to an agreement with Tippu Tib, whose influence was travelling down the river at a staggering pace.

The public and media engagement in the case quickly escalated, resulting in a narrative about the British government's obligation to intervene in order to save Emin Pasha from the merciless savages and avoid a "second Gordon". The Anti-Slavery Society supported the idea and pressurised the government, adding to a plot that thrived on the stories about Livingstone and explorers who must find their way through the desert. Meanwhile, Mackinnon, Léopold and many other stakeholders began to perceive Emin Pasha and Equatoria as the keys to their grand plans; however, their focus was not on rescuing Emin

Pasha and leading his trapped people back to Egypt but hiring him and paying him to stay in the province, working as an administrator in their service and covering up their business. The rescue mission received financial support from the Egyptian government, which had political reasons - principally the pressure of the Mahdi jihad, which had isolated the province from the rest of Sudan - for wanting to contribute to the evacuation of Egyptian envoys in the area. For Mackinnon and Léopold, the Egyptian withdrawal would result in a power vacuum, leaving a new square open in the African board game. The consequence was an increased administrative mandate, which led to confusion and rebellion when Stanley arrived in the area, and in the end wore down the already fragile management. The Egyptians and their families had no intentions of leaving the area; they mistrusted Stanley, and when he finally set out towards the coast, the group who had been talked into following him at the last minute was plagued by internal disputes.

Stanley's negotiations of the expedition's objectives with Mackinnon and Léopold were held in separate locations, and he kept their intentions from each other. The rescue plot portrayed Emin Pasha as a hero, while presenting his circumstances in the worst possible light; nevertheless, Mackinnon and Léopold saw him as an obedient tool for their private ambitions, which, incidentally, were based on exaggerated notions of Equatoria's administrative and economic potential. This situation was partly the result of Emin Pasha's carefully balanced letters, which stressed the need for help while at the same time portraying Equatoria as a well-organised and prosperous colony. Emin even contributed to spreading exaggerated rumours about the vast supplies of ivory, possibly as a calculated spin to stimulate the dreams of unimaginable wealth, which in the end resulted in the launch of the rescue expedition.

Aided by the media's demand for a spectacular rescue expedition, which caused the British foreign ministry reluctantly to drop their objections, the key players set up an expedition which would be led by the obvious choice, Stanley, who hastily returned from lecture tour in America. After lengthy negotiations it was decided that the route should go from the Congo to Equatoria, and from there to Africa's east coast and Zanzibar, instead of the more obvious, tried and tested route to Lake Victoria, which Stanley had helped to open. Stanley's official argument for the decision was that following the well-known route would result in many more desertions among the soldiers and carriers than following the unknown and presumably hostile route would, although rumours about the unrest and persecution of missionaries in Buganda were also relevant. In the end, the route along the Congo River was chosen in consideration of the veiled politico-economic goals behind the rescue mission. As mentioned above, King Léopold would only support the

From *How Stanley Found Emin Pasha*. Apparently two opposites: Jephson describes Emin as gentle and considerate and Stanley as half Arab, half white man. Deceitfulness, malice, greed, and ruthlessness make up Stanley's Arab side, while power, energy, spiritual strength, decisiveness, leadership, and writing skills constitute the European side. Stanley describes Emin as nearsighted, fickle, and far removed from reality. However, the two main characters are similar in the way they change identities and nationalities.

project – and release Stanley from the contract that still bound him to work in the Congo Free State – if the route opened up the north-eastern, completely unexplored Ituri District, thus connecting the transportation network of the Congo River with that of the Nile. This would ensure that the vast amounts of ivory and other goods from the prosperous Central African area could be transported to Europe through the Congo. If the expedition chose to travel along the Congo River, Léopold would furthermore put steamboats at its disposal until it reached Stanley Falls, where the infamous slave trader and recently appointed 'governor' of the Free State, Tippu Tib, would take over responsibility for supplies.

Tippu Tib was an important part of the plan, which entailed that Stanley, on behalf of Léopold, would enter into a contract with Tib, who was staying on

Zanzibar at the same time as Stanley was hiring the necessary Zanzibar soldiers for the expedition. Part of the contract was that Tib would be employed by King Léopold as ambassador of the northern part of the Congo, based at Stanley Falls, the post that had fallen to the Arabian expansion anyway. The idea was that with Tippu Tibs' authority and control over the largest number of Arabian groups in Central Africa, and given his double role as an Arabian authority and governor for Léopold, it would be possible to direct the Arabs' activities into the north-eastern part of the Congo, thus keeping clear the western and south-western parts, as well as creating a barrier against the French who were advancing from the north. Fearing that the alternative was a devastating war with Léopold, Tippu Tib accepted the terms, which also required him to supply Stanley with 600 carriers and an escort for the strenuous trek through the Ituri Forest to Emin Pasha.

Iain Smith and Dorothy Middleton include more details and nuances concerning the political game; however, the outline presented here adequately illustrates the dream-like basis on which the expedition was launched.[70] First, as far as Léopold's, Mackinnon's and Emin's engagement went, it was based on completely unrealistic expectations of the prospects in Equatoria – a place that was, in reality, caught up in a chaotic political and economic situation, and thus far far from being the key to colonial expansionist plans. Secondly, the motives were both conflicting and obscure. The expedition funding was secured with two aims: on the one hand, Léopold's dream of expanding his kingdom to the Nile, annexing Equatoria and employing Emin Pasha as governor in the Congo Free State's service; on the other, Mackinnon's plans of convincing Emin to create a new province as a base for a prospective East African company. Stanley presented both these offers to Emin Pasha, who was tempted but found it difficult to decide on one. Both plans required Emin to stay in Equatoria, possibly in headquarters farther to the east, while the media and public expected a spectacular rescue operation bringing him to the coast, and the captured Egyptians back to Cairo. That scenario was not far from Stanley's personal motives: bringing the distressed party home from the heart of Africa would be a welcome satisfaction after the failed Livingstone expedition. As usual, Stanley apparently had no plans for personal gain, with the exception of the earnings from the travel account already stipulated by the committee and the hope of making some final, sensational scientific discoveries. Of course, it was significant that the media had already prepared the scene for Stanley to play his role of national hero. Stanley was no doubt aware of the expedition's economic and political interests, but his account leaves the impression that he was employed on the usual terms, i.e. to deliver a message and carry out a task without asking problematic questions.

These obscure expectations resulted in a number of complications on an organisational level. Because Léopold's engagement was to a great extent founded on secret agreements with Stanley that had not been passed on to the Congo State officers, they were very surprised when the expedition arrived and demanded steam ships and supplies that did not even exist in the hard-pressed colony. Léopold's inauguration of Tippu Tib as governor had similarly not been stipulated or fully accepted by the administration in the Congo, which found it difficult to acknowledge the notorious slave trader as an ally against slave trading. Furthermore, Stanley's European officers were unaware of the majority of the expedition's real aims, which led to frustration that was only compounded by the unavoidable disintegration of their naïve ideas of an honourable and heroic rescue operation.

The March

As early as the infamous march around the cataracts to Stanley Pool, the expedition's expectations were considerably diminished. The journey was extremely strenuous, and the European officers complained that they had to whip the carriers to make them proceed, as if it were a slave caravan and not a well-organised European expedition with humanitarian goals. They also discovered Stanley's no-nonsense leadership style, which was to be more understanding towards the dedicated soldiers from Zanzibar that the inexperienced Europeans. The first of many unexpected hurdles came when the expedition was unable to mobilise the steam ship capacity needed to carry their huge freight. Stanley decided to split the crew and supplies for Emin Pasha and Tippu Tib into two sections that were to meet at the planned camp of Yambuya by the Aruwimi River, a tributary of the Congo River. The transportation problems made Stanley adopt a plan that had been considered at an earlier date: splitting the expedition into a vanguard and a rear column. The vanguard, made up of the best trained Zanzibaris, was to follow Stanley to Lake Albert, clear the passage through the difficult terrain and enter into an agreement with Emin Pasha. There, they were to wait for the rear column, which would simply follow in Stanley's trail when he had reached Yambuya and Tippu Tib had provided the 600 carriers in accordance with his contract with Léopold.

The decision to split the expedition into a vanguard and a rear column was the first step towards disaster. Stanley took all the elite troops in his own section, leaving the least trained – e.g. the Sudanese who had been included in the expedition for ethnic reasons along with all the ill and weak – behind in the Yambuya camp under very difficult circumstances, as the camp had been established after a hostile takeover of a village, a fact that stood in the

"The relief of Nelson and survivors at starvation camp", from *In Darkest Africa* (1890).

way of trade with the local population. The camp was cut off from vital food supplies, with the exception of a manioc plantation, which, however, poisoned the crew, who did not know the right way to prepare the root. Furthermore, Tippu Tib did not provide the necessary number of carriers; there were already rumours about the extensive casualties on Stanley's march, and the area was feared by the local Manuyema carriers. In addition, Stanley had not met his part of the deal, which was to provide ammunition to Tippu Tib, who in reality held a weak military position at Stanley Falls, threatened both from outside and within. Because the collaboration with the Congo State steam ships had not been prepared by Léopold, and his strategy of inaugurating Tippu Tib as governor has not been communicated properly, the supplies for Stanley Falls were delayed by all the parties intended to aid the expedition. This had disastrous consequences for the rear column, which suffered huge casualties and demoralisation, resulting in the ultimate scandal when the hour of reckoning came back in London.

Stanley's order to the rear column was to follow when everybody was gathered and Tippu Tib's carriers had joined them. Stanley would continue through the extremely difficult terrain, where it was often impossible to find food. Stanley's supply units burned down villages, stole anything edible in the area, several

"Emerging from the forest", from *In Darkest Africa*.

times killed natives who put up resistance and took hostages from among the women and children, who were only released when they had provided Stanley with useful information regarding the locations and expected strength of populations in the unknown areas ahead. The locals were mainly hunter-gatherers, farming and trade were scarce, and so the expedition saw no other solution than the ruthless approach of violence and pillage.

When the vanguard reached Lake Albert, after five months instead of the expected two, Emin Pasha was not there; on the second attempt he was the one who found the expedition, not the other way round. All parties were disappointed. Emin Pasha and his supporters did not receive the supplies they needed, and they found it difficult to accept Stanley's miserable delegation as a helping European hand, which caused Emin's officers to see the entire project as dubious and to lose faith in his authority. Stanley, on the other hand, was annoyed with Emin Pasha's laid-back manner and relatively safe position; he obviously did not want to be 'saved', but had been hoping to receive supplies, especially ammunition, to reinforce his position. Stanley delivered the proposals from Léopold and Mackinnon and began the march back to meet the rear column, who would bring new supplies and carriers for the journey to Zanzibar. In the meantime, Emin was encouraged to consider the two offers.

"Meeting with the rear column at Banalya". Stanley finds the rearguard in a miserable state; only the subordinate Bonny is present. Barttelot has been killed, and Stanley questions Bonny about why the rearguard did not follow the front guard long ago. What Bonny actually tells Stanley, and whether Stanley later writes the truth about it, are questions that will come to haunt all the survivors of the expedition and occupy the foreground of the conflicting testimonies of the travel books, as well as their reception in the newspapers.

When Stanley arrived back at Banalaya on 17 August 1888, the rear column, led by Barttelot and Jameson, had been waiting for almost twelve months. The camp was disintegrating. An extremely irregular group of carriers had only just arrived from Tippu Tib, despite the diplomatic delegations that had many times been sent to Stanley Falls by the increasingly desperate commanders. Discipline and order in the camp had been undermined by desertion, looming mutiny, thefts and escalating punishments. There had been many deaths from starvation and disease, and the camp was cut off from reliable information – from the Congo administration, Tippu Tib, the expedition committee back in London and not least from Stanley, whose fate must have seemed uncertain and definitely far from what was planned. According to the diaries, there was an atmosphere of absurd stagnation in this no man's land. Shortly before Stanley's arrival, Barttelot had decided to follow after him, but on 19 July he had been shot and killed by one of the natives whilst in a random fit of rage – according to some sources because of the Manuyema carriers' incessant singing and

"Emin and Casati arrive at our lakeshore camp", from *In Darkest Africa*.

drumming during a festival that he failed to understand. Later reports claim that the killing was connected to the white officers' kidnapping and abuse of women as sex slaves. Jameson died of a fever on his way to Stanley Falls, where he had intended to report Barttelot's death.

The original plan had been to evacuate women, children and Emin Pasha's ivory back through the Ituri Forest and down the Congo River; however, this had proved impossible now the conditions in the forest were known, which on several occasions brought even Stanley to breaking point. Instead, he decided to lead an even more mixed bunch of worn-down, sick carriers and soldiers from different tribes to Emin Pasha, and from there hopefully escort him and his entire entourage to the east coast. It did not make the journey easier that the expedition had to pillage their way through the already ravaged and hostile terrain for a third time. In addition there was then the disappointment of the realisation that after all their trouble, Emin Pasha had in the meantime fallen victim to a *coup d'état*; he had been deposed by his officers, who had no faith in Stanley's staggering rescue mission. Emin Pasha's, Mackinnon's and King Léopold's spectacular plans for possessions in Central Africa were now obsolete, and Stanley decided to take over the command of the irresolute Emin Pasha, escorting him to the coast in order to complete at least one objective of the failed expedition.

When the odd party of Europeans, Sudanese, Egyptians, Turks, Zanzibar soldiers and Congolese Mauyema carriers, a total of approximately 3000 people, arrived at Bagamoyo on the coast across from Zanzibar on the 5 December 1889, they were initially received with triumph that was only enhanced by the rumours that had travelled ahead, about the rear column's disastrous fate and the journey's incomprehensible endeavours and likely collapse. It is a fair assumption that the mere fact that Stanley managed to complete the expedition and present Emin Pasha as a living trophy was enough to cause a sensation. The basis of the project, however, was immediately questioned, and when Stanley and Emin reached a missionary post, before they even arrived at the coast, they received reports of the scandalous accusations that were gaining foothold especially in Britain. Before they even had time to celebrate the fact that they had made it out alive, they were each in their way deeply involved in trying to dodge the scandal and provide *their* version of the course of events.

The expedition was received with huge publicity and promoted in advertisements for travel books, exhibitions, shows, tea, suitcases and typewriters. Stanley spoke in front of 15,000 people at the Royal Albert Hall, and the dissemination of the travel narrative brought him – and to a lesser degree the other officers – new journeys. In the newspapers, discussions about morality and responsibility, and the conflict between differing testimonies, was taking place. The battle's fronts were defined by two different narratives: one that created heroes on the basis of popular culture's identification mechanisms, and another that was doubtful and desperate, based on standards in the public sphere and Victorian culture. The dual consequences of the expedition were worldwide success and the fracturing of basic values in the culture that had initiated it.

We find a similar duality in the appraisal of the expedition's results, held up against its original objectives. In spite of its sweeping success in the context of popular culture, positive as well as critical appraisals of Stanley agreed that the mission had been a failure with regard to some important objectives. Although Stanley had succeeded in taking the reluctant Emin Pasha to the coast together with a ragged group of fatigued, starved and sick soldiers, carriers, women and children – an impressive achievement that bore witness to his unsurpassed resilience and technical ingenuity – it was not possible in the long term for him or the Emin Pasha Relief Committee to present this achievement as a triumphant completion of the expedition's goals.

Emin Pasha was not prepared to put up with his role as rescuee, nor did he want to take on administrative positions under Mackinnon or Léopold. Little by little he came to realise that the rescue operation was not intended to reinforce his position in Equatoria, but to include him as a factor in others' political ambitions. Emin Pasha became a victim of his own letters to Europe, in which he had painted a far too promising picture of Equatoria's riches. The letters were intended to secure new deliveries; instead, they spurred ill-founded hopes of quick profit and, on Léopold's part, fantasies of greater power.

All the parties' motives were based on dreams of power, but it is significant how the clash of their differing illusions does not seem to have been an explicit realisation on anyone's part – be it Stanley, Emin, Léopold or the rescue committee. Stanley and Jephson present Emin's increasing reluctance towards the expedition and his eventual entering into a contract with the rival German stakeholders in East Africa as treason, though Emin had never requested any part in the British or Belgian colonial projects. However, it is symptomatic of the veils and illusions that obscured the expedition from beginning to end, and the participants' nightmarish experiences, that Emin's reaction is described as an inconceivable defect of character. Jephson admired Emin's respectful leadership style, his friendliness and his intelligent and openhearted conversation; however, he dissociated himself completely from what he perceived to be Emin's utter lack of authority and resoluteness. At the end of Jephson's official account from 1890, Emin's 'betrayal' is mentioned as "curious forgetfulness": "Emin suffered from a singular defect of memory" (Jephson, *The Rebellion*, p. 468). It is an actual physical disability that keeps him from following a goal and realising plans in a forward-looking way – very much in contrast to Stanley's resilience and formidable ability to structure a plot. Emin simply lacks the "straightforwardness" that the British possess in both character and behaviour, and Jephson summarises the portrait of Emin as "A Curious Combination" of incompatible characteristics: "a generous mind"; "morally a coward"; "enthusiastic about science", but lacking "that firm temper required to lead men"; possessing "kindness of heart", which, however, is spoiled by "childlike vanity". He is, in short, a man whose "European directness and accuracy has been warped by a too long residence among Orientals" (p. 479).

Stanley's portrayal is mainly in agreement. Emin's scientific interests are linked to an image of "sensibility" and nearsightedness, indicating a noble character who is nevertheless floating in some intangible space outside reality, either too close to insects and plants or too far removed from practical, harsh reality. Like the rear column, Emin is portrayed as a mystery – an anachronistic wanderer who is both too scientific and too romantic (i.e. too German) and at the same time too Oriental in his nature to meet the expedition's expectations.

The criticism of Emin also represents an attack on the classical nineteenth-

century explorer who comprehends the world through scientific descriptions and labelling nature's inexhaustible resources of blank places and species – each one reflecting, and adding to, the entire system. Emin is a traveller who completes his tasks in slow, absent-minded movements through the terrain, in direct contrast with Stanley's straightforward plots. However, the final tally after the expedition does not add up to an uncritical stereotyping of Emin Pasha as a noble and sensible, romantic learned traveller and Stanley as an ignorant, ruthless representative of the rabble.

Emin was also a master of disguise, who in his life took on numerous identities, roles and nationalities. Born in Germany, he was christened Eduard Schnitzer; later he graduated as a doctor, converted to Islam and changed his name to Emin, 'the loyal one', after which he worked for the Egyptian army in Sudan where he was recruited as governor or 'pasha' as Gordon's successor.

Emin's contributions to science, especially ornithological collections and fanciful comments on German philosophy, are characterised by grandiose dreams of establishing his own kingdom in the middle of Africa. His apparent unworldliness concealed his extremely selfish motives; his passivity was a deliberate attempt to drag out the rescue operation and hold on to his position of power, and the combination of sensibility and scientific "skinning" and "collecting" were – as we will see in Jameson's dramatic version – symptoms of his disavowal of responsibility. The disastrous events in Equatoria happened, to a large extent, because of Emin Pasha's detachment, just as it was his rhetorical duplicity that fuelled the media scandal in Britain.

Emin Pasha fell from a balcony, presumably because of his nearsightedness, and suffered a fractured skull during a big banquet in Bagamoyo to celebrate the arrival on the east coast. His decision to enter into German service has therefore been linked to suggestions that he was not only eccentric and 'Oriental' in nature, but actually suffering some mental illness. Stanley's accounts of Emin's subsequent fate, which can be found in *Autobiography and other works*, describe an aimless and short-sighted course of coincidences which, considering the area's changing, but always perilous, circumstances, was bound to end in disaster. Emin Pasha was still – sometimes without any support – concocting completely unrealistic plans of rebuilding an army based on the Egyptian and Sudanese soldiers he had left behind at Lake Albert, in order to make it back to the Atlantic coast through the Congo. However, Emin and his shabby entourage never succeeded in establishing a stable base; instead they lived as a band of highwaymen whose methods were every bit as ruthless as those of the Arab slave traders who ransacked the area. Emin is said to have robbed and drowned four Arabs without hesitation, only to run into a relative of one of the victims in October 1892, by which time he had gone blind; the man decapitated him. "What a strange, eventful history, for this commonplace epoch of ours!", Stanley concludes his account (*Autobiography*, p. 375).

Stanley's first trans-African journey, which is described in *Through the Dark Continent* and in his enthusiastic letters about Mutesa's Buganda as a ripe fruit for missionaries and capitalists to pick, led to his service for King Léopold and a large-scale deployment of missionaries that served as justification for the actual colonisation and subsequent creation of the colony of Uganda. In comparison, it may appear on first sight that the Emin Pasha operation stood out from former expeditions by causing nothing but strife and shattered illusions.

It is worth noting that the Emin Pasha Relief Expedition's illusory circumstances and absurd course of events did not put a stop to colonial expansion in the area, but rather sped up the pace of the race for Africa. On his way home to Europe, Stanley reported to Léopold about the abundant resources of the Ituri Forest, including rubber, and suggested building a railway all the way up to the Nile. Léopold responded that Stanley should immediately arm 30,000 men in order to conquer the vast territory from the Free State to Khartoum and Lake Victoria – a proposal that Stanley regarded as unrealistic and declined straight away. Impervious to Stanley's advice and warnings, Léopold deployed a second expedition that reached the watershed between the Congo and the Nile in 1892, and managed to establish an extremely frail and provisional province. On behalf of the Imperial British East Africa Company, Frederick Lugard, on the other hand, succeeded over the course of a number of expeditions in gaining control over the British zone of interest in East Africa, and resolved the religious disputes between Muslims, Protestants and Catholics in Buganda. Another expedition for the same company, led by Frederick Jackson, began in the early months of 1890 a race against a German expedition led by Carl Peters, who, in the service of Deutsch-Ostafrikanische Gesellschaft, became the first to reach Mwengo, modern day Kampala, and managed to sign a colonial contract with Mutesa's successor, King Mwanga. However, the race also led to a new "Anglo-German Agreement", signed in July 1890 as a replacement for an older, looser agreement from 1886 regarding zones of interest. Despite the Germans' head start, Buganda was subjected to British interests, and what were previously vague spheres and zones became well-defined boundaries drawn on the map of Central and East Africa.

The idea of Africa as one big free trading zone had played an important role in the initial phases of its colonisation. It had justified semi-military business ventures, who could operate freely because they were not controlled by national governments, as well as ideological support for the expropriation of property: even if the Europeans had to use force in order to secure their pres-

ence, they still contributed to an increase in trade, production and prosperity, and consequently an undermining of the oppressive institutions of isolated, hostile societies – including the slave trade. Free trade was among the items on the agenda of the Berlin Conference and it was an important aspect in the justification for economic and military intervention. However, the Emin Pasha Relief Expedition revealed free trade to be a hazardous adventure, in which clashes between private interests could escalate to international political conflicts. From the beginning of the Emin Pasha Relief Expedition – when the British government interfered as little as possible in accordance with the established Victorian colonial policy in Africa – to its sad end, the European engagement in Africa changed gear as governments and foreign ministries took control. And like the earlier expeditions that had prepared the initial stages of the race, the Emin Pasha Relief Expedition was an important factor in phasing it out – paradoxically, because the goals were not met.

Before we continue to the conflicting accounts of the expedition, let us conclude the analysis with a passage from a long article by Sidney Low, July 1894, linking Stanley's discoveries and mapping to the division of Africa. Low begins with the words "The map of Africa is a monument to Stanley", and continues:

"It is not merely on geographical science that Stanley has left a permanent impress, so that, while civilised records last, his name can no more be forgotten than those of Columbus and the Cabots, of Hudson and Bartolomeo Diaz. His life has had a lasting effect upon the course of international politics. The partitioning of Africa, and its definite division into formal areas of administration or influence, might have been delayed for many decades but for his sudden and startling revelation of the Continent. He initiated, unconsciously, no doubt, and involuntarily, the "scramble for Africa" in which Germany, France, Great Britain, Italy, Belgium, and Portugal have taken part. The opening up of the Congo region, by his two great expeditions of 1874 and 1879, precipitated a result which may have been ultimately inevitable, but would perhaps have been long delayed without his quickening touch. The political map of Africa, as it now appears, and is likely to appear for many generations to come, was not the work of Stanley: but without Stanley it would not have assumed its present shape. His place is among those who have set the landmarks of nations and moulded their destinies" (cited from *Autobiography*, p. 395).

Mt. Stanley

The distance between Stanley and Emin grew wider on the last part of the journey from Lake Albert to the coast. The differences between the energetic, ruthless Stanley, who loved dramatic orchestration, and the unworldly, sensitive

Emin became clear in the new distribution of roles to which Emin reluctantly had to submit. In *In Darkest Africa*, Stanley complains that the near-sighted botanist slowed down the march, as if he did not want to be rescued at all, and saw the whole thing as a magnificent outing (*IDA* II, p. 246). When they reach their destination, however, Emin realised that the expedition's agenda was far from philanthropic, and that he was a pawn in Léopold's and Mackinnon's game of dominance over the region and its ivory traffic – including the depots the expedition had to leave behind, hardly able to carry its own weight. The situation was not made easier by the expedition's arrival in the German part of East Africa, which Bismarck was working eagerly to expand via the energetic work of Carl Peters, Stanley's German counterpart.

Emin was received more courteously by his many compatriots than Stanley, who felt left out and failed in his attempts to convince Emin to accept some form of service for the British or Belgians. The two men parted as adversaries, and yet another layer of meaninglessness was added to the expedition when the news came out that Emin Pasha had signed a contract with the Germans who – in spite of the Anglo-German Agreement, which was meant to regulate the competition between the two colonial powers – pushed hard to honour Bismarck's dreams of an African empire. The essential motive behind the British media and public's pressure to rescue Emin Pasha and avoid national humiliation in Sudan – a "second Gordon" – thus fell flat in a manner that sent tremors through the foundation of the British empire, and the same newspapers that had hyped the launch of the expedition did not hesitate to exploit what became one of the biggest scandals of the era.

Before it was even completed, the accusations against the expedition were well under way in the newspapers, which put Stanley under pressure to finish his own account of the events. Although the contract between the other officers and the Emin Pasha Relief Committee included a clause stipulating that they were not allowed to publish their travel accounts earlier than six months after Stanley's authorised version had been published, snatches began to appear early on in the media. In "Author's and publishers' note" to the first edition of *In Darkest Africa*, the publication is announced as a sensation in the history of books: "It may safely be asserted, without fear of the assertion being questioned, that no work of travel of this magnitude was ever before produced in so short a space and time".[71] The end of the almost 1,000 pages of *In Darkest Africa* describes how Stanley, after having handed over the 260 refugees from Equatoria to the Egyptian authorities, shuts himself in a villa in Cairo in order to write the book. The writing process proves almost as hard as the journey itself:

"on January 25th I seized my pen to do a day's work. But I knew not how to begin. Like Elihu, my memory was full of matter, and I desired to write that I might be refreshed; but there was no vent. My right hand had forgotten its cunning, and the art of composition was lost by long disuse. Wherefore, putting firm restraint against the crowds of reminiscences that clamoured for issue, I let slip one after another with painful deliberation into the light, and thus, while one day my pen would fairly race over the paper at the rate of nine folios an hour, at other times it could scarcely frame 100 words. But finally, after fifty days' close labour, in obedience to an irresistible impulse I have succeeded in reaching this page 903 of foolscap manuscript, besides writing 400 letters and about 100 telegrams, and am compelled from over-weariness to beg the reader's permission to conclude" (*In Darkest Africa* II, p. 430).

The ensuing conclusion is quite similar to the conclusion of *Through the Dark Continent* in that it is a rhetorical farewell to both the writing of the account and to the story, illuminated one last time by Stanley's favourite tropes. The memories Stanley struggled to place at the beginning of the book – which, with its lengthy historical accounts of the relationship between England and Egypt and lists of the expedition's supplies of goods and weapons, is very heavy going – finally flow willingly from the pen. This is related to the fact that the memories are no longer bound to the chronological order of the expedition's countless obstacles and entanglements through which Stanley struggled to maintain his style. The final pages sum up the story in an impressive light show, banishing the powers of darkness, and the mind is elevated to an Olympic, panoramic perspective while violence, meaninglessness and political intrigue disappear into thin air.

It begins in darkness, initially related to the forests, but soon seeming to take over memory itself. Scenes from "the wonderful land of Inner Africa" will always be remembered; the eternal forests "will stand in their far-away loneliness for ever", falling and growing up again in the darkness and silence, "shadowy as ghosts in the twilight". And "athwart the memory will glide spectres of men cowering in the rainy gloom, shivering with cold, gaunt and sad-eyed through hunger; we shall hear the moaning of dying men, see the stark forms of the dead". Ultimately, the darkness is penetrated by light and a multitude of changing perspectives that reveal the landscape, "the prospects of the grassland", "the vistas of green bossy hills", "the receding view of uplifting and subsiding land waves rolling in the distance" (II, p. 430). His thoughts can fly at

"aërial heights over sere plain, blue water, vivid green land and silver lake, and sail along the lengthy line of colossal mountain shoulders turned towards the Semliki, and around the congregation of white heads seated in glory far above the African

"Ruwenzori, from Karimi (from a photograph)". When Jephson, one month before Stanley, claimed to have discovered the snow-clad peaks, Stanley refuted it as ramblings; this made it possible for him to claim the discovery as his own and crown his journeys by having his name inscribed in the legendary Mountains of the Moon.

From *My Early Travels*. Stanley photographed immediately after the Emin Pasha expedition, fully decorated and with 'snow' on top.

world, and listen to the dropping waters as they tumble down along the winding grooves of Ruwenzori" (pp. 430-31).

In *Through the Dark Continent* we examined other aspects of this rhetorical *tour de force*. In this context, the trope is even more dramatic and effective, partly because it encompasses stronger contrasts and spans the vast distance between the expedition's meaningless course of events and the reader's expectation of triumph, and partly because it is the last of its kind, concluding the narrative about what has been termed "the last expedition".[72] In the final passage, the terror is employed dramatically, while its causes are veiled. The profound twilight perspective of the journey's horizontal impenetrability changes one last time to the pyramidal panorama, in which the entire African world is unified in one single gaze. In this passage, the pure perspective of cartography also makes an important point of the few, indisputable results achieved by the expedition: the

mapping of Semliki, the last of the Nile's sources, and Ruwenzori, the long-sought legendary Mountains of the Moon, which had been described, among others, by Ptolemy. With the prosopopeia of the mountains' "white heads", Stanley also inserts his own, well-known likeness, his white hair as a kind of signature for the discovery of this ultimate goal of all expeditions to Africa since the dawn of time. Mount Stanley in the Ruwenzori Mountains rises 5,109 metres, and in the concluding passage Stanley hovers above it, discovering and signing it one last time before leaving the journey and the book. However, the book is also, as mentioned in the introductory chapter "Traveller on Global Terms", a self-portrait.

The rhetoric in the concluding passage is similar to that in *Through the Dark Continent*, but the narrative is different. In retrospect, it is difficult for Stanley to reconstruct the course of events as an epos with himself in the role of hero, saviour and discoverer. His disappointment is noticeable throughout the text, and he struggles immensely to restrain his aggression towards Emin and other implicated parties in the last pages, where the score is settled. The resistance he encounters when trying to convert the notes into artful composition is not only due to time pressure and fatigue; it is also a result of his difficulties with a narrative that resists the established conventions of Victorian travel writing. Only by mustering the same superhuman and ruthless resilience that helped him complete the journey, despite all its obstacles and meaninglessness, does Stanley manage to write the book.

Through the Dark Continent plays on a series of established ideas and images, intertwined with a mix of sweeping rivers, sunny kingdoms and well-known figures, such as the abolitionist rhetoric's shifts between romanticisation and terror. *In Darkest Africa* is less enthusiastic in plot and description, which also makes it even more challenging: Stanley desperately clings to the chivalrous quest tale about the honourable, heroic and perilous rescue of the noble Emin Pasha – the story everyone prefers. Nevertheless, he speaks the truth – or his version of the truth – and gives vent to his frustrations. The quest tale is merely the narrative carcass, marked as it is by soul-searching, attempted justification, doubt and gothic gloom. This endows the text with rhetorical shifts, though they are of a different nature from those in *Through the Dark Continent*. It also adds a pervading ambience of bitterness and doom that causes the book to appear stylistically consistent, paradoxically because of its surprising shifts. This happens, for instance, when Stanley suddenly tells us – without having mentioned it in the lengthy background story, and without it affecting the chivalrous staging – that he is running an errand for Léopold and Mackinnon in order to generate lucrative business. Another shift in the epic narrative occurs in the account of a court case in which Stanley brings charges against Tippu

Tib, accusing him of a breach of contract because he has not delivered the carriers on time. Tib, on his part, accuses Stanley of being the first to breach the contract, for not having delivered the ammunition as agreed. While Stanley is writing his travel account in Cairo, the context has already grown so distressing – though he tries to keep all disturbances at bay – that the journey's chronology in some passages is completely ignored, and other passages are clearly edited in consideration of the pending disputes in London.

The most important factor in the accelerating scandal, obviously, was *In Darkest Africa*'s harsh accusations of incompetence and madness among the rear column officers – in particular Barttelot and Jameson. These breaches of code indicate a completely different story about, and context for, the expedition, encompassing both the race for Africa and the equally important strategic battle of opinion regarding nation and empire towards the end of the nineteenth century. While Stanley in Cairo braved the impossible, writing at breakneck pace, he was well aware that his authority would be attacked even more eagerly than when he returned home without Livingstone. The breaches cannot therefore be interpreted as conscious attempts to anticipate and create the terms for the media craze he had already been warned about upon his arrival in Bagayomo. Furthermore, many passages in *In Darkest Africa* are directed at Stanley's autobiography; they are introverted reflections that correspond to the shifts between exterior and interior landscapes as seen in the gothic romances of *fin de siècle* literature.

"Mystery" and "Misery"

The main background for the disputes about the events was what Stanley calls a "mystery" in a letter to the Emin Pasha Relief Committee. The letter is enclosed in *In Darkest Africa*, serving as a preface to the book. As such, the travel account is more than an account of the expedition: it is just as much – or even more so – a comment on the public dispute, arranged as a court case with presentations of testimonies and appraisals of the witnesses' credibility and the readers as judges. The travel book's function as affidavit runs through its presentation and influences its materiality, which to a large extent is characterised by sworn statements in changing, imagined courtrooms within the already fragmented prose.

Rhetorically, Stanley pretends to be completely mystified and puzzled by the fact that the rear column did not try to follow the front column through the Ituri Forest, instead of wasting twelve months in an apparent paralysis, unable to do anything. Subsequently, he repeats and expands on this "mystery" figure, which does not explicitly identify the ultimate cause of the rear

column's disastrous fate, but nevertheless clearly places the responsibility on Barttelot and Jameson, the two commanding officers. Within the narrative, Stanley is far more direct in his criticism of the blatantly poor command in the Yambuya camp: their repeated attempts to create the conditions for departure are ridiculed in descriptions of how Jameson and Barttelot shuttled back and forth between the camp and Tippu Tib (I, p. 480-85). It is inexplicable – "uncanny", as Stanley writes with irony. And when, on the same date, Emin Pasha was captured by rebels at Lake Albert and Jameson dropped dead, after which misfortune followed misfortune, the expedition apparently becomes a victim of "supernatural *diablerie* operating, which surpasses the conception and attainment of a mortal man" (I, p. 483). As becomes clear in these examples, Stanley launched a rhetorical counter-attack which, while exposing the rumours in the London newspapers as lies and superstition, managed also to repeat a number of the major accusations of violence and cannibalism in relation to the officers:

"In addition to all these mischiefs a vast crop of lying is germinated in these darksome shades in the vicinity of Stanley Falls, or along the course of the Upper Congo, demonstrating measureless cunning and an insatiable love of horror. My own murder appears to be a favourite theme, quantities of human bones are said to be discovered by some reconnoitring party, human limbs are said to be found in cooking-pots, sketches by an amateur artist are reported to have been made of whole families indulging in cannibal repasts; it is more than hinted that Englishmen are implicated in raids, murder, and cannibalism, that they have been making targets of native fugitives while swimming in the Aruwimi, all for the mere sake of infusing terror, alarm, and grief among quiet British people, and to plague our friends at home.

The instruments that this dark power selects for the dissemination of these calumnious fables are as various in their professions as in their nationality. It is a deserter one day, and the next an engineer of a steamer; it is now a slave-trader, or a slave; it is a guileless missionary in search of work, or a dismissed Syrian; it is a young artist with morbid tastes, or it is an officer of the Congo Free State. Each in his turn becomes possessed with an insane desire to say or write something which overwhelms common sense, and exceeds ordinary belief" (I, p. 483).

Here, Stanley suspends chronology in order to address the controversies in London directly from his desk in Cairo. The passage is remarkable because it so explicitly – in a manner that is both refined and problematic – highlights the issue of credibility as crucial to the appraisal of the expedition's central "mystery". The rumours about cannibalism and terror in the camp were, according to Stanley, started by rumour-mongers without any authority who merely exploited tragic events to conjure up fantastic tales of terror. However, by passing on the rumours, after having listed all the officers' undoubted virtues and then rejecting any understanding of their deeds, Stanley gives support to the suspicion that the rear column's story should, in fact, be perceived as a horror story. He thus creates distance from the authority of other versions, maintaining decorum and yet substantiating his attack against Barttelot and Jameson. Living up to the expectations of a good leader, Stanley defends his officers while simultaneously reminding his readers about the rumours of cannibalism that were in circulation both before and after the expedition's authorised version.

In Cairo, while Stanley was writing, and shortly after having appealed to "facts" as a cure against the unrestrained imagination of rumours, he found himself entangled in the very fascinated horror from which he had created an ironic distance. This takes place in a detailed description of the misery of the journey, turning the figure of credibility on its head.

"Pen cannot picture nor tongue relate the full horrors witnessed within that dreadful pest-hold. The nameless scourge of barbarians was visible in the faces and bodies of many a hideous-looking human being, who, disfigured, bloated, marred and scarred, came, impelled by curiosity, to hear and see us who had come from the forest land east, and who were reckless of the terror they inspired by the death embodied in them. There were six dead bodies lying unburied, and the smitten living, with their festers, lounged in front of us by the dozen. Others worn to thin skin and staring bone from dysentery and anæmia, and ulcers as large as saucers, crawled about and hollowly sounded their dismal welcome – a welcome to this charnel yard! Weak, wearied, and jaded in body and mind, I scarcely know how I endured the first few hours, the ceaseless story of calamity vexed my ears, a deadly stench of disease hung in the air, and the most repellent sights moved and surged before my dazed eyes. I heard of murder and death, of sickness and sorrow, anguish and grief, and wherever I looked the hollow eyes of dying men met my own with such trusting, pleading regard, such far-away yearning looks, that it seemed to me if but one sob was uttered my heart would break. I sat stupefied under a suffocating sense of despondency, yet the harrowing story moved on in a dismal cadence that had nought else in it but death and disaster, disaster and death" (I, p. 493).

Stanley leaves out any possible consideration that he might be responsible for the course of events, without mentioning how, specifically, the rear column was expected to have acted differently and followed the front column. His affidavit is accompanied by copies of letters and excerpts from logs and reports by Barttelot, Ward and Jameson, who were all witnesses to the desperate situation in

the camp. In this context, the documents also serve to substantiate Stanley's indirect allegation that the officers' lack of determination was the sole reason for the disastrous development.

Other weighty circumstances, however, point to Stanley as the responsible figure: as the expedition leader, his decision to leave the rear column under impossible conditions, without having met his part of the contract with Tippu Tib, was a grave mistake. His decision to split the expedition into two camps was based on a combination of insufficient resources – first and foremost the lack of steamships for the transport on the Congo River – and the unresolved situation with Tippu Tib, and, what was no less pressing, Stanley's forward-looking attempt to complete the operation by rescuing Emin Pasha. From this forward-looking perspective, the decision was the right one, but in retrospect, the consequences were disastrous, and no one – not even Stanley – was willing to take responsibility for it, which only triggered and intensified the rumours and accusations against all the parties involved. Stanley was accused of having opted for the solution out of sheer egoism, intending to garner all the glory for rescuing Emin Pasha. Allegedly, that was why he disposed of the ill and incompetent in order to speed up the pace, leaving the rear column behind in a hostile territory without supplies.

The sarcastic and elliptic touch in these rhetorical constructions is not, however, purely the result of Stanley's attempt to cover up his responsibility for the events; rather, it reveals the impossibility of placing the blame decisively or deciding what was right or wrong, true or false. Initially, Stanley calls the camp a "mystery", a breeding ground for horror fictions; he then lists a number of incontestable facts that do not bring him closer to an explanation; finally, he presents a lengthy, compassionate passage in a sentimental, pathetic tone. By doing so, he exploits the dominant discourses associated with the event, but he also demonstrates the impotence of these discourses. We will return to this later; for now we can note that the "mystery" discourse forestalls Conrad, who ten years later would use the description of "darksome shades in the vicinity of Stanley Falls" as the very origin of nameless terror, while the "misery" discourse reaches back to the rhetoric of the abolitionist movement and points forwards to the Congo Reform Association's tales of terror. Stanley's *In Darkest Africa* contributed to this trajectory, although it remains unresolved – shaken and composed at the same time – in the book. It took a great effort to bring together all the antitheses that ultimately turn out also to be antitheses within Stanley himself.

In the "misery" passage, Stanley reasserts his caring and paternal character as a responsible leader and the only reliable witness. This aspect follows a familiar pattern from his other travel accounts: objections to his choices and

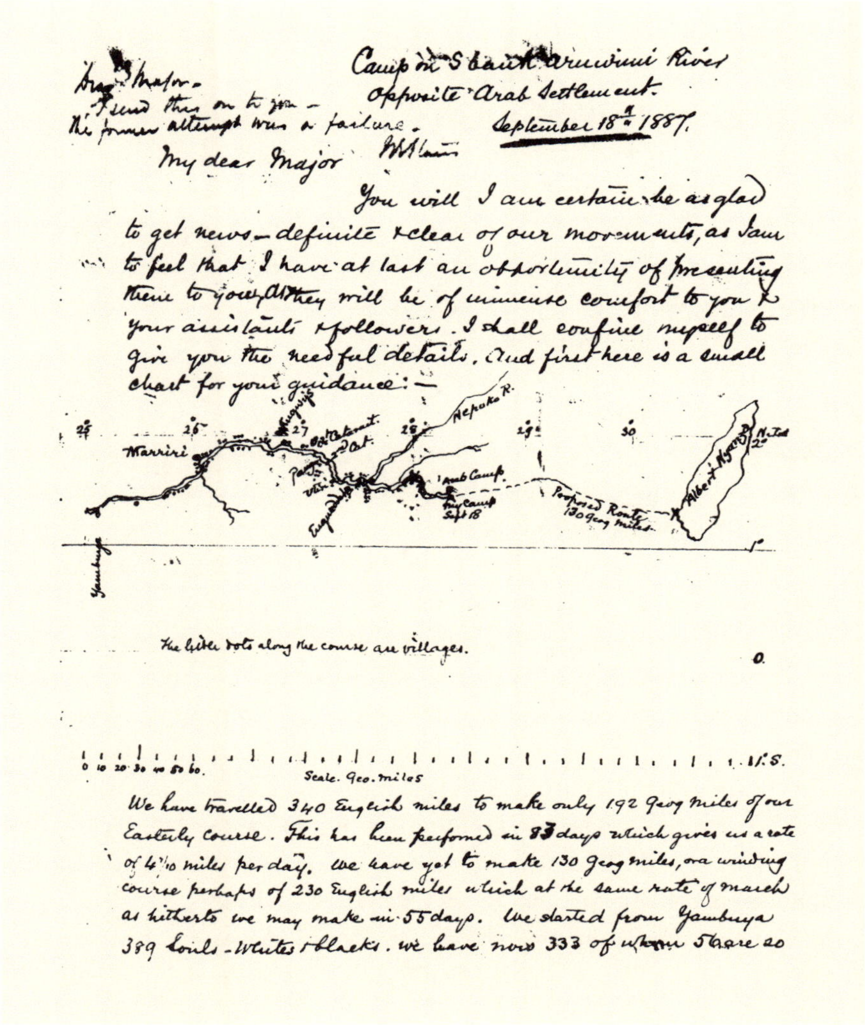

Camp on S bank Aruwimi River
Opposite Arab Settlement.
September 18th 1887.

Dear Major – I send this on to you – the former attempt was a failure. HMS

My dear Major

You will I am certain be as glad to get news – definite & clear of our movements, as I am to feel that I have at last an opportunity of presenting them to you, & they will be of immense comfort to you & your assistants & followers. I shall confine myself to give you the needful details. And first here is a small chart for your guidance:–

We have travelled 340 English miles to make only 192 Geog miles of our Easterly course. This has been performed in 83 days which gives us a rate of 4 1/10 miles per day. We have yet to make 130 Geog miles, or a winding course perhaps of 230 English miles which at the same rate of march as hitherto we may make in 55 days. We started from Yambuya 389 souls – Whites & blacks. We have now 333 of whom 56 are so

Draft of a letter to Barttelot, urging him to follow the front guard, with a sketch of the route. The letter to Barttelot in *How I Found Emin Pasha* is very detailed in regard to leading the rear-guard around hostile villages and avoiding the mistakes Stanley made. The letters show that Stanley was in good faith. The officers in the Yambuya camp impatiently awaited news from the expedition leader, but Stanley's voluntary messengers never reached them. From Stanley's travel diary (SA no. 56).

methods, put forward by his European travel companions and the public, are rejected with reference to the critics' lack of knowledge about the conditions in Africa, their spoiled behaviour and sentimentality. Stanley, on the other hand, is positioned outside binding human relationships. He is the leader appointed to solve the task, regardless of the cost, and he basically perceives all Europeans as obstacles. Stanley prefers the company of his Zanzibar soldiers, among whom his ethical codex of work, obligation and discipline goes hand in hand with a fatherly care for his devoted children. However, his distance from his British subordinate officers and all the resulting misunderstandings also represent the clashes in the British public between Stanley's American pragmatism and national ideas about the officers' class-related privileges regarding rightful behaviour and truthful accounts.

By means of a few rhetorical techniques, Stanley manages to distance himself from the sensational stories about the rear column – stories with no more credibility than the fabrications of deserters and slave traders. The actual facts and their causes are referred to as a mystery; these omissions are justified by the discretion expected of an expedition leader and considerations regarding the officers' ideological grounding. Stanley's account does not allow "the full horrors witnessed" to be presented in the light of rationality; instead, it simultaneously rejects and enhances the rumours about his subordinates' decadent excesses. Responsibility is not placed on anyone, which only adds to the travel account's incoherent, contradictory and introverted form. In particular, this becomes apparent in the way descriptions from the journey are displaced as *fin de siècle* tropes in which the terror is stripped of its concrete, historical conditions, only to become aestheticised and sentimental, e.g. in the final chiasmus of the "misery" passage: "the harrowing story moved on in a dismal cadence that had nought else in it but death and disaster, disaster and death".

Looking at supplementary archival material will facilitate an enhanced understanding of the reasons behind Stanley's hesitation to enter the space he summarises and seals off with the term "mystery". First, though, there is a need for more background information. We will begin with an overview of the book's reception in the newspapers, followed by a reading of Jephson's and Jameson's diaries, which both offer illuminating insights.

Testimonies under Pressure

While Stanley was writing *In Darkest Africa* in Cairo, he, the Emin Pasha Relief Committee, the publishers, the Royal Geographical Society, the Anti-Slavery Association and the public in Britain, Germany, Portugal, Belgium, America and soon the entire world, were aware of the rumours, especially those concerning the rear column, about the both horrible and farcical fate of the expedition. The "Author's and Publishers' Note" mentions that all parties involved have tried "to meet as speedily as possible the extraordinary and unprecedented demand that has been made upon them by the public" (*IDA* I, p. iv). Stanley's *In Darkest Africa* was written as a contribution to a dispute about the proper version of the account – a dispute that was incited by the newspapers' handling of the news, but would soon come to occupy national opinion.

Stanley's mention of rumour-mongers and false witnesses reflects the fact that the newspapers were pressing for new information without waiting for his authorised version; the publication of other accounts of the expedition was prohibited by legal contracts until six months after Stanley's had appeared. His attempts to discredit the rumours that abounded were also part of a comprehensive effort to maximise profits via authorised copyright, and secure the expedition's reputation for posterity – linked to one single voice and subjected to the same discipline and ethos as the expedition itself. The Emin Pasha Relief Committee had control over all information regarding the expedition, and on several occasions Mackinnon censored facts that he thought would offend the public – including in Stanley's text. The committee had established detailed agreements with newspapers about how and when the material could be published, for instance in the case of simultaneous publications of Stanley's travel letters. The committee could also intervene if other publishers marketed similar travel accounts from Africa with titles or covers that referred to the Emin Pasha Relief Expedition.

These attempts to monopolise and authorise the travel accounts, however, proved futile. As early as 1888, Herbert Ward and John Rose Troup – two of the officers who did not manage to follow suit when the rear column finally set out – leaked letters and reports to the press. Naturally, this was detrimental to Stanley's and the committee's authority, but Tim Youngs has also described it as a typical symptom of the fundamental crisis in Victorian society's distribution of public voices and mouthpieces.[73] While the explorations had previously been national projects, supported by the Royal Geographical Society and characterised by an unwavering spirit of patriotism and imperialism, this foundation cracked towards the end of the nineteenth century concurrently with the value crisis that permeated the entire culture during this period. In Tim Youngs' words, "the travellers themselves were now explored".[74]

At this early stage, different players and stakeholders were already involved in a risky game of rights. The correspondence between John Rose Troup and Stanley – and their legal advisors – sheds light on the connection between copyrights, credibility, rights and recognition, and we find parallels in the relationship between Herbert Ward and William Bonny, the latter of whom held a special position as the only European left in the camp upon Stanley's arrival, and thus the star witness in piecing together the rear column's story. In a letter to Stanley dated 4 December 1889, Troup mentions Sir Francis de Winton's lawsuit against him in relation to his public statements about the expedition and plans to publish a book. Winton was acting as member and secretary of

the relief committee, using the lawsuit to try to enforce the stipulation that no one was allowed to publish material from the expedition until six months after the release of the authorised account. In the letter, Troup appeals to Stanley, asking him to make an exemption, given that Troup's account will by no means affect the sales of Stanley's – the idea that his book would be able to "compete with yours" (SA, No. 1351) is unthinkable. In a letter dated 4 March 1890, Troup outlines what happened in Yambuya in Stanley's absence, placing the blame on Barttelot's "reckless conduct" and offering his testimony (SA, No. 1352). Stanley's answer (13 March 1890) is initially forthcoming; however, he does not yield to Troup's implied demand to be publically recognised by Stanley and allowed to publish his account. On the contrary, he is reprimanded for trying to dodge his responsibility: in Stanley's opinion, all the rear column officers, not only Barttelot and Jameson but also Bonny, Ward and Troup, are guilty as charged for not having followed Stanley's order to follow the front column – unless they can produce written material that proves otherwise.

Furthermore, Stanley warns Troup that his attack on Barttelot will backfire. In his next letter, Troup offers to write "the sort of statement you would like me to make for insertion in your forthcoming volume". This statement will "adopt the moderate language you suggest & it would be more in consonance, probably, with the rest of your book" (SA, No. 1354). Stanley chose to ignore Troup's offer and published *In Darkest Africa* without modifying his accusations against any of the officers, which caused Troup to write a fuming letter (3 July 1890) in which he demanded that Stanley withdrew the accusations. He also wrote to William Mackinnon, the chairman of the committee, requesting that he use his influence to convince Stanley to soften his criticism and highlight Troup's accomplishments. If he refused, Troup would not refrain from handing over the information the public had pushed hard to gain possession of since he returned from Africa.

Troup was prepared to support Stanley's version of events in return for being exempted from charges and allowed to publish his own travel account. Stanley, for his part, was attempting a difficult balancing act, not wanting to let Troup off the hook and publish an unauthorised, autonomous version or take his criticism of Barttelot and the rear column too far. He was at immediate risk of being thrown off balance, which would result in criticism of his own decisions – e.g. having appointed incompetent officers for the task. Meanwhile, Troup's, the committee's and Stanley's lawyers were preparing an impending court case about rights and the rightful interpretation of the committee's stipulations regarding the publication of alternative accounts. The question was whether the term "the official report" was to be understood as the brief summary that Stanley sent to the committee immediately after the expedition ended, included in *In Darkest Africa* as a preface, or if it meant the entire account. On 25 March 1890, Stanley's lawyers suggest that Stanley uses the term "the official publication" as the book's subtitle, and on 7 May 1890 they request additional material to prepare the case against Troup, including an "Affidavit" in which Stanley accounts for the documents in his possession that mention changes to the expedition, e.g. in relation to the travel route. Enclosed in their letter is a copy of another letter posted to all the surviving officers, impressing on them the copyright restriction:

"Dear Sir,
As you are bound under the terms of your agreement with Mr. Stanley not to publish anything connected with the Emin Pasha Relief Expedition for 6 months after the issue of the official publication by Mr. Stanley we think it due to you to inform you that this official publication will be issued in a book entitled "In Darkest Africa" which is now being advertised by Messrs. Sampson Low Marston & Co. And that after the expiration of 6 months from the publication of that book you will be free from the restriction imposed by the Agreement" (SA, No. 1359).

Troup's lawyer refused to give in, insisting that one must at least be allowed to defend oneself against public accusations. The right to publish the travel account was inextricably linked to the right to speak out for oneself, which in retrospect positioned the travel accounts less as descriptions of places and travels in Africa, and more as testimonies in a London courtroom. In a private letter to Stanley (6 December 1890), Troup's solicitor emphasises, in relation to various "recent publications", the travel accounts' function as affidavit:

"For myself I do not think that the case requires any further lifting and that the less said about the conduct of the Officers under you the better but events may induce me to alter this opinion.

Mr. Bonny's and Mr. Troup's evidence is quite sufficient as regards Major Barttelot and nothing can add to Mr. Jameson's own confession. As regards the newspapers, if I may say so, there is no one who can afford to despise them better than yourself.

The sole question which affects you is in your capacity as chief of the Expedition and of this you are responsible to the Relief Committee and to the Relief Committee alone" (SA, No. 1359).

In Bonny's case, the dispute did not concern a court case and the right to publish a book, but negotiations via letters with similar things at stake. As early as 1 September 1889 there were signs that Stanley was preparing for the legal consequences of the rear column scandal. When the expedition arrived at the

east coast and received the first "newspaper clippings" about the controversy in London, Stanley made sure that Bonny wrote a statement which could be used to keep him from criticising Stanley later. The statement reads:

"I certify that during the stay at the Yambuya Camp Aruwimi River I received plenty of food of various kinds – kinds of foods purchased at Yambuya Camp for officers from November '87 to August 1888.

This food was purchased by the officers at the Yambuya Camp, Aruwimi River. Below is a list of kinds of food purchased: Bananas, Fish etc." (SA, No. 1282).

Bonny concludes by verifying the document's authenticity. We will return to his role as a witness in the camp in the last chapter about Stanley. For now, let us focus on the extortion that Stanley performed after returning to Britain, following Troup's example. Like Troup, Bonny promised to write a loyal account of the events; in a letter dated 25 March 1890, for instance, he asks Stanley to disregard an earlier report from the expedition's arrival in Babalaya, since it contains far too many "regrettable expressions" (SA, No. 1287). In other words, Bonny offers to modify his testimony to suit Stanley's wishes in return for Stanley modifying *his* criticism of, among other things, Bonny's dealing out a punishment of 100 lashes with a whip (SA, No. 1284). Bonny was apparently not as brutal as the other officers, and the criticism would not benefit the expedition: "I am sorry the idea has taken place & you know Sir that prejudice is the spider of the mind", writes Bonny, ending with a threat disguised as a promise: "I shall not be the first to throw the stone". The theme is repeated and varied in the following letters, referring to the fact that Bonny might feel compelled to correct various errors in *In Darkest Africa* – especially if Stanley refuses to write a reference for Bonny to the Duke of Cambridge, among others. While Bonny becomes increasingly demanding, Stanley replies in a professional tone and refuses to be threatened into changing his appraisal of Bonny's character or getting involved in editing testimonies.

Much of the newspapers' continuous criticism concentrated on brutality. Since other explorers, like Livingstone, had managed to reach their goals peacefully – this was the prevailing, although not entirely true, belief – then why, asks e.g. the *Daily Telegraph* (10 November 1890), did Barttelot reserve the moral right to treat the Africans like animals, whip and beat them and sometimes even execute them, for the ultimate aim of making money? On 29 October 1890, the *Times Weekly Edition* printed an interview with Troup, who claimed that Stanley had only undertaken the expedition for personal gain, and fame: "He has no more philanthropy than my boot". The officers, claims Troup, took part in the hope of earning a share of Emin Pasha's ivory. The general tendency in the newspapers was that they did not wait for – or did not accept – Stanley's account as the authorised version, and they did not hesitate to contribute to the confusion by drawing on a variety of conflicting sources.

In this respect, it could be said that the reception mimicked Stanley's strategy in *In Darkest Africa*. The newspapers avoided conclusions, as if the truth could not be localised or would have too broad a consequence on the legitimacy of the empire. Instead, we find a theme similar to Stanley's "mystery" figure, infinitely changeable and similarly contradictory, in which an explicit distance is created from the sensationalistic tendencies – especially other newspapers' – while at the same time a suggestive, scandalising discourse is implied, hinting that the case is unsolvable and beyond comprehension.

On 8 November 1890, for example, *The Times* wrote: "the issues are so confused and confusing, and the evidence is so conflicting and so inconclusive, that a satisfactory settlement could only be obtained by a strict and exhaustive judicial investigation". Apparently, this is an appeal to reason; however, in reality it is a continuation and emphasis of the rhetorical construction of an inexplicable mystery. The implication of the "mystery" discourse is that everything has been said, yet it still hovers in an equivocal twilight that prevents testimonies from being accepted or excluded with reference to facts or the witness' authority. On the same day, *The Times* printed an accusation written by Stanley against Barttelot of having kicked a ten-year-old boy to death. This accusation was intended to subvert the officer's credibility in relation to the publication of his notes from the expedition.

No one took responsibility, and no one had the necessary authority to stop the stream of exposés, none of which were focused on the truth, instead aimed solely at subverting the credibility of someone else's testimony. Bonny, the only surviving European from the rear column and the source of the most scandalous stories, told *The Times* (10 November 1890) that Barttelot sentenced the interpreter John Henry to three hundred lashes of a whip, resulting in actual strips of flesh being torn off Henry's back and his body swelling to twice its normal size before he eventually died. Bonny's stories about Barttelot's cruelty and Jameson's cannibalism were immediately called into question with reference to the fact that Bonny was not an officer but a servant to Doctor Parke. Other statements highlighted Bonny's uncomplicated nature and straightforward, unpretentious language to vouch for his honesty, compared to the officers' elaborate reconstructions of the story.

Other newspapers, such as *The Spectator*, added another twist to the question of credibility: while it was impossible, on the basis of class and family relations, to believe the stories about Barttelot's acts of cruelty, they would be understandable and excusable if the man had gone insane – something that

would also exempt the newspaper from further investigating the legitimacy of the expedition as such. In Jameson's case, it was impossible to trust his own statements. His diary, published posthumously by his family, contained elements that could not possibly be true, taking his high moral standards into consideration: "Moral impossibilities do exist, and the crime confessed in this story is one of them, and one of the least credible we recall ever having seen". Even critical newspapers found it impossible to accept testimonies that so radically pulled the rug from under the moral basis of Victorian culture. As for Stanley, the criticism of his decisions and management style often balanced on the same edge that he had created in *In Darkest Africa.* The scandalous material is suggested and exploited as entertainment, and the crisis of conscience caused by the affair aestheticised as a *fin de siècle* gloom instigated by a decay of values, as everybody closes their eyes to the truths that actually appear mysterious or inaccessible, or are so profound that they cannot be spoken.

While Stanley's European companions on his previous expeditions had all died in the course of the journey, preventing them from controlling his authorised account, the Emin Pasha Relief Expedition turned into a quarrel about credibility in which the style and genre of the contesting testimonies formed part of the criticism. Edited travel accounts, such as *In Darkest Africa* and A. J. Mounteney Jephson's *Emin Pasha and the Rebellion at the Equator* (1890), can be compared with private documents such as diaries and letters that have become accessible to the public, though also in edited – e.g. abridged – versions, which again calls for critical reflections on the relationship between genre, form, style and credibility.

When it became clear that the debate was not coming any closer to a conclusion, but rather drawing an increasing number of people and institutions into a bottomless morass, several newspapers requested that it be shelved in consideration of public morale. It is thought-provoking in this context that the criticism in the last phase of the scandal was aimed at the messengers – those who had contributed to the suspicions of fathomless madness with accounts that had not edited out any and every hint of scandal. Initially, the unedited eyewitness accounts, such as Troup's, Ward's and Bonny's, had been perceived as nearer the truth than the officially recognised accounts, which were, in turn, suspected of fabricating the most convenient versions. Towards the end, however, the newspapers appealed to decorum and common sense, and favoured the travel accounts that refrained from presenting truths that had *not* been filtered through considerations of the nations' moral reputation.

Realism and Loyalty: Mounteney Jephson

In 1890, A. J. Mounteney Jephson published a travel account that focused on the description of his captivity together with Emin Pasha in Equatoria while Stanley journeyed back to Yambuya to catch up with the rear column. Jephson was very loyal towards Stanley, and in the book he clearly tries to avoid straying into his territory – presumably in accordance with an agreement with both the Emin Pasha Relief Committee and the publishers who announced the publication of Jephson's book in the first edition of *In Darkest Africa.* The book's style and design are inspired by Stanley's epic model, although lacking his brilliant rhetorical talent, and it was encouraged by Stanley and the committee who saw it as a much-needed support of his threatened authority. However, in 1969 Jephson's diary was published, which left a different impression of the expedition and illuminated both Stanley's and Jephson's own previous accounts.

Jephson's diary is extremely detailed, an impressive feat considering the practical circumstances under which it was written and a surprise even to the author himself, for instance when on 28 May 1888 at Lake Albert he realises that he has already filled all the pages in his journal and must wait several months to get a new one from the camp in Yambuya or obtain some paper from Emin Pasha.

"There must be a great lot of nonsense in this journal for one has kept it in just a helter skelter kind of fashion putting down facts in a disconnected way without much regard to grammar or spelling I'm afraid. It must be recollected however that it has been written under very trying circumstances, often I would much sooner have laid down & slept after a long & fatiguing march than sit up & write my journal. I have however kept it pretty regularly thus far, & hope it will answer its purpose which is to tell a true & exact story of the expedition, of how we found & relieved Emin Pasha & of the trials & difficulties we met on the road & how through the strong determination of our leader & the hardiness of our Zanzibaris we overcame them all & arrived a small handful of men on the shores of Nyanza & reached Emin Pasha after fourteen months' continual marching."[75]

Shortly before, Jephson had parted with Stanley, who was headed back to the rear column from whom there had been no news for a whole year. He was relieved to have made it through the forest alive and even more optimistic about a glorious end to the story. Like the other officers, Jephson had from the beginning viewed the expedition as an opportunity to perform honourable deeds; however, he stood out as the participant who held on most persistently to this naïve hope. The concluding lines of the passage above make this clear, as the expedition's progress so far is summarised in an epic structure that would later come to characterise both his and Stanley's travel books. This desire for epic

Instead of publishing his diaries, Jephson published the travel book *Emin Pasha and the Rebellion at the Equator* (1890), which – partly due to copyright – had Stanley as its co-author. The diary, which appeared in 1969, was not written for publication, and Jephson describes it as messy nonsense. However, the prose is actually clearer than that of most testimonies about the expedition – often shockingly clear. The advertisement for the book was found among adverts for typewriters and travel equipment in Marston's *How Stanley Wrote "In Darkest Africa"* (1890).

coherence expresses a hope that, post festum, meaning will be ascribed to what he sees as disconnected nonsense. Jephson's writings describe the journey's chaos and meaninglessness, as well as the wide gap between expectations and reality. When we read the diary, there are no linguistic hindrances to understanding the text, but the events appear hazardous and irrational, lacking a clear pattern or a comprehensible plot.

Jephson's deliberations forestall the crisis of credibility of which his later travel account would become part; however, testimonies and truth are already an issue in his diary. It is as if he is unable to trust his own words, or does not dare rely on what he has seen and heard. As is always the case in the private genres of letters and diaries, we also encounter a mixture of monologic and dialogic discourses. Jephson is commenting on his own diary – the authenticity of which as private, uncensored notes there is no reason to question – at the same time as addressing the reader, who at some point is going to open it in order to gain insight into the factual situation. The diary can tell us more than the travel account, which was subject to a vast array of rules regarding public discourse; however, it cannot necessarily tell us everything. The idea that the genre offers a natural and unaffected presentation of an individual's personal truth can often lead to even more confusion and impenetrability.

Jephson's comment about keeping the diary in "a helter skelter kind of fashion putting down facts in a disconnected way" is telling since it shows that the diary is not a composition, but a log of the events and the writer's thoughts in the order in which they were hastily written. The link between what Jephson wanted to see and what he actually wrote is therefore often weak or completely absent. Two days before he concludes the book with his loyal declaration of "the strong determination of our leader", he mentions how Stanley has stolen what would prove to be the expedition's most important geographical discovery: the Ruwenzori Mountains, including Mount Stanley, the triumphant conclusion of *In Darkest Africa.* When Jephson had reported the mountain range and its snow-clad peaks a month earlier, Stanley had rejected it as rambling, only to steal the glory for its discovery later, and have his name added to Ptolemy's renowned Mountains of the Moon.

Within the nineteenth-century ethos of explorations, stealing someone else's discovery was the worst thing imaginable; yet Jephson remained loyal to Stanley to the end, even after their return to Great Britain. Numerous passages in the diary, however, launch severe attacks on Stanley's management and unfriendly behaviour. Stanley several times during the expedition feels compelled to leave the ill and dying behind in so-called "starvation camps", without even taking minimal measures to protect them, which in Jephson's opinion is not only a sign of Stanley's ruthlessness, but also a breach of his fundamental responsibilities – especially towards the officers that are given the thankless task of staying with those who are abandoned without supplies in a hostile hunger zone.

"Stanley himself, so Parke tells me, took quantities of food & great numbers of chickens. He did not even take the trouble to say goodbye to Parke when he went, which to put it mildly was ungracious. It is really quite wonderful how little Stanley seems to care about the welfare of his officers, he seems to take no interest whatever in what they do or how they manage to get on" (p. 181).

On 26 February 1888, Jephson writes a lengthy description of one of the rare occasions when Stanley engages in private conversation with the officers about private matters. Stanley has just overcome a critical illness during which he draws a sketch of Jephson, who has been looking after him, and compares it to a self-portrait. According to the note, the sketch of Jephson is not flattering. He is everything that a man should not be, according to Stanley: overly enthusiastic, prone to exaggeration, prejudiced and – worst of all – endowed with an "overweening pride – pride of birth & pride of self". Even when Jephson has uncomplainingly taken upon himself the most humble and unrewarding tasks, according to Stanley he has done so with an annoying pride "in every movement" and "turn of body". Stanley also accuses Jephson of having only experienced "the soft side of life", and although at the time he puts up with these humiliations, Jephson responds in his diary; Stanley's wild, self-praising "sketch of his own character" is "rubbish":

"He made out to be a St John for gentleness, a Solomon for wisdom, a Job for patience & a model of truth. Whereas I do not suppose a more impatient, a more ungentle, a more untruthful man than Stanley could exist. He is most violent in his words & actions, the slightest little thing is sufficient to work him into a frenzy of rage, his sense of what is honourable is of the haziest description & he is certainly a most untruthful character" (Jephson, p. 229).

Jephson's conviction that Stanley is the only person in the expedition who has the skills and determination to complete it often causes him to play down in public the criticism divulged in the confidence of the diary. After Stanley's humiliations, however, his rather simple sense of loyalty does not keep him from making serious accusations. Other passages in the diary directly mention Stanley's hot temper, for example he once shot at two carriers because they were working too slowly (p. 235). He also criticises Stanley's tendency to romanticise his experience of Africa, thus betraying the travel accounts' main goal of informing the public, such as when dirty villages in Stanley's "flowery descriptions" are made into fairytale castles peopled by emperors, princes and princesses (p. 390).

Jephson's diary is "disconnected" in the sense that one sentence may complain about irritating ticks, while the next describes the forest as a place where "a supernatural fairy" awaits around the next corner with her legs dangling and her feet in the clear stream, "exactly like the pictures in fairy tales" (p. 120). However, this disconnectedness and uncontrolled registration also allows for descriptions of how terror becomes part of the journey's practical, everyday chores: "We burned our camp on leaving it & the village we had occupied below

Jephson with gun and potted plant in a studio. According to the diary, Stanley once described Jephson as a spoilt upper-class dandy, which the loyal Jephson found difficult to accept, considering all the gruelling events of the expedition. From *Emin Pasha and the Rebellion at the Equator*.

& left the head of one of the natives we had killed suspended from a tree close to camp" (p. 205). In another description, the terrors take place during one of the "foraging expeditions" Stanley ordered Jephson to go on:

"I collected all the men silently & we made a rush into the village. Every man woman & child left everything and ran as hard as they could leaving bows, arrows, knives everything they possessed just as they were, the cooking pots full of bananas yams etc were left on the fires so that one had a dinner ready cooked if one cared about that sort of food. We chased the natives from village to village – there was a perfect network of them – & drove everything before us. One man only made a stand & shot one of our men through his shirt but he paid dearly for it for a bullet through his head gave him his quietus" (Jephson, pp. 225-26).

Jephson does not question the method, although he feels sorry that it has such a harsh impact on the people who do not invite the expedition to dinner and barely have enough for themselves in the famine-ridden area. Hostage taking, pillage and the burning of villages make sorry sights that play on Jephson's conscience, especially when he considers the expedition's complete technical superiority and how the men shoot escapees in the back and attack small children. In particular the realistic descriptions of village life Jephson can give because he secretly watches the unsuspecting villagers just minutes before the attack indirectly indicate how the writer is moved by the scene, while hastily making his notes. At the same time they reveal voyeuristic tendencies in the way the events are perceived, for instance in the description of a logistics platoon who "were watching a village on an island about 50 yds from the bank in which the natives were all working away & laughing & talking in happy ignorance of the 250 odd enemies watching them at so short a distance. (...) As we fired a volley two men fell & Parke shot two who were escaping in a canoe" (p. 155).

Jephson's own conception of the natives is limited to the classical idea of Africans as children with changeable minds, "like an unwritten sheet". They may be lying and deceitful but not impossible to reach. Jephson believes he has noticed an anthropological pattern in which the two most developed tribes are found in Uganda and in Bangala by the Congo River. Between these places live the ugliest and least developed tribes, and the pattern also continues outwards to the east and west of Africa (pp. 304-5). He does not believe the Africans can be colonised by white people conquering the land; the only path to colonisation is by mixing whites and blacks, possibly by importing vast numbers of Chinese who will ensure a mix of "cheap labour & intelligence". Towards the end of the diary, he returns to his "ideas of Africa", accounting for his own position between Burton and Stanley:

> "I always condemn Stanley's optimistic views as being exceedingly misleading to people who have never been to Africa; on the other hand I equally condemn Burton's pessimistic idea & deny most emphatically the truth of his saying 'The African has neither love, gratitude nor affection'" (p. 408).

Jephson is proud to position himself in the middle, as a friend of Africa. His centrist view may seem both sympathetic and naïve, but it corresponds well with the diary's notes on carriers who fall to the ground from starvation and exhaustion and are left for dead, as well as the entire expedition's unjust use of violence, which he preserves and neutralises at the same time in the diary's testimony.

We find the same balance in Jephson's appraisals of Stanley's accusations

"Entering Andikumu". In the accompanying text in *In Darkest Africa*, Stanley describes how the expedition with its many starving and dying members reached the village; the front guard pushes through fallen trees and a "lively confrontation" takes place, before the rest of the caravan follows suit and requisitions the village store of extra large bananas. Jephson's diary provides a better impression of the spying that happened before the attack and the chaos caused by the pillaging.

of the rear column officers' "perverseness", received via letter before the expedition's different sections are finally gathered again in Equatoria in February 1889. In Jephson's mind, there is no doubt that Stanley wrongs the officers; however, he withholds his appraisal until he has had the chance to talk to Bonny, the most important witness from the rear column.

"But his letter to me is in many ways greatly wanting in common sense & I think the way he speaks about officers of the rear column is not very pleasant. He seems to forget he told them he would be away at the outside 6 months & in point of fact was gone 14 months, meanwhile these people were left encumbered with loads, unable to move, & the men, from his description, dying like flies, they could have hardly anything moreover to eat. (...) Stanley's stories are never very just in matters of this kind & I suspect there is a good deal more in the real story than meets the eye in his letters" (p. 329).

Jephson does not trust Stanley's explanation, believing that there is more to it than he lets on; "the whole story is a very dark one, as dark as any of the dark stories connected with African travel" (p. 329). However, when on 18 February he has the opportunity to hear Bonny's version, he is just as keen to undermine its credibility. For instance, it is not to Bonny's advantage that he is trying to tell a story in which he is the only character in his right mind. Jephson also suggests that Bonny might have stolen from Barttelot's and Jameson's personal equipment. Worst of all, Bonny obviously *enjoys* telling the dreadful tales:

"The thing which is so bad is that Bonny seems to take such a pleasure in telling all the most dark & disreputable stories of the officers & he has certainly done his best to blacken their characters as much as possible, for even were all the stories true – which we all of us doubt – still there is no necessity to repeat them with such pleasure. He says he thinks Barttelot became insane, & he tells a story of his running after a woman & seizing her by the cheek with his teeth, & relates a story of Jameson having bought a slave woman & handed her over to the Manuyema on condition that they would kill & eat her before him. Stories like these are incredible ..." (p. 337).

On the one hand, Jephson believes that there is more to the story than Stanley's version suggests. On the other hand, his mind boggles at the gall of Bonny's stories, and he tries to distance himself from them as vulgar pulp fiction. In both cases, his objections are made in solidarity with officers of the same rank as himself.

This brings us back to some of the correlations between testimonies, authorities and genres mentioned in relation to the newspaper debate in London. Jephson's rejection of Bonny's stories is based on a class-related appraisal of the witness' credibility. In Stanley's diary (SA, No. 58), however, we are informed that Bonny's official account of the rear column's story is splendid, a "well written report" that forms the basis of Stanley's own reconstruction in *In Darkest Africa*. And Bonny's own, unpublished diary (SA, No. 69) is a highly credible text that is both less censured and more detailed and vividly narrated than the others. Furthermore, the diary contains the most exhaustive descriptions of Barttelot's brutality in particular, which destroyed any attempt to build connections between the crew and natives. Contrary to Jameson, who views the pillaging of the villages as dramas, and Jephson, who takes part in them and describes them as a necessary aspect of his job as a soldier, Bonny is critical and sceptical towards the expedition, naming it "Bully Matady's Slave Caravan". When Jephson discredits Bonny as a witness for his allegedly vulgar pleasure in telling the graphic stories, it is an indication of the code of discretion that became clear in the subsequent newspaper debate, as well as the considerable importance ascribed to position and class. Bonny, who can muster neither, is disqualified in advance.

Sentimental Aesthete, Cannibalistic Voyeur: James Jameson

Jameson died in delirium on his way to Bangala, where he was going to receive his final orders before the rear column set out to find Stanley. It was his wife, Ethel Jameson, who in 1890 surprisingly chose to publish his book, *Story of the Rear Column of the Emin Pasha Relief Expedition by the late James S. Jameson. Naturalist to the expedition*. The book was published in an attempt to refute the accusations of the rear column's inhumane behaviour, which were made by Troup and Ward and subsequently reaffirmed by Bonny and others prior to Stanley's official version. As mentioned, Stanley's version neither substantiated nor refuted the worst stories, instead conceding the formal criticism that the officers did not follow orders and lacked discipline – leaving the stories lingering in a mysterious twilight zone. With the book, Jameson's family wanted to present uncensored letters and diary entries that would prove the sensitive, selfless and respectable nature of the deceased – including during the expedition.

In the preface, Andrew Jameson argues that the diary speaks for itself as a total acquittal of his brother James Jameson. The reader is promised that they will see how tirelessly Jameson, as opposed to Stanley, strived to create the conditions necessary for the rear column to follow the front column. However, addressing the many discussions of responsibility, Andrew Jameson sees fit to spend quite a lot of space on pulling the rug from under the witnesses supporting Stanley's account. He does so using a proper legal discourse: Stanley must only later have come into possession of the information which he, in *In Darkest Africa*, presents as the results of his enquiries on the return to the rear column, and the testimonies that confirmed them retroactively must have come even later still. By drawing in other materials that question the witnesses' credibility, and by comparing these with passages in which Stanley contradicts himself, Andrew Jameson claims, with a good deal of irony, to have shed light on Stanley's motto for *In Darkest Africa*: "Let There Be Light".

With particular regard to the accusation of cannibalism, the most controversial point in relation to Jameson's reputation, his brother repudiates the eyewitness accounts – even though the story had the Congo State considering the arrest of Jameson, according to Stanley. These stories, claims Andrew Jameson, are false rumours started by second-rate participants such as Bonny or "coloured witnesses". Andrew Jameson thus believes that he can throw Stanley's satire of the rumour-mongers in London back in the author's face:

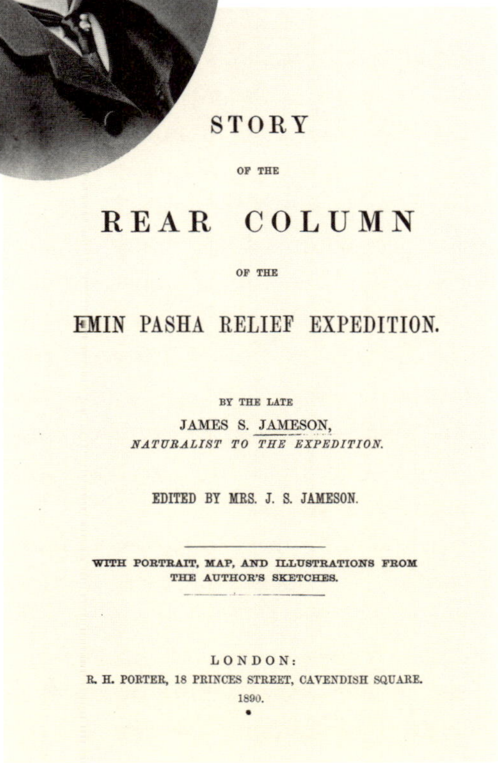

STORY

OF THE

REAR COLUMN

OF THE

EMIN PASHA RELIEF EXPEDITION.

BY THE LATE

JAMES S. JAMESON,

NATURALIST TO THE EXPEDITION.

EDITED BY MRS. J. S. JAMESON.

WITH PORTRAIT, MAP, AND ILLUSTRATIONS FROM THE AUTHOR'S SKETCHES.

LONDON:

R. H. PORTER, 18 PRINCES STREET, CAVENDISH SQUARE.

1890.

Jameson's diary, *Story of the Rear Column of the Emin Pasha Relief Expedition* (1890), caused a scandal due to the so-called 'cannibal story' about a cannibalistic killing of a young girl. Jameson bought the girl for the purpose and drew sketches of the deed. However, the upheaval caused by the diary was also due to the fact that Jameson told the story rather than concealing it, and that his family chose to publish the account in order to save the reputation of the sentimental natural historian.

James Jameson's portrait in *Story of the Rear Column of the Emin Pasha Relief Expedition*.

"But in what light does all this place the author of 'In Darkest Africa'? Is it the pure light, which shines round a man striving to make the truth known? Or is it the baneful gleam of those darksome shades in which Mr. Stanley tells us a vast crop of lying is germinated?"[76]

Jameson's diary, however, was interpreted differently from how his wife and brother had imagined it. Andrew makes a detailed account of their sentimental understanding of the text. They read Jameson's extensive notes of how sick and tired he is of whipping the natives – the carriers on the march and the guards in the camp when they fall asleep from starvation and exhaustion – as the complaints of a sensitive soul and as proof of his "kind, helpful, and unselfish nature" (Jameson, p. xxiv). The public, on the other hand, was more prone to see Jameson's loathing of the punishments as a sign of moral weakness, associated with suspected sadism and an unhealthy curiosity about cannibalism indicated numerous times in the diary.

While Jephson's diary was incoherent in its hasty assembling of everyday elements, Jameson's appears, both stylistically and as process, to be written with a strategic aim. This is not to say that the text appears inauthentic, but that it was more than the notes for a travel book. Jameson's text is curiously polished, and even its confused passages are testimonies to a profound division that shed important light on the Emin Pasha Relief Expedition and the crisis in travel literature in a more general perspective.

The thing that initially surprises the reader is how Jameson mentions his passion for "collecting". On the march to Yambuya he is very frustrated that there is no time to collect birds and insects due to all the energy spent whipping the carriers forward: "Nothing but beating niggers with a stick (...), and day after day the same disgusting work" (p. 30). And though he is terribly disappointed about not being part of the glorious 'rescue' operation, he is looking forward to the prospect of having unlimited time to collect animals and insects from the camp.

"The natives are a bad lot, and I believe we will have to fight for food for the men by looting villages. The bright side of the whole thing is the splendid opportunity it gives me of collecting in a country never collected in before, and altogether, as far as I can make out, we shall have rather an exciting time of it" (p. 43).

This combination of "looting" and "collecting" is a consistent and characteristic trait in Jameson's diary. Both activities contribute to his anticipating an "exciting time" in Yambuya, and they fill a considerable number of pages, alongside considerations of how the rear column might move on, and how to interpret the conflicting rumours delivered by deserters from the front column about Stanley's progress or spectacular death. Looting and collecting are represented by the accounts of ceaseless misery, starvation, whippings, executions, hostage-taking to provide food and pointless fights with natives, and Jameson's field trips on which he shoots and skins birds and collects and prepares insects for his collection as described in the diary's appendix. Often, these phenomena are recorded in close proximity: "Two more deaths. Shot two very handsome plovers, chocolate-coloured breasts, and bright lemon-coloured wattles over the eyes" (p. 167).

It is tempting to see Jameson's "collecting" as a liberating pastime away from the depressing responsibilities of the camp, and he does in fact mention its therapeutic function: "Had it not been for odd little bits of collecting and drawing, which filled up a lot of time, I think I certainly should have become an idiot here" (p. 175).

For the reader – we must assume that Jameson had his wife in mind if no one else – the collecting discourse works as embellishment and distraction from the unpleasant lists of deaths and disasters.

In this sense, we are dealing with an explicit and striking continuation of the eighteenth-century link between sentimental aesthetics and ornithological collection, preservation, sketching and typology, only in this context it is far more desperate and dramatic. Emma Spary has studied a relevant paradigm shift in the way natural science exhibited and described preserved and live birds. A "gallant" system dominated the natural history of birds in the first half of the eighteenth century, so that the birds' 'infidelity' and "interspecies copulation" were perceived positively. Later this was replaced by a system of sensibility within which the world of birds became a model of chastity and virtue in the bourgeois family.[77] Spary also points out that the paradigm of sensitivity distinguished between virtuous free birds and captive birds that developed libertinism, laziness and infidelity. From this perspective, it is possible to read Jameson's aesthetic delight in the birds' colours as a shifted expression of forbidden sexuality – the "interspecies copulation", which all the officers, except Stanley, practiced. The connection is striking in Jameson's letters to his wife, Ethel, which are included in the publishers' edited version of the diary and form part of the whole in the same way as the illustrations of artfully crafted weapons and kitchen utensils. They function like the diary's passages on "collecting" which, for a while, distract Jameson and the reader from the desperate situation, even offering a brief moment of triumph over the surroundings that have fundamentally left him powerless. Ornithological sensitivity is, as Spary mentions, a discourse of domination in which the viewer, preservation artist and illustrator takes on giant proportions, while his surroundings are reduced to preserved, manipulable, powerless objects. We can see this in Jameson's diary entry of 27 January:

"Had a most successful day's collecting. In the morning I shot two cock sunbirds, quite new to me, one of them the most beautiful I think I have ever seen. The throat and the upper half of breast are bright metallic golden green, and below this, on the breast, is a line of prussian blue, edged with carmine. The lower part of the breast, belly, and vent are a rich, dark velvety brown. There is a small patch on

Jameson's pastime during the early days in the Yambuya camp was collecting, sketching, and skinning birds. Later on, this interest took a more artistic direction, as he began to sketch natives and situations. In the monotony of camp life, the different activities began to overlap, which is one of the explanations of why he arranged to live out one of his cannibalistic fantasies. Ward, who mentions in *Five Years with Stanley's Rear Guard* that he got on well with Jameson because they shared interests, contributed with illustrations for the book. Ward also associated collecting, skinning, sketching, and cannibalism. The slave girl portraits were done by a Mr Charles Whymper after Jameson's sketch. The portrait of Barttelot is the only example of Jameson's own art in the book.

the crown of dark green and purple, and on the cheeks a line of dark green. The rest of the bird is a rich golden olive-brown in dark and light shades. The other is much smaller, and not nearly so beautiful. Painted and skinned them. In the evening I shot a very handsome pair of weaver-birds. Selim Mahommed's men attacked Ungungu's brother's village this morning. It lies lower down the river, on the opposite bank. We heard the firing quite distinctly. They killed the chief, and brought back his right hand with them" (pp. 199-200).

The work of skinning, drawing and describing the colourful plumage of the birds appears to be Jameson's attempt both at self-preservation and domination of a world that disintegrates around him more and more each day; however, the juxtaposition of natural science and aesthetic activities on the one hand and the decadence and violence of the camp on the other is merely superficial. What is truly striking about Jameson's diary is the ho-

mology between killing and preserving birds and killing and preserving natives; in this case, a hand is brought back as a trophy. Both acts are hunts, and their homology is emphasised through their increasing convergence in Jameson's writing. It is already prepared by the indifference with which Jameson moves from one field to the other, but, as the situation deteriorates and the unbearable paralysis continues, everything simply becomes part of the same monotony: "14.12. Not a single thing of interest to make a note of. The monotony of this camp life, without one atom of sport or excitement of any kind to relieve it, is becoming perfectly sickening" (p. 168).

Jameson's scope is more or less limited to the camp area, and he complains that there are hardly any new species left to skin and draw. In the same way that the incessant "floggings" of starved, living skeletons are tiring and monotonous, camp life's lack of "sport or excitement of any kind" is sickening. The only stimulating incidents are the whippings and field trips that stand out from the ordinary, such as when Jameson shoots two birds of the same species, which enables him to replace one's broken tail feathers with the other's. Then there are the incidents of 4 December:

"Burgari Mahommed was flogged today, before all the men. The Soudanese are wonderfully plucky in bearing pain, for although he received 150 strokes, which cut him very much, he never uttered a sound. One of the Zanzibaris from Bolobo died, making thirty deaths. Had my first good night's sleep for a long time, and woke up quite a new man" (p. 165).

The convergence of the two types of activities, and the experience of both as monotonous, lead to Jameson recommencing another pastime that towards his death seems to occupy more of his attention than his collecting trips and even his responsibilities in the camp. During the march to Yambuya, Jameson comments several times that a particularly splendid view ought to have been drawn by a painter who the expedition unfortunately has not brought along: "one longed for the skill of an artist to give to the people at home an idea of this magnificent river (...) – all these scenes furnished splendid subjects for the artist – who is not with us!" (p. 41). After a few months in the camp, Jameson starts to draw more than birds and beetles, determined to become the expedition illustrator. In the diary, he writes that his sketches are beginning to take up more space than notes in his notebooks, and that he is looking forward to showing them to Ethel when he returns home.

The first step in this new direction, in which earlier parallel discourses converge to form a new trajectory, is described in the entry for 4 February. With no apparent moral qualms, Jameson manages to bring back the head of a native after a raid against a village, which he draws, skins and preserves with the intention of taking it to London.

"A number of natives were shot, but I cannot tell how many, as most of them sank in the water; however they captured one man, and brought back one head with them, which Ward and I sketched. Afterwards I skinned and preserved it, and I shall try to get it home with me. (...) The Arabs had burnt the whole of the village, which now made a beautiful picture, with the smoke and flames rising up from under the dark foliage of the forest, and reflected as in a mirror across the sunlit waters, while higher up the river the canoes were disappearing into the mist which still hung over the rapids" (p. 204).

Facsimile of a Pen-and-Ink Sketch by J. S. Jameson.

Naturally, the fact that Jameson would treat a fellow human being this way was shocking, but when the head arrived in England, it started a raging media storm. Ethel refers to it in a detached footnote: "This head reached home safely, and was the one which gave rise to the atrocious attacks in the Press on the late Mr. Jameson. – Ed." (p. 204). What is truly remarkable about the diary, however, is the indifference with which the scientific and aesthetic discourses are both merged and transcended. Jameson refers to the head in the same manner as the birds he draws, skins and preserves, seeing in it a continuation of what he calls "a beautiful picture", exemplifying an aesthetic ideal concerning the best use of light and shadow in the landscape painting of the jungle. On 21 March, for instance, he writes: "The whole picture should lie in deep shadow, with a streak of bright sunlight falling through the trees, from high up in the cleft, on the dark forms of the natives as they sit or stand round the bases of the giant stems" (p. 229). Immediately after the episode of the preserved head, we find still more evidence for Jameson's increasing interest in symmetries between scientific and aesthetic discourses on the one hand and the natives' cannibalistic practices on the other. On 6 February, two days later, Jameson notes:

"I painted a lovely snake which a man brought in, and a fish, which I had in a large earthenware jar. Selim Mahommed says that when they reached the place, yesterday, where the ten Arabs had been killed by the natives, they found the native fires still burning, and a lot of dead men's flesh left in the pots. The natives had eaten nearly all the bodies, and had nailed their fingers to the surrounding trees" (p. 206).

Every time Jameson hears one of these constantly circulating stories of cannibalism, he reaches back to the curiosity expressed at the very beginning of the diary. However, the cannibalism trace is now subtly connected with his expanding collection, and the practice of attaching insects with pins is paralleled in the natives' inclination to nail severed fingers to surfaces or display heads on spits. Meanwhile, these tendencies and ideas start to convene around his "sketching" of the natives – Jameson's new favourite pastime in the growing meaninglessness of the camp: "After breakfast Farani brought me a splendid specimen of a savage to sketch" (p. 269).

The most striking convergence of the different discursive traces, as well as the main focus of the criticism of the "atrocious attacks" (with the exception of the preserved head), appears in the so-called "cannibal story". On 11 May, Jameson writes about a fantastic party at which the native Wacusu tribe celebrates two months of "medicine-making" by dancing and drumming all night long. This takes place during a visit to Tippu Tib's camp, where Tib tells Jameson that two Wasucus can easily consume an entire person in one night, along with several other old wives' tales. Tib also says that once he found the water in the well greasy and undrinkable because the natives had rinsed human meat in it. Jameson mentions that people where he comes from usually regard those sorts of stories as "only travellers' tales" – "or in other words lies".

"He then said something to an Arab called Ali, seated next to him, who turned round to me and said, "Give me a bit of cloth, and see". I sent my boy for six handkerchiefs, thinking it was all a joke, and that they were not in earnest, but presently a man appeared, leading a young girl of about ten years old by the hand and I witnessed the most horrible sight I am ever likely to see in my life. He plunged a knife quickly into her breast twice, and she fell on her face, turning on her side. Three men then ran forward, and began to cut up the body of the girl; finally her head was cut off, and not a particle remained, each man taking his piece away down to the river to wash it. The most extraordinary thing was that the girl never uttered a sound, nor struggled, until she fell. Until the last moment, I could not believe that they were in earnest. I have heard many stories of this kind since I have been in this country, but never could believe them, and I never would be such a beast as to witness this, but I could not bring myself to believe that it was anything save a ruse to get money out of me, until the last moment. (...) When I went home I tried to make some small sketches of the scene while still fresh in my memory, not that it is ever likely to fade from it. No one here seemed to be in the least astonished at it" (p. 291).

As mentioned, this was the story that led some critics to the backward conclusion that Jameson could not possibly be telling the truth, since it was a moral impossibility. Jameson, however, did not doubt the rumours about cannibalism, and earlier in the diary he writes with fascination: "They told me that one of the chiefs, who was very rich, is now quite poor from buying nice, fat, young women to eat; this I know to be a fact" (p. 31). Relevant documents in the Stanley Archives not only support the truthfulness of Jameson's account, they add still graver details to the incident, which Jameson chose to leave out.

The main witness - apart from Jameson - was his interpreter, Assan Farran. In his introduction to the diary, Andrew Jameson tries to discredit Bonny with reference to his class, while Assad Farran is discredited on the basis of his nationality and job as a Syrian interpreter - in other words, an undignified and non-British position. However, while Assad Farran was being publically discredited, he was blackmailed by Sir Francis de Winton, the secretary of the Emin Pasha Relief Committee, possibly under pressure from the influential and extremely wealthy whiskey-producing family of the deceased Jameson. From his exile in Cairo, Assad Farran sent the following letter on 15 January 1890 to an unknown but very important recipient:

"Sir,
Captain Vangele who was on board Le Stanley with me, told me that Mr. Jameson showed him, as well as to other officers, some sketches of a girl which has been killed by cannibals, and the flesh was divided in your (sic) presence on your way back from Casongo. I told Captain Vangele the whole story when I saw that Mr. Jameson himself did not keep it secret. Captain Vangele had examined the story from the Arabs before leaving the camp, he therefore related it in every station we came to, confirming his reports by saying here is the interpreter who was with him and Mr. Troup has also seen the sketches" (SA, No. 1340).

The letter continues with an account of the blackmail exerted on his arrival in London. He was contacted by a Mr McDermott, who - on behalf of Sir Francis de Winton, with reference to "the serenity of Major Barttelot and the story of Mr. Jameson with the girl" - demanded that Assad Farran signed "declarations" that the stories he had presented earlier were untrue. Farran opposed the demand, stating that he could not "contradict the truth", but he yielded to the pressure when he was threatened with imprisonment and demands to

pay back his salary in accordance with his contract of employment. If, on the other hand, he signed the declarations, he would be paid a considerable sum of money in instalments, "as long as he does not repeat those stories again".

The reason Farran wrote the letter and ran the risk of breaking the agreement was his situation in Cairo: ill and indebted, he was unable to live off the instalments. However, the letter did not result in the desired assistance – quite possibly the opposite – and the anonymous recipient probably handed it over to the committee or to Stanley, after which it ended up in the archives in Tervuren. Today, it is significant in illuminating Jameson's cannibalism story and particularly the unconcerned and almost vain way in which he handled the tale and the sketches – as if he were proud to have finally provided proof of this horror.

Farran's account is supported by Bonny's testimony, which is also central to the story, although it appears in different versions according to context. In Bonny's official report to Stanley about the fate of the rear column, there was – according to both Stanley's and Bonny's own diaries – no mention of the cannibalism story, while Jephson's diary on 18 February 1889, immediately after the expedition was gathered again, recounts and condemns Bonny's "story of Jameson having bought a slave woman & handed her over to the Manuyema on condition that they would kill & eat her before him" (Jephson p. 337). When Stanley received a newspaper clipping about the subject in September 1889, he made Bonny sign a statement that everything had been satisfactory in regard to food and supplies; however, his diary expresses surprise that stories were circulating in London about cannibalistic excesses on the expedition. This, however, is contradicted by another version of the events in Stanley's strange, unpublished "Personal Journal of the Emin Pasha Relief Expedition", probably

---

The fact that Jameson also drew sketches of the cannibalistic killing he ordered contributed heavily to scandalising the expedition. The linking of established myths about cannibalism with an explorer's extravagant purchase of services, coupled with a gaze that was at the same time sentimental and distantly aesthetic, was impossible for the British public to accept and therefore also difficult to place in a normal frame of understanding. Bonny mentions the drawings, as does the Syrian interpreter who was threatened into silence; Stanley probably saw them when, breaking normal rules of conduct, he opened Jameson's personal travelling crates. However, they were not shown to the public, and they are still not accessible today. The so-called 'copies' of the drawings in Buel's *Heroes of the Dark Continent* (1890) were therefore a bold scoop, probably based on rumours rather than Jameson's original sketches. Buel did not refrain, either, from providing illustrations of the shooting drama surrounding Barttelot's death, even though the official account had not yet been published and the circulating rumours were very doubtful.

COPY OF SKETCHES MADE BY JAMESON, ILLUSTRATING THE KILLING AND CUTTING UP OF A SLAVE GIRL.

written after *In Darkest Africa*, to which we will return later. In this account, Stanley writes that he instigated a cross-examination of Bonny upon arrival at the Yambuya camp. Allegedly, Bonny said that the cannibalistic incident was known of in the camp because Jameson boasted about it to everybody. Bonny described what each sketch depicted, and Stanley asked him what Jameson had actually done since Bonny seemed unwilling to reveal it:

"Has showed some sketches as he called them. There were six of them, representing the act of cannibalism in his presence. The first--- a naked little girl. There was another picture showing the men driving the knife into the little girl, and the blood seems splashing out – another picture shows the savages cutting up the body, others---pieces to cook. I asked him how he came to sketch in so real a fashion – then he told me the story of how ---- the thing was seen by his own eyes.

I asked him when he had finished, what he thought the people in England would say when they heard such a terrible story. He seemed rather taken aback by that as if it had never struck him before. Ah, he said after a while. I would deny it all.

I found that the story was all over the camp, Assad Farran---- has spread everywhere. Jameson had shown the sketches to Troup. Stanley: My dear Bonny, I said, this story is so incredible, I utterly refuse to believe it" (SA, No. 64 B).

At this point, Jameson's own identity was rapidly disintegrating, and his request to witness firsthand the ultimate combination of "skinning", "eating", "collecting" and "sketching" may have been representative of his desire to enter a world that was completely absurd and did not allow him to get away. The diary displays none of the moral crises present in most travel accounts' descriptions of violence and human disasters. Instead, the desperate situation leads the normally reflective Jameson to self-critical considerations of the rationale behind his presence and the Yambuya camp's destructive influence on the area. It is understandable that Jameson – like the other officers – does not disclose the abuse of native women as sex slaves, for example, but it is striking that there is no trace of moral concern given his understanding of social standing and his role as a representative of Victorian culture. His writing style is aestheticised sensitivity while his attitude is detached and insensitive, and even at the end there is no sign of doubt or panic: Stanley's conclusive characterisation of the rear column's "perverseness" in *In Darkest Africa* seems apt.

Barttelot was shot in a confrontation about one of his kidnapped sex slaves – or perhaps because he could not stand the noise from a celebration and ran amok as he had done so many times before. In Jameson's and Jephson's diaries, he is described as hot-headed and ruthless, full of hatred of the Africans and lacking the ability to socialise with anyone except a small circle of officers. Furthermore,

Barttelot was completely lacking in relevant language competences, which only added to his isolation, suspicion and paranoia until he assumed everyone to be liars and murderers. Jameson, on the other hand, engaged with his surroundings; his "collecting" and "sketching" were both activities that involve contracts with the native population. However, he appears to lack the will or ability to reflect on his actions or interpret his situation; there is no suggestion of conscience, and he is not critically selective regarding the rumours about Stanley's fate in the land of the Pygmies or the savage customs of the natives. His recording and preservation of birds and insects, and the later sketches of natives, seem to be his only strategy of self-preservation, and it is significant that this strategy reflects his and Barttelot's involuntarily static situation – attached with pins, sealed in a box, watched coolly by native Congolese, Sudanese and Tippu Tib's Arabs. Jameson's pathological defiance and perverseness stemmed from his static situation, inside and out. This immobility resulted in an obsession with the discourses that ought to have shielded him against the world's unintelligibility; instead these discourses became uncritically intertwined, with the ultimate consequence that he went insane. On 17 February Jameson describes one of the many drawings he has not had time to do, but which still meets his imagined ideal of the distribution of foreground and background, light and shadow:

"One scene on the march formed a very beautiful picture. As the carriers wound their way in a long line over the white sand, now thickly strewn with brown dead leaves, and up the high wooded banks, gleams of sunshine fell upon them through the dark tropical foliage. In the foreground lay an old log across the stream, over which crept mosses and large ferns, and far away through the depths of the forest, every now and again gleamed patches of sunlight on water and figures, while from bough to bough, hanging in graceful festoons, clung giant creepers" (p. 211).

On 9 March 1888, Jameson writes that ignorant Muslims view "picture-drawing" as a kind of "sorcery", which explains their unwillingness to be drawn: "They say, if you wish to kill the person you have drawn, you have only to tear off the head in the picture, when the subject of the sketch will certainly lose his or her head" (p. 220). On 17 March, in a letter to Mrs Jameson, he writes:

"This hope deferred, and weary waiting, month after month, with no brighter outlook, is horrible work, far, far worse than any amount of hardship and fighting. No steamer has been up the Congo since the one that came to us in August, so that we are completely shut off from all the world ... When I look ahead and see nothing but darkness, and no signs of its brightening, it drives me nearly mad at times" (p. 225).

Jameson's artistic attempts were not successful, and he himself was perfectly aware of the fact; however, they still served as more than pastime. His lack of practical skill did not stand in the way of his imagining wonderful paintings, realising an aesthetic ideal in which the tropical details are fixed in the lighting and distribution of foreground and background, seen from a single coherent perspective; the "dark tropical foliage" is not impenetrable or chaotic but organised and permeated by "gleams of sunshine" and "patches of sunlight". It is from this perspective that Jameson prefers to view the natives: dark shadows in an aestheticised landscape, or black bodies with light gleaming on the surface of the skin. It could thus be said that their fear of Jameson's sorcery is well-founded: his pictures *do* in fact steal the lives of his models, and his illustrative example of the ignorant belief in a connection between cutting the head off a portrait and decapitating the portrayed is stumblingly close to his own scandalous drawing, skinning and preservation of a severed head. Furthermore, the example foreshadows the cannibalism episode, which illustrates Jameson's inability to interpret critically the stories he hears; it also shows his will – and perhaps desire – to cement the rumours and collect tangible evidence for the transgressions that form the basis of his sense of reality. However, Jameson's reality is, as he writes to his wife, "nothing but darkness", and his aesthetic and discursive strategies only condense the paralysis and "perverseness" of which his diary is the ultimate legacy.

As one story among many about the expedition's internal battles, the cannibalism incident is noteworthy for several reasons. First, the publication intended to clear his name and reputation of this particular accusation, but it can only be read as a confirmation of the rumours. The publication is based on a major fallacy, disclosing profound contradictions in Victorian self-understanding, which surface via Andrew Jameson's sarcastic attitude towards the accusations that judge his brother by putting the testimony "in the mouth of Jameson himself" (Jameson p. xix). Andrew calls instead for an "eye-witness" – disregarding the Syrian interpreter Assad Farran.

An extenuating circumstance in the criticism of Jameson's cannibalism story is the description of the contractual background for the girl's murder. For six handkerchiefs, Jameson makes a deal that allows him to live out his dream of making real what might only be "travellers' tales". By paying for the murder as a service, Jameson violates his private, anecdotal sphere, linking the act to the usual practice of expeditions in which natives are paid with pieces of clothing for devoting their lives to the work of carriers or soldiers. Jameson's act, and the description of it, thus implicates Stanley and the entire expedition, which is one of the reasons why Stanley hesitated to tell the whole story, though he was tempted. It also explains why the committee took the risky step of threatening

"A Cannibal scene with human flesh roasting over the fire". From Herbert Ward's *Five Years with the Congo Cannibals* (1890). Cannibals and cannibalism are mentioned in almost all the accounts of the era from the Congo; however, they are usually loose labels applied to foreign, hostile natives, or second-hand rumours and wild stories. The books rarely contain images of consumption of human flesh. Ward's sketches are therefore exceptions, often reproduced in other accounts, such as Jenssen-Tusch's *Scandinavians in the Congo*.

and blackmailing Assad Farran to give false evidence and then disappear from the public eye. In a wider context, the act implicated all expeditions, becoming a parable and formula for the trade and negotiations that were central to all journeys: what were mere rumours of cannibalism now became cool facts about how explorers could pay to satisfy their curiosity, getting natives to act out their own secret fantasies and so they could be recorded in twisted, aestheticised or sensational sketches. Jameson's diary illuminates the link between sensitivity, aestheticisation and violence. We will soon return to the related activities of "collecting", "sketching" and "skinning".

Double Perspective

In relation to a sketch of a chieftain that Jameson considered fairly successful, he points out a difference between himself and the natives. that in his own mind was a fundamental one. In the light of what we have seen, however, it should instead be read as a self-projection:

the poor victim is brutally beaten to death with sticks, and the body bound to a small tree, far away from the village, generally on some hill top, where the ghastly figure stands out in bold relief against the clear tropical sky.

THE FIGURE OF A MURDERED MAN.

Once, after a weary day's march, I became separated from my followers, and completely lost my way in the maze of native paths. It happened to be in a district where the people had for some time past been hostile to the officers of the Congo State. In order to obtain a more extensive view of the surrounding country, I climbed to the summit of an adjacent hill. Upon reaching the top, I was horrified to find, crowning the height before me, the figure of a murdered man bound to a rough branch that had been driven into the ground. His head had been crushed in by a heavy stone, and three hawks circled in the air around the ghastly scene. While gazing at this horrible sight, I could hear the sound of firing in the valley beneath. The

"It is a curious fact that the Arabs, and I may say all the natives, hold a picture sideways when they look at it, even after they understand it. Landscape is quite beyond them; with any amount of explanation they do not understand a picture as a whole, although they will recognize trees and figures in it" (Jameson, pp. 241-42).

What is distinctive about Jameson is precisely the fact that the coherent, singular perspective is only a cherished dream that he cannot realise, either in art or life. First and foremost, he lacks the ability to balance his world around an understanding of correlation and entirety. While we can easily read the individual "trees and figures" in the crystal clear text of the diary, *we* are forced to understand the text by looking at it sideways - just as the natives look at pictures. We are not dealing with a narrative - a biographical self-portrait of a coherent author subject that convinces us its descriptions are anchored in a unified perspective - but a peculiar dramatisation of shifts and collapses of

sun was sinking, and I should soon be surrounded by darkness. I was unarmed, and my mind was agitated with fears for my followers. I knew not but what the sounds I heard might be a message to me of their fate. But the scene and its surroundings had so strange fascination for me that I could not leave it without making a rough sketch in my note-book. Steering my course for a fire that I saw flickering about two hundred feet beneath me, I descended the hillside in the darkness, and was glad to find that I had chanced upon the camp fire of my own followers. The Bakongo week consists of four days, *Nkandu*, *Nkonsu*, *Nkenge* and *Nsona*. The market places, which are usually situated on hill tops, are named after these days, and the markets follow in rotation. On *Nkandu* all the people of the neighboring villages assemble in the *Nkandu* market, and on the following day they again assemble on an adjacent hill, which is the market place of *Nkonsu*. These markets are usually situated about two or three miles apart and are presided over by the neighboring chiefs, who settle all disputes and see that their laws are not infringed. No guns are permitted in the markets, and summary punishment is visited upon any one who draws a knife in anger. There is no recognized price for their wares, which consist of all kinds of vegetable food in sea-

Image layout and composition. From Ward's *Five Years with the Congo Cannibals*.

a discursive nature, the collected performative trajectory of which creates a cannibalistic act.

If we look at the expedition as a whole, we face a similar conclusion. From beginning to end, the project was veiled in delusional ambition and illusory ideas about more or less every aspect of the reality it was to confront. Mackinnon, Léopold and Emin Pasha were dreamers, all obsessed with the idea of conquering African territories. The main goal of the endeavours, Equatoria, was based on a highly idealised notion of order and prosperity that was contradicted by the chaos of the province's brief existence. Obviously, there are common motives here such as colonisation, conquering and profit, but less rational elements appear to have played an equally important role, such as King Léopold's dream of connecting the transportation system of the Congo River with that of the Nile. On the other hand, the expedition had considerable impact on British

self-understanding in the wake of scandalous disclosures and the escalating race for Africa in the 1890s.

The discursive shifts and collapses we can trace in Jameson's text, and their challenge to our accepted notions of textual and cultural totalities, also apply to the role of the expedition and travel literature in the *fin de siècle* value crisis. When Jameson writes "This waiting here in utter darkness is sickening, and the men are dying off like rotten sheep" (p. 206), it serves as a fairly accurate account of the state of the Yambuya camp, somewhere deep in the heart of Africa; however, it is also describes history as repetition and decadence, as it was portrayed in European literature and art towards the turn of the century. The search for answers to the questions of guilt and responsibility is similarly rendered impossible because the individual elements do not fit into a coherent perspective; we can only trace fragments of the intricate processes and motives.

With the exception of Tim Jeal's aforementioned biography, most recent books place the responsibility for the disastrous fate of the expedition, in particular that of the rear column, on Stanley. It was Stanley who chose an irresponsible travel route out of political considerations arising from his collaboration with Léopold. They should have taken tried and tested routes from the east coast, or at least have made use of the pre-existing caravan network rather than clearing a completely new path through the Ituri Forest and an area that was already suffering a famine.[78] Furthermore, it was Stanley who chose to leave the rear column behind under unacceptable circumstances. Stanley's side in the dispute tried subsequently to redirect the blame to Tippu Tib, who supposedly had not met his obligations and had hindered the rear column's planned progress by exacerbating the officers' indecisiveness. However, it was also true that Stanley had not met his part of the contract, leaving Tib – who was under additional pressure from his own suspicious government officers in the Congo Free State – unable to act.

Barttelot and Jameson come across as the worst possible commanders of the rear column, and in that respect they are to blame for the increasing demoralisation and decadence that subverted the moral basis for their presence and action. Perhaps the harshest accusation that can be made is that Stanley must have realised early on in the course of events that he had made the wrong choices, which implies that the rear column commanders were left behind with the intention of getting rid of them or showing them in a bad light.

Stanley did not select the best qualified of the many people who applied to accompany the expedition. All the officers' diaries express great surprise with Stanley's coldness and rudeness immediately after their arrival in Congo. They interpret it as stemming from his fear first of rivals and second of witnesses from higher ranks and prestigious families that – when compared to his own shady past – may give them an advantage in the anticipated disputes about credibility. On the expedition, Stanley preferred his Zanzibari soldiers to his European officers, and took their side in conflicts when the officers caught them or the carriers looting natives. Jephson complains that Stanley gives orders to the natives that he does not communicate to the officers, who are – in all fairness – the commanders, thus deliberately causing chaos and hostility in the parties of which he is not the direct commander. Furthermore, Stanley makes sure that he has the best and most loyal people, while the other parties are patched together from groups of ethnically incompatible natives. Barttelot's, Jameson's and Jephson's diaries all express great admiration for Stanley's resilience and superhuman energy, which are the engines behind the incredible journey and explain how the expedition reached its goal against all odds. But they also agree that Stanley ought never to have Europeans with him on his expeditions, and that his conduct as commander is unreasonable. All three men mention an episode during the march to Yambuya in which Stairs and Jephson search some men suspected of theft, causing Stanley to burst into rage. Jameson's account is the most detailed:

"Mr. Stanley takes the word of the Zanzibaris on every occasion before that of the white men, and when he saw that he had hold of rather the wrong end of this stick, he attacked them about their tyranny of the men. He attacked them in a frantic state, stamping up and down the deck of the *Peace*. He called Jephson all sorts of names, a "G-d d-n son of a sea-cook", "You d- -d ass, you're tired of me, of the Expedition, and of my men. Go into the bush, get, I've done with you. And you too, Lieutenant Stairs, you and I will part to-day; you're tired of me, Sir, I can see. Get; away into the bush". Then he turned round to the men (about 150) sitting down, and spoke Swahili to the effect that the men were to obey us no more, and that if Lieutenant Stairs or Jephson issued any orders to them, or dared to lift a hand, they were to tie them up to trees. He had already told Stairs that he had only to lift his hand for the men to throw him into the Sea. He last offered to fight Jephson, "If you want to fight, G-d d-n you, I'll give you a bellyful." (...) As for Stairs or Jephson being tired of the Expedition, no men could work harder or have their hearts more in it. I should think a repetition of this kind of thing would make them both pretty sick of Mr. Stanley and the Exhibition. He also called Jephson, "G-d d-d impudent puppy." (...) I had no idea until to-day what an extremely dangerous man Stanley was. Could there be anything more inciting to mutiny than what he had told the Zanzibaris?" (pp. 47-48).

This is the first of several diary entries that present Stanley as a "dangerous man". An important reason for Stanley's rushing ahead with the front column was obviously his ambition to reach his goal in time – both in regard to the

Chapter vignette in Ward's *Five Years with the Congo Cannibals*. The ring in the drawing makes a capital O – the beginning letter in the first word, "Opposite ...".

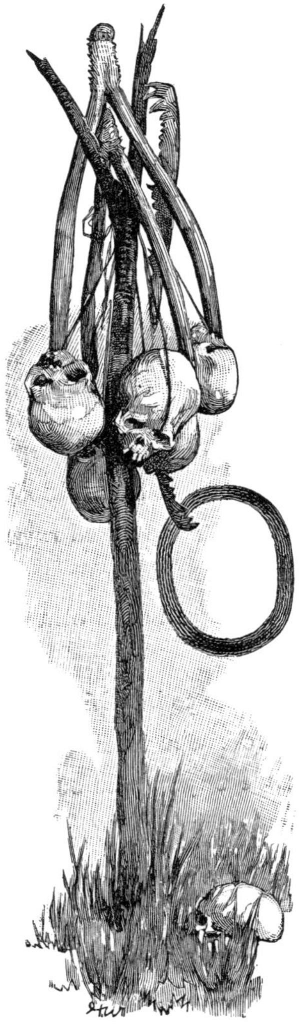

relief objective and the grand political plans. However, the suspicion remains that he was hoping his story of the triumphant rescue would shine even brighter if it was viewed on the background of bad luck and incompetent commanders. It would also have been unbearable for him to have to share the anticipated glory with people he perceived to be complacent upper class fops who had bought their way into the expedition without any of the underlying ethical qualifications – "work" – that Stanley possessed.

If we pursue this suspicion, the most interesting implication is that the rear column's fate was the consequence of choices made early on with regard to authorship, credibility and testimony. As opposed to the common notion that the rear column's demoralisation resulted in a dispute that subsequently found its way into the newspapers, the *expected effect* of the travel accounts on public opinion was in fact determining both the actual events of the journey and the design of the texts about it. Conversely, the narratives that were also motivating factors for the expedition also constituted a concrete framework for the crucial decisions taken on the march in the forest. If we follow this theory to its conclusion, Stanley's inability to write a triumphant account that overshadowed all the other testimonies appears particularly ironic; his carefully considered actions resulted in a completely unstable expedition context that is seen most clearly in the aforementioned "mystery" passage, which even today continues to produce testimonies that subvert Stanley's authority.

However, if we look at this patchwork of narratives and testimonies from an angle that does not involve any predetermined moral condemnation of

Stanley, a different picture emerges. A number of the alleged misjudgements were based on knowledge that was only gradually acquired. Stanley did not know beforehand, for instance, that his route went through an area of famine; he had to adjust to this unforeseen situation. Furthermore, his latitude for alternative planning was very limited, as the expedition's objectives and routes were wholly defined by his employers. It is fair to conclude that under these near impossible conditions, Stanley did well to complete the expedition in a disciplined and defensible manner.

Among the Europeans, only Stanley – and to some degree Jephson – managed to maintain the self-discipline required to keep up the moral leadership of an expedition that went on for years, every day threatening to disintegrate into a state that would lead to even more destruction. Viewed in this light, Stanley did the right thing under the given circumstances, while his officers' morals deteriorated from the moment he left them; this also applies to Parke and Stairs, who were left behind in a famine camp during the first march to find Emin. We are thus left with the impression that Stanley was within his rights to prefer the company of his Zanzibari soldiers to that of the Europeans, who isolated themselves from their surroundings and refused to learn local languages or gain vital knowledge. Stanley's party did what caravans have always done on long marches in Africa, while the European officers took to meaningless violence in order to maintain a façade of colonial and military order and discipline. Barttelot, and in particular Jameson, can be seen as extending and corrupting British colonial ideas of dominance as well as sustaining a sentimental, romantic, orientalist discourse on 'the other'. Jameson's collapse, to which his diary is a chilling testimony, more generally marks a collapse in the travel account's legitimacy and a contestation of the imperial world view. However, the connection between thejustificatory scientific and aesthetic discourses and the brutalisation, depravation and violence discovered in Jameson's report was so profound and problematic that the British public was unable to digest it with any rhetorical consequence, and instead chose to suppress and close the case.

The events of the expedition, and the rhetorical background for *In Darkest Africa* and the diaries, were strongly influenced by a pre-defined discursive structure that positioned testimonies and credibility in relation to the literary market, legal-moral discourses and justifiability in the political public sphere. The great national narratives about Britain's reputation around the world, and the relief committee's attempt to establish a contractual monopoly, were predetermined influences on the expedition's testimonies that were already active when the events were being played out and the stories told. However, the reception of the expedition testimonies was also subject to a number of discursive terms for what *could* be expressed – regardless of whether or not they

were true. The readerly focus was thus redirected to aspects of the rhetoric that involved decorum: ethical, aesthetic and rhetoric rules of "appropriateness" or "bienséance". In the context of explorations, these factors were to a large extent defined by Victorian codes of duty and honour, home ground for the officers and their class but one of Stanley's weak points. Stanley's strongest card, on the other hand, was the market, which we shall investigate in more detail below.

As mentioned, the diaries offer an oblique illumination of *In Darkest Africa* and the expedition as a whole that is crucial since their many threads are intertwined and very difficult to organise into a coherent perspective. Among other things, the diaries emphasise the chillingly desperate, chaotic and futile situation in which the expedition found itself. Furthermore, Jephson's and Jameson's day-to-day notes on provision expeditions, raids and abuse paint a picture of a decidedly inglorious reality, which official reports and authorised travel accounts have always tried to veil and suppress.

On a general level, however, the diaries – especially Jameson's – highlight one of the fundamental causes of colonial violence and subsequent suppression in the nineteenth century. In the guise of aesthetic sensibility, a scene was set where the suppression of the reality of foreign places was combined with a perverse pleasure in watching the suffering of others. In Jameson's case we are dealing with a scandalous transgression, where in Jephson's writing there is merely voyeuristic fascination. However, the transgression – formalised through payment, completion, writing and drawing – indicates a deep structure of the sentimental and affective narratives about the Congo of which we will see examples in the reform movement campaigns and other nineteenth-century travel accounts. At this discursive level there is no doubt that Jameson and Jephson were far more responsible for the scandal than Stanley with his insensitive pragmatism.

The Forest

Towards the end of *In Darkest Africa*, Stanley mentions the difficulty he had getting started – something that was unusual given his normal speed and facility. It has been suggested that the problem was that the events themselves did not fit into Stanley's usually energetic rhetoric or the finished book's attempt to silence the dispute over credibility. From Stanley's autobiography it appears that the process finally fell into place with the chapter about the Ituri Forest, "The Great Central African Forest" (chapter 23, volume II). It therefore makes sense to use this as the final piece in the Emin Pasha puzzle, before we return to the book's market and public reception. Stanley's release from his uncharacteristic writer's block seems to be the key to important conflicts in the material – the complex mix of his and others' experiences and documents, facts, suspicions, inklings and beliefs. The present analysis of 'the forest' will compare a number of dimensions in Stanley's prose by reflecting on his autobiographical account of the episode and the writing process in Cairo. This reading will be elaborated in the subsequent section, "The Marketplace". Let us begin with a sketch of the text's unique phenomenology, in which the forest becomes the backdrop for projections and confessions that implicate completely disparate spaces.

Grandiose in design, the chapter in question is a highly eclectic catalogue of the spirit and events of the forest – from its vast area, equivalent to France and Spain combined, to chimpanzees and Pygmies, to how to make arrow poison, to "A few secrets of the woods" and "The queer feeling of loneliness" it inspires. The chapter ends with a hope that one day the Congo railway will come to transport all the forest's treasures to the coast. It begins, however, with a satire of one Professor Drummond, who – despite his academic achievements – has admitted that he is only "a minor traveller" and has therefore probably got the wrong end of the stick when it comes to the African forests. Drummond claims that the fauna and vegetation lack the fertility and tropical luxuriousness expected of them. Stanley's criticism takes as its starting point the professor's limited armchair perspective: "if this is honest description, the reader had better toss my books aside, for this chapter goes to prove that I differ in toto with the learned Professor's views respecting tropical Africa" (*IDA* II, p. 68).

The learned professor has no understanding of Africa's variation and diversity. Nyasaland, the Masai areas and the Sahara are not the entire story of the continent, but merely parts of the enormous diversity that encompasses the rest of the whole world: the Russian steppes in the Masai areas, parts of France in Egypt, Switzerland in Ukonju, the Alps in Ruwenzori, Brazil in the Congo River Delta and the Amazon in the Congo River. The Ituri Forest alone is so vast and diverse, yet so homogenous in appearance, that it would require many books to describe it correctly: "Nay, if we regard it too closely, a legion of specialists would be needed" (II, p. 69). In contrast to "scientific analysis" and the specialists' either very detached or myopic descriptions, Stanley intends to offer "a real idea of what it is like". There simply is not enough time to investigate "the buds and flowers", or compare different types of liquids that drip "in milky tears or amber globules, or opaline pastils" or watch "the industrious ants", "the insect armies", etc. Nor is there time to delve deeper into the enormous masses of dead, spongy wood that are swarming with "minute tribes".

"Put your ear to it, and you hear a distinct murmurous hum. It is the stir and movement of insect life in many forms, matchless in size, glorious in colour, radiant in livery, rejoicing in their occupations, exultant in their fierce but brief life, most insa-

tiate of their kind, ravaging, foraging, fighting, destroying, building, and swarming everywhere and exploring everything" (II, p. 70).

Stanley's nature descriptions do not intend to "examine", "observe" or "compare", but to invite the reader to imagine the forest through a long series of images that together make up the insect parable we saw exemplified above in the account of the happy island in *Through the Dark Continent*. The insects initially look like shiny, colourful native "tribes"; later, they seem to reflect the expedition's own march through the forest, "fighting", "foraging", "destroying" and "swarming everywhere and exploring everything". In order to depict the impenetrability of the forest, Stanley invites the reader to partake in the weaving of a gigantic tapestry as the lianas form Ws and Ms and the epiphytes are ropes that fall down from high above, "with open thread-work at the ends". The reader must incorporate other threads in an intricate manner – "with absolute disregard of material" – eventually draping the tapestry with orchids and decorative ferns and mosses. Around the tapestry there are numerous glades, where all the smaller plants are fighting their way up, suffocating each other in their endeavours. The forest is "a mixture of these scenes", where life and evolution are governed by tough, Darwinian selection:

"There is also death from wounds, sickness, decay, hereditary disease and old age, and various accidents thinning the forest, removing the unfit, the weakly, the inadaptable, as among humanity. Let us suppose a tall chief among the giants, like an insolent son

The chapter in *In Darkest Africa* where Stanley describes the vast Ituri Forests is an addition to the travel book. It communicates his intense sensory perception of the forests and, on a different level, signifies the collapse of the expedition and the labyrinthine mirror images of Stanley's autobiography and the mapping of Africa. The sketch was made by Joseph Bell, the main artist in the team of illustrators for *In Darkest Africa*. While Stanley was writing the travel book in Cairo, Bell created, according to Stanley's instructions – and often following much discussion – a representation of the forest in which tree trunks and human figures are loosely drawn in the same entangled composition as they are in textual body of the forest chapter. Stanley's publisher, Marston, would take the sketch to Paris, where Eduard Riou developed it into the finished illustration entitled "Gymnastics in a Forest Clearing". From *In Darkest Africa*.

of Anak. By a head he lifts himself above his fellows – the monarch of all he surveys; but his pride attracts the lightning, and he becomes shivered to the roots, he topples, declines, and wounds half a dozen other trees in his fall" (II, p. 71).

In this enchanted forest, where Stanley in desperation often resorts to biblical passages and finds relief in the belief that God sees him as a Moses, one parable follows another, most referring to the analogy between man and forest. The parables are more than descriptions of the forest: they also illuminate Stanley's understanding of his role in the expedition. The previous chapter, "Our Starvation Camp", which – according to the autobiography – was written *after* the chapter about the forest, describes one of the most desperate situations on the

"In the night and rain in the Forest", from *In Darkest Africa*.

journey, momentarily causing Stanley to doubt himself and "the Great Deliverer": "too many memories crowded about me; too many dying forms haunted me in the darkness; my lively fancies were too distorted by dread, which painted them with dismal colours" (II, p. 64). These vivid imaginings only add to the profound darkness and diminished hope and faith. They are linked to blurred vision and deafness turning the senses inward to listen to what is several times described as "mute witnesses" (II, p. 64).

In "Our Starvation Camp" the expedition is at its lowest ebb, and Stanley even considers taking his own life. Typically of his self-portrayal, the situation is finally resolved through a gothic, *fin de siècle* combination of inner, ghostly memories and divine revelation. The forest chapter is a supplement that does not recount the journey's events, but tries to collect different impressions of the endless forest in a complete picture, thus creating a platform or opening for the writing process. In that sense, it constitutes both the last and the first part of the finished travel book, and the two chapters appear to be opposites. In the earlier one, descriptions of the forest are completely absent though it is the basic reality for everyone on the expedition – many of whom die or lose their way – and the whole focus is on death, which Stanley himself only just escapes. In the one that follows, the forest is full of life, vegetation and variation, and the text invites the reader to take part in its intricate embroidery, creating texture and writing the text with liana letters. The description and the descriptive strategy are intertwined, but the forest also serves as a mirror for a vast number of other images that wind around each other and live off the forest's bounty.

In this context, we can only see a self-portrait when Stanley describes the tallest tree in the forest as "a tall chief", a head taller than his companions and "the monarch of all he surveys". And when Stanley imagines that the tree's pride attracts lightning and takes the smaller trees down in its fall, it is a paraphrase of a profound crisis in Stanley's confidence that his endeavours will have a meaningful result – presented in an uncharacteristically chilling style in the previous chapter. The fall of proud trees contributes to the image of the forest as an intertwined mass of "great goitrous swellings" and "deformed trunks". The trees are wounded, infected, ill and deformed, attacked by parasites – like the famished camp: "too many memories crowded about me; too many dying forms haunted me in the darkness; my lively fancies were too distorted by dread, which painted them with dismal colours".

What Stanley calls a "mental picture" of "the ruthless forest" is expanded in lengthy, detailed descriptions of density and light, entangled growths and forms that destroy and live off each other in a savage but vital interplay, including a scene in which a raging storm becomes a "wild war", expressed like one of Stanley's dramatic war reports. Preoccupied with the expedition's struggle to survive, Stanley has no time for "fine sentiments about the forest"; however, if he were to wander off into its depths, he would recognise its "eerie strangeness" and experience a "queer feeling of loneliness". This feeling is related to the way in which the trees momentarily appear to be inhabitants of another world, existing outside and independently of Stanley's own: "it did seem curious that the two lives, so like in some sense, were yet so incommunicable" (II, p. 75).

The portrayal of the dense forest is followed by that of glades which have been created by storms or humans, whose homes, tools, tendencies and crops are described in Stanley's scenic-anthropological discourse. The narrative sketches an evolutionary process in which the pure, dense jungle is gradually replaced by control and civilisation, with the Pygmy as the link, and the dream that natives "will easily be induced to collect rubber" and produce export that will someday be transported along the imagined "Congo Railway" to the coast. However, this vision of the future is contrasted with a passage that sponges off its optimism, telling a very different story:

"As I have already said, the forest is typical of the life of humanity. No single glance can be taken of it without becoming conscious that decay, and death, and life, are at work there as with us. I never could cast a leisurely look at it but I found myself, unconsciously, wondering at some feature which reminded me of some scene in the

civilised world. It has suggested a morning when I went to see the human tide flowing into the city over London Bridge between half-past seven and half-past eight, where I saw the pale, overworked, dwarfed, stoop-shouldered, on their way to their dismal struggle for existence. They were represented here faithfully, in all their youth, vigour, and decrepitude; one is prematurely aged and blanched, another is goitrous, another is organically weak, another is a hunchback, another suffers from poor nutrition (...). And as there is nothing so ugly and distasteful to me as the mob on a Derby day, so there is nothing so ugly in forest nature as when I am reminded of it by the visible selfish rush towards the sky in a clearing, after it has been abandoned a few years. Hark! the bell strikes, the race is about to begin. I seem to hear the uproar of the rush, the fierce, heartless jostling and trampling, the cry, "Self for self, the devil takes the weakest!" To see the white-hot excitement, the noisy fume and flutter, the curious inequalities of vigour, and the shameless disregard for order and decency! (...) The melancholy sound of the wind fluttering the leafy world aloft, and the sad rustle of the foliage reminded me vividly of a night spent at --- House, where I passed half the time listening to the dreadful sighing of the rooky grove, which filled my mind with forlornness and discomfort. Here again, as I lay in my tent, were suggested memories of ocean gales, and general cold, pitiful wretchedness, and when the rain fell in an earnest shower and the heavy fall of raindrops roused the deep and funereal dirge that sounded round about me, it seemed to me I heard sad and doleful echoes of sad and unsatisfied longings, and crowds of unworded thoughts, and past aspirations, unbreathed sentiments of love, friendship, and unuttered sympathies advancing with awful distinctness to the sharpened imagination, until one seemed ready to dissolve in tears and gasp sobbingly, "Oh, my friends, the good God is above all, and knows all things!" (II, pp. 80-81).

The forest chapter is the opening and facilitator of Stanley's last great travel book. At first sight, it looks like a supplement of the kind that is characteristic of classical travel accounts, offering a safe opportunity to order the chaotic experience and give it a unified meaning. However, in this instance the material ultimately resists such an ordering, which becomes clear through the closely knit patchwork of explanations and intentions. Not even Stanley could orchestrate the bitter, contrasting events in the forest, the fate of the rear column, the starvation, punishments and pillage, the months of trekking through the forest. The addition contains many hints of fictionalisation and sublime aestheticisation, along with references that establish an alternative textual space which is neither purely scientific nor quite intimate enough to be confessional. It can be read as hypothetical prose in which apparent contradictions merge in an allegorical form, each part of which is a readable representation, while the close-knit whole does not represent any identifiable reality.

Various species of the forest's trees, which Stanley explicitly refrains from describing scientifically, comparatively or analytically, become in the passage a gothic repertoire of crippled people on London Bridge, mirroring the catalogue of degrees and forms of human disintegration that constantly haunts Stanley throughout the expedition's own chamber of horrors. Once again he sees himself as "prematurely aged and blanched", an old, noble tree that will soon be toppled by "insolent youth". This is a parable of Jephson and Stanley's exchange regarding youth and experience in another situation when the old explorer came close to dying. The two passages, and the one cited above in which Stanley portrays himself as a "monarch-of-all-I-survey" tree in the forest whose pride is punished by lightning, are – in the simultaneously veiled and obvious forest allegory – tales that both conceal and confess Stanley's part in the expedition's chilling events.

However, the passage about the forest and humanity remains self-contradictory to the end. On the one hand, Darwinian selection is recognised as a principle of nature and life that in an extended form justifies colonisation and the expedition's conduct, clearing forests to allow for paradisiacal plenitude, growth and light. On the other hand, Stanley is full of fear and loathing when, in glimpses, he sees himself as part of the brutality, as if "the mob on a Derby day" one day will clear him from their path too. Darwinian vitality is also a shameless disregard of order and "decency", and the struggle for life is a chaotic "white-hot excitement" and "noisy fume and flutter" – everything that has previously been associated with "darkness". And, in accordance with the perception in decadence literature of progress and industrialism as destruction and decay, the Darwinian idea of the survival of the fittest is accompanied by a looming suspicion that it is actually the least fit who procreate the most. Racial and genetic degeneration is an important theme in decadence; however, in this example of travel literature, which has traditionally been classified as shameless, imperialistic adventure, it is also an introspective theme.

This first European description of one of the world's greatest forests lists observations on Pygmies, tree species, and so on, but its most distinctive quality is that it consists of a vast number of elements that are irreconcilable, in a rhetorical-textual sense as well as in the context of Stanley's self-image. The passage's final melancholy echoes throw the reader back and forth between "an out of the way place" in Africa and then Britain. Sad memories of loss, unfulfilled desires and unspoken emotions end with Stanley characteristically addressing a reconciling God. Embedded in Stanley's thorough descriptions of the forest's phenomenology, this peculiar passage is a testimony to his intimate, secret biography, which – at the sound of "the wind fluttering the leafy world aloft" – points towards a completely different set of explanations for his pres-

ence deep within the darkness of the forest. This book's introduction, "Traveller on Global Terms", has followed this trace, so let us just briefly repeat that an important motivation behind Stanley's actions, and the eventual completion of the Emin Pasha Relief Expedition, is to be found in his compound identity and character formation: it was not Stanley who created the journeys – the journeys created Stanley, and when he was sitting at his writing desk in Cairo, settling the score, the journey's crises were also crises of his writing and identity.

In the *Autobiography*, he often reflects on the events in the great forest with a focus on superhuman endeavours, while also returning to the accusations in relation to his decisions. The most striking element, however, is his forced forgetfulness:

"For my protection against despair and madness, I had to resort to self-forgetfulness; to the interest which my task brought; to the content which I felt that every ounce of energy, and every atom of self had been already given to my duty, and that, no matter what followed, nothing more could be extracted from me" (*Autobiography*, p. 387).

Besides forgetfulness, there was a need for extraordinary "self-control" in the "epical experiences of the Great Forest" (p. 390), which is described as a timeless and unreal limbo:

"We began now to re-date our time. What happened in the Forest was an old, old story, not to be remembered; it was like the story of toddling childhood; it is what happened *after* the Forest days that they loved to be reminded of! 'Ah! Master,' they would say, 'why recall the time when we were "wayingo" (fools, or raw youths)?" (p. 391).

Retrospectively, Stanley writes – perhaps surprisingly –that he subsequently found himself longing for the forest's cool shadow, loneliness and "and the large acquaintance I made with our own ever-friendly selves, with whom there was never any quarrelling, and not a trace of insincere affection" (p. 409). The encounter with the luxury of Cairo intensifies the shock-like confrontation in which Stanley's "dreaming temper" and "castles in the air" are mercilessly destroyed. What he himself has described as horrifying challenges of stamina and self-control are later, in the autobiography, mentioned as "meditations in the wilds" (p. 410). This is followed by a request for forgiveness for the explorer returned from Africa: "His opinions are too much his own. Then, again, his vitals are wholly disorganised. (...), and his mind harks back to the strange scenes he has just left (...)." (p. 410). In this state, naturally Stanley is incapable of writing:

"Stanley at work", from Marston's *How Stanley Wrote 'In Darkest Africa'*.

"I could not, immediately, dash off two consecutive sentences that were readable. A thousand scenes floated promiscuously through my head, but, when one came to my pen-point, it was a farrago of nonsense, incoherent, yet confusedly intense. (...). What to say first, and how to say it, was as disturbing as a pathless forest would be to a man who had never stirred from Whitechapel. My thoughts massed themselves into a huge organ like that at the Crystal Palace, from which a master-hand could evoke Handel's 'Messiah' or Wagner's *Walküre*, but which to me would only give deep discords.

The days went by, and I feared I should have to relegate my book to the uncertain future. At last I started on the 'Forest' chapter, the writing of which relieved me of the acute feeling. Then I began the 'March from Yambuya'; and presently, I warmed to the work, flung off page after page, and never halted until I reached 'The Albert'. My stronger emotions being thus relieved, I essayed the beginning, and found by re-reading that I was not over-fantastic, and had got into the swing of narrative" (p. 411).

The forest chapter pretends to be a phenomenological presentation of sensory perception, and the highly evocative imagery invites the reader on an imagined trek through the dense foliage, embroidered "with absolute disregard of material". The forest is "a mixture of these scenes", but, as we have seen, it also

includes ghostly emanations of Stanley himself, alongside images and parables covering both confession and concealment of responsibility for the journey's hazardous events. The discourse is explicitly not based on scientific observations and comparisons, but rather on a patchwork of practical knowledge and pure dream and fantasy – a form that is always prominent in Stanley's texts but here reaches its climax. Timothy Reiss has termed it a "patterning" discourse in which the "analytico-referential" element only plays a passing role as the creator of some measure of recognisability and background for the text's dreamlike passages.[79] Perhaps Stanley did not personally find the text "over-fantastic", but it remains difficult for the reader to imagine what the forest and the Pygmies really look like, and yet the total effect is an extremely effective impression of the forest space.

The reader is drawn into a fierce drama in which destruction and powerlessness are raging in both the internal and external descriptions of Stanley's experiences; each event culminates in a kind of epiphany as the solid contours dissolve, the sensory perception of the world is dulled and his companions appear as ghostly figures on an inner screen. Here, they connect with vague, unspoken memories in a form of repetition that is described as emptying and resetting, atonement and release. However, in accordance with Stanley's religious belief, they do not explain or point in any direction; they merely purge. These epiphanies are coherent with Stanley's declared method in the field, which basically consisted of exercising maximal self-control by cutting off anything that was irrelevant to completing the task. They are involuntary responses to Stanley's ruthless determination and control.

When Stanley loses his self-control, the uninvited memories, "crowds of unspoken thoughts" and "dumb witnesses of past mercies" pour out in a sentimental dream that is apparently far removed from the dynamic explorer. However, the textual rhetoric has a therapeutic function and communicates a sensibility that is very different from that of the sentimental travellers' aestheticism. In the sentimental travel account, the ego is expanded without being fundamentally questioned, and in equivalent nature observations, the text assumes the aesthetics of the sublime – the forest is worshipped as incomprehensible. Stanley's descriptions, in contrast, are written in a realistic style, albeit characterised by a vast number of doublings that destabilise the ego and, from a wider perspective, indicate an understanding of the journey as formative.

For Stanley, the accepted boundaries between internal and external reality seem to be suspended in the forest, and he dreams of being able to communicate with the trees. We may interpret this as a rhetorical attempt to organise the chaotic, meaningless and ultimately identity-threatening experience – the fear of surviving as the living dead, having lost sight of any meaning in life. It may also, however, be interpreted as an apt description of a reality of which the single components are not interrelated in accordance with normal proportions. The cited passages are profoundly conflicting – which cannot be a result of carelessness, given that the forest chapter is the result of a lengthy process – and this is subsequently confirmed in Stanley's retrospect, where he also emphasises that there were things he was unable or unwilling to express. The loneliness of the forest, a space where man is engulfed and time stands completely still, causing the paths to become labyrinthine, is in Stanley's account populated by figures of the metropolis, pushing and shoving from all directions. And what in the retrospect are termed "epic experiences" – presupposing both plot and hero – are several times characterised as states of "self-forgetfulness". This self-forgetfulness paradoxically provides the opportunity for uninterrupted conversations with the author's "own ever-friendly selves".

The surprising comparison of the travel account with Wagner's *The Valkyrie* and the organ at the Crystal Palace, which in Stanley's ears sounds out of tune and inharmonious, is telling in relation to the *fin de siècle* culture to which it alludes, as well as to the book's role in the empire's exposure and marketing discourse. Another striking characteristic is the correlation between the forest and the book. Both are "pathless forests", and when Stanley finally gets out into the light, the march through both forest and book is headed towards a happy end. The lianas become Ws and Ms, the book is the forest and the people are trees, and when Stanley invites the reader to create the images of the forest "with absolute disregard of material", he also characterises the assemblage of highly varied materials that is his writing style.

Nuanced reading not only brings Stanley closer to the decadence of 1890s high literature, and thus closer to the centre of our usual understanding of literary history, it also questions the well-established juxtaposition of Victorian and imperialist sensational literature on the one hand and literary decadence's experimentation with consciousness on the other. In many respects, both literatures can be perceived as reactions to the same fundamental experiences of decay and historical vacuum, played out in separate, parallel spaces. *Fin de siècle* is often described as the experience of a zero: time stands still while events are perceived as repetitions and representations reflected on expanding, unreal spaces. Similarly, the forest is described as a time warp, a paranoid space that is completely empty yet full of objects and memories from throughout history – just like a Wagnerian *Gesamtkunstwerk*. What Stanley perceives as pipe dreams, "toddling childhood" or "wayingo", beyond control and reason, is torn down upon his arrival in Cairo and subsequently rebuilt in the travel book's reconstruction of his all-encompassing castles in the air and a surrealistic atlas that represents unknown regions of Africa's geography and Stanley's inner life.

Basically, the style is realistic; however, Stanley's reservations about scientific methodology, and his enthusiastic expectations of Africa's opportunities, often lead him to romantic ideas of a lonely, spiritual fusion with majestic, enchanted nature. However, as the forest only offers glimpses of sanctuary and stability for Stanley's projections, it soon transforms back into the threatening and ghostly backdrop for a procession of deaf and blind witnesses of the past. Realism as form and romanticism as inspiration collapse in his gothic and decadent style, which – with its fascinating descriptions of decay and parasitic insects – dominates the chapter. The forest chapter displays an almost complete catalogue of the motives and stylistic characteristics of *fin de siècle* literature: the *Doppelgänger* and the splitting of the ego; the fascination with neuro-pathological and mental anomalies on the one hand and hallucinatory sensory perceptions of natural phenomena on the other; the growth and decay of plants; and blurred contours in internal and external landscapes.

Romanticism is present in the quest figure to which Stanley often returns, promising reconciliation between man and nature, organic growth and human identity. Realism is present in the text's fixed narrative position, which confidently distinguishes between the subjective and the objective world. Both models, however, collapse in the textual experience of what Jan Gordon has called "decadent spaces", characterised by intertwined spatiotemporal figures such as the apocalypse, the mirror, the ruin, etc.[80] As a prominent metaphor for the transparent, rational hyper-space of Victorianism and industrialism, the Crystal Palace is only a dream in Stanley's text, in which the spaces are opaque and self-reflectively labyrinthine; however, for that very reason they are strong phenomenological communicators of the experience of the forest and the journey, as well as reflections of the travel account's creation and performativity. The concluding chapter will return to this connection between the Crystal Palace and Stanley's prose.

There can be little doubt that somewhere in his fragmented self-understanding, Stanley wanted to express the truth about the forest and the expedition as a whole. His journeys can be seen as attempts to anchor a fluid identity in unchallengeable reality, and the travel account's credibility is therefore strongly connected to his identity project as indicated via the overlapping experiences of his being engulfed by and emerging from both the book and the forest. The forest chapter as addition or supplement to the travel description constitutes a strategy and authority that enables Stanley to repress everything he does not want to tell, while connecting everything that suits him, allowing him to write the rest of the book in one big, elegant sweep from coast to coast. However, we are not told what the supplement actually represents. It remains unsaid in Stanley's chains of "unworded thoughts", and what he describes as an "out of the way place in Africa" is not in any way encompassed by our normal standards of knowledge. The text's authority is inscribed in, not raised above, the "mystery" – a term that Stanley uses several times for the rear column's abnormal and inexplicable defiance and "perverseness", and one that can be read into his own labyrinthine journey in forest and text.

In the context of *fin de siècle* literature, the chapter can be read as a refined piece of fiction in which we follow reflections and reversals between a fluid and fragmented ego and an unstable world. The text can also be read from an anthropological perspective, its fluid and collage-like mix of autobiography and anthropology presaging Michel Leiris' *L'Afrique fantôme* (1934).

We can only perceive the text as a desperate attempt to navigate and anchor a fluid ego, and to edit a narrative about experiences that resist integration into any of the discourses and genres offered by travel accounts at the time. Stanley's use of the "mystery" figure is thus linked to real and profound perplexity regarding where he has been, where he has come to and how, in the travel account, he can repeat the expedition's meaningless marches as rational and directional movement – and consequently regain control of his own body. The text is an outstanding example of its genre, for many reasons. With its hints of suspense and horror, it offered qualified entertainment to the mass consumers of books, while at the same time fascinating the elitist recipients' decadent taste for decay, sadomasochism and gothic aesthetics. Furthermore, it managed to bridge the gap between fatalities and destruction on the one hand and the mercantile-colonial purpose and heroism on the other.

Subject to enormous time pressure, and weighed down by the crisis of credibility that had already arisen in London because of the conflicting, scandalous testimonies, Stanley developed a number of stylistic and rhetorical techniques that – in the travel account's desperate testing of time, place and identity – gave birth to a unique prose. The strategies of contemporary travel literature is exposed as insufficient and transcended in the book's key passages. In that respect, *In Darkest Africa* marked the completion of a genre and an era.

The Marketplace

In the peculiar little book *How Stanley wrote 'In Darkest Africa': A trip to Egypt & back* (1890), Stanley's publisher Edward Marston provides a different view of the book's creation and design. *In Darkest Africa* advertises that Marston, who published all Stanley's travel accounts, also published titles such as *The Amateur Angler's Days* and *Fresh Woods and Pastures*, as well as *Copyright, National and International, from a Publisher's Point of View*. Marston's book is an account of his own journey to Cairo to offer advice and guidance to Stanley in his work on

Marston's book about *In Darkest Africa* is a triumphant, enthusiastic, and ironic tale of the media globalisation of the book market at the end of the nineteenth century. Stanley's travel book is described as a statistical wonder – a record-breaking leap in the history of books that surpasses everything else, while at the same time functioning as a marketplace where books, typewriters, and electrical lighting are traded.

In Darkest Africa. It gives an insight into Stanley's legendary writer's workshop from a commercial publishing perspective – as suggested by the advertisements for The Remington Standard Typewriter, Fisher's Gladstone Bag and Apollinaris, of which Stanley drank bucketloads while in Cairo. Related publications, such as *Books on African Travel, by H.M. Stanley and Others*, further add to the impression of a veritable marketplace. Furthermore, the commercial angle is manifest in the book's style – a pastiche of Laurence Sterne's amusingly confused *Sentimental Journey* and Phileas Fogg's struggle against time in Jules Verne's *Le tour du monde en quatre-vingts jours* (1873): we are dealing with an intimate and ironic text that is clearly aware of the international scene but still ready to be anecdotally confessional.

Marston presents his journey as an extraordinary event in the history of books: a publisher goes on an expensive journey to secure the maximal production speed for a book that is eagerly anticipated by a worldwide audience. However, it is also highly unusual because Marston has promised himself he will obtain some feathers from Egyptian wild geese, which are allegedly invaluable to fly fishers. This leads him into burlesque situations due to language confusion between Russian, French, Arabic and English; it also raises the reader's suspicion that this part of the journey might prove to be a "wild goose chase". In contrast to Stanley, Marston is interested in puns and coincidences, and he has an eye for the comical in the few trips he takes to the city and the Pyramids. It therefore seems fair to interpret his joke about the journey being a wild goose chase as equally applicable to Stanley's frantic pursuit of his story. Throughout his account, Marston processes this trope of wildness and frenetic determination – an unreal, untruthful or inflated dimension in the book project as well as a literal hunt for a bird – for example where the feathers of Egyptian "wild-geese" are described as the raw material for creating a superb "*facsimile*" for an English, "natural May-fly" (Marston, p. 38).

Despite his joking attitude, Marston stresses the seriousness of the situation – if Stanley does not finish the book before the deadline, it will probably never be written at all. This comment presumably hints at the stipulation in his contract with the Emin Pasha Relief Committee that allowed him a six-month headstart, but which – even before his arrival in Cairo – was undermined by the scandalous disclosures in London. If Stanley did not finish the official account in time, they would have missed their chance to publish a version that was backed by the committee's institutional authority, legitimacy and marketing.

Stanley's shock at the encounter with the city's luxury after three years on the expedition, described in his *Autobiography*, and his immense difficulties with transforming "a farrago of nonsense, incoherent, yet confusedly intense" into a harmonious organ composition or a magnificent construction in glass and steel similar to the Crystal Palace, in addition to the time pressure to provide the first authoritative account, are all factors that are confirmed by Marston's account. Stanley takes to throwing things at a waiter, who consequently invents a bamboo pole system with which he can deliver the many hundreds of telegrams that – much to Stanley's annoyance – keep arriving from all over the world. Except for a brief trip to the Nile, whose sources to the west he had discovered shortly before at the no longer "fabulous 'Mountains of the Moon'", he did not leave Hotel Villa Victoria before he had finished the book. When the two friends are contemplating the Nile, Stanley laconically comments that now that Marston has discovered its *mouth*, they might as well get on with the book (p. 23).

The process was hard work, given that Marston was determined to take back with him a finished manuscript and all the sketches and maps. The photographs that Stanley took on the expedition were especially valuable; however, most of them prove to be useless as anything but vague guides for the illustrator who transforms them into sketches. Many of them were either over or underexposed because of the extreme climatic conditions under which they were taken; a few, however, represented "scenes of greatest value, artistically and geographically". They were all carefully copied, so that Marston could bring one set back to London in an insured suitcase, which indicates the value ascribed to the manuscript that would later be published in hundreds of thousands of copies and come to redefine the scales of targeted production for the global literary market.

The market perspective is emphasised through Marston's anecdotes about the truckloads of letters that arrive "from all parts of the world", with distinc-

tions, nominations, blackmail, invitations and congratulations – among many others from Mark Twain, one of Stanley's devout admirers. One rich American wants at "a fanny price" to buy Stanley's "old cap" – the peculiar headgear with net and air holes that Stanley designed – as part of a "collection of curiosities". The bidder promises Stanley that it "shall be preserved in a glass case with your name on same" (p. 53). The producers of various commodities also seek permission to use Stanley's name, e.g. in the marketing of a "first-class quality of cigar" (Stanley's only vice was cigars). The marketing of Stanley himself and of tents, suitcases, medicine, typewriters, and so on were seen as parts of the same international marketing strategy.

Marston writes about the American publishers' tricks and scams in the stiff competition to obtain "the copyright and entire control of his great work for the United States and Canada", a competition that would ultimately be won by Scribner's Sons. Even before Stanley had arrived in Zanzibar, innumerable plagiaristic works and compilations of older material, letters and articles had each been announced as the long-awaited account of the Emin Pasha Relief Expedition. One of these titles was called "Heroes of the Dark Continent. – The Great and Only Genuine and Complete History of Africa and African Exploration, including Stanley's Last Expedition. – Tremendous Success of this Great Standard Work. New Plates! New Edition!! Everything New!!!"

For the legitimate publishers waiting for Stanley to finish the real thing, the situation was unbearable. Arthur Scribner therefore travelled the thousands of kilometres to Cairo to obtain a letter from Stanley: "Notice to the American Public", which was printed in American newspapers as a warning against forgeries, and to authorise Scribner's exclusive rights to the announced work entitled "In Darkest Africa".

In Stanley's both complimentary and patronising preface to Jephson's travel account, which had a full-page advert in Marston's book, an important passage is devoted to discussion of the insufficient protection of authors' copyrights. Particularly in Jephson's case, since he personally donated £1,000 to the expedition and will expect to receive the profits of the sales, the need for an "International Copyright Law" is strong, writes Stanley. The situation for Jephson is that if he does not become an American citizen, or explicitly write the book in collaboration with an American, he will not be entitled to the American rights. In the preface Stanley states he assisted Jephson in the writing process; this acknowledgement is an attempt to establish an informal basis for prosecuting "unauthorized imitations" on both sides of the Atlantic.

In Stanley's case, we are dealing with an even closer link between copyright and the weight of testimonies. In the dispute of authenticity around *How I Found Livingstone*, an audience with Queen Victoria was decisive for the Royal

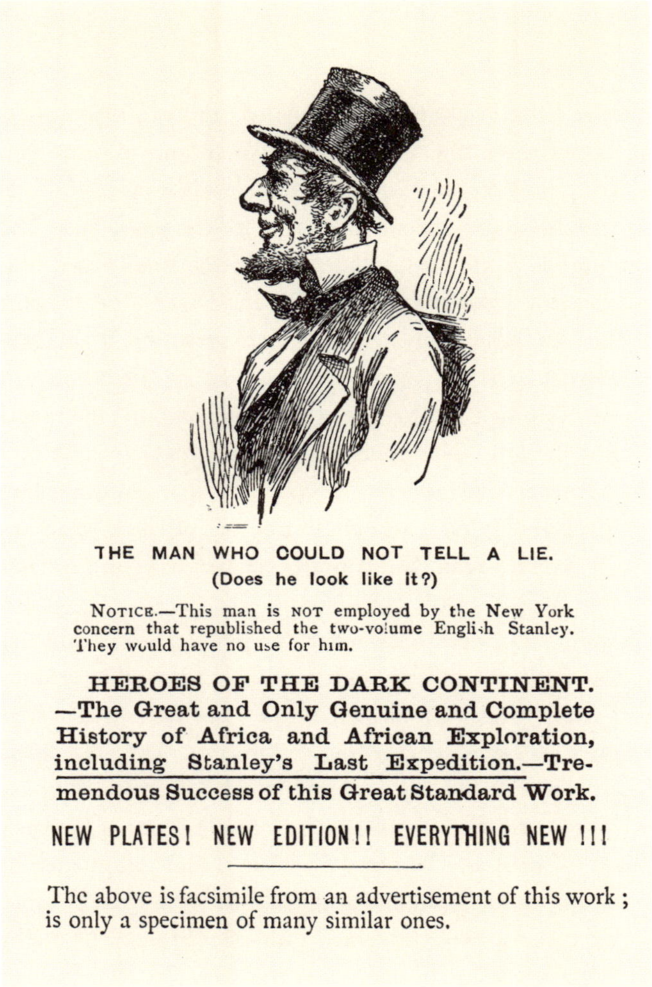

Many of Marston's and Stanley's strategic considerations about the editing of the book pertain to copyrights in the European and American markets. However, copyrights did not only relate to sales numbers and, e.g., specific dates of release in the different markets; they also played a role in the planning and organising of the expedition and the reception of the testimonies, for instance in relation to credibility. Stanley maintained his American citizenship in order to protect his copyrights, the consequence of which was that he could not accept an order from Queen Victoria – though it would have boosted his authority in relation to the disputes in London. Marston's illustration is a fake advertisement for Buel's *Heroes of the Dark Continent*, which was printed in two editions during 1890. It is a cleverly made pirate version with well-written accounts of all the famous expeditions in Africa, focusing on the most spectacular and dramatic elements with lots of illustrations in full colour. "New Edition" was published before Stanley's official account, updated with the latest rumours from the Emin Pasha Relief Expedition, excerpts from diaries, and the infamous drawings of Jameson's cannibal story: Marston was facing fierce competition.

Geographical Society's reluctant acknowledgement of Stanley's discoveries. Although the queen herself was rather reserved, her acceptance prompted a number of important compromises between the venerable, although obdurate, institution and the successful, uneducated journalist with the shady past. The media storm surrounding the Emin Pasha Relief Expedition finally died out, among other reasons because both the newspapers and Stanley once again managed to sustain the inexplicable mystery that had surrounded the case from the beginning. However, Stanley could have secured a good headstart in the dispute of testimonies had he not – to Queen Victoria's astonishment and regret – chosen to decline the offer of ennoblement and distinction as GCMG and *Sir* Stanley. He had become an American citizen in 1885 in order to protect his books against unauthorised copies, and could not accept the distinction without changing his citizenship again and running the risk of losing considerable royalties.

While Stanley's position was weak with regard to prestige, class and nationality, the market forces were definitely on his side in the conflict around the Emin Pasha Relief Expedition. None of the moral questions were solved through legal proceedings, as noted with regret in *The Times*. They remained in a twilight zone, where they – as Stanley had predicted – continued to breed new, authority-subverting horror fictions of which Conrad's *Heart of Darkness* was to become the most influential. The focus on what actually happened in the Yambuya camp – the question of Stanley's responsibility, as well as the more dangerous and profound disclosure of the sentimental decadence of Barttelot and Jameson – was overshadowed by the success of the sales figures. Marston often mentions this in his letters to Stanley. In an early example, responding to the attacks against Stanley caused by the telegrams' dramatised version of the punishment of Bumbireh in the trans-African expedition, Marston offers reassurance: "Your assumed cruelties in slaughtering inoffensive natives (...). Never mind them. Come home and write a good book as quick as possible and it will sell well". Presumably, good sales figures would subdue the critics (SA, No. 5521, 18 October 1877).

In Darkest Africa's rhetorical power and scope, along with the unprecedented media hype surrounding it, established him as an international icon. In Berlin, the hastily written *Stanley in Africa* was performed before a full house; in Reykjavik, a welcome tune was printed; and in London, Stanley and Emin were portrayed on mugs and plates, in spite of their embittered relationship. Richard Hall mentions several examples of the penetration of the 'Stanley' brand in *Stanley: An Adventurer Explorer*. These include an advertisement for tea, showing Emin and Stanley sitting together in the forest. Stanley says: "Well, Emin, old fellow, this cup of the United Kingdom Tea Company's Delicious Tea makes us forget all our troubles", and Emin answers: "So it does, old boy" (Hall, p. 335). All ethical and political obstacles are evened out in the simultaneous marketing of the travel account *In Darkest Africa*, Stanley-related products and Stanley himself as a product. Tim Youngs mentions a jigsaw puzzle, "Stanley in Africa", which contains scenes with titles such as "During this period we lost 69 men from starvation and sickness" and "Camp fire at night, Stanley talking to his men". None of the scenes, however, are called "Mr Jameson witnessing a cannibalistic murder" or "Major Barttelot shot dead" (Youngs, p. 173).

The Stanley products, including *In Darkest Africa*, were marketed in numerous sophisticated ways, Marston's little book being one of them and Stanley's lecture tour another. On his tours of Britain, the European continent and the USA, Stanley sold his message to a market that had already been prepared by considerable media hype. The marketing of *In Darkest Africa*, however, was not only a sales activity addressing the finished product; it also played a part in the actual creation of the travel account, which functioned as an advertising space from which a long list of products were marketed to a vast audience. The book's lengthy introduction contained a kind of shopping list, presented as an acknowledgement of companies who sponsored the journey by putting custom-made products at the expedition's disposal, e.g.:

"Messrs. Burroughs, Welcome & Co., of Snowhill Buildings, London, the well-known chemists, furnished gratis nine beautiful chests replete with every medicament necessary to combat the endemic diseases peculiar to Africa" (*IDA* I, p. 38);

"Messrs. John Edginton & Co., of Duke Street, London, took charge of our tents, and made them out of canvas dipped in a preservative of sulphate of copper, which preserved them for three years" (I, p. 38);

"Messrs. Fortnum & Mason, of Piccadilly: Every article was superb, the tea retained its flavour to the last, the coffee was of the purest Mocha, the Liebig Company's Extract was of the choicest, and the packing of all was excellent" (I, p. 39).

Stanley's purpose-built steel boat and his Maxim machine gun are also mentioned as recommendable products, tested under extreme conditions. Everything was an interplay between sponsorships, advertisements for products in the book and advertisements for the book via the products. The pharmaceutical company Welcome used excerpts from Stanley's and Parke's travel books about the Emin Pasha Relief Expedition to promote their products, for instance with a full-page advertisement in Marston's *How Stanley wrote 'In Darkest Africa'*. With *In Darkest Africa* acknowledging and integrating various products, different values

were exchanged and counterbalanced, resulting in an effective assimilation and acceptance of the expedition that Stanley could never have hoped to achieve through the newspapers' moral disputes.

Under the headline "Advertisements" in Marston's book, there are two in particular that exemplify the expedition's integration into popular culture. One of these is for Gilbert and Rivingston Ltd, regarding "An Interesting Memento" on the occasion of the Stanley and African Exhibition, an anthropological exhibition that was arranged in the wake of the expedition. It displayed various items from the exhibition, such as "Map of Africa, showing Mr. Stanley's route during the recent Emin Pasha Relief Expedition" – "The whole reproduced from the Copyright Originals by special permission". The other advertisement is for Woodrise & Rawson United Ltd, producers of electric light. It is an impressive collage of text and images from Africa and Stanley's expedition, creating a link between the expedition's and colonialism's staple trope of bringing light to Africa, the title of Stanley's book and commercial electric lights – the culmination of European technology and know-how. The text reads: "What is wanted in Darkest Africa is the Electric Light".

Edward Marston's book goes to great lengths to emphasise the international scope of this market. His and Scribner's journeys around the world make use of a Phileas Fogg-inspired race against time, in which metropolises and cultural highlights are mere coordinates in time and space, only significant for their relation to the completion of Stanley's book. They are publishers for a worldwide market, not tourists or travellers, and when the book is finished and on its way through the printing process, a complicated network of travels has ensured simultaneous publication in a vast number of countries. At a banquet two days before the publication, Marston declares "the statistics of the work" as follows:

"The work contains, roughly speaking, a thousand pages of forty lines each. On January 25 of this year, not a line of it had been written. Then it was that Mr. Stanley sat down at the Villa Victoria in Cairo, with a firm determination that nothing earthly should stop him till he had finished it. In fifty days he completed his self-imposed task, or rather the task which he says I imposed upon him. This means that he not merely wrote out, but he had to think out, twenty pages, say, 8000 words, a day. Gentlemen, if you wish to know what an amount of endurance and perseverance that means, I recommend you to try the experiment yourselves. It is easy enough to write twenty very long pages a day, for one, two, or three days, but to keep on doing so for fifty days consecutively, without any break or relaxation whatever to speak of, is quite another matter. Now let me glance at the manufacture of these volumes. In view of the enormous amount of public interest felt in this book I see no objection for once to depart from our usual reticence in such matters, and to say that we have

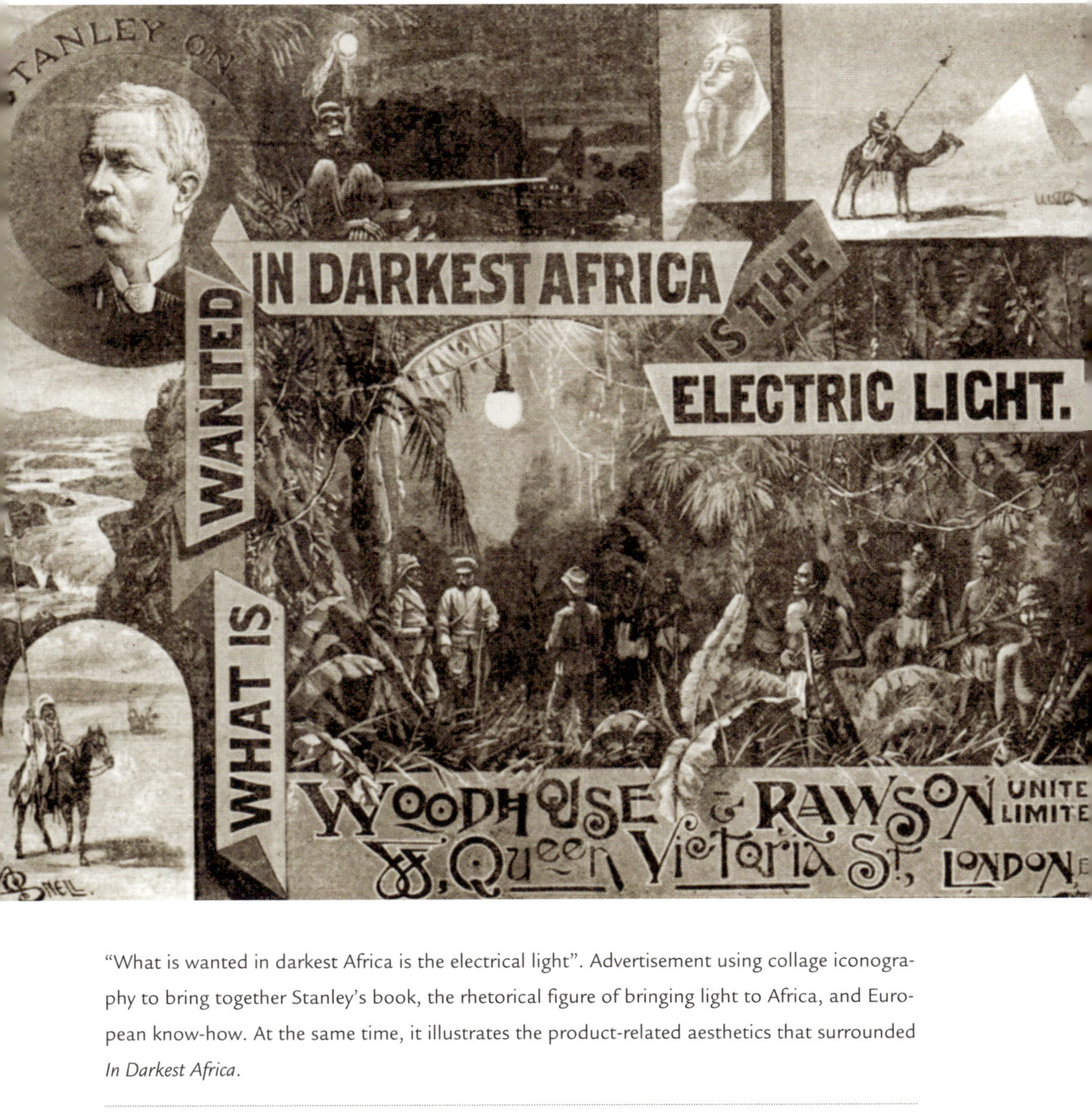

"What is wanted in darkest Africa is the electrical light". Advertisement using collage iconography to bring together Stanley's book, the rhetorical figure of bringing light to Africa, and European know-how. At the same time, it illustrates the product-related aesthetics that surrounded *In Darkest Africa*.

orders in the house for, and on Saturday morning we shall despatch, over 16,000 copies, besides 6000 of a colonial edition, and other issues. You know the whole thing had to be rushed through the press, and I assure you it has taxed the resources of Messrs. Clowes' vast establishment for many weeks. To produce this book in the way it has been produced required something more than mere routine work. It required a thoughtful guiding spirit – one who would devote heart and soul to the work, and

Stanley gave a talk on the Emin Pasha expedition at the Royal Albert Hall. It was a multimedia show in which he described "the great forest" and addressed a large audience like a professional performer in the old-fashioned style. After the Livingstone expedition, Stanley had addressed the Royal Geographical Society in a gesticulatory and 'American' style that was far too populist for the audience of British academics, and later he had to cancel a large-scale tour in the USA after disappointing American audiences with a dry, scientific talk. After that, he learned to captivate his audiences wherever they were, and he earned large sums on royalties by touring both Europe and the USA in the wake of his travel book successes. From *The Graphic*, 10 May 1890.

we cannot feel too grateful to Captain Clowes for the extraordinary devotion and personal attention he has given to the accomplishment of this task. In the printing department the work has found employment for many weeks for 60 compositors, 17 readers, 12 reading boys, and about 200 machine-pressmen and warehousemen. The paper consumed in printing the *édition de luxe*, the colonial edition, the canvassing edition, and the trade edition weighs 65 ½ tons. This paper, if it had been laid out in single sheets, would have formed a white carpet for Mr. Stanley to have walked upon from the Congo to Zanzibar, or if laid sheet upon sheet it would have formed a tower something like the Tour Eiffel. The type and material used weighed 7 ½ tons, and there were 2,500,000 types used in each of the above editions. Eighteen steam printing machines and ten hand presses consumed 1 ½ tons of printing ink. Then as to the binding, we had to get bound in a fortnight, in all, about 40,000 volumes. These have given employment to over 500 men and 600 women. About 4,500 yards, or nearly 2 ½ miles of binder's cloth were consumed on these editions. Now, as there have been produced simultaneously in America and on the Continent about ten other editions, I think I should not be far out in stating that it would be quite within the mark to multiply all the figures I have mentioned by 7 or 8. Taking the latter estimate, Mr. Stanley may comfort himself with the reflection that during the last four months his fifty days' labour of brain and pen has given employment to an army of probably seven thousand men and at least as many women and girls, and probably the aggregate weight of all the editions which will be issued simultaneously on Saturday will exceed three hundred tons" (Marston, pp. 72-74).

The correspondence between Stanley and Marston tells a similar story of extravagant figures and new breakthroughs on the book market. *Through the Dark Continent* and *The Congo and the Founding of its Free State* had both been best-sellers, the latter breaking records upon its launch on the worldwide market. In a letter from 28 January 1885, Marston had written to Stanley that he – in consideration of the American and Canadian markets – must be quick in getting his American citizenship, as Marston had already arranged the publication and rights in Germany, Spain, France, Scandinavia, etc., and was only waiting for the sign to arrange simultaneous publication across the Atlantic (SA, No. 1585). The expectations of earnings from *In Darkest Africa* on the world market were even greater: even before the book was finished, Marston assured Stanley that "You will produce a book surpassing in interest and in sale anything you yet have done" (SA, No. 1597, 30.11.1889), and he encouraged Stanley to lock the door behind him, so he will not be tempted by other publishers' less serious offers. In a telegram to Zanzibar Station on 6 December 1889, Marston requests authorisation to arrange the "worldwide" publication of the book. Not long after its release, *In Darkest Africa* had exceeded even Marston's wildest hopes:

"I confess that the result of *I.D.A.* has exceeded my most sanguine expectations, your profit amounts to £ 21,006. Suppose Scribner's will do at least as much to you, I should not be surprised to learn that your total profit from the Book and your lectures will approach £ 60,000 - probably the largest amount ever made by one book in so short a period of time" (SA, No. 1626, 7.2.1891).

Aftermath

Stanley's officers thought of him as unpredictable, uncommunicative and ruthless. Jephson's account of Stanley's attempt to humiliate and patronise his younger subordinate in order to create a ridiculously glorified image of himself offers insight into a person whose self-understanding lacked a basis in reality, and whose authority to a great degree was founded on unacknowledged rhetorical father figures. The Africans were all lumped together as children, the Zanzibaris were his own children, and it was impossible for him to acknowledge equal, European men, unless they complied with their roles as sons who must be reared and encouraged within the paternalistic discourse of honour and duty. After becoming acquainted with Emin Pasha in April 1888, Jephson compares the two men's characters and styles:

"It is wonderful with what love and affection his people speak of him (Emin) & how they all look up to & revere him - what a difference from our leader with whom things are done by sheer brute force only. Murabo my chief amused me very much yesterday, he said 'the Bwana M'kubwa - Stanley - is half a white man & half an Arab'. That describes Stanley very well. All the falseness & double dealing, the indifference to breaking his word, the meanness, brutality & greediness, are the Arab side. The wonderful powers of resource, the indomitable energy & strength of mind, the dogged determination to carry through to successful issue all that he takes in hand, his cleverness in mapping, writing, conversation etc. all belong to the European side. He has two distinct characters, one cannot be too much admired & praised the other is contemptible in the extreme" (Jephson, p. 248).

It has been mentioned that it is tempting to understand Jephson's, Jameson's and Parke's attacks on Stanley as signs of their own weaknesses and doubtful fitness for the task. Nevertheless, they all express unconditional respect for Stanley, and their mistrust is often based on paranoia on account of their lack of relevant knowledge and linguistic abilities; they tend to stick to the tight-knit group of Europeans, while Stanley camps with his native carriers. As the reading of the forest chapter suggested, what Jephson, in a striking characterisation, presents as two conflicting aspects of Stanley's nature can be understood as reactions to the same problem: Stanley's fluid identity. His impressive writing skills, however, are not in conflict with his "falseness and double dealing", and his determination to complete tasks is but another aspect of the self-control that is nothing more than a veneer to conceal the chaos that the expedition, the mapping and the travel account all aim to resolve into something meaningful.

In the preface to Monteney Jephson's *Emin Pasha and the Rebellion at the Equator: A Story of nine Months' Experiences in the last of the Soudan Provinces* (1890), Stanley appears friendly when he expresses his understanding that all his fellow officers will probably print their own accounts – having noticed that they have been making "valuable notes of the expedition" (Jephson, p. vii). He is, however, particularly pleased with Jephson's book, because it will "not in the least traverse my ground". In the preface, Stanley acknowledges the fact that one of the other participants "no doubt is describing what he has seen and done from his own point of view", and he admits that a matter can contain different truths, depending on the point of view. According to Marston, this moderated statement from Stanley had a beneficial influence on the media storm (SA, No. 1622, 22 November 1890).

In the retrospective *Autobiography*, Stanley assesses the competing testimonies with a lot more scepticism. In response to the criticism of his terrible temper he reminds the reader that it is unfair to expect a man who finds himself in Africa, suffering unbearable pain and fever, pumped full of quinine, to "smile like a full-dreamer at home". Then he offers an explanation for one of the precautionary measures the officers found difficult to accept: in "intermittent periods of gloom and bitterness, when the temper is tindery", Stanley preferred to locate his camp apart from the others, knowing from bitter experience that his random comments far too often had given rise to

"too much 'copy' for note-books, and that my friends were in the habit of indiscriminately setting down every word, too often in a perverted sense, and continually taking snap-shots at me, without the usual formula of the photographer, 'Look pleasant, please!' On the Congo, it is too hot to stand on an open-air pedestal for long! One *must* be in 'undress', occasionally; and during such times he is not supposed to be posing for the benefit of Fleet Street! Then, upon the strength of table acquaintance, I found that the young men were apt to become overweening, familiar, and oblivious of etiquette and discipline. From that date, I took to living alone, by which my judgment of my subordinates was in no danger of being biased by their convivial discourse; and I was preserved from the contempt which too often proceeds from familiarity" (*Autobiography*, p. 384).

"Henry M. Stanley and his officers 1890", from *Autobiography*. Parke, Nelson, Stairs, and Jephson were loyal to Stanley and did not become involved in the conflicts about the aftermath of the expeditions. Parke's and Jephson's published travel accounts follow the course pointed out in the official account; only their diaries provide an impression of Stanley in 'undress' – situations in which he loses self-control, takes rash decisions, or reveals himself as vain and vulnerable behind the tough exterior. The image does not reveal that Barttelot had bitten a native woman on the cheek and used other natives as shooting targets; neither does it reveal Jameson's excesses. The official expedition photo is this well-kempt palm garden; however, even before the expedition had returned home, this impression was counteracted when those voices referred to by Stanley as "silent witnesses" started telling the most inconceivable stories.

This passage is more restrained than the satirical passage in *In Darkest Africa*, where Stanley raved against the horror fictions that emerged from the Yambuya camp. But it picks up on several leads we have followed through the Emin Pasha material. Stanley seems to think that his judgement is enhanced by his distance from the other officers, while their notebooks claim the opposite. In the officers' view, many of the expedition's errors are due to Stanley's inability to empathise with and acknowledge other people's experiences. The passage also highlights Stanley's dedication to avoiding exposure that might put him in a bad light. On a more general level, it indicates a conflict between the journey's reality in "undress" and the edited version presented to the reader in the travel books – something that is simultaneously hinted at as a conflict between Stanley's and the officers' points of view. Once more we can see how Stanley acted and reflected on the basis of the travel account's discursive terms, while his companions' understanding was generally very limited and certainly more naïve. Furthermore, it emphasises the above-mentioned difference between the officers' tendency to travel through Africa inside a sealed, self-sufficient container, defined by European values, and Stanley's ability to distinguish between the theoretical and practical aspects of the journey. The conditions for completing the latter were to a large extent defined by the ability and will to abandon European habits and expectation, instead accepting a state of "undress" to imitate native languages and practices. The testimony is dependent on point of view, but it is also a staged or theatrical pose for the camera.

We have lingered over Stanley's allegorical strategy and the "mystery" shrouding the expedition; however, Jameson's, Jephson's, Barttelot's and the other testimonies are obviously also framed in rhetoric that constitutes certain challenges and limitations. In Jameson's and Barttelot's diaries, we are dealing with testimonies that have been given without knowledge or intention. Their families only used the diaries in one last attempt to save the honour and morale of their late relatives after Stanley's accusations of betrayal and defiance. In Jameson's brother's preface – in which, ironically, he repeats Stanley's motto "Let there be light" – the posthumous circumstances are used as rhetorical support of the testimony's credibility, albeit in a paradoxical form that also has a subversive effect:

"The charges are brought against Jameson when he is in his grave, when the common usage of humanity suggests silence, and when a man of noble and honourable cast of nature would altogether prefer to lie under an unjust suspicion rather than asperse and defame the voiceless dead" (Jameson, p. xvi).

In defence of Jameson it is also stated that because the diary was not written for publication but "self-revelation," his "true personality" is portrayed – "no man lies to himself" – and the diary is one, long testimony to "duty, kindliness, and hard work". Stanley, on the other hand, uses all kinds of rhetorical means to exploit his readers' unreserved admiration in order to destroy others' reputations, according to Andrew Jameson. Blinded by his faith in the persuasive power of his own celebrity, Stanley does not imagine that the dead someday will

respond. The publication of the diary is an attempt to give voice to "the voiceless dead" who cannot tell anything but the truth, while Stanley with his journalistic rhetoric is capable of appearing credible even when he is lying. In any case, in Andrew Jameson's view Stanley ought to have resorted to lies, whether or not the suspicions were well-founded, rather than breaching decorum – here, the unwritten rule that you cannot accuse someone who cannot defend himself. With this argument, Jameson reaches back to another critical internal conflict in nineteenth-century sentimental travel literature.

The arguments behind the presentation of Jameson's testimony are far-fetched, to say the least. Furthermore, it is striking that the preface tries to question the cannibal story by discrediting the Syrian interpreter's eyewitness account, which he presented to the Congolese authorities, on the grounds that the testimony in Jameson's diary presents roughly the same story. The differences are that Farran leaves no doubt that Jameson was completely aware that he ordered the murder and consumption of the girl – something he had allegedly been planning long before they arrived in the village – and that Jameson drew the acts *while* they were taking place, not later the same day as Jameson claims.[81] Andrew Jameson's point is that the portrait of his brother's *character* is so strong and unquestionable that it counteracts what both the eyewitness and Jameson *himself* have said about the episode. Because Jameson is dead and "voiceless", consideration for what is 'appropriate' – his class, character and decorum – outweigh any other testimony.

In the public opinion, however, the payment for the cannibalistic murder was a grievous fact. The handkerchief currency shocked Victorian England by exposing and making literal the hidden link between the market and colonialism on the one hand and the perversion of sensitivity into voyeuristic and sadistic pleasure on the other – as we have seen in Jameson's vague distinctions between "looting", "collecting", "skinning" and "sketching".

On the other side of the Atlantic, the newspapers had no problem with being explicit and critical in relation to Jameson's character, given that it could be associated with un-American 'Britishness'. A review in the *New York Times* does not mince words, reading the diary as a strangely blind, shameless self-revelation of the double moral standards behind the Victorian façade.[82] The review mentions the cannibalism story, which was notorious at the time of publication, but also reads the whole diary as a testimony to a pervasive decadence. Despite his contract, Jameson acted out his idea of the expedition as a hunting trip. The text's confessions show little consideration of duty and sacrifice, but rather a detached preoccupation with pleasure, pastime and sport, and the reviewer also notices Jameson's failing sense of reality which is both romantic and brutally insensitive. Jameson, in other words, is a typical "English gentleman".

Above, the expedition's mute, internal conflicts regarding central events of the journey, and in the accounts and their reception, have been traced through a number of prose texts, on different levels of explanation and interpretation. The letters, diaries and accounts are conflicting, both in enunciative position and genre; however, that only makes their testimonies of a disintegrating world more convincing as real experiences of internal collapse expressed through prose experiments. The classic discourse of extroverted discovery is replaced by introverted doubt about identity and place. The authority and credibility of Stanley's previous travel accounts, although they were under fire, could still be discussed within the decorum regulated by conservative institutions, such as the Royal Geographical Society. Acknowledgement of the Emin Pasha Relief Expedition, on the contrary, depended on two, partly contradictory, factors: the British newspaper-reading public and the international literary market.

The link between court cases and copyrights, which is visible on all levels of the material, indicates the difficulty of interpreting, in the sense of *assimilating*, the account of the expedition when the old institutions have lost their power and the new ones have yet to gain a solid footing. In that respect, the British newspapers' coverage of the events is telling: first, it contributed to the staging of the dream-like plot; second, it helped subvert the expedition's credibility; third, it appealed either for silence or for settling the matter via a court case – terrified that the seemingly never-ending stream of horror tales would tear the decorum of the upper classes and the foundation of the nation apart. The reception of Jameson's diary highlighted, in particular, the clash between class privilege decorum and a public sphere based on mass media, without fully acknowledging it. The reception of Stanley's *In Darkest Africa* furthermore emphasised the conflicts between one camp among the British public, whose self-understanding was changing as the empire disintegrated, and another whose conditions were defined by the global market, itself increasingly controlled by American interests.

The following, conclusive chapter will return to Jameson's and Stanley's contributions to the dominant western literary-historical understanding of Africa and the Congo. The two texts come from two very different traditions. Jameson's diary belongs to the sentimental tradition's problematic repression of place and displays the ruthless underside of sentimentality. Stanley's, on the other hand, shows an effort to overcome sentimental discourse, although it never manages to escape it completely. *Through the Dark Continent* is organised in accordance with the antithesis between light and logos on the one hand and darkness and pathos on the other; *In Darkest Africa* contains a similar structure. In the last passages of the book, Stanley allows the light and sun to dissolve all the ghostly, pathetic testimonies, while at the same time making sure that

they will live on by shrouding them in the mystery/misery discourse. In doing so, Stanley paved the way for the pathetic and mystifying rhetoric of exclusion that characterises twentieth-century narratives about the Congo. At the same time, his pragmatic attitude and modern prose represent a model alternative, which will be examined at the end of the following chapter.

3 The Space of Prose: Magic and Pragmatism

The chapter "Anthropoetic Narrative and Method" ended with a discussion of Claude Lévi-Strauss' and Paul Ricœur's positions on the writing of history and the suggestion that the narratives about the Congo be read from a prose perspective. Reference was made to the point that one of the routes away from literary history's internal contradictions, which have threatened to paralyse the field, is to adopt Lévi-Strauss' ideas about historical studies as field studies, where there is no distinction between different types of sources, but rather between their density of information. Biographies and travel accounts, for example, are rich in varied information, while historical accounts, for instance, explain more but contain less information. This type of field work would facilitate a bridge between formalistic analysis and studies of the works' contexts. In the same vein, Paul Ricœur has described historic archival material as a continuous field of text forms, in which the same basic aporia apply to the construction of both primary sources and historical narrative – and in continuation whereof he has emphasised the importance of historic testimonies, including the contemporary criticism of testimonies.

This book's reading of Stanley's autobiography, *Through the Dark Continent* and *In Darkest Africa* have been attempts to construct a literary-historical narrative about Stanley's prose under the conditions of field work, by using a broad selection of texts and archival material with different degrees of information density and explanatory power. The effort has consisted in explaining – and thereby reducing – the density of meaning in texts such as the autobiography and the forest chapter, which, read separately, are completely valid testimonies about what, in the introduction, were termed anthropoetic narratives. Furthermore, the travel books have been compared with sources and primary testimonies, mainly found in the Stanley Archives in Tervuren. The letters and diaries are parts of the prose, rather than its firm ground or explanation. On the contrary, it has been the experience – one that is obviously not unique to the topic of this book – that the deeper one delves down in the explanatory hierarchy, the more inexplicable matters are raised. It is possible to reach certain conclusions by including the correspondence and diaries, but they really only emphasise the lacunae. Where, for instance, are the crucial sketches Jameson drew of the cannibalistic incident? Are they in the family's care, or did Stanley destroy them on his arrival at the Yambuya camp or later, when he realised that a scandal was in the offing? Was Bonny's account of Jameson's

"Stanley and Joseph Bell, the artist, preparing sketches", from Marston's *How Stanley Wrote 'In Darkest Africa'*. A lot of effort was put into the travel book illustrations, and the many contributors and processes required thorough discussions. Rather than aiming to illustrate situations with 100 per cent accuracy, the artwork was intended to recreate the sensory perception of the journey in a performatively effectual manner. In this way, illustrations and maps contribute to creating the many different spaces of the book – what can be defined as its 'magic'.

encounter with cannibalism and Barttelot's inclination to extreme violence only overheard by Jephson, who did not savour Bonny's vulgar pleasure in telling it, or did Stanley hear it too – and was thus prepared when Bonny reported it to him?

The previous chapters have mapped different spaces in Stanley's prose that are conflicting and constitute the heterotopic conditions which, in the introduction, were mentioned as an early characteristic of travel literature. The following, final chapter on Stanley will investigate how these spaces are interlinked and how Stanley's texts appear from within the prose perspective described in the introduction.

The antithesis between light and darkness functions as a compositional principle, as well as defining the distribution of rationality and pathos and structuring the text's constructions of space and place. It is a classical composition; however, in the beginning of the nineteenth century it was applied to

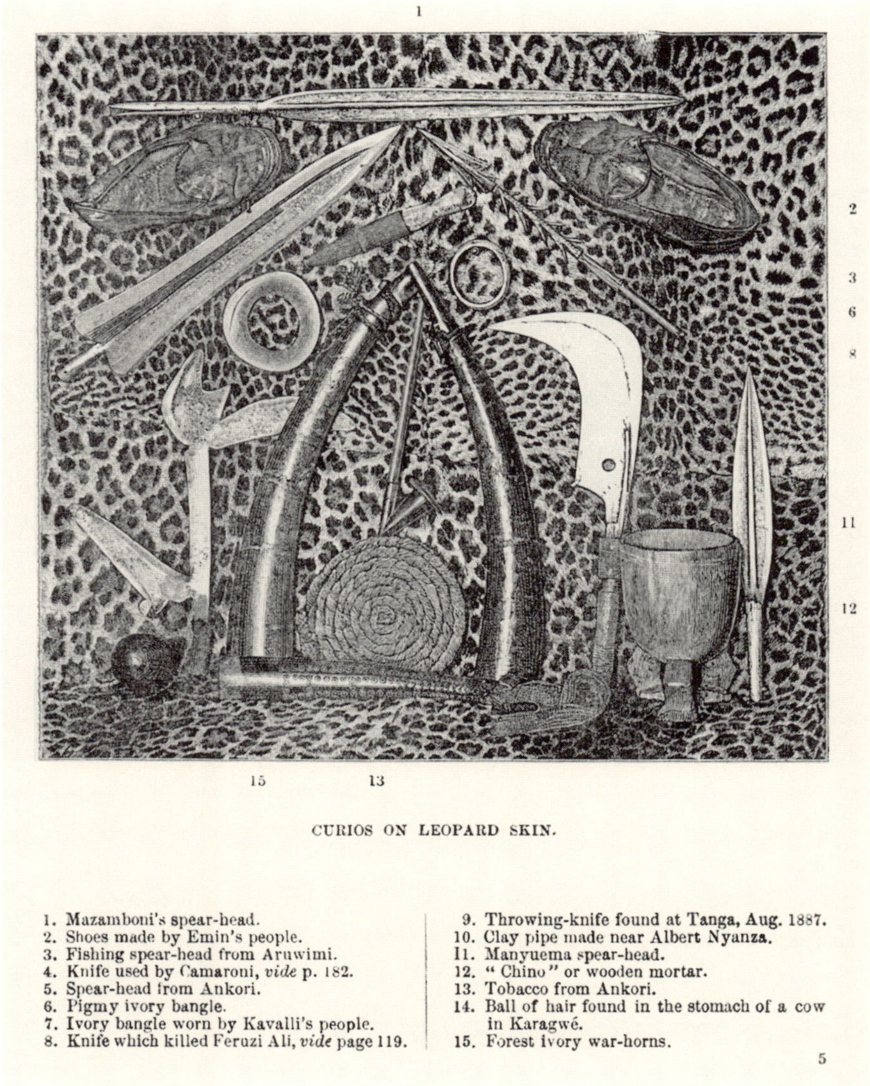

"Curios on leopard skin", from Parke's *My Personal Experiences in Equatorial Africa* (1891). Parke's book includes a supplement about the progresses of modern science in the fields of bacteriology and tropical illnesses; in light of that, it is difficult to place the photographic fascination of unique, powerful objects that belongs somewhere between European curiosity and African fetish.

the abolitionist movements' descriptions of Africa, from which it moved on to Victorian travel accounts. To Stanley, it was also the recognisable form in which the texts encountered their readers. Stanley's prose, however, is written in globalised terms and far removed from classical rhetoric. The first part of the next chapter will examine what has been called the texts' 'magical properties' in this book – mentioned, for instance, in relation to the natives' description

of Stanley's field notebook as a fetish. The terms "magical" and "fetish" are not meant to indicate that Stanley or the travel accounts possess supernatural properties. Instead, they are used as collective terms for the texts' amazing scope and performative strength, as generators of history with relation both to public opinion and to the literary market. It is highly unusual, and in some ways unnatural, for books to have such a massive effect over such long distances, though it was obviously in part due to a number of mechanisms in both their rhetorical and material design – for example the function of illustrations and maps.

The second part will identify what may superficially look like the opposite of magic – Stanley's pragmatism. His determination and leadership was supported by resilience and a talent for negotiation; his invocations of God and descriptions of epiphanic or apocalyptic experiences are exceptions in an otherwise non-metaphysical universe. His pragmatic attitude had two conflicting expressions that would come to influence the long-term effect of the travel books. One was his attempt to obtain maximal control of the public reception of the final, scandalous expedition, which kept him from shedding ultimate light on its involuntary, but important, 'discovery' – the gloomy, sealed space of cannibalism. The other was Stanley's confident, exaggerated campaigning for free trade, demonstratively exhibited in these radically accessible textual spaces.

The following two chapters also serve as a summary of the main points of this book's section about Stanley.

The Book as Fetish: Stanley's Magic

When we compare the finished travel books with the articles Stanley sent to the *New York Herald*, and later to other sponsoring newspapers, we come across significant differences due to the conditions and recipients of these texts, but also obviously the aspect of time. The intense reactions in Britain to the telegram's descriptions of Stanley's "punishment" of hostile natives on the island of Bumbireh led to a government ban on using the British flag on expeditions – something that Stanley for obvious reasons was unaware of. Subsequently, the account of the punishment was heavily edited and toned down in the travel book itself. When we compare Stanley's field notebooks and travel diaries, to which researchers have recently been granted access in the Stanley Archives at the Musée Royal de l'Afrique Centrale in Tervuren, there are also divergences.

In the extensive description of the stay with Mutesa, we find a development from field notes to letters and telegrams in the travel book that reveals an extensive editing process. Several of the reappraisals and modifications of the portrayal of Mutesa are directly linked to the sceptical reception of Stanley's initial, unreservedly admiring letters and telegrams which indicated that he had been caught up in the role of "dupe of the artful savage" (*Despatches*, p. 227). As early as the presentation of Mutesa in *Through the Dark Continent*, Stanley added a self-ironic omen of his revised perception, thus maintaining the reader's feeling of changing points of view while indicating his retrospective editing. In his first, hastily written telegram, Stanley boasts of having undermined Mutesa's newly adopted faith in Islam through only one conversation, and he summons all missionaries to Buganda while guaranteeing that the wealthy "Emperor" is willing to give the Europeans everything they want. Via Mutesa, whose subjects imitate his every movement, all of Africa could – according to Stanley – be colonised at one fell swoop. Stanley refers to another European, the Frenchman Linant de Bellefonds, as a witness to the fact: "Colonel Linant de Bellefonds is my witness that I speak the truth, and I know he will corroborate all I say" (*Despatches*, p. 227). Furthermore, Bellefonds becomes Stanley's courier of precious messages to the Christian, civilised world; however, he is killed during this duty, which only boosts the media's focus on the expedition, seizing the opportunity to create the canard that the telegrams were soaked in Bellefonds' blood.

The point is that Stanley's elaborated, yet witnessed, conversion of Mutesa, although it was only nominal, actually urged a vast number of missionary movements to focus on Buganda, which – in the long run – led to the colonisation that Stanley had predicted with little basis in reality. In spite of the reservations towards Stanley's apparently excessive admiration for Mutesa, the telegrams had a convincing effect and world-changing consequences. In the hasty telegram style of syntactical jumps and hurried summaries, sudden insertions and detailed instructions as to what the missionaries ought to bring with them on the journey, the impression is given that the missionaries are *already* on their way, and that Mutesa has already been converted and baptised.

In Stanley's notebook from this period we can identify keywords that are used in his later work, but also longer, detailed sketches of this plot, which was initially launched in the telegram and then expanded and refined for the travel book. Different tellings are prepared on the basis of their intended use in the two public versions, and several preliminary sketches are in evidence, such as "Notes on Uganda army, products, medicine", "A bit of history of Uganda" and "A peasant of Uganda", as well as brief statements such as "Mtesa (sic) is the most intelligent African (who owes his intelligence to his own natural capacity) in and out of Africa". In *Through the Dark Continent*, the conversion, baptism and transformation theme forms the basic structure of the entire Mutesa section;

it goes through a great number of variations with the same performative function. Figuratively, a colonial acquisition is created through writing; however, movement and emphasis on reversible mechanisms also highlight the narrator's unstable identity, which is rooted in Stanley's incoherent biography and the discursive terms constituted by New Journalism as genre.

The notebooks are never confessional, in contrast to those of the classic sentimental traveller. Rather, they can be characterised as sober and realistic, the many descriptive passages directed towards registrations of particular, primarily visual phenomena and landscapes. The degree of empathy and interpretation, on the other hand, is fairly limited. However, they are more than mere registrations of data to be developed in the narrative form of the travel books. The notebooks' materiality, and the preceptible effect of Stanley's surroundings and fatigue on his handwriting constitute additional layers – both in the margin and the text – that show signs of his active reading and editing of his notes *during* the journey. Several passages about Buganda are written after the stay with Mutesa, and parts of the text are drafts for the finished travel book, already addressed to an imagined reader. Throughout the entire journey, for instance, Stanley works on a chapter called "A journey into Africa", which clearly causes him trouble. Uncharacteristically, he struggles to write in the tradition of introductions from classical, so-called "apodemic" travel literature, providing educated reflections and instructions to the traveller who wants to follow in the writer's footsteps. As was the case with Carsten Niebuhr, the drafts appeal to the traveller to keep an open mind and avoid referring to European standards, because they will prevent him discovering Africa:

"If he is too much attached to home, and home pleasures, to the luxuries, refinements, and graces of civilized life it may be that he will yearn for them to such a degree that he will regret ever having left home, and his usings of Africa will become tinged with a sinly prejudice + his credibility as a witness for things African may be impeached" (SA, No. 3, December 1876).

Later, during the transfer of the notes to the edited version of the travel diary, which Stanley completed during the expedition, stylistic details were introduced that warned travellers against bringing their European expectations with them, which will only lead to "melancholy & depression", while travellers who are capable of leaving Europe behind will find great pleasure in the experience of something new. There are references to the passage again in notes from 27 April, where the apodemic instructions are supplemented with educated references to Shakespeare, which seem very far removed from the urgent challenges of the journey's present. The notebooks are not only raw material for the travel books –

and therefore closer to the immediate experience of the journey: they already articulate the plurality of incommensurable spaces which, in the introduction, was mentioned as a basic, heterotopic characteristic of travel literature. Even the field work's preliminary sorting of the data points in different directions at the same time.

In *Through the Dark Continent* we saw a figurative evocation of ancient Greek and Jewish-Biblical colonisations that were part of the paraphrasing of Buganda's history and the descriptions of the organisation of the royal court and the war against the Wavumas. This was an archaisation in which the *Odyssey* and the *Iliad* – presumably the versions Stanley found refuge in as a child – were incorporated into the notebooks and telegrams. They add complex historicising dimensions while simultaneously creating spaces in the text where elements of Stanley's autobiography and romanticised versions of the ancient epics could merge. One important consequence was the theatricalisation in which Mutesa's "Trojan fields" become a stage on which Stanley can perform his Homeric tricks – e.g. with the mysterious fort that even in the field notes take a magical turn. It is tempting to conclude that the series of revisions resulted in increased fictionalisations with each new layer, and on that basis brush the story aside as a typical "newspaper stunt". From the prose perspective, however, it is important to maintain that the increased theatricalisation, and the layers of asynchronous spaces, produce rather than impede performativity. If *Through the Dark Continent* in these passages removes itself from what we usually associate with credible representation, it still magically or figuratively creates a world, just as the narrator creates a portrait of a great explorer who transforms myth to scientific fact with unprecedented efficiency. With the dramatisation of the Trojan fort that is equipped with an invisible deep voice demanding peace, the text even pinpoints its own magical effect.

In the travel books, Stanley often explicitly makes use of long passages from his notebooks, specified as citations and on further inspection they prove more or less accurate. Obviously, this has an effect of increased authenticity, both because the citations from the notebooks substantiate a temporal link to the experiences of the journey, and because they facilitate stylistic closeness between travel book and notebook, thus counteracting the impression of revised orchestration. In *Through the Dark Continent*, the 'opening' of the heart of Africa, which in Stanley's prospectus is a medieval bestiary of curiosities and legends, is the effect of rhetorical magical formulae and shibboleths that force darkness to vanish. However, this also emphasises the book's own magical effect as a shibboleth that brings light to Africa.

The story about the superstitious natives who see his notebook as a fetish with terrifying powers is interesting in this context. First, its different versions

vary a great deal depending on where we look: the notebook, the fake citation in *Through the Dark Continent*, the telegram about the episode or the later version in the travel book. In the notebook, only one line is devoted to the episode; in the fake citation the description is expanded; the telegram turns the story into a drama; and in *Through the Dark Continent* it is played out in full force. The first versions note the natives' well-known curiosity about written language, and their association between "strong medicine" and the notebook, which they call "tara-tara, or looking-glass". In the telegram these notes are dramatised in a scene in which Stanley pretends to burn the notebook, having cunningly replaced it with a volume of Shakespeare (*Despatches*, p. 387). The version in *Through the Dark Continent* is full-blown, including dialogue that covers several pages, as the natives call the book a "fetish" and Stanley elaborates on its value, since it contains, in concentrate, the two volumes that essentialise all knowledge about Africa, anxiously expected by readers, and the historic changes that the travel book will come to instigate (*TDC* II, p. 386).

To Stanley, the notebook's magic is related to its function as *pars pro toto* of the travel book that will change Africa forever. To the natives, its magic consists in its power to destroy their existence: "This is very bad. Our country will waste, our goats will die, our bananas will rot, and our women will dry up. (...) Why is the Mundelé so wicked?"(*TDC* II, p. 385). In the notebook this is less elaborate: "The Malenis of East Mora became considerably excited to-day because I took my note book out, and wrote the names of things in their dialect. They say I make strong medicine to kill etc. their country" (SA, No. 19, 2.6.1877). Again: the episode expresses the precise effect of the two octavo volumes as fetishes in circulation on the literary market.

The series of editing processes incorporate a number of rhetorical techniques that respond to the demands of testimony and credibility without detracting from the text's authority, but rather installing it at other levels. Other revisions include the textual strategy that has been mentioned as supplement. The strategy is a classical one, also in the context of eighteenth-century travel accounts: chronology is dissolved to allow for chapters to be added after the return, often based on completely different material from the observations made on the journey.

These supplements often serve as mirrors for the questions of conscience that haunt Stanley during the journey, but also – and perhaps in particular – in the retrospective process of writing the account, in the light of new knowledge. In the forest chapter in *In Darkest Africa*, this mirror effect is used to such a degree that not only are the trees personified and Stanley's self-portrait merged with the landscape: any normal separating line between inner consciousness and outer observation, and between past memories, the presence of the journey

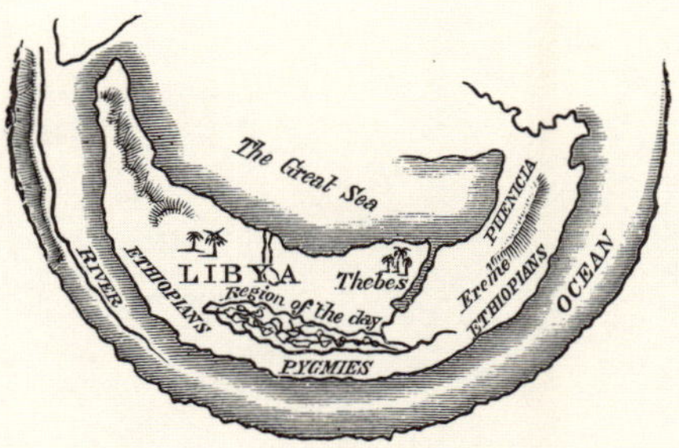

AFRICA IN HOMER'S WORLD.

An entire series of maps is inserted in Stanley's chapter "Map-makers in general". The aim was to demonstrate that the geographers of Antiquity possessed knowledge that was forgotten by later map makers. For centuries, explorers had arduously been plotting in places and coordinates, only for mapmakers to erase them. The maps in *In Darkest Africa* are, according to Stanley, above this irony of the era; however, the interesting and detailed account in the chapter suggests that Stanley's maps utilised existing local knowledge that was similarly erased in the completed European maps. In this manner, the maps perform a kind of magic trick that enhances the value of the book as fetish. The historical maps are copies from "old books in the Khedive's library in Cairo".

and the time of writing melt together in an impenetrable mystery. This happens even though the chapter begins with the intention of acting as a phenomenological correction of scientific fallacies. While it is possible to decode the parts of the allegory, its totality cannot be read as a representation of a real context, and yet this book contests that it supports a specific figure for the journey, which functions effectively in correlation with the book's rhetoric in general. This simultaneous process, in which the landscape is emptied of meaning and subsequently filled up anew – something that has religious connotations in Stanley's writing – is in some sense magical and therefore a continuation of the travel book's character of fetish; however, it is also related to the specific category of supplements found in the travel book's cartography.

In Stanley's militant geography, the cartographic aspect of the journeys constitutes the ultimate authority in the many disputes regarding the credibility of his accounts. Important controversies in the media and in relation to the Royal Geographical Society concerned cartography and naming. Apart from the obvious rivalry regarding who discovered what, the debate concerned the differences between field cartographers such as Stanley and Livingstone and cartographers who drew the locations of rivers and maps on the basis of second hand information from travel books. Stanley went so far as to defend Livingstone's errors in relation to the Nile's sources on account of their being based on personal experience, and he emphasised Speke's correct guess about Lake Victoria being the Nile's main source as an example of the fact that he who has been there knows better – in spite of Speke's *not* having actually seen it. In Stanley's travel books there are numerous lengthy digressions regarding

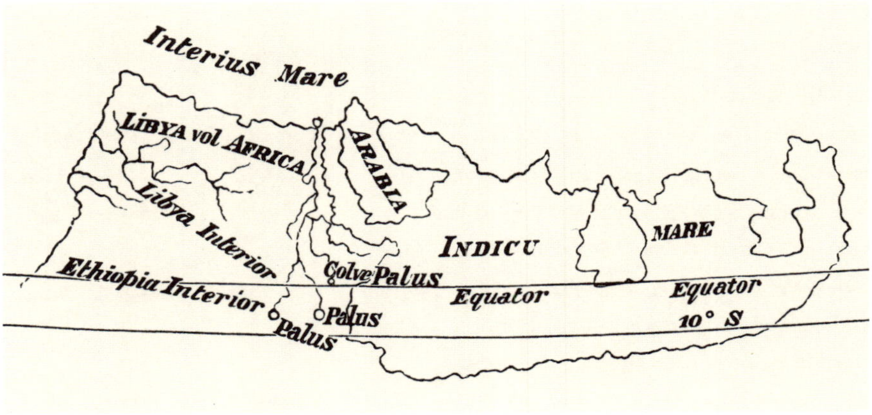

place names that diverge between local languages; in several passages they develop into purely philological studies in which etymologies in many cases lead to discovery, rather than the other way round. Because Stanley's interest in nature and society was non-sentimental and only anthropological to a certain degree, he was more purposeful and effective than his predecessors in his search for the answers to the great geographical riddles of Central Africa. In the dispute about his authority, cartography was therefore one of his trump cards, and he played it every time he was seriously challenged as Livingstone's heir.

All Stanley's European predecessors had been wrong, while his own field observations corrected the map and added the right names. However, in Stanley's description of an African "Royal Geographical Society" in Karakwe, the reversibility of the anecdote's satirical and self-parodic style is pinpointed. Offhand, we might read the anecdote as a rhetorical appreciation of authority; however, compared with other Victorian travel accounts there is a striking openness that casts ironic light on the formalistic procedures and accepted rules for science in the British Royal Geographical Society, thus exposing the society as remote and overly academic. At the same time, the anecdote literally points out the source of Stanley's discoveries as the already existing, highly accurate local cartography, only waiting to be translated into a standardised, European cartographic representation.

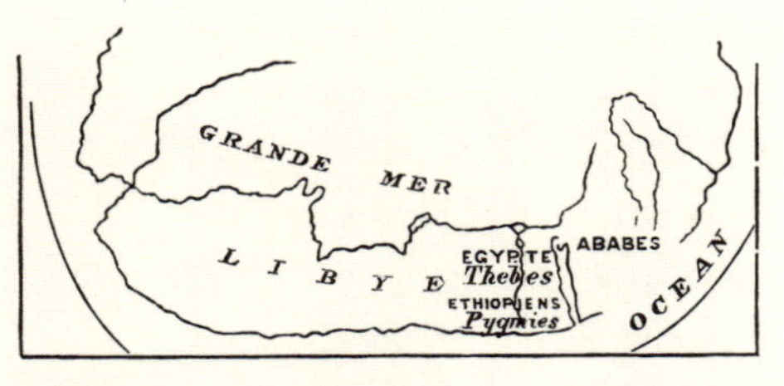

AFRICA IN MAP OF HEKATÆUS.
500 B.C

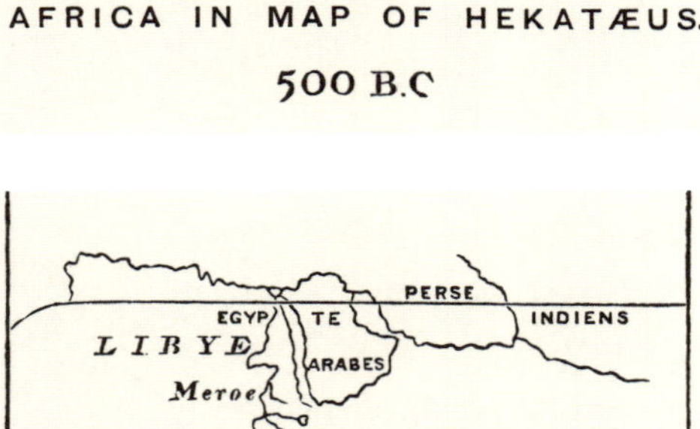

HIPPARCHUS.
100 B.C.

Compared with Bruno Latour's analysis of Lapérouse's discoveries in the Pacific Ocean, the anecdote about Karakwe's "Royal Geographical Society" is also an explication of Stanley's dependency on local knowledge, which grants access to a different understanding of the earliest expeditions' vulnerability.[83] Latour claims that a pre-established attitude towards the balance of power between natives and Europeans, determined by profound differences in culture, rationality and cognitive capacity – the ideological assumption he calls "the Great Divide" – will result in the notion that Stanley's cartography was a rationalisation of dormant, local, savage knowledge: the natives' implicit and local geography translated into the explorer's explicit, universal geography; the natives' beliefs and intuition transformed into European knowledge and reflection. Viewed from "the Great Divide", the explorer assumes a favoured, powerful position in relation to local knowledge – a point of view that is often repeated and perpetuated in postcolonial criticism. If, on the other hand, the relation is viewed in the light of Latour's structural parameters – the observation's movement, angle, direction and scale – what is striking is the vulnerability of Stanley's position. He was in every respect dependent on intermediaries, middlemen and translators of local knowledge to clear the way for the expedition *within* unstable, fragile networks, in contrast to our usual concept of a grandiose clash between different cultures.

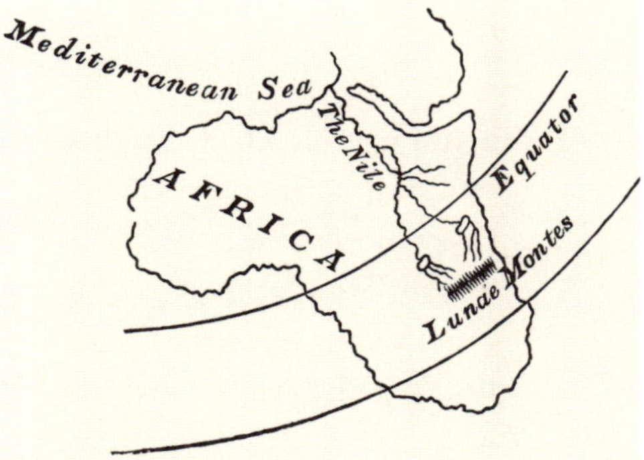

JOHN RUYSCH
A.D. 1508.

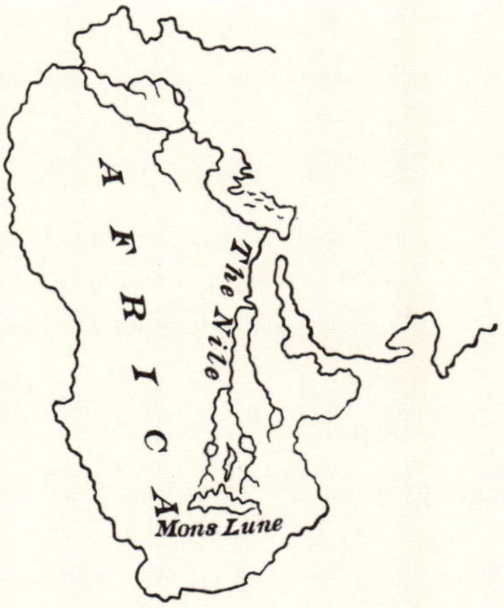

SYLVANNUS' MAP
A.D.1511

The balance of power, however, is altered owing to the Europeans' extraordinary mechanisms for combining and accumulating knowledge in their centres. These factors make it possible, subsequently, to calculate and – most importantly – predict the course of a journey. Cartography in the eighteenth and nineteenth centuries was one of the most important mechanisms in this

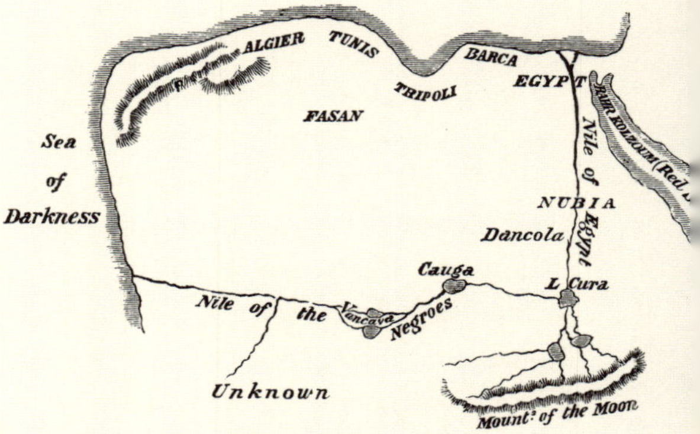

CENTRAL AFRICA
according to
EDRISI. 1154 A.D.

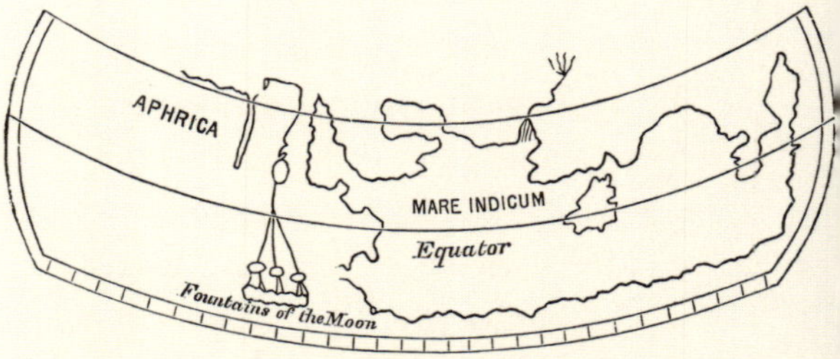

MAP OF THE MARGARITA PHILOSOPHICA
A.D. 1503

accumulation, which enabled centres to affect many different points on the globe *from a distance*. Stanley's exploration of Africa mostly took place in unmapped areas from which he gathered knowledge that had not yet been accumulated. His own journey was unpredictable and dependent on local knowledge, and his records in the notebooks and maps *after* the journey were invaluable for the European centres of knowledge. The travel account's span between cartographic uncertainty and faith in the almost demonic power of cartography and geography expresses this basic challenge for any first-time traveller; in Stanley's case, because he was travelling inland in hostile territories, it was so much more intense than for the explorers who sailed on the great oceans. Stanley's linguistic and rhetorical talents enabled him to draw his routes on the basis of exchanges with the natives, which minimised risk and vulnerability. The same talents were also used in the design of the travel books' cartography and the text's metaphoric appreciation of the value of maps, related to the magic of maps – their crucial ability to affect far-away objects, just like fetishes. This adds another magical element to the book.

The most significant cartographic supplement is found in chapter 29 of *In Darkest Africa*, a lengthy, historiographic account of the discovery of the Nile and the localisation of the Mountains of the Moon. The chapter bears the mark of the supplement, written in the light of the many errors and meagre geographical results of the expedition. Several times, Stanley gives vent to his annoyance at the fact his discoveries will inevitably be erased by the travellers of the future, who will move and rename the localities he has just plotted on the map. However, his melancholia, interrupted by angry, sarcastic attacks against all the know-it-alls who are sitting by the "sparkling fire and under the light of the parlour lamp" (*IDA* II, p. 267), is actually caused by the fact that his cartographic review clearly shows that what he has just 'discovered' has been common knowledge for two thousand years. His famous answers to the riddles of the Nile and the Mountains of the Moon – which he stole from Jephson – are in fact *rediscoveries* of traditional knowledge that European "map-makers" erased through the successive distortions of the previous couple of centuries. And the "tribe" of "modern cartographers" have also erased Stanley's own discoveries of a bay and an island in Lake Victoria: "The bay has been wiped out, the great island has been shifted elsewhere, and the picturesque channels are not in existence on his latest maps, and they will not be restored until some other traveller, years hence, replaces them as they stood in 1875" (p. 269).

Stanley suspects that the same fate will befall the new maps published in *In Darkest Africa*; however, he finds comfort in the knowledge that the British Museum has a copy of the book, where it can always be found "as an honest witness of truth". It is clear from Stanley's deliberations that the authority of maps is not evident but must be created and recreated in a never-ending process as one map is superimposed on another without the landscape fitting into any final, cartographic representation. The series of maps and accompanying text material from early Greek and Arabic sources display great precision; in changing iconographic codes, and with much use of oral and written knowledge, they appear as testimonies equal to Stanley's own maps, which he tries to present as the ultimate climax of the series. Stanley's maps are – in contrast to the Greek and Arabic ones – without myth or history, but his accompanying text reinstates the myths.

Contrary to Stanley's intention of

HIERONIMUS DE VERRAZANO
1529

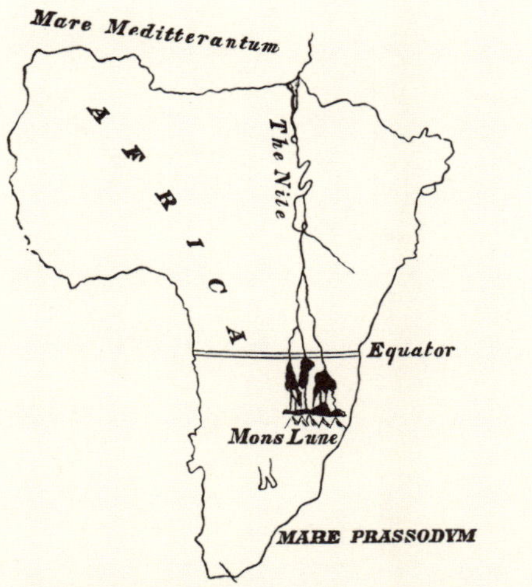

SEBASTIAN CABOT'S MAP OF THE WORLD
16th Century

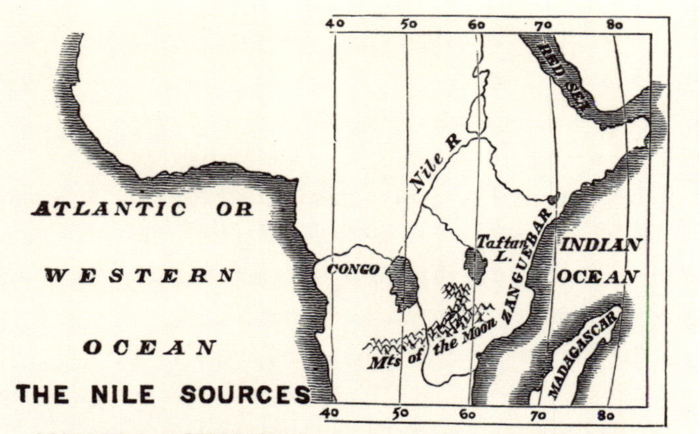

THE NILE SOURCES
ACCORDING TO GEOGRAPHERS OF THE 16TH & 17TH CENTURIES

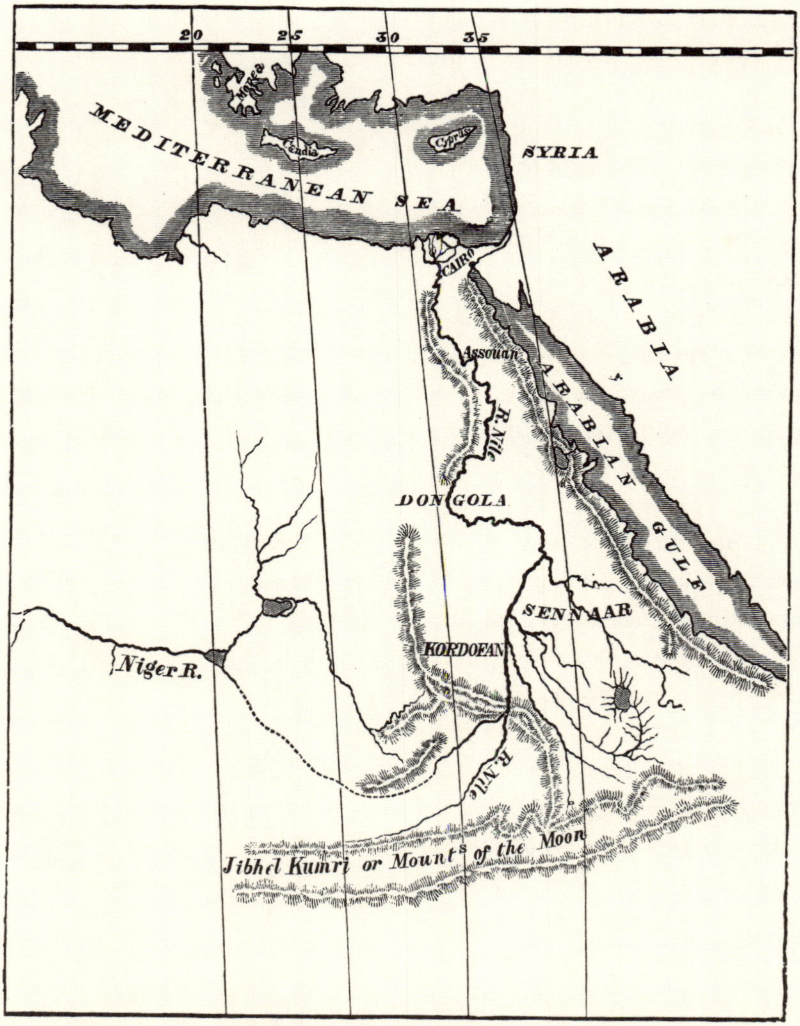

MAP OF THE NILE BASIN. 1819.A.D.

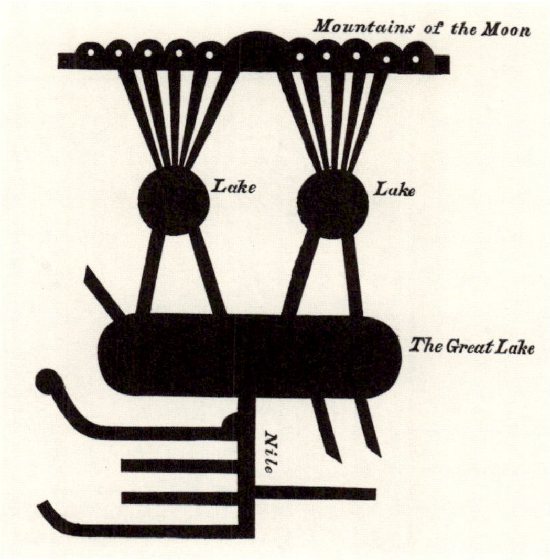

re-establishing the Emin Pasha Relief Expedition's faltering authority, the supplement displays fundamental doubts buried deep in Victorianism and Stanley's own cartography, the exploration discourse more or less depending on tricks that postulate a complete lack of previous knowledge which – with a snap of the fingers – is transformed into absolute knowledge. The prerequisite for inscribing names into the landscape that can subsequently be represented in cartography is a clean slate. However, Stanley's supplement also problematically demonstrates the frailty of both discovery and naming if they are not based on local knowledge and language.

Characteristically of this type of change in perspective and knowledge, in a lengthy passage at the end of volume one of *Through the Dark Continent* Stanley presents a detailed anthropological sketch of the Watutas migrations, followed by a declaration that his knowledge is based on a complete coincidence: Wadi Safeni's wife has overheard a couple of gossiping Watutas: "The dialect and accent sounding familiar to her, she listened, and a few moments after she was herself volubly discussing with them the geography of the locality inhabited by the Mafitté between Lake Nyassa and Tanganika" (*TDC* I, p. 501).

The expedition actually navigated on the basis of this sort of local knowledge, without which it would have been doomed, and Stanley's texts are – as mentioned above in relation to the "Royal Geographical Society" in Karakwe – unique in that they mention these sources. Local knowledge, however, is moulded to comply with cartographic conventions during the retrospective editing of the travel book. The Watutas' famous achievements are associated with the word "Mono-Matapa", "that great African word, which from antiquity and its persistent appearance on our maps" has resulted in conflicting hypotheses among geographers and "learned travellers". However, Stanley is able to solve the riddle by combining the local knowledge provided by Safeni's wife with his linguistic understanding of the word's probable migration, thus locating the legendary place in a stable geographical context:

"It ought to be mentioned here that Mani, Mana, Mono, Moeni, Muini, Muinyi, are all prefixes, synonymous with lord, prince, and sometimes son: for example, Mana-Koos, Mani-Ema, now called Manyema and Mana-Mputu, lord of the sea; Mono-Matapa,

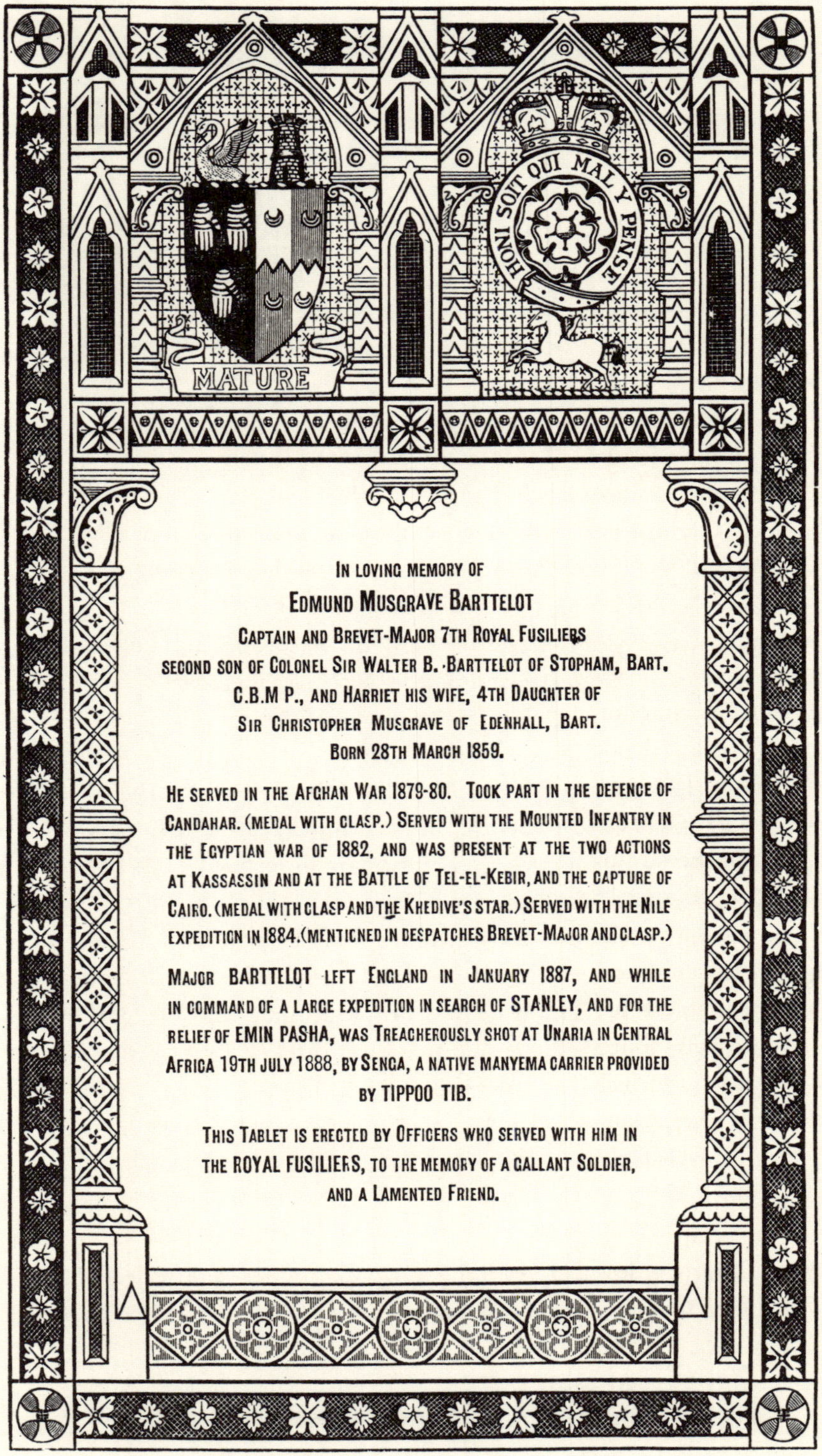

TABLET ERECTED IN STOPHAM CHURCH.

From *The Life of Edmund Musgrave Barttelot. From his letters and diary by Walter George Barttelot* (1890). From a tablet erected in Stopham Church, copied in the diary; also included is a two-column appendix with Stanley's instructions and letters in one column and Barttelot's critical comments in the other. Barttelot's rhetorical strategy is an appeal to decorum, expecting the reader to acknowledge the fact that a man with an honourable and immaculate career in the military cannot possibly be guilty of amoral conduct. The heraldry of the copied tablet is part of the ancient magic, "Honi soit qui mal y pense".

Mana-Ndenga, Mana-Butti, Mana-Kirembu, Mana-Mamba, and so forth. In Uregga the prefix becomes Wana, or Wane, as in Wane-Mbeza, Wane-Kirumbu, Wane Kamankua, Wane-Kipangu, Wana-Mukwa, and Wana-Rukura" (*TDC* I, p. 502).

Maps and cartographic supplements raise questions as much as answering them. They compound the uncertainty in the text, contesting the intended superiority of Stanley's metaphoric map, for instance the panoramic prospectus from the peak of Musira Island described in *Through the Dark Continent*. The map's names and markings designate conquests – such as Stanley Pools, Léopoldville or the peak named "Gordon Bennett" after the unscrupulous editor of the *New York Herald*, but they are also inscriptions that are challenged and incite opposition.

The map as supplement is a foreign body in the travel text, at the same time as it is its very nature. In its unassailable, mathematical notation, the map conveys the text and the author's authority, but it is also vertiginously fascinating and inexplicable. It provides hints of etymological and mythological knowledge, but conceals its sources. It is empty in the forward-looking perspective of the journey, and as such characteristic of the traveller's powerlessness and ignorance, while, in the retrospective of the travel book, it holds a fetishistic power that allows for magical changes of perspective and scale between local and global, giving the centres of Europe influence across time and space. In Stanley's travel books, the map's authority is therefore subject to modern doubt, which – according to Latour – reflects the actual balance of power on the journey, while also constituting an important factor in Stanley's appreciation of the book as fetish.

The travel book's appreciation of magical value, created in the supplements and the rhetorical additions introduced in the editing process, are manifest in the book's materiality. This is most obvious in the aesthetics of the maps, with precious colourings, bindings and frontispieces shaped as monuments with heraldic inscriptions and peculiar scenarios that counteract the monumental

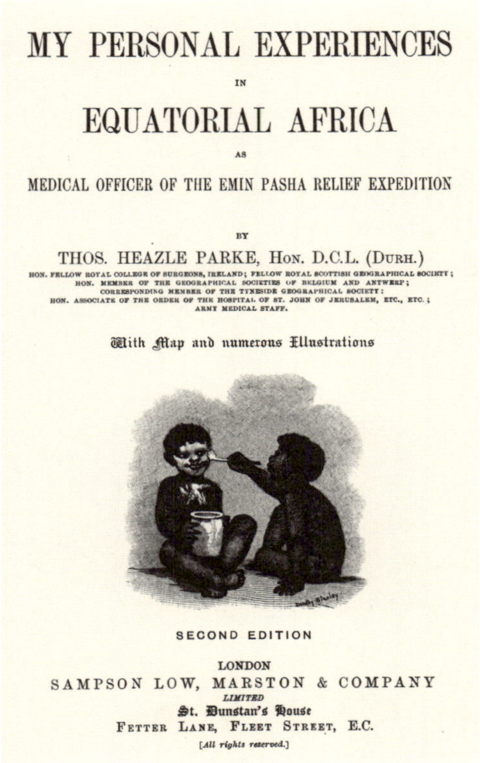
MY PERSONAL EXPERIENCES
IN
EQUATORIAL AFRICA
AS
MEDICAL OFFICER OF THE EMIN PASHA RELIEF EXPEDITION

BY
THOS. HEAZLE PARKE, HON. D.C.L. (DURH.)
HON. FELLOW ROYAL COLLEGE OF SURGEONS, IRELAND; FELLOW ROYAL SCOTTISH GEOGRAPHICAL SOCIETY;
HON. MEMBER OF THE GEOGRAPHICAL SOCIETIES OF BELGIUM AND ANTWERP;
CORRESPONDING MEMBER OF THE TYNESIDE GEOGRAPHICAL SOCIETY:
HON. ASSOCIATE OF THE ORDER OF THE HOSPITAL OF ST. JOHN OF JERUSALEM, ETC., ETC.;
ARMY MEDICAL STAFF.

With Map and numerous Illustrations

SECOND EDITION

LONDON
SAMPSON LOW, MARSTON & COMPANY
LIMITED
St. Dunstan's House
FETTER LANE, FLEET STREET, E.C.
[All rights reserved.]

The illustration was made by Dorothy Stanley who also drew the two cupids on the green cover of Parke's book and the small, dancing, black cupids on Jephson's. Inside the books are ironic texts like "Pigmy damsel, changing her dress", accompanying an image of two native women wearing nothing. In conjunction with the vignettes and covers, they suggest frivolity behind the strict discipline, which refers both to the Europeans' sexual relationships with natives that were never mentioned openly, and to the reversals of identities caused by the journey, which were sometimes counteractive to formation and maturation.

impression. Portraits of determined Victorian travellers, for instance, are often accompanied by vignettes of small black satyrs or cupids, indicating a magical transformation in the direction of the mystical and primitive, rather than a formative and civilising journey. While the symbols on the binding of Stanley's *Autobiography* were attempts to express the author's determination, the binding and vignettes of the editions of both Barttelot's and Jameson's books are ironic, apt declarations of the texts' enchanted stories of transformation.

The images add to the magic of the books. Marston, who is usually quite ironic and pragmatic, describes with almost religious reverence in *How Stanley Wrote 'In Darkest Africa'* how Stanley's precious but damaged photographs were developed, as well as the illustrators' meticulous work using his blurred photographs and sketches:

"It is needless to say that these negatives, taken with infinite care, by Stanley himself, of scenes all through the journey, were regarded by him and by me with the utmost jealousy. I therefore took upon myself to watch the whole process from beginning to end, and I never lost sight of these precious negatives till I carried them back to the hotel. Alas I am sorry to say that many of the pictures had almost disappeared from the glass, and at best could only serve our artist. These had been over-exposed or not sufficiently exposed in the blazing sun of the tropics. Others, I was delighted to find came out quite clearly, and represented great value artistically and geographically, as well as conveying accurately the types of new races in the interior" (Marston, p. 27).

It is clear from Marston's description that the books' illustrations were based on the photographs, but that they went through an extensive editing process when Stanley and the illustrator, in close collaboration, produced pictures of dramatic situations that – according to Marston – no longer needed to resemble the photograph, although they were not to counteract the text or the real events.

The illustrations are often independent ornamentation or curiosities that add an aesthetic or anthropological dimension to the text's combination of technical descriptions and dramatic New Journalism. In other instances, they depict views and dramatic climaxes in the text, but in a processed and developed manner that corresponds to the text's development from notebook to travel book and adds a similar fetishistic value. The perspective, framing and location of the illustrations operate with the same tensions between light and darkness and voyeuristic pleasure as the text, either by mastering the landscape ("Monarch of all I survey") or shuddering at the sight of the traveller's body and identity being threatened by darkened or shadowy surroundings.

A characteristic of the illustrations in *In Darkest Africa* is their congenial, often subtle interpretations of Stanley's text, containing various levels of voyeurism and dominance in their perspective. Furthermore, they are often placed and framed in the textual course of events in a way that makes the description of a view a literal *vista* in the text – from either the traveller's perspective or the imagined bird's-eye view that plays such an important role in Stanley's performative rhetoric. In other travel books – by Stanley, as well as others – we find a different but equally magical use of illustrations, e.g. in Parke's *My Personal Experiences in Equatorial Africa*. A long supplementary chapter about the ultramodern prospects of bacteriology-based tropical medicine, "A Study of Bacteriology", is illustrated with a photograph of "*curios* on leopard skin" (Parke, p. 183). The illustration's linkage of western "wonder" and native fetish

"The Pygmies at home. A Zanzibar scout taking notes", from *In Darkest Africa*. A number of illustrations show situations of surveillance, described in the diaries with voyeuristic characteristics.

is in contrast to the modern scientific paradigm on which the military doctor insists. However, it also directs the reader's attention back to Parkes' extremely detailed descriptions of sores, boils and parasitic diseases – descriptions that serve as highly visual, renaissance-inspired displays of anatomical curiosities rather than medical examples.

The illustrations are based either on Stanley's drawings and sketches or on his photographs, meticulously processed and with layers of interpretation added at every stage from original to finished etching. The photographs in particular form part of the travel book's construction of credibility and authority, on a par with citations from the notebooks and geographical maps; however, they also form part of the text's performative endeavour. The photographs' blurriness and unsuitability as realistic representations, highlighted by Mathilde Leduc-Grimaldi among others,[84] underpin their contribution to the complete text's entire performative act. The photographs' primary function is not to show the reader how landscapes or Pygmies looked, but to relate a story about the explorer who was present and performed a magical action with a wondrous

"The Pigmies under the Lens, as Compared to Captain Casati's Servant, Okili (from a Photograph Taken by Albert Nyanza)", from *In Darkest Africa*. In the accompanying text, Stanley explains that Emin Pasha is obsessed with measuring and weighing, scientifically mapping the anatomy of the natives, to the extent that he is prepared to boil the heads he can procure and send them to a museum in Berlin. Stanley finds this scientific indifference provoking and emphasises his own method: noticing the life of the face; the movement of language; the expressions and inner nature, thus getting to know the human characteristics of the natives while consciously abstaining from explaining their ethnic distinctiveness, clan systems, etc. The photograph, however, often entails dehumanisation of the same kind as dissection and measuring: the pose appears phantom-like, soulless.

technological device. A great deal of the original photographs, many of which are collected in the so-called *Album bleu* – a present from Marston to Stanley's widow, Dorothy, containing 175 original photographs, maps and illustrations from the work on *In Darkest Africa* – express this phantomisation of photographs and photographed. This applies to the subjects' dehumanised poses and the distortion of light and shadow caused by over or underexposure. These effects are often developed further in the artistic process, especially by illustrators whose style – as demonstrated by Leduc-Grimaldi – was inspired by the fantastic romanticism of the day. From its original role as valuable documentary registration of data, the photograph assumes the role of fetish, which nevertheless does

not weaken its power and influence on the creation of authority and credibility. What happens is that the textual field work inaugurates several spaces at the same time: the photographs address decadent spaces for metropolitan readers, while creating another space defined by superposition of a specific media technology, the traveller's biography and a place in Africa.

The illustrations' pinpointing of competing spaces in the text is especially clear in the framings that are experimental in style, which are particularly evident in *In Darkest Africa*. In one case, the image is a vertical pillar, the motive a section of the expedition climbing an almost vertical cliff, which suggests to the reader the experience of climbing up inside a chimney. Other images are framed in rounded, irregular shapes in an attempt to materialise a sense of the lush nature depicted. The travel book illustrations contain rich varieties of geometrically shaped framings, which – in interplay with the profusion of perspectives – can be interpreted as correlating with the prose's presentation of simultaneous spaces that are not unified into one overriding representational or discursive artifice.

Similar to the correlation between Cubism and aerial photographs, including their military uses, studied by Paul K. Saint-Amour,[85] *In Darkest Africa* contains striking parallels between the multi-perspectival textual prose and the book's experiments with new visual technologies. The aim is not only to reproduce what was seen on the journey, but to reproduce the perception of the journey – which, in turn, can be seen in relation to Stanley's instruction to his illustrators to stay true to the phenomenological experience rather than the factual aspects. The restless, changeable gaze of the expedition is incorporated into both the prose and magical images in the book.

In the travel book's editing, and in the supplement, the textual materiality is inscribed as a fetish value, which – depending on the context – can have either a fortifying or eroding effect on authority and testimony. The fetish value, like the value of the testimony, is dependent on market value. Marston's book about *In Darkest Africa* clearly demonstrates the connection between the travel book as fetish, commodity and testimony. His "statistics of the work" is a celebration of the industrial design of an exceptional event on the literary world market, while at the same time functioning as a powerful fetishisation of the book. Stanley's authority as an author and traveller is inseparable from the magical figures that appear to imitate his recurrent statistics of the expedition's dead, sick and starving members. Furthermore, Marston's witty comment that the initial editions of the book would have enabled Stanley to walk on paper from Congo to Zanzibar creates a link between the expedition's purely numeric achievements and the book market. The industrial aspect of the production required Stanley to write the book exceptionally quickly. What

Framings and perspectives interact with the multitude of textual perspectives. The examples are from *In Darkest Africa*.

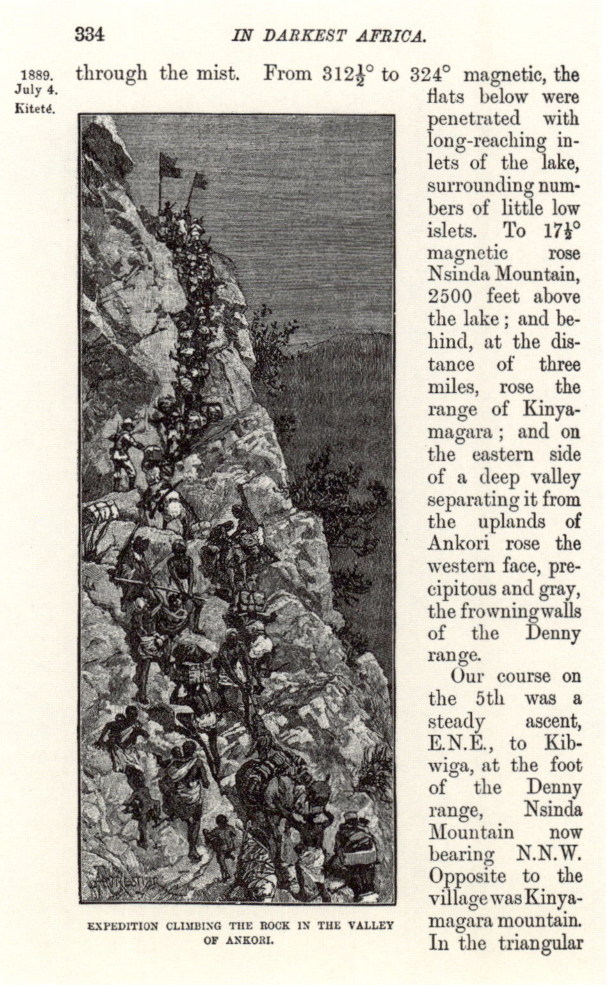

334 *IN DARKEST AFRICA.*

1889. July 4. Kiteté.

through the mist. From $312\frac{1}{2}°$ to 324° magnetic, the flats below were penetrated with long-reaching inlets of the lake, surrounding numbers of little low islets. To $17\frac{1}{2}°$ magnetic rose Nsinda Mountain, 2500 feet above the lake; and behind, at the distance of three miles, rose the range of Kinyamagara; and on the eastern side of a deep valley separating it from the uplands of Ankori rose the western face, precipitous and gray, the frowning walls of the Denny range.

Our course on the 5th was a steady ascent, E.N.E., to Kibwiga, at the foot of the Denny range, Nsinda Mountain now bearing N.N.W. Opposite to the village was Kinyamagara mountain. In the triangular

EXPEDITION CLIMBING THE ROCK IN THE VALLEY OF ANKORI.

he did can be characterised as a fusion of travelling and writing, in which the forest supplement becomes a magical shibboleth that creates access to the rest of the book but also demonstrates that the authority of the testimony is inscribed in the book's double position as commodity and fetish.

The advertisement "What Africa Needs is Electric Light" shows Stanley in the light cast by an electric bulb on the Dark Continent, resulting in both illumination and comfort and allowing the explorer to type out the notes from his "tara-tara". However, the advertisement's reification and the electrical light cannot suppress the book's fetishistic character; rather, it leeches off and continues it, while the impact of the book's discoveries, testimonies and message proliferate apace with its increased exposure and circulation. After the collapse of Victorian culture's decorum in relation to negotiations about testimony and credibility – in this instance exemplified by the public resistance to assimilating Jameson's fundamentally incomprehensible account – the authority of travel literature depended on the ability to create the book as both fetish and commodity.

The Livingstone expedition had already established Stanley as a brand, a global media phenomenon who was the first – both in his description of the internal organisation of time and space and in his marketing – to take advantage of the changing terms for the production and distribution of travel

literature. Livingstone's iconographic status was continued and inherited by Stanley's telegram articles and travel books, although in a completely novel style which – in contrast to his predecessor's sentimental and romantic traits – was characterised by modern, pragmatic, goal-orientated forms and New Journalism. Livingstone's message was conveyed through lectures via traditional channels such as the Anti-Slavery Society, the Aborigines' Protection Society and the Royal Geographical Society. Stanley's expeditions and travel book, on the other hand, were marketed via an unprecedented utilisation of modern media, popular culture and the nineteenth-century development of commodity aesthetics, in which marketing increasingly used ideological and aesthetic values that were only loosely related to the product – for example the use of the Stanley iconography in soap advertisements. Generally, advertisements were directed at the world market, as is made clear in Marston's correspondence with Stanley regarding the launch of "Railway book instalments" and use of posters "worldwide" (SA, No. 1627). This shift in primary receiving institutions, audiences, means of dissemination and marketing aesthetics is part of the travel books' rhetoric in the form of tense conflicts and very innovative formal techniques. We have seen how Stanley's prospects of scientific recognition by institutions such as the Royal Geographical Society depended on his citizenship, which was also critical to his copyrights on the American market until the USA ratified the Berne Convention for the Protection of Literary and Artistic Works in 1891. However, the travel books were not only *disseminated* on the existing world market; Stanley's accounts contributed to

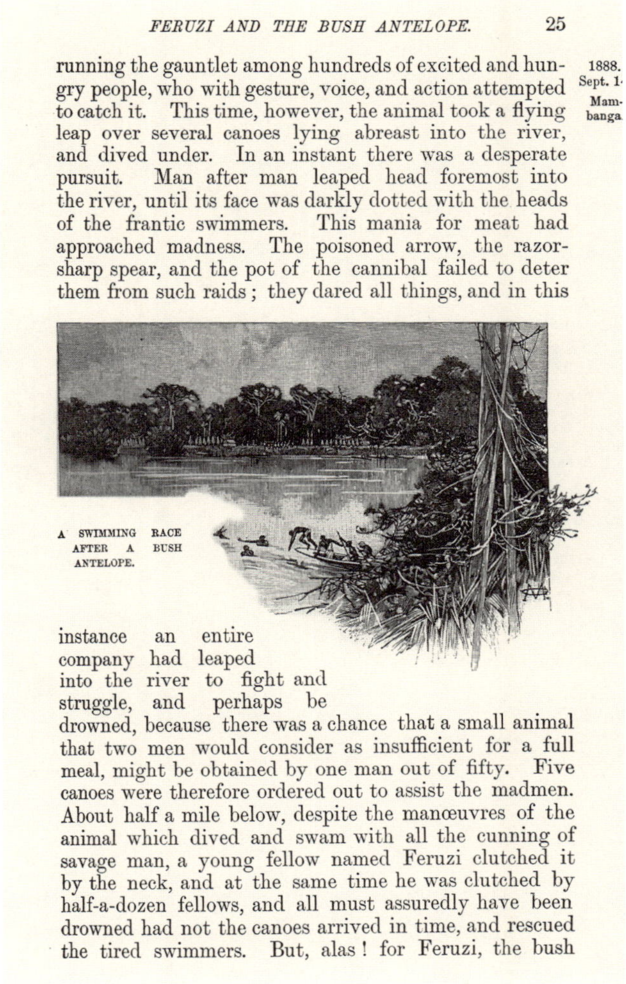

running the gauntlet among hundreds of excited and hungry people, who with gesture, voice, and action attempted to catch it. This time, however, the animal took a flying leap over several canoes lying abreast into the river, and dived under. In an instant there was a desperate pursuit. Man after man leaped head foremost into the river, until its face was darkly dotted with the heads of the frantic swimmers. This mania for meat had approached madness. The poisoned arrow, the razor-sharp spear, and the pot of the cannibal failed to deter them from such raids; they dared all things, and in this instance an entire company had leaped into the river to fight and struggle, and perhaps be drowned, because there was a chance that a small animal that two men would consider as insufficient for a full meal, might be obtained by one man out of fifty. Five canoes were therefore ordered out to assist the madmen. About half a mile below, despite the manœuvres of the animal which dived and swam with all the cunning of savage man, a young fellow named Feruzi clutched it by the neck, and at the same time he was clutched by half-a-dozen fellows, and all must assuredly have been drowned had not the canoes arrived in time, and rescued the tired swimmers. But, alas! for Feruzi, the bush

1888. Sept. 1[illegible]
Mambanga.

A SWIMMING RACE AFTER A BUSH ANTELOPE.

creating this international space that began with the Livingstone expedition's scoop on both sides of the Atlantic and culminated with *In Darkest Africa.*

Nineteenth-century USA saw a tremendous increase in its reading audience, first and foremost due to the proliferation of newspapers. This paved the way for cheap, unauthorised publications of books that were only protected by copyrights on the British market, where they maintained high prices and small print runs. Stanley's travel books were directed at both markets, making use of two very different prose forms: New Journalism, with which the American audience was familiar, and the Victorian travel account as inspired by Livingstone, Speke and Burton.

Stanley's travel books contributed to creating a world that facilitated the texts' combination of different styles. In the article "The Globalization of the Book 1800-1970",[86] David Finkelstein describes the globalisation of the book market in the second half of the nineteenth century as a result of industrialised production methods with the steam press, increased transnational communication via telegraph, and the development of postal services, increased global trade and the new consciousness of a global scene for travel and exchange of accounts and information. Stanley, in particular, played a central role in the establishment and utilisation of this psychological and market-orientated global space. Finkelstein mentions a vast number of international standardisations, such as the establishment of postal services in 1874, international measurements in 1875 and an international calendar in 1884, as signs of the need for systems for predictable and safe handling of information exchange.

The literary market's contribution to the process was international copyright and the export of industrialised standards for book production, including recognisable fiction formats. According to Finkelstein, travel literature also played a prominent role with its accumulation and dissemination of knowledge between distant places. With his sensational publishing success, his dissemination of intercontinental knowledge and his unique, transnational biography, Stanley in many ways incarnates this heterogeneous space in which national literatures were challenged by transnational markets, and high literature was challenged by popular literature.

In the section about Stanley's description of the great Ituri Forest, there was mention of Jan Gordon's "'Decadent Spaces': Notes for a Phenomenology of the Fin de Siècle", which provides a description of literary decadence's internal and external spaces that corresponds to Stanley's 'phenomenology'. Gordon sets these transformations of classical literary spaces in relation to the collapse of the romantic quest figure and the nineteenth-century *Bildungsroman*, in which the journey must end with the hero returning home to find himself. If we add the correspondence between the *Bildungsroman* and nation states, suggested in Franco Moretti's *Atlas of the European Novel 1800-1900* (1999), it is tempting to associate the collapse of the *Bildungsroman* with the establishment of transnational literature. In this sense, it is yet another configuration of Stanley's 'multidirectional' field work, which unfolds in a global space, determined by factors such as intensified transnational communication, the European nation states' crises and the threat of wars between superpowers. This provides further explanation of the scandals that surrounded Stanley from beginning to end. First and foremost they bear witness to the clash between conservative, Victorian institutions and American New Journalism, in which Livingstone and Stanley were prominent figures, and which was given free rein because there was no authority to sanction one version or the other. The scandals, however, were also – as suggested by Gordon regarding the gossip surrounding bohemians such as John Gray and Oscar Wilde – substitutes for the sense of community that had been sustained by the *Bildungsroman* and other media. Celebrities became projection screens and objects for the same type of voyeuristic transgression of the boundaries between public and private spaces that was promoted through their literature.

In Darkest Africa contains shopping lists and product catalogues of various brands, while the book proper is promoted as a statistical wonder, a sensational combination of information design, art and commodity, which resulted in surprising shifts and reversals of classical relationships between space and time. The field work took place in different 'places' at the same 'time': legitimisation and institutional conflicts on the domestic front constituted a field before the journey even began and continued on the expedition to define route decisions with fateful consequences that subsequently, in the travel account, established decisive terms for what *could* be written and what *was* in fact written. At home and abroad, the travel accounts were changeable scenes, often occurring simultaneously in Africa, London, New York and Cairo, and the convention that the reader must sense the here-and-now of the journey was counteracted by Stanley's introverted field work on his autobiographical project, as well as by the rhetorical processing of the text's many different recipients. In some instances, fictitious or highly theatricalised topographies appear that are not directly linked to real places but still, despite their independence from the representative function, serve to strengthen the text's credibility as a performative act. As readers we are never confined to the author's sentimental and wild interpretations; instead, the prose points us in the direction of the traveller's modern and mundane world, which cannot be anything but this simultaneity of incompatible spaces in motion.

It is natural to compare this simultaneity of competing space and time – what Michel Foucault calls "heterotopia" – with similarly incompatible spaces in the Stanley and African Exhibition, which took place at the Victoria Gallery in Regent Street, London, between March and November 1890, partly to take

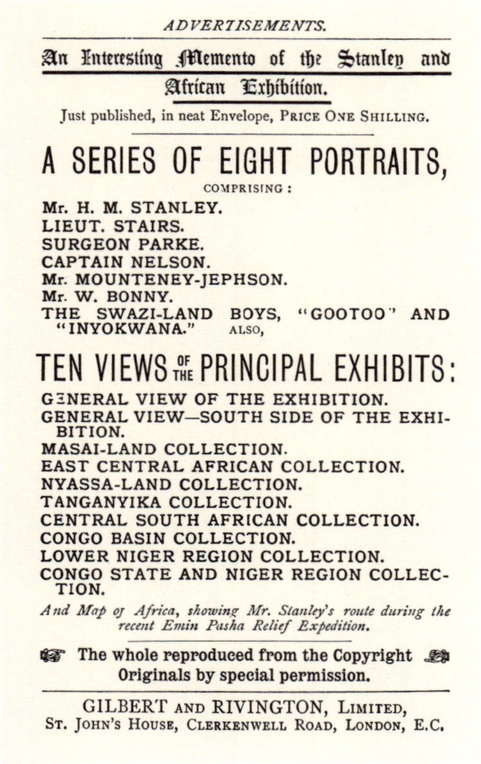

For one shilling, a souvenir could be bought that showed prospects from *The Stanley and African Exhibition* (1890), which collected and exhibited various objects that were loosely linked to the Emin Pasha expedition; the aim was to exploit the media attention to make propaganda for the Royal Geographical Society, investments in businesses in Africa, abolitionist and missionary movements, and much more. The advertisement for the "interesting memento" is from Marston's *How Stanley Wrote 'In Darkest Africa'*. The demand for images from Africa was apparently insatiable.

advantage of the worldwide media hype surrounding the return of the Emin Pasha Relief Expedition. The Stanley and African Exhibition has been analysed by Felix Driver in *Geography Militant* and Annie E. Coombe in *Reinventing Africa: Museums, Material Culture and Popular Imagination in Late Victorian and Edwardian England* (1994). Both emphasise the exhibition's representations as a result of random, conflicting interests and discourses. In other words, the exhibition did not represent one coherent, colonial discourse on Africa – which became clear through the subsequent notorious court case about the legal position, history and origin of two African boys who were 'displayed' – but rather gathered many tangled threads in nineteenth-century colonial history under the same roof.

The exhibition formed part of a pervasive nineteenth-century preference for entertaining shows, world's fairs, dioramas and panoramas encompassing science, technology, industry and commerce, alongside the promotion of products and ideologies, providing the audience with unusual sensory and aesthetic experiences. Though the exhibition aimed at some form of organisation, partly along the lines of the participating parties – such as the Royal Geographical Society, a vast number of African businesses and the abolitionist and missionary movements – the dominant interest was entertainment over information, and the museal representation principles were therefore disregarded, or rather they were orchestrated in a multitude of incongruent

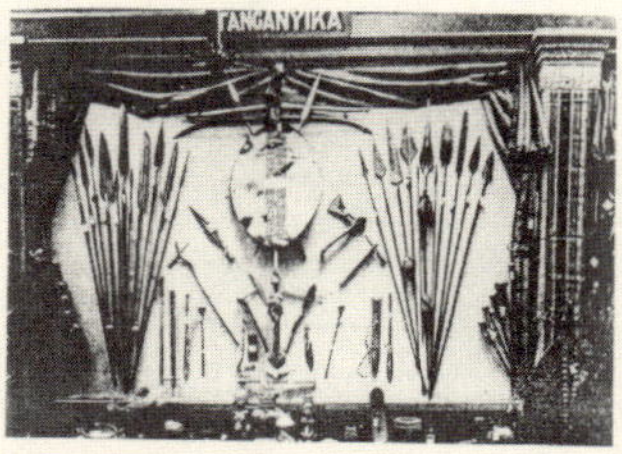

27. The Stanley and African Exhibition display from Tanganyika.

30. The Stanley and African Exhibition display from 'Nyassaland'.

28. The Stanley and African Exhibition display from Lower Niger Region.

29. The Stanley and African Exhibition display from the Congo Basin.

31. The Stanley and African Exhibition display from Central South Africa.

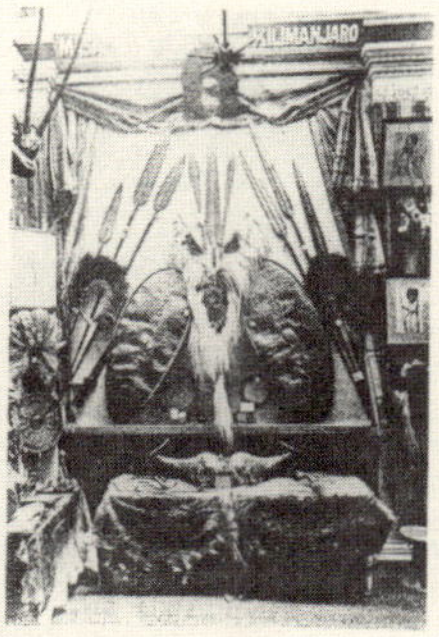

32. The Stanley and African Exhibition display from 'Masailand, Kilimanjaro'.

Exhibition prospects from *The Stanley and African Exhibition* (1890). The prospects do not express any clear anthropological intention; rather, they are related to the heraldic style according to which big game hunters and explorers organised their collections of trophies and objects of art. The exhibition was organised as an entertaining experience rather than a dry presentation of scientific results. The visitor was welcomed by a palisade entrance with the inscription "in the heart of wild Africa", and the journey presented the opportunity to see African villages and moving scenes in which slaves were captured. This eclectic and entertaining dissemination of knowledge was a parallel to Stanley's changeable, multidirectional prose.

classifications. African weapons in heraldic and ornamental combinations that represented the gatherer as hunter, rather than the ethnography of the native hunter, were exhibited side by side with busts depicting Stanley and other explorers, skeletons of hippopotamuses and monkeys, dioramic landscapes showing scenes from East Africa, the Congo River and Mount Ruwenzori in the same prospect, as well as randomly placed drums, kitchen utensils and fetishes. Furthermore, there were reconstructions of African villages and a touching 'slave capturing scene'. The exhibition was organised as a journey for the visitor, who was greeted at the entrance by a palisade ornamented with skulls and the inscription "Into the Heart of Wildest Africa". Immediately

inside the palisade was shown an expedition camp with tents, natives and so on, thus inviting the visitor to imagine themselves in the role of Stanley – whose ventilated cap was on display for the first time.

Visitors were not invited to partake in a monolithic representation of the British Empire's colonial possessions, as the most biased branch of postcolonial criticism would claim, but to create their own narrative via their journey through the exhibition's fragmented landscape, in which they were fascinated by the strange materiality and decontextualisation of various scenes and objects. The exhibition pre-empted a long series of shifts, both by heralding the paradigm of the leisure economy and by mixing audience segments that were usually separate, in a joint effort of science and entertainment. As pointed out by Coombes and Driver, the popular turn had radical consequences for former expressions of legitimisation and authority, as both the Royal Geographical Society and philanthropic and humanitarian organisations were compromised following the intensive exposure of the exhibition and subsequent court case. The exhibition's massive branding of the colonial project included elements that de-legitimised the scientific, humanitarian and national ideologies on which the project had been based throughout the nineteenth century; this was unintended but inevitable, considering the aesthetic and sensational marketing that – in many respects – was a continuation of the discourse of wonder.

When Stanley was not posing as "gentleman traveller" or writing like Livingstone, but giving voice to the mixed audience that encompassed the middle class, the lower middle class, and – through the distribution of cheap pamphlets – also the working class, he was playing with a similar de-legitimisation of the travel account's dominant institutions. Stanley's New Journalism is the stylistic equivalent of the Stanley and African Exhibition; his visualising "graphic scraps" reflect the superficiality of fragmented modernity without representing class, nation or culture. The criticism of the travel books' sensationalism, and the claims of Stanley's extraordinary ruthlessness posed by a united front of geographical and humanitarian societies, was on closer inspection rooted in their loss of discursive control caused by Stanley's popularity. In turn, this led to a disclosure of sensationalism, exaggeration and betrayal *within* these discourses.[87]

A brief remark on another of the nineteenth century's great exhibitions serves to illuminate other aspects of Stanley's performative and spectacular textual strategy: the opening of the Crystal Palace in London, 1851, started a series of world's fairs that would come to play an important role in the history of travel literature, both as the motivation and starting point for journeys and as the stage for exhibiting the objects they brought back. The new glass and steel architecture with open, partly transparent galleries was a culmination of the nineteenth-century preference for theatre and a turn towards the commer-

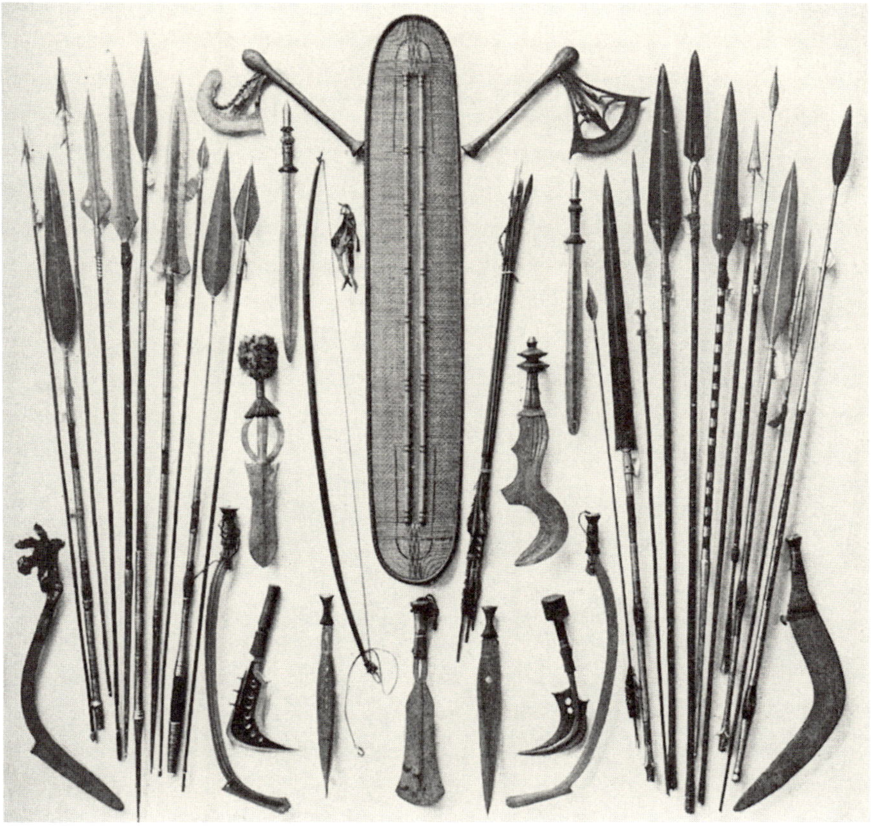

"Congolese weapons". The second edition of the French version of Ward's book about his years of service during Stanley's colonisation of the Congo 1884-89, *Chez les cannibals de l'Afrique Centrale* (1910), contains a number of photographs of Ward's collections of weapons, ethnographic objects, and sculptures. Ward's collection, amounting to several thousand objects, was handed over to the Smithsonian, where they – partly because Ward had catalogued them so meticulously – became the basis of the 'African Collections' of the museum. In his studio in Paris, both the green walls and the windows were completely covered in fetishes, sculptures, a stuffed python, gorilla skeletons, and ferocious weapons. Utilising dimmed lighting to recreate dark Africa in the flat, his own sculptures and African motifs were exhibited in a gloomy combination of the museum, the curiosity cabinet of wonders, and the commercial studio.

cialisation that is self-evident in contemporary culture. In *The Commodity Culture of Victorian England. Advertising and Spectacle 1851-1914* (1990), Thomas Richards highlights some characteristics of the world's fairs and the Crystal Palace that supplement this book's analysis of Stanley's distinct use of theatrical techniques in his description of Africa.[88]

Richards sees the preference for the aesthetics of show at the Crystal Palace as a continuation of autocratic forms of representation under "l'ancien regime" – forms whose transparency was a nostalgic ideal at the same time as the exhibition's rhetoric was updated to fit the "commodifying tropes" of the day (p. 54). The eighteenth-century predilection for exaggeration and sentimentality was rediscovered as a basic element of the nineteenth-century music halls and dioramas, characterised by movement and visual pleasure rather than reference to the real world. According to Richards, this loss of referentiality took place in pace with the display of shiny commodities from all domains and for all kinds of purposes, including the special attraction of objects without any purpose. "'Gadgets' became a way in which the *material* world could be 'produced'". The greenhouse lighting on the objects, exhibited in a labyrinthine order as in a *Wunderkammer*, where lions and Amazons, clasp knives and locomotives were laid out in an abundance that was inexhaustible to the eye, while at the same time the gaze had unrestricted access to great, transparent spaces: all this resulted in the objects being aestheticised, representing the world as magical and full of promise.

The combination of department store and representation of the world seen at the Crystal Palace has striking parallels in Stanley's travel books, parallels which, as mentioned above, the author was also aware of. *In Darkest Africa* especially is a magical world's fair that disenchants and re-enchants itself and the objects it finds, which, in turn, no longer represent foreign cultures but become electrified commodities on the global market. Stanley's favouring of presentational and performative strategies at the expense of representation, condensed in the mundane style of New Journalism, is also an endeavour to *produce* the material world in its totality in one textual stroke. The rhetorical shifts between light and darkness, especially in *Through the Dark Continent*, and the consistent scenic structure signal a specific version of natural science's obsession with vision, including fascinating, changing displays of impenetrability and transparency – which have been described in detail by Barbara M. Stafford in *Voyage into Substance* (1984) and *Devices of Wonder: From the World in a Box to Images on a Screen* (2001).[89] Stanley's variety of perspectives and focus on vision are reminiscent of the renaissance cabinets of curiosities, in which the objects were not placed within collective terms of culture or nature but rather illuminated from many different angles in an essayistic, visualising discourse. However, Stanley also forestalls the anthropological literature of surrealism, in which the peculiar phenomena of everyday life are subject to similar optical exposure in a similar interplay between impenetrable darkness and transparent light. The nostalgic dimension of Stanley's admiration for the transparency in Mutesa's regime and form of representation, which – apart from the references to antiquity – has traits in common with spectacular forms of representation in the "ancien régime", is rooted in a forward-looking and utopian dimension in which the texts dream of a world that is one great funfair or Crystal Palace, where ordinary everyday life becomes extraordinary through commodification – a very apt characterisation of modern travel literature.

Open and Closed Spaces: Stanley's Oblivion

Let us briefly return to the writing desk in Cairo, where Stanley is struggling to write *In Darkest Africa*. The book is resisting the architectural design of the Crystal Palace or the *Valkyrie* until the forest chapter allows all the pieces to fall into place; the remaining text can be written in one fell swoop, and we can glimpse the outline of the many competing spaces that fill the study. Scientific institutions, markets, celebrities, publishers, lawyers, hawkers and blackmailers from all over the world are knocking on the door to obtain permission to use Stanley's name, exhibit his hat, take his money, borrow his prestige or subvert it in any way possible. These intrusive spaces are manifest in the telegrams and letters that Stanley's servant must hand to him with a bamboo pole in order to avoid the tea mugs and water bottles that are flung at him in return.

In Darkest Africa had to be finished quickly out of consideration for the contract with the committee and all the competing testimonies that had already popped up in the media, threatening to create a scandal that included Stanley, his name, identity and – from a broader perspective – all nineteenth-century explorers and the ideologies that carried them forward. Stanley writes twenty pages a day for fifty successive days. He is not fully concentrated on reconstructing the events, since all the alternative spaces constituted by the intrusions are present in his hasty scribbling – they are not secondary or subsequent but simultaneous, for instance, with the trek through the Ituri Forest. They are present in the text's globally-oriented prose and the subjects of the journey's field work, keeping them open, moving and visible from ever-changing perspectives. Stanley's travel accounts are in this sense as exemplary as Bougainville's, Diderot's and Niebuhr's. However, there is one space that Stanley cannot open and set in motion without risking the entire crystal palace shattering – the space that constitutes the conditions for all the others: the Jameson affair.

On 24 February 1890, Andrew Jameson posted a letter to Sir Francis de Winton, requesting that Stanley hand over all James Jameson's notes and diaries to the family without using any part of them in the planned book. The request is put forward not only for "sentimental reasons, but in view of the real value which lies in the right of access to publication of such interesting documents" (SA, No. 1341). Considering that de Winton had already, a month

SALI DELIVERING TELEGRAM.

In Cairo, Stanley was working at full throttle to finish the official account of the Emin Pasha expedition for publication before the deadline set by the committee, and before Stanley's authority was undermined by scandalous rumours and conflicting testimonies. Once he got going, he wrote *In Darkest Africa* in one great "swing" from coast to coast at a staggering pace, which Marston listed in his statistical account of the impressive data related to the work. While Stanley was writing, however, he was not only in Cairo, remembering the expedition and writing up his notes; he was already involved in other spaces, places, and circumstances: representatives of the media in London, the book market, and looming court cases were knocking on the door to his study with telegrams and declarations, demands and promises, offers and threats, all of which became parts of the travel account. In order to avoid flying Apollinaris bottles, his servant, Sali, delivered the telegrams with a long bamboo pole. From Marston's *How Stanley Wrote 'In Darkest Africa'*.

before, been involved in blackmailing Assad Farran to make him withdraw his highly compromising testimony – presumably prompted by the Jameson family – the wording "interesting documents" is indicative of the outspoken and twisted way in which the family approached the cannibalism incident. Andrew Jameson presented the case to his lawyers, and they made the grave accusation against Stanley that he had "broken the seals" and discussed Jameson's diary with the other officers (SA, No. 1342), subsequently threatening to bring a proper court case against him. Andrew Jameson and his lawyers knew that Stanley was writing his account in Cairo, and they were clearly trying to prevent him from publishing the controversial material: "The diaries in question are strictly private property, and, unless we are misinformed, they were sealed up when they came into your possession; Mr. Jameson's Executor objects to you making any use of these diaries for the purposes of your book or otherwise" (SA, No. 1342).

Stanley's lawyers assured Jameson's that no material from the diary would be used, and that all Jameson's personal belongings were still in a pewter box that was opened in 2 October 1888, then shut again after "a casual glance". Not until the expedition arrived at the east coast and received news about Jameson's death and other stories did Stanley open the diary in order to read selected parts that might explain urgent questions about the rear column's fate. However, Stanley also mentions in his letter to the lawyers, as if in passing, that a couple of sketches accidentally fell out of the diary, but that he immediately put them back. The letter ends with Stanley's puzzlement as to the family's assumption that there would be "serious matters connected with Mr. James Jameson's name and the reputation of his family, of which a law Court alone could elicit the truth"; Stanley cautions against "that clear broad light obtainable in a Law Court", which the family "in the most unwise manner wish to shed" (SA, No. 1344).

At this point, Stanley considers bringing charges against Jameson - or at least he uses it as a threat. A draft of another letter to Jameson's lawyers recounts the entire cannibal story, beginning with Jameson's preservation of the head of a native man, followed by a detailed description of the six drawings and Jameson's purchase of a girl "for the purpose of seeing her butchered and sketched". He concludes by assuring the receivers that the entire course of events was repeated under oath and signed by credible witnesses (SA, No. 1345). In a letter to de Winton, Stanley asks for advice in relation to bringing charges against the Jamesons, thus beating them to it. The problem is that "the very least thing will explode the whole secret which I have wished to keep down - you are yourself aware of what Assad Farran had to say - what he did say I am firmly persuaded is true and can be proved at a very small expense" (SA, No. 1346).

In the end, both the Jameson's family and Stanley refrained from bringing charges that would harm both parties by legally reaffirming what were still only rumours. Andrew and Ethel Jameson chose to publish James Jameson's diary in the conviction that the text was a strong testimony to the author's morals and would therefore gainsay his actual words, while Stanley in *In Darkest Africa* settled for the combination of hints and veilings that make up the book's

"mystery" discourse. The correspondence between Stanley's and Jameson's lawyers exposes the narrow margin within which Stanley could write about Jameson's cannibal story. Like the rhetoric in the letters – illustrating both parties' delicate handling of the unspoken secret, which they knew the adversary knew – Stanley's account of the rear column's fate is balanced so that it could subsequently be escalated or toned down, according to the opponent's reaction. Stanley did not wish to do anything that would "explode the whole secret", which would automatically show his own leadership in a bad light. In this way he makes Andrew Jameson aware that he is ready to expose the entire scandal if Jameson's lawyers do not cease their attacks.

An article on 17 November 1890 in the *New York Times* – "Stanley Strikes Back"[90], with the lead paragraph "He tells his own story of the rear column. The details of that terrible tale will in all probability be related in a British Court" – demonstrates the importance of the case as a public affair, followed closely by American reporters and disseminated through the world's press. The interview is conducted in the drawing room of Everett House, Stanley's London residence, and the reporter continuously emphasises the American interest in the infamous case. As mentioned earlier, the American reception of Jameson's diary did not hesitate to pass the sentence the British newspapers had refrained from passing – that the rear column's collapse was a symptom of the failure of the British "Gentleman" culture, Victorian morals and "Englishness". *The Times* had already recommended a court case to halt the avalanche of rumours and scandalous disclosures, possibly in the form of a parliamentary commission, which underlines the seriousness of the matter. When the *New York Times* strongly recommended this approach it was also because the dispute did not only involve Jameson and Barttelot on one side and Stanley on the other; it encompassed the dispute between decadent, noncommittal Britishness on one side and American willpower and determination on the other. In this generalised perception, it was a case of one empire in decline and another on the rise.

It is characteristic of Stanley's comments in the interview that he still hesitates to take this ultimate step in order to be right. He insists that he has not wished to bring anything compromising to light about the expedition's officers; on the contrary, he has recommended discretion. Stanley threatens – publically – to agree to take the case to court and mentions that he is in possession of well-attested evidence for the verity of the cannibal story, that is, "Assad Farran's affidavit"; however, he also emphasises that he has only heard the story in parts at different times, and that he has yet to compile the information into a whole. Stanley stresses his respect for Barttelot and Jameson, thus counterbalancing promises of discretion with threats of disclosing everything. Stanley, too, would prefer to avoid the court.

This implied court case constituted the circumstances for *In Darkest Africa* as testimony and affidavit, as well as for a vast number of similar disputes with other officers, among them Troup and Bonny. They tried to blackmail Stanley by threatening to tell the whole story, but Stanley convinced them to modify their criticism of Barttelot and Jameson in accordance with his own version, thus preventing the case from getting out of hand and dragging his own name into the horror of cannibalism. This cautious behaviour was rather unusual for Stanley, who had not in his former disputes hesitated to bare all, explicating even the most controversial and taboo subjects. His caution indicates how grave Jameson's acts and specifically their circumstances were: paying for the experience with clothing that normally symbolised the travellers' peaceful interaction with natives; staging his fantasy and realising it with the aim of using it as a motive for his artistic endeavours; and, according to the accounts, showing no sign of moral regret – on the contrary, expressing unashamed pleasure.

Surrounded by *fin de siècle* culture's fluid and reflective spaces, the Jameson affair was a secret box, made inaccessible by a vast number of discursive seals that nevertheless could not prevent the story from production and circulation in a series of variations. Jameson's violation reveals the general terms for conveying meaningless or radically self-destructive evidence about the expedition. While *In Darkest Africa*, according to Marston, became the quickest bestselling book of the era, in principle for *everyone* to read, it is interesting that *no one* was allowed to read the most important testimony, while, at the same time, its central significance was stressed in almost every single polemic comment. When the experiences resist logic and reason, Stanley's hesitation is expressed in a pathetic mystery/misery discourse, which penetrates the text's predominantly pragmatic style. It is characteristic of Stanley's use of language in these passages that he refers to ghostly apparitions and mute witnesses, which emphasise the double nature of the testimonies: they are ever-present but do not speak.

For Stanley's part, the expedition's black box was also inaccessible due to facts of his biography outlined in the chapter "Traveller on Global Terms". It was not only the risk of public defamation, but of a sweeping collapse of the autobiographical construction that was Stanley's identity, inextricably linked with the journeys in Africa, which kept him from playing the ultimate trump – that the rear column's leaders were, in fact, perverse. Even during the expedition, Stanley was striving to achieve this balance; his initial reaction, for example, to the newspaper clippings he received after his arrival at the missionary station on the east coast was to draw two portraits of Jameson and Barttelot in his notebook, showing them as "gentlemen" with high morals

who had sadly misunderstood his orders. However, he also notes: "But there are worse things yet which will have to be thoroughly investigated .... Tales of raids, rumours of cannibalism – in which it will be a relief for me that the Britons---- continued to be passive" (SA, No. 58). In these notes, Stanley is already bracing himself for the court cases and public disputes that would soon become a reality in the telegrams handed to him with a bamboo pole. On his way to the coast, Stanley copied selected parts of Jameson' diary; however, three pages have since been torn out that might very well have been the cannibal story. And later on, presumably in 1895, long after the publication of *In Darkest Africa* and the public scandal, Stanley found it necessary to write another version of the Emin Pasha account in the form of the peculiar, unpublished "Personal Journey of the Emin Pasha Relief Expedition" in two volumes of 1270 pages in total (SA No. 64).

This bulky work is a cross between an encyclopaedia with a table of contents and index, an interrogation or court case protocol and a travel diary. Under the entry "Barttelot" are 80 references, including "falls into a rage", "lets matters slide", "major's temper varying to extremes" and "Barttelot not insane but spoiled boy", along with a number of others to passages about the commanding officer's savage punishments, his "biting of a woman on the cheek" and so on. Similarly, there are several hundred references to passages about Jameson, which describe him in detail not as "gentleman" but as the unworldly and perverse man he has unwillingly described himself as. The form of presentation imitates court records, with long interrogations in which "Stanley" questions Bonny and others; he also acts as doubtful bystander, expressing scepticism towards the atrocities presented, thus heightening suspicion without apparently advancing his own case. Stanley's main concern here is not – remarkably enough – to present evidence that Barttelot and Jameson in numerous concrete instances were guilty of wrongful and cruel conduct. Rather, he writes they were guilty of having a spoiled upbringing, understood as their class background, or – as the *New York Times* wrote – their "Englishness"; they were not "insane", as the London newspapers wrote to pardon their conduct in 1890.

This asynchronous and massive justification project shows that Stanley would have liked to be able to relate all of this before a court of law that would have agreed, but knew it would have undermined the journeys' legitimacy as such, thus shattering the foundation of his own biography and identity, which consisted of his late nationalisation of a number of "un-British" drafts. For once, he chose to cover up the real reasons for his decision, and the published passages, both insinuating and making light of the gravity of the situation, formed the basis of the subsequent radicalisation and continuation of the mystery/misery discourse in the Congo Reform Association's campaigns, in which the "mute witnesses" were presented in the ghostly light of slide projectors all over Europe and the USA.

This closed space was, as we have seen, an exception for Stanley, whose discourse strived for transparency inspired by Homeric epic and New Journalism. Through the essayistic prose form, many spaces are put in motion, aided by the texts' perspectival rhetoric. This book's positive angle on Stanley's rhetoric is opposed to the branch of postcolonial criticism that focuses solely on the "monarch-of-all-I-survey" trope, neglecting conflicting and reversible perspectival play to justify a problematic, panoptical reading of the texts as an unambiguous discourse of dominance. This is the approach of Mary-Louise Pratt, but it is even more clear-cut in Daniel Bivona's *British Imperial Literature, 1870-1940: Writing and the administration of empire* (1998), in which the chapter on Stanley places him as a matter of course in the role of scapegoat for every colonial error. Bivona's reading particularly emphasises Stanley's utopian fantasies and his propaganda for free trade, which – in this ideological tradition – can only be a cloak for cruel exploitation of the native population.

Stanley's utopian passages, like the ones we have read about the fertile Bugunda, are not free of internal contradictions, and Bivona lists some of them, such as why it was necessary to convince the Bugandans about the advantages of international trade when they apparently had everything they needed. Likewise, Stanley's tendency to draw his conclusions on different tribes' readiness to trade on the basis of their either hostile or friendly attitudes towards the expedition is *petitio principia* and led to a problematic distinction between open and closed societies.

In the present prose perspective, however, the conclusion is not definitively dismissive of Stanley's ideas of free trade. His insistent plea that trade should not be limited by narrow national interests, protectionism and sectional interest may appear naïve if we judge it based on later knowledge; however, in Stanley's pioneer position, ideas of free trade had not yet been compromised by Léopold's misuse of it or by the nation states' unscrupulous division of Africa, which he regards critically in *In Darkest Africa* and other works. Stanley based his opinion on his own experiences as a traveller in the Congo, which told him that trade was the path to peace, development and prosperity, and a far better weapon in the fight against the slave trade than the missionary movements' appeal to global compassion for the natives, which kept them in a degrading position. When Stanley addressed nations around the world, arguing for the advantages of free trade for Europeans as well as Africans, it was a parallel to the travel books' constant arguments for free movement, flexibility and transparency. The free trade doctrine was the ultimate and most comprehensive formulation of Stanley's utopia – a borderless space for free

Stanley's commercial success with *In Darkest Africa* temporarily gave him the upper hand in the dispute about who was responsible for the accidents on the expedition, but in the long haul, the success of the books and Stanley's position as 'celebrity' paved the way for the books sinking into oblivion and Stanley becoming the scapegoat of twentieth-century postcolonial criticism. Countless retellings of the explorations in Africa replaced Stanley's own accounts, which were only available in edited, extremely abridged versions that favoured descriptions of violent events. Today, Stanley's changeable, multidirectional prose, open textual spaces, and perspectives on free trade can be extracted as a model example of one way of describing Africa.

movement and equal exchange. In the economical discourse that pervaded everything related to Stanley, free trade is the term that sums up the meaning of his transnational biography and the travel books' world literary space. Stanley's biography, and the creation and reception of the travel books, is to a great extent a story about conflicts and tensions between nation states and the new, transnational and globalised conditions for life and literature. Time after time, the travel books' success on the global market, especially in the USA, brushed aside the nationally rooted criticism of Stanley's credibility. For that very reason, he avoided the court case about the Emin Pasha Relief Expedition, placing his trust in the market instead.

Stanley's decision to keep the Jameson affair off-limits is one of the reasons why reception history has forgotten or underestimated his significance. His hesitation to go to court earned him great short-term success, while in the long run it paved the way for the mystery discourse, which would come to dominate western descriptions of the Congo from Conrad all the way up through the twentieth century, and stood out through its exposure of Stanley's American, pragmatic and direct New Journalism as dubious.

Stanley's utopian ideas of free trade are orchestrated as perspectival abundance in literary history's most spectacular and effective example of what today we call media globalisation. The travel books thematise, employ as material and are in themselves contributors to these new globalised conditions, while their hyperbolic and fantastic promotion of the potentials of free trade and globalisation explains why the books have been forgotten or suppressed by history. There are even contemporary reviews of *In Darkest Africa*, for instance in *The Edinburgh Review*, October 1890, that attack Stanley's far too optimistic estimates and calculations of the advantageous effects of free trade.[91] The recipients of the travel books were far removed from Stanley's transnational position; instead, they expanded in all the areas that might reinforce national interests, often followed by nationalistic ideology in the increasing competition between Germany, Great Britain and France for territories, and especially for Africa. While today we can acknowledge the vision in Stanley's insistence upon free trade, his contemporaries saw it as naïve and fantastic, and in the period that led up to the First World War also as anti-national. Since the 1960s postcolonial criticism has used Stanley's utopia as an example of pure imperialism, substantiating the claim with reference to his not officially dissociating himself from Léopold's regime when critical reports began to circulate around 1900.

The most inaccessible and the most open spaces in Stanley's prose contributed, each in their way, to preparing the future suppression of a unique work in book history and world literature. Bernard Piniau mentions in *Congo-Zaïre 1874-1981. La perception du lointain* (1992) other, more tangible reasons, in-

Stanley's grandson placing a wreath on a memorial for the 50th anniversary of the explorer's death in Kinshasa, 1954. A few years later the statue was pulled down and dumped on a scrapyard; it is still there.

cluding the fact that Stanley is perceived by many as Conrad's opposite, and that the comparison usually favours Conrad; we will return to this in the next section. Compared with Conrad's mystifying discourse, Stanley's is non-metaphysical, non-literary and "non-fabulating"; rather, he is practical and pragmatic, negotiating landscapes, beings and objects, which shows in the texts' realistic presentation of individualised, particular phenomena in the Congo. There is no cultural relativism or wild anthropological theory of unique cosmogony – "This world is human, plant-like, mineral, and to him [Stanley] first and foremost a real world, a synchronous world whose existence he – in a way that is as immediate as it is indisputable – proves in a physical, sensory and intellectual manner" (*Congo-Zaïre*, p. 40).

Stanley's texts represent a powerful alternative to the dominant images of the Congo found in the literature, media and political rhetoric of the twentieth century. According to Piniau, Stanley discovered the Congo and described it in all its diversity, while Conrad founded its topography by overwriting and outmatching Stanley. Conrad drew the Congo into Europe's own literature: Stanley drew the Congo nearer to Europe, while Conrad drew it further away. And the reception of Conrad caused the Congo to lose its historicity so effectively that future criticism censured Stanley, who – owing to his expeditions – was a key figure in the country's history.

However, Stanley's own texts also contributed to this suppression: the combination of his fame in his age, the books' status as bestsellers and the monstrosity of detail and magnitude – enhanced by the development of the book market - meant that Stanley's works in posterity were read in abridged, compiled versions that did not show his prosaic realism in presentation and ethics, but focused mainly on the most dramatic episodes. The titles and spectacular passages were cited time after time, positioning Stanley's works as reaffirmations of the twentieth-century Hegelian myth about the Dark Continent, though they actually strived for the opposite.

In the introduction to his book, Piniau argues that a study of literature and the media's iconographies of the Congo can be exemplary for our understanding of globalisation. The Congo's status as a non-topos in the world - an apparent exception from worldwide communicative networks - makes the study relevant for understanding the relationship between literature, the media and geopolitical power relations. The contraction of the world, often mentioned as a symptom of the effects of media globalisation, leaves places behind - the Congo being the most striking example - that do not move any closer to the global power centres and metropolises; rather, they are given distant positions, justified by the Conrad discourse, according to Piniau's analysis. The question is how the Congo can once again become "synchronous", part of our present, global communication: a real place in the world. One of the answers could be to re-read Stanley in the unabridged version. Not because his prose is a more suited representation of the place, but because the performative power the books wield as fetishes - i.e. the effects they have over great distances in time and space - position the Congo as an equal part of a boundlessly open, synchronous world. As Bernard Piniau points out, Stanley's prose not only drew the map of Africa; it created, for the first time, a common space for Central Africa, Europe and America.

III

To understand Heart of Darkness as a testimony about Red Rubber – King Léopold's reign of terror – we also need to consider the different contexts, genres and institutions of which the novel is part. Its effect as event and action occurs within a broad field of prose narratives that represent competing testimonies.

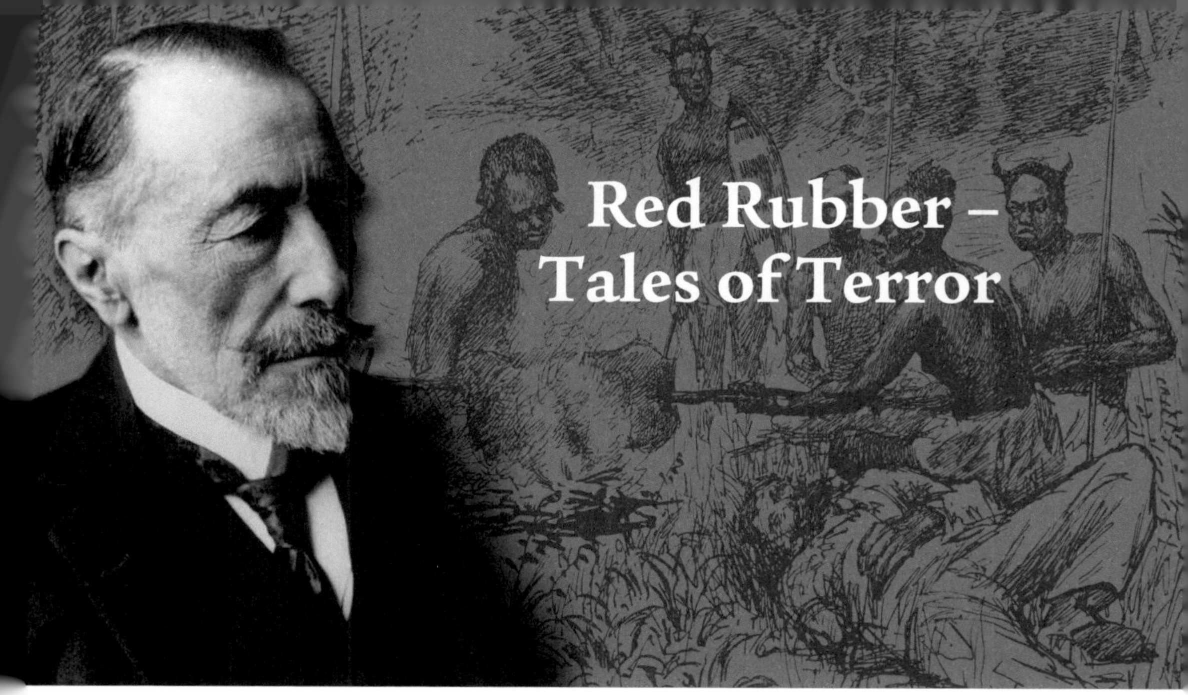

Red Rubber – Tales of Terror

The third section of this book is about the period of terror in the Congo's colonisation known as 'Red Rubber', and the highly diverse texts related to it. The thread followed through the material will be the double significance of testimony in the writing of history – a theme that has already been mentioned several times: ultimately, all we have is testimonies and the *criticism* of testimonies. From the perspective of history and literary history, understanding the Red Rubber period requires, on a concrete level, that we investigate *different* testimonies and view them as different prose strategies that convey the fluctuating relationship between the complexity of experience and interpretation. Contrary to the dominant tendency in research and debate, which allows a few testimonies to achieve monopoly status, this argument will present an alternative. A text's authority and credibility as a description of place cannot be illuminated on the basis of a perception of it as a singular event; it needs to be compared with other competing testimonies. Nevertheless, Joseph Conrad's *Heart of Darkness* inhabits a central position; let us therefore begin by investigating it.

The novel's first scene is set aboard the ship *Nellie,* which is moored while waiting for the tide to change at the mouth of the Thames. We are presented with the frame narrator, who introduces the place, situation and the four other men on the deck: "The Director", "The Lawyer", The Accountant" and Marlow, who is sitting cross-legged, looking like "an idol". The frame narrator remembers an incredible amount of detail, though there must be quite a gap between the time of the event and the account. He describes the atmosphere aboard as hesitant and meditative, completely in harmony with nature, the sunset and the play of colours that shrouds the twilit landscape in a hazy mist.

The narrator quotes Marlow commenting that this place used to be one of

From Marcus Bleasdale's *100 Years of Darkness* (2002). The book is an anniversary publication celebrating the best known narrative about the Congo, Conrad's *Heart of Darkness*, which was published in a serialised format in three parts in 1899 in the conservative, imperialistic *Blackwood's Magazine* and subsequently as a book in 1902. Bleasdale's book is printed in a large format, each entry laid out so that one side shows his black-and-white photographs and the other a quotation from Conrad's narrative. *100 Years of Darkness* is an example of a widespread understanding of Conrad's text as a morally indignant and colonialism-critical testimony. A review in *Time Magazine* praised Bleasdale for this take on the meaningless nightmare that has befallen the Congo.

the dark places on Earth, before giving a more thorough presentation of him; as opposed to most sailors, who have a preference for "a sedentary life", Marlow is a "wanderer". His tales are also atypical, when compared with most sailors' simple, direct canards, "the whole meaning of which lies within the shell of a cracked nut". In Marlow's tales "the meaning of an episode was not inside like a kernel but outside, enveloping the tale which brought it out only as a glow brings out a haze, in the likeness of one of these misty halos that sometimes are made visible by the spectral illumination of moonshine" (p. 9).[92]

After this presentation, Marlow takes over and maintains the narrative all the way to the end, only occasionally interrupted by comments from the frame narrator. The novel ends with Marlow quietly leant back, positioned as a meditating Buddha, and *Nellie* being taken out to sea by the tide. The location of the frame narrative is the deck of the ship. We are told where the ship is moored, but also that all contours are dissolved in the deepening darkness surrounding Marlow's narrative. In the concluding lines, the darkness seems to have reached a more universal, mysterious and dense significance: while the frame narrator in the beginning imagines how the tide, together with the great explorers, brings the torch of progress to the darkest corners of the world, the end is bereft of any faith that the tide will bring *Nellie* out on a mission of enlightenment.

Marlow begins by saying that the English coasts used to be dark places in the world too, where once upon a time the Roman Empire had its outposts, and lonesome men far away from home were confronted with mysteries and savagery. The difference between them and the company on the deck, Marlow points out, is that the latter are far more effective colonisers, guided by an idea. The frame narrator warns the reader that they will encounter a tale about one of Marlow's "inconclusive experiences", concerning the time when he signed up as a freshwater sailor on a great river in Africa: "how I got out there, what I saw, how I went up that river to the place where I met that poor chap. It was the farthest point of navigation and the culmination point of my experience" (p. 11).

He cried whisperingly at some image, at some vision – he cried twice, with a cry that was no more than a breath – 'The horror! The horror!'

Children flee soldiers in Kinshasa. Fear is a constant throughout the Congo, as are rumours of rebel attacks, assassination attempts, and daily civil rights abuses.

... the sun sank low, and from glowing white changed to a dull red without rays and without heat, as if about to go out suddenly, striken to death by the touch of that gloom brooding over a crowd of men.

After a forced march from their home in the neighbouring DRC, children watch their mother die in a hospital in the Republic of Congo. Here, as in many countries along its borders, medical aid is non-existent.

Marlow's narrative follows in the same vein, with detailed descriptions of the individual stops on the journey. On the way down along the coast, toward the country with the great river, Marlow encounters, from a distance, the colonial presence of the French as an absurd farce. On his arrival, he notes the railway workers' wretched state and the completely meaningless nature of their work. Except for one European who has "backbone", everybody is in a state of moral disintegration and acting strangely. Here, he hears about Mr Kurtz for the first time – "a first-class agent" who collects more ivory than anyone else, "a very remarkable person" – before continuing on a dreary journey by foot, accompa-

nied by another white man who must be carried in a hammock due to a fever.

When he reaches the outpost, he encounters another absurdity: the river steamer, which he was supposed to use, is an upside-down wreck. Secretly, he overhears several conversations between the manager and one of his spies about the mysterious Mr Kurtz, and when the manager subsequently lectures him about his major influence on the central administration, Marlow pumps him for information about Kurtz:

> "'He is an emissary of pity, and Science, and progress, and devil knows what else. We want,' he began to declaim suddenly, 'for the guidance of the cause entrusted to us by Europe, so to speak, higher intelligence, wide sympathies, a singleness of purpose.' 'Who says that?' I asked. 'Lots of them,' he replied. 'Some even write that; and so *he* comes here, a special being, as you ought to know.' 'Why ought I to know?' I interrupted, really surprised. (...) 'You are one of the new gang – the gang of virtue. The same people who sent him specially also recommended you'" (p. 28).

Marlow continues describing the state of the boat, how he leads the manager to believe that he has connections with great powers in Europe and how he is growing more and more obsessed with Kurtz. Once in a while he breaks off the narration in order to ask his audience whether they can picture the story, or whether it also appears as a dream to them. Marlow overhears another confidential conversation that indicates that the manager and his assistant have decided to get rid of Kurtz, who has proven to be too much competition for them.

The narrative about the journey up the river constitutes the second part of the novel, while the third and last part accounts for the encounter with Kurtz and the return to London. The journey into the country is described by Marlow as a journey into darkness, back to the earliest times. This weakens his ability to sense the difference between "surface truth" and "inner truth"; only the navigation of the river offers a fixed point of reference. The frame narrator interrupts to describe Marlow's increasing excitement as he draws nearer the story's goal, which results in a more disconnected, fragmented narration. After a pause, Marlow mentions how he was longing to hear Kurtz's voice, and he explains that even before the meeting he felt some kind of admiration for the extraordinary man – even after he received confirmation of his inkling that Kurtz had gone mad and yet exercised complete power over the engulfing darkness. Kurtz may be mad, but he is also incredibly rhetorically talented – something that Marlow can deduce from a report to "The International Society for the Suppression of Savage Customs", written by Kurtz. The report exhorts readers to "Exterminate all the brutes!" (p. 51), which is rather inconsistent with the pamphlet's humanist preaching. After attacks on natives and an interview with a Russian loner, who prepares Marlow for the encounter with Kurtz by providing more fragmented anecdotes about the man's greatness and cruelty, the small expedition finally reaches the sick and spiritually blackened Kurtz. His voice and eloquence, however, command Marlow's respect and admiration, while the manager and the other "pilgrims" only see him as insane. Their business is determined by envy and veiled, selfish motives, from which Marlow distances himself. Before meeting Kurtz, he denies being a great admirer, and after the meeting he eagerly emphasises that Kurtz – despite his practising "unspeakable rites" (Marlow sees with his own eyes, for instance, the skulls on the palisades around the station), and his blatant lack of purpose in his actions – acts with consequence, based on moral strength and untouchable truth or principle. In Marlow's mind, Kurtz possesses the "inner truth" missing in the other Europeans and – what becomes increasing clear – in himself as well. Reluctantly, and plagued by inner conflict because he realises that Kurtz has transgressed a dangerous limit, Marlow takes it upon himself to protect Kurtz's posthumous reputation as "a remarkable man": someone who had something to say and said it.

When Marlow returns to London, representatives of different interests request that he hand over Kurtz's writings. A company representative is satisfied with the report about "the Suppression of Savage Customs"; however, Marlow tears the addition "Exterminate all the brutes!" off it. One of Kurtz's journalist colleagues, who believes that Kurtz's unique eloquence could have earned him a prominent political career in one of the extreme wings, is handed a similar report, while Marlow keeps the real story to himself. In Marlow's last passage, he pays a visit to Kurtz's fiancée, where he – a man who hates lying – honours Kurtz's last words in the gathering darkness that surrounded them both. Instead of repeating Kurtz's real last words, "the horror, the horror", he tells her what she longs to hear most: "The last word he pronounced was – your name" (p. 75).

Heart of Darkness is a work of fiction with a powerful core that exerts an immense, long-term impact on readers, critics and authors, who continue to be challenged by, and enter into dialogue with, the text – aiming to learn from, outmatch or surpass it. Olof Lagercrantz's *A journey with the Heart of Darkness* (1987) is one of many examples of how an author may perceive Conrad's short novel as a substrate for lifelong identity formation – a master text that enigmatically contains the answers to life's great questions while providing moral and artistic guidance. To Lagercrantz, the relationship is characterised by rivalry, a conflict with the predecessor that allows him to escape its influence and discover his own originality. This far from uncomplicated legacy affects many third world writers, but also, as we will see, Graham Greene's, V. S. Naipaul's and Urs Widmer's Congo novels.[93] As part of the English, European, postcolonial and later world literature canon, the text has had a wide-ranging influence on

the history of literature and criticism, challenging readers' sense of morals and aesthetics, and continuously instigating strong reactions.

Conrad's own experiences from his journey up the Congo River in 1890 form part of the novel and are, without doubt, partly the reason behind its strong moral and aesthetic appeal. These experiences are disseminated in a language that is highly suggestive and draws the reader into a fascinating and mysterious space, speaking the senses and luring interpreters from all schools of thought into looking for meaning in the novel and the literary-aesthetic conditions it defines as an institution.

Reading *Heart of Darkness* from the prose perspective, the same degree of attention is not paid to the novel's role within the art literature tradition. The subject below will be the novel's dialogue with a broad field of prose forms. *Heart of Darkness* is also a travel account that contributes to a long series of descriptions of space and place in nineteenth-century literature about Africa. Texts such as Stanley's travel books, abolitionist literature, adventure fiction and Conrad's own travel diaries are not outside or prior to the novel's space but parts of it, in that they produce the conditions for the novel's function within a literary-historical transformative field, and for the understanding of Congo as a place, with effects that are still perceptible today. This diversity of texts and prose genres that surround *Heart of Darkness* is carefully pinpointed by the text through Marlow's relatively detailed account of the way in which he takes responsibility for Kurtz's documents, garbles them and hands them over to politicians and journalists back in London, where they are used as testimonies, though completely removed from their original context.

The current prose perspective will foreground the novel's dialogue with, and creation of, these spaces; its universal, moral qualities will play a less important part. The focus will rather be on the text's description and understanding of place, and the type of experience Conrad confronts in his famous novel. In recent years, the discussion has considered how - and to what extent - Conrad aesthetically shapes the journey's experiences of terror - i.e. violations against natives, racism and colonial violence. The hypothesis that will form the basis of the following appraisals is, on the contrary, that Conrad did not experience acts of terror on his journey, or at least that he did not perceive, experience, understand or communicate them as terrible. The experience we read about in the relevant diaries and letters is rather one of disappointment and illness, and first and foremost it is the distance, secrecy and doubt that is conveyed and superbly expressed in an authentic, aesthetic form in the novel. Arguments will be made for this correction, and for reading Conrad's novel from the prose perspective. It will become clear that both aspects encompass a revision of events and primary causal relations in relation to the novel's creation and initial reception, reaching beyond the narrow scope of literary studies. What type of 'reality work' does the text contribute in a broad field of prose narratives?

Franco Moretti, one of the leading figures in the re-launch of 'world literature' as a focus for reading transnational exchange of literature and genres from a current and retrospective perspective, has suggested "distant reading" as a method to approach the immense body of world literature.[94] New Criticism's "close reading" keeps to formalistic analyses of isolated, autonomous works within well-defined, limited national canons. Distant reading, on the other hand, takes into account the actual immeasurability of world literature, and instead of close reading primary texts, it makes sense to extract primary patterns in world literary developments through studies of how genres have travelled, as well as of others' readings. We will return to this principle below; for now, let us simply note that the strategy cannot stand alone: without close reading, the previous section could not, for instance, have argued the case that Stanley's texts hold a key position in important patterns in world literature.

Nevertheless, distant reading will be employed in some measure in the following discussions of patterns in travel literature from the period in Congo's history known as 'Red Rubber', named after the Free State's intensified and ruthless extraction of crude rubber from the middle of the 1880s. Joseph Conrad's short novel *Heart of Darkness* will be the central point of departure. Not through close readings of the text, of which thousands have been presented throughout the lengthy, complicatedly ramified interpretative play in the novel's reception history, but through distant readings of a number of responses to the text an investigation will be made into which mechanisms underlie different types of readings of the text to illuminate Conrad's role in the mythology surrounding the so-called "atrocities".

Adam Hochschild's bestseller *King Leopold's Ghost* has received international recognition as the first work to present complete documentation for what Hochschild calls a forgotten "holocaust" or "genocide". In his dramatic narrative – "a work of history that reads like a novel", as one review put it – Stanley's journeys are portrayed as crimes against humanity, and Conrad's novel as a detailed and shocking testimony based directly on the author's personal experiences, while Edmund Morel's involvement in the reform movement's campaigns against the Free State is seen as a heroic model of self-sacrifice and altruism for later human rights organisations. These organisations have repaid Hochschild by taking his book to heart as a powerful justification for their international activities, thus linking them to a glorious past and an unquestionably good cause in which a coordinated, voluntary and international campaigning effort led to justice.[95] Hochschild's book is, as the title suggests, an attempt to let the skeletons out of the closet. In the epilogue to later editions, and in interviews, the author is

very keen to emphasise that the story has been completely wiped clean from the memory of both the Belgian and international communities. He also lashes out at the attitude of literary studies towards Conrad's novel as a tale of universal evil rather than a description of concrete, localised historical events.

In the following, reference will be made to Conrad's novel, letters and diaries in Robert Kimbrough's *Heart of Darkness: an authoritative text, backgrounds and sources criticism* (1971), supplemented with primary materials from *The collected letters of Joseph Conrad* (1983-2008), Roger Casement's report and diaries in Séamas Ó Síochain and Michael O'Sullivan's *The Eyes of Another Race: Roger Casement's Congo report and 1903 diary* (2004) and Edmund Morel's published pamphlets. In addition to the three major works on *Heart of Darkness* discussed in the first chapter of this section, the study of Conrad's novel is based on a number of articles that illuminate the text's function as testimony. The outline of colonial history is based on primary materials supplemented with the documents in Barbara Harlow and Mia Carter's *Archives of Empire* (2003), as well as general texts about the Red Rubber period, including Adam Hochschild's *King Leopold's Ghost*, Samuel Nelson's balanced *Colonialism in the Congo Basin 1880-1940* (1994), Jean Stenger's *Congo. Mythes et réalités. 100 ans d'histoire* (1989) and a number of articles about the magnitude of terrors and tales of terror in an anthology edited by Jean-Luc Vellut, *La mémoire du Congo. Le temps colonial* (2005). Susanne Gehrmann's *Kongo-Greuel. Zur literarischen Konfiguration eines kolonialkritischen Diskurses (1890-1910)* (2003) balanced account of the terror campaign and the link between Conrad and the reform movement has contributed important aspects to the conclusion reached here.

In the previous chapter, it was rendered probable that Hochschild's use of Stanley as a scapegoat is historically fallible and results in problematic simplifications of the history of the Free State. A contention of the following will be that not only historians like Hochschild, but also vast numbers of international critics and literary researchers use Joseph Conrad in a faulty and twisted manner, resulting in significant historical blind spots. If we wish to understand the text as a testimony, we need to look at the different contexts, genres and institutions of which it is part, which are inseparable from its effect as event and action. There is not space in this book to analyse these institutions exhaustively, but some of the most important ones will be outlined first in relation to the novel's place in travel literature, second in relation to its effect in and on the Congo Reform Association and finally in a comparison with selected prose narratives that present competing testimonies about the Red Rubber period. Together, these elements will constitute the prose field in which *Heart of Darkness* operates.

1 *Heart of Darkness* in Travel Literature

In 1890, Joseph Conrad took a job in Léopold's service as a ship's mate on one of the steam ships that freighted passengers and goods between the Congo Free State's trade stations north of Stanley Pool. In several respects, Stanley was the background for and context of Conrad's journey, as well as his novel. Stanley had paved the way for the steamer traffic, and it was also he who founded most of the outposts during the colonisation process described in his immense work *The Congo and the Founding of its Free State* (1885), which was published in eight languages. In the book's preface, Stanley does not resist the opportunity to mock the British for not accepting his proposal in 1878 of engaging actively in the colonisation of Congo. As will become clear from the book's descriptions, he writes, Léopold, through Stanley's immense effort, has succeeded in establishing infrastructure and administration across a vast area. This has facilitated trade with a completely new and unexploited market, which the investors, however, will only really profit from when a railway has been built on the very difficult stretch from Matadi to Stanley Pool. The basic motivation is still the ideal of free trade, established at the international conference in Berlin. The book's description of a "history of a great and successful political and diplomatical achievement" is dedicated to "His Majesty Léopold II, the King of the Belgians, the generous monarch who so nobly conceived, ably conducted, and munificently sustained the enterprise which has obtained the recognition of all the great powers of the world". Stanley expresses the view that he will be surprised if the railway has not been built within one year, and he concludes his preface by handing over his "work to the public, in the hope that it will effect a happy change for Africa, and give a greater impetus to the true civilising influences which are seen in the advancement of commerce and in the vitality of Christian missions" (p. 15).

Furthermore, the preface lays out these perspectives as part of a Christian obligation to promote work and trade as the route to progress, and as such it is a manifestation of imperialist ideology – a crystal clear example of the promotion of "Christianity", "commerce" and "civilisation". The contents of the book, however, are not nearly as unambiguous, in rhetoric or ideology; rather, it continues, to some degree, the composite form of *Through the Dark Continent* – partly because *The Congo* is not as much a travel account as it is a text about the river, work and colonisation. In the preface, the two books are connected: *Through the Dark Continent* led to the colonisation of Africa –the annexation not only of Congo but also of West Africa, the Niger Delta and the rest of

the continent. *The Congo* describes the consequences of the first book; *Through the Dark Continent* is performative, while *The Congo* is descriptive. Stanley cites Léon Gambetta, who would subsequently become foreign minister for France, making the following "prediction" in July 1878 after having read the account of the Anglo-American expedition: "Not only, sir, have you opened up a new Continent to our view, but you have given impulse to scientific and philanthropic enterprise which will have material effect on the progress of the world. It is not only in the action of private individuals that that is seen. What you have done has influenced Governments – proverbially so difficult to be moved – and the impulse you have imparted upon them will, I am convinced, go on growing year after year" (p. 6). In 1885 the prediction, according to Stanley's preface, had more or less come true, though *The Congo* also tells a different story – one of chaos and corruption, illnesses and rebellion, not to mention the landscape putting up a fight against the attempt to construct roads.

While Conrad stayed in Belgium's "city of death" in 1890, Stanley was being enthusiastically received in Antwerp and Brussels following his return from the Emin Pasha Relief Expedition. There were parades through the city to the castle, where Léopold was trying in vain to get Stanley to embark on even wilder adventures. The king's intention was that Stanley would train and lead 20,000 Congolese warriors to conquer Khartoum. In 1890, *Through the Dark Continent* was republished simultaneously all over Europe, becoming a significant factor in the creation of the Congo as "the rage of Europe".[96] Both *Through the Dark Continent* and *The Congo* were factors in Léopold's large-scale recruitment campaign to get European soldiers, administrators, mariners and so on to the Free State, where they would handle his private interests under strict stipulations of secrecy. However, it is important to distinguish between Stanley's and Léopold's very different projects, especially considering their subsequent, uncritical confusion. Stanley was first and foremost an enthusiastic supporter of the creation of transnational free trade zones, and for a long time he believed that this was the cause he was working for. This was also the case for one of his friends and employees, Roger Casement, who would later become a prominent member of the Congo Reform Association, and for most of the other participants in the first phase of the colonisation.[97]

Joseph Conrad had been granted British citizenship in 1886. He had passed his British ship's mate exam and was waiting for his diploma to become captain, but even before he finished his education, he realised that his eagerly expected career as a captain on large intercontinental ships was threatened by new technology: steamers were gaining footing, and to Conrad that was the *coup de grace* for an era in which the aristocratic ideals of honour and plight were still linked with real achievements, travels and adventures. The Suez Canal had been opened in 1869, which he saw as a curse, and he later wrote how French and Egyptian engineers had dug an ugly but profitable ditch and let countless steamers spread their steam over "the restless mirror of the Infinite": "The hand of the engineer tore down the veil of the terrible beauty in order that greedy and faithless landlubbers might pocket dividends. The mystery was destroyed".[98]

Joseph Conrad was in Brussels when Stanley was being celebrated for his 'rescue' of Emin, who – like Kurtz in *Heart of Darkness* – had no desire to be rescued. Conrad was in the city to sign a three-year contract with Societé Anonyme pour le Commerce du Haut-Congo to become a ship's mate on what he expected would become an expedition to make additional discoveries about the upper parts of the Congo River – equivalent to the novel's "Eldorado Exploring Expedition". It appears from his letters of the period that his ambition was to create a situation in which he might rediscover the romantic journeys he had read about, for instance in Stevenson's romances from the islands in the southern oceans. Later, Conrad writes in *A Personal Record*[99] that as early as 1868, when he was nine years old, he had put his finger on a "blank space representing the unsolved mystery of the continent" and said to himself: "when I grow up I shall go *there*". Later in his life – with far fewer unbroken illusions – he would find himself in this place, "as if the sin of childish audacity was to be visited on my mature head. Yes. I did go there: *there* being the region of Stanley Falls, which in '68 was the blankest of blank spaces on the earth's figured surface" (p. 13). Conrad's turn towards Congo is in accordance with the mid-nineteenth-century turn towards inland expeditions, especially in Africa, which had replaced the great fleet expeditions to the Pacific Ocean in James Cook's wake. The young Polish-born man's dream to partake in a "civilizing mission" was based on a romantic hope of rediscovering the mystery that modern technology had eliminated and finding "truths" that were not compromised by what he – presumably with reference to Stanley – called "newspaper stunts".

Conrad's expectations were strikingly unrealistic, nostalgic, desperate and illogical, for example when he decided – despite his aforementioned attitudes – to sail with a steamer and enter into a contract with a company whose activities he was not blind to (according to his letters from the journey to Boma), and which made the Suez Canal appear philanthropic in comparison. Other expectations, however, might have been more important: though Conrad was discreet about it, he was planning a career that involved neither sails nor steam, but had to do with the hope of being able to write travel romances in the style of Stevenson's *Treasure Island* (1883). On the journey in Congo, Conrad brought along the half-finished manuscript of *Almayer's Folly*, his literary debut. In a letter to his cousin, Karol Zagórski, sent from Sierra Leone on the way down, Conrad puts into words his desperate hopes and anxieties regarding both the

expedition and his prospects of becoming a writer. The letter is written as a small stylistic exercise for Zagórski, revealing the poetic shifts that led Conrad from reading Flaubert's *Madame Bovary* to writing *Almayer's Folly*, which – according to a biographical note – he began on the cover of Flaubert's ironic romance. Conrad's description of his rushed departure from Brussels is a kind of poetics *en miniature*:

"If you had only seen all the tin boxes and revolvers, the high boots and the tender farewells; just another handshake and just another pair of trousers! – and if you knew all the bottles of medicine and all the affectionate wishes I took away with me, you would understand in what a typhoon, cyclone, hurricane, earthquake – no! – in what a universal cataclysm, in what a fantastic atmosphere of mixed shopping, business, and affecting scenes, I passed two whole weeks" (Kimbrough, p. 152).

The "universal cataclysm" of "bottles of medicine" and "affectionate wishes" corresponds with the way Flaubert wrote about the discovery of his new style in a travel account from Egypt: his writing, when he became a real author – because he, too, planned a career in literature – would generate just such a clash between the trivial and the beautiful. Conrad's ironic style also resembles the young Flaubert's when it reveals his insecurity rather than showing off his status as a fearless traveller and author in the making. In the letter, Conrad sums up the bleak employment statistics in Congo – including that 60 % of colonists are sent home within six months in order not to burden the territory with casualties, and that only 7 % complete the three-year contract. He adds with irony: "To tell the truth, they are French! Des nevrosés! (C'est très chic d'être nevrosé – one winks and speaks through the nose)". Meanwhile, Conrad pretends to be invulnerable in his unique, international transvestism – "a Polish nobleman, cased in British tar" – and he finishes ironically and yet seriously by referring to himself as "the distinguished personage who is penning this autograph (...). Future generations will read it with admiration (and I hope with profit). In the meantime, trêves de bêtises!" (p. 153).

Only three weeks later, on 10 June 1890, Conrad's letter to his aunt is written in a different, disillusioned language, complaining that there is nothing new under the sun, "no new events. As to feelings, also nothing new, and there is the trouble". If only one was able to empty one's soul, memory and brain and thereby achieve "a whole new set of these things, life would become perfectly diverting. As this is impossible, life is not diverting. It is abominably sad!" (p. 153). Conrad's mixed expectations about his new position in Congo had been lowered even more on the way there, and on 15 May 1890 he reports from Tenerife:

"One doubts the future. For indeed – I ask myself – why should anyone believe in it? And, consequently, why be sad about it? A little illusion, many dreams, a rare flash of happiness followed by disillusionment, a little anger and much suffering, and then the end. Peace! That is the programme, and we must see this tragi-comedy to the end. One must play one's part in it" (p. 152).

What Conrad describes in his poetic letter to his cousin as a cataclysm of productive juxtapositions in this "wicked world", is, in his moralistic and confessional letters to his aunt, presented as a clash between idealism and scepticism – with an emphasis on the latter. This corresponds with what critics agree on viewing as a dominant and consistent tendency in his writing, although they rarely associate it with the nineteenth-century tradition of romance and travel literature or with Flaubert.

During his stay in Congo from 12 June to 4 December 1890, Conrad wrote a diary ("The Congo Diary") about the strenuous trek from Matadi to Léopoldville, which everyone who was serving in Upper Congo must complete, given that Stanley's vision of a railway had still not become reality in 1890. The work was initiated three months before Conrad's arrival and finished in 1898. Furthermore, he took notes on his brief spell as a ship's hand aboard the river steamer *Roi des Belges* – "The Up-river Book". When he returned to London, he was ill and devastated. During a long hospital stay he continued writing the first five chapters of *Almayer's Folly*, which was published in 1895 and followed by *Outcast of the Islands* in 1896. In the interim period, he went on several long journeys – to Australia, Malaysia and Thailand – as a ship's mate and captain, before becoming a full-time author in 1896. In spring 1899, *Heart of Darkness* was published; according to most critics it is his best work, although its reception at the time was more sceptical. It was thought that *Heart of Darkness* was inconsistent with Conrad's other novels, showing he was "ready to experiment artistically with very private material" (Kimbrough p. ix); its suggestive and impressionistic style was very different from the former works' descriptively and thematically clear narratives. Robert Kimbrough writes in his introduction that *Heart of Darkness*, according to Ian Watt, was Conrad's first and only "symbolic work". He also notes, however, that Conrad himself responded to reader's criticisms of the overly symbolic representation of Kurtz, recognising that it was an error on his part as "mental laziness took the line of least resistance". *Heart of Darkness* was first published in *Blackwood's Magazine* in three parts in February, March and April 1899 and republished in 1902, alongside two other stories.

These comments, which raise the question of how the texts could simultaneously be an experiment with private material and Conrad's most symbolic work, sum up the extremes in the novel's reception history. One tendency

among critics has been to admire the book for its universalistic and aesthetic characteristics, substantiating interpretations achieved via analyses of the textual form and emphasis on its many stylistic and narrative layers. Another school has attached special importance to the context of *Heart of Darkness*, particularly the fact that it was written on the basis of Conrad's own experiences in Congo.[100] However, this fact leads the 'contextualists' to two different appraisals, either condemning Conrad as a racist because of the text's descriptions of Congo as an indefinable hell populated by mute beasts, or praising him as one of the period's few critics of imperialism, which is supported by observations of Marlow's criticism of the Belgian administration. The focus in the following investigation will be on the novel's impressionistic or suggestive style, which all critics agree is important, although they assess it very differently. The question will be studied with specific attention to the novel's use of "The Congo Diary" and "The Up-river Book", which will be viewed in the context of Conrad's place in nineteenth-century travel and adventure fiction. The aim is to bring the discussion to a comparison with Stanley and to the collapse of the classical travel genre represented by the two authors. Initially, this will be achieved through the presentation and comparison of three books' interpretations of *Heart of Darkness*, which emphasise in different ways the links between the diaries, the novel and travel literature as a genre.

Modernist Form and Embodied Experience

Jakob Lothe's 2002 book *Joseph Conrad* is a comprehensive portrait of the author and an introduction to his works, while at the same time taking stock of twenty years of Conrad studies. In the preface, Lothe identifies one of the reasons for his fascination with the author as the travel motif that pervades both his biography and works. When *Heart of Darkness* appeared on Lothe's curriculum at the University of Bergen in the 1970s, he found the novel difficult and dreary, but the travel descriptions made him read on, perhaps because, as he writes, he had not travelled much: "For someone who does not travel much, the ideas of travelling usually become stronger". In Lothe's broad presentation, the travel motif and *Heart of Darkness* occupy central positions.

In the preface, Lothe assumes the view of literature that supports his arguments throughout. He belongs to a generation of literary researchers who were "brought up to emphasise the form of literature rather than the author's life". Form is crucial to content, though biographical information is not rejected as a means of shedding light on important aspects of the text. The important thing is to keep a keen eye on their complex relationship. In Conrad's case, biographical detail is "highly informative, *because* it is indirect and complicated" (Lothe,

p. 10). Part of Lothe's book places his authorship in the history of ideas and literature with regard to the main European currents in the period; another part emphasises textual analysis as the main works, including *Heart of Darkness*, are interpreted to give a comprehensive understanding of Conrad's art. Precise and balanced, Lothe's account is particularly interesting because, apart from focusing on the general influence of the travel motif, it puts more emphasis than is usual on "The Congo Diary" and "The Up-river Book" – works that he has studied previously.[101]

In Lothe's understanding, the diaries – primarily "The Congo Diary" – can be seen as intermediate stages in Conrad's writing becoming literature. The diary is fragmented, more directed at the writer than the reader, but still communicates the disappointment Conrad experienced as harsh reality shattered his dreams, expressed mainly through his criticism of the Belgian administration, though there are also racist comments regarding the native population. The latter are partly explained with reference to Conrad's feeling of being distant from everything and everyone during his stay in Congo, and partly with reference to his reaction to the violence against the natives, which was stronger than that of most Europeans. "In this undetermined combination of ignorance and insight lies a form of literary potential which Conrad could later employ in *Heart of Darkness*" (p. 38).

In Lothe's interpretation, this is a central clue. Conrad is not only "homo duplex", he is also "scriptor duplex", and the tensions and paradoxes that characterise his life experiences are expressed through his fiction. Conrad's distinct stretch between idealism, scepticism and pragmatism, his triple identity regarding language and nationality, and his extreme conservatism and solidarity with the poor and persecuted are all factors that influenced his modernism. The period's tensions are also the author's, expressed in an increasingly clear modernist form. Similarly, his attitude towards imperialism is ambivalent. It is a significant part of his own past experience, due to Russia's occupation of Poland; however, his scepticism does not bring him to reject the concept, only to distinguish between the ways different nations go about it. British colonialism was preferable by far to Russian or Belgian. Once again, the point of view is that the literary work profits from Conrad's ambivalence, retrospectively adding nuance to the author's attitude towards imperialism. The overall description of Conrad is as an early modernist. He inherited Flaubert's perception of the author as both a critic of society and an artist, as well as his simultaneously ironic and sympathetic style and his experiments with the narrative shaping of time and causality.

Leading up to the interpretation of *Heart of Darkness*, travel literature is considered as one of Conrad's inspirations. Lothe mentions Mungo Park's and Livingstone's travel books, although he concedes that Conrad's text is not consistent

with either. Likewise, the novel does not appear to fit naturally into the distinction between "representing" and "nomadic" forms, which Lothe takes from Syed Islam's *The Ethics of Travel*.[102] A travel book in the representing form perceives its own culture as more civilised than another and does not learn anything from the journey, while the nomadic form is more open and dialogical. Conrad's diary, however, is closer to Park's subjective style than to Livingstone's – which, according to Mary Louise Pratt, is devoid of descriptions of natives – because Conrad describes and makes visible the use of force against natives.

The relationship between diary and fiction can, according to Lothe, be characterised with Adorno's term "embodied experience", i.e. the processing and distancing of experience into a literary form. Form thus becomes the focus for Lothe, who traces the incorporation as a subtle, shifting process via a detailed analysis of the novel's narrative mechanisms. The frame narrator's relation to Marlow, and their respective relations to the story told and their audience of fellow passengers are described as obscuring measures that have similarities with impressionist painting. The narrative situation in which Marlow uses the wait for the tide to tell his strange tale is compared with Claude Monet's painting of a riverboat on the Thames with the vague outline of the parliament building in the background. The painting communicates an interpretation that "highlights the close relationship between the observed and the observer, between the external world of reality and man's (the subject's) attempt to navigate in this world" (p. 107). There are similarities in the construction of space and time in the novel's complex doublings and repetitions, in which linear and circular movements are interwoven in paradoxical patterns; it is not clear whether different sequences – for instance, the parallel between Marlow's narrative about the Roman colonisation of the British Isles and the journey up the Congo River shaped as a journey back in time – substantiate or subvert each other.

Lothe, however, distinguishes between Conrad's different uses of the two narrators. First-time readers of the novel will probably accept the frame narrator's imperialist phrases as if they express the attitude of the novel itself. The frame narrator invites the reader to approve of the imperialist ideology that was dominant among the majority of the readers who encountered the novel in *Blackwood's Magazine* alongside other imperialist propaganda. Conrad assured Blackwood of his complete solidarity with the magazine's position, and in his letters he made sure to avoid anything that might be perceived as ideologically offensive, just as it was important to him that the text appealed to the readers. In Lothe's interpretation, the frame narrator has this assimilating function, while Marlow introduces doubts about the frame narrator's and the reader's values, thus carrying out a critical function. When Marlow points out that Britain also used to be one of the dark places on Earth, in Lothe's opinion we are dealing with a significant ideological point that positions the frame narrator's given assumption that London is the centre of the empire in a relativistic and historicising context. From this shifted perspective, London is positioned on the barbaric periphery of the Roman Empire. The novel's narrative structure thus manipulates the reader into a situation where they are forced to navigate their way into the novel's problem complex, searching for meaning within the text. This process is exposed with irony in the naïve frame narrator's insightful warning to the reader that with Marlow one cannot expect to find meaning *in* a nutshell, as is the case in normal sailors' tales; rather, it is to be found *around* the story, like the rings of mist around the moon.

Lothe refers to Tzvetan Todorov's, Peter Brooks' and J. Hillis Miller's interpretations of *Heart of Darkness*, which concurrently conclude that the narrative dynamics both deter the reader from and lure them towards a centre - a heart of darkness in the text - which turns out to be empty or illegible. In relation to Conrad's experiences in Congo, Lothe writes:

"Behind Marlow stands Conrad: as the text's most important narrator, Marlow presents facets of the experiences which the captain and future author had in the Congo. However, we cannot conclude on that background that Marlow 'is', or represents, Conrad in any simple or unambiguous manner. Conrad's narrative method is indirect and composite - in other words literary" (p. 116).

Correspondingly, Conrad's obscuring of specific names and places is interpreted as another aspect of "the literary generalisation process" - explicit naming would have fatal consequences for Conrad's art. The intertextual references to Virgil and Dante point in the same direction: to Lothe, Conrad's and Marlow's experiences are included in a literary intertextuality that collaborates with impressionism in the depiction of Marlow's uncertainty and doubt.

In Lothe's understanding, the aesthetic form supports the critical function of the text. Addressing the objection that Marlow's explicitly positive assessment of the British colonisation as "real work" denotes clear limits to both his and Conrad's criticism, writes Lothe: "As literature, the novel presents a criticism of European imperialism which is, simultaneously, specific and general: specific in the criticism of what the Belgians did in Congo; doubtful and questioning in regard to imperialism as a historical phenomenon and activity". (p. 132). Addressing Chinua Achebe's criticism of Conrad as a racist because he depicts the native Congolese as dehumanised, Lothe refers to specific passages in which the violence against black people is explicit, as well as to the text's general scepticism towards the imperialistic project in Africa. Though it is not consistent, the novel is - according to Lothe - "extremely critical" towards the

imperial use of violence, and because it is a piece of literature, it overcomes its own tendencies to become racist:

"Given that the book is a literary text, its criticism possesses a persuasive power that is not eliminated by the hints of racism contained in the same text. The content of ideas in *Heart of Darkness* is composite and partly conflicting: The book is a modernist novel that expresses doubt, preferring to ask questions rather than providing definite answers" (p. 145).

With his focus on form, Lothe extracts a balanced and nuanced interpretation of the novel that is among the most convincing interpretations within the aesthetic-formalist tradition in Conrad criticism. And because his theoretical starting point does not isolate the text, but rather places it in the contexts of the history of ideas, Congo and imperialism, while also including Conrad's personal experiences, it is far more challenged and challenging than, for instance, Todorov's and Hillis Miller's. However, problems are also revealed in relation to the link between experience and literary form. These questions are difficult to solve, and Lothe prefers to ask questions rather than provide answers – like the novel, in his interpretation. This manifests itself as a difficulty in the argumentation that leads Lothe to the conclusion that the novel is extremely critical towards imperialism, specifically because it is written in an aesthetic, modernistic form.

The assumption concerning the modernistic text's tense, enigmatic values gives present-day interpreters leeway to switch back and forth between specific and general textual levels in their argumentation. Marlow's specific imperialistic characteristics are rejected with general reference to his doubts, while reservations about the text's impressionistic tendency to blur its references and raise questions about its position – thus obscuring its criticism – is reputed by highlighting specific details in the text such as Marlow's focus on violence against the natives. Similarly, the frame narrator's imperialistic attitude is initially read as an adaptation to the attitude of the readers of *Blackwood's Magazine* and subsequently as a subtle criticism of this attitude, admitting that first-time readers will probably read the text in the former manner rather than the latter. Alternatively, Conrad's explicit endeavours to meet his readers' expectations can be read as part of his struggle to become recognised as an artist, rather than an attempt to sneak ideology criticism contraband into the imperialistic stronghold. In David Finkelstein's *The House of Blackwood: Author-Publisher Relations in the Victorian Era* (2005), the magazine is described as downright militaristic in the period around the turn of the century. In his preface to another study, Finkelstein writes:

"Thus *Maga*'s readers, finding *Heart of Darkness* alongside pieces on mountain exploration in the Canadian Rockies, the struggle between France & Great Britain for control of Nigeria, and a narrative of a Malaysian woman caring for her leprous husband, would not have seen it first as anything less than standard 'Blackwoodian' imperial adventure anecdote. Its criticism of imperialism would have been accepted as a critique of Belgian behaviour, having little to do with the British imperial mission upheld and defended strongly in *Maga*'s pages".[103]

What becomes clear in Lothe's reading, however, is that Conrad's experiences in Congo and his travel diaries were transformed into literature in a way that meant their significance as criticism and testimonies could be suppressed or reduced. The fact that the text in a short passage describes violence against natives does not make it "extremely critical", given that Marlow's attitude towards violence is far from clear. Also, the detail cannot be seen in isolation from the text's scepticism and doubt – as if this specific passage were an exception providing clear criticism of imperialist ideology. The experimentation with private material in *Heart of Darkness* to a large extent blurs the concrete basis of the experiences, as if the text were trying explicitly to *avoid* being perceived as a testimony. The impressionistically blurred boundaries between internal and external spaces, and the circular composition of events, results instead in a universal, all-pervading darkness that expresses the text's scepticism. Lothe's focus on Marlow's doubts, on the other hand, can be viewed in relation to the travel books and a localisation of the experience that the text's aesthetics of doubt attempt to express. We will return to this matter later on.

Heart of Darkness as Adventure Fiction

Andrea White's *Joseph Conrad and the Adventure Tradition. Constructing and deconstructing the imperial subject* (1993) follows Lothe's consideration of a critical potential in *Heart of Darkness*, but on a genre historical basis that argues for a closer link between eighteenth-century travel literature and adventure fiction. White's thesis is that Conrad's novels, through their simultaneous continuation and deconstruction of these popular genres, also demythologise imperialism. This happens in a complex, modernist process which on the one hand expresses admiration for people's ability to dream, while on the other it distances itself from the practical consequences of those dreams, equivalent to Lothe's description of the author as both *homo duplex* and *scriptor duplex*.

White points out that Conrad was redeemed by the academic tradition relatively late, particularly thanks to F. R. Leavis' *The Great Tradition* (1948), which emphasised the works' modernist characteristics, including the link to Flaubert, as those of a "serious art of fiction". The tradition, from which Conrad himself

admitted to having inherited significant elements – the popular romances by Trollope, Marryat and Stevenson, and travel books by Cook, Mungo Park and Livingstone – was obliterated in the process. To White, this literature played a dominant role in the creation of Victorian imperial myths: it was from them that Britain gathered knowledge and created images of the world which, in combination with cultural and scientific movements – especially abolitionism and Darwinism – made up the imperial myth.

These genres contributed to the upholding of the nineteenth century's dominant ideology, and the break from them in literary history towards the end of the century was both the effect and cause of the upsetting of the imperial myth – a process that many consider to have been completed with the coronation of Victoria as Empress of India in 1876. The genre shift also resulted in a shift in the prevalent perceptions of the outside world. In his time, Conrad's works were usually read in relation to adventure fiction and travel writing, although often with regret, because they did not live up to the expectations of these genres. White reinterprets this deficiency as Conrad's hallmark – a subversive effect of the novels' destabilisation of narrative clarity and authority.

Andrea White argues for the popularity of the genres by quoting impressive sales figures: Mayne Reid's *The Scalp Hunter* (1851) sold more than a million copies in Great Britain alone; Charles Kingsley's *Westward Ho!* sold 500, 000 in 1889; G.A. Henty is said to have sold 3.5 million books; and so on. White substantiates her claim for the importance of these genres by highlighting their role in the education system, where travel literature, in particular, held a prominent position after The Reform Bill in 1867. Novels and historical romances were considered to be bad taste and perverting, while travel literature had an instructive effect on a par with geography and history. The close partnership in literary history between travel literature and adventure fiction, each borrowing from the other, also ironically suggests that adventure fiction could achieve almost the same degree of prestige and authority as travel literature, although it was to a large extent based on the same 'tasteless' and fantastic elements as romances. Travel literature borrowed narrative models from adventure fiction, while adventure fictions exploited the authority of travel literature to build authenticity and credibility, often simply by disguising themselves as fantastical travel accounts – just as Defoe's *Robinson Crusoe* in the beginning of the eighteenth century faked a real testimony, which qualified it as novel. Magazines such as *Blackwood's Magazine*, *The Graphic*, *Illustrated London News*, *Cosmopolis*, *Longman's* and many others printed adventure fiction, travel accounts and articles about Jamaica, Borneo, India and Malaysia, which portrayed the colonial project in triumphant, exoticised terms. Both genres enjoyed authority and vast distribution throughout the century, even compared with the novel.

In the chapter "Travel writing and adventure fiction as shaping discourses for Conrad", White mentions a number of linkage points between the genres and Conrad's works and biography. Both James Cook and Marryat were significant sources of influence. From Marryat's adventures, Conrad inherited romantic, heroic and idealised characteristics, as well as the profession as a sailor on the seven seas, which provided him with his raw material. From Cook, he inherited a similar dream of travelling, but rather in order to describe the world as it was. According to White, Conrad's journey to Congo, which was largely motivated by these role models, resulted in his recognising an incredibly wide gap between the literary fictions that had shaped his ideas and the reality he witnessed firsthand. This resulted in the scepticism of his authorial attitudes, and particularly in *Heart of Darkness* the genres are therefore reconfigured in a modernist poetics that uses them against their original imperialistic potential.

Andrea White's genre critical perspective is concise and leads to a different localisation of the authorship's tensions than Jakob Lothe's. White's perspective puts more emphasis on Conrad's dependency on the codes of popular literature, and the novel's modernist turn is interpreted as a leap from popular literature to high literature rather than a condensation of disparate experiences into a fragmented, literary form.

The focus on genre, however, is more convincing in White's literary-historical framework than in the textual analysis and interpretation of Conrad's novel. Here, genre is not part of the work but rather something institutional, created in the context of literary history in publications such as *Maga*. White's analysis of *Heart of Darkness* as an attack against genre is therefore invalidated by the fact that no one perceived the text as a breach of genre – at most they saw it as "adventure fiction *manqué*" (p. 172). The detailed account of the novel as "most unconvincing", because it was not "vigorous, direct, effective, like that of Mr Kipling" or "clear and fresh like that of Stevenson", indicates an institutional framework for the reading of the novel, not a breach of genre.[104] Furthermore, White stresses Conrad's developed sense of his audience (p. 176), making it difficult to argue that Conrad's configuration of the genre had any subversive or critical *effect* in relation to the public's attention to violations in the Congo.

Heart of Darkness contains both the adventure genre, in the form of Marlow's sailors' tale, and travel literature, in the form of references to great explorations. In this respect it resembles countless other popular fictions from the nineteenth century. The hesitant and incomplete use of the genres is the result of Conrad's conservative nostalgia towards a world in which adventure and exploration were still possible, rather than a critique of imperialism that he did not articulate anywhere else. The blurring of references can be perceived as a step in his transformation of travel literature, rejecting the traditional genre

preference for communicating testimonies about the world and brushing aside Cook's realistic presentation of facts – all in order to inscribe himself in the 'Great Tradition' of prose literature.

This book shares White's opinion that *Heart of Darkness* marks a breach of genre: it is not a breach directed towards the ideological preconditions of the genre, however, but a forward-looking hope that the innovation would canonise the novel in the high literary tradition of the English novel. White notes that Conrad's relationship with adventure fiction was fundamentally nostalgic and uncritical; to him, Stevenson was the real deal, while he criticised literary forgeries – what he called "masquerade", in which the noble genre was misused with suspect motives (p. 165). If we read the novel's genre mix in connection with Conrad's ambitions as an author, however, we are bound to see *Heart of Darkness* as a masquerade in which the ends justify the means. Furthermore, it is problematic that White treats the popular genres as if they were all, without exception, promoters of the imperialistic project until Conrad entered the scene. The utopias of adventure fiction and travel literature reports could be employed either to confirm or reject prejudices about the ideological basis of colonial annexations, and they were often subject to controversy and profound public disputes (cf. Stanley). In the popular genres, the internal conflicts of imperialism were often expressed far more explicitly. The many publications that followed in the wake of the Emin Pasha Relief Expedition, for instance, had a far more shocking effect on the public than *Heart of Darkness*. One example White mentions, without drawing this conclusion, is the author of *King Solomon's Mines*, Henry Rider Haggard, whose popular fictions are simultaneously triumphantly imperialistic and explicitly critical of the internal barbarianism of European civilisation.

Heart of Darkness as Gothic Romance

Patrick Brantlinger's *Rule of Darkness. British Literature and imperialism, 1830-1914* (1988) has, in contrast to White, a very keen eye for the often paradoxical forms in which imperialism was expressed. The book is literary history that also encompasses history and the history of ideas, including elements of discourse analysis inspired by Michel Foucault. Conrad's *Heart of Darkness* also plays a key role throughout the book's discussions and as the final work that Brantlinger analyses. His reading of is quite different from the two discussed above, and closer to this book's position, partly because he unearths the genealogy of the trope, figure and image of "darkness" throughout the literature, criticism and science of the nineteenth century. This facilitates an appraisal of the aesthetic and ideological facets of the novel's central trope, in terms of their connection and their place in literary history. The advantage of Brantlinger's method is, in other words, what has been termed 'the prose perspective' in this book.

"Darkness" gained footing in romanticism as a figure to describe unknown places on Earth populated by underdeveloped, primitive, barbaric natives outside the reach of civilisation's light. The content of the figure changed over the course of the nineteenth century in concert with the changes in the imperialistic project. The "darkness" figure and imperialism were both paradoxically results of abolitionism, the influential eighteenth- and nineteenth-century British and American political campaign against slavery – the motives of which were not purely altruistic but also linked to the effort to win market shares. Abolitionism led to increasing British involvement in Africa, as the abolition of slavery in non-colonised districts became the new goal after The Emancipation Act of 1833. The abolitionist movement's humanitarian ideals provided ideological backup to the great Victorian expeditions to Africa, and as Darwinian ideals were combined with evolutionist and later racist doctrines, the moral, scientific and religious justification for imperialism – what Brantlinger calls the myth of "The Dark Continent" – was created. While the battle against slavery was won in the British imperial territories, abolitionism's emancipation rhetoric led to racist views of black people who, in the British consciousness, were still perceived as slaves (p. 175). Several Romantics, such as Wordsworth, Byron and Shelley, contributed to the abolitionist movement's propaganda with poems and pamphlets that detailed the terrors of the slave trade and produced the rhetorical figure of "Dark Horror". Brantlinger mentions in this context two points regarding the influence of anti-slavery literature. First, the propaganda included displays of atrocities, so that detailed descriptions in text and images maintained a constant association between inhumane violence and Africa, which was generalised to become the image of The Dark Continent. Second, anti-slavery literature at the beginning of the century started to describe Africa as in terms of pastoral bliss, where noble savages had lived in innocence and freedom until the Europeans introduced them to greed, war and slavery. Both these elements worked together to create the idea of the natives as underdeveloped children and enhance the impact of the "darkness" metaphor.

The disastrous events during the first British expeditions into Africa, for example the Niger expedition in 1841, resulted in Dickens, Carlyle and many others perceiving Africa as so wild and barbaric that it was better left alone, at least until poverty and darkness had been overcome in Britain. Others, however, saw these setbacks as reasons to intensify the effort: there was truly work needing to be done. From 1850, the great era of exploration was launched with Burton, Speke and Grant's exploration of the Nile, followed by Baker, Livingstone and Stanley. Livingstone's *Missionary Travels* sold 70, 000 copies in a few months in

The symbolism is clear in this illustration accompanying a collection of poems on the 1809 abolition of slavery: literature can bring light to the savage, dark corners of the Earth, and the enslaved native can rise and follow the light towards freedom, sense, and sensibility. The literature of the abolitionist movement established a problematic formula in which the propagandistic aim led to descriptions of natives as helpless children in need of saving and Africa as the Dark Continent. The formula was continued in the effort of the Congo Reform Association against King Léopold's reign of terror after 1900, and it continues to structure our conceptions of Africa. Printed from Brantlinger's *Rule of Darkness*.

1857; Stanley sold 150, 000 copies in England alone, and vast numbers of less famous travel accounts and imitations were circulating among the seemingly insatiable audience. One reviewer of Stanley's *In Darkest Africa* believed that the book "has been read more universally and with deeper interest than any other publication of 1890" (p. 180). In Brantlinger's emphasis of the link between humanitarian projects and imperialism, Livingstone plays a central role in this phase of the myth's history. Because Livingstone was seen as pilgrim and a saint, spreading light in the darkest corner on Earth, and because of his self-proclaimed view of the natives as savages and children leading lives under constant threats that could only be alleviated by European civilisation, he became one of the most prominent communicators of the notion of Africa as a dark continent – not despite, but due to, his humanitarian rhetoric.

Similarly, the missionary movements' propaganda in books such as *Dawn in the Dark Continent* supplied a plethora of terrifying tales of cannibalism and human sacrifices – myths that were perpetuated and reaffirmed in travel accounts and incorporated into evolutionistic models that positioned black people as a different species, close to gorillas and chimpanzees.[105] These models were explored in the fiction of the era; however, they were usually ultimately confirmed, regardless of the attitude of the texts towards Africa and the native population. When Victorianism was in its prime, there existed a stable juxtaposition of Europe as the sphere of light and civilisation and Africa as the sphere of darkness and primitiveness. Towards the turn of the century, however, the extreme poles of this model started to become less stable. With the decline of imperialism, "darkness" assumed the ghostly associations which Conrad used to such effect in *Heart of Darkness*. However, "darkness" was no longer reserved for a distant continent; it became a symbol that pervaded the entire *fin de siècle* culture, including its self images.[106]

Brantlinger places *Heart of Darkness* in this *fin de siècle* context, thus understanding the text as part of a general turn, in which a number of the ideological projections that earlier in the century had been directed out towards the expanding empire were now directed inwards, towards the world of Victorianism, in the form of experiments with the culture's own hidden primitiveness. Brantlinger demonstrates combinations of occultism, spiritualism, scientific materialism and imperialism within the same fiction field in works by Stevenson, Doyle, Stoker, Haggard and Kipling. The theme of the gothic romance is the reversal and reversibility of civilisation and barbarianism, linked with dangerous experiments in telepathy and occultism. In this context, the motif of the discovery of the Dark Continent changed. It was no longer a question of filling white blanks on the map, but of exploring the traveller's descent into mystical, primitive, subconscious layers under the civilised surface, subsequently to be described as the text's encounter with the traveller's own ghosts.

In his reading of *Heart of Darkness*, Brantlinger immediately approaches the debate surrounding Conrad's alleged racism, fuelled by Achebe's attack on the novel in 1975. Conrad's defenders claim that his critical attitude toward imperialism raises the text above its racist elements, which can only be perceived as part of the era's typical repertoire. We have already become acquainted with the initial discussion via Lothe; however, Brantlinger directs our attention to the implications of Marlow's distinguishing between British and Belgian imperialism and the impressionist style.

Emphasis is put on the fact that Conrad's criticism does not implicate imperialism as such, but rather the discrepancy between its ideals and practice, as well as the misinformation that was spread via the Belgian administration's philanthropic rhetoric. In this sense, it is more just to claim that the novel plays out a nostalgic and romantic longing for a past in which heroism and discovery were still prestigious, not yet eroded by technology and commercialism. In the novel's attack against the decline of ideals, however, all ideals become "idols". Kurtz is put on a pedestal as a fetish god; the white pilgrims' worship of ivory is fetishistic; furthermore, Marlow assumes the position of the Buddha on the deck; and Kurtz's fiancée is elevated as a generalised, universal expression of the trope of "darkness" and textual fetishism. On par with Brantlinger's genealogical unravelling of the history of the "darkness" figure, this equation of African and

European fetishism is read as the text's contribution to imperialistic rhetoric, which conceals the economical and political motives behind apparently mysterious and magical events.

According to Brantlinger, Conrad's diaries and experiences were not only based on his journey to the Congo, but also on reports about atrocities published during the period between his journey in 1890 and the publication of the novel in 1899/1902. What is important, however, is that his experience and sources were significantly simplified, and employed in the same manner that was found in countless other imperialistic romances of the time. *Heart of Darkness* is, in every important aspect, a confirmation of the genre of gothic romance, but it also displays a "will-to-style", the total effect of which can be described via the double nature of the text, wavering between mass culture and modernist art.[107] This double nature did not obstruct, but rather *promoted*, the novel's subsequent acceptance into the literary canon through an institution in which critics, reviewers and lecturers increasingly focused on the internal, organic form of closed works of art. This contributed to the appreciation of the text's will-to-style and completed the erasure of references to the historical context begun by Conrad himself. Simultaneously, there was an insistence on the text's authenticity – not as a testimony but as a work of art in which moral and artistic integrity are one and the same.

Brantlinger has a keen eye for elements in the novel that – if viewed in isolation – can be interpreted as critical, or at least sceptical, of imperialism. However, he argues convincingly for the idea that Conrad's nostalgic and romantic investment in the myth of the Dark Continent places *Heart of Darkness* in close proximity to the gothic romance and *fin de siècle* culture's pessimistic, occult projections of the journey as a descent into archaeological strata of consciousness and evolutionary history. The novel's incorporation of various temporal sequences and spatial formations are not, in this interpretation, deconstructive protests against the genre conventions within which Conrad wrote; rather, they are positively reaffirming utilisations of the possibilities the genre permits. In other words, the novel is not critical of the "darkness" figure or imperialism as such. It is a reworked idea of the Dark Continent in unstable constellations in time and space – and the overall function is to create rather than criticise myths. Brantlinger's conclusion is unambiguous: "Conrad does not debunk the myth of the Dark Continent" (p. 193).

"The Congo Diary" and "The Up-river Book"

On a fundamental level, the travel literature context invites us to emphasise Conrad's own claim that the novel in all important details follows his experiences as ship's mate on the Congo River. And as we have seen, it is a common notion among the text's critics that *Heart of Darkness* is a personal, broad but detailed account of the conditions in Congo towards the turn of the century.

The introduction's description of the Roman occupation of England is interpreted as a mirror image of the Belgians' scattered outposts of progress. The text's lacking references are supplied, even in interpretations that are otherwise sceptical of an uncritical understanding of the text as a realistic representation. The autobiographical material is added in the paraphrase, so that data from Conrad's own journey fills the blanks when the frame narrator and Marlow are silent: the contract in the offices of death is signed in Brussels, while the sea journey's omens of the adventure's tough reality and the details of the skipper's encounter with the dark river and his employers are read as direct references to the Congo Free State's secretive and brutal administration. Critics acknowledge that Conrad's private material is transformed in the text's orchestration. Nevertheless, it is still being read as a testimony of concrete, historical injustice and destruction. This happens through retrospective linkages which isolate the testimonies from the novel's general context and exempt them from the sophisticated aesthetic analysis otherwise characteristic of Conrad criticism.

Admittedly, this is tempting, given that Conrad's desperate letters written during his journey to the Congo provide a sketch of the narrator who appears, years later, in the guise of Marlow. Before he even reached the Congo, Conrad came to realise that his adventure was naïve – like Marlow's: a young man's realisation of a boy's dream of becoming an explorer. Upon his employment in Brussels, he promised not to tell anyone about his work; however, it soon became clear that the mission was secret even to him. He was, however, in possession of the shocking statistics of casualties and therefore – understandably – fantasised about being two people at once: while one was on his way towards the unknown in Africa, the other was headed back to Europe. "Another me who moves about with great ease; who can even be in two places at once. Don't laugh! I believe it has happened" (Kimbrough, p. 152). In his increasingly desperate letters from the Congo, he urges his aunt to use her connections in Brussels to get him out, discreetly and without revealing his true state as a fatally ill, mentally broken man. As his uncle comments in a letter, Conrad's language and style have changed worryingly, and the family put all their energy into getting the young Korzeniowski out alive. However, it was probably the Free State's policy of sending their employees out of the country before they died that resulted in the fever-ridden Conrad being transported first down the river and then, on 4 December 1890, back to Europe on a steamer, after six months' service.

The letters express the internal conflict between *homo duplex* and *scriptor duplex* through which all critics view Conrad's authorship, although with very different

conclusions. In this book, it has been highlighted how the letters' cataclysms indicate the young sailor's dream of becoming an author like Flaubert, while he fought the same unresolved conflict between nostalgic idealism and scepticism – and between romanticism and realism – as his famous role model. Conrad was not just any traveller when he arrived in Congo. He was planning to become an author, and he brought five chapters of *Almayer's Folly* with him in his travel bag. This, however, sheds new light on the relation between, on the one hand, "The Congo Diary" and "The Up-river Book", and, on the other, *Heart of Darkness*. "The Congo Diary" is written in a traditional, if incoherent and fragmented form, covering Conrad's journey in July 1890 from Matadi to Kinshasa on the caravan trail through hell, which most of the recently employed had to travel to reach the steamers above the waterfalls. Offhand, "The Congo Diary" resembles countless other diaries from the same trail, with its tales of illnesses, chaos, lonely despair and skeletons along the paths. "The Up-river Book" contains Conrad's notes from his job as second officer aboard the *Roi des Belges*. It is not written as a diary, but rather consists of brief, telegram-like notes on whirlpools, reefs and points of orientation in the huge, largely unknown river system.

"The Congo Diary", however, stands out from other diaries of this death route because Conrad also notes settings, colours and perspectives in the landscape, even when, after a few days, he became so weak from fever that he had to be carried in a hammock. Many critics, especially Lothe and Zdzislaw Najder, are of the opinion that the notes from the caravan trail were prepared as raw material for a novel or Conrad's own contribution to travel literature. Najder writes, for instance:

"As a beginning author and realizing well the thematic possibilities offered by his African journey, he apparently wished to put down some distinct and concrete impressions – in order to be able later to bolster his memories with hard data. After arriving at Kinshasa he was, by turns, either too busy or too sick to continue. Such a purpose in writing a diary would explain the limitations of its content. Some critics have noted that Conrad's remarks do not contain any condemnation of, or any expression of resentment against, atrocities which he must have observed – if we are to believe *Heart of Darkness* – during his stay in Matadi and on his walk to Kinshasa" (Kimbrough, p. 157).

In relation to the discussion of the link between the travel material and the novel, it is striking that Najder with the insertion "if we are to believe *Heart of* Darkness" refers to the *novel* as a reference to what Conrad might have seen but not noted in the diary. This is particularly interesting because Najder carefully warns us that the diaries should not mislead critics to read *Heart of Darkness* biographically or psychologically; it should first and foremost be read and appraised as a work of art. Still, the art work is apparently authentic enough as a source that the fictitious Marlow's suggested experiences on an unpleasant journey in some undefined place in the world still serves to fill blanks and correct observations that the author Conrad does not describe on his own journey. Secondly, it is difficult to see how we can be dealing with "hard facts" when both novel and diary appear extremely averse to localising and describing atrocities.

Najder is right in claiming that there is no "resentment" in "The Congo Diary", but it is not clear in his introduction how this lack is connected to the diary being the preparation for a work of literature; if we read the diary more closely, it soon proves difficult to perceive it as such. There are few sketches and descriptions, often only with diminutive hints of artistic potential. The following example from 3 July 1890 is unique in that it actually does hint at a scene or perspective:

> "General tone of landscape gray-yellowish (dry grass), with reddish patches (soil) and clumps of dark-green vegetation scattered sparsely about, mostly in steep gorges between the high mountains or in ravines cutting the plain. Noticed Palma Christi -Oil Palm. Very straight, tall and thick trees in some places. Name not known to me. Villages quite invisible. Infer their existence from calabashes suspended from palm trees for the "malafu". Good many caravans and travellers. No women unless on the market place.
>
> Bird notes charming. One especially, a flute-like note. Another kind of "boom" resembling the very distant baying of a hound. Saw only pigeons and a few green parroquets; very small and not many. No birds of prey seen by me. Up to 9 a.m. sky clouded and calm. Afterwards gentle breeze from the North generally and sky clearing. Nights damp and cool. White mists on the hills up about the halfway. Water effects very beautiful this morning. Mists generally raising before sky clears" (Kimbrough, p. 161).

Notes like these bear witness to a writer who is distanced, rather than one who is looking for and holding on to impressions for later use, although there are hints in the recording of the landscape's mist formations and the sounds of birds. Similarly, it would be misrepresentative to view the diary's few examples of violence and abuse as testimonies of atrocities. Also on 3 July: "Met an officer of the State inspecting; a few minutes afterwards saw at a camping place the dead body of a Backongo. Shot? Horrid smell. Crossed mountains (...)". On 4 July: "Saw another dead body lying by the path in an attitude of meditative repose" (Kimbrough, pp. 160-61). The final lines of the diary on 28 July read:

"Chief came with a youth 13 suffering from gunshot wound in the head. Bullet entered about an inch above the right eyebrow and came out a little inside. The roots of the hair, fairly in the middle of the brow in a line with the bridge of the nose. Bone not damaged apparently. Gave him a little glycerine to put on the wound made by the bullet on coming out. Harou not very well. Mosquitos. Frogs. Beastly. Glad to see the end of this stupid tramp. Feel rather seedy. Sun rose red. Very hot day. Wind South" (Kimbrough, p. 166).

The notes do not place these observations in any context that would lead to understanding, condemnation or the placing of responsibility. They are completely equal to mosquitoes, frogs, fever and heat, and leave no deeper impression on the text. It is striking, however, that the description of the dead body is supplemented with "Horrid smell" and "in a meditative pose", just as the gunshot wound receives unusually detailed attention: "the roots of the hair, fairly in the middle of the brow in a line with the bridge of the nose". This, however, is an indication of aesthetic potential, which only serves to highlight the lack of indignation or criticism in the text.

If we compare these notes with Marlow's narrative about the arrival and the trek from Matadi to Stanley Pool, there are several corresponding elements. From the beginning, we are told that there is "no use in telling you much of that" (p. 23). The country is deserted, and Marlow seems keen to transform his lack of knowledge about the terrain and nature into sarcastic superiority: "There's something pathetically childish in the ruins of grass walls". On the subject of the native he finds with a bullet through his head: "Can't say I saw any road or any upkeep, unless the body of a middle-aged negro, with a bullet-hole in the forehead, upon which I absolutely stumbled three miles farther on, may be considered as a permanent improvement" (p. 23). Such sights become familiar: "Now and then a carrier dead in harness, at rest in the long grass near the path, with an empty water-gourd and his long staff lying by his side" (p. 23).

The diary's detailing the sounds of the forest may be reflected in Marlow's comment on distant drumming – "a sound weird, appealing, suggestive, and wild – and perhaps as profound a meaning as the sounds of bells in a Christian country" (p. 23). The aesthetic distance of the diary, however, is reflected in Marlow's repetitions of the figure in "a meditative pose", in the passage about the trek as well as before and after, with the natives described as if they were posing in the landscape as pensive or meditating sculptures before the traveller's eyes. A consistent trope, it is also expanded to include the group aboard the *Nellie*, especially Marlow, who is characterised by the frame narrator as meditative and enigmatic. The distance is all-pervading, even in the description of the railroad workers' starved, mistreated bodies that are seen as effects of the all-encompassing meaninglessness but also as enigmatic, sculptural ghosts: "Near the same tree two more bundles of acute angles sat with their legs drawn up" (p. 21).

"The Up-river Book" directs the reader's attention to the part of the novel about a book Marlow finds in a deserted hut on his way to Kurtz: *An Inquiry into some Points of Seamanship*, the "humble pages" of which are "luminous with another than a professional light" (Kimbrough, p. 39). The book helps Marlow to distance himself from the nightmare around him, because it gives him the feeling of something "unmistakably real", which is also "wonderful" and "astounding", since he finds some comments pencilled in the margin, written in what he initially assumes is encrypted writing. Marlow can hardly tear himself away from this "mystery" – at the same time a simple guide to seamanship and an intelligible text. It is later revealed that the book used to belong to a Russian wanderer, and that what Marlow thought was an encoded message is in fact merely Cyrillic writing. The event forms part of the novel's construction of an ambiguous field surrounding Marlow's references to the "truth".

In the essay "Geography and Some Explorers", Conrad expresses his admiration for James Cook's and similar expeditions, the ambition of which was not conquest but "facts". The essay's mention of Conrad's early fascination with the blanks in the atlas, especially Central Africa and the great lakes, however, illustrates that facts only interest him if they arouse his imagination:

> "I have no doubt that star-gazing is a fine occupation, for it leads you within the borders of the unattainable. But map-gazing, to which I became addicted so early, brings the problems of the great spaces of the earth into stimulating and direct contact with a sane curiosity and gives an honest precision to one's imaginative faculty. And the honest maps of the nineteenth century nourished in me a passionate interest in the truth of geographical facts and the desire for precise knowledge which was extended later to other subjects" (Kimbrough, p. 145).

In the same way that the stars draw a map of the sky and indicate infinity, precise knowledge and facts appear to have both limiting and stimulating effects on the imagination. Still, it seems to be the case that Conrad's facts very quickly disappear and are replaced by a fascination with "exciting spaces of white paper" – his metaphor for the explorations' maps of Africa, dotted with "dull imaginary wonders of the dark ages".

In *Heart of Darkness*, the narrative – until Marlow journeys out to find Kurtz – can be perceived as a detailed rewriting of the diary, from the caravan journey and the mutual enmity with the Manager to the trouble with salvaging and repairing the river steamer, while the textual processing of facts from "The Up-river Book" is more subtle. Together, they form a text in which narrative and

reality work together in a paradoxical reversal of the traditional dynamics of travel literature. While the great explorers fill the blanks on the map with facts, Conrad's endeavour seems to move from the incontestable facts of the notes towards increasing cartographical uncertainty. The journey upriver is presented as a journey back in time. The distances covered do not add facts to the "exciting spaces of white paper"; on the contrary, they transform facts to "dull imaginary wonders of the dark ages". Marlow's modern recourse to fact only enhances the estrangement wrought in the textual rhetoric. Every detail which – in Marlow's pondering on "surface truth" – was supposed to create linkage with reality is instead dislodged from the context, which causes it to refer to a borderless, infinite, unfathomable darkness, rather than serving as lodestar for the desperate navigator. And what is more, it is not only the beautiful Amazon or the skulls on the palisade around Kurtz's station that appear as "wonders". Absolutely everything, from Marlow's shoe and the Russian's clothes to the sound of the steamer's whistle, is rhetorically decontextualised and appears fascinating and extraordinary. Discursively, *Heart of Darkness* describes a movement not towards modern discovery but back to the early renaissance and its focus on wonders. Furthermore – and this is a significant characteristic – Conrad's recycling of the discourse of wonder is fundamentally different from the prosaic realism mentioned in this book. While the discourse of wonder attempted, by means of essayistic and descriptive techniques, to grasp extraordinary phenomena within the field of reality, Conrad's strategy works in the opposite direction, towards the fantastical, sublime and unfathomable.

Conrad's criticism often refers to "The Congo Diary" when it wants to expose the novel as a testimony, usually based on the argument that the reader – despite the novel's ambiguity – is involved in the assessment of, for example, Marlow's observation of the dying railway workers along the caravan trail. "The Up-river Book", on the other hand, exposes the critical strategy that Homi Bhabha has called "Signs Taken for Wonders".[108] It is therefore difficult to use as an argument for the novel's contribution of significant testimonies about the state of Congo. "The Up-river Book" resonates with the increasing dislocation from reality that Conrad reports in his letters, making various phenomena appear fascinating, unintelligible and frightening. Critics who wish to champion a critical dimension within the novel usually suppress this strategy, while others including Tzvetan Todorov and J. Hillis Miller, whose aim it is to canonise the text in the modernist tradition, generalise this partial strategy to the whole text, characterising the novel as "unreadable", engulfed by darkness or some mysterious, lurking 'it'.

Todorov's article "Knowledge in the Void: *Heart of Darkness*"[109] mentions, by means of introduction, the novel's similarities with and differences from adventure fiction. Conrad's use of traits from the popular genre variants is, according to Todorov, only superficial, given that all suspense is shifted from the narrative to the interpretation. The result of Marlow's quest is first and foremost disappointment and lack of adventure. Unintelligible information and interminable waiting without purpose characterise Marlow's tale from the very beginning:

"Nothing happens; and even when something does happen, the story does not tell us about it: for instance, the departure for Kurtz's Inner Station, the meeting between Kurtz and the manager of the Central Station, Marlow's return and his dealings with the "pilgrims" after Kurtz's death. During the key scene when he arrives at Kurtz's camp, Marlow remains on board the steamer talking to an enigmatic Russian; we learn nothing about what takes place on shore. Or take what is traditionally the high point in adventure tales: the battle scene, here between Blacks and Whites. The only casualty deemed worthy of mention is the helmsman, and Marlow only mentions him because his shoes are filled with the blood of the dying man, thus forcing him to throw them overboard" (p. 162).

Crucial scenes are veiled in smoke and mist, just as the black Amazon has no significance beyond that of "an enigmatic sign". The events are blurry, while the interpretation takes centre stage.

Todorov's intention, however, is not, like White's, to demonstrate a deconstructive and critical use of the adventure genre; nor is it to accentuate the text's racist traits detected in the dehumanising effect of the omissions, as Achebe does. In Todorov's view, the text's enigmatic nature is what makes it distinctively literary and a valuable object for literary-critical scrutiny. The fact that it challenges Todorov's narrative terminology qualifies it for such an analysis, whilst the motivation behind the text's secretive nature is not questioned.

An essay by Hunt Hawkins illustrates the internal conflicts among those who try to defend the text's critical dimension. In "Conrad and Congolese Exploitation", Hawkins gives a detailed account of the historical situation in Congo at the time when Conrad was in the country.[110] The essay is written in response to Norman Sherry's *Conrad's Western World* (1971), which Hawkins, apart from one point of criticism, praises for its thoroughness. Sherry writes: "Conrad's journey did not, I believe, bring him face to face with the cruelty that was traditionally part of the history of the Congo", and he "very probably saw little of the actual exploitation which he uses as a basis for 'Heart of Darkness'"(Hawkins, p. 94).

Hawkins lists a number of phenomena that Conrad *must* have seen, such as the railroad workers' appalling working conditions: the Free State's official statistics list 900 dead Africans in the period 1890 to 1892, which resulted in the area's native Bakongo population fleeing or hiding in the hinterland. Conrad

"probably" encountered these circumstances, or heard about them, even though he was very ill; he must at least have heard about them after his return to London. Unfounded assumptions, however, do not prevent Hawkins from concluding:

> "Conrad's personal observation of exploitation in the Congo contributed to the depth of feeling he expressed in his art, and may even have confirmed his motivation to become an artist. His outrage against what he later called 'the vilest scramble for loot that ever disfigured the history of human conscience' made *Heart of Darkness* one of literature's most powerful statements about imperialism" (p. 99).

This canonisation of the text in the tradition of imperialist criticism, however, is done without wondering why "The Congo Diary" and *Heart of Darkness* do not describe the atrocities in any extent worth mentioning.

While both articles – on the basis of a formal-aesthetic and a critical-historical approach respectively – inadvertently demonstrate Conrad's conspicuous silence when it comes to violations and destruction, neither Todorov nor Hawkins focus on the relationship between Conrad as witness and the novel as text. In Todorov's argumentation it is irrelevant, and in Hawkins' the novel is subject to the failure we have witnessed several times: Hawkins' admiration for Conrad's moral integrity and the novel's aesthetic integrity lead to unfounded assumptions that Conrad based his text on profound experiences and first-hand knowledge.

In letters to his cousin and aunt, Conrad poses as an author. Ray Stevens' "Three Voices of Conrad's Narrative Journey" compares the language and style of these letters and the two very different diaries Conrad wrote during his stay.[III] The main focus is on the letters to his aunt, Marguerite Poradowska, who used her connections in Brussels to get Conrad the job, and who was herself an established author. According to Stevens, the letters address the authority the aunt represents for Conrad, as the person who might be able to get him out of hot water, while at the same time being the stage on which he can play out his dreams of becoming an author. The letters contain conventional figures associated with a gentlemanly, chivalrous, witty and philosophical style; however, they also the rehearse main characteristics of his future work: the clash between noble ideals and profane reality, melancholia and disillusion, ironic comparisons of high and low and a unique mix of nostalgia and scepticism. The letters bear witness to Conrad's dream of becoming an author, influenced by Flaubert's *Madame Bovary*.

There were two motivating factors behind Conrad's hazardous involvement in the Congo. One was a romantic expectation of taking part in a civilising mission – an opportunity to play out the great explorers' quest for uncompromised truth before modern technology eradicated every mystery. The other was to find the material and form for an ironic romance inspired by Flaubert. The two motives were obviously interlinked and would later become a staple formula in Conrad's use of the adventure romance.

If we read "The Congo Diary" from this perspective, the lack of a moral stance and the text's characteristic distance are hardly surprising. The diary expresses massive disappointment that adventure has long since disappeared from the Congo. Conrad's anger is directed at monotony and repetition, which steals material from the future author (cf. the novel's "No use telling you much about that"), and erodes all truth. It is not directed at atrocities; they are merely presented as signs of the expedition's all-pervading meaninglessness, on par with the unidentified sounds of the forest. The expectation of a civilising mission and heroic discoveries is confronted with a reality that is stale, meaningless and trivial. The ambition to become an author can be traced in the ironic comparisons and additions, such as the corpse's "meditative pose", in accordance with the letters' indication of a poetics based on the clash between idealism and scepticism, the elevated and the profane. However, it is also clear that this endeavour is only present as a trace of a dream that has been shattered and shamed by the monotony, sickness and stupidity of trivial reality. "The Congo Diary" is by no means a record of atrocities; rather, it is a powerful testimony about the experience of the secretive organisation of the colony and Conrad's desperate realisation that he had embarked on a journey that was anything but heroic.

The diary documents the collapse of Conrad's expectations of a double career as explorer and author. It barely attempts even to be a diary – it is a text that does not seem to address anyone or be interested in anything. The initial brushstrokes of sketches indicate the futility of completing the picture, and the text painfully reveals the naïve nature of the hopeful young author's romantic ambitions. In this light, it is no surprise that Conrad put the diary down almost as soon as he had started it, dedicating himself rather to the navigation notes' indications of indisputable surface truths. At this point, the comparison with Flaubert, Conrad's early role model, becomes particularly relevant.

In Flaubert's *Voyage en Égypte* we encounter a split between the first part, which attempts to be a proper travel diary in the style of countless period descriptions of the Orient, and the second part, in which this attempt is given up in favour of a coarse, fragmented style, aiming only to grasp things via their "mutual precise differences". In Egypt, and in the travel diary, Flaubert discovered a poetics: a synthesis between incompatible elements that contains beauty as well as ugliness, even stupidity, while attacking all stereotypes from within. This poetics later became the foundation of *Madame Bovary*, a major work in romanticism, realism and modernism, and in Flaubert's career as an author. His poetics was rooted in the experience of two kinds of repetition: one was that everyone had 'been there' before, that everything was engulfed by a

nauseating *déjà-vu* and contaminated by European clichés, no matter how far away one fled; the other was that patterns and repetitions are formed in the desert sand, erased and reformed as signs of beauty and truth beyond man. He synthesises these repetitions in an aesthetic form, but in order to further his career he had to suppress his experience of collapse.

There are also similarities between Conrad's and Flaubert's early travelling experiences and their significance to their future writings. The contrast between "The Congo Diary" and "The Up-river Book" is parallel to Flaubert's shift from travel book to coarse text in *Voyage en Égypte*, and both shifts express the collapse of artistic expectations in the romanticist tradition. The diaries' striking indifference towards moral questions corresponds to Flaubert's ironic and sceptical attitude. While Flaubert's first attempt to write a travel book tries to stay within genre confines, "The Congo Diary" is fragmented and disillusioned from the very first page. As it appears from the letters, Conrad had already acknowledged the absurdity of the project before he reached his destination. In a letter to his aunt from Tenerife on 15 May 1890, he writes: "The screw turns and carries me off to the unknown. Happily, there is another me who prowls through Europe, who is with you at this moment" (Kimbrough, p. 152). When Conrad imagines being someone other than the person who has signed up for three years of contractual work – someone who can move freely and be in several places at the same time – it is his signal to Marguerite Poradowska that the author Conrad is imagining being on the way to anywhere except the destination awaiting him.

When critics refer to Conrad's own statements about the Congo journey as landmarks for the author, they interpret them as if he had been exposed to a moral shock that he failed to process until he wrote *Heart of Darkness*. However, if we read the diaries without any preconceived aesthetic or moral frame of reference from the future novel, the shock is not of a moral nature but rather a combination of physical fatigue, illness, mental disintegration and artistic disappointment, which, from the beginning, isolated Conrad from his surroundings – with one important exception.

The exception was Roger Casement, who Conrad met in Matadi in June 1890, and who in 1904, together with E.D. Morel, founded the Congo Reform Association. In 1903, Casement and Morel encouraged Conrad to support the Reform Association. Conrad declared his moral support for the humanitarian cause but refused to step forward as a public activist. He would not take part in Casement's "crusade". What the Reform Association needed were eyewitness accounts of atrocities, but all the people who were able to relate these accounts, especially the missionaries, were dependent on Léopold's goodwill; and, as Allan Simmonds writes in his article "The Language of Atrocity: Representing the Congo of Conrad and Casement", it was very difficult to establish who saw what and where.[112]

A few eyewitness accounts of atrocities, e.g. George Washington Williams' in 1890, reported the severing of hands and feet as one of the Congo Free State's ways of disciplining uncooperative natives, but it would be thirteen years before Casement could report similar acts. Simmons shows that Casement, as well as Conrad, either had not witnessed these acts, or did not ascribe any particular significance to them until the Reform Association had built up some steam.

When *Heart of Darkness* mentions unspeakable rituals, we are dealing with a feature shared with other reports from Congo, which do not specify atrocities but refer to a vague sphere of indeterminable evil. Simmons perceives this as an indication that Conrad had no first-hand knowledge about these events, or that he only began to see them as important *after* the publication of *Heart of Darkness*. According to Simmons, however, the novel played a role in the Reform Association, because it discreetly prepared the public – within the confines of acceptable language – for the Reform Association's presentation of images and detailed descriptions of terrors that would otherwise have been rejected as improbable. It is Simmons' opinion that the fiction of *Heart of Darkness* thus had a function *complementary* to Casement's direct descriptions and documented reports.

Simmons does not refer to Conrad's letters and diaries, and he does not consider *Heart of Darkness* in relation to its kinship either with travel literature and adventure fiction on one side or Flaubert's scepticism on the other. The diaries might have helped clarify one of his questions, since they confirm that Conrad did not witness atrocities or at least chose not to focus on them, and the indeterminate form of the "unspeakable rites" is therefore rather, as Richard Kuppel suggests in "*Heart of Darkness* and the Popular Exotic Stories of the 1890s", a conventional figure taken from the exotic popular fiction of the era.[113] Kuppel mentions F.R. Leavis' attack against Conrad for borrowing popular writers' techniques, such as letting the exotic float in "unspeakable secrets". Furthermore, he supports the theory about the novel's close relationship with popular literature by comparing it with C. J. Cutcliffe Hyne's "The Transfer", which was published fifteen months before *Heart of Darkness* in *Pall Mall Magazine*, and is conspicuous in that it both thematically and structurally tells the same story.

Viewed in this light, and supported by Simmons' mapping of the temporal changes to which Conrad's and Casement's testimonies are subject, we can only conclude that the moral and critical content of Conrad's testimony from the journey to the Congo were constructed as part of the Reform Association's strategy *after* the publication of *Heart of Darkness*, which subsequently, through critical history, has been endowed with the aesthetic and moral authenticity of the eyewitness account. It is possible, as Simmons writes, that "Conrad's contribution to the movement for reform in the Congo is precisely the provision of this (fictionalised) context which enabled the subsequent transmission of

uncomfortable facts" (Simmons, p. 101). However, Simmons is uncritical when he claims – partly with reference to Morel's statement about the novel providing a "powerful picture of Congo life" – that *Heart of Darkness* was also a powerful testimony about actual conditions. Morel's statement is in fact a testament to how the novel became a piece in a political game with which it had no connection originally – either via its basis in experience or its aesthetic form.

The connection between the diaries and *Heart of Darkness* is not a shared critical attitude towards imperialism. Their common traits are not based on critical testimonies handed over from one text to the other, but on their basis in nostalgia and scepticism. In the diary we can detect the classic expectation of discovery, movement and action, as well as Conrad's naïve posing as author, all of which capsize on the reefs of reality's empty repetitions. *Heart of Darkness* plays out the roles that Conrad rehearsed in the letters' scenic composition of "a wicked world", continuing the ironically self-subverting style that comes from Flaubert. However, nostalgia in Conrad is far stronger than in Flaubert. The shattered illusions in *Heart of Darkness* are not directed inwards as critical investigation and rejected ideals, as in Flaubert's *Madam Bovary* or *L'Éducation Sentimentale*; they are maintained in the novel's ambiguous and nostalgic aesthetics, for example in the sailor Marlow's enigmatic meditation as the text's Buddha.

In the light of *fin de siècle* culture and the very close links between adventure fiction and gothic romances, the novel's ingenious narrative construction and overlapping temporal and spatial sequences – the journey into Africa is a journey back in time, while the wait on the Thames provides an opportunity to rehearse the Roman colonisation of the British Isles – are not examples of a critical contraband in *Blackwood's Magazine*, but rather of strategic dislocations of the narrative material that draw it into a gothic frame of reference with which readers were both familiar and tantalisingly unfamiliar. The indefinable nature of *Heart of Darkness* made it possible for the readers of *Maga* to assimilate the text into the genre of gothic romance, while at the same time paving its way into the literary canon.

Flaubert's literary success depended, in some senses, on deceit, because the poetics on which his career was based stemmed from insights that could not be integrated into his authorship and were therefore rejected. However, all of his works show that he is aware of this deceit, which is why he undermines his own poetics and any idealistic notion of literature and art in an infinite, downward spiral. With Conrad, on the other hand, the radical negativity that can be traced in the diaries is transformed into *fin de siècle* spleen and impressionist aesthetics, indicating his meticulous adaptation to his audience's literary expectations, and apparently positioning his project far away from Flaubert's critical and self-critical literature.

If, however, we direct our attention to the novel's own explication of the *discursive terms* for its testimony, it is possible at this meta-level to read a more subtle, but also more radical, critical point. Through several references to his promise not to reveal business secrets, Marlow provides a concise and concrete explanation of the novel's strategy of obscuring and veiling. The meaning of the novel is thus not found in "the heart of darkness" like a nut in a shell, but outside the narrative – just as the frame narrator warn us it is before Marlow takes over the narrative. From this perspective, the darkness is not a mystical property of the place, but the discursive precondition for narrating it. From the initial scene on the deck to the meetings in the company's front office and with the influential aunt, the Manager, and so on, there are numerous meticulously arranged hints as to the colony's institutionalised and all-pervading fraud, conspiracies and suspect use of information, which ends up in the hands of the wrong people. Herein lies the explanation for Marlow's complex web of confessions, omissions and testimonies. Marlow's lie to Kurtz's fiancée – that the dying man's last words were not "the horror, the horror", but his fiancée's name – is a conclusion to the novel that simultaneously reveals its limit and breaks it. By lying, Marlow avoids destroying the fiancée's philanthropic ideas of Africa, but as readers we have heard another story, and we know that he is lying. We must thus ask the question, why? The novel explicitly informs us, here and elsewhere, about its own lies and omissions. These paradoxes and meta-paradoxes are the topic of Ermien van Pletzen's "'Mine is the Speech that cannot be Silenced': Confession and Testimony in "Heart of Darkness".[114]

Pletzen's focus is on Marlow's confessions and testimonies, the diffuse and rhetorically twisted and evasive nature of which is perceived as the novel thematising the way in which atrocities were talked about at the time, rather than the atrocities themselves, which are not discussed. Marlow's confessions are read in the style of Paul de Man's deconstructive readings of Rousseau, and *Heart of Darkness* is perceived as a performative speech act, which demonstrates – through its own lies – the silence, ignorance and the circulation of false and twisted testimonies that constituted the public's response to Congo around 1900.

Pletzen mentions a number of instances in which Marlow's narrative appears to be a testimony to historical circumstances; however, he emphasises that the discursive presentation of testimonies is inseparable from the discourse of confession, which dominates Marlow's narrative. The confession of an inner truth, even – as with Rousseau – when it is the confession of a lie, always assumes the form of self-delusion, as the confessing subject shifts the truth to ever-new narratives that ultimately destabilise the concept of an inner, authentic self. It is also in accordance with conventional characteristics of the discourse of confession when Marlow numerous times tries to substantiate his credibility by admitting his lies.

In this "framework of professing honesty by confessing dishonesty" (p. 153) lies Marlow's innermost truth: in the heart of Africa, in spite of all the European disguises and lies, he glimpses the wild, original truth to which Kurtz has unique access, and which initially paves the way for Marlow's solidarity with him. Furthermore, it justifies Marlow concealing Kurtz's "unspeakable rites" from the public and lying to his fiancée. Pletzen mentions several examples of how Marlow's narrative tries to avoid shared responsibility, partly by juxtaposing lies and truth, partly by shifting to farce or sarcasm before the text reaches the atrocities. Pletzen subsequently links Marlow's veiling to the historical-political circumstances of the era by drawing a parallel between the novel's internal and external terms of communication:

"Thus Marlow's narrative dramatizes the dilemma of being told when the listener does not really want to be held accountable, as well as the dilemma of being told when the listener does not want to be implicated by hearing the story" (p. 168).

In Pletzen's analysis, it is significant that Marlow's listeners on the boat are typical 'pillars of society', representatives of the reigning imperialistic ideology. They are in possession of the right authority to receive the confession without protest, because they themselves are involved in the same pact of secrecy as Marlow. In this sense, the novel demonstrates from beginning to end, and on all levels,

"human beings' inability to face up to the atrocious; it changes course, tone and focus to foreground the halo of idealistic, hazy, or ridiculous constructions which most of us come up with when we feel implicated, whether individually or collectively" (p. 172).

If we summarise the partial conclusions presented above, comparing them with Pletzen's point, and furthermore read the novel as performative prose rather than representing literature, it makes sense to perceive *Heart of Darkness* as a criticism of the era's fetish relationship with testimonies rather than a testimony about "atrocities". The novel authentically conveys Conrad's doubt and paranoia in relation to his experiences of secrecy and misinformation, while at the same time criticising the very terms for giving evidence. However, the novel itself is designed in accordance with these terms, and contributes to the feeling of guilt that marks Marlow's confessions and smokescreens. Just as the activities in the colony are without any moral purpose (they are a "masquerade"), the documents that mention them are abridged and corrupted, though they are presented to the public as testimonies, like Marlow's distribution of Kurtz's manuscripts. In a historical context, the extraordinary scope and influence of *Heart of Darkness* is due to its precise communication of the discomfort experienced when both author and reader are aware of the necessary non-disclosure that is, paradoxically, the precondition for the communicative act. Furthermore, the text warns against interpreting it hermeneutically – following its clues towards a mystical centre; instead, it recommends looking for meaning in the surrounding prose field.

Stanley's forest chapter in *In Darkest Africa* can be described as gothic romance, encompassing the entire *fin de siècle* repertoire of reversals and shifts between internal and external worlds in a timeless, ghostly continuum, where silent witnesses from the past approach the narrator, threatening to subvert his authority – both as one who confesses an inner truth, and as one who presents a testimony from the journey. The representation of the forest is characteristically devoid of history, a blind alley in which everything seems to repeat itself in labyrinthine confusion.

Significant characteristics of *Heart of Darkness* are kindred with Stanley's travel descriptions, though it has become a habit in criticism to refer to Stanley's travel books as the diabolical antipole to Conrad's emancipating text, without further explanation. In terms of ideology, both authors supported free trade and were critical of the inefficiency and moral decline among the Europeans in the Congo. In terms of literature, *In Darkest Africa* and *Heart of Darkness* both contributed to *fin de siècle* culture's boundary-pushing investigations of the darkness that exists in the self but was recreated in Africa, without being confined to Africa only. Both are quasi-spiritualistic experiments in continuation of a long-lasting genealogy of the trope of "darkness", which towards the turn of the century was no longer used chiefly to characterise the barbarism of strange, primitive cultures, but became localised in the centre of rationalism and civilisation. Anxiety and suspicion are prevalent in the texts. They both simultaneously declare and renounce their role in the primitive, and it is not definitively removed from the narrators' attempts to justify themselves morally. Furthermore, both mark a farewell to travel literature, in the dual sense of heroic discoveries of facts in the style of Cook, and the romantic idea of strange worlds that were also adventurous and wondrous. The link between Stanley and Conrad is not the huge contrast claimed by critics from all camps. The works circulated in different institutions and encountered very different fates in the histories of their reception, but they were reactions to the same transformations of travel literature: a loss of innocence in the public reception of testimonies that occurred alongside similar changes in the literary market. While Stanley's *In Darkest Africa* can be read as a final celebration of testimony, which – via its heterotopic prose – also discloses the conflicting construction of testimonies, Conrad's *Heart of Darkness* is a critique of the discursive circumstances to which the credibility of travel literature, including Stanley's, was subject.

From Guy Burrows' *The Land of the Pygmies* (1898). The image of the spectacular method of execution appears in several travel accounts from the turn of the century, for example in the Scandinavian *Three Years in the Congo*. The conception of the particularly violent culture of the native Congolese population was a defining one for the images of Africa that dominated around and after the time, focusing on rumours of cannibalism, which have a central position in travel accounts and narratives like *Heart of Darkness*, in which they are referred to as "unspeakable rites". However, in colonialist rhetoric, the image of the savage must be kept in balance: the savagery was an important argument for the European presence, but in order to justify the project of civilisation it was important that such savagery was represented as something that could be cured, i.e. as part of the native culture rather than nature. Nevertheless, the accounts often succumb to the temptation to describe savagery as an intrinsic part of the nature of the place – an unchangeable destiny that basically exposes the European mission as a meaningless, absurd, and dismal farce. The accounts of Léopold's atrocious violations, and the counterattacks of the Free State against the reform movement, are positioned in this grey area: can the stories about severed hands, for example, be ascribed to the barbaric customs among the natives, still unmanageable for European officers, or are they atrocities carried out as part of the authorities' systematic terror? Historical studies show that spectacular violence, such as theatricalised displays of public punishment, played a central role in the cultures of the Congo long before the European intervention – and continue to do so today as an efficient deterrent in the civil wars in the Kivu Province. And they work: media reports of decapitations or cannibalism help to prevent outsiders from meddling.

2 Atrocity Accounts

The use of *Heart of Darkness* as a source for criticising the historical conditions in Congo, and "The Congo Diary" as a shocking moral testimony to atrocities, is based on a number of fallacies. Typically, we are dealing with an aesthetic and moral appraisal of the novel as a work of art that leads to the text's topographical, historical and ethical blanks being filled in with historical data so that conclusions can be made about the text's status as testimony.

Heart of Darkness stands on the shoulders of popular literary genres such as gothic romance and adventure, while also being profoundly entangled in *fin de siècle* culture's decadence and occult soul-searching; its artistic point of departure, after all, was inspired by Flaubert's sceptical modernism and Cook's travel literature realism. Characteristics of these very different inspirations are traceable in the novel's reception history – on a general level in the schizoid position between high and mass literature that Frederic Jameson has pointed out, but also in the continuous dispute about the importance of its organic unity and universal ethics versus its context and historical function as testimony.

This book has identified an alternative to both dominant traditions, suggesting, instead, that we read the novel from a prose perspective with emphasis on its performative aspects. In this light, *Heart of Darkness* is not a text about an unspoken, sublime and universal truth that can never be uncovered but only examined in an infinite downward spiral – as a powerful academic tradition has claimed. Neither can it be presented as a testimony to atrocities, or – in an expanded and hypostatic sense, through a retrospective interpretation – as an eyewitness account of genocide. The novel's impressionistic technique and scepticism endows it with an openness that has paved the way for these dominant tendencies in reception history, but at the same time these qualities have impeded its critical potential – first and foremost for the discursive criticism of testimonies – within the prose field outlined above. In what follows, other aspects of this prose field will be outlined via a closer look at Conrad's and his novel's position in relation to the Congo Reform Association and the campaign against Léopold's regime.

In 1879, Stanley launched a systematic colonisation of Congo. It was begun through contracts with local chieftains, and the establishment of a 1, 500-kilometre line of trading stations along the river. Due to the carriers' immense effort, Stanley managed in 1881 to transport the paddle steamer *En avant* above

the waterfalls, where it was launched in 1882. While the region was in principle open to other European trading companies, in reality Léopold had monopolised all European traffic, information and trade. At the Berlin Conference in 1884-85 – following clever negotiations with France, England and Germany, during which he indicated that his interests were purely philanthropic – the king had acquired what would come to be called *L'État Independent du Congo* (EIC) as his personal property.

Until the Belgian state was given responsibility for the colony following strong international pressure, King Léopold sustained 20 years of colonial rule for his own gain; this period was the most extensive and violent example of the exploitation of nature and people in the black book of colonialism. Initially, EIC was drained of ivory and other luxury products, and then of natural rubber. Dunlop and Michelin had just developed the pneumatic rubber tyre, and the demand for natural rubber exploded along with the demand for bicycles and cars. Since there were no rubber plantations at the time, the price of the rubber that was collected in the forests increased rapidly. According to Samuel Nelson's *Colonialism in the Congo Basin 1880-1940* (1994), one of the most balanced historical expositions, the world market price of rubber doubled between 1869 and 1880, and again between 1900 and 1906.

Léopold's method included three basic measures. First, he extended his property right to include all the country's natural resources. Second, he launched a detailed, effective payment system that encompassed all activities related to work, production and trade, and in 1889 he banned all Africans from selling ivory and crude rubber to agents other than his own. Thirdly, he divided the area into a number of districts or concession areas in which the state's agents, without offering quid pro quo in the form of products, could simply demand the amount of rubber, ivory, work etc. they wanted; furthermore, they received bonuses from the state according to the amount of resources collected. In practice, the system was beyond legal control and led to dreadful forced labour, which could only be carried out through extreme repression, for example by taking hostages from villages in order to make the men collect even more rubber. Any attempt to avoid this exploitation was punished with the burning of entire villages. The use of military units in the so-called 'Force publique', and the annexation of the country as a whole, was justified with reference to Léopold's claim that he wanted to put a stop to the barbaric slave trade. However, his widespread tax and bonus system resulted in a system of slavery that was far more violent than before. It escalated after 1892, when Léopold allocated vast areas to private trading consortiums, allowing them to establish military units and use force to recruit workers and collect 'taxes' in the form of rubber. The fifteen years of colonial rule that followed became known as the period

A chieftain captured by a unit of Danish Knud Jespersen's native force. 'La Force publique' was, in principle, meant to ensure public order, but in reality they were beyond jurisdiction and took part in hostage taking, terrorism, and blackmail, partly in order to increase rubber collection. In his memoirs, *A Danish Officer's Journey to the Congo* (1930), Jespersen gave an impression of being balanced and just; however, his work as a soldier was no different to that of any other.

of 'Red Rubber', the name often printed in red by the reform movement that spread across most of Europe from 1904, until the Belgian government was forced to seize control in 1908. In relation to Stanley's, Conrad's and Casement's participation in the colonisation of Congo, it is crucial to distinguish between the different phases of Léopold's regime.

The first phase did not involve forced labour or systematic repression and exploitation, only an increased exchange of products. This no doubt resulted in conflicts and combative negotiations, but there were both Europeans and Congolese who saw it as progress and prospered. This situation had potential for what the excited Stanley described as a successful realisation of the free trade doctrine's philanthropic and civilising ideals. When Stanley returned to Congo in 1887, in the context of the Emin Pasha Relief Expedition, he observed

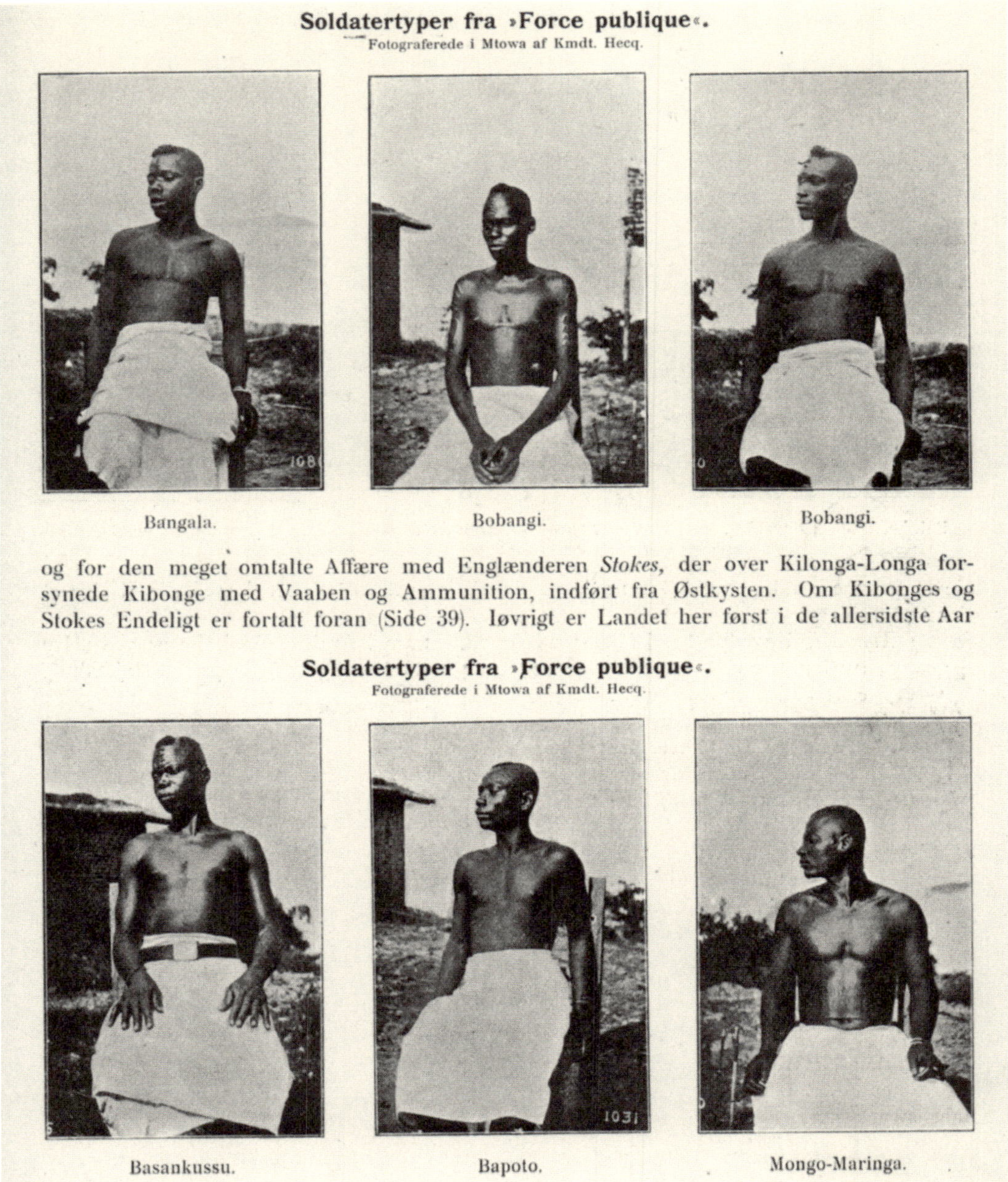

Soldatertyper fra »Force publique«.

Fotograferede i Mtowa af Kmdt. Hecq.

Bangala. Bobangi. Bobangi.

og for den meget omtalte Affære med Englænderen *Stokes*, der over Kilonga-Longa forsynede Kibonge med Vaaben og Ammunition, indført fra Østkysten. Om Kibonges og Stokes Endeligt er fortalt foran (Side 39). Iøvrigt er Landet her først i de allersidste Aar

Soldatertyper fra »Force publique«.

Fotograferede i Mtowa af Kmdt. Hecq.

Basankussu. Bapoto. Mongo-Maringa.

Types of soldiers from 'Force publique', from Jenssen-Tusch's *Scandinavians in the Congo*. The native soldiers were officially enrolled as volunteers, but in reality they were forcefully relocated as part of a hostage treaty. They had to collect crude rubber far from their homes, using the same methods that were used in their own villages. The photography makes use of the same aesthetics as the reform association's atrocity photographs.

with anger and disappointment the disrepair of the trade stations and the slave trade's destruction of whole districts around Stanley Pool.

Conrad's brief stay in 1890 took place in a period when the administration was under intense economic pressure because the expenses of the EIC were exceeding its profits. There was a serious lack of skilled labour, and most of the colony's districts were, in reality, beyond political control. His experience, therefore, was one of disappointment that the philanthropic marketing of the Free State towards investors and contract employees, including him, was a cover for the chaos of rival consortiums, misinformation and inefficiency. Compared with Stanley's precise and critical assessments of the state of the colony a few years before in *In Darkest Africa*, which expressed concern for the well-being of the natives, Conrad remained silent, which is particularly striking in relation to his boat journey through the racked areas around Stanley Pool.

Casement's first involvement in Congo was between 1884 and 1890, when he – like Stanley – worked for the international company of which Léopold was increasingly seizing control. However, Casement, Stanley and a number of nations and trading consortiums still thought of the company as a free trade organisation, and when Casement left it in 1890, it was not because he wanted to distance himself from the Free State's treatment of natives, but due to his disappointment with the Free State's effective monopoly of the region, which had also disappointed Stanley. When Casement, in his capacity of British consul to the EIC between 1901 and 1904, wrote the critical Red Rubber report, which forced Léopold to hand the colony over to the Belgian state, he characteristically did so with reference to the early phase's prosperity and thriving trade, which had been undermined during the 1890s by the rubber work. This is an important distinction, given that it later became common practice to confuse these different situations, for examples by claiming that Casement's report gives evidence for violations that were carried out by Stanley and described in Conrad's diary and novel.[115]

King Léopold made enormous profits. After the completion of the railway between Matadi and Léopoldville in 1898, and the expansion of the network of trading stations, money invested in EIC was returned twelve times. The effects on Congo were devastating. Old trade routes and production systems were destroyed and whole regions deserted, the population reduced by two thirds as the result of illness, slavery, war and famine. Léopold's administrative and military apparatus in the Congo State was organised in a strict hierarchy, within which all communication was surrounded by the utmost confidence and discretion. Orders from Brussels came direct to the state agents even in the outermost districts, who returned their products, taxes and secret reports back to the centre. The system resulted in extreme rivalry between the individual stations,

King Léopold wanted to appear as a philanthropic and altruistic champion of science and progress. He initiated the Berlin Conference, where the European colonial powers divided Africa between them; Léopold secured a large piece of the pie for himself. According to the treaty, the Congo was meant to be a free trade zone and the object of an ambitious philanthropic programme, while in reality it became the private property of the king and subject to ruthless exploitation, the proceeds of which funded the 'business king's' luxury buildings and playboy lifestyle.

which were all monitored by other state agents in the network. Because the official ambition of the project was philanthropic – promoting science, trade and civilisation among the 'savages' – extreme care was taken to prevent information leaks that political opponents and competing trading interests might use to subvert Léopold's administration.

According to the Berlin Conference, EIC was to be a free trade area. However, in reality trade was monopolised and the country made inaccessible – particularly after the defeat of the Afro-Arab slave traders in north-east Congo in 1896. Explorers, missionaries and non-Belgian trading agents and observers, who were not subject to the confidentiality provisos all employees in EIC had to sign upon their employment, started to release critical reports about the true state of the country.

The criticism was directed at irregularities in the government administration, especially the courts of law and Léopold's tax system and protectionism, which were seen as the main causes of the atrocities that featured in vast numbers in European newspapers after the turn of the century. The criticism did not address colonial exploitation as such, but rather the un-British administration (cf. Marlow) and the fact that Léopold impeded the free trade that – according to the accepted doctrine – in itself would result in development and civilisation. The reports led to concerted international campaigning, headed by Edmund Morel, and with Roger Casement as the ideological mastermind. The campaign was very effectively countered by King Léopold's propaganda unit, *l'Association pour la Défense des Interêts Belges à l'Étranger*, which used bribes, political pressure and anti-campaigns that reported atrocities in other colonies. In the sleeping-carriages owned by Léopold's *Compagnie Internationale de Wagons-Lits*, Europe's elite could read the Congo State's version of the truth in French, German and English in the free monthly magazine *La vérité du Congo.*

The area around the Congo River has witnessed several waves of colonisation, the earliest being around 2, 000 years ago when the Bantu people forced the Pygmies to take refuge in the north-eastern Ituri Forests, where they are still living today. Compared with the colonisation of North and South America, India and North and South Africa, however, the European colonisation of Central Africa took place very late and proceeded with an unprecedented programme of efficient and methodical repression, due to the colony's initial, highly unusual governmental and administrative organisation. It also needs to be viewed in relation to the country's unique history, especially the global slave trade's influence on the existing societal structures for trade and work, as well as the region's unique geo-physical conditions. Polemic expositions that aim to promote contemporary postcolonial and anti-racist agendas, for instance Adam Hochschild's and Sven Lindqvist's, portray the Red Rubber phase as a "holocaust" or "genocide", which is misleading, though the deaths of an estimated ten million natives suggest otherwise. These gloomy statistics,

however, are not proof of the systematic elimination of a people based on ethnic discrimination, but mainly the result of famine, illnesses and a decrease in the birth rate, though there were also considerable casualties and killings as direct consequences of forced labour.[116] The chapter on Congo in *The Black Book of Colonialism* is fully deserved, but the reference to Hochschild's use of the terms 'holocaust' and 'genocide' to describe the forms of repression as indisputable fact, is, regrettably, characteristic of the uncritical reception of Hochschild's book.[117]

During EIC's twenty-year exploitation of the country, its presence, in the form of administrative stations, was distributed over the entire, colossal network of the river system. Stations were often manned by only one European agent, who lived without any contact with other white people, except for in situations related to the transport of rubber and ivory, the secret reports sent up and down the river and the mail, which could be months apart. In a vast part of Upper Congo, the exploitation thus took place under circumstances that resembled permanent guerrilla war, with no stable positions or balance of power – a constant stream of confrontations, hostage situations and fleeting alliances with the area's chieftains. Furthermore, the colonisation took place in a critical period of European history. On the one hand, there was a culmination of national currents, resulting in a parallel culmination of colonial projects, expressed, for instance, through the world's fairs' overt demonstrations of colonial power. On the other, Western European culture was pervaded by self-criticism regarding ideas of progress and formation, the very foundation of the concept of the European civilising mission, in a crisis loosely described as *fin de siècle*.

This outline of the colonial-historical background for the dispute about *Heart of Darkness* – which continues unabated today – provides an almost too convincing explanatory background for many of the novel's fictitious events. Critics have had no trouble providing models for the portrait of Kurtz, often mentioning Stanley, but also the vast number of station managers who having begun their work with noble artistic ideals concerning the great civilising projects quickly succumbed to the permanent paranoia created by the EIC system and the hostile surroundings. Critics have paid less attention to the fact that the secrecy, corruption and withholding of information in the EIC chain also play an important role in the novel. This in fact constitutes a far more consistent link between Conrad's biography, the diaries and the novel, whose own omissions and confessional lies can be read as a meta-discursive disclosure of EIC's information control, reflected in the author's self censorship and masquerade. The *fin de siècle* motifs, which appear in much of the Congo literature after *Heart of Darkness*, have their basis in the nervous breakdowns and fevers that plagued the European contract employees, who often turned the established ideas of barbarism versus civilisation upside-down. The agents' use of native soldiers to repress other natives, and of informers and renegades who were hostile towards their own people, enabled managing Europeans to distance themselves from the terror, although they themselves gave orders under violent pressure. One of the traces in Congo literature, therefore, is a decadent fascination with dissolving boundaries and the reversal of moral values. The Danish author Jürgen Jürgensen's novel *Christian Svarre's Journey to the Congo* (1909) is one of many examples to which we will return.

It is remarkable that EIC's methods, bar a few exceptions, did not receive critical attention for such a long time. As Susanne Gehrmann points out in her introduction to *Kongo-Greul. Zur literarischen Konfiguration eines Kolonial kritischen Diskurses (1890-1910)*, the period has predominantly been described in a positive light in Belgium until fifteen or twenty years ago, something that is evident, for instance, from the exhibitions at the Musée Royal de l'Afrique Centrale.[118] Outside Belgium, some critical books have been published that pick up where the Congo Reform Association left off – e.g. Adam Hochschild's *King Leopold's Ghost. A Story of Greed, Terror and Heroism in Colonial Africa* and Sven Lindqvist's *Exterminate All the Brutes*. One of the reasons behind this delay in colonial criticism is, according to Gehrmann, the chaotic course of events surrounding Congolese independence in 1960, and the subsequent, bloody civil war. Gehrmann's theory is that Mobutu's cleptocracy, combined with the West's conduct towards the Congo based on its interest in the country's raw materials, resulted in the repression and forgetting of colonial violence – a topic that in other postcolonial countries often became the object of renewed historical interest, especially in the beginning. This is also a question to which we will return.

The Congo Reform Association: Morel, Casement, Twain

Until Roger Casement's report to the British government of 1903, by which time he had spent almost twenty years in the Congo including a period as consul, only very restrained criticism of the regime reached the public. Missionaries were dependent on EIC's goodwill, and when they breached the censorship rules their area of responsibility was immediately decreased. In Europe, the public's impression until the turn of the century was concurrent with Léopold's image of the enterprise as a philanthropic project, supported by EIC's propaganda magazines. *Le Mouvement Géographique*, for instance, published illustrated articles about the great advances in the colony. Critical elements had throughout the century been closely related to the abolitionist

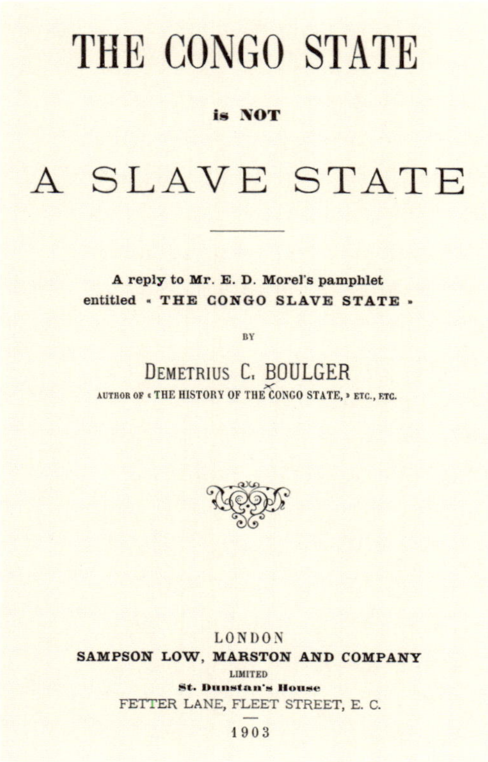
THE CONGO STATE

is NOT

A SLAVE STATE

A reply to Mr. E. D. Morel's pamphlet
entitled « THE CONGO SLAVE STATE »

BY

DEMETRIUS C. BOULGER

AUTHOR OF « THE HISTORY OF THE CONGO STATE, » ETC., ETC.

LONDON
SAMPSON LOW, MARSTON AND COMPANY
LIMITED
St. Dunstan's House
FETTER LANE, FLEET STREET, E. C.
1903

The book market was flooded with pamphlets from both parties in the conflict, making the Free State a public issue in which politicians, in the beginning, only hesitantly involved themselves. However, it would remain a hot topic, and European readers had to make up their minds. The colonial powers were involved due to the fact that King Léopold's system had been approved at the Berlin Conference, and a vast number of other countries were present in the Congo in the form of the large contingents of contractual workers they had contributed. Danish publications, including *Scandinavians in the Congo*, also had to address the accusations. The dispute about the Congo became an issue for all of Europe.

movements, and given that the main goal declared by Léopold, next to free trade, was to fight the Arab slave traders, it was difficult for early critics such as George Washington Williams and the Swedish missionary Sjöblom to gain authority and find institutional support. Williams' reports are written in the form of public letters, making rhetorical use of his position as what he calls an "eyewitness" on long journeys up the river, while the many crimes he witnesses and accuses Léopold of are themselves expressed through racist stereotypes and philanthropic figures that subtract from his credibility.[119] Sjöblom's reports are also written as eyewitness accounts. They were first printed in *The Times* in 1897 at the request of the Aborigines' Protection Society. Sjöblom's style is detailed and matter-of-fact and his almost pedantic accounts of violations were perceived as credible testimonies, paving the way for subsequent accounts such as Edward Glave's "Cruelty in the Congo Free State" (1897), published in *Century Magazine*.

Roger Casement's position as envoy for the British Foreign Ministry and his considerable experience of Africa and EIC, not to mention the fact that he had no personal interest in the affair, endowed his 1903 report with great authority and impact in the public sphere. It came to be seen as the truth about the Congo, which was refuted by the Belgian newspapers, who – partly with just cause – accused the British of acting on the basis of financial interests in the colony. Meanwhile, the Belgian press was also beginning to show doubt, with

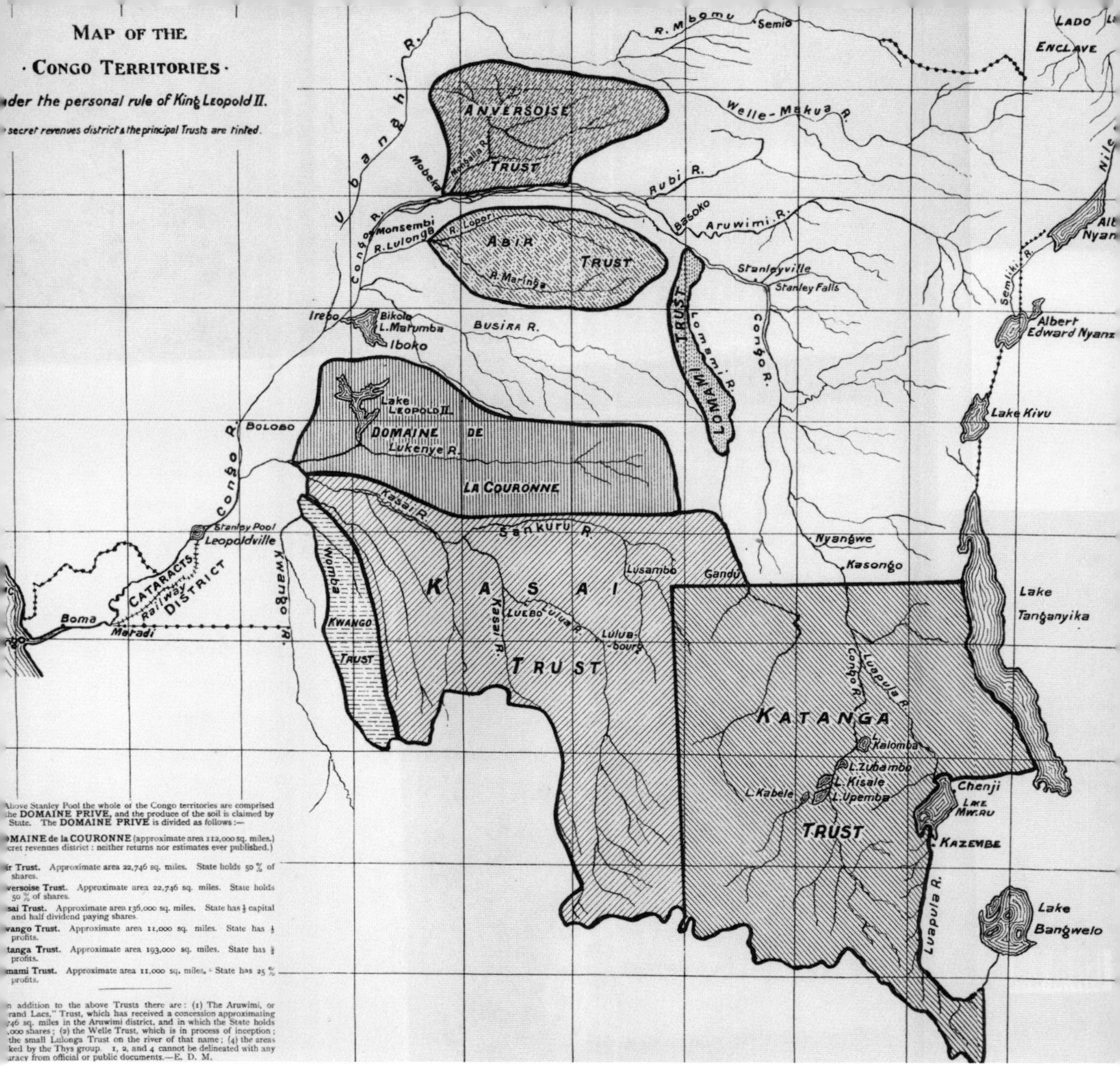

Edmund Morel's campaign against Léopold's Congo began when he noticed discrepancies between account books and deliveries to the warehouses in Anvers, where he was employed as bookkeeper. His criticism was first and foremost directed at Léopold's breaches of the free trade treaty, based on statistical and economical analysis. However, in order to agitate public opinion, he increasingly made use of atrocity photographs, combined with brief accounts of atrocities and violations. The books, especially *Red Rubber* (1906), and the so-called 'Atrocity Meetings' – pre-produced 'packages' of slides and 'testimonies' shown around Europe – defined a basic form that would come to be used by subsequent human rights movements. To Morel and Casement, the issue was political rather than humanitarian: basically, it addressed the fact that Léopold's protectionism resulted in England missing out on rightful earnings from the declared free trade zone.

socialist newspapers and even pro-colonial periodicals such as *Le Mouvement Géographique* printing critical comments. Following international pressure, an independent investigative committee was set up, the Commission d'Enquête. After 370 protocols in all, it published its report in 1905, supporting every significant point made by Casement. In Belgium, this changed the public's attitude to Léopold's involvement in Congo. The first step was the formation of the Commission des Réformes, but the pressure increased, and after a debate in the parliament in which the socialists suggested that all members, regardless of their political affiliations, should engage in a "concerted humanitarian action: the annexation of Congo, in order to put an end to the wretched state of affairs" (Gehrmann, p. 84), Léopold was forced to face his defeat. EIC was annexed by the Belgian government in 1908, and the colonial government was reorganised to fit in with British and French norms.

The journalist Edmund Morel was sceptical of reports like Sjöblom's and defended EIC against the attacks. Later, however, he became the campaign's main writer and strategist, authoring the association's best known works, including *The Congo Slave State. A Protest against the new African Slavery and an Appeal to the British Public* (1903) and *Red Rubber. The Story of the Rubber Slave Trade Flourishing on the Congo in the Year of Grace 1906* (1906). According to Gehrmann, Morel's change of mind happened after a meeting in 1899 with Mary Kingsley, who – against the background of two long journeys in West Africa – had developed a special variety of the free trade concept that made an impression on Morel. Kingsley's main point was that the colonisers ought to acknowledge and respect African societies as rational and effective on their own terms, instead of – in Gehrmann's words – forcing upon them a "pseudo-civilising re-educational programme" (p. 88). This was an expansion both of the free trade doctrine and the British formula of "indirect rule", in that it emphasised first that free trade also implicated the natives' right to trade with whomever they wanted, and second the shared interest of colonists and colonised in developing the existing forms of production and trade, instead of destroying them.

As it appears from the final chapter in *Affairs of West Africa* (1902), Morel's attack against EIC was based on statistical and financial analysis of the Free State's own accounts, compared with accessible information from the trading companies that had concessions in the area. Morel's meticulous, detailed exposure of Léopold's circumvention of the free trade agreements from the Berlin Conference in 1884-1885 was the Reform Association's strongest card in relation to the governments and trading interests involved, who had been fooled by Léopold's countless shell corporations that all made profit for him personally. The testimonies of atrocities were of less importance to Morel, but they contributed effectively to a rhetorical strategy in which indisputable, scientifically

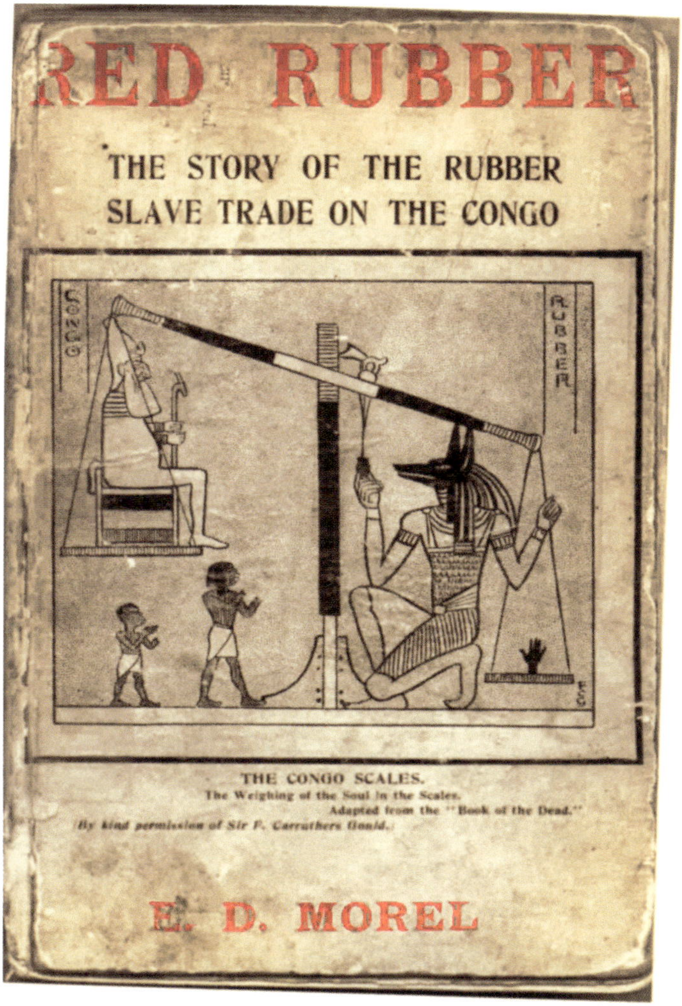

The cover of Morel's book, which provided the name for the brutal rubber collection methods of the 1890s. King Léopold is weighed on the scale of souls and found lighter than a severed hand. Both parties in the conflict made use of every means available: lots of caricature drawings of Léopold were in circulation, while Léopold, on his part, bribed newspaper editors and founded his own publications to promote "La Verité du Congo".

supported data were presented side by side with testimonies of violations and massacres. In Morel's retrospective analysis of the campaign, he emphasised that the British public was sceptical of "missionary evidence", which convinced him of "the impracticability of leading a crusade against the Congo Free State by invoking humanitarian sentiment alone". His main goal, therefore, became the exposure of "the whole infernal system, its legal bases, its monstrous claims, its fraudulent accounts and fraudulent statistics".[120]

Morel continued the rhetoric of the abolitionist movements, but updated it in response to the development of modern mass media. *Red Rubber* is a paperback edition of *King Leopold's Rule in Africa* from 1904, and Morel writes in the preface: "This book is written with the object of putting into the hands of the British public, at a cost which places it within the reach of many, a brief and up-to-date narrative of the Congo tragedy, avoiding side issues, and dealing with the main features of the story" (*Red Rubber*, p. xix).[121] While *King Leopold's Rule* was a 466-page long, detailed account addressing readers who valued scientific documentation, in which detail in itself functioned as rhetorical support of credibility, *Red Rubber* first and foremost appealed to a mass audience through emotional means. It is a narrative about the tragedy, written to promote the just cause. Simultaneously, it is implied that the atrocities in the Congo had become part of a public drama in which the excitement of watching others suffering was inseparable from the moral and political discourse. The Reform Association's increasing use of photographs and slide shows of mutilated Congolese at so-called "atrocity meetings", which spread all over Europe, highlighted this rhetorical-aesthetic dimension of the campaign.[122] The audience reacted very strongly to these images as an early example of mass communication within a new media, but there was not a clear understanding of their connection to the reality in the Congo.

In a discussion of the role of these images, Gehrmann points out that a key element in the campaign's strategy was to propagate photographs of children with severed hands and feet, without any link to the complexity of the context, which would only interfere with the desired effect on the viewers. Regardless, the images were often more ambiguous and disturbing than Gehrmann suggests. She demonstrates how the photographs of the mutilations were framed and staged with a view to the campaign, and argues that the consequently problematic linkage of voyeuristic desire and moral indignation also degraded the subjects. Many of the photographs even raise the suspicion that the mutilations were carried out as part of the photographic staging. For instance, the type of photographs that show severed hands and feet contradicts the argument: they were part of testimonies to Force Publique's infamous practice of severing the hands of their dead victims to show them to their superiors in return for new ammunition. This testimony is counteracted and subverted by the photographic documentation of the severed hands, which are clearly *not* in the soldiers' possession, therefore raising the unpleasant question of how they ended up in the photograph. The hallucinatory reception of the images in darkened rooms in local halls and mission houses problematise their status as testimonies: they were standardised with an eye to mass distribution, and their effect relied on oblivion and repression, rather than remembrance of the conflict's historical

"Nsala of Wala in the Nsongo District (ABIR Concession), with the hand and foot of his little girl of five years old – all that remained of a cannibal feast by armed rubber sentries. The sentries killed his wife, his daughter, and a son, cutting up the bodies, cooking and eating them." Photographed by Mr John H. Harris in May 1904. From Morel's *King Léopold's Rule in Africa* (1904).

complexities. The next section will return to the consequences of the rhetoric and prose strategy of the Reform Association's campaign in relation to contemporary human rights campaigns.

Side by side with the statistical observations in Morel's campaign text are a number of testimonies that are – like the financial analysis – listed according to geographical districts. Their historical contextualisation, on the other hand, is rudimentary, and they are abridged and edited. The excerpt below from Sjöblom's 1896-1897 diary about the beginning of the rubber terror regime, for example, jumps between Sjöblom's own text and Morel's interjections:

"Within his knowledge 45 towns have been burnt down. Describes the sentry-system, the soldiers stationed in the villages, living on the people, and driving the adult males into the forest to gather india-rubber. Narrates how he visited a village at sunset. The people had never seen a white man and had returned from their hunt for rubber. As he was speaking to the chief, a soldier rushed in among the crowd, and seized an old man guilty of having been fishing in the river instead of gathering rubber; shoots

Caption: "Natives of the Nsongo district (ABIR Concession) (with hands of two of their countrymen, Lingomo and Bolengo, murdered by rubber sentries, May 1904. The white men are Mr Stannard and Mr Harris from the Congo Balolo Mission in Baringa. See letter from Mr Stannard in appendix)." From Morel's *King Léopold's Rule in Africa* (1904). The Kodak became a standard piece of equipment for all travellers in Africa, especially the missionaries who started sending compromising pictures home to Europe – something that Mark Twain used in his satire about Léopold in which the king is foaming with rage over the great effect of the small device. Many of the photographs are staged, including the characteristic black-and-white dress, and their value as evidence is doubtful.

Natives shot and mutilated by Congo soldiery, from *King Léopold's Rule in Africa*. >

him before Sjöblom's eyes. Right hand cut off. People flee out of town. "All except the old chiefs are forced to go away and work for rubber". The sentries are "from the vilest tribes". "When they get to this work they are many times worse". They are really small kings in the towns and often kill the people for the sake of the rubber. If the rubber does not reach the full amount required the sentries attack the natives. They kill some and bring the hands to the Commissioner" (*Red Rubber*, p. 47).

Morel's exposition of the 'testimonies' follows this formula, defining them in relation to time and geographical location, noted in a specific system, including comments in brackets such as "(Area: river banks, north and central region, *Domaine Privé*)". However, they are never provided with a context that explains the reason behind the atrocities, which become increasingly macabre as the

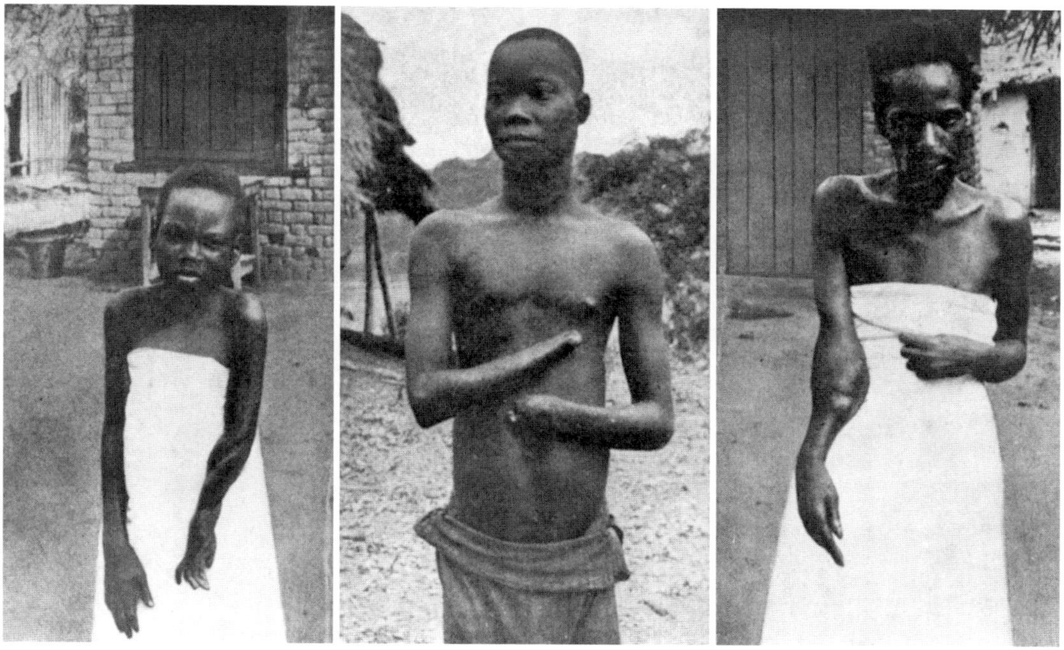

story progresses. The following is the testimony of four missionaries from the British Baptist Society in the town of Yandjali, 1903:

"The town was occupied by a party of Congo Government soldiers under two white officers. The four missionaries on board were horrified to see the native soldiers of the administration, under the very eyes of their officers, engaged in mutilating dead bodies of natives who had just been killed. Three native bodies were lying near the river's edge as the *Goodwill* put into the banks, and human limbs were lying within a few yards of the steamer as she sought to make fast. One of the slaughtered natives was a child. A State soldier was seen drawing away the legs and other portions of a human body. Another soldier was standing by a large basket in which were the viscera of a human body. The missionaries were promptly ordered off the beach by the two officers presiding over this human shambles" (*Red Rubber*, p. 69).

The text is introduced as an eyewitness account in which the missionaries come upon a scene by chance, "when turning a bend of the river". In reality it is not a testimony but a paraphrase, which Morel backs up with direct quotation from one of the missionaries involved, Mr Frame, who

"in a letter to the author confirms the accuracy of the above account: "Time can never wipe the barbarous scene from our memory. The mutilated dead, the mad rushing and firing of the soldiers let loose, and the hasty flight of the poor people, hunted from their homes, like wild beasts, made us sick at heart, and when we looked into

the faces of our black crew we were ashamed, for were not these things done in the name of the State, and under the eyes of its white officers?"" (*Red Rubber*, p. 70).

Rather than supporting Morel's paraphrase of the initial testimony, this statement actually sows additional doubt. The introductory statement that "time can never erase the barbarous scene from our memory" already indicates a rhetorical arrangement of the account, while the emphasis on the fighting and escape scenes is glaringly incongruous with Morel's focus on the macabre details *after* the fight. It is not possible for both versions to be true, since it is also mentioned that the boat is sent on its way by the two white officers immediately after the events; the missionaries cannot have witnessed both incidents. The supporting witness thus does not support the credibility of Morel's account, but rather serves to demonstrate his rhetorical manipulation of the gruelling material. The effect grows stronger when testimonies are removed further from their contexts, directing attention to the rhetorical appeal to emotion and pathos at the expense of reason and logos. Mr Frame's statement is less about the incident, of which he apparently has only a vague impression, and more about the shame and remorse the memory sparks. As we will see, this rhetorical mechanism is significant for the way in which Conrad's *Heart of Darkness* was integrated into the Reform Association's campaign, and for the long-term effects the relationship had on them both.

Both Roger Casement's and Mark Twain's contributions to the criticism of Léopold's regime diverge from the dominant tendency in the campaign rhetoric, which essentially followed Morel's collage of statistics and disparate testimonies, coupled with highly visualised presentations of violence and mutilation. Casement's report was obviously written by a diplomat who knew how to create a strong political argument for Britain's strategic and financial interests in the region. The report begins by defining the writer and the receiver of the report, as well as the task and the journey, which it is admitted was brief. This is Casement's opportunity to introduce the main foundation of his authority: he had visited the same villages in 1887, which allowed him to compare the early days' "savage lives in anarchic and disorderly communities, uncontrolled by Europeans" to the present state, after "a decade of very energetic European intervention".[123] Brief mention is made here of the Belgians' admirable transportation system and well-organised district stations. There follows a section on sleeping sickness, which has reduced the population considerably in the entire region, for which the Belgians are not directly to blame. On the contrary, they are commended for having carried out thorough bacteriological studies of the phenomenon, "worthy of much praise", and for quality of the hospital for Europeans in Léopoldville. This, however, is quickly contrasted with the hospital for natives – "three mud huts" (p. 53) with no roofs – where the patients lie dying and helpless on the bare ground, "in a somewhat striking contrast" (p. 53) to the state hospital's disciplined and effective organisation.

This rhetorical technique is characteristic of Casement's report. He invites the reader into an unpolemic and broadly descriptive frame narration, where his testimonies are included without emphasis or comment. Into the diplomatic introduction, however, Casement manages to sneak horrifying facts into the flattery: what on first sight appears to be a contrast between the natives' anarchy and the energetic order of the Belgians instead becomes a contrast between the area's vibrancy fifteen years earlier and the huge numbers of fatalities in 1903. Casement states in passing that a specific area used to be populated by more than 5,000 people, while there are now less than a hundred left. He uses an almost ironic strategy, the admiring style filling the foreground while it is negated by the realistic, critically descriptive style in the background. For instance, he praises the director of the Société Anonyme Belge du Haut-Congo for the magnificent hospitality and luxury he met with in his dealings with the local authorities. In apparent solidarity with the Free State he also praises it for having brought the slave trade to an end, though he mentions in the same sentence that all other native trade has also been eliminated from a formerly busy centre. All the big cargo canoes, which were the basis of the native trading community, have simply disappeared and been replaced by steamers, which confirms and supports the report's main objection to the Free State – that its unlimited monopoly on all trade and labour, together with the commission system, is the primary cause of the regime's terror methods.

Casement encloses testimonies in the form of interviews, edited according to the same strategy as in the main text:

"Three of the men sat down in front of me, and told a tale which I cannot think can be true, but it seemed to come straight from their hearts. I repeatedly asked certain parts to be gone over again while I wrote in my notebook" (p. 118).

Casement assumes the reader's sceptical position until the testimonies of forced labour, prosecution, kidnapping, the burning of villages and so on are presented in a form that simulates the examination of a witness in a court of law – for instance in Casement's frequent interruptions and sceptical questions to the witness. As it appears from a letter sent by Casement on 16 December, the journey did not go unnoticed by the natives:

"From far and near people were coming in to beg that I would help and protect them. On Monday, the 7th there must have been close on 100 wild forest savages on the mission beach at Boginda waiting or hoping to see the "Bonkunzi" to pour out their tale of wrong. (...) I was rapidly ceasing to be a Consul travelling in a foreign country, and had become a Criminal Investigation Department" (p. 37).

Casement's text seizes every opportunity provided by the diplomatic and legal discourse to alternate direct and indirect appeals, mutually reaffirming each other's authority. Without saying it directly, and with no suggestion of controversy or macabre evidence, Casement leaves an irrefutable impression of how the entire region's former wealth of people and resources have been destroyed by EIC's ruthless repression of free trade and the natives' property and labour rights. The short report is consequently more convincing and more effective than Morel's reports of several thousand pages, and in the years that followed it became the one text to which all others, including that of the independent investigative commission, were compared.

However, as has been suggested, Roger Casement's report was not a legal document in the proper sense, although it aims at building rhetorical authority. His stay was brief, and the information is only partly based on first-hand observation, relying also on reports from missionaries and other sources who were deeply involved in the cause. The natives saw the Irishman as an instrument in local conflicts and told him the stories they knew he had come to hear. Casement was caught up, to some extent, in the idea of being a "protector", and his diary – the so-called "Black Diary" – leaves the impression of a feverish and stressed man labouring under countless difficulties and expectations that were disproportionate in relation to his actual power, many of them communicated in the hundreds of telegrams from Europe he must answer from his cramped, primitive office aboard the small steamer. He becomes increasingly tense after reading Morel's periodical and Burrow's book, as well as meeting with Mrs Sjöblom, which manifests itself in his gambling, drinking and frequent visits to male prostitutes.

The most convincing part of the report concerns Casement's own experiences as a former employee, when he witnessed a drastic population crash following illnesses and the destruction of the natives' own trade and traffic networks in favour of monopolisation and forced labour. In contrast, his testimony to atrocities is weaker and marked by the campaign he was already on the way to joining, outside the foreign ministry commission. This campaign would lead him to speak for other repressed peoples, first for native South Americans and later for the Irish, which ended in his being sentenced and executed for high treason against Great Britain.

A central element of both the official report and the secret diary is the case of the boy Epondo, in which Casement feels like the head of a criminal investigation. According to testimonies enclosed in the documents added to the report proper, a local guard, Kelengo, allegedly chopped off Epondo's left hand. The entire village supported the boy's story and condemned the guard. After the publication of the report, the administration in Brussels claimed – with compelling evidence – that the boy's hand had withered as the result of an attack by a wild boar, and that the story was a fabrication in a plot against Kelengo. This raised serious doubts about Casement's investigation in general. EIC's response to Casement's report hardly addressed any other point than this, and the British Foreign Ministry partly accepted their argument, while stressing that the files and the villagers' motive clearly demonstrated the level of repression and brutality. Casement felt let down by his employers, considered resigning and intensified his activities within CRA, an organisation outside the government's control; later he took to 'anti-British' activities.

Casement's report was mentioned as the direct cause of the increased pressure from the international public, and especially from the British government; however, the pressure from government was carefully adjusted to the political situation in Europe and mainly focused on Léopold's monopoly. Morel and Casement, however, wanted to take it further. Casement was an instrument, so to speak, in local power struggles in the Congo as well as in the high-stakes European political game. His testimony had been produced under extremely strange circumstances, which the biographical fragments in the "Black Diary" witness, but this has not prevented recent reconstructions from portraying him as a heroic model for investigators of repression and genocide, supported by the idea of his intrinsic compassion for the repressed – a notion that is quite idealised. W. G. Sebald's coolly melancholic portrait of Casement in a chapter of *Die Ringe des Saturn. Eine englische Wallfahrt* (1995) approaches a more nuanced historical appraisal. Sebald maintains the image of the stubborn human rights advocate, but places him as an unheroic piece in a cruel, unchangeable historical game in which he is both involved and ultimately sacrificed. The chapter ends with the discovery of Casement's black diary, his execution for high treason and a suggestion that his solidarity with repressed peoples was clearly linked to his homosexuality and close contact with men who sold themselves, thus removing him as far from the centre of power as can be imagined.

Mark Twain contributed to the campaign by supporting the formation of the American Congo Reform Association and publishing the satirical text *King Leopold's Soliloquy. A Defense of His Congo Rule* (1905). The soliloquy is used here as an elegant rhetorical frame for a caricature of Léopold, portraying the un-

scrupulous king as a wild animal or a witchdoctor who squeezes all the life out of his colony in order to fund extravagant constructions and amorous adventures. In the context of this book, it is especially noteworthy how Twain inserts quotations from Morel's and Casement's reports in a fictitious monologue in Léopold's hysterical self-defence. Their comments, which provoke the king's restless, gesticulating, aggressive reading of the pamphlets against his rule, obviously subvert trust in his authority and judgment. Furthermore, Twain plays on Léopold's infamous statement that his ownership of the Congo resembles an author's ownership of his writings: "There is no more legitimate or respectable right than that of an author over his own work, the product of his own labour" (Nelson, p. 85).[124]

Léopold's attacks against the pamphlets aim, in particular, at undermining their credibility, but in the process Twain lets him get overly excited and *admit* to their accusations. Léopold enunciates the hidden misdeeds, presents his strategies for manipulating the public and through his use of language and gesticulation reveals the brutality behind the philanthropic façade – "If I had them by the throat!" (Twain, p. 781).[125] Within this satirical form, which is very different from Morel's double appeal to economic sense and compassion, Twain includes selected quotations from testimonies to atrocities, the fragmented and incomplete characteristics of which are not hidden but revealed. *King Leopold's Soliloquy* is a montage, with visible ruptures between the satirical and pathetic text elements, exposing both the king's and the reader's relation to what is made visible as a confusing, colossal torrent of highly diverse documents concerning the Congo. Twain's polemic is obvious, but in addition the text directs the reader's attention to the genre and media context of testimonies, as well as a meta-discourse that relates to authority and credibility – something we will investigate more thoroughly in Octave Mirbeau's writings. In a passage in which Léopold boasts about how easy it is to bribe newspapers or prevent the publication of critical books, Twain mentions another medium – "the Kodak" – which has far-reaching consequences for the documentation of eyewitness accounts:

"*(Studies some photographs of mutilated negroes – throws them down. Sighs).* The Kodak has been a sore calamity to us. The most powerful enemy that has confronted us, indeed. (...) Then all of a sudden came the crash! That is to say, the incorruptible *Kodak* – and all the harmony went to hell! The only witness I have encountered in my long experience that I couldn't bribe. Every Yankee missionary and every interrupted trader sent home and got one; and now – oh, well, the pictures get sneaked around everywhere, in spite of all we can do to ferret them out and suppress them. Ten thousand pulpits and ten thousand presses are saying the good word for me all the time and placidly and convincingly denying the mutilations. Then that trivial little Kodak, that a child can carry in its pocket, gets up, uttering never a word, and knocks them dumb!" (pp. 798-99).

The Reform Association's Construction of Conrad as Eyewitness

Susanne Gehrmann's *Kongo-Greul* emphasises two specific circumstances surrounding Conrad's incorporation into the Congo Reform Association. The first is that Conrad's discursive authority as a famous and recognised author at the turn of the century was of use to the campaign; the second, that the novel's indeterminate nature meant that it could easily be transposed into a completely different context and associated with concrete testimonies to atrocities. The novel prefigures certain textual strategies that subsequent campaign texts could use in their disposition and style. Gehrmann mentions Morel's connection of Casement's factographic testimonies with Conrad's fictitious text:

"When he [Morel] made Roger Casement's acquaintance and overheard his story about his unpublished experiences from the journey into EIC's rubber districts, he associated Casement's story with Conrad's text: 'we turned again to that tortured African world, to the 'heart of darkness', as Joseph Conrad described it in his memorable story'" (p. 121).

Gehrmann further shows how Morel adopted Conrad's suggestively indeterminate style and the use of the frame narration from *Heart of Darkness.*

The few letters exchanged between Casement and Conrad concerning the author's experiences and possible involvement in the Reform Association are often included in Morel's published collages of quotations, though their value as testimonies is highly questionable. Although Conrad was introverted and ill for most of his journey, and therefore – according to Norman Sherry's investigation – cannot have obtained much knowledge, he still allowed himself to be enrolled as eyewitness, partly due to the impression Morel's *The Congo Slave State* made on him. Subsequently, Conrad was integrated into Morel's main work, *King Leopold's Rule in Africa*, as a guarantor for the authority of the other compiled testimonies.[126]

The circumstances surrounding the exchange of letters suggest that Conrad was included as a result of serious misrepresentation of his testimony. After Conrad's return, Casement contacted him for confirmation of the rumour that severing hands was a widespread practice, which was the main focus of the public interest, and which Casement believed he had proof of in the Epondo case. However, Conrad did not provide such a confirmation:

"17th Dec 1903
My dear Casement
Under my sojourn in the interior, keeping my eyes and ears well open too, I've never heard of the alleged custom of cutting off hands amongst natives; and I am convinced that no such custom ever existed along the whole course of the main river to which my experience is limited. Neither in the casual talk of white men nor in the course of definite inquiries as to the tribal customs was ever such a practice hinted at; certainly not among the Bangalas who at that time formed the bulk of State troops. My informants were numerous, of all sorts – and many of them possessed of abundant knowledge.

I have to thank you for Morel's pamphlet which reached me from L'pool a few days ago. There can be no doubt that his presentation of the commercial methods of the Congo State is absolutely true. It is a most brazen breach of faith as to Europe. It is in every aspect an enormous and atrocious lie in action. If it were not rather appalling the cool completeness of it would be amusing.

My best wishes and cordial regards
Yours Jph. Conrad".[127]

Casement's reaction can be deduced indirectly in an answer from Conrad, 21 December 1903, which begins: "You cannot doubt that I form the warmest wishes for your success". This is followed by a list of all Léopold's flaws, in continuation of the first letter – that is, with a focus on his breach of the free trade obligation and a description of the regime as a masquerade, against which Europe apparently no longer feels compelled to react. The letter is written in the ironically mocking tone found at the end of the first letter, with interpolations such as "This is very funny". It ends with Conrad giving Casement permission to use his letters in the Reform Association's campaign: "Once more my best wishes go with you on your crusade. Of course you may make any use you like of what I write to you" (p. 97).

Conrad's second letter contains no new statements about atrocities, keeping instead to the criticism of the Congo State as masquerade monopoly; however, it is written as a public letter, which Morel may copy directly into his books and articles. Three factors, however, are striking. First, probably in response to the ongoing debate, Conrad presents himself as an eyewitness with "eyes and ears well open" and access to further detail from informants, in the style of Casement's investigative expedition – despite the fact of his well-documented illness. Secondly, Conrad *denies* the atrocities on which the Reform Association insists, but which must have happened ten years after Conrad's brief stay. Thirdly, and crucially, Morel edits the two letters together in his writing, so that Conrad is made to seem an eyewitness to the atrocities.

There is a complex interplay here between Conrad and Morel, who use each others' formulations in a process by which Conrad is gradually integrated as an eyewitness into the Reform Association's propaganda. Conrad's "personal observations" and status as a recognised author adds moral authority to the many unknown voices in Morel's collage of quotations. All this despite the fact that Conrad's statement – claiming that his brief visit to the Congo in 1890 was more or less a reconnaissance and reporting mission on a par with Casement's – is presumably a lie, not to mention that Conrad contradicts the cardinal point and most effective argument of CRA's campaign: the photographic 'evidence' for the practice of severing hands.

Conrad put the two letters at the association's disposal, but he refrained from participating actively in what he, in his decadent *fin de siècle* pessimism, perceived to be a meaningless, didactic-moral project. Conrad supported the theory that an impending cooling of the planet would soon put all human actions in an absurd light anyway. Correspondingly, his statements about his stay in Congo demonstrated that his focus was not on the factual circumstances but his personal disappointment: "All the bitterness of those days, all my puzzled wonder as to the meaning of all I saw" (Conrad, in Kimbrough, p. 199).[128]

Conrad's "puzzled wonder" was subsequently, with the author's reluctant acceptance, reconstructed as a testimony for the Reform Association. Rhetorical traits from the novel were also transferred to Morel's pamphlets, meaning subsequent texts about Congo were organised in a way that was historically fallible and rhetorically problematic. The author's and the novel's aesthetic integrity continued to be confused with moral integrity, obstructing a more objective understanding of the link between Conrad's own journey, the diary, the novel and the Reform Association. Although Susanne Gehrmann presents several crucial pieces of the puzzle, she refrains from drawing the obvious conclusions. On the one hand, she demonstrates the problem in Adam Hochschild's polemic use of Conrad as a "historical document", and his insistence on the "eyewitness's discursive power", which has no basis in reality. On the other hand, in her own reading of *Heart of Darkness* Gehrmann succumbs to the temptation to fill all "blanks" with the potential for criticism of the Congo situation: "Although the text's topography is imaginary, the historical contexts can be reconstructed as Congo specific" (p. 138). As we will see in relation to polemic writings such as Hochschild's *King Leopold's Ghost* and Sven Lindqvist's *Exterminate All the Brutes*, this fallacy is particularly problematic when Conrad's novel is presented as a shocking eyewitness account.

Morel's use of testimonies in *Red Rubber* adopts the rhetorical aspect of Conrad's novel by which suggestive descriptions of "unspeakable rites" serve

as powerful appeals to pathos rather than logos, and to a general, unspecific feeling of guilt, while repressing another aspect of its rhetoric that warns against putting faith in handed-down testimonies. For instance, the final passage in the novel, in which Marlow distributes Kurtz's writings in edited editions, makes a critical point about the public treatment of colonial material. The novel's thematisation of the discursive conditions for Marlow's own testimony contradicts the campaign's use of the novel in conjunction with the display of 'eyewitnesses' and photographs of mutilations that were both heavily arranged and edited and devoid of any elucidating context - and therefore also simulated documentarism.

The effect of the campaign's rhetoric was the same as the effect of the abolitionist movement's, namely that the Congolese were presented as dumb, savage and blunted - or as defenceless, passive children. Furthermore, the rhetoric reinforced the image of the Congo as a place of nameless, unfathomable terror, as it appeared in Conrad's novel. Samuel Nelson's chapter on the Red Rubber period begins by expressing regret that Conrad's novel, as well as Morel's writings, resulted in the complete obliteration of the Congolese's own role in their country's history. This is not to say that "horrible atrocities" did not take place - Nelson provides many examples based on African accounts - but that the massive scare campaign left a biased impression of the natives as helpless victims, which is inconsistent with their actual participation, both as active opponents against the oppression and in some cases active contributors to it. Samuel Nelson's research provides a nuanced picture of a society that was, in fact, very quick to adapt to severe and violent changes. From this perspective, the Reform Association's rhetoric contributed to consolidating and enhancing the myth of the Dark Continent that the abolitionist movement had developed throughout the nineteenth century. Furthermore, the Congo Reform Association had a decisive effect on modern human rights organisations such as Amnesty International and Human Rights Watch. The international aspects of the course of events, the formation of an independent investigative commission and the display of statistics, atrocities and testimonies created a basic pattern that is recognisable in the media campaigns of our time, and entails the same problems.

Previously, it was concluded that the way in which *Heart of Darkness* deals with the conditions for Marlow's narrative contains elements of discourse criticism. With its inclusion in the Reform Association's campaign, this aspect of the novel was repressed, only for it to reappear as an eyewitness account of atrocities. Through this transformation, the novel ended up consolidating the myth about the heart of darkness, alluding to a darkened, unspecific, allegorical attitude towards the Congo and Africa that perceived them as places outside history and the reach of reason. According to Pierre Halen, responding to Bernard Piniau's *Congo-Zaïre 1874-1981. La perception du lointain* (1992), we are dealing with a long-term effect of the metaphor, which permeates all levels of our understanding of Africa: "As soon as it is possible, we return with pleasure to the Conrad tradition: a famine, a coup d'état, a civil war – there is no shortage of tragedies to make the notion of catastrophe penetrate the 'literary' representations on the one hand and media on the other" (Halen, p. 64).[129]

Bernard Piniau formulates the novel's reception history as an annexation of the Congo of a greater power and with a more profound and lasting effect than any military or diplomatic intervention. He defines the publication of the novel as the pivotal event in the country's history, because its "formal perfection" and "stylistic abundance" paved "the way for a strange and surprising 'gaze drift' [dérive du regard]" (Piniau, p. 25). According to Piniau, this drift, established paradigmatically in Conrad's novel, is not only replicated as mystification in twentieth-century literary and mass media representations of the Congo, but has also had a crucial influence on political decisions in the region. Opposing Susanne Gehrmann, and the main conclusions of both formal and postcolonial criticism, Pierre Halen and Bernard Piniau respond sceptically to Conrad's alleged colonial criticism. They both view Conrad's project as an investigation of a European subject in crisis, making the Congo merely a dramatic backdrop for exploring a darkness of galactic dimensions. This book agrees with Halen and Piniau that the intrinsic qualities of *Heart of Darkness* are of less importance than the historical effects of the novel's topographic reduction.

"It [the Conrad tradition] should be understood less as a testimony about colonial and postcolonial Africa than about a literature in crisis, devoted to illustrating the collapse and uselessness of humanism and materialistic positivism. In this sense, one could just as well name this tradition 'radical exoticism', given that it is true that everything there is constructed according to the assertion of alterity" (Halen, p. 88).

The concluding paragraphs of the previous section raised awareness of the biased and extremely reductive image of Stanley that was created in the beginning of the twentieth century and marginalised his works in literary history. The ground was prepared for this image by certain traits in the travel books, in particular Stanley's use of the mystery discourse in *In Darkest Africa*. The canonisation of *Heart of Darkness* either as high literature or historical eyewitness account, and posterity's repression of its discourse critical potential, was similarly prepared by traits in the novel, of which its impressionistic technique and scepticism have been highlighted here. Together, these traits result in

contours and values being evened out, which makes all positions fluid and unclear, including the subtle critical illumination of the conditions surrounding the testimony. Between them, they forestall the topographical comparison of "darkness" and Congo – a fusion that would become standard in the literary tradition, as well as in the use of Conrad as eyewitness.

3 "The Espionage System": Red Rubber in Prose

We have already seen how a number of alternative testimonies from Morel, Casement and Twain serve to illuminate and modify Conrad's text, which today is often put forward as crown witness. The field of investigation will be broadened in the following, with more prose types and approaches illuminating the problem of the historical reconstruction of the terror regime and the role literature played in it. The examples are mainly contemporary, with the exception of the one that opens the chapter. Sven Lindqvist's *Exterminate All the Brutes* (1992) is written as a reconstruction in the archive and a travel account. Lindqvist reads *Heart of Darkness* as a testimony of genocide, and he thus provides an illustrative example of historical and literary misinterpretations that have had wide-ranging consequences – not least because his well-composed essays have enjoyed vast distribution and international recognition. The text in question is a travel account that in several respects can be read as a qualified example of the tendency in travel literature – particularly Congo literature – referred to in this chapter under the term "prose". However, as will become clear, Lindqvist's essay is *not* a model example, which highlights the general and rather obvious point that prose experiments and mixed genres do not hold any privileged position in regard to credibility and authority.

Exterminate All the Brutes follows two main tracks: the first is that of a travel account in the traditional sense, describing the author's journey to godforsaken destinations in the Sahara Desert; the other is an exploration of the archives, in which answers are sought to questions pertaining to history, literary history and the history of ideas raised by the sentence in Conrad's novel that provided the title: "Exterminate all the brutes!" Throughout the book, the two routes gradually converge, which is an important rhetorical point. Furthermore, like Sven Lindqvist's other travel books, it is made up of short, numbered pieces of writing, varying in length from a few lines of aphoristic fiction or description of epiphanic visions on the computer screen to reasoned essays several pages long. The book's prosaic mix of fiction, travel description, literary science and history points to a dialogical openness towards the material and the reader.

The first track – the journey – leads the author to the sites of European massacres of natives, telling a tale about a French officer whose bloodlust has made him insane and another French officer whose objective it is to take him home. In a blend of harsh realism and desert romanticism, red sand drifting

Svend Lindquist's *Exterminate All the Brutes* (Danish translation 1993) is exhibited in the museum in Tervuren, Belgium, as an example of modern myths about the colony under King Léopold's rule. The book is an indignant attempt to transcend the myths of the white man, but the outcome is equally demagogical and xenophobic. In relation to *Heart of Darkness*, it is one example of many, including Adam Hochschild's *King Léopold's Ghost* (1998), that retrospectively construct stories of "greed, terror and heroism", employing Conrad's narrative as a shocking testimony of genocide.

across the roads and evenings when the narrator's computer screen glows green in the pitch-black night, he reflects on his archival work. Like the great explorers' desire to solve geographical mysteries and determination to reach their goals no matter what happens, the narrator's work is described as an exhausting and heroic pursuit of the truth. The other track, the objective reconstruction, presents the results of this work, organised for the reader as a continuation of the heroic narrative of the travel account. The aim is for the reader to experience the detective work in the archives, while at the same time gaining insight into Lindqvist's perception of historical processes as labyrinthine and characterised by great uncertainty, both in their development forward in time and in their historical, backward-looking reconstruction.

The narrator's search for the origin of the genocide leads to his archival work posing new questions to established knowledge, including the narrator's own, until the truth is discovered. The closer he comes to the truth, the closer the tracks get, until they converge when the narrator arrives at the scene of the French massacre. Conrad's novel, a Central African expedition on the Niger River in 1898 and the relief motif in the French story are hereby juxtaposed as each others' truths. According to Lindqvist, it is thus proven that *Heart of Darkness* is a merciless criticism of imperialism's attempt to exterminate other peoples, while history's countless examples of ethnically motivated violations and massacres simultaneously all become examples of genocide. The limited number of concrete references to repression in *Heart of Darkness* is, according to Lindqvist, due to the novel's impressionism, and it was unnecessary anyway to name the terrors that readers already knew about. In this way, Lindqvist can read the novel both as a specific criticism of colonial terror in the Congo and a universal accusation. Through similar shifts between descriptions of specific massacres, often in both gruelling detail and generalised, very broad historical accounts, from Cuvier and Darwin to the Nazi holocaust, his theory about civilisation's inherent xenophobia is supported.

The technique of *Exterminate All the Brutes*, in which pieces from normally separate disciplines and discourses contribute to the same puzzle, results in surprising and insightful combinations, especially concerning the linkage of political theory and natural science. Critics regarded Lindqvist's use of a vast, unusual source material as a sign of credibility and documentarism, which made the shocking claims about our civilisation's participation in genocides even more shocking. The critical objections that followed its publication in Sweden, and subsequently in England, Belgium and France, mainly addressed the book's tendency to draw all-encompassing generalisations at the expense of historical analysis. This was the case, for instance, in a fierce debate in Sweden led by Per Ahlmark, who criticised Lindqvist for completely disregarding anti-Semitism as a crucial factor in the Holocaust; Ahlmark considered the book one of the most destructive of its age. In addition, the book's composition raises other issues that go beyond form, making clear its problematic use of the material.

First, the use of Conrad, who plays a decisive role in the composition as well as the argumentation, is misleading and manipulative. As detailed above, Lindqvist's interpretation of *Heart of Darkness*, which was probably inspired by Olof Lagercrantz's apocalyptic reading, is fallible.[130] Genocide is the wrong term for the violations committed against the natives in the colonies, and its adoption here indicates an extremely ahistorical use of the exemplary material. This has deservedly earned the book a place in the museum in Tervuren as a modern example of the *mythologisation* of the Congo, rather than its historicisation. Furthermore, colonial "atrocities", in the sense of extermination and terror, were *not* known to the public when Conrad's book was published. The predominant image of the colonies, including Belgium's, was positive, with the exception of the after-effects of the scandals that followed in the wake of the Emin Pasha Relief Expedition. However, these scandals did not expose genocides of natives, but powerless British officers' moral decay. Only later was the link constructed between Conrad's novel and the Reform Association's display of atrocities. Lindqvist exploits the novel's gothic as a demagogical means of appealing to

the reader's anger, shame and anxiety, while the novel's indeterminate nature is exploited to increase the flexibility of the field of argumentation, helping individual quotations and cases to fit in with Lindqvist's universal vision of man as monster.

In this case, the prose encourages false openness and dialogue. In one passage, the reader is explicitly invited into a critical dialogue with the book's 'I', and to take a critical look at the enunuciation; Lindqvist drops numerous hints that the reading, the journey and the research in the archive are all part of the same labyrinthine, erratic process. However, if we look at the book's rhetorical refinements as a whole, a different pattern appears: the pieces are precisely arranged with the aim of convincing the reader of one thing only – the thesis behind the archival work and the reconstruction of the story for the reader. The aphoristic and fragmented characteristics are a cloak for a solid determinism that leaves no room for the reader's doubt or independent decision. Even the book's construction ultimately results in a xenophobic and misanthropic attitude.

On a general level, it is obviously problematic that *Exterminate All the Brutes* extends the concept of genocide to include almost all European violations and violent conflicts. The concept ought to be reserved for actual genocides such as the Nazi holocaust and the mass killings on the basis of ethnicity in Rwanda. In the present context, we are also dealing with a serious misuse of *Heart of Darkness*, which was not a testimony to atrocities but rather a warning not to fetishise testimony, which is exactly what Lindqvist does. The reasoning behind this fallible interpretation, as mentioned above, is based on the connection between Conrad's novel and Morel's pathetic use of isolated testimonies – a method which Lindqvist copies to create a link between his demagogical, apocalyptic argumentation and the abolitionist myth about the Dark Continent. Lindqvist's and Adam Hochschild's pamphlets thus help us shed critical light back on the early attitudes to the novel that paved the way for such fallible interpretations.

Another critical aspect also becomes clear in this respect: Lindqvist's archival studies include a broad range of texts and genres, which plays an important role in the text's building of authority and a documentary ethos. However, he does not reflect critically on the individual testimonies – which merely become parts of the text collage – or on the discourse of testimony as such. The archive and the testimonies are employed as if they in themselves, due to their discursive or rhetorical characteristics, are 'evidence' to the truth. This is extremely misleading. Furthermore, it is a rejection of the possibility that we might find real knowledge in archives and the prose they preserve.

Consulting one of the many databases of the Red Rubber period, one encounters a rich body of prose narratives that illuminate significant points of *Heart of Darkness*, which provide a different, more nuanced understanding of the European presence in Congo during Léopold's rule of terror. Lindqvist's polemic essay thus highlights a problematic, yet popular, use of Conrad's novel, not only as one testimony among others but as the crown witness, which ultimately, and uniquely, has guaranteed access to the truth.

The following chapter will present some of these many alternative narratives about the Red Rubber period in order to identify the prose field of which *Heart of Darkness* is part. It begins with "The Transfer", a short narrative that might have been the inspiration for Conrad's novel. Via "An Outpost of Progress", Conrad's first of two stories about Congo, the Danish author Jürgen Jürgensen's literary prose is investigated, and the chapter ends with a travel account written by two Danish employees in EIC.

Both Andrea White and Patrick Brantlinger emphasise that the outpost motif is far from unique to Conrad's writing; around the turn of the century it was a constituting trait of other genres, such as the *Bildungsroman*, adventure fiction, gothic romance and travel literature. Kurtz would later become the epitome of the aesthetically cultured European who transforms into his opposite during a stay at a distant outpost of civilisation. This takes place through a process of reversed cultivation, in which the traveller's inner primitiveness unfolds in unspeakable rites and a particularly decadent version of what has subsequently been termed "going native". Conrad's short stories about outpost decadence became templates for countless successors, but according to Richard Ruppel, they themselves were palimpsests of an existing popular literary formula.[131] Ruppel mentions Cutcliffe Hyne's "The Transfer" from 1897 as the inspiration for *Heart of Darkness*.[132] The outpost theme is treated in the same manner, the plot and organisation of narrators are strikingly similar, and the overall decadent decline of the outpost's values not to mention the intrinsic system of values in the story are shared traits in the two texts. The last part of the following chapter investigates Octave Mirbeau's travel description *La 628-E8* (1907), about a journey in Europe by car. The focus will be on Mirbeau's criticism of colonialism in his prose, which is similar in some respects to Conrad's, but differs in ways that can help illuminate *Heart of Darkness*.

"The Transfer"

Cutcliffe Hyne's "The Transfer" is almost forgotten today, which means it very difficult to get hold of. Ruppel believes that this once popular, exotic text was Conrad's inspiration for *Heart of Darkness*, and while no certain proof exists, this author tends to agree. Hyne's narrative, like Conrad's, is organised into

three parts. The equivalent to Marlow's account of the text's anonymous frame narrator in Hyne's novel is Cecil Gering's account of Calvert, a ship's mate aboard a ship on its way from England to Africa. The story is narrated aboard the ship, not on the Thames, but by a small trading station at the coast, while the crew is waiting for Cecil Gering's ivory to be loaded. The ivory comes from the area around the Kurtz figure's "Inner Station", and the role is played by an equally demonic figure, the Belgian Baron Caissier, who has been searching for the enormous stock of ivory which Emin Pasha, according to rumour, has hidden and forgotten in some secret place in Central Africa.

Gering and Caissier meet here and realise that they are after not only the same treasure, but also the same girl, Marion Kennedy, to whom Gering became engaged just before he left for Africa. Gering suffers from fever and ends up saying too much, about both the girl and the treasure. The infamous, barbarous Caissier lays a trap for Gering, luring him into offering to sell him a British weapon, which enables him to sentence Gering to death with reference to international law and the principles of the Free State. However, the execution is stopped at the last minute; the British agent hangs the Belgian instead, and the entire caravan travels to the coast where the reader, and the narrator Calvert, meet Cecil Gering for the first time and hear the incredible story, which is indirectly confirmed by the Free State's official, opposing version in which Gering is wanted for murder.

There are many similarities in structure and content between the two texts, including rather specific facts. One example is the presence of a fiancée who is better off not knowing about Africa, how the treasures are obtained or the strange coincidences in "the Interior". There are also similarities between Gering's and Marlow's presentations of the story – "I might spin you a queerish yarn" – to pass time aboard. Both texts accentuate the outpost decadence theme and take place in a political context in which the boundaries between British efficiency – symbolised by the rifles – and Belgian incompetence are clearly drawn. Furthermore, both Hyne and Conrad create suspense via an all-pervading paranoia in the portrayed universe, achieved by playing on the Free State's secretive and terrorising communications, and by reproducing this strategy in the texts' own information structure. Hints, unfounded rumours, betrayal and unreliable narrators create uncertain terms for the reader, who cannot tell what is true and what is false.

In relation to the critical appraisal of *Heart of Darkness* presented above, the most interesting aspect of "The Transfer" is that it is extremely clear and explicit when it comes to the Congo's geography and historical-political situation in the 1890s, the so-called Red Rubber period. EIC's breach of the free trade agreements are foregrounded in the text, and atrocities such as the burning of villages and forced labour - often accentuated through the contradiction in terms "the Free State forced labourers" - are described explicitly as consequences of the shareholders' pressure on the colony's employees to increase profits in conjunction with an unskilled, demoralised labour force. The Gordian knot of the plot is tied and untied via the theme of the Free State's lawlessness, its "philanthropic excuses" which cover "filibustering expeditions", presented as a breach of the administration of "International Law". The moral seems to be that the British vigilantism in the Free State territory was justified, because the Free State disregarded legal procedures for law and conviction - which are sarcastically portrayed in Caissier's pedantic, explicitly fake performance of a legal case as a play:

"he was the jealous guardian of the International Law; and as such he formed himself into judge, accuser, and jury, all in one. The trial was the baldest of farces. Caissier sat on a hammock chair under the shade of a mango tree, with an ammunition box to serve as table, and the margins of a novel (the only available paper, it seemed) to take his notes on" (p. 212).

"The Transfer" was published in 1897, two years prior to the serialised version of *Heart of Darkness*. It deals with the period after the Emin Pasha Relief Expedition, clearly inspired by a well-publicised scandal in 1895: Charles Stokes, a British trading agent with a sullied reputation was arrested at Stanley Falls, accused of weapon smuggling, and hanged after a summary procedure carried out by a Belgian officer, H. J. Lothaire, who had received special attention during the war against the Arab slave traders in 1896-1897 for his unprecedented brutality. "The Transfer" uses the skipper's tale as a popular literary form in which to stage the high political conflict, and like *Heart of Darkness* it celebrates the advantages of British imperialism compared with the inefficient and corrupt Belgian administration.

If we compare the two texts, it is striking that Conrad does *not* mention 'atrocities' or, for instance, the Free State's legitimisation crisis in relation to Léopold's increasing enforcement of the colony as his "domaine privée". On the other hand, we become aware of the form in which Conrad's experiences from the journey to the Congo are presented: *Heart of Darkness* can be read as Conrad's Congo diary, combined with Cutcliffe Hyne's "The Transfer", supplemented with the impressionism that influences style, figurative language and the veiled narrative situation. As mentioned in the previous chapter, this veiling is also a "will-to-style" that secured Conrad's position in the national and, subsequently, international canon. However, Hyne's tale also appears to codify a pattern that reaches far beyond Conrad's novel, which we will see exempli-

fied in many variations in twentieth-century travel literature about the Congo. The relief motive is replicated in E. R. Burroughs' novels about Tarzan and in *Trader Horn*; we find it in the form of Arne Falk-Rønne's relief of a mercenary, a so-called 'mutilator', who is helped to escape "the Interior"; we also find it in Jürgen Jürgensen's stories. Wrong masked as right, and the collision between the idea of the free state and international law on the one hand and a state of emergency on the other, are recurrent themes that appear in connection with clusters of other exceptions from generally accepted rules of rhetoric and history. Finally, most of these texts, including "The Transfer", appear to adhere to a topographic model that distinguishes between coastal areas, in which light and sense reign, and inland areas, where all hell is let loose.

"An Outpost of Progress"

Joseph Conrad's "An Outpost of Progress" was published in two parts in *Cosmopolis* in June and July 1897, the year before "The Transfer". It begins with two dreamers, Kayerts and Carlier, arriving at the outpost full of illusions that are soon exposed and shattered by "fateful complications" in the surrounding forests. The gullible gentlemen become involved in the slave trade, which is arranged by their black servant in order to fill their shrinking stock with ivory and thus save face when their superiors come to check up on their work after six months. They gradually become aware that their workers are being sold as slaves, and slowly but steadily they are dragged into complete moral decay, beyond all standards of civilised behaviour.

Conrad's story is emotionally detached and its style is sarcastic from the very beginning. The narrator never becomes involved in the events, which are described as absurd comedy. It is a masquerade in which all the participants may be unmasked, while the narrator and reader keep their distance. This impression is emphasised by the stereotypical portraits both of the two Europeans and of the natives who are either indolent, comical fops, like the area's chieftain, or silent and stoic, like the servant.

The description of Kayert and Carlier's partnership is strikingly reminiscent of Flaubert's unfinished farce *Bouvard et Pécuchet* (1881), and highlights the sceptical position mentioned above in relation to *Heart of Darkness*. As is the case with Flaubert's main characters, the wretched state of affairs in Conrad's story is caused by Kayerts' and Carlier's excessive reading of fiction. For want of company in the forest, they take Balzac's *Père Goriot*, Dumas' *D'Artagnan* and Cooper's *Hawk's Eye* to be "living friends". The style is unmistakably Flaubertian; even the content sometimes seems to be copied from *Bouvard et Pécuchet*:

"All these imaginary personages became subjects for gossip as if they had been living friends. They discounted their virtues, suspected their motives, decried their successes; were scandalized at their duplicity or were doubtful about their courage. The accounts of crimes filled them with indignation, while tender or pathetic passages moved them deeply" (*An Outpost*, p. 44).

Carlier and Kayerts furthermore appear to copy Flaubert's imitators in the sense that they repeat the clichés about progress that Bouvard and Pécuchet try to realise at *their* post in the middle of nowhere in Normandy, comically confusing them because they cannot read properly and therefore becoming victims of "déja vu" and "bêtise", Flaubert's own formula for stupidity. For example:

"Carlier said one evening, waving his hand about, "In a hundred years, there will be perhaps a town here. Quays, and warehouses, and barracks, and - and - billiard-rooms. Civilization, my boy, and virtue - and all. And then, chaps will read that two good fellows, Kayerts and Carlier, were the first civilized men to live in this very spot!" Kayerts nodded, "Yes, it is a consolation to think of that"" (p. 44).

Although Conrad concludes his story with Kayerts sticking his tongue out at the manager, who arrives at that very moment - too late - it is a farce that does *not* turn the "bêtise" inwards, like Flaubert's, to include the narrator and the reader. Numerous distancing mechanisms place the events in a thoroughly strange and absurd sphere, unrelated to historical circumstances and unaffected by scepticism. Rather than being a crime, slave trade is an act of stupidity, and the place - "the very spot" - is, like in *Heart of Darkness*, first and foremost described as the meaningless scenery of the comic play, which the narrator and reader can enjoy in comfort from a distance.

The Danish Congo Novels of Jürgen Jürgensen

The Danish author Jürgen Jürgensen's Congo novels and Congo tales are also outpost literature, but they are more closely based on the author's own experiences of Congo than either Conrad's or Hyne's. Jürgensen was in Congo in 1898, spending some time as the district manager of the post in Belondo - where he was the only European in an area of over 10,000 square miles. In 1909, he published the novel *Christian Svarre's journey to the Congo*, followed by *Fills the Earth* (1910) and the collections of short stories, *Fever* (1911) and *The big and the small river* (1913). Later, Jürgensen wrote other contributions to the new genre of "Congo novels" or "Congo tales", which together were referred to as "the Danish Congo literature". Jürgensen also enjoyed international success; some

of his books were translated into many languages and published concurrently with the Danish versions. As a phenomenon in literary history, this Congo literature, and specifically Jürgensen role in it, is interesting, not least because it has been completely erased from literary memory until recently. Its rediscovery – in which Peter Tygesen's *The Congo – I Presume. Narratives from Dreamland* (2001) was seminal – will be investigated later. For now, we will focus on the textual traits that are revealed by the prose perspective, which can be seen as exemplary in the same way as Octave Mirbeau's forgotten travel book, the topic of the next paragraph.

The positive reviews that are often cited on the covers of Jürgensen's books generally tell us that we are dealing with something unique.[133] Sven Lange wrote in the Danish newspaper *Politiken*: "A poet has written this book, and his absolute poetic power has resulted in one of the strangest and most important works published in Denmark in recent years". *Socialdemokraten* also highlighted the experience of something strange, however with a reservation:

> "Because of its theme, this book is as exceptional in Danish literature as its treatment of the theme is strange and captivating. It is not the dream of a poet, but the experience of a man of action, whose strength – and weakness – could be found in his imagination. Without it, the description of his internal and external experiences – nature's peculiarity, the childishness and savagery of the native people – would not have formed such curious images as the ones that fill Captain Jürgen Jürgensen's books. No Danish author before him has given us a similar account".

The reviewers were very taken with the novel and the author, who is described as an "experienced, clever and compassionate guide into the mysteries that are the lives of white people and the encounter of races in the innermost, dark mainland".

It is also noticeable that the reviews emphasise this as "honest" and "truthful" literature, based on personal experience, which adds a guarantee of realism to the otherwise impressionistic style. From *Nationaltidende*: "The author describes their silhouettes with a few, firmly and sharply drawn lines; his method is, in that respect, quite impressionistic, but it is based on his own experience, which always provides a guarantee for the credibility of the observations". This appraisal corresponds with the text on the back of the debut novel, which links its impressionistic form with its geography: "The descriptions are shrouded in a light dream haze, leaving the reader with an impression of a veil of unreality through which a northerner sees the tropical regions, saturated and trembling with sun".

One final fact worth noting by way of introduction is that several reviewers

Jürgen Jürgensen's narratives about the Congo are unique because they were not promoted by means of the stable, recognisable types, titillating suggestions of white men's relationships with black women, or fantasies about boundless possessions and distant provinces. The tales often include several, opposing views of conflicts in which the narrator is involved *while* narrating. Even though they address a large audience and were translated into several languages, their morals and aesthetics are more unpredictable, challenging, and complex than those of other contemporary prose texts about the Congo.

took the opportunity to address the audience of readers who were assumed to be abandoning books, especially high literature. Jürgensen's novels were highlighted as an example, on par with Kipling, of the partnership between popular and quality literature. Some reviewers emphasised their popular qualities: "It meets all the requirements for becoming popular", wrote *Politiken*, while the majority perceived Jürgensen's experimental novels as a solution to the division between the way high literature and mass literature were distributed – something that was seen as an increasingly urgent cultural problem, as discussed above in relation to Conrad. Oluf Bang in *Vort Land* wrote: "In a time when audiences with good taste, who should and must be reproached despite their excuses, turn away from heavy, less digestible art and towards the more easily accessible, it is a pleasure to encounter this book. It is good enough to be perceived as art, under any circumstance". And Helge Rode in *Illustreret Tidende* judged Jürgensen "A splendid author who has rare prerequisites for gaining the favour of the select few, as well as the broad, educated audience – if indeed an audience exists that can be termed as such in these times, when one must often ask oneself whether literary education has passed away".

Christian Svarre's Journey to the Congo (1909) contains many of the same motifs

as *Heart of Darkness* and "An Outpost of Progress". The novel's attitude towards the idea of civilisation is ironic, and Jürgensen, like Conrad, cultivates simile and prosopopeia – i.e. comparing and personifying tropes – as a means to conjure up an image of nature as animate and equipped with its own unpredictable and evil will, while humans are described as beings that are very close to descending into pure biology. And like Marlow, Christian Svarre's internal pendulum swings between hard, Kiplingesque fact and an escape into poetic imagination.

Christian Svarre succeeds in founding a new district with an extraordinarily good yield of rubber: an organised society of villages and a disciplined team of willing workers. The catastrophe occurs when new orders arrive from Brussels. The point is that new philanthropic currents from Europe – what *Heart of Darkness* calls "the gang of virtue", which includes, according to the Manager, both Marlow and Kurtz – will have apocalyptic consequences if the reforms are introduced too quickly. When Svarre refuses to follow the command, he is persecuted in the same way as Kurtz. An important aspect of the story is the endeavour to gain as much influence as possible using information in the form of rumours and secret reports – the "Espionage System" – carried up and down the river. After an exhausting battle fought anlongside the chieftain's trusted men, the novel ends with a description of a utopian reconciliation in which Svarre listens for the first time to the natives' tales and experiences a new working community.

These twists and turns take the novel to bursting point, while also making it entertaining, wild and unpredictable. It is not free from unpleasanr stereotypes, as when Svarre's engagement with a native girl is excused by the fact that her beauty is "the fruit of an error of memory in the race, a living reminder of the time when the Bantu lived far to the north and had eastern features".[134] Compared with Conrad, however, it is based less on guesswork and observations of coastal areas, and the adventure element is not secretive or sublime but supported by knowledge of inland nature and ethnography; it is "rich in experience" and close to the autobiographical material.

The novel *Fills the Earth* (1910) appeared in the immediate wake of the debut's success; however, it is far more gloomy and pessimistic. *Christian Svarre's Journey to The Congo* may contain many violent episodes from life on the plantations, as well as examples of atrocities, but these stories are mostly offshoots from the main story of Svarre's formative experiences. *Fills the Earth*, on the other hand, makes violence and atrocities its theme. The book's hero is Commandant François Germain, but the narrative follows many other characters who each carry the point of view through lengthy passages until they die, one by one, in the rebel war in Upper Congo's great forests. The composition resembles the collective novel, which gives Jürgensen the opportunity to describe the different war

parties from within, for example the native rebellion leaders are described through an empathic identification that is in stark contrast to their opponent's views in the subsequent chapter. After many bloody clashes, a miraculous reversal allows François Germain to crush the rebellion. This happens because of an impulsive and uncharacteristic decision to grant safe conduct to a Pygmy girl who has been captured by one of his scouts. He is subsequently rewarded by the girl's chieftain, whose invincible forest warriors enter into an alliance with the Free State against the rampaging Bantu tribes.

The terrors and chaos of war are described in blood-soaked detail, and there is no doubt that Germain is the story's hero. Still, changing perspectives contribute to a highly complex presentation of the moral conflicts, which, throughout the novel, are in the foreground. In this sense, the war adventure appears to be an opportunity to describe and discuss the moral implications of the conflicts rather than vice versa. This is especially evident in the intense clashes between different perspectives and points of view. The narrative is often interrupted by different narrators, who are divided and ambiguous in their appraisal of the narration: "We who work hard for a living at our workbenches or writing desks at home" are, according to the narrator's overarching idea, *related* to the native rebels as well as the punitive expedition in one great community of fate called "The parasite century of expansion fever". From this constructed vantage point, the narrator deals merciless blows to the notions of colonisation and civilisation:

"In addition to the crops of their own fields, the Europeans devoured the fruit of others'. They ploughed down entire foreign races into their ancestral soil with armies of farming machines. They listed the results of their exploitations in the statistics, without mentioning one single word about the cost of the wares that had been

obtained with cannons and machine guns, that the foreign coasts were besieged by ironclad warships that dominated the world market in Europe's favour. The Europeans protested from time to time in the name of international law and charity, but the protest was always powerless, because the law and charity only applied to themselves and they still received the wares. No one rejected coffee, tea, tobacco, cocoa, sugar, salt, exotic fruit, rice, maize, wheat, fuel and manure – in short, all the living and dead native peoples and the staggering contribution of their soil to the sustenance of the European races. No one was asking: How can we have come by all these things honestly? (...) Nevertheless, Europe, led by an internal instinct, acted protectively towards its primitive working species, particularly in the places on Earth where their ultimate extermination would result in economic losses; where their existence was necessary to ensure the complete exploitation of the land" (pp. 76-77).

The passage continues a good deal further with what we can only perceive as a detailed and precise analysis of the colonial question, clearly substantiated by Jürgensen's own experiences from the Congo. We are dealing with some of the most concise descriptions of the complicated systems of exploitation, work contracts, deportations of natives to foreign districts to serve as soldiers against other natives, regulations for hostage-taking, forms of punishment and so on – everything that both Casement and Morel had trouble penetrating and understanding. The concise and sarcastic description of Europe's "groaning expansion mania" is, however, inserted into another figure that diverts its polemic impact: this expansion fever is linked with the Europeans' excessive desire to procreate and their "hypersexuality". The bloody colonisation and "uncontrolled consumption of coffee" is, in the narrator's opinion, caused by Europeans lacking the ability to define and respect boundaries for their expansion, consumption and ideas. First and foremost, men have ceased to limit their sexual desire, taking pleasure instead in the new women of easy virtue who are breaking the old chains.

The responsibility for the terrors is not unambiguously placed with the colonisers; they are merely the enzymes of a far more comprehensive metabolism. The catalysts are, as with Conrad, comedians, in as far as they do not realise their situation; in the novel they become victims of their own philanthropic illusions, often described as a manic, feverish disintegration of their connections with place and reality. Unlike Conrad, however, Jürgensen wrote his masquerade of the disintegration of place in close conjunction with his experience of place. Furthermore, his heroes are exceptions who see through the colonisers' *and* humanists' hypocrisy and still manage to hold their heads high, courageously pursuing justice amidst the chaos, even when it is clear that they – like Christian Svarre and François Germain – are contributing to the exploitation and atrocities that the novels clearly expose as unjustifiable.

François Germain's noble act towards the Pygmy girl, and their platonic love, are significant fictional additions to the novel's non-fictional background. As in his debut novel, it is interesting that Jürgensen installs an antipole to the description of the conflict and contact zone between Europeans and natives. Svarre acknowledges the wisdom of the natives' stories, which he – despite all western ideals of cultured behaviour – ends up identifying with, and Germain has a similar encounter with the Kilima people, who have achieved insight that surpasses his own but is on par with the narrator's. The Kilima live peacefully with their neighbours and have plenty, though there are many of them. This is due to a legal measure which proscribes the men having intercourse with a woman during her pregnancy and the two years after the birth. This supposedly results in stronger children and, in the novel's fantasy, solves a number of demographic problems in the region.

The mindset is ecological, attempting to understand the relationship between the sexes and between cultures as vulnerable metabolisms that are either unbalanced by interventions from the outside – as is the case with the natives – or destroyed by uncontrolled desire from within – as is the case with the Europeans. The problem in the novels' presentation of these metabolisms, which today we can only recognise as surprisingly precise and forward-looking, is that the literary images employed to illustrate the expansion fever also grow and expand uncontrollably. At the same time, it is this lack of narrative control that makes Jürgensen's Congo narratives so interesting.

We saw that Jürgensen's reviewers – in spite of all their praise – also expressed reservations about his unusual and peculiar style, which was perceived as "captivating" and "fascinating" but also as a breach of literary conventions that could not be satisfactorily assessed. These reservations are absent when it comes to the short stories, which Helge Rode in *Illustreret Tidende* calls "genuine pearls of short fiction art", and about which *Berlingske Tidende* writes: "Several of the stories are absolutely exquisite – perhaps the author reaches higher in these concise short stories than in the two above mentioned extensive novels; at any rate, the effect and impression they cause are equally strong". The form of the short stories is much simpler than that of the novels, and at first sight they do not seem to challenge the reader's values to the same extent.

The first story in the collection *Fever*, "The white bacterium", is – as the title suggests – framed in the same biological imagery as the novels. Like many of the other stories it is about a young, naïve man who arrives at his outpost with great expectations of being about to civilise the world and excel; however, Hendrickx soon succumbs to fever, loneliness and all-encompassing misinterpretations. The bacterium image has been mentioned earlier in connection with the "medical officer" on the Emin Pasha Relief Expedition, T. Heazle Parke,

who discussed the paradigm shift in microbiology caused by tropical medicine. Here, the image introduces a link between the young man's feverish collapse and colonialism's penetration of "the dark mainland" which had, until then, been "a kind of sanctuary from the disease".[135]

"[The bacterium] penetrates the body of the forest along the Congo River. It spreads in the opposite direction of the hundred river forks' pulsating liquid, out into the forest's capillary network. It eats its way into river banks and digs holes in the tissue. Everywhere it arrives, diseased blotches appear, and the disease spreads over the Stream of Time, as it has done in Europe and America. But the forest defends itself. Inside the disease-ridden vein walls it secretes healing substances which, here and there, enables the tissue to expel the intruding organism to the bloodstream, where it is flushed away or killed" (pp. 5-6).

The image of the bacterium's penetration of the forest's body is so consistent that it is just to claim that the entire text is, in reality, a literal representation and deterministic exposition of the implications of that one figure. Hendrickx is the bacterium who tries to penetrate the forest but is expelled and disappears into the same circulatory system that brought the disease. Together the characters form a comprehensive, pulsating metabolism that works beyond good and evil, and the reader is situated within a relatively familiar frame of reference in which bacteriology and decadent-gothic ideas of bodily decay and genre boundaries intertwine as aspects of the same parasitic contagion.

Most of the stories, however, are much less unambiguous; they are composed as open, challenging narratives, in which changes are not linked to singular events or summarised in a simple moral. "The white bacterium" is an exception: in other stories – partly because they deal with colonial conflicts in historical and concrete forms – the narrator and reader are involved in the narrative in a challenging, unresolved manner.

The story titled "Vitelli" describes how a naïve Italian soldier without any knowledge of the country and the people in EIC's service suddenly transforms into a devastating monster. Because of the demoralisation and cowardice of the people around him, his illusions are not countered; rather, he is encouraged to live them. The narrator is far removed from Vitelli, the prototypical European who is given the chance to realise his romantic fantasies in the Congo with horrifying consequences, as all his accomplices fail to stop him, instead pragmatically using his warmongering energy in their own interest – or enjoying the course of events as a drama with an ending they already know but will not give away before it is too late. As the narrator is clearly one of the spectators who should have intervened, telling the story in a retrospect that discloses ev-

eryone's responsibility for the devastating spiral of violence, the story is highly self-critical. In the Congo, the romantic idea of war as a drama is allowed to develop into a simulacrum: at one and the same time both farce and extreme subversive violence.

"Iron hunger", also from *Fever*, is more subtle, but similarly investigates perceptions of the conflict and contact zone between colonists and natives with an understanding of their complexity that is unique for its time. The story describes Lieutenant Johansen's early days among the natives, whose language he does not understand. This story, however, does not develop into the classical degeneration model, leaving Johansen to perish in moral decay, but depicts a coloniser who manages to survive because he acknowledges his own limitations and tries to overcome them by learning to master the natives' language and mentality. Johansen starts by knowing nothing and being aware of that, slowly building an identity in the foreign surroundings on the basis of a pragmatic strategy for surviving and understanding them. He concentrates on single words and isolated gestures, gradually figuring out their semantic content. He does not perceive his situation as a clash between two cultures, but as a long learning process in which misunderstandings are unavoidable steps on the way.

This is the case with the word "efeko", which Johansen initially interprets as "weapon", because all the natives point towards arrows, spears, knives, etc. when he says it. Subsequently, its meaning is expanded with ideas about violence, cannibalism and mysterious rituals. This method of interpretation exemplifies paranoid hermeneutics. Later, when he goes on a mission through a famished area, he comes upon the correct meaning of "efeko", "iron", which is linked to the poverty in the area: the remaining natives have not been able to cultivate the land due to a lack of iron tools. It turns out that a mad district manager, Moron, has stolen all the iron in the area on violent raids, convinced that he could con-

trol the entire district by preventing the natives from forging weapons. Unlike Johansen, he maintains and cultivates his paranoid ideas, which lead to absurd measures and extreme repression, actually making these violent fantasies a reality. It is a clever story that analyses basic mechanisms in the West's relationship with Africa. However, the story's most striking feature is that at the beginning Johansen and Moron are in the same position, and the point is expressed not through fixed ideas about heroes and villains but through one character's ability to change his preconceived ideas. "Now, when in the villages he heard the word, the perpetual efeko, it was not, like a few days ago, an impenetrable concept, the mute, animalistic, raw idea of a savage. It was iron, nothing more" (p. 108).

The next example is the titular story from Jürgensen's second collection of Congo stories, *The big and the small river* (1913). The debut novel's sub-plot about a complicated, unresolved moral dispute surrounding a trading agent's violations of natives is central to this story. As in *Christian Svarre's journey to the Congo*, the narrator distances himself from the hell of rubber production and forced labour, instead focusing his sarcastic and precise analyses on the rigid control apparatus and the secrecy of the "Espionage System" that cause paranoia and exacerbate the spiral of violence. On the other hand, the new humanistic demands from Europe, once again wanting to enforce laws and regulations that, according to a mutual, unspoken agreement, have been suspended in Upper Congo and along the tributaries of the great river, are characterised as both unrealistic and unjust. Europeans who have met their obligations under impossible conditions in Congo are now suddenly termed criminals because of these changing attitudes. Humanism's criticism of colonialism and colonialism's deceitful philanthropy are perceived from the outpost as two sides of the same coin, both lacking any understanding of the "frontier" situation.

Viewed from the prose perspective, the story is interesting because it is written on the basis of a perceived idea of the fluid and changeable nature of attitudes and positions. The narrator has recently arrived at the outpost of Molenga, by a tributary of a tributary of the Congo River. He wishes to remain neutral, aloof from the activities of his superior, Justin, whose informants report accusations against a trading agent who handles the task of collecting rubber on the other side of the river with excessive determination and effective brutality. Early in the course of events, Justin describes a chance encounter with a useless wretch, Pelgrims, who suffered a complete, humiliating downfall in the Congo before returning to a life of poverty in Belgium. When the trading agent – against whom Justin has prepared a detailed and documented court case but has still not met in person – suddenly pays a visit, Justin's self-assured opinion of the question of guilt changes. The narrator is puzzled by this change, but he has also listened to the trading agent's account with admiration and felt ashamed to be cognisant of the accusations Justin has compiled but not presented to the agent. The narrator initially reckons that this must be due to a cheap trick on Justin's part, encouraging the trading agent to say too much and thus admit to the accusations in good faith. However, the following morning he realises that Justin has allowed the criminal to escape.

Throughout the entire course of events, the narrator has been sceptical about Justin's preparation of the court case against the trading agent; it is interpreted as a symptom of jealousy and rivalry between the two posts, rather than the consequence of a profound sense of justice. Justin's sudden change of attitude, on the other hand, is interpreted as a result of several more complex factors. It is revealed that the trading agent is Pelgrims, who has apparently returned with a more humane approach to frontier conditions; Justin's change of mind might therefore be a continuation of his previous compassion. Alternatively, he might have been convinced that Pelgrims' straightforward account justifies his violations. Or perhaps Justin's change of mind is simply an acknowledgement that the confession is a result of his own feigned hospitality, and that an arrest would breach the laws of this hospitality. His commander is convinced that Pelgrims must be captured and sentenced to set an example; however, this eagerness is shown as pure opportunism.

Several times the narrator makes the reader aware that he has misinterpreted a situation or character, or that unexpected events have taken the story in a completely unpredictable direction. When finally the intelligence arrives that Pelgrims has escaped prosecution by the skin of his teeth, Justin and the narrator celebrate the news with a bottle of champagne. This does not mean, however, that they accept the terror he has perpetrated, but rather that they relieve the individual of a guilt that should be placed on the entire system. The narrator tries to remain detached, but ends up being involved as a witness to the extensive evidence of the agent's methods, and he spends a great deal of energy considering who he would support if it came to a court case. Although he fully acknowledges that many atrocious violations have taken place, he regards Justin's legal preparations as a flagrant manipulation of the natives' testimonies, which include stories about severed hands. Faltering and doubtful about what is right and wrong, he finally encourages Justin to write a false report about Pelgrims' visit that will throw a smokescreen over the man's confessions. In this way, the narrator makes visible his own part in the Espionage System's misuse of testimonies, while at the same time shedding critical light on colonialism's and humanism's acquisition and use of testimonies to atrocities. And uniquely in the Congo literature, the narrator admits to his own doubt, expressed, for example, in an "embarrassing" inability to "classify a fellow man" (p. 24), and in his changeable attitudes, which give vent to all his initial prejudices about

the "Negroes" while retrospectively recognising such prejudices as limitations and unavoidable blind spots that no one involved can escape.

"Roi" from *Fever* is a story about a river skipper whose world disappears completely, eaten up by his caprice that he must always beat his own records. He navigates in accordance with the rationale of the sail plan and the charts, ignoring the conditions on the river, and is doomed because he inherits and incarnates the exploitative system's blind efficiency measures. The story thus exemplifies the analytical dimension that makes Jürgensen's texts so effective, directing attention to two essential aspects of the European history of colonisation in Africa. First, the fundamental, systematic mechanisms of colonisation are laid bare, e.g. the bureaucratisation of forced labour, the administration of information in a demoralising Espionage System and the dehumanising effects of the colonial regime's economic and statistical basis. In this sense, Jürgensen's stories forestalled Hannah Arendt's controversial hypothesis about a link between deployed Europeans' colonial experiences around the turn of the century and Nazism.[136] Second, he explores the narrator's and reader's own contributions to, and knowledge of, the corruption of testimonies, which for some reason or other thwarts the understanding that begins with realising that "efeko" means "iron", not "weapon".

Jürgen Jürgensen's writings have been highlighted here because they attend to the complexity of place and landscape, they show the Europeans' dealings with natives and, crucially, they allow narrators to appear insecure, changeable and contradictory in the learning processes of the text. They are far removed from the exoticism that is the texts' point of departure, whether the distancing and supercilious gaze represents greedy capitalists or empathic humanists. With Jürgensen, Europe is also seen from the Congo, as the knowledge communicated to European readers is forced to seek new literary forms: it calls for recognition of the text's daring execution, which also, however, makes it difficult to understand and assess. The attempt, praised by reviewers, to build a bridge between high and popular literature was probably one of the reasons why the novels were forgotten by both – including in the education system. The effect of Jürgen Jürgensen's texts today is an ominous one – too strange and challenging, both for aesthetically educated readers and for postcolonial critics – and they will probably never become part of any canon, though the recent emphasis on the global terms of literature, perspectives of world literature and the renewed interest in travel literature of course make them highly relevant.

Conrad's *Heart of Darkness* was the result of a long, troublesome process and did everything in its power to appear as art, while Jürgensen's stories, bar a few exceptions, are far closer to complex experiences that have not been fully stylised aesthetically. Rather, they insert changing, conflicting and overlapping perspectives *between* narrators and *within* each narrator's own changeable attitudes. The peculiarity of Jürgensen's Congo literature, which his reviewers thought of as highly significant, should be seen in relation to the texts' unschooled form, which allows literary images to be developed and moral judgments to be shifted – and what is more, without undermining the texts' authority. Instead, these wild, compound and changeable characteristics enhance the impression of testimony to real experience being included and preserved in literary fiction, where it challenges conventions of style and narrative organisation. With Conrad, conversely, experience is erased in order to ensure the highest degree of refinement in style and narration. Similarly, the impressionistic, flickering light of Jürgensen's feverish stories serves a specific and concrete purpose. While the impressionism in Conrad's writing erases any references to identifiable locations, Jürgensen's impressionistic style and allegorical images of global metabolisms thrive on a concrete knowledge of nature and people. Jürgensen's veiling mechanisms are directly related to the terror, paranoia and corruption of testimonies in which both imperialistic colonialism and humanistic anti-colonialism took part.

Two Danish Travellers to the Congo

In addition to milestones such as Stanley's *Through the Dark Continent* and Joseph Conrad's *Heart of Darkness*, there exists a comprehensive, largely unknown body of literature, that was, however, fairly popular in the colonial period. A good deal of these texts aimed primarily at entertainment, presenting captivating and sensational adventures or plain macabre horror. Depending on the context, these texts could assume significance either as proof of the horrors of the place such as cannibalism – a classical topos in more or less all the stories – or as an exhibition of the colonial administration's cruel violations. The latter includes tales of ammunition only being handed over in exchange for severed hands – smoked, so they would last in the heat. Others are personal narratives, often surprisingly cool and bleak, as if harsh reality has already faded the exotic expectations of the travel writer or correspondent. The texts are, on the one hand, rooted in personal, often very dramatic, conflicts of conscience that exert an influence regardless of any explicit attitude taken, while on the other, they fulfil the reader's expectations of thrilling adventures.

These texts were written by missionaries, district managers, mercenaries, trading agents and sailors, who – like Conrad – entered into three-year contracts with the Congo Free State to do service in the steam ship traffic above Léopoldville. Most of the employees died or had to return before the three years had passed, and those who returned often died shortly after of untreatable tropical diseases. Only a few lasted the entire period; they were employed permanently

Schønberg and Martini's travel account from 1890, the same year Conrad made his journey, is the first in a long series of reports written by Danish contractual workers in the Congo. In terms of prose, it is an odd mix of travel account, letters, and jovial workplace jargon. It combines jolly anecdotes with terrifying accounts and naïve credibility, which is related to the fact that the authors have no qualms and nothing to hide. They see themselves as subordinates who merely follow orders, for example in burning down villages, and must put up with the circumstances. The book provides an alternative glance at the Emin Pasha expedition and an unadorned description of the results of the Arab slave traders' ravaging along the shore of the Congo River – something that Conrad must have witnessed but never mentions.

in high positions in the Belgian administration. However, the Congo literature does not only relate the stories of the survivors; the dead are often represented in the form of diaries and letters addressed to relatives, who compile these testimonies into narratives aimed at explaining away, apologising for or justifying their authors' actions.

These texts were usually written by untrained writers who seized the opportunity to relate things that they had experienced themselves to an eager audience. They were based on this most simple and fundamental narrative contract, and do not appear to have been driven by any particular urge to chronicle extraordinary events or present testimonies in relation to the political and moral debates about the Congo. They are similar to letters and the primary material of travel diaries. Everyday life is described chronologically; it is extraordinary enough to deserve a story, but rarely enough for the narrator to question the observations or show signs of emotion, conflict or worry.

Together with the Royal Danish Library's own database, the catalogue material for exhibitions on the Congo in recent years in the Nordic countries includes hundreds of titles in this unpretentious genre, which does not claim to present new discoveries or literary art, but rather imitates and confirms the

From *Two Danish Travellers to the Congo* (1890).

figures and ideas that had become part of the standard repertoire long before, especially through Stanley's texts, and were thus familiar to everyone. The audience's interest cannot therefore have been due to curiosity about the unknown; rather, it was a result of a skewed fascination with everything being the same. Furthermore, the Danish Congo literature encompasses an extra dimension of national and class-related significance: the colonisers of Africa were mainly unemployed, or people with little education, which ensured authenticity and identification among the mass audience. This is not to say that there are no links between recognised literary history and the travel accounts, although in many cases they appear as nothing more than expanded letters to loved ones.

The Danish Captain Duhst's diary provides an insight into the dangerous work of sailing, punitive expeditions, burning villages and purchasing "curiosities", but there is also an observation from the sideline of "an English Captain, Joseph Conrad".[137] Ill from dysentery and fever, Duhst and Conrad travelled together for five days down the dreaded caravan route, both fatigued and being carried in hammocks. There is a special Danish thread to this story, evident here and in other coincidences of Danish travellers to the Congo coming close to Conrad, both on their way there and back and on the ship journey itself, where Conrad was second in command under the Danish Captain Koch. Conrad's

novel, for instance, relates the story of the Danish Captain Freiesleben, called Freesleven in the novel, who was killed at Tschumbiri because of a dispute about the right to collect firewood – an event that Duhst helped revenge by burning the villages in the area.

In Christian Martini and Christian Schønberg's *Two Danish Travellers to Congo. Memoirs from our first stay in the Congo State* (1890), there are glimpses of other celebrities, including Stanley and Tippu Tib, in connection with the Emin Pasha Relief Expedition's march up along the Congo River. Martini and Schønberg were both commanders of steamers on the usual three-year contracts, which they spent transporting goods, mail and people on the stretch between Léopoldville and Stanleyville. They also took part in several explorations on the tributaries of the Congo River and eagerly contributed to crushing the Congolese opposition. The narrative follows the classical pattern by describing the hellish journey on foot from Matadi to Léopoldville, an ordeal that everybody had to complete before the railway was completd. From the first chapters, the text gives rise to a sense of wonder that is difficult to place: is it because we, as modern readers, are unfamiliar with the form of address, or is it caused by other narrative characteristics that shine through the chummy jargon and jovial style?

The narrative is obviously intended to be a humorous, oral account that extends the jesting tone between the two men to the relationship between narrator and reader. In the beginning, several anecdotic and mildly naughty stories are told, which bear witness to the adventurers' unimpressed attitude and status as free men who are not ready to put up with anything. The stories support this narrative authority and mandate a taunting, unpretentious dimension that includes both employers and employees, without it ever developing into a critical discourse.

When Schønberg describes Martini's fit of fever, which soon results in him needing to be carried in a hammock like Conrad, it is presented as a joke: "Meanwhile, Martini lay there explaining to me that his head was the centre of a roundabout, spinning twenty miles a shift". The style resembles Marlow's sailor's jargon, especially in the passage about the three-hundred kilometre trek. However, the joke is followed, only a few lines below, by the first of many descriptions of atrocities:

"On the way we had passed a town, which, some months ago, had been burned down by the Congo State soldiers, because the inhabitants would never let the caravans pass in peace. The graves lay untouched, and we saw there all the strange ornaments with which the Negroes embellished the last resting places of their dead – old potsherds, glass bottles, old musket barrels and other such pretty things. At the other side of the town the road led through a field of grass, the grass more than fifteen feet tall".[138]

"In that case, undoubtedly we would have been eaten", from *Two Danish Travellers to the Congo*.

This description is as far removed from Conrad's sceptical, fragmented diary as it is from Morel's cultivation of terrifying tableaux. Characteristic of Martini and Schønberg's many depictions of punishments, shootings and burnings of towns are the references to tactical considerations and the light, ironic tone, as if the bloody events have taken place in a shooting gallery or at a funfair:

"Messrs Negroes, however, had reckoned without the Krupp cannon, which Schønberg had brought with him. Quicker than it can be told, I saw my friend rush over to the blunderbuss and fire a canister shot up into the trees. Down fell the Negroes, with guns and rags hanging in the branches, and their sprint towards the forest would have amused any respectable monkey" (p. 89).

Contrary to what one might expect, this distancing irony – concentrated in the expression "enticing pantomimes" (p. 23) – also endows the two narrators with a certain innocence, partly because it never allows for justifications of violence, though the reader cannot help questioning the reasonableness of burning all the villages in a large area because of a minor dispute over a hippopotamus. On the contrary, we perceive the narrators' ignorance as gullible innocence, not least because they suffer life-threatening fevers and their medical treatment is wholly ineffective. We see them neither as villains nor victims, but as employees who do not ask questions; they merely carry out a job, making a point of the

Danes on the bridge of the steamship *Ville du Bruxelles*. From the left: Engineer Petersen, Captain Jessen, and Captain Martini. From *Scandinavians in the Congo*.

food being edible and the working conditions bearable, offering opportunities to unwind once in a while. This neutrality, combined with the ethos conveyed to the reader in the loyal relationship between the two narrators, lends a large degree of credibility to their stories, whether they deal with chance encounters with incomprehensible rituals or their duties as soldiers.

Completely meaningless destruction, for instance the cutting down of a suspension bridge on an important caravan route, is described with shameless objectivity. Compared with other testimonies, this text therefore appears particularly earnest when – in its detached, unsentimental style – it recounts in detail the Emin Pasha Relief Expedition's march up the Congo River to Yambuya, and the sight of devastation caused by the slave traders. Here, the massacres have not been filtered through the justifying discourse often used by the English officers; they are exposed as pure fact. Similarly, the portraits of leading officers and post managers from Martini and Schønberg's subordinate, yet rude and unrepentant, perspective are more revealing than Morel's subsequent disclosures of atrocities. It is striking, for instance, that Glave, who would years later become one of the earliest contributors to the Red Rubber campaign, features several times in the text partaking in the callous prosecution of natives which the officers appear to view as a sport. Compared with Conrad, the text furthermore provides an interesting description of the entire area around Stanley Falls, sacked and destroyed either by EIC soldiers or Arab slave trading gangs, the latter having seized the opportunity provided by Tippu Tib's absence to fight their way down the Congo River, exterminating vast parts of the population or taking them as slaves. Martini describes this devastation of the area as an eyewitness, while Joseph Conrad, who travelled along the same routes a few years later, reveals nothing about the signs or stories of this destruction.

Stanley's *Through the Dark Continent* is presumed to be a shared reference between the reader and the narrator; it is as an authority on the Congo to which frequent reference is made. From the very beginning, Martini and Schønberg are aware that they are not in any position to add to Stanley's authorised version. While they both visit unmapped areas, they do not associate them with any particular excitement or adventure. In their view, everything has been discovered before them, but still they insist on putting forward their uneducated and immoral perspective on the place, which appears honest and human. At the same time, its effect on the reader is deeply disturbing, because the text's exposure of inhumane conduct is never linked with or softened by aesthetic or humanistic discourses.

Their text's prosaic ethics endow Martini and Schønberg with great credibility as witnesses. The place and events are neither dystopian nor utopian; but the text does not provide explanations or attempt to see things from a wider perspective. Along with thousands of similar travel descriptions in letter or book form written by contractual employees in the Free State, this text occupies the biographical and anecdotic level of Lévi-Strauss' aforementioned information pyramid: they are rich in information but provide little explanation. *Heart of Darkness* and *In Darkest Africa* are positioned on a higher level, where the profusion of experience is explained or interpreted, and the biographical "information is schematised, erased and obliterated, as we move on gradually to 'stronger' stories".

The few examples from the Red Rubber period presented here, as viewed from the prose perspective, will enable us to distinguish between different types of literary testimonies in a way that does not necessarily question their authenticity, but rather clarifies what it is they witness. *Heart of Darkness* is a "strong story" about the impact and significance of its own and others' testimonies. It contains minimal information, but universal explanatory power. Martini and Schønberg's testimony is of the type that quantitatively fills the archive; it is incredibly rich in information, something that is clear from Jenssen-Tusch's impressively encyclo-

paedic and absurdly monumental work *Scandinavians in Congo*. In Lévi-Strauss' model, Jürgen Jürgensen's stories are somewhere in the middle: they are rich in information, saturated with biographical and anecdotal material and contain nuanced descriptions of the characters and "their complicated motives, the development of their mindset"; they are also explanatory and interpretative on many levels. This complexity of both experience and interpretation endow the texts with a testimonial quality that surpasses both "strong" stories, such as Conrad's or Lindqvist's, and "weak" ones, such as Martini and Schønberg's.

In order to understand history, we must - according to Ricœur - go back to the sources, which are "the testimonies offered by the archive": "We have nothing better than testimonies and the criticism of testimonies"; everything depends on "the credibility of the witnesses". From the prose perspective, which constitutes the horizon for this book's treatment of the Red Rubber material, it is important to compare texts that collectively constitute a critical field of conditions for testimonies. Reaching back to the testimonies in the archives, writes Ricœur, might allow us to hear the voices of witnesses saying: "I was present - believe me or not - and if you do not believe me, ask someone else". In the case of Conrad, asking someone else who was present will not provide clear answers; however, it does turn up fragments with varying levels of explanatory power. Some support the testimony, such as the stories about the "Espionage System", while others subvert it, especially the ones about atrocities. As opposed to biased, formalistic-literary or historical-polemic approaches, the prose perspective has the advantage of foregrounding this complexity of experience and interpretation, which facilitates a recognition of the literary and historical qualities of Jürgensen's stories, as well as revealing a text such as *Heart of Darkness* as both performative act and reality work.

Transnational Colonial Criticism in Mirbeau's "Red Caoutchouc"

In this section of the book, which is named after the most brutal period in Congo's colonial history, *Heart of Darkness* has been the centre around which a number of other prose texts have been analysed. The intention has been to highlight the text's unique qualities and explain why it remains popular today. However, an objective attempt has also been made to define its role in the literary field that was undergoing transformations around 1900 and, in addition, its role as historical testimony. On a meta-discursive level, the text criticises its own conditions, making it a unique testimony to the problematic fetish status of the testimony itself as a rhetorically uncontested bearer of historical truth, and to the public's inability to assess accounts that counteract the accepted doxa. Nevertheless, the text is still so influenced by *fin de siècle* decadence that

Octave Mirbeau's *La 628-E8* (1907) was published in many editions and versions, including a luxury edition illustrated by Pierre Bonnard, who was one of the artists promoted through Mirbeau's art criticism. The main character in the novel is the car, as the narrative rushes through Belgium, the Netherlands, and Germany. The travel account can be read as a futurist manifesto of progress and speed, albeit one that does not beat around the bush when it comes to describing the costs for both Europe and Africa. The narrator, for instance, points out that the rubber from which the tyres are made probably comes from Léopold's 'red caoutchouc'. The narrative upends traditional conceptions of place, so that the Congo is no longer a different place, far removed from Europe, and pogroms against Jews are no longer a barbaric Russian pastime: together with nationalism, xenophobia is also knocking on the doors of France and Germany.

locations and spaces become engulfed in a darkness Conrad assumed was an astronomical phenomenon – a forewarning about the planet's cooling and ultimate doom. The text's topographical indications do not, therefore, result in heterotopic prose like Stanley's, where spaces are 'present' and 'simultaneous'. All the novel's spaces are accorded the same enigmatic qualities from beginning

to end, and the text as field work is folded around itself and the national context in which it is told.

In 1908 Léopold was pressurised into handing over the Free State to Belgium, mainly as a result of Casement's report, but the Reform Association's campaign also played a part. At the same time, a travel book was published in France that included in its plot a visit to Belgium. Like *Heart of Darkness* a few years earlier, the book was a criticism of the discourses that organised the colonial reality, only in a more comprehensive form. Octave Mirbeau's *La 628-E8* (1907) is situated on the other side of the turn of the century's pessimism and paranoia, linking its colonial criticism with an avant-garde, transnational openness towards the possibility of redrawing the old maps. At the centre of *La 628-E8* is a chapter titled "Red Caoutchouc", which relates to the spectrum of prose texts about the Congo mentioned above. This reading of Mirbeau's travel book will further illustrate the potentials and limitations of *Heart of Darkness*, in which the critique of discourse is only negatively defined in the sense that it points out its own limitations – the reason behind its secrecy.

Octave Mirbeau's travel novel *La 628-E8* (1907) is an account of the author's journey through Belgium, the Netherlands and Germany in his Charron automobile, which had the number plate 628-E8.[139] The composition follows the journey, introducing and describing landscapes, people and customs; on first sight it resembles the era's Baedeker guides, addressing the increasing numbers of tourists who travelled by car, using the improved roads to draw new travel routes through Europe. However, on closer inspection, *La 628-E8* is both a barbed parody of tourism and the travel book of its time, and an anti-novel that tries to break out of the existing frameworks of literature and genre, thus inventing a new, unique form of aesthetic and social criticism.

As the title indicates, the novel's main character is the automobile, which is fast creating a new form of perception that in the book's terminology is "cinematographic". In the foreground is literary experimentation, expressing changing forms of perception and a critique of travel and tourism's traditional form and content. The experiment is so radical that the text breaks down the classifications and genres of the travel novel and account from within, providing the carcass for what the anthropologist James Clifford has called "surrealist ethnography".[140] As the text simulates the cinematographic stream of images caused by speed, breaking away from literary and anthropological convention in an avant-garde, it also draws a map of Europe in which the individual countries' "hidden ways and customs" and "ideas in motion" are taken beyond nationalistic prejudices, instead being understood in relation to an open system of differences. Under the threat of a great European war, Mirbeau's *La 628-E8* tries to dismantle nationalism with every partisan strategy imaginable.

Octave Mirbeau was a highly paid journalist, anarchist and recognised art critic who had contributed to the dissemination of impressionism. He was very influential in his age, and his experimental novels were – unlike those of the later avant-garde – widely read outside France too. The argument here will be that although Mirbeau is completely absent from recent literary history, *La 628-E8* represents a model innovation of literature as world art, which qualifies it as "world literature"; or, rather, world art as a methodological perspective will expose traits in Mirbeau's book – anthropoetic, transnational traits – that place it at the centre of current attempts to map the historical and literary terms for globalisation.

Mirbeau's journey never took him to the Congo, but the book's use of the Belgian colonial power as a theme, the numerous attacks on King Léopold and the chapter about 'red rubber', "Red Caoutchouc" ("Le caoutchouc rouge"), create a link to critical discourses around colonial atrocities, which was explosive and scandalous material in the European newspapers of that age. An important aspect of Mirbeau's strategy was to expand the existing concepts of travel, space, movement and place in order to rediscover the forgotten or hidden rhetorical conditions for cultural criticism that had always been part of travel literature. One of many effects of this strategy was the realisation that the exploitation of the Congo – like the pogroms in Russia and the stock market crash in the USA – was not something that was happening in a distant part of the world, but had been plotted on the readers' unstable map of Europe as a critical 'location'. Although Mirbeau's text might appear marginal and peripheral to this discussion of the Congo, what follows will place it at the centre.

La 628-E8 is more than a futuristic étude. The suspension of usual literary genre boundaries, combined with a critical rearrangement of the world map's political, geographical and anthropological boundaries of nations and cultures, result in a prose that is more than a new genre: it is a field of new potential for political and literary criticism. Within the critical horizon of prose, Europe, for example, can be imagined as something other than accumulated national histories, and colonialism and imperialism can be perceived through far more complex contexts than the postcolonial alterity model.

When read from the prose perspective, *La 628-E8*'s kinship with surrealism's anthropoetic use of "everyday wonders" becomes clear. However, a broader in-

vestigation will also detect a kinship with the renaissance and an eighteenth-century tradition of prose that addresses the world while presenting a discourse critical analysis of the dominant, simple-minded images of the world. The overall argument is that Mirbeau's post-literary, transnational prose can be seen as a model for anti-colonialist prose about places in the world in a different way from texts like *Heart of Darkness*, while also being a critical reflection on globalisation.

In the dedication to Fernand Charron – who designed the car – at the very beginning of the book, we catch a glimpse of Mirbeau's unusual and controversial concept of theme and style. Not only does the automobile allow us to perceive landscapes in constant change – "through endless shapes" – it also leads us through "hidden ways and customs, ideas in motion, across history; our continually living history" (p. vi). The automobile allows the narrator to see the world in a completely different manner from the railway's prisonlike tracks; this "this completely new feeling" of speed resulting in concentrated time and perception is sensed as a journey on which experiences that took place over several months are compressed into a single day, and the spectrum of customs representing very different cultures is perceived as simultaneous. The introductory dialogues are presented as fragments of conversations, overheard in passing, while narrator and vehicle seem to merge into one unified perspective. They appear unfinished, a textual demonstration of the principle of movement in which coordinates have only a loose and temporary significance for the narration, the focal point being the movement of the car and the perspective. The period's fascination with the consequences of a fusion of man and machine is expressed in another juxtaposition: while the staggering speed of the car facilitates a perception of the world in flux, it also results in an all-encompassing oblivion – "l'oubli de tout" – which is characterised as a "superhuman" dimension of speed.

The "Reader's guide" expresses a few reservations: "Are we actually dealing with a diary? Is this even a journey?" (p. 1). The reader cannot expect the historical, geographical, political, economical and statistical comments of traditional travel guides. This book relates memories, perhaps dreams, and dreams which are – perhaps – real. They might take the narrator to the scheduled cities in

Europe, but there will be stops in America, Russia, China and "the lakes in Africa". His stories also resemble memories and dreams and have, he warns us, "no visible connection whatsoever to the countries visited" (p. 1); they will probably shock the reader's feelings and sense of logic, because they will be full of coincidence, incoherence and contradiction. What Paul Bourget calls "stages of the spirit" should, according to the narrator, rather be described as "stages of the matter", which precede and influence imagination and sensibility. This is why changes of weather and conditions will result in changes in the text's attitudes and appraisals, which thus reserves the right to be contradictory. Unlike the traveller who is subjected to a country's institutions and customs for a long period of time, and therefore able to describe the culture in detailed catalogues of the military structure, parliament, universities, etc., the narrator's aim is to capture culture in motion – "hidden ways and customs", "ideas in motion" – which cannot be found in the museums and institutions, but must be conceived through a narrative that is, in itself, in motion and subject to constant change.

Speed, therefore, should be perceived not only as the mechanical movement of the vehicle; it is also a psychological phenomenon. Automobilism is a kind of "insanity":

"It is not about the mechanical speed that carries the vehicle forward on the roads through one country or other, but rather about a kind of neuropathic speed that drives man through all actions and distractions ... He is no longer able to remain calm; he is restless, his nerves tense like springs, after his arrival always impatient to leave again, constantly longing to be somewhere else, incessantly somewhere else, farther away still than somewhere else ... His brain is an endless lane, where thoughts, images, perceptions rotate and drive around at a speed of a hundred kilometres an hour. A hundred kilometres, that is the standard for his activities. He races past like a tornado, lives like a tornado. Life rushes and pushes forward from all sides, commenced by an insane movement, like a salvo from an entire cavalry troop, and disappears cinematographically out of sight, like trees, windbreaks, dikes, silhouettes standing along the road ... Everything around him and inside him is jumping and dancing, is moving, a movement opposite his own. Now and then: a painful feeling, but strong, fantastic and intoxicating, as of dizziness or fever" (pp. 6-7).

40

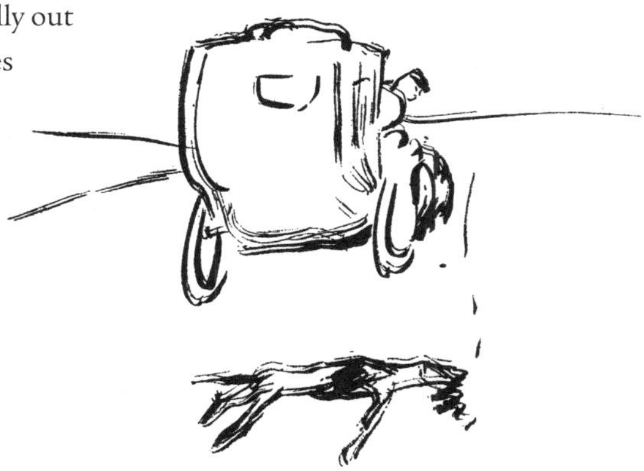

When the driver stops to stroll on foot, for instance in Amsterdam, the cinematographic movement and pace continues. It is a form of perception that is also related to the flickering visual impressions of "slide shows" (p. 11), very much part of the body, so that the *flâneur* must jump in every direction to catch himself: "my hips have new elastic bands; on the cobbles, the pavements my soles jump backwards, in front of me, behind me, like tennis balls ... I must run to catch up with them ... I am running ... I am running ..." (p. 9).

In a passage about this sort of walk in Amsterdam, *fin de siècle* culture's idolisation of Baudelaire's *flâneur* is deconstructed. The first-person narrator bumps into people, knocking them over; he overhears fragments of conversations, detects body odours and perceives the crowd in incoherent details which gradually, in filmic waves, succeed one another. And when he stops to gaze at his own reflection in the window of a department store – in typical *flâneur* style – he does not see a blasé artist but "an image of vertigo and speed" (p. 10). The narrative position of the 'I' is also subject to this movement; not only does it contain a multitude of perspectives, but it challenges conventional concepts of unity and authority in relation to the work, the 'I' and the narrator. *La 628-E8* is a literary innovation, as suggested in the peculiar title, which breaks with the decadent worship of psychology – the book contains many satirical attacks on the psychological novel – and counters the period's worship of spirituality and aesthetics with radicalised materialism, which also constitutes a break with the concept of the organic unity of art works.

The concerns Octave Mirbeau addressed in his extensive work as an art critic and a critic of society, for instance as a prominent debater on Émile Zola's side in the Dreyfus affair, a bleeding heart anarchist and polemicist against all forms of nationalism, become, in the travel book, textual forewarnings of surrealist works such as André Breton's *Nadja* (1928) and Louis Aragon's *Le Paysan de Paris* (1926). However, Mirbeau's book is, in many respects, more radical and richer in perspective than these later texts, for example with regard to literary form and anthropological thinking.[141]

La 628-E8 can be seen as an unyielding attempt to write a post-national literature which, in trying to argue against the European war looming on the horizon, is bound to deconstruct all forms of nationalism, including its own, by enunciating and renouncing them. While the text simulates the speedy, cinematographic stream of images and visual perceptions, it also aims to give access to a map of Europe where prejudice may still exist, but is no longer linked to nationalistic typologies.

As we will see in Mirbeau's Congo criticism, an alliance exists between, on the one hand, the *post-literary form*, in which it is unclear when and where the text is a novel, autobiography, travel account, journalistic pamphlet, art criticism or cultural analysis, and, on the other hand, the *post-national perspective*, which is an important aspect of the book's criticism of the European powers' colonial policy. The elegance and speed of the car belong in the transnational flux of the future, crossing borders and cultural expressions that are contrasted with nationalistic 'form': juxtaposed with the car is the balloon – a huge, clumsy being, only capable of bouncing uselessly on the spot. Balloon nationalists, "these strange animals called nationalists" (p. 135), are disproportionate beings who have obstructed development and evolution, reaching a historical dead end.

The Album and World Art

In a series of images, like an album, the narrator describes life on the quays of Anvers – the French word for Antwerp – in a form that imitates the typical travel book repertoire of colourful displays of life's diversity, but its organisation quickly turns in one direction, then another. It begins with the short part "Tapirs", which is about twenty tapirs that the narrator helps to get ashore from a ship from Africa. They are admirably modern animals, he writes, because they are not surprised by the crowd and the noise of the city; rather, they look like a group of banking executives returning from a tour of observation or a "business expedition" (p. 151). After this follows "Singers", about two "poor Negroes" in black suits and top hats, one dancing comically, the other singing; in other words, they are exactly how Negroes should look and act on the quay in Antwerp. Next comes "The evangelist", about a missionary who wants to use the gramophone as a means to convert the heathens in Africa. He has heard from a friend that after just three records "... pop! ... they are Christians". Caruso, Strauss and military marches will work better than promises of Paradise and booze. In these images, the style is grotesque and exaggerated; the next images in the series are different in tone, perspective and style.

Leaving behind irony and the grotesque, these images display a peculiar mix of pathos, expressed through solidarity with the persecuted, and a fascination with macabre, bloody violence. "Emigrants" is an indignant, detailed description of poverty, starvation and humiliation among the hordes of workers and proletarians from Hungary, Romania, Bulgaria, Serbia and Russia who are crammed together in the hulls of the ships setting out for America. In this miserable crowd, the Jews stand out as the most persecuted and miserable – "they are massacred in barbaric countries, such as Russia, and boycotted in civilised countries, such as France" (p. 155). This is illustrated in the subsequent part, "Pogroms", as a Russian-Jewish lawyer gives an account of how he fled from

anti-Semitic pogroms in Russia, where his family was killed, and was later sent packing due to anti-Semitism in France.

Mirbeau's criticism was effective, considering the shocked reactions it received in patriotic circles at the time. However, it is also strategically positioned in a series of images that at first sight resemble the classical repertoire of the travel book's picture album, only later revealing its monstrous mix of tapirs, dancing and singing Negroes, persecuted emigrants and genocides, not to mention "Prostitution", which contains scandalous descriptions of huge whorehouses pretending to be "colonial exhibitions", where the wares on sale are women from all parts of the world: "Let us colonise ... there will always be something left" (p. 172). The style is explicitly critical, but what is unique about Mirbeau's strategy is the narrator's ambivalent attitude, which is a consequence of the detached, machinelike view from the automobile.

The series of images from Antwerp ends with a night-time tableau in which the narrator is smoking a cigarette, lying next to a black prostitute, "une Dahoméenne", who is telling an incredible story about massacres and tyranny in her home country; the story is overtly linked to sexual excess and violence. The tableau draws both on Manet's painting *Olympia* and Flaubert's mistresses, showing a different image of the narrator indulging in decadent pleasure rather than reflecting on a critical condemnation. Pogroms, colonial repression and violence are, in these images, ranked alongside tapirs and singing Negroes, and the series ends with a tableau in which the narrator emphasises his own blasé position. He offers a concise criticism of the international trafficking of women – "I have seen, at night, in the heated streets, the pantomime of international luxury and unbridled greed, heard the shouting and screaming when girls of all races are herded along – in the narrow streets I have seen sailors from all countries, with naked upper arms, shouting and babbling like big children who have gone insane" (p. 173). Soon, however, the narrator adopts a decadent, pleasure-seeking position, in which the woman is reduced to a Baudelairean tableau: "She was resting on a surface of yellow silk, naked, completely covered in strong perfume, so that one could hardly breathe. A big, scarlet dahlia was blooming in her woolly hair" (p. 173).

The picture album thus displays a broad and colourful palette, which seems initially to correspond with the Baedeker guide that Mirbeau caricatures in the book's beginning. On the world map in the mind of European readers around the turn of the century, Antwerp was first and foremost a centre of colonial capitalism, where the biggest corporations that collected ivory and caoutchouc from Congo – such as *ABIR* and *Société Anversoise de Commerce au Congo* – had their domiciles. The latter had become infamous due to an article in *Kölnische Zeitung* in 1897, which revealed – with photographic documentation – that one of the corporation's managers was in possession of a collection of 1308 severed hands. The first major demonstration of King Léopold's colonial exploitation of Central Africa took place at l'Exposition Universelle in Antwerp in 1885, and Mirbeau's album appears to follow in the wake of the period's popular travel accounts and guide books from the world's fairs.[142]

The series of images in *La 628-E8* imitates and deconstructs the travel book as picture book or album, in which we find similar, grotesquely compiled images and photographs aiming at presenting the world in all its kaleidoscopic, colourful – and innocent – diversity. The combination of the transnational perspective and the montage form furthermore imitates and deconstructs anthropology's systems of classifying curiosities. The tapirs, the singing and dancing Negroes, the prostitute and the persecuted Jeware all phenomena which the narrator – with great empirical care and exaggerated, microscopic detail – records in his report of the field studies on the Antwerp quays. However, the transnational perspective and montage form are simultaneously combined with the narrator's propensity for change, inspired by the speed of the automobile. And with no solid authority to define the relationships between phenomena, profound chasms between classifications are revealed; the phenomena once again appear as "curiosities", or what the surrealists termed "merveilles du quotidien", everyday wonders.

The anthropology we can detect in Mirbeau's strategy, the search for what he calls "hidden ways and customs" and "ideas in motion", is thus close to the anthropological ideal James Clifford finds in the so-called "surrealist ethnography", exemplified by the periodical *Documents*, the surrealistic museum strategy of which merges genres, discourses and high and low culture, thus reclassifying the 'exhibited' objects – African fetishes, cartoons, Parisian abattoirs, Hollywood sets, photographs of Picasso's paintings and deformed bodies. Similarly, Mirbeau's guide to an imaginary world's fair in Antwerp does not map cultures as unified, delimited collections of customs and cultures, but rather shows their movement through an global system of differences. This system is, furthermore, placed in a critical, self-deconstructing discourse, where the fascination with the exotic, curious and culturally 'impure' is linked to the repression that created the curiosities, thus denoting – as Georges Bataille would later – a link between aesthetic pleasure and violence. This kinship with later surrealism often becomes evident through diction, e.g. in a description of the harbour in Antwerp and "la mer surnaturelle" (s. 9), where the narrator states that as a child he discovered the principle of "connected vessels", "des *vases communicants*", which is a precise characterisation of an important principle for the form and anthropology in *La 628-E8* and would subsequently become the title of a chief work in surrealism.[143]

The critical essays about modern art and literature included in the text mention Maurice Maeterlinck, Henrik Ibsen, Claude Monet, Pierre Bonnard and Gauguin as truly modern, while distancing themselves from the aestheticism, egocentricity and spirituality of the posing and withdrawn self-sufficiency of the *fin de siècle*. The manifest criticism of colonialism and nationalism is thus linked with the original access points to the art that is closest to Mirbeau's heart. In accordance with the text's automobile strategy, however, this takes place in a form in which the Parisian art centre is moved to the periphery, subsequently to be linked with other centres of world art history.

These analyses emerge at various points in the midst of the staggering speed of the journey. Monet, for instance, is the theme while a Dutch canal landscape is being observed in "Claude Monet's discovery". Previously, the narrator has noticed a pastoral idyll with blonde women who do not know what to think about the strange vehicle - or perhaps they do not care. On their cheeks he sees a play of colours, "where the Far East yellow competes against the European rose" (p. 205). This is a further expansion of the narrator's typical attention to detail, as when, faced with a Dutch prospect, he notes "this Oriental or Far Eastern aspect, which one finds in most Dutch cities and villages, without being able to say what, exactly, constitutes it". (p. 207). The Dutch cities' Oriental character - reminiscent of Japanese, Chinese and Indian art - is presented as a fact that leads to more hypothetical contemplations on the source of this effect.

Perhaps the link is the result of the Dutch fleet's close contact with the Far East; perhaps the navigators have brought these colours back with them, along with the goods that have enriched the country. This brings the narrator to develop a theory about the influences on, and historical development of, thinking: we are dealing with an "oscillation of ideas, which is fully graspable" yet difficult to get understand because it is derived from arbitrary, mechanical influences. The idea is illustrated with an anecdote, one of the "historiettes", about Monet's journey to the Netherlands fifty years before; while visiting Zaandam - according to the narrator the most Japanese place in the country - he allegedly by coincidence saw his first Japanese copperplate on some wrapping paper, and in a split second, grasped the secret behind Oriental art's ability to contain "the entire existence, any movement" (p. 208) in one single stroke. In this sudden recognition of his kinship with Oriental artists, the exhilarated Monet runs back to the small grocery shop, where the grocer is obliviously wrapping coffee and pepper in "glorious pictures brought home from the Far East". Monet buys the grocer's entire stock of cheap wrapping paper, and when later he unfolds these images of the sea, bathing women, birds and flowering trees, impressionism and modern art is born - providing perpetual meaning to the anecdote, which according to the narrator contains "true historic value" (p. 209).[144]

As we will see in an anecdote below, which begins in a shop with samples from the Congo and expands into a sketch of a global system of connections, the story about Monet also contains a vast expansion of perspective. According to Mirbeau's hypothesis about the historical development of ideas as the result of random mechanical clashes, the modern breakthrough in painting was the result of a chance encounter between a historically delayed influence from the East and the artist's stay in a Japanised Dutch environment. The combination of Japanese classicism that Monet discovered on the wrapping paper, the impression of the landscape, the decorations and the omnipresent water, prepared and predisposed the breakthrough discovery which Mirbeau, among others, would subsequently introduce as impressionism. The point is that only anecdotal history is capable of preserving knowledge about coincidences that connect distant destinations in world art.

"Red Caoutchouc"

In the chapter "Among the Belgians", after "The king of commerce", in which the narrator, in the role of reporter, in vain tries to trace information about King Léopold's *positive* qualities, we find the heading "Red Caoutchouc". The narrator stops in front of a small shop, where he watches a strange display of pyramids or cylinders of grey or black material. "Nothing else. No explanation. No tag. [...] On the sign only this name, written in red: "Blothair et Cie" (p. 118). When the narrator steps inside the shop to enquire, he is informed that the objects are samples of crude rubber. He describes in detail his impression of the shop: it appears empty and has an atmosphere of quiet resignation; however, a glimpse through a door that is ajar reveals that the backroom is full of old raincoats, pieces of cable and car tyres. "Congo, I presume?" asks the narrator, which the proprietor proudly confirms.

Although the display window and the shop "appear unobtrusive", the narrator becomes increasingly interested in the product samples. "Why are there no explanatory images, photographs, in this display window? My imagination could add them soon enough" (p. 119) – which is exactly what it does. With impressive rhetorical refinement, the narrator lists everything that is unsaid and not on display in the shop, basically within the same demonstrative and discourse critical form as the passage mentioned above. In a lengthy interpolation, the narrator fills in the missing labels, explanations and photographs in the shop with an exhilarated, dreamlike repetition of the worst colonial clichés about Africa:

"I am dreaming about forests, about lakes, about fairytale worlds in this paradise of sun and flowers ... I am dreaming about childlike Negroes, graceful Negro women, who are capable of committing the same cruelties as children. I remind myself about this sentence, written by an explorer: 'They are lovely and sweet, like rabbits seen in the evening, at the edge of the wood, making their toilet of playing amongst fragrant herbs'. Which, by the way, does not keep him from killing them" (p. 119).

After this dramatic change of tone, the self-caricaturing comparison of Negroes and rabbits taken from Mirbeau's novel *Le jardin des supplices* (1899),[145] the idyllic image continues to dominate a passage that could have been taken from any of the many campaign contributions defending the Congo State, or from the countless critical contributions that continued the abolitionist movement's rhetoric and painted an idyllic, infantile picture of the natives in a state of unworried, paradisiacal bliss. However, as a powerful contrast, "I am dreaming" is replaced, in the following passage, with the clear vision of "I see":

"I see the executions, massacres, torture, the helter-skelter of roaring, hogtied and crucified athletes, women whose torments create an abominable and sensuous play, children fleeing with their hands in front of their faces, their small legs under the distended stomachs. In a crude rubber slab, in a black bullet, I have been able to discern the far too beautiful torso of a raped and beheaded Negro woman, and I have also seen mutilated and dying elderly with dry, crackling limbs. And I must shut my eyes to escape all these terrors which the samples of caoutchouc, lying there completely motionless and unsympathetic, have set in motion with sudden intensity. Such are the images that more or less any car tyre and cable, covered with its insulating lagging, ought to evoke. One does not always know where the rubber comes from. Here, one does: It comes from Congo. Yes, it is in fact 'red rubber', the red caoutchouc. In Antwerp not a single gram arrives that is not soiled with blood" (pp. 120-21).

What ensues is not presented as a vision, where imagined pictures and photographs replace the exhibited objects' missing labels. Rather, it is formulated in a documentary style, like a news report from the Congo. It describes how the rubber is produced, the forced labour and the punishments, but without the gothic or decadent effects used in the previous photographic passages: "an abominable and sensuous play", "the far too beautiful torso". The production of rubber, and the methods with which it is obtained, is then linked to the increasing demand for car tyres, insulation material and telephone cables, fading out in yet another change of style and position – an ironic passage about King Léopold's propaganda apparatus, his consumption of women and luxury and his thoroughly corrupt rule.

"Red Caoutchouc" is only two or three pages long, but it leads the reader through a surprising number of levels and positions in one of the first and largest international humanitarian crises: the conflict surrounding King Léopold's administration of a private colony in Africa, and particularly the methods used to obtain rubber in a time that saw an escalating demand and ever-increasing profits for it. The first passage is, as mentioned, a parody of the abolitionist movement's form of colonial criticism that had been dominant throughout the nineteenth century, with its propensity for archaic rhetoric in which atrocities are contrasted with idyll, and the natives are portrayed as children or rabbits. The next passage imitates the rhetoric of the Congo Reform Association, which was founded by a former bookkeeper who worked on the quays of Antwerp, Edmund Morel, and counted among its members Arthur Conan Doyle, Mark Twain and, in the background, Joseph Conrad. The text sticks to the form of documentary prose that characterised Roger Casement's report from 1903 about the Red Rubber regime in central Congo – the text that had the most direct impact on Léopold having to hand over his domain to the Belgian state in 1908. Finally, the concluding passage, with its scornful and ironic style, shares similarities with Mark Twain's polemical pamphlet *King Léopold's Soliloquy* of 1905.

The sign outside the shop, "Blothair et Cie", is written in red, and the proprietor's name is a paraphrase of one of the most notorious Belgian officers in the Congo, infamous for his brutality and sadism: Hubert Lothaire. The fact that there are no explanatory photographs in the shop is a direct reference to the prominent role this new media played in international propaganda's display of mutilations. We saw in Mark Twain's parody how Léopold fears the new, easily accessible "Kodaks"; here, the narrator must create his own images. The shop's unobtrusiveness and its motionless, neutral samples set the images in cinematographic motion, the lack of explanation sparking the narrator's own account, which is, however, presented in several parallel rhetorical registers that at the time would have been perceived as antagonistic.[146]

Octave Mirbeau's refined adaptation of the Congo campaign's conflicting positions is exceptional in European literature about the Congo. The text is an extremely precise criticism of Belgian colonialism, basically perceiving it anthropologically as a question of commerce: industrialism's technological revolution and the consequent demand for rubber, for instance for the tyres of Mirbeau's wondrous automobile. However, the criticism distances itself – through the use of conflicting discourses – from both the colonial idyll and the Reform Association's pathetic display of terrors ripped out of their contexts, without denying its part in either clichés or fascination with the terrors. The narrator changes perspective, style and tone, but is still exceptionally objective and consistent in his criticism, even to the extent of carrying through a devastating *self*-criticism in

relation to the facilitator of the book's project. The car tyres and the lagging on the wires are directly linked to the violations against the native population of the Congo, and the modern perception based on speed – the key to the book's style and anthropology – is seen in its dependency on bloody, colonial exploitation.

This passage, and *La 628-E8* in its entirety, thus establishes a critical anthropology that turns away from the idea of alterity – i.e. the tendency to perceive primitive cultures as situated in a different place in space and time – and static juxtapositions, instead focusing on the differences in a transnational, changeable global system. The text acknowledges its own part in the discourses it criticises without establishing authority over or outside the "change of perspective" that comes from the idea of alterity.[147] In the text's gliding motion, near and far swap places to such a degree that alterity collapses and endows "Red Caoutchouc" with an unsettling intimacy that implicates the reader, making us indignant as well as accomplices. The quiet shop and the immobile samples give rise to animated images that expand the textual space and time; the narrator's chance opening of a door in a European city simultaneously opens a door to Africa, and an understanding of the products' and images' circulation on the world market.

By expressing, distinguishing between and critically processing media and literature images of the Congo as competing discourses, each one fighting for dominance – but collectively contributing to, and reinforcing the country's position as 'another place', 'otherness in another world' – Octave Mirbeau organises his material on a meta-textual and discourse critical level. In "The king of commerce", the chapter preceding "Red Caoutchouc", Mirbeau imitates and criticises both the reform campaign's and Léopold's propagandistic use of statistical documentation and testimonies, which is aimed less at arguing the case in question than at starting rumours. The narrator puts on an exaggerated role as a reporter who is supposedly searching for positive stories, statements or documents that can prove that the king is a real king, not just an unscrupulous businessman and philanderer. Mirbeau's feigned survey, unsurprisingly, only discovers rumours and scandalous anecdotes about the king's debauchery, fully consistent with the caricaturists' satirical simplifications. In this way, the text manages to present criticism of Léopold while also mocking the reform movement's smear campaign. Later, Mirbeau leaves it to a German colonial official to criticise the Belgian administration, simultaneously satirising German efficiency. Most importantly, in a long chapter that is an exhaustive catalogue of the animals inevitably killed by the automobile – the vehicle that helps the narrator escape the trammels of straitlaced nationalism – a young girl is killed by a reckless driver, who sees the accident merely as an unwelcome delay on the journey, and thus a delay for progress in general.

The book's internal context, expressed in "Red Caoutchouc", clarifies the textual process of maintaining conflicting critical perspectives. The blood-stained rubber is also the raw material of the narrator's rubber hips and rubber soles as he bounces along in the modern bustle of the city like a tennis ball. *La 628-E8* both forestalls and looks back at many aspects of Congo criticism; for instance, it mentions "these fine rubber factories" as soon as the story arrives in Belgium, and "Red Caoutchouc" is integrated into the book as a whole, whose consistent theme is the pacifistic criticism of nationalism and colonialism. At the same time, however, this part appears as one random interpolation among many other extremely diverse genres and causes – not only digressions but independent expansions of the book's transnational project. A peculiar encounter, for instance, with a fictitious, odd character – a former great capitalist with huge investments in the energy sector, now betting his money on investments in global risk – develops into a manifesto in which Mirbeau's criticism of both capitalism and socialism is implemented in an anarchistic agenda.

La 628-E8 consistently insists on high speed in thought and movement, accompanied by ideas that break down time and space with anecdotes about Monet, Balzac, Maupassant and others. These ideas counteract the linear trajectory of speed and forward movement; however, they do not result in a standstill, but rather cause the textual time and space to expand at great speed. The strategy of textual expansion of time and space is the literary correlation to Octave Mirbeau's declared internationalism, expressed both in the surrounding European context by his constantly transcending prejudices and borders between European nation states, and in his colonial criticism, which is neither nationalistic nor postcolonial. With this distinctive correlation between formal, post-literary techniques and the use of radically subversive strategies to deal with basic ideas about nation states, borders and cultures, the criticism in *La 628-E8* is so far-reaching that Mirbeau's project can no longer be described merely as 'international'. The agenda for the book's innovative form and endeavour is the end of nation states, and in relation to the looming conflicts between European states the book insists on anarchistic and individualistic vessels that are connected across borders – "vases communicants" – in a project which, collectively, is better described as 'transnational'.

With regard to the book's position in literary history, this interpretation results in similar transformations. According to a number of formal factors, *La 628-E8* is a forerunner of avant-garde works such as Aragon's *Le Paysan de Paris* and Breton's *Nadja*. These works also avoid stable narrators or 'I' authorities, allowing their narrators to assume numerous positions that are logically inconsistent. The 'I' cannot be identified as a defined psychological entity or character; it is subject to the terms of the speed, and therefore only defined in

vague outlines in the anecdotal web. Chapters and parts are interlinked and parasitic, feeding on each other through leaps in style and genre that are so big the work approaches the avant-garde movement's dissolution of the art work's organic unity. In relation to the fundamental anthropological endeavour to describe and map differences in customs through the scientific, microscopic description of everyday wonders, while those very systems of classification are undermined from within, the book is also related to surrealism.

However, Octave Mirbeau's political anarchism, and his role as a journalist and popular author, influences the book in a direction that makes it far more attentive and critical towards the media than later avant-garde works. The criticism of discourse is particularly noticeable in the subtle treatment of the ongoing media campaign against King Léopold's colony in the Congo. While surrealist experiments to a large degree resulted in unintelligibility, causing the authors to lose sight of their readers and obstruct their own critical projects both in art and everyday life, *La 628-E8* is highly accessible and radically subversive in relation to politics, art and anthropology.

While it borrows traits from the literary decadence of the turn of the century – a movement to which Mirbeau himself had contributed with books such as *Le jardin des supplices* (1899) and *Le journal d'une femme de chambre* (1900) – *La 628-E8* explicitly breaks with the *fin de siècle* narrowing of culture, which in many respects links it to the experimental, rationality-based, critical end engaged literature of the eighteenth century. For instance, the text is not far removed from Diderot's addition to Bougainville's account from Tahiti – a text which, like Octave Mirbeau's modern high-speed text, manages to put our preconceived conceptions of the world and the relationship between near and far into motion. Mirbeau, too, was one of the most popular, wide-ranging, original and feared intellectuals of his time, writing for all the biggest newspapers in France and being paid the equivalent of £1,000 per article. He attacked all society's institutions with scorching criticism, often unleashing angry reactions from the relevant parties, with the first being the nationalists following a brutal satire of the army's miserable effort in the war against Germany after the fall of the empire in 1870. Mirbeau's entire career was scandal-ridden because of the extraordinary correlation between his anarchism – which he declared officially in 1890, but pursued throughout his authorship, for example by urging people to boycott elections for parliament – his ultramodern literary and journalistic forms, such as fictitious interviews that picked apart the people in power, and his vast audience.

Opposing both the mainstream and the avant-garde, Mirbeau's radical political and artistic experiments had extraordinary impact. *La 628-E8* was published in many editions, including a luxury edition with Pierre Bonnard's illustrations; it was translated into many languages and sold well in the European countries he addressed with his transnational and pacifistic message. In Russia, two editions of his collected works were published between 1908 and 1912. *La 628-E8* does not belong in the realm of 'fiction' in the limited sense of the word, and at first sight it might appear both historically marginal and geographically peripheral; yet due to its mixed form and will to critical reflection it is central to the movement termed 'prose' in this book. It drew a new map of Europe in which the demarcations of zones of interest and communities did not adhere to national borders, and coordinates of place and time in the world atlas of African, Russian, Japanese and American locations were identified as nerve centres in actual, *critical* cartography. A broad spectrum of critical and apologetic discourses were incorporated and transcended in Mirbeau's transnational, media critical and post-literary reflections. The globally conscious prose of *La 628-E8* thus serves as an example for a critical approach to images of the world on globalised terms.

The process of globalisation challenges anthropological theory, which – according to James Clifford – is left stranded with its travel accounts and its basic literary-historical assumptions of national identity. As mentioned in the introduction, the literary historian Wlad Godzich has coined the term "anthropoetic narrative" to reflect these conditions – that is, personalised, stylised, anecdotal and global narratives about questions of borders and cultural identity, what human beings are in a global sense and the individual's sense of belonging and place. The intention here has been to read *La 628-E8* as an anthropoetic narrative that challenges our fundamental conceptions of identity, nationality, literature and what it is to be human. The book, work, novel or travel account – the prose – captures the coming into being and the transformation of the world through the speed of the vehicle and the text; however, speed also – according to the narrator – results in oblivion, a "superhuman" fusion of man and machine that forces readers of *La 628-E8* to ask themselves not only *who*, but *where* they are.

4 The Field: Red Rubber and *Heart of Darkness* between Nationalism and World Literature

Compared with the two key texts *Heart of Darkness* and *In Darkest Africa*, *La 628-E8* shares traits with the discourse critical agenda of the former, whereas the perception of space and the text's multidimensional field work is closer to Stanley's heterotopic prose and its juxtaposed, changeable perspectives. Mirbeau's dialogical and journalistic reportage style, and his visualisations of wondrous *faits divers* of everyday life, is a continuation of the tradition in travel writing that dates back to the eighteenth century and reached its climax with Stanley. From the prose perspective, and in comparison with other narratives about Red Rubber, especially *La 628-E8*, *Heart of Darkness* is the strongest as discourse criticism; however, it is equally weak as reality work. The summary in this final part about the Red Rubber period will take its starting point in the unique position Conrad's text has enjoyed in world literature.

The reception of *Heart of Darkness* has emphasised two main tendencies. One has been the textual form, for example the internal conflict between different narrators and the impressionistic style, which blurs the contours of descriptions. The text has been seen as a messenger of universal truth, either about human evil or the fact that any reading invariably ends with an "unreadable report". The other tendency has placed emphasis on the novel's context, especially Conrad's own journey to the Congo, either criticising the author for racism or praising the text for being one of the earliest and strongest examples of anti-imperialist criticism. Many interpreters of the novel, among them the prominent postcolonial critic Edward Said and to a lesser degree Patrick Brantlinger, combine the formalistic and contextualistic approaches in sophisticated analyses that typically include the fact that the novel, despite itself, contains a layer of subversive contraband that saves it a place in the poststructuralist and postcolonial canon of great literature.[148]

In anthologies directed at the increasing number of university courses in world literature, Conrad and *Heart of Darkness* enjoy a similar key position. Not only are author and text listed among the most important subjects in literary history, they also help legitimise the world literature approach and method as such. In *The Bedford Anthology of World Literature* (2003), an ambitious work of several volumes which is meticulously designed to meet the demand of the popular courses in world literature, Conrad is a central example in the anthology's illustration of its method and perspective. His works are already part of the western canon of masterpieces, which is on a par with the anthology's dominant material and view on literature. In addition, Conrad is a "hybrid author" who brought Polish, French and British culture together, and thus the first author in the nineteenth century to represent the "global perspective". Furthermore, his material came from Asia, Africa and South America, thus helping the anthology to expand the term 'world literature' to accommodate non-western literature. *Heart of Darkness* is a perfect example of the anthology's desire to be inclusive – transcending not only the boundaries of national literature, but also the methodological disputes within literary studies. The novel invites both formalistic close reading and attention to historical and biographical background material. In this sense, it becomes a unique stage on which literary studies' normally irreconcilable juxtapositions can play out a drama *within* the text, while the juxtapositions avoid becoming themes in political and institutional conflicts. The introduction to Bedford's volume of twentieth-century world literature elevates *Heart of Darkness* as the most outstanding multicultural and transnational example of the globalised perspective. Nevertheless, this does not prevent Chinua Achebe's caustic criticism of Conrad's racism from being praised in the same introduction as a clever, fully justified postcolonial response. The interpretation drama works as a centrifugal force that draws the novel ever closer to the centre of a new world literature canon. The process is apparently irreversible, and no protest, however well-founded, can change it. On the contrary, there is much to suggest that negative opinions will only spawn positive ones in an infinite cycle that keeps the book in anthologies and teaching rooms across the world.[149]

The positioning of *Heart of Darkness* in the world literature canon is mainly a result of critics agreeing that it is a suitable battlefield for ritualised academic disputes, rather than readers or student finding the book relevant or inspiring. Lennard Davis is among the few to express doubt as to whether it still makes sense to read and teach the text. In the article "The Value of Teaching From a Racist Classic" he presents a problem that is well-known today, of students – especially Afro-Americans – being averse to reading the novel.[150] Davis emphasises that their reactions are not the result of postcolonial "resentment"; rather, they signal uncertainty, confusion and nervousness. Why must students, not only once, but several times during their educations, drag themselves through this unappealing text? Davis presents an overview of the many different emphases he has noted in his own worn copy, following changing trends in literary studies – new criticism, post-colonialism, feminism and deconstructivism – before concluding that he will no longer be teaching *Heart of Darkness*. The point is *not*, as Davis points out, that it should not be taught because some students

find it racist. In fact, he lists all the classical arguments against that type of protest: if we were to yield to such a demand, we would subject ourselves to self-censorship, thus eradicating vast parts of world literature from before 1900 from our understanding of history, tradition and education. Also, it is an important educational task to have to process basic conflict patterns in our culture as they appear in aesthetic forms. The point is that we should not feel obliged to read and teach the novel simply because the text itself does not justify our being tired of its massive exposure in the educational system. Lennard Davis' resignation entails the possibility of putting the book down without first having to discuss one's way out of the infinite, all-consuming game of interpretation – and any consequent accusations of denying the holocaust.

If we compare the frequency of references to Conrad's *Heart of Darkness* with Shakespeare's *King Lear* or other prominent works in the canon of world literature, Conrad's book stands out as one of the most frequently discussed in criticism and literary studies; it is also one of the most taught texts worldwide. The novel has served as an example of high literary modernism and impressionistic style, universal existential-psychological themes, anti-imperialist criticism, racism and – most recently – holocaust and genocide related literature.[151] It has been published in countless editions, each establishing its own context by comparing the original with selected critical articles, comments and background sources from the enormous archives in the world's libraries. The accompanying texts typically praise the novel's aesthetic, moral and critical value as both high literary art and shocking testimony to colonial atrocities. There is no doubt that the novel holds a unique position in world literature, from which it – via powerful institutions – exercises a great deal of influence on the way the West perceives the rest of the world, most crucially and obviously the Congo and Africa as a whole.

This book's distant reading of *Heart of Darkness*, which deliberately avoids the close reading of literary analysis in order to concentrate on the novel's relationship with genres and its critical reception, arrives at a more sceptical appraisal of the novel's position in world literature. From the perspective of travel literature, and alongside Joseph Conrad's own travel account of his brief stay in Congo, *Heart of Darkness* is placed in a different field of transformation. Conrad does not break with his ideological masquerade; rather, he continues it in textual double agendas. In the novel this is done by concealing his moral co-responsibility, as Pletzen noted in the analysis of Marlow's confessions and lies; in his dealings with the Reform Association it is done by misrepresenting his travels in the Congo as a human rights expedition, and his novel as a report about it.

The transformation from travel book to serialised novel in *Blackwood's Maga-*

zine, and then into a classic of world literature, is the result of coincident historical mechanisms of which two, in particular, have been mentioned. During Conrad's journey to the Congo, there was already a conflict between his inspiration from popular literature – romance and adventure fiction – and a nihilistic modernism inspired by Flaubert and others. This duality has been defined as the key characteristic of his authorship by Fredric Jameson. The texts are not only placed between high literary modernism and popular literature in terms of their form, style and narratives; they also generate a synchronicity of "distinct but as yet imperfectly differentiated cultural 'spaces'"[152]. *Heart of Darkness* is at one and the same time sensational adventure travel literature and impressionistic art – or, rather, it took part in both literary circulations, which helped its propagation among readers and critics and resulted in "cultural spaces" *within* the text. The broad scope for interpretation created by the impressionistic style facilitated its reception's investment in, and actualisation of, these spaces in polemic disputes across the 'great divide' between high and popular literature in the twentieth century.

The second mechanism in the novel's transformational field is related to its part in two apparently very different tendencies in the nineteenth century: the history of literature, and ideas of imperialism and abolitionism. As Patrick Brantlinger has demonstrated, the novel's captivating title shares close genealogical ties both with the abolitionist metaphor of romantic figures such as "dark terror" and with the fundamental juxtaposition in imperialism of civilisation's light and barbarism's darkness. In the novel's *fin de siècle* theme, where internal and external spaces overlap in unstable configurations, the two movements' associative fields converge in an ambiguous, hazy form that carries on the mythologies about Africa as a dystopian place out of reach of rationalism, while remaining open towards both types of interpretation – those that reaffirm and those that criticise imperialism. However, the interpretations have no actual basis in reports from the Congo; they rely solely on the manipulative construction of the Reform Association.

This book has argued for the crucial significance of *Blackwood's Magazine* as the institutional context in which the novel was first published, and in the thousandth anniversary edition of which it held a prominent position as the introductory text and only work of fiction. William Atkinson's article "Bound in Blackwood's: The imperialism of 'The Heart of Darkness' in Its Immediate Context" expands on the discussion above presented in connection with Jakob Lothe and Andrea White.[153] Atkinson gives a solid argument for the notion that Conrad was by no means trying to smuggle subversive anti-imperialist criticism into Great Britain's leading imperialist periodical. On the contrary, Conrad had studied the recent volumes of the magazine in order to adapt to

its ideological line and style, which he concurrently followed up through questions to, and an exchange of letters with, the editor whose job it was to ensure that the novel adhered to the readers' expectations of imperialist rhetoric and entertainment. *Blackwood's Magazine* vouched for a clear, ideologically controlled form that addressed a well-defined, well-off, influential audience in the so-called 'gentlemen's clubs', where romances and novels were resented, but fictions in the traditions of adventure and travel literature were accepted. In this context, Atkinson also supports something other critics have pointed out: the novel promotes efficient British imperialism via the satirical exposure of inefficient Belgian and French imperialism – the exact same ambition we can detect later in E.R. Burroughs' *Tarzan*. However, Atkinson further links this pro-British and anti-Belgian/French tendency to the diplomatic crisis with France in 1898-1899 concerning the colonial rule of South Sudan. *Heart of Darkness* can be seen as a part of *Blackwood Magazine*'s nationalistic campaign against France and other users of the French language.

F.R. Leavis' adoption of Conrad as one of the founders of the "Great Tradition" in English literature was seen by most critics as his final and decisive step into the canon, after Leavis had weeded out both the strong original influence of popular literature and anything un-British.[154] Regarding the latter, Atkinson's "Literary archaeology" points out that Conrad's eagerness to adapt and make a career from the beginning was not only an imperialist, but also a nationalistic, project. Viewed in this light, Conrad's "Britishness" was not an invention that took place in Leavis' canonisation, as Terry Collits suggests in the book *Postcolonial Conrad*.[155] On the contrary, the re-launch in the last forty or fifty years of Conrad as a hybrid and multicultural author seems to rely on a superficial observation of his double-cultural and multi-lingual background. Conrad was ultra-British, and *Heart of Darkness* was as far from propagandising internationalism or trans-nationalism as it was possible to be. Actually, the introduction to Norman Sherry's *Conrad, The Critical Heritage* suggests that his being a foreigner was a significant positive factor in his integration into English literature: the combination of declared nationalism and conservatism, the author's personal background and the exotic quality of his works all resulted in a perfect brand for the British Empire's increasingly nostalgic understanding of self.[156]

If, furthermore, we consider *Blackwood's Magazine* by attending to the Arabic meaning of the word *makhazin* – "storehouse" – a so-called "commodity reading" of the wares offered to the reader by *Heart of Darkness* will first and foremost point towards British efficiency in imperialistic business, conservative British nationalism in relationships with other countries and an attitude towards colonial scandals that values discretion over publicity.[157] The similarities between Stanley's *In Darkest Africa* and Conrad's *Heart of Darkness* have already been pointed out, mentioning both texts' overlapping internal and external spaces, gothic qualities and examinations of *fin de siècle* culture via an unstable identity. The texts also share an inheritance from, and break with, the sentimental tradition of travel literature and its kinship with popular literature.

The texts' modernity, however, is expressed in very different forms. Stanley's New Journalism accentuates a world in motion, which – in accordance with the explorer's transnational biography and ideology – is visualised and made present through fragmented "graphic scraps" that were received and experienced as subversions of established Victorian institutions. Conrad's aesthetic modernism, on the other hand, is vague in form and style; it is ambiguous, indirect and secretive, aiming at inclusion in a nationalistic community of values. Stanley's texts spurred controversy, partly because they transgressed the norms for what can and cannot be said, thus challenging the dominant codes of travel accounts. Conrad's travel diary, like his novel, is strikingly quiet about the destruction in the Congo that other travellers noticed along the same routes, and it completely disregards more pressing colonial scandals. It is possible to perceive the novel's thematisation of the discursive terms for Marlow's testimony as a subtle, meta-critical dimension in the novel, which the reader experiences as an uncomfortably disturbance in the textual message, but it is exactly that – an interpretation that cannot be located or put into exact words in the public sphere.

The novel's tendency to veil Marlow's expedition in "mystery" evokes the creation of unfounded rumours surrounding the Emin Pasha Relief Expedition, which Stanley disdainfully refers to in *In Darkest Africa* with the term "horror fiction" but nevertheless contributes to them himself. Stanley, Emin Pasha and Jameson have all been mentioned as the models for Kurtz. However, Stanley was the only one of the expedition's European officers to stay level-headed and effectively ensure that the effects of the disastrous expedition were minimised. In that respect, he has more in common with Marlow than Jameson or Emin, who both fit rather into the book's description of a hyper-developed sentimental culture which, outside the domain of civilisation, crumbles and 'turns native'. Observers who wish to see a link between the novel and criticism of colonial Congo will therefore notice with interest that the scandal which marred the *British* officers' sexual and cannibalistic excesses in 1890 is *not* included in Conrad's material, even though it was the biggest – and, in the imperial self-understanding, most shocking – media story of the era. In comparison, Stanley's account is an explicit exposure of the scandal, presented to the public, while *Heart of Darkness* is on a par with the British officers' families', and the newspapers', defence of decorum, discretion and seemliness, which caused them to banish the affair to the realm of mystery. The novel's silence about the media scandal that followed in the

wake of the Emin Pasha Relief Expedition, as well as about other revelations of atrocities in the Congo in the 1890s, should also be understood in the context of its own paradoxical criticism of the status of testimonies.

This section began by announcing that the Red Rubber prose would be read through the perspective of Franco Moretti's term 'distant reading'. We might describe it as a return to the method of comparative literature, now on globalised terms. One difference in relation to Moretti is that he studies the migration of genres in world literature, especially the novel, while this book has argued for the advantages of studying a broader and more continuous field of forms and strategies, termed 'prose'. Within this field, Conrad's novel, Morel's collages, Twain's satire, Casement's report, Lindqvist's essay, Cutcliffe Hynes' short story, Martini and Schønberg's travel account, Jürgensen's stories and Mirbeau's automobile novel can all be compared as different forms of prose and testimonies to the same transgressions of "international law". They express different understandings of place, establish different audiences and form parts of different strategic contexts. However, they can still be compared and appraised in the light of each other, in accordance with the assumption that historical knowledge cannot rely solely on canonised testimonies and that criticism of testimonies cannot be established from a position *outside* the archive.

This expanded perspective entails a different appraisal of the historical situation – here, the terror regime from the 1890s until the Belgian government's takeover of Léopold's private business – and thus the European perceptions of the Congo at the time. However, it also entails a different appraisal of *literary* history, as we have witnessed in the case of Octave Mirbeau. In his novel, criticism of discourse and of nationalism are two sides of the same coin, and his transnational perspective places the Congo as a location in the European and world atlas – just as Stanley plaes the Congo in a shared European-American-African space. The reading of Mirbeau's novel from the prose perspective, and in relation to the Congo, produces a transformed understanding of its position in literary history, somewhere between *fin de siècle* and avant-garde, while the book's insistence on movement and interrelated places constitutes an important alternative to the rhetoric of exclusion that dominated twentieth-century European descriptions of the Congo. What is more, it is not a purely academic matter, but reveals mechanisms that play a significant role for example in the EU's global policies today, in which territories and sectors for strategic security are defined – for instance Kosovo – while the Congo remains outside this system, despite the fact that it was a Belgian colony longer than it has been an independent state.

As for the problem of testimony, *Heart of Darkness* has been compared with

Conrad's own letters and diaries, as well as with Mirbeau and Jürgensen. Influential research has presented Conrad's novel as the archival crown witness, and on that reasoning has arrived at fallible conclusions which have been propagated as the truth about Red Rubber. The canonisations of Conrad's text as novel and testimony have supported each other in a reception history that ultimately contributes to forgetting and repressing an important chapter in the shared history of Africa and Europe. This book's reading of Mirbeau's chapter about red rubber illustrated the discourse critical traits in *Heart of Darkness*, which the Reform Association can be accused of having covered up. In contrast, Martini and Schønberg's travel account, and in particular Jürgensen's stories, have been used as examples of far stronger testimonies about the *place* that address the complexity of both its experience and interpretation.

IV

An understanding of history on global terms is also an understanding on prose's terms. It needs to pass through anthropoetic narratives that are never purely fiction, eyewitness account or report. Atrocity accounts about the Congo are not closer to the truth and cannot stand alone.

The Twentieth Century

In recent years Danish literary history has taken a national perspective, with the works analysed mostly enjoying central positions in the established fiction canon. Danish literature about the Congo remains understudied, though it has played a role in Danish readers' perceptions of the world and can offer historical and literary accounts of the Danes' involvement in a unique example of what today we would term an "international operation". Even attempts to employ a total perspective on the history of literature that included hitherto marginalised and 'common' literary forms have not uttered one word about colonial literature or literature about the Congo.

In the following section, a selection of texts will be presented and analysed in order to open a path into the literature of a forgotten era and a repressed historical period. Unlike the current attempts by publications and exhibitions to specifically address the latter, i.e. to recount stories about *what* Scandinavians experienced during their time in the Congo, this book will focus on literary history: the way in which these stories are narrated and the patterns they form when viewed in a broader literary context. These readings will not concern criticism of what today we can distance ourselves from as the texts' racism and European prejudices about Africa. Rather, critical light will be shed on more fundamental rhetorical mechanisms that are profound, lasting characteristics of our culture, playing an important role in Danish self-understanding as well as in perceptions in literature and the media of Denmark's relationship with the world today. A number of these rhetorical mechanisms were inherited from major predecessors, such as Stanley and Conrad, and since then have naturally changed according to the contexts in which they were used. The texts examined are not limited to Danish travel accounts and travel novels from the

Congo; these are read alongside other examples of so-called "tragic tourism" and placed in a broad field of texts. V.S. Naipaul's, Graham Greene's and Urs Widmer's travel books and novels from the Congo are read as examples of the continuation of the inheritance from high literature following *Heart of Darkness*, while Dian Fossey's gorilla romance and world bestsellers such as *Tintin au Congo*, *Tarzan and the Leopard Men* and *Trader Horn* are read as examples of the enormous fascination the Congo has held in popular culture.

Although it is not a matter of course for the prose perspective that was established in the introduction, the investigation of patterns in twentieth-century literature about the Congo will follow three tracks for the sake of clarity. The first addresses a number of travel descriptions that all contribute to the figure of the Congo as a state of emergency. The second will investigate three novels that all explicitly address *Heart of Darkness* and the Congo as a place. Naipaul's, Greene's and Urs Widmer's novels all wrestle with the great predecessor, trying to come to terms with it. The third track follows Tintin, Tarzan and other popular cultural after-effects of the fundamental patterns in the understanding of the Congo, which were roughly outlined in Stanley's and Conrad's texts.

Towards the end of the nineteenth century, science, travel reports, art and mass literature were discourses and institutions in relation to which individual prose narratives took an enquiring stance. They were poles in the fields of transformation to which Stanley and Conrad each contributed, but they were not yet specialised sub-sections. Stanley's travel descriptions were, in his own time, read as serious works of scientific authority, news reportage and popular literature. Conrad's *Heart of Darkness* addressed a similar area of tension concerning mass literature and art. Such tensions are present in all the twentieth-century prose narratives presented below – for example, Graham Greene's fear of his novels becoming *too* popular, thus becoming mass literature rather than world literature; or the travel report's apologetic, paranoid form, which distinguishes it from the open, globally conscious and dialogical prose of which Mirbeau is a primary example. The last chapter of this section will return to an interdisciplinary enquiry about Congo literature from the prose perspective.

Mirbeau's travel book is, at one and the same time, reportage, autobiography, anthropological self-reflection, political satire and much more, leading admirers of the text to place it within the tradition of avant-garde art, supported by the book's futuristic approach. Viewed in this context, *La 628-E8* is an attack on the organic art work and the montage form is a parallel to Picasso's early collages, while the prose perspective points to the pre-history of the text, which goes much further back in time. The profusion of readerly and narrative positions – including conflicting and partly neutralising ones – and the text's extraordinary hospitality towards foreign discourses, which are layered on top of and next to one other but effortlessly held together, are characteristics found in eighteenth-century prose. These are the same characteristics that, according to Godzich and Kittay, characterised prose's significance as a separate domain during the fourteenth century. Instead of reading *La 628-E8* from a postmodern or avant-garde perspective, it is possible to describe it as actualising possibilities hidden in prose's past, which have been given a form in a specific historical and cultural context. This makes both Martini and Schønberg's and Jürgen Jürgensen's narratives differentiated prose experiments that mirror a fundamental uncertainty. Read from a 'novel' or canon perspective, these texts are bound to be perceived as unfinished and unschooled – Jürgensen's faltering and conflicting enunciation, for instance, will be criticised as artistic weakness, whereas the prose perspective is able to pick up on the strength of the construction and describe it as an adequate communication of the complexity of experience in a refined literary form. Similarly, what we may perceive as an almost offensive lack of emotion in the catalogues of death and disease in the letters to Denmark investigated below is not telling of the writers' lack of ability; rather, they are prose forms that reach back to the dry objectivity of medieval chronicles, where a lack of ornamentation and stylistic finesse, together with the writer's humble position as a secretary for history, would support the truth even in the most unlikely events.

By using categories such as travel account, novel and popular culture, what follows aims to create an overview of a broad field of texts about the Congo. We are looking at the ramifications of the narrative structure of literary history referred to when Conrad's and Stanley's texts were characterised as parts of the same transformational field. The above readings give reason to assume that around 1900 the prose field was not nearly as differentiated according to codified norms as twentieth-century literature about the Congo. Travel accounts and travel reports were separated from scientific ethnography and anthropology, which were elevated above their predecessors, even to the degree that they based their scientific merits on a ritual exorcism of the travel account – as we see in Malinowski and Lévi-Strauss.[158] After the mapping of Earth's remaining 'blank spots' around the turn of the century, travel reporters had nothing to write about except their disappointment and guilty consciences, and the dominant tendency was for the traditional travel account to become unfaithful to its origin in prose. It became a separate genre that was more interested in defending and justifying itself than in the surrounding world, which was viewed in terms of collapse, negativity and apocalyptic visions of ruin as it happened in 'tragic tourism'. Novels about the Congo in this period may appear as nothing but reaffirmations of Bernard Piniau's claim that they carry on the catastrophic

scenery of *Heart of Darkness*, while on closer inspection their endeavour to break the spell of the novel format and rediscover themselves as prose becomes apparent. Consequently, what from a general perspective seems to be a pattern of ramifications, specialisations and codifications will appear more nuanced in the individual analyses. Innovative potentials of prose will be discovered, particularly in popular culture's media constellations, as narratives and images of Tintin, Tarzan, leopard men and mountain gorillas repeat patterns from the earliest stories in new prose forms.

1 The Congo in Travel Literature: History and Oblivion

H. Jenssen-Tusch's mammoth work *Scandinavians in Congo* (1902-1905), in two volumes, is dedicated to the memory of the author's brother who died as an officer in the service of the Congo State. "Car on y crèv' commes des mouches / Dans tout l'Congo", "They die like flies all over the Congo" states a line from a Belgian song from the 1880s, which Jenssen-Tusch quotes at the end of the preface to his monumental tome. *Scandinavians in Congo* demonstrates the enormous attention paid to the Congo by the European and Scandinavian public at the time, but it also inadvertently reveals that the colonisation of the Congo was in the middle of a profound crisis, exposed through the controversies surrounding Red Rubber, and happening in concert with the *fin de siècle* cultural crisis, including the collapse of the legitimacy of travel accounts.

On the one hand, Jenssen-Tusch's work expresses the era's ideal of sticking to the facts. Considering that he had never set foot in Africa, this resulted in an absurd degree of detail that resembled earlier forms of "Erdbeschreibungen". The book contains a rich repertoire of contradictory definitions of slavery; ethnographic categorisations of noble, wild, talented and beautiful Negroes juxtaposed with "bewildered, degenerate" people living in caves without any form of "societal order"; and classical discussions of questions such as the Negro's craving for flesh, which sometimes brings him to eat rotten human flesh, his kleptomania, his "astonishing memory" and the question of whether or not he was "lazy".

The part about "The foolishness of the Negro" expresses concern about how easy it is for white people to exploit the natives' ignorance and vanity. "In particular, this has become clear every time the Negroes have been presented with European industrial objects, tools and machinery, which may appear beautiful or wondrous; not least have they been the laughing stock in those cases when they have been taken to Europe to feature at the exhibitions in Antwerp and Brussels" (p. 145). After this, Jenssen-Tusch inserts excerpts from letters that document diverse experiences from foreign places. In 1894, for example, Lieutenant Schou travelled from Belgium to the Congo with 35 Congolese who had been exhibited in Antwerp. He writes about the departure:

Cover of the serialised edition of Jenssen-Tusch's *Scandinavians in the Congo* (1902-5), a monumental, encyclopaedic publication that attempted to collect all existing material that might shed light on the work of Nordic migrant workers in the Congo; it is also a book of the dead, commemorating all those who died, including the author's brother. It is richly illustrated and contains hundreds of quotations from unpublished letters and diaries, thus providing a mixed and varied impression of the experiences of Scandinavians in Africa and the ideas they gave rise to. Jenssen-Tusch's point of departure is triumphant – a celebration of the progress of the colony, despite setbacks and challenging climatic conditions; however, vast parts of the account are made up of chilling stories of death, disease, and despondency. The cultural pessimism often associated with the fin de siècle influences the work from beginning to end.

"They showed up in the most amusing procession, wearing old uniforms, with long sabres, feather hats, gloves, collars and smoking long cigars. The brief stay of 5 months in Europe had been enough for them to pick up a lot of European manners, European dress and a certain conceited importance and arrogance (...) I saw several ladies – nice ladies, I was assured – practically begging for or forcing kisses from these fellows, and, in short, acting up, as if they were a group of demigods going away, instead of considering that the same persons might have eaten their last meal of human flesh only half a year before, and that they would probably start again as soon as they reached their native soil" (p. 246).

Once Schou gets started, he cannot stop; he continues to cultivate his priceless little scene, the Negro ladies' dress "à la grotesque", with Pompadour hats and colourful pieces of uniforms, their chieftain in boots that are far too small and "plumage" in his top hat, waddling in front of the procession with uncomfortable dignity.

Initially, the Congolese are brought to the exhibition in Antwerp as tangible support for King Léopold's civilisation project and attract attention due to their unfathomable, decontextualised status of phenomena from another world. Subsequently, their acquisition of symbols of dignity is ridiculed, because it transcends this decontextualisation and appears 'childish' and 'vain'. This criticism backfires, unintentionally applying to the World's Fairs' *own* fascination with wonders, whether they are technological or anthropological. Finally, the description distances itself from the European ladies' attraction to Congolese men, which is criticised for being overly curious and out of context, although in the letter's own discourse it is in itself a curiosity addressed to the hopefully shocked readers back in Denmark. Jenssen-Tusch continues, as if it were completely natural, with a passage about "The Negro's polite forms", which are often "highly complicated".

Scandinavians in Congo was written as a defence of the Congo Free State, the "proud legacy" of King Léopold. However, it reads like a book of the dead. In the numerous incorporated letters, the histories of disease at different posts up and down the river system, of transporting patients in unbearable suffering and of funerals for friends and acquaintances are usually written as objective accounts of incontestable facts – chilling but natural consequences of the work in the colony. Manager Herløv writes:

"The first time I was seriously ill was in Lutete, where in Feb. 85 I was sent on convalescence from Manyanga South. The manager in Lutete, Edwards, died a few days after my arrival, and the day after the brilliant missionary from the nearby mission post [died], the Scotsman Cruikshank, who had just performed the funeral ritual.

Just behind the glass facades of the exhibition building at the exposition in Anvers/Antwerp 1894 was a Congolese village, including its inhabitants, imported to Belgium by, among others, the Danish Lieutenant Schou.

(...) However, I suffered sunstroke, was treated in Manyanga South again, and after this new delay I left, with the Belgian Destrain, who came from the famine camp, and Van Gèle, who also came from Upper Congo, for Isangila, from which 8 days later I left for Vivi with my own caravan without hardly any provision for me and my men (...) Destrain suffered a terrible death here" (p. 353).

So it continues, for 750 pages. *Scandinavians in Congo* is a chilling read, even today. It compiles numerous unadorned, objective testimonies of dead and dying people who – like Jenssen-Tusch's brother – present a very different, bleaker version of the truth than the one laboriously wrought by the author. The work thus becomes a witness box in which the mere quantity of chilling testimonies becomes the weightiest criticism of Léopold's grandiose project.

However, in some passages, even Jenssen-Tusch is hesitant in his dogged admiration. He writes, for instance, that the EIC is too clearly the dream of one man, more "scaffold" than state, and he also hints that Stanley is more preoccupied with entertainment than truth. From his desk, he feels within his rights to correct Stanley's exaggerated descriptions of the Equatorial forests' "savageness and eeriness". According to Jenssen-Tusch, Stanley's assumptions of an impenetrable, dark continent are based on a fallacy caused by the so-called "gallery forests" that stretch in belts along the rivers, whereas the rest of the landscape is open savannah. Despite the promise in the preface that the book will not intervene in the current polemic about the Congo Free State, throughout the book Jenssen-Tusch comments on various rumours of violations in the form of instructive or corrective remarks, which generally refute the accusations as exaggerations or explain the episodes with reference to the natives' inherent brutality or lack of compassion. A lengthy passage is dedicated to the Red Rubber campaign. Sjöblom's, Fox Bourne's and Edward Glave's criticisms are presented in a fairly detailed way and accompanied by photographs of atrocities, only to be refuted, partly with reference to *La Vérité sur la Civilisation au Congo*, one of King Léopold's propaganda periodicals. What is remarkable is not that Jenssen-Tusch refutes the criticism – after all, the book's colossal project was first and foremost to create a reverent memorial to all the Danes who died in the colony – but the fact that he mentions it at all, and in such detail. The critics' statements are termed "testimonies", and the reproduced photographs have greater accusative power than the defensive quotations, resulting in an overall effect that destabilises the declared project. The many pages of the two volumes thus present two kinds of testimony – to the mutilation of natives and the suffering of Europeans – which together counteract the ideal view of civilisation and progress in the colony. This adds to the work the same period 'spleen' that we find in the texts of Stanley and Conrad. Furthermore, it raises fundamental doubt in the reader's mind regarding what kind of story this catalogue of testimonies actually communicates.

Today, the diaries and letters can be read as historical documentation of working life in the EIC and the tasks that soldiers, post managers and sailors performed. These texts are the basic material of the great exhibitions about the Congo at the National Museum of Denmark and the Bornholm Museum, and were used in the joint Nordic museum project about "Scandinavians in the Congo". They have been the raw material for curators, ethnographers and historians, who have edited them or written explanatory notes so that they can be incorporated into the exhibition's concerted representation strategy and give nuance and authenticity to the museal collage. This indicates a tendency to use the archive's travel accounts, which Jenssen-Tusch was the first to organise, as historical witnesses of a coherent truth, while in reality, the accounts are fragmented – both because they are more concerned with forgetting than remembering and because Jenssen-Tusch, and subsequently exhibition curators, have cut them up into small sections. In this light, *Scandinavians in the Congo* was not a monument to the achievements of the Free State and colonialism, but to the collapse of imperialism as an ideology. The positivistic and encyclopaedic method exposes so many internal conflicts in the project that it can be compared with the Orphic poetry of Apollinaire or James Joyce's *Dubliners*, in which the beauty of distant places and lost times revisited can for a brief moment be enjoyed and commemorated in the texts' passing ghosts of half real, half mythological figures.

The Whip and the Pointer

Viggo Jungsbøll's *Per Just on Congo adventures* (1944) is an example of an important speciality in the vast collection of Danish and European travel accounts from the Congo. In this book, the journey and testimony are combined with a popular cultural fascination with the curious, framed by unambiguous didactics. Per Just is restless and lazy, and he struggles to finish his studies in his native town of Ordrup. His father, the wholesale dealer Carl Just, therefore decides to send him on a journey to the Congo, "the proper country for real men" (p. 23), so that he can take charge of his life and see what he can achieve in the world if he pulls himself together. The book ends with Per back in the classroom, ready to account for what he has learnt, but the clear didactic framework is also part of the plot and narrative composition, which is built around Per asking questions of different representatives of the Belgian colony. This results in short lectures about the excellence of the colony or trips that demonstrate it brilliant results. The didactic trajectory is disturbed and halted from time to time by "curious" events: a crocodile hunt elevates Per to a god in the natives' eyes, a group of native girls are ready to tear each others' arms and legs off in order to marry him and so on. In the beginning of the book, a vague outline is made of the colony's earliest history through a portrait of General Olsen, whose elite troops showed outstanding skill in crushing an uprising; however, the book's rhetoric in these passages imitates the summaries of schoolbooks, and pure colonial ideology is presented with massive apologetic confidence. Per is told that it is necessary to punish the Negroes because they are lazy, dishonest, etc. - besides, they prefer it that way. The forest must be destroyed in order to meet the demand for rubber in Europe; otherwise progress will be impeded, which will, in turn, affect the natives. In the book's climactic scene, Per Just must demonstrate the man he has become by heroically intervening in the natives' rebellion against a tough plantation owner. When the leader of the rebels is taken away to be punished with the dreaded hippopotamus whip, Per feels compelled to question the method. He receives the straightforward answer that as it is against the law to use the whip, it has to take place in secret - Per ought to be able to understand that.

From *Per Just on Congo Adventures* (1944). The adventuring young man gets the opportunity to crush a rebellion in a rubber plantation and participate in the punishment using the infamous and illegal hippopotamus whip. The narrator informs the reader that this kind of justice is necessary, though it is illegal.

Per Just on Congo adventures is an example of a didactic exposition of colonialism that sheds light on the repression of the early history of the Congo – an illumination that has only recently taken place in Scandinavia, and also in Belgium, where an active effort was made in textbooks and popular fiction to forget the past. Jungsbøll repeats the testimonies and the wonders of travel literature in a form that apologetically constructs testimonies as forgeries and a repression of history, while wonders are reduced to adventure, understood as stereotypical images of unusual events. In this sense, the book qualifies as fiction – a trivial transformation of the staple elements of travel literature and the *Bildungsroman*. At the same time, Jungsbøll gives the book authenticity by illustrating it with his own photographs, which seems illogical and counterintuitive in relation to its explicitly fictional approach. Furthermore, it sows doubt about whether it is the author's or Per Just's journey that is illustrated, thus implying that Per Just

The cover of Jungsbøll's *Black Man's Land* (1943) features one of the infamous leopard men, a theme that is also found in *Tintin au Congo* and *Tarzan and the Leopard Men*. Jungsbøll writes how he was successful in exposing members of the Anioto sect and made sure they were hanged, although "the case was legally difficult" and all evidence was shrouded in a dreamlike and hallucinatory twilight. The account also shows that emergency laws were continuously widespread long after Léopold handed over the Congo to Belgian colonial rule.

is a projection of the author's fantasies of repeating his journey to the Congo, albeit without the real journey's conflicts, doubts and obstacles.

Jungsbøll's travel book *Black man's land* was published in 1943, the year before *Per Just on Congo adventures*. It exemplifies various other fundamental mechanisms of the repression of the Congo's early history, which would become a rule with very few exceptions in later travel accounts. A comparison of this book of adulthood with the book of youth makes it clear that although they share material, they arrange it in two different contexts and communicative situations. The former is presented as the testimony of a man who has seen everything, enduring the greatest exertions, and therefore has the courage to expose the truth about the Congo even when the public do not want to hear it. The explicit motivation behind the book is a familiar one: an admonition to "the brave, dynamic youth who, after the war, must continue the work where we left it, and justify it in the same way that I wish and hope the war will be" (p. 10). The later book, on the other hand, is presented as the story of the innocent and ignorant Candide who gullibly perseveres, but is eventually forced to face the harsh facts of reality, such as the need to use the chicote – the hippopotamus whip. Both books, however, build on the same repressive and responsibility-evading discourse to propagate untruths, infantilising and fetishising the curious, which is neither wondered at nor reflected upon but reduced to the object of a vain desire for possession.

The two books' didactic presentations of attitudes towards the colonial project are overlapping. Jungsbøll's brutal career as a soldier is described as foolhardy bravery in *Black man's land*, while Per Just is guided by a masked narrator who, by virtue of his mature, cosmopolitan experience, is capable of filtering the story through humanistic ideals and the complex Congolese reality. This opposition of youthful innocence and mature deliberation is a much-used figure that defines the framework for the questions and answers of twentieth-century travel literature and governs the transformation of the traditional rhetorical traits of the genre: realism and orientalism.

The narrator's introduction about leaving Europe and arriving in the Congo in 1923 is described as a crossing into a completely different world. In Antwerp, the cultured behaviour in the state administrative offices of the colony, the "seraphic music" of the Notre Dame Cathedral and Rubens' paintings are compared with the rewards that Jungsbøll will be granted on his return, once he has proved his courage, willpower and strength. When he sails into Boma, it is as if "Africa has closed around us!" and the scene is set for an "initiation, as if we were setting foot in a shrine" (p. 20). Then follows a chapter in which, while sailing along the river, the narrator resumes the history of the Congo's conquest; this accords with the general formula for travel descriptions of the country, and includes references to Léopold and Stanley. The perspective adheres entirely to that of colonial rule, and the point of the story is that because the initial years in the Congo Free State "demanded a tremendous effort of both the king and his officials" (p. 27), any man who signs a contract with the Belgian administration must uphold the principles of the initial rule as much as possible. In 1923 and then again in 1943, when the story was written, the horrors of King Léopold's "Red Rubber" appear to have been totally forgotten, and the story can be told with natural heroic depictions of the Free State's pioneers.

On the journey up to Stanleyville, another standard element from the travel accounts of the era is added to the story: Jungsbøll relates that he used to be very sceptical of the stories his travel companion told, but that now, having spent many years in the Congo, he has "become much more gullible than before" (p. 30). To illustrate this, he mentions an anecdote about the chieftain Lubanga, who is feared by everyone "because of his animal savagery": for instance, he is said to carry out human sacrifices on his dead wife's grave "by slowly slitting the throat and letting the blood flow" (p. 30). Jungsbøll's rehearsal of this story shows that he initially offends the person telling it with his overt disbelief, only to have to apologise for his behaviour the following day, after having seen "some

"Many are under the impression that African women cannot be shapely. Asha, for example, whose marriage controversy is mentioned, could compete with many of her European sisters." From *Black Man's Land*. The pinup image of native women is a staple element in both travel reports and novels. Before 1900, they are usually justified as anthropological representations of ethnic types, while images after 1900 more blatantly reveal a sexual interest, highlighted through the dubious allegations of black women's promiscuous nature in the accompanying texts.

of Lubanga's very unappealing subjects with filed teeth" (p. 31) – which apparently gives him reason enough to believe the tale. This is a common feature of twentieth-century literature about the Congo: a sound mistrust and scepticism of rumours about cannibalism soon give way to the unfounded recognition of even the wildest tales of terror.

As in Conrad's novel, the inland journey on the Congo River is described as a geographical closure that leaves civilisation behind. This is a repression of history that erases the life, conflicts and diversity of the place, replacing them with a few classical figures of conquest and acquisition and, eventually, a rhetorical transformation in which decisions regarding right and wrong and true and false, can no longer be built on the same rationale as in Europe. Unlike the rhetoric of orientalist travel writing, this exclusivity is not associated with ideas of origin, abundance and harmony, but rather describes a state of emergency in which guidelines for justice and societal organisation cannot depend either on European customs and tradition oror on the natives' superstition; they must be reinvented by the in-post plantation manager. The narrator spends several chapters relating with great pleasure how he has established a reservation and kingdom of his own on the Island of Bertha, where, instead of an office chair in Copenhagen, he occupies the position of judge over life and death, marriage, childbirth and so on. The adventurous Jungsbøll may find his subordinates' daily disputes and conflicts trivial, but his system of absolute power is more than enough compensation, and constitutes an important aspect of the self-image he tries to project throughout his narrative.

The natives are described as descendants of cannibals who are still savage at heart. Their hunts, for example, are described as awakening their "dormant savagery", which "was relieved in the imminent bloodbath": "nothing could stop them. They had only one thing on their mind: Blood, blood, blood!" (p. 63). The natives are coquettish, childish and completely ruled by their desires; women are incapable of rejecting men, for example. Jungsbøll's own role is, naturally, to create disciplined and capable manpower by way of the means he sees as necessary. In this respect, his account resembles thousands of others, and it is extremely tempting to respond with postcolonial criticism of its oppressive, stereotypical distortions. Let us focus instead on two of Jungsbøll's stories that will help illuminate the literary-historical traces in the material, as well as the mechanisms in the experiences of the Congo that support Hannah Arendt's theory of a link between colonial terror and fascism. Both stories are inspired by the classical genre discourse of wonder, which permeates the whole book, though in degenerate forms that use it to stigmatise and exclude the natives, ultimately justifying their reduction to the status of animals or brutes – products of the narrator's manipulative imagination.

On his first encounter with the Pygmies, Jungsbøll's first impulse is to take out his travel gramophone to amuse himself at the expense of the natives, who are initially shocked but then begin to dance with a "rhythmical wriggle" that makes them seem like children or "some people such as pixies or dwarves, who had stepped out of the fairytale book to dance for me in a glade in the middle of the African jungle, where the yellow disc of the moon was the only lighting" (p. 93). This double staging of the wondrous, first on the journeys in the Congo and then in the book's repetition, remains unchallenged by the narrator's and reader's image of the world; it is a manipulated drama in which the movement of bodies is savoured with voyeuristic pleasure, while at the same time the savagery of the natives is met with disgust. The scene with the gramophone is repeated in every village Jungsbøll visits, and every time the narrator enjoys the natives' surprised reaction, though it ought no longer to be new to him. The dance is described as an evocation of the "primitive Africa", which in other passages he assures us he is trying to subdue and, in time, obliterate. The dancers are described as being "possessed by the demon of dance", as if they are brought by "autosuggestion" or hallucinogens into a form of "hypnosis" and "satanic possession" – though in reality it is Jungsbøll who is possessed by his feeling of power and perverse pleasure, which lasts until he turns the gramophone off and the natives "shuffle away" (p. 97) in disappointment.

This contradictory structure is continued in the descriptions of rituals and hunts, but also in more serious cases concerning justice. The most striking part of the book is a story about how Jungsbøll miraculously manages to find irrefutable proof of the Leopard Societies' gruesome activities in the Congo – something that had hitherto been a much-discussed question, suspended between myth and reality. Jungsbøll explains that primitive societies everywhere have secret societies, the origins of which are "lost in a distant past" (p. 159). Science has not been able to penetrate these mysteries, and the Leopard Societies in particular have remained impenetrable. Under "gruesome torment and torture", young boys are initiated as leopard men, apparently with no other goal than to spread fear in the area in which Jungsbøll finds himself. According to the rumours the narrator passes on, the leopard men attack their victims in the middle of the night, tearing their aortas with an iron hook. They are clad in leopard skins, with black hoods over their heads, and so no one has been able to identify them. Until now, writes Jungsbøll, every attempt to solve these cases has ended in conflicting testimonies and eroded evidence, and the judges have been forced to let the defendants off. Jungsbøll reports his suspicions about the neighbouring village's chieftain, Wambamba, to the district governor, believing that he is behind – or at least knows something about – the increasing number of Leopard Society murders in the region. A commission reluctantly arrives at the place. Extremely doubtful that the case will hold water, they refuse to drag Wambamba to Stanleyville with no legitimate reason. Jungsbøll admits that the case is difficult from a "legal perspective": "Obviously, the judge was right, in a legal sense, but still! There was so much that pointed in that direction, or was it merely an inexplicable feeling I had, which seemed to me proof enough? Only time would tell" (p. 161).

That same evening, however, a Lieutenant Barnabé arrives, who has overheard "fragments of a conversation" between the native suspects in the village, whom "unfortunately he could not see, but the conversation regarded 'members of the Aniotos Society, he did not doubt that for a second'" (p. 162). The narrator and Jungsbøll immediately rush to conclusions: "My assumptions were true, but how can we prove the attacks? The proof which any conscientious judge would always require" (p. 162). Wambamba, is summoned as a suspect, only to refute it all as malicious and vengeful gossip. It soon appears that Jungsbøll has many other, more concrete unresolved issues with the chieftain: he has complained before that the chieftain does not follow government orders, something Jungsbøll is responsible for ensuring; Wambamba's sons have abducted women from Jungsbøll's village; Wambamba's village neglect the cultivation of rice; and so on. However, the narrator immediately moves from these concrete disputes to a sphere of mystery, blurring the boundary between real and fantastical: Wambamba looks like "A god of cruelty and savagery, as he might be expressed in primitive Negro sculpture. It was as if his features became supernatural, the muscles bulging, the chest arching, the jaw muscles working with animal power" (p. 163).

With no confession from Wambamba, the case stalls, and Jungsbøll, according to his own description, becomes more and more excited and "agitated"; "the Aniotos riddle was getting on our nerves" (p. 165). He has put himself in danger by summoning the commission, and if it leaves without a sentence being passed, he will be left unprotected. Luckily for him, all the riddles are solved one night when soldiers shoot a man dressed in a leopard skin, black hood and iron claws, who turns out to be Wambamba's eldest son. This stroke of luck takes place because Lieutenant Barnabé sleeps fitfully, dreaming that a figure wearing a leopard skin was bent over him with his iron claws. In fright he woke from his dream, only to see a real leopard man ready to kill the person he believed to be our narrator. The leopard man fled at Barnabé's terrible screams. "A strange coincidence of luck and premonition" thus saves the narrator's life, while at the same time providing the coveted proof that the secret sect really exists.

We are told that Wambamba and a number of the village's men were arrested the next morning and taken to Stanleyville, but that the case was difficult "because the arrested Negroes' black souls were black in more than one sense. One got the impression of heathen superstition combined with satanic savagery and supernatural power, which emanated from the leopard men's societies. It was the dark, unfathomable soul of Africa that was laid bare". The process drags on, "with countless interrogations", but "one morning, at half six, six gallows were erected in Stanleyville's prison yard, and at exactly twelve o'clock twelve black bodies were dangling from them as an example" (p. 167). Jungsbøll continues on new adventures, though not without some regret: "Sadly, I never witnessed the killing of more than one Anioto".

The story is uncanny, and it is presented in quite different terms from those of the sensationalism the narrator of *Black man's land* carefully applies: it still seems highly doubtful from a "legal perspective". It appears that the accusation is based solely on a feeling of hatred and mistrust of Wambamba, who refuses to follow orders because his domain is outside Jungsbøll's district. He is therefore described with the classic repertoire of animalistic attributes and placed outside the reach of reason and law. Simultaneously, however, the narrator and the legal discourse are brought to a state of emergency, which paves the way for the narrator's and colonial rule's revenge. It appears that the legal basis for letting the "twelve black bodies" dangle from the gallows is extremely fragile. If we choose to believe this part of the story, the killing of the leopard man in itself

does not prove the guilt of the others, and the strange coincidence that leads to the tangible evidence is left in the same twilight zone Jungsbøll constantly accuses the natives of occupying. What is described as a peculiar coincidence of luck and premonition is more precisely a combination of superstition and delirium, hypnotic hypertension and autosuggestion, as well as the narrator's unnatural obsession with macabre details. It is also, therefore, the narrator who is characterised when there is talk of exposing the "unfathomable soul of Africa" and the bestial desire to "see the victim's red, warm blood flowing from the gruesome gashes on the side of the neck" (p. 167).

Nevertheless, Jungsbøll achieves what he aimed for. Wambamba is forcefully relocated with reference to one of the controversial special laws the Belgian colonial rule still upholds in the Congo, and the text acquires a legal basis for what looks – to more objective eyes – like the lynching of natives who resist the military discipline Jungsbøll boasts of having implemented everywhere. The state of emergency paves the way for the textual rhetoric of unnatural demonisation, and the legal discourse prepares a verdict which is, in reality, based on purely circumstantial evidence. It is fuelled not by justice but by strong, instinctive aversion, revenge and fear.

The book's next chapter is a repetition of this textual game in which the narrator once again seems keen to influence the reader's sense of justice and expectation of sadistic, voyeuristic entertainment. The main character here is Djendya, who looks like an "old male gorilla" with his "flat, retracted forehead, the small, vicious eyes and the projecting cheek bones", and has an "animal sexual desire, which did not allow any woman over the age of twelve to avoid his wild libido" (p. 168). Djendya is uncontrollable, and Jungsbøll assigns him to extremely hard labour in the forest with the other "scum from the plantation – with similar unpleasant attributes". In Jungsbøll's eyes, these workers are particularly lazy and the wages they demand are exorbitant; when Djendya pressurises his fellow workers into striking, the result is open conflict. In addition to his animal attributes, Djendya has the ability to put his enemies to a magical sleep called "Lisombo", and it is the threat of this that makes people follow him. An inspector, Tongonginda, writes a "brief, objective report" of the case, which leads Jungsbøll to deport Djendya to another district. Again, Jungsbøll sleeps fitfully, "the uncanny screech of an owl was an ill omen", while he ponders the form of revenge Djendya, "a personified devil in the shape of a man", might conjure up. The next morning he is woken by the "hysterical screaming of a Negro woman" and is told that Tongonginda is in a coma, struck down by Lisombo.

Jungsbøll cannot decide whether the coma is caused by hypnosis, autosuggestion or poisoning, but he summons Djendya, who refutes both Tongonginda's report and the accusation of having performed Lisombo. Jungsbøll, however, arranges for Djendya to be tortured with the chicote in order to make him break the spell. In this extraordinary situation "I had to put aside all humanitarian feelings, resorting to raw and brutal Africa's own methods of punishment (...) I was seething with rage against him who had used black African magic to which we Europeans still have not found a cure, but whose tragic, inevitable result we knew" (p. 175). In the "primitive, brutal Negro's blunted emotional life", only "crudeness and violence" command respect (p. 176), and although Jungsbøll was supposedly "disgusted by the brutal incident" the narrator does not refrain from describing the punishment in minute detail. Djendya's nakedness is mentioned several times, as well as the torturer's careful placing of his lashes in the same wounds, despite the legal prohibition of that very practice. Finally, "evil had been flogged out of him", and Djendya wakes Tongonginda, who rises from his bed like a sleepwalker.

Jungsbøll rounds off the story by saying that he would have preferred to see the events sink into oblivion, and that he was surprised when the state labour inspector arrived at the plantation to investigate the rumour about his "abuse of a native". The inspector summons all the natives in order to give them the opportunity to present their complaints and questions. But they answer in unison: "The fat master is a good master. He is a papa to us all!" (p. 181). Jungsbøll gives them an extra day off work and extra rations of rice and tobacco, and the labour inspector apologises "that an innocent man could be accused of something as unpleasant as abuse of the natives. He was glad to find that it was all lies from one end to the other" (p. 181). Finally, the narrator assures us that he is aware some readers will condemn his behaviour, insisting however that he did not act on "sadistic tendencies" but a desire for justice, which he believes to have been confirmed by the fact that Djendya, with "the primitive Negro's instinctive feeling of what is just", chose not to testify despite the labour inspector's encouragement (p. 182).

The pattern here is the same as in the story about the leopard men. Initially it is a question of a labour conflict, which Jungsbøll tries to solve with the infamous special law that legalised deportations of recalcitrant workers to other provinces. But this is not enough for Jungsbøll, who then chooses to use the chicote for an illegal and extremely violent punishment, in which he appears to take much pleasure – both at the time and long after, in the narrator's retelling. At the same time, the retelling is a lengthy, laborious justification, initially of the use of special laws and, subsequently, of the exceptions from these laws. The narrator employs the terror ascribed to the natives, while at the same time lulling the reader into a state like Lisombo, waking us in time to realise that Jungsbøll is absolved of his crime.

The cover of Jungsbøll's *Zanga* (1960), a dramatic story of revenge and valour that ends with Zanga being eaten by army ants, enduring terrible pain and suffering. Like his other works of fiction, the book – novel? – is illustrated with the author's own photographs.

Thus, the text is cleverly designed so that the narrator simultaneously admits to his guilt and acquits himself, while several times repeating the first crime in the voyeuristic display of violence for the reader. This can take place because the reader is hypnotised by Jungsbøll's magical use of a broad repertoire of numbing, intoxicating and terror-evoking rhetorical effects, preventing the reader from even questioning the reasonableness of the text's extremely peculiar claims, for instance about Djendya's power of Lisombo or the interpretation of the group of natives' silence as an unconditional acquittal. Justice works in close partnership with fictionalisation, and it is difficult to judge whether it is "lies from one end to the other", or which elements are so important to Jungsbøll that he needs to tell them in order to buy indulgences and which are used as smokescreens around the textual witness box. Which of his actions are fictitious displays of perverted fantasies of power, and which are real crimes?

Through the use of legal discourse and themes of credibility and testimony, *Black man's land* employs the travel genre tradition for the realistic presentation of factual events. At the same time, the book adopts the genre's fascination with the curious, which – in the renaissance tradition – was the starting point for phenomenological wonder. Both rhetorical traditions, however, are transformed in this book into displays of the superior power's perverse and infantile pleasure in the native as a decontextualised object of manipulation and violence. By simultaneously revealing and concealing violence, and carrying out a rhetorical hypnosis, the book also misrepresents and represses the Congo's history while justifying the practice of a permanent state of emergency in the legal field. What is more, history itself – in the sense of concrete, dynamic social forces – is absorbed by the concept of a timeless, animalistic darkness, which the text involuntarily situates within the narrator himself.

In the chapter "Dismal fates", immediately after the two stories investigated above, Jungsbøll gives a series of classic examples of colleagues who are destroyed by their stay in the Congo. "[T]he Congo is a Moloch that destroys weak characters. Brutally it strips them of the sense of shame, lets human inhibition disappear and leaves only animal instincts. (...) The graces of tolerance and forgiveness disappear, and from the sick, tormented imagination grows megalomania and self-importance, both assuming enormous proportion" (p. 183). Jungsbøll wishes to distance himself from those to whom "Virtue and order are abominable", those who have lost "the sense of shame and ability to regard themselves critically" (p. 190), in the same way that he has distanced himself from the natives' desire-fuelled animalism. Perhaps he identifies a key question for himself, too, when he asks "Towards whom would they feel shame?"

In this reading, Jungsbøll is not portrayed as decisively different from his decadent colleagues; the only difference is that his concepts of virtue and order seem to provide opportunities to enact perverse, uncontrolled fantasies. His travel book – which, as mentioned, also functions as a work of repression – can be perceived as a twisted, veiled attempt to atone for his unrestrained desire by publically confessing and expressing shame.

The didactic framework of Jungsbøll's novel *Per Just on Congo adventures* takes a similar form. If we compare the photographs in the two books, the main character in both is the author, who is prevented from returning to the Congo by the Second World War and must instead write about his noble deeds there as an innocent youth and then a mature adult. In fiction, Jungsbøll is able to assume the roles both of the young Per Just, whose lack of historical knowledge allows him to live through the events in stylised innocence, and of an adult supervisor like the plantation owner Brouwers, who will say and do what is necessary to manage the real conditions in the Congo. The filtering of reality takes place behind Per Just's back, based on an agreement with a hypothetical adult reader: though Per's journey is a formational project, which will ultimately make him a man who knows about the world, there are many things he does *not* need to know. Nevertheless, the book hints at its own non-disclosure, like a guilty person who cannot keep his mouth shut. Per Just is puzzled by the schedule for the delegation assigned to collect the leader of the rebellion at the plantation: "The administration explained that they would have safe-conduct in the forest,

The cover of Freiesleben's *The Congo is Calling* (1944). Both Freiesleben and Jungsbøll distance themselves from the unjustified use of violence and savage conduct among natives as well as Europeans. Nevertheless, encapsulated in the text are fascist power fantasies and a fascination with the inhumane.

because they would administer a good thrashing to the chieftain with the hippopotamus whip. They knew they were not allowed to, because it was against the law, but as long as everybody agreed, no-one would tell. The chieftain would certainly keep his mouth shut, or he would be flogged even more" (p. 101).

If we compare the two books, it becomes clear that *Black man's land* makes use of the same infantilised innocence as *Per Just on Congo adventures* in order to justify the combination of sensationalistic wonder and fictitious shrouding in what pretends to be the earnest talk of an experienced man. The simulated innocence in the book of youth exposes the real contract with the reader of the book of manhood: both narrator and reader not only accept the violations – they also find childish satisfaction in sharing this knowledge about unrestrained power in a state of legal emergency.

Viktor Freiesleben's *The Congo is calling* (1944) uses many similar figures in relation to stories about the chicote. The beginning of this travel book gives a detailed description of Freiesleben's first, shocking encounter with this method of punishment: "I was shaking as from sickness at the sight of the torture". At the same time he assures readers that not only the commanders but also the victims would find it unfair if "a disobedient soldier did not have his backside spanked"; they would perceive it as cowardice. "The flogging must therefore not be seen as a symptom of savagery or sadistic tendencies in the Congo army officers – quite the contrary!" (p. 19). In an episode that strikingly resembles Jungsbøll's story about the Lisombo rebellion, Freiesleben issues orders to use the chicote against a disobedient medicine man who refuses to administer an antidote to one of Freiesleben's allies who has been poisoned. And like Jungsbøll's story, the narrative is organised as a peculiar mix of sadistic desire and justification: "At that very moment, the hideous torture instrument, the 'chicote', lashed against the medicine man's backside. (...) I felt that this was a battle between a savage, primitive Congo Negro's reluctance and a white man's selfless attempt to save a friend. No mercy must be shown, because the second it was, the battle would be lost" (p. 107).

Freiesleben's detailed description of how he plunders the villages of fetishes and humiliates the local authorities is written in a similar, undisguised ridicule of the natives' religion – something that gives the narrator great pleasure and increases his own power and influence. It is not "easy to get hold of the good old Negro sculptures. Obviously, the natives were not keen to let go of them", so it could prove dangerous to "go fetish hunting" (p. 127). There are thus many "exciting experiences and interesting stories" related to the stolen fetishes. In one, a chieftain hides a valuable fetish with particular care, and Freiesleben must

"The author, ready to crush the rebel Kasongo-Niembo", from *The Congo is Calling*.

"Illunga, Kasongo-Niembo's subordinate chieftain, rolled around in the dust for me, promising that he did not know of his master's whereabouts. Illunga means – My little darling! Actually, his brutal mug did not inspire pet names." From *The Congo is Calling.*

go to a lot of trouble to find the hiding place and retrieve the fetish. This "stolen idol" turns out to be an artistic "masterpiece", and the narrator's knowledge of the fetish's crucial importance to the natives, and their deep sense of loss, only makes the trophy even more valuable:

"He and his medicine man were without doubt infuriated by the abduction of the village shrine. Through many years, perhaps generations, it had guarded his people (...) Now it sat on my table in the tent. I looked at it from all angles, admiring the artist's imagination and skill. This was indeed a sculpture far beyond the usual; the face had life – yes, exactly, life – that which had meant so much to the villagers" (pp. 130-31).

One chapter about the promiscuity of black women is – like the book in general – spiced up with erotic anecdotes about having unlimited access to sex with girls of tender age or about the dangerous but tempting aspect of having a Negro woman as "menagère". Here, Freiesleben expresses his fundamental perception of the natives: "In general, they only know of two feelings: Hunger and sexual desire, and both are satisfied without consideration, in vast quantities" (p. 116). As with other figures that ascribe to the natives brutality,

"Is there not wonderful life in this face? The quest for her almost cost me my life". From the beginning of the colonisation, it was common that travellers brought back religious, artistic, and ethnographic objects to Europe, where they were kept in private collections, often ending up in Congo exhibitions at museums or archives of local history. The labels rarely tell anything except how they were acquired. Some travellers, such as Herbert Ward, were more or less professional art collectors, who systematically purchased large quantities of items and thus contributed to founding a market for produced curios and fetishes especially for export. Others, like Stanley, appear to have been relatively uninterested in this aspect of exploration. Travel accounts by Martini/Schønberg and Freiesleben, however, mention proudly how weapons and fetishes were seen as legitimate trophies after battles, or simply stolen from the natives. Particularly shocking is Freiesleben's bragging about how he managed to steal a fetish to which the village ascribed great value and had therefore hidden from the European fetish-hunter. From *The Congo is Calling*.

impertinence or childish behaviour, we are dealing with the narrator's desire to live out a fantasy of being an admired and respected authority, king or god, at the same time as being an infant whose every desire is satisfied. The figure of the promiscuous African woman is contradicted by the stories about faithful Africans and decadent Europeans who – as Freiesleben reveals in a daring story about an affair on the steam ship to the Congo – have not experienced a real relationship with a European woman, but let their sexual fantasies loose in Africa: "The word no never crosses her lips when a man calls" (p. 117).

Both Jungsbøll and Freiesleben distance themselves from the unjustified use of violence and express strong moral condemnation of both natives and Europeans who act like animals. Nevertheless, through this normalising system of values a fascination with the beastly aspects of human behaviour is expressed – which is also a projection of the narrators' own fascist fantasies of domination. Behind the demand for "virtue and order" looms a lawless abandon, legitimised with geographical, biological and legal arguments. Furthermore, the stories are told with no shame, which – on a deeper textual level – is a cause of shame in relation to the reader, who is made complicit. The plundering of fetishes is justified by exposing the natives' superstitiousness, where the shamelessness in itself is made a conciliatory element. The stories that the plundering gives rise to are in themselves reasons enough for the theft, just as the travel account on the whole excuses the crimes it recounts by allowing the reader to share in the pleasure of the violations and humiliations required to turn it all into a good story. The terror, which characterises this type of travel description from beginning to end, is, in this sense, not found among the natives, but rather in the texts' strategic oblivion of the world they pretend to describe. As Freiesleben's fetish stories openly show, the profound nature of the book is linked to the shameless plundering of life, which in the textual retelling neither conveys beauty nor bears witness to the power and influence of the owner of the trophy: it merely reveals the narrators' desire as an infantile fantasy.

Indignation and Pathos: Feminisation and Non-disclosure

Jungsbøll and Freiesleben have purposely not been analysed within the framework of postcolonialism, though that would have allowed the identification of a vast number of mechanisms in the texts' use of colonial stereotypes. This decision is based on the fact that the logic of alterity that postcolonialism tends to both criticise and be rooted in obstructs an understanding of other, equally pervasive rhetorical characteristics that are also found in the colonial and humanistic discourses. Their acknowledgement of guilt, accusations and displays of atrocities often employ the same problematic mechanisms as Jungsbøll and

I DE SVARTAS LAND

AV

ELIN BÖRRISSON

S T O C K H O L M

SVENSKA MISSIONSFÖRBUNDETS FÖRLAG

Elin Börrison's account *In the Land of the Blacks* (1922), describing her missionary activities in the Congo, is one example of the thousands of missionary texts that carried on the abolitionist movement's representation of the natives as children who on the one hand were in need of help, and, on the other, were not so savage that they were beyond the reach of the gospel. The text is pathetically indignant and romanticising, seeing the place through a blur of plant vignettes and dream-like or misty images.

Freiesleben do, though such texts explicitly declare their critical attitude towards colonial exploitation and aim to provide justice for the oppressed.

Elin Börrisson's *In the Country of the Blacks* (1922), for instance, is fuelled by indignant pathos. The introductory chapter takes its starting point in Møller, Pagel and Gleerup's *Three Years in the Congo* (1887). In this account by three Swedish officers, Börrisson finds examples of both colonial violence and the cynical and humiliating ridicule of natives. "Robbed of everything and mocked as well!" is her comment on the comparison of a captured native, who expresses his longing for home by constantly turning towards his village, and a turtle's instinctive longing for water. However, what from her missionary point of view she calls "heartless cynicism" is based on a quotation from Møller in which the unmistakable point is that the officer has to intervene in the soldiers' brutality when they treat the native with methods from the time of the slave caravans. In Møller's account, what is shocking is that he feels compelled to punish the soldiers for their brutality towards members of their own race – with the dubious moral "That is the Negro; he has no compassion for the suffering of his neighbour" (*Three Years in the Congo*, I, p. 236). However, this complexity naturally interferes with Börrisson's agenda, which is – like that of hundreds of other

missionary tales from the Congo – to maintain a boundary between the colonial rule's use of force and the dissemination of Christianity, though the two factors are usually not juxtaposed but seen as mutually dependent. A further ironic dimension may be added to the aforementioned passage when we recall that, in the initial years of the Free State, the mission posts bought unwilling natives who they then educated and converted, thus actively contributing to the slavery they had sworn to fight.

Börrisson's use of the quotation supports the travel book's general effort to communicate a balanced image of the Congo, appealing to compassion while keeping silent about everything that is either too terrifying or complicated to comprehend. Although the travel book was published in 1922, its basic framework is a continuation of the eighteenth-century abolitionist movement's texts, in which the description of Africa as dark and barbaric is balanced with an archaising portrayal of it as a paradisiacal, pastoral landscape. The intention is to justify the missionaries' presence by emphasising the darkness of the place while avoiding any suggestion that it is beyond the missionaries' reach, emphasising the existing light that must be protected so it can spread.

The book's use of metaphors in relation to its journeys, places and peoples – "caravan journeys", "desert" and "Bedouins" – introduces the evangelic text as a staple element, combined with a romantic composition of the changing seasons and landscapes. As opposed to Stanley's omniscient gaze in his descriptions of houses and everyday life in Uganda, Börrisson's field of vision is always blurred by mist or the "foliage in the window". A scriptural passage about "the Lord Jesus Christ, who will transform the body of our humble state into conformity with the body of His glory" (p. 30) is linked to a reading of misshapen acacia trees as "deformed cripples" that transform into "glory": "Every leaf and every flower is a masterpiece of beauty". The gospel is thus inscribed in the landscape, which is "rich in changing expressions" and stunningly beautiful in its "changing forms", opening onto panoramas that are both "misty images" and "dream images" (p. 40). An exception to these dream images is found in the concluding chapter, "People", which returns to criticising the state of affairs during the colony's first years; however, the narrative is still filtered, as atrocities become tales from "old times", which are now almost overcome, and therefore deserve no more attention than the changing light caused by the foliage outside the writer's window. "Surely, there is still oppression and violence in the world, but individuals have been dragged up from the reeking morass, whether it was vice, ignorance or heathenism that held them captives" (p. 197).

When Elin Börrisson and her husband returned to Sweden in 1921, she published *In the country of the blacks*, which, according to the preface, was written during her stay in Africa at her Swedish friends' request: "Write about everything out there. We know so little about the Congo" (p. 5). The Börrisons continued telling their stories in the missionary society's travelling museum, a refurbished bus, which brought collections of ethnographica, fetishes, plants and animals to the country's congregations. The travel book's amateur scientific descriptions of plants and animals combined with the influence of the gospel and romantic nature poetry would fundamentally result in a history of replacement that had nothing to do with the Börrisons' friends' request. Promoted by the missionary society's propaganda bus, in conjunction with numerous similar tales and exhibitions about the Congo, they contributed significantly to the obliviating "gaze drift" that Conrad's novel, and subsequently the Reform Association's propaganda, established as staple figures.

There is no doubt that through their missionary work the Börrisons acquired detailed knowledge that surpassed that of the plantation owners' and officers' limited scope, and their ethnographic and botanical observations have several times proved to contain valid scientific results. This only makes it more conspicuous that they keep silent about the human conflicts in the region; they may be detectable in the texts' pathetic indignation, but it is also fair to say that these issues are relocated in the impenetrable web of plants. It is as if the narrator is equally keen to reveal and conceal, presenting a version to the reader that, like later travel descriptions undertaken for humanitarian organisations, is edited mainly with an eye to the overall good intention, thus avoiding confronting more complex and demotivating issues.

Honeymoon in Belgian Congo (1950), by the fashion designer Saga Roos, makes full use of the melodramatic potential of the exotic material provided by her marriage to the handsome Klas Roos, who was a captain on one of the Congo's river steamers. With detailed descriptions of elite society and modern and fashionable perspectives, Roos' travel book appears to be in direct contrast to Börrisson's missionary story; however, on closer inspection we are dealing with the same fundamental attitudes and rhetorical figures, only they are addressed to very different readers. In Roos' book, attention is not directed towards landscape and botany, but towards dress and etiquette among the different classes of colonisers and native tribes which she, with fervent curiosity, sets out to photograph. Her both professional and erotically fascinated gaze at the carnival held to celebrate the "Equatorial party" on the steamer on the way to the Congo, with its elegant and exotic costumes, is similar to her fascination with the African world's profusion of colours and shapes, which, however, are merely perceived as a backdrop for changing scenes of festivity and terror.

In the Congo of the thirties, the lives of the reigning class of officials and businessmen was one of prosperity, luxury, protected idyll, exotic trips, elegant parties and drinks and dancing in the tropical night, while the surrounding

ANVERS-CONGO
LÉGENDE
CH. DE FER EN EXPL^ON
" CONST^ON
NAVIGATION MARIT^ME
FLUV^LE
LIGNES AÉR^IENNES
VERS
PORT SOUDAN
BONDO
AKETI
BUTA
NIANGARA
BUMBA
IRUMU
STANLEYVILLE
COQUILHATVILLE
PONTHIERSVILLE
JINJA
INONGO
BANDUNDU
KINDU
COSTERMANSVILLE
UVIRA
BRAZZAVILLE
LEOPOLDVILLE
MOMBASA
TSHELA
BANANA
P^T FRANCQUI
LUSAMBO
KONGOLO
KIGOMA
ANVERS
BOMA
MATADI
LUEBO
TSHIKAPA
KABALO
ALBERTVILLE
DAR-ES-SALAAM
BUKAMA
DILOLO
ELISABETHVILLE
LOBITO
SAKANA
BEIRA
VERS CAPETOWN
LÉOPOLDVILLE
Cie Belge Maritime du Congo
Lamoyon

country, sealed off from "les colons", is described as a marketplace that can provide all kinds of pleasure and entertainment. "One could see many a raffia dress swaying on wide hips, a thin brass ring adorning a steady ankle or a green bead ribbon, the so-called 'majakka', around a voluptuous waist" (*Honeymoon*, p. 41). Like Börrison's use of flickering "misty images" and "dream images", the descriptions in Roos' travel book stray from one striking detail to the next, never attempting to contextualise individual elements or define a foreground and background. The method is common in exoticising travel accounts from the middle of the twentieth century, in which sometimes every last page is dedicated to this special double-layered, weaving metaphoricity.

The travellers are aware that they have arrived too late to perform a meaningful search for an origin, and they have given up hope of saving the natives from the destruction of their civilisations, which is usually perceived deterministically as a necessary consequence of progress. The travellers, therefore, keep their distance from the experience; unlike earlier orientalist travellers they do not see their journey as a formative project, but merely as a passing, compensatory pleasure. The consequence of this lack of involvement is an artificial objectification of the country as a show or a lavish, luxuriant, colourful work of art, which is completely detached from any historical context. In this conception, the landscape has coloured itself and the natives have dressed up for the benefit of the tourists. All the observed details, whether they relate to the everyday inconveniences of thieving servants or adventurous journeys, are blurred together in the flickering, stale narrative image of the colourful natives. Noses, bellies, breasts, hips, clothing, tattoos, uniforms, hippopotamuses, calabashes and slender palms are all employed simply to contribute to the image, which the narrators pretend to record passively like their cameras.

Although Saga Roos' husband gives her "courses in Negro mentality" (p. 69), she admits that she does not understand the natives, except for the fact that

Poster from the 1920s, advertising luxury trips to the Congo. Saga Roos's *Honeymoon in Belgian Congo* (1950) accounts for the fashion designer's observations of the lush lives of the colonisers and the fascinating contrast with the colourful natives. Both cultures are described as exotic carnivals, staged with the aim to entertain Roos on her journey through a colony in splendid progress, despite the emergency laws that allow for forced relocation of rebellious natives.

they – because of their childish nature – must be "treated strictly but fairly". This admission, however, does not change her view of the natives as an inexhaustible source of entertainment, for instance in the anecdotes about the servant Joseph, who must be rebuked because he is caught in the kitchen making Swedish meatballs by rolling them on his "round, impressively shiny belly" (p. 68). In this kind of account the historical context has collapsed or disappeared completely. When the narrator, for instance, hears "interesting details about the Negro rebellion two years ago", these are communicated to the reader like a fireside tale, and summed up with the conclusion "Those were exciting and scary times" (p. 164).

Saga Roos is mundane and, in her own self-understanding, emancipated. Like Elin Börrisson, she often expresses sympathy for the natives, especially the women. However, both women's accounts fall victim to a sentimental and aestheticised discourse that in its intention to leave a positive impression of the Congo, where the forces of darkness are contained by civilisation or the missionary movement, indulges in the tourist's narcissistic representation of a world that exists solely for their sake. At a general level, these texts leave the impression of an immense repression of the period's actual political tensions. They illustrate the prevailing misconception that post-war Belgian Congo was a blissful oasis – a notion that was primarily based on the colonisers' own isolation.

Reports: The Collapse of the Travel Account

In this series of travel accounts that facilitate the obliviating repression of Congolese history, two additional travel books will be mentioned, both of which were written to commemorate historical anniversaries and both of which explicitly claimed to address their age on the basis of critical, historical analyses. Both were also written in the genre of the journalistic report, while allowing for digressions in forms familiar from Jungsbøll and Freiesleben. Edvard Andersen's *Adventurous Congo* was published in 1957 on the occasion of the 50th anniversary of the Belgian state's takeover of the Congo from King Léopold. Arne Falk-Rønne's *In Stanley's footsteps through Africa. 100 years after his encounter with Livingstone* of 1972 bears the strong mark of the political climate in the period following independence in the 1960s.

Edvard Andersen's journey is explicitly designed as a kind of balance sheet, listing achieved results and remaining challenges in the Belgian colony. However, despite the critical and inquisitive rhetoric on the textual surface, it soon becomes clear that the book should rather be read as a loyal celebration of the colony on its anniversary – an admiring little gesture from one small European

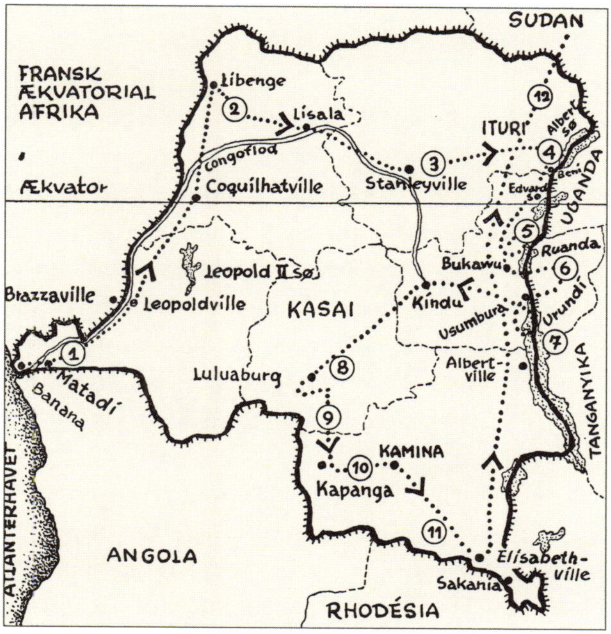

Edvard Andersen's *Adventurous Congo* (1957) was written as a celebration of the 50th anniversary of the Belgian takeover of the colony from King Léopold. The account pretends to be a critical report aiming at measuring and evaluating the results of the colony, and assessing the living conditions of the natives in light of the independence movements in other African countries. However, the report format is merely a facade to cover the textual cold-war demagogy and argumentation for the necessity of defending Western possessions in Africa. The balanced style is fake, and the evaluation of pros and cons is formulated in the same problematic rhetoric as Hawkesworth's additions to James Cook's diary account from Tahiti: it apparently reconciles and erases the differences between 'them' and 'us', but in reality they are enhanced, becoming massive, insuperable cultural antitheses.

nation to another. At the same time, the book wants to share the credit for the successful colonial experiment "in one of the world's treasure chambers" (p. 7), by including stories about the heroic contributions of Danish travellers.

Andersen describes a visit to "Kawa, Hans Christensen's jungle kingdom" – a strictly managed plantation where the sixty-year-old Viggo Jungsbøll had the coveted position of manager. He also describes the leopard men's assumed haunts in north-east Congo; the Pygmies in the Ituri Forest; ultra-modern model plantations where the links between colony and colonised are rationalised in

big, sterile labour camps; diamond and uranium mines in the south-eastern provinces; and a detour to the Rwandan highlands where he met the extremely tall, beautiful and aristocratic Tutsis.

Other African countries' relationships with their respective European colonial rulers are explicitly drawn into the journey's political context. The journey and narrative approach the colony's future with implied concern, presenting it in a manner that is both tantalising and frightening: "at the Congo's borders, hatred is burning, but within the Congo the concept of Mau-Mau is unknown. Why is it so, and how will Central Africa's future turn out?" Furthermore, the narrator wants the reader to see the book as "a complete picture of Central African society today, where black and white work together without hostility"; the mysteries of the past coexist just as peacefully with the modern Congo "on the threshold of the atomic age" (p. 8).

However, the answers to the introductory questions, as well as the promised complete picture, disappear in the elliptical rhetoric, where key questions and sensitive issues are barely touched upon before they are obscured by conspicuous leaps and diversions. The introductory summary of the history of the Congo, which – contrary to tradition – comes before the account of the departure and arrival, is organised around Stanley's friendship with the Dane Albert Christophersen, who was a member of Stanley's colonising expedition in 1879. Already, the declared criticism of such projects is contradicted by the account's crude representation of the colonisation as a merry game. After the description of his arrival in the Congo, the narrator establishes a double role for himself and the reader: partly a reporter who makes superficial inquiries before drawing his superficial conclusions, and partly a fake, naïve "guest", exemplifying his own superficial questions and answers. The "guest" asks whether it can really be true that "black people plainly accept that they are subject and inferior without feeling oppressed", or whether it is really not a sign of race discrimination when "the highly praised Belgian Congo" does not allow political parties, pays black people lesser wages than whites, divides cities sharply between white and black districts, and so on. The "reporter", having denied the first, most obvious answer, insists that complicated circumstances must be considered before hasty conclusions are drawn. And when he later directs the question to an anonymous representative of the Belgian authorities, he is told that the blacks are locked in separate quarters at night-time in order to "protect the natives against white undesirables" and to "accommodate the blacks' own wish" (p. 39). Other questions from the reporter regarding similarly sensitive issues are answered just as readily by the representative, who also encourages anyone who might want to carry out their own investigation. During other visits to the authorities, the reporter is given equally good answers

“Standing there before us, the witch doctor looked fantastic ...”, from *Adventurous Congo*.

to his compromising questions: the crime rate is insignificant and the Congo’s infamous punitive system is going through extensive reforms “governed by modern, educational methods” (p. 41).

Edvard Andersen’s particular use of the reportage structure of problem-question-answer is linked to a temporal argument according to which the new Congo, when compared with the old, can only be true and just as a result of implied syllogistic logic. “Compared to the new and good, one recalls a glimpse of the dark chapter in the history of the Congo, when the *chicote* and the *iron chains* were part of the punitive system” (p. 42, Andersen’s emphasis). “The Belgians refused to believe what was told about cruelties. However, it all came to an end with a number of reforms” (p. 42). The prisons of today have “modern workshops”, and can “happily state that *absolutely no race discrimination takes place*” (p. 43). An account of the “guest’s” astonishment when encountering apparent apartheid-like phenomena in the city is thus summarised in italics with a complete acquittal of “the highly praised Belgian Congo”. Both the criticism and the hint of sarcasm in the phrase “highly praised” is only make-believe, preparing the ground for a presentation of the colony as an unrivalled successful experiment.

A key element in this peculiar but widespread rhetoric is the use of a temporal mirroring of the Congo’s “medieval” past, which accentuates the colony’s present and future as bright, transparent and just in contrast with its previous

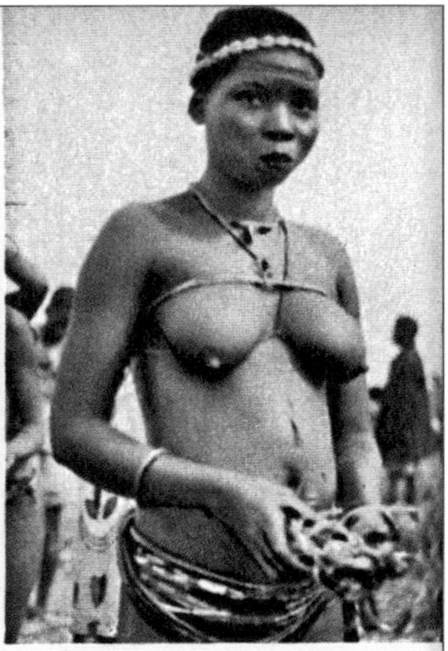

I de sorte damers omklædningshytte. Den slanke kvindę i forgrunden skal netop til at ryge en pibe tobak. — Til højre: Basala-pige, yndig og naturlig

»...få meter fra mig stod en af Basala M'Pasus meget omtalte suppegryder...«

From *Adventurous Congo*.

impenetrability. It is basically the same figure we encounter in Jungsbøll's and Freiesleben's texts; however, in Andersen's, guilt and innocence, disclosure and non-disclosure are injected as a simulated critical discourse which only serves the text's apologetic aim. The gullible guest believes that the dance in Congo is jazz, but the cosmopolitan reporter can inform him that it is samba and rumba, performed in "an uncivilized manner" (p. 44). In the implied dialogue of narrator and reader, every possible protest is turned into an affirmation of the Belgian administration as a model for other African countries and a corrective for all the continent's independence movements.

The narrator, like all the travellers in the Congo in this period, distances himself from tourism's effect on the original culture in the zoological gardens, displays of Pygmies and so on, and mentioning completely uncritically the planned World's Fair in Belgium in 1958, where "shiploads of tropical trees, plants and flowers, even an entire village, will be brought to Brussels" (p. 117). The mining industry, the general government, the missionary activities and folklore will have each their showroom, and the natives themselves will create the decorations. Edvard Andersen views the exhibition as a "sensation" that will repeat and surpass the earlier World's Fair in Antwerp, where Lieutenant Schou was amused by the conduct and dress of the native Congolese for whose homeward journey he was responsible. The stories about the leopard men are told with the same faked scepticism, which only helps confirm the series of unfounded rumours and suspicions. "That type of thing sounds like cock-and-bull-stories, and as an outsider one can barely conceal one's scepticism" (p. 128), reads the beginning of the sensational chapter about the secret societies' murder methods. However, the reporter then presents the facts: in the period between 1918 and 1938, about fifty leopard men were "strung up in gallows", following 112 unsolved leopard murders. And although he admits that "there is a wall of silence around the phenomenon", he nevertheless sees fit to dramatise the leopard men's gruelling initiation rituals with dialogue and stage directions, claws and all. Finally, he summarises the initial scepticism and the final proof by referring to the Tervuren museum's exhibition of a sculpture that depicts a leopard man. "Is the description exaggerated? It is objective. Talk to the Belgian police in the Congo or look at the collection of 'leopard equipment' in Tervuren" (p. 130).

Edvard Andersen's style is balanced, and his approach always aims at compromise: the magic of the old Africa must be contained where it poses a threat to societal order, while at the same time an attempt must be made to save the best elements of the traditions, for instance the Aru'unda people's matriarchal culture, which can help facilitate equal rights for women in modern Africa. Andersen's method of scepticism followed by affirmation anticipates all the

reader's objections in a manner that ultimately lends balance in both style and attitude to the colonial rule's defence. The narrator's own division into naïve guest and critical reporter is a purely rhetorical construction, the ultimate purpose of which is a shrouded reversal of the tourist's and reporter's traditional roles. This results in the impression that any critical attitude towards the colony is, in fact, superficial and touristic, while the positive attitude is both profound and well-founded. The introductory question of why there are no bloody confrontations between whites and blacks in the Congo, and no Mau-Mau as in other African countries, is therefore answered by the casual conclusion that the Congo is the African country in "which there is the best understanding between black and whites" (p. 243). Belgium will do anything to avoid "the usual follies", because "the Belgians are a people who, due to their attitude to life, combine down-to-earth realism with true humanism" (p. 245). While other colonies have given countries their independence only to witness the natives squander all the benefits of the colonial era, letting society dissolve in internal battles or become subject to foreign economical and political powers, the Congo has a unique opportunity to achieve "peace and understanding between two cultures" (p. 244). In the chapter before this celebration of the anniversary of Belgian colonial rule – which we now know came immediately before the Armageddon of independence – Andersen points out the actual reason why Belgium goes to such extensive lengths in order to continue the balanced approach.

In "Belgium's giant base in the desert – Egypt's shadow", a Belgian air force officer's surprised question finally gives a believable answer to the author's initial question: "Did you really think that, in the age of the jet fighter and the nuclear bomb, we would leave it in the hands of our distinguished, black Congo corps to protect this prosperous country?" (p. 227). As the narrator innocently remarks, the enormous military base protects the diamond and uranium mines nearby, as well as being the "outermost redoubt of civilisation", in case Egypt's Soviet imperialist President Nasser ventured south to annex the mineral rich Central Africa. In other words, it is the Iron Curtain and the cold war that dictate the requirements of Edvard Andersen's apparently balanced style. The western powers' fighter planes and nuclear bombs create safety for the writer and ensure that the exploitation can continue, despite Nasser's revolutionary promises to Africa's native population and the leopard men's blind terror, which looms in the background of the contrived image of peace and understanding. The rhetorical reversal of tourist and reporter, and the presentation of the Congo as a success, aims at maintaining this cold war organisation of the world. The travel book is, in reality, a strategic remodelling of the reader's possible reservations about the cold war ideology,

With his 50 published titles, Arne Falk-Rønne is the most productive author of travel books in Denmark. Together with Aage Krarup Nielsen, he founded the mix of scepticism and nostalgia, guilty conscience and adventure, which characterised twentieth-century travel accounts. In principle, the world had already been mapped; thrill and innocence had evaporated, but in the narrative form it was recreated with cleverly staged dramas or dreams. *In Stanley's Footsteps* (1972) is, like Edvard Andersen's book, an anniversary text; however, it was written after the Congo became independent, and was influenced by the related bloody conflicts, especially in the area around Stanleyville/Kisangani. The style is that of a hardboiled journalistic report that will do anything to expose the truth. When the journey and narrative both collapse, because the basis of the project turns out to be meaningless, the contradictory nature of text and era in relation to Africa are exposed in a manner that is uniquely blunt and undisguised.

which – relocated at outposts in Africa – once again feed on the myth that Patrick Brantlinger has called "the rule of darkness".

Like Edvard Andersen's *Adventurous Congo*, Arne Falk-Rønne's *In Stanley's footsteps through Africa. 100 years after his encounter with Livingstone* aims to take stock on the occasion of an anniversary. Much of the text consists of comparisons

between then and now and lengthy paraphrases of Stanley's travel accounts, mixed with the popular travel reporter's own observations in the same locations. His political and rhetorical point of departure, however, is very different from Edvard Andersen's. The Congo did not develop in a peaceful balance between the two cultures, as Edvard Andersen hoped it would; rather, the period leading up to independence in 1960 was increasingly chaotic and for a long time lacking any stable societal organisation. Falk-Rønne's travel routes are therefore limited to the parts of Stanley's journeys that lay outside the frontiers of the Congo, that is, the route from Zanzibar through East Africa to Southern Sudan taken by Stanley on the Emin Pasha Relief Expedition. Falk-Rønne's rhetorical adaptation of Stanley and his legacy becomes increasingly marked by the collapse of the Congo throughout the book – simultaneously causing a collapse of the book's project and form.

In the beginning, *In Stanley's footsteps* maintains a balance. Stanley's achievements, the design of modern, independent African nations, assumptions about the soul of the African people, reflections on Central African links with "the forgotten tribe of Israel" and Falk-Rønne's visits to nightclubs all merge in a narrative that may be very colourful but is held together by the tough reporter's style and attitude. The narrator is still willing to consider conflicts in his experiences and the historical material, and his narrative is close to being a critical exposition. Falk-Rønne's culture-sceptical style is based on insights from his many years as a globetrotter, as well as his thorough research and keen eye for detail, which also manifests itself in his language – though he does not refrain from repeating the most tired clichés, for example about Africa's lack of history: "The shroud of oblivion" covers the centuries, "Yesterday has never been. Tomorrow will never come" (p. 61). Here, history has been reset, and Herodotus and the Old Testament provide the background material for the descriptions of natives and landscape alongside Speke's, Burton's and Stanley's texts and Falk-Rønne's descriptions and photographs on location; all are part of the image of an unchangeable continuum. Africa remains the same, and all these texts can therefore be used freely, regardless of their original context.

On this basis, Falk-Rønne can invent a situation in which he is Stanley's peer and contemporary; at the same time he can make Stanley's discoveries anew, tracing his route with a broader horizon facilitated by retrospect and knowledge of which steps initially looked like progress but turned out to be errors. He is keenly aware of the fact that Stanley's successes were due to his inferiority complex, and he critically assesses Stanley's management skills with the objectivity of a professional, experienced traveller – which also leads him to attack other critics of Stanley for their complete lack of experience in the field. The text thus convincingly constructs a narrator who, on land and at sea, in the archives and in language, is first and foremost a professional – a traveller who is completely confident in every situation, who the reader can safely trust.

Later on in the book, when the descriptions approach the unsafe and insecure border regions of Uganda and South Sudan, the narrator's authority collapses. The reporter's stylistic nihilism and his feigned, self-assured resolution to see everything through leads him into a number of paradoxes that are not solved in the text, but rather carried with him to the next destination and the subsequent chapter. The correct observation, for instance, that Livingstone's story about the battle against the slave trade – the one single event that was the most important 'opener' of Africa – in practice paved the way for new hunting grounds for the slave traders cannot be incorporated into the travel book's fundamentally positive perception of colonialism; instead it grows, together with numerous other unpleasant paradoxes, into a nagging doubt about the journey's and book's project. The conflict between South Sudan's black population and North Sudanese Muslims about a Christian, independent Anyidi republic, which even in the 1970s seemed desperately unsolvable, is analysed part of the way, only for the reporter to give up. Unlike the foreign policy reporters back home, his liberal-mindedness and prejudices are influenced by his experiences as a traveller: "Here I come strolling into the area, starry-eyed, wanting to make up my mind about all sorts of things, while people around me die of sleeping sickness and malaria"; "everything is boggled in my mind" (p. 203). The reporter's professional authority is tested by the persistent meaningless of his experiences, which makes it impossible "to express an opinion" or "make up one's mind and express something absolute and universal" (p. 203). The countless conflicts, ethnic and clan differences and geographical, religious and demographic indeterminacies prevent him gathering the impressions into an experience that could adequately express the text's critical balance between disillusioned scepticism and confidence that the steps Stanley once took in Africa still feel like progress today.

At this point, not only the book's concept, but the entire journey seems to collapse. Despite its critical style, the book was meant to be a celebration of Stanley on the occasion of the anniversary of his meeting with Livingstone. The usual pattern is that the independent African states' combination of totalitarian ideology, Maoism and corruption is criticised more severely than the colonial powers' oppression of native populations, but Falk-Rønne's crisis in Sudan also destabilises this overriding system of values. His stance becomes changeable, often harsh and aggressive, as if he is trying to rebuild moral backbone and rhetorical authority by articulating all the unpleasant truths he has held back until then. Similarly, the travel route and destinations disappear along random tracks into the unknown – at least for the reader. We are no longer following in

Stanley's footsteps, but wandering aimlessly in a Central African zone bordering on the Congo, which is not geographically defined but shrouded in a twilight of terror, meaningless violence, Pygmies and "Pygmy bastards"; everything is described with a mixture of fascination and disgust.

The book's and journey's collapse coincides with Falk-Rønne's attempt to find an acceptable solution to the embarrassing fact that he is not allowed into the Congo, though this was the most important territory on Stanley's exploration. This modern travel reporter, who has found fame by staging himself as a fearless investigator and imitating his predecessor's legendary courage – Stanley never yielded to hostile resistance – must now rely on constructed second hand sources, which he can edit at a safe distance from the conflicts in the Congo. In order not to compromise what is left of his credibility, Falk-Rønne arranges a hazardous rescue of one of the infamous European mercenaries, the so-called "jungle soldiers". The transaction takes place in the Congo's north-eastern border region; it is a peculiar trade-off in which the soldier is granted safe conduct in exchange for his story about the battles in the Congo – the bloody crushing of rebellions, Simbas and leopard men. Falk-Rønne conceals the mercenary's identity and recounts, in indirect speech, his story about the terrors in and around Stanleyville – the heart of darkness Falk-Rønne cannot experience first-hand.

The reporter also arranges an interview with a person who passes himself off as a leopard man who has fled from the Congo; however, this part of the narrative is similarly mysterious. When the two men approach the leopard man's hut, the surroundings grow increasingly "bewitched"; it is "like driving through a tunnel that becomes ever narrower" (p. 333). At the same time, Falk-

Arne Falk-Rønne's selection of images reflects the desperation of the book: photographs like the following, of a victim of cannibalism during rebellions in Stanleyville; bodies driven away in wheelbarrows; drunken Pygmies; or, like on the opposite page, ritualistic dances which the reporter has given up trying to understand, even though the caption suggests an anthropological explanation. In this way, the narrator contributes to the image of Africa as a non-place, which is emphasised by the ironic fact that the journey in Stanley's footsteps does *not* allow for entrance into Zaïre because it is too dangerous; therefore, the reporter is forced to buy second-hand knowledge. On the other hand, Arne Falk-Rønne's wandering takes him to the centre of the conflict between ethnic Africans and Muslim Arabs in South Sudan, which was the indirect trigger of the Emin Pasha expedition, and which is still raging.

"African from the Congo, tortured during the rebellions and a victim of cannibalism", from *In Stanley's Footsteps*.

Rønne makes a detailed account of the credibility of the testimony: he brings with him some Congolese civilians and representatives of the authorities who would be able to verify the story, and only if the leopard man speaks the truth will he receive the agreed payment. The testimony is communicated via an interpreter who struggles a great deal in translating the Swahili into broken English and French, often falling into discussions with the leopard man. The presence of the authorities, and the threats of punishment and promises of reward, must also have influenced the fragmented interview, which the narrator nevertheless ensures is recorded on tape. The leopard man's tale about secret rituals and atrocious acts against white people is rounded off by the narrator's description of long screams in the night and a curse being cast on him, because the leopard man felt forced to tell a story to the detested white man for money.

In the stories about the mercenary and the alleged leopard man, the reporter thus buys testimonies to the Congo's chaotic conflicts, and in both cases there is an implied connection between money, terror, magic and narrative. When the reporter inquires about the rumoured collaboration between Eastern Europeans and leopard men, the witness answers that it is nothing but politics:

"Politics, monsieur! I collaborate with you at this moment for a couple of hundred shillings!" (p. 336). Despite the fact that the story is bought for money, and the myth that the leopard men are a political brand, the reporter is more terrified by the leopard men's magic than the mercenaries' extermination of unwanted elements. Neither the mercenary's feigned first-person narrative nor the narrator's comments attempt to conceal the jungle soldiers' brutality and sadistic pleasure in killing the natives; they are called "mutilators". Nevertheless, Falk-Rønne chooses to place his sympathy with the mercenaries, because despite their profoundly warped sense of morals, they master some measure of technical rationality, which makes it possible to negotiate with them – in contrast with the leopard men's unconditional lust for revenge.

The mercenary's story is bought for 100 dollars, but it takes a long time before the narrator is even on speaking terms with him and can begin taking notes. The action-packed present tense narrative, with filmic descriptions of the bloody, ravaging war, replaces the reporter's own journey and travel account. The leopard man's story, bought for 200 shillings, replaces any real judgement of what is myth and what is politics in the many rumours – even though the story is acquired by means of threats and promises. In other words, these two accounts replace the narrator's own account after it has collapsed. They fill a rhetorical and critical vacuum in the book, enabling Falk-Rønne to communicate by proxy a way out of the journey's labyrinthine wanderings far away from Stanley's footprints, towards an end to the book. However, a logical consequence of this design is that the last part of the book lacks both a narrator and a traveller; it merely consists of repetitions of points about gorillas, Pygmies and Stanley's final, failed expedition. The travel account has compromised its credibility and collapsed as a valid form, whether of history, phenomenological challenge or testimony about the world. The testimony of an eyewitness who also makes critical enquiries about the things he encounters on his journey, was one aspect of the ethos and raison d'être of the classical genre, while the other was the ability and will to capture a genuine source of wonder and formulate new questions. Both aspects degenerate when the eyewitness is bought and his testimony passed off in place of the travel writer's own experience.

Tragic Tourism and Gothic Science: *The Black Heart* and *The River*

The term 'tragic tourism' is usually associated with a fairly recent phenomenon, often characterised as a trait of postmodern culture, in which travellers visit historic locations that possess some special power of attraction because their close or distant relatives have been subjected to abuse or massacres there. Afro-Americans visit places in Africa from where slaves were shipped; Jews visit

concentration camps to commemorate the dead and memorialise the events as unique and unrepeatable. The tragic element is obviously directly linked to the nature of the event, but it is also linked to the fact that the traveller is often unable to identify exactly what happened, or where and to whom it happened. The traveller is thus confronted with a crisis their search for identity and origin. The apparent paradox of the term 'tourism' in this context is due to the fact that this traffic is organised as mass culture: the traveller will remain in a superficial relation to the place in question for reasons that are both tragic and postmodern.

With very few exceptions, this is the formula for all travel accounts from the Congo; the journey up the river to Stanleyville or Kisangani is nearly always accompanied by the story of the colony from the arrival of the first Portuguese to the traveller's present. This classical characteristic of the accounts serves to dramatise a situation in which the traveller is presented as knowledgeable and determined, following in the footsteps of others and claiming authority and credibility from predecessors' observations. The traveller also becomes someone who daringly transcends these predecessors' beaten paths by making or inventing new wondrous discoveries.

However, most of the travel accounts that have an eye for the bloody past of the Congo, faithfully paraphrasing Conrad or Casement for example when they pass Stanley Falls, invoke the past in heroic versions, which we have seen exemplified in Edvard Andersen's and Arne Falk-Rønne's texts – although the collapse in the latter brings it close to tragic tourism. Our two final examples of popular cultural 'readings' of the Congo as a fascinating place in literature and geography put the tragic elements in the foreground of their narratives.

Paul Hyland's *The Black Heart. A Voyage into Central Africa* (1988) is a typical variety of the postmodern travel account, which is closely related to the phenomenon of tragic tourism, though its journey does not address any single, specific historical tragedy. Together with his wife, Noëlle, Hyland wants to travel from the mouth of the Congo River to its sources, ending with a detour to Shaba, the district around the Elisabethville of colonial times – present day Lubumbashi – and the minefield of Katanga, where Dan Crawford, Hyland's great-uncle, wrote and conducted research at the end of the nineteenth century. As was the case with Andersen and Falk-Rønne, the occasion is an anniversary – the 100th anniversary of the foundation of the EIC Free State – and Hyland's plan is to follow Conrad's, Casement's and Crawford's travel routes by using their travel books, letters and diaries as 'maps' on the journey. *The Black Heart* aims to trawl through the history and present-day culture of the Congo in order both to celebrate and criticise the country to which the author feels personally attached, through the family connection and gifts that are rich in memories, for

The Black Heart (1988) is another anniversary text, about a journey not in Stanley's footsteps but rather in Conrad's and Casement's, 100 years after the foundation of the Free State. The journey takes place in the form of 'tragic tourism', seeking out places and bits of text that express terror and misery particularly aptly. The text pretends to be an existential quest for meaning and origin, but the result is mere repetition and kitsch.

instance a comb from Katanga and an arrow from Equateur. Hyland "wanted to look at the old white myths of the Dark Continent in today's light" (p. 12), but also longs to visit the place where Conrad's Kurtz is buried and see where "Casement investigated Congo Free State atrocities".

By way of introduction, Hyland describes his concerns and speculations about the forthcoming journey; will his marriage for instance survive the endeavours? He then recounts a nightmare that has been tormenting him for some time:

"As a child I had a recurring nightmare: the world rolled towards me. It was not a school globe with clear-cut coloured counties but all clouds and oceans and half-hidden continents, massive and ethereal. It spun heavily, rolled onwards, nearer, nearer, never reaching me but always crushing me with horror. Recently I woke from another dream: I am chasing three men into darkness. I follow them into the night and at dawn I am still running. But now they are chasing me. I look over my shoulder; still I can't see them, the sun is behind them, they are back-lit ghosts. I shorten my stride, weary, utterly visible, defenseless against the burning light" (Hyland, p. 12).

Effectively placing the literary rather than believable nightmare as a portal to the travel account, Hyland defines a personal, existential motive for his journey, which is more profound than external circumstances such as anniversaries and family souvenirs. The nightmare is related to the author's initiation as traveller and travel writer, in the form of a tragic, paranoid vision of the world and the world map. In the subsequent passage, the three men in the nightmare are introduced as Conrad, Casement and Crawford, who were all in the Congo in 1890. At first, the author is chasing them, then later they are chasing him, while he feels exposed and defenceless. This part of the dream about the globe seems paraphrase Conrad's famous anecdote about a time when, as a child, he would look at the world map, putting his finger on the blank spot – inner Congo – and confidently promise himself that he would go there. As we know, the journey turned out to be a disappointment for the adult Conrad; however, in Hyland's case, disappointment has become a tragic basic condition for the child, which the adult aims to mend through travelling and writing. The nineteenth-century completion of the renaissance and enlightenment era's mapping project had made the world a strange and hostile place, and a new beginning must involve the rewriting of the myths about "the Dark Continent in today's light", which in the dream are reworked as a merciless illumination of the author himself.

In Hyland's text, the rhetorical antithesis between light and darkness – the figure around which most travel accounts from Africa are organised – is unfolded with a particular fascination for the dark pole, as is evident in the title "*The Black Heart*". Hyland's journey, which – with reference to the comb from Katanga, the arrow from Equateur and the 100th anniversary – is a kind of tourism, is thus introduced as tragic and black: Crawford's travel book *Thinking Black*, Conrad's *Heart of Darkness* and Casement's *"Black Diaries"* are the maps, and the main travel destinations are sites of massacres and atrocities. Although it is difficult to follow the author's attempt to present the journey as necessary and attractive – "The plan was seductive enough. Now Noëlle and I had to live it" – the journey and travel description are linked to a peculiarly intriguing, misanthropic search for and description of memorials to the terrors of the past. Its discoveries facilitate a view of the present as a meaningless dissolution of the connections between culture, history and traditions: either expressed through the empty mundanity of the brothels, or through sudden, sporadic admiration of natives as 'noble savages' – for example in when people rowing on the river appear to the author as if they had just emerged from a reservation.

The composition of the book follows the classic formula of the geography of the river, including in this structure the individual memorials as 'dense' points of geography and history, reflected in chapter titles like "Black Gold", "The Haunted Path", "Journeying Deep", "A Muddy Hole", "The Inner Station", "Black Thoughts" and so on. The descriptions of the actual travel experiences and contemporary culture are limited to lists of views and meals, which appear to be merely a backdrop for the proper course of events that takes place in dialogue with Conrad, Casement and Crawford – and, in addition, long passages from and paraphrases of Stanley's travel books, supplemented with André Gide. Whenever Hyland sketches a view or visits a village, they are compared with far longer passages from Stanley's description of the same view, Casement's report about diseases and depopulation in the area or the cryptic notes of *"The Black Diary"*. And when Hyland watches the river, he immediately replaces his own observation with Gide's: "If you look over the gunwale and peer downwards the water it is opaque and, as André Gide observed, of a frightening thickness, however it sparkles off the blade of a paddle" (p. 22). In this sense, it is a dense and impenetrable web of other texts, which replace Hyland's own story – not only interrupting him, but also feeling things in his place, because the tragic, existential motivation is always in the foreground: Hyland feels Graham Greene's spleen as a "burnt-out case". We receive no information about the reason for his gloom; instead we are told about Gide's existential angst and Casement's indignation in his diaries, rather than his cool analysis in the report to the foreign ministry. Conrad's most embittered passages become speech bubbles in the travel book's endeavour to surpass its predecessors' mythology about the continent in 'darkness'.

The compositional linkage of river and history lead to a representation of past and present as simultaneous aspects of a uniform stream in which Hyland, for example, takes *Heart of Darkness* with him to bed, dreams about it and in the daytime does not see – or at least relate – anything that Conrad has not already related. Hyland's introductory nightmare is therefore a precise omen of the fact that his "chase" of the three dark authors is reversed, so that they are chasing him. On the one hand, Hyland is shrivelling in the shadow of his predecessors; on the other, he is exposed and illuminated as a charlatan, who merely stages the terror and undertakes the journey in order to lend a profundity to his authorship which it does not in reality possess.

Paul Hyland's introductory description of the nightmare indicates his fear of being exposed, while at the same time displaying the deceit on the basis of which the book is written. In other passages, the author suggests that the tragedy of the travel book is due not to his obligation to some existential conflict, nor to the historical dimension of the journey and the archival material, but rather to the author's difficulties with writing a travel account at all.

"Now I watch Noëlle watching Africa. Like the explorers, we have to hack our way into the heart. We cannot overfly ourselves to see where we are. We are too close. The observer affects the observed, attracts and repels the spirit's elementary particles. The uncertainty principle. The past is easier than the present, and the future only lasts so long" (p. 209).

With reference to Heisenberg's uncertainty principle, the author appears to provide a sophisticated explanation of the travellers' difficulty in perceiving themselves as travellers; however, it also precisely defines the book's difficulties with describing and relating to the world in which the Hylands find themselves. The problem is not that they are influencing the world they want to describe, but that they are doing everything they can to keep their distance instead of delving into the future, which is easier than delving into the past; other people's travel accounts are safe space which they can sample without committing to anything except diffuse, pathetic statements about "black thoughts".

Prompted, among other things, by dreams in which Conrad's heart of darkness is supplanted by Rider Haggard's more promising descriptions of twin mountains as the breasts of the earth, the ending of the book is a dedication to Hyland's relative, Dan Crawford, who was known for his "goodness, strength and love", and whose reputation as a poet, visionary, pioneer and explorer finally turns out to be the trophy that the author has coveted from the beginning. When he finds himself in a museum in Crawford's former home, he himself feels at home, even though he is "as far from home as I have been, in the house of my great-uncle. I, the youngest of thirty-six cousins, part of a tribe tight-knit by its sense of self, scattered across the world - Australia, Tasmania, New Zealand, India, America, England - but no longer on African soil" (p. 256). The home is a library full of travel books, and the ending thus becomes the beginning, where Hyland can write his account both as tragic tourism and as a work of travel literature in the tradition of his canonised predecessors. The travel plan has reached a satisfactory point of completion; Hyland has found himself and united his family, whose chronicle is now inscribed in the history of literature and exploration. The tragedy seems to have been survived and even conquered.

The element of the tragic, however, is never more than an excuse for recounting the predecessors' accounts of atrocities - the evil dreams. This literary design adds existential depth to the account and conceals its actual meaninglessness, which is rooted in the fact that Hyland has nothing to tell and no one to chase. Whereas Conrad mythologised the Congo by condensing its significance in the metaphor of the "heart of darkness", we encounter not condensation but thickening in Hyland's dense, multi-layered paraphrases that replace independent observation. Even from the outset, the travel writer has renounced the authority which is a precondition for the credibility of the genre and the traveller's ability to set his own course. The result is a repetitious text haunted by literary "ghosts", who are not associated with wonder, and challenge neither the traveller nor the reader. Similarly, the world becomes a globe that threatens to catch up with the traveller, rather than vice versa. If Conrad's novel can be characterised as an "unreadable report" because the ending does not shed retrospective light on the events – the plot deconstructing itself – *The Black Heart* is unreadable because the text's ambition to become literature ends up in "black thoughts" and kitsch.

Paul Hyland's 1988 travel book provides an example of a recent tendency in such accounts of introducing the reader to a more or less feigned value crisis from the outset, which functions as an excuse to go on a journey that is chiefly defined by the author's reading of selected predecessors. These elements are either overtly or implicitly employed as the travel book's main motivation, while the journey itself plays a secondary part as a mere opportunity for dramatising the historical accounts. We are dealing with a devaluation of the classic genre characteristics of the travel account, which prescribed a dual focus on expectations based on an orthodox knowledge about the other, and on transgressions and obstacles that legitimised the journey as meaningful. Tragic tourism, as found in *The Black Heart* and Jeffrey Taylor's *Facing the Congo* (2000) – another 'dark travelogue' containing the same series of desperate, crisis-ridden visits to the most tragic memorials on the great river – imitates the conventions of its predecessors without, however, contributing or learning anything new, and it therefore remains purely an exercise in style.

Central Africa – especially the area by the great waterfalls around Stanleyville, present day Kisangani, where Stanley overcame some of his hardest struggles on his way across the continent and in his 'opening' of Africa – has since Conrad's *Heart of Darkness* been described as a unique territory. It has been depicted through special rhetorical mechanisms, which – via a vast number of literary, historical, legal, geographical and anthropological discourses – define a state of emergency in which neither evil nor irrationality can be disciplined. While this topography is an unnatural construct, though founded on geo-physical structures in the landscape, it is so persistent that it appears to be an essential condition. One final, particularly striking, example of the area's availability for hypotheses about the origin of evil is a controversial, although influential, doctrine pertaining to the origin of AIDS.

Edward Hooper's *The River. A Journey back to the source of HIV and AIDS* (1999) is a detailed, thoroughly researched 1000-page contribution to support the claim that AIDS is the result of a series of experiments conducted during

the development of the polio vaccine. The experiments were carried out in the Stanleyville area, and, according to the theory, the virus spread from there to the Central African region including the eastern and northern districts of the Congo, Uganda and Rwanda, which today witness the world's most extensive epidemics with up to 75 % of the population ill and 12 million children orphaned by the disease. The theory is controversial and has been rejected by the medical establishment, who persistently incline towards the so-called 'hunter' hypothesis, according to which the HIV virus was transferred from chimpanzees to humans during the natives' hunting and butchering of them – a theory that has since then been substantiated via a number of studies. One of Edward Hooper's insistent claims, which justifies the extensive magnitude and documentary meticulousness of the book – and furthermore makes it read as a thriller – is that the transfer of the virus to humans via an experimental oral polio vaccine, the so-called OPV hypothesis, is the subject of a conspiracy between the pharmaceutical industry and researchers, who refuse to admit that the worldwide epidemic is a result of disastrously careless animal testing and vaccination programmes. The book's plot is determined by Hooper's endeavour to find, substantiate and present evidence for the OPV hypothesis. Alternating between historical, legal and medical discourses, the book presents disclosures of the opponents' conspiracy, covert agreements, concealment and disposal of evidence from the laboratory reports, and so on. Everything is treated from within a mixture of journalistic and literary genres – gothic romance and detective novel being the most striking.

Nevertheless, the book manages to unite the scientific exposition, two major plots and many genres in its composition, which organises the vast material in accordance with a classical structure: the journey back to the source. This is a repetition of a formula we have already examined, in which explorers and travellers who have visited the sources of the Nile have regarded them as the cradle of both culture and history. However, Edward Hooper reverses the figure so that the source is not the beginning of civilisation, but its destruction. The reversal is a powerful rhetorical effect in the book's effort to persuade the reader. There is much at stake: the global pharmaceutical industry and the global disease. According to the author, however, the reversal is based on facts. Hilary Koprowski's research centre is located just outside Stanleyville – a place which, in the rhetorical tradition, has been inextricably linked with Conrad's "inner station" or "heart of darkness". This allows Hooper to describe his own actual journey back to the crime scene to interview the locals who captured the chimpanzees for the vaccine development programme, while employing a metaphoric structure that, in the middle of the medical argumentation, contains permanent reference to Conrad's decadence and gothic. The implication is obviously, although it is not said in so many words, that Koprowski is a Kurtz who has transgressed the original, civilising aim of the project and transformed it into its barbaric opposite. The chapter titles guide this metaphorical reading by structuring the argument like posts on a river journey – "The Passage through the pools", "Whirlpools and sinkholes", "From trickle to flood: The early spread of AIDS", etc. – and the research centre, Le Laboratoire Médical de Stanleyville, is described as a reinforced, inaccessible fort in the middle of the wilderness, where the border between animal and human is being transgressed. The medical, legal and critical-journalistic discourses, all of which use empirical evidence, tests, testimonies and archival materials, are thus entrenched in a gothic and decadent reading, where the element of fascination is no longer determined by true and false, but facilitated by uncanny allusions to the transmission of the virus from animals to humans, parasites penetrating the body's septum and membranes, the immune system being destroyed, and so on.

We have seen multiple examples of the gothic pathology that permeated travel accounts around the turn of the century, both in medical discourses such as Parke's – Stanley's field physician during the Emin Pasha Relief Expedition – and in the form of literary metaphors about the advance of civilisation as a bacterial infection along the capillary network of the river in Jürgensen's text. In Hooper's book, this becomes an apocalyptic vision of man's self-inflicted downfall.[159] According to the book, the rejection of the OPV hypothesis is preventing effective measures being implemented to stop the disease from spreading, as well as effective preventatives being applied in similar experiments involving gene technology and animal testing. The *fin de siècle* motif that sees the end of the century as the end of history and humankind is made concrete, not in the form of Conrad's exaggerated ideas of the cooling of the Earth, but in a terrifying vision of viral aliens who invade and take over the human body. In his search for the origin of AIDS, Edward Hooper may have done nothing but follow leads recognised by the medical establishment, which take him to Central Africa and the Congo, where the first documented case of HIV-1 was found in 1959. This is the region of the world where contact between chimpanzee and human is most common, and contamination therefore most likely – the region which happens to be known as the heart of darkness. Another possibility, however, in this literary reading of the book, is that he has followed leads from Conrad's *Heart of Darkness*, which take him to Hilary Koprowski's "inner station" and a paranoid interpretation of the impenetrable web of reports, testimonies and rumours of exchanges between man and animal.

Gothic pathology and literary rhetoric play important roles in *The River*, indicating the significance of *Heart of Darkness* as a background for Hooper's "conspiracy theory".[160] Furthermore, it builds on a century of popular fiction about the place and the notion that at this very location on Earth, the conditions favour transformations of humans to apes or leopards – or vice versa. This notion is already there in Professor Bill Hamilton's preface, in which Hooper is presented as an "explorer" who follows in the footsteps of Burton and Livingstone, but with the intention of delving even deeper into our past. Reading this book is like following an explorer

"making his halting progress toward some centre of mystery that is far inland from the obvious coastal hills which we have all been seeing. Most strangely, as it may seem at first, his story wends toward exactly the same centre of Africa as those Victorian explorers sought. This comes to seem a little less strange, however, once we reflect on our evolutionary origins" (*The River*, p. xxxiv).

Just before this passage, Hamilton has recommended that Hooper be given the Nobel Prize for his effort to uncover a great void of ignorance behind science's knowledge, subsequently expanding this image with the repetition of Conrad's figure of the visible coastal areas and the hidden hinterland. However, this mysterious centre behind science's "obvious coastal hills" is tself embedded in an even more profound figure, in which myth and science converge in the same trope: the area that includes Uganda, Rwanda and the eastern part of the Congo is also thought of as the origin of man, though paleoanthropologists locate the place of origin farther south. "Upright we became ... trying for new social structures, for tools, for speech, for fire ... finally out of Africa, our home, there came this new disease and on its heels, in this case, a *written* drama of *how* it came" (p. xxxiv, Hamilton's ellipses and emphasis). The first human drama takes place at the dawn of time, with no critical reporters to follow the event closely. However, it is also a success story that has culminated in mankind's scientific and technological domination of the world. The second drama is the spreading of AIDS from the same mysterious centre in the borderland between savannah and jungle, the place where evolutionary leaps are made. Here, the first drama is reversed: in biotechnological hubris, technology and science have interfered with the nature of species, transgressing their own ethos and causing their own fall. The journalist gets revenge on the scientist as the animal catches up with the human.

Laboratory tests on tissue from lungs, testicles and kidneys from elephants, turtles and in particular chimpanzees are mentioned almost in the same breath as descriptions of meals that include meat from apes and discussions about corruption and deleted archives. The people Hooper contacts for interviews in Belgium or the Congo disappear under suspicious circumstances, die because of war or disease – including AIDS and new, unexplained diseases. 300-400 chimpanzees are captured with the help of 150-200 natives, mostly Pygmies. The apes die from pneumonia and other diseases, which they get from humans, and the dead animals have the flesh melted off their bones – if the natives do not eat it first – so that the remains can be kept as scientific material in the cellars under the colonial museum in Tervuren. Everything is described in gruelling detail, including how the entire industry in the wisdom of hindsight raises ethical issues relating to those involved, who admit that hunting chimpanzees is a violation of the principles of protection of endangered species, and that it is unpleasant because the animals look like human beings.

The fundamental themes of *The River* are not far from those of thriller films, such as *Congo*, which we will investigate below. In several respects, the book can even be perceived as a radical exploitation of the myths about Central Africa as the origin of both life and evil, in which the connections between corrupt science and the rhetorical superposition of chimpanzees, Pygmies, natives and degenerate scientists seem never-ending. The last page of the book gathers the clues into the single image of the river, which is first "our great river of Science"; second, it is a metaphor for the passage of time, where the past is shrouded in darkness, the present is a flickering "heat-haze" of "sizzle and glimmer" and the future is apocalyptically "suffused with red"; third, it is the transport route via which Hooper finally leaves the Congo; and fourth, of course, it is the literary river that Conrad created in his novel a hundred years before. Like the camp in which the experiments took place, the river boat is described as a defiled Noah's ark: "This great floating community, with its own doctors and traders and cooks and prostitutes, this body of crushed humanity, is one of the means whereby the virus may have been transported down to the capital, and onward to the world at large" (*The River*, p. 825). The captain navigates among water hyacinths, which were once introduced to beautify the river, but today only poison it with dangerous, impenetrable isles of tangled tissue. He sticks to the course, taking no "shortcuts" or "bold initiatives" that might put his entrusted "community" at risk. "He knows that the well-being and safe passage of the people on board are his responsibility, and he takes his job seriously" (p. 826).

Hooper ends his book with a pathetic, apocalyptic vision that reaches back to the rhetorical patterns of the myth about the Dark Continent, and is particularly influenced by Conrad's novel. It is a cultivation of the unexplained as mysterious and impenetrable, and the nostalgic longing for a captain who sticks to his "simple truths".

An alternative hypothesis about the origin of AIDS that is both more probable and closer to the colonial problem is only implicitly and rhetorically present in Hooper's quest. The so-called "colonialism theory" or "*Heart of Darkness* theory" – an expansion of the orthodox "hunter" hypothesis – attempts to

explain how the transmission could take place between the hunter and his prey. The man behind the theory, primatologist Jim Moore, suggested in 2000 that the transfer of SIV from chimpanzees, and its transformation into the HIV virus, was caused by the labour camps that were built in the Congo around 1900 and were for many years inhabited by forced labourers in remote areas of the Ituri Forest. The lack of food led to intensive ape hunting, and the weakness of the labourers' immune systems, which had deteriorated due to slavery, starvation and disease, facilitated the transfer of the virus. Furthermore, the cases were not detected or registered quickly enough, because the number of deaths was already very large.

The Congo in Oblivion

In recent years, there have been significant exhibitions in the Nordic region of objects and stories that bear witness to Scandinavians' contribution to the colonisation of the Congo. Naturally, these exhibitions have not been intended as propaganda, like those of the museum in Tervuren or Börrison's travelling missionary museum; instead, they have tried to communicate both the fascination with and critical distance from the historical images presented to the modern audience. Travel accounts and original photographs convey a strong sense of authenticity and realism, while it is rightly emphasised that all such testimonies are historical and therefore rooted in the attitudes of their time. Even critical accounts do not distance themselves from colonialism as such, but demonstrate the writers' positions in the colony as missionaries, officers, privates or prominent officials. Another key feature of the exhibitions has been the fact that they are dealing with forgotten, perhaps repressed, history. The function of the museums is to administrate national cultural heritage, which in this case means reintroducing material that was initially discarded through historical processes while at the same time meeting the globalised demand for national histories to be contextualised within the dynamics of Nordic and international developments.[161]

A brief look at the National Museum of Denmark's databases will reveal the vastness of the material available to the curators of exhibitions on the Congo. A large part of it consists of travel accounts from the founding of the Free State, and later, from the period as a Belgian colony, diaries written by doctors and nurses at the Danish hospital in Kinshasa - which was Denmark's first active development aid effort; still later, there are accounts from Danish UN soldiers stationed in Congo in the chaotic period after independence. By exhibiting this material, the museums contribute to the commemorative effort made in books such as Peter Tygesen's *The Congo – I Presume* and the highly praised *Congo. A*

History by David Reybrouck, to which we will return. However, the exhibitions do not have the same options that particularly Tygesen makes use of in his prose, surmounting a number of the limitations that have been highlighted in this part of the book. In comparison, the exhibitions are often strikingly silent or discreet, in relation both to their material's internal conflicts and their own selection criteria. Curators appear to have defined a balance between, on the one hand, maintaining a curiosity towards the foreign, including the shocking effect of hinting at unimaginable horror, and, on the other hand, establishing a constructive, forward-looking and hopeful expectation of a better future, based among other factors on the first UN-monitored democratic general election in 2006. The creation of this overriding narrative balance, however, sheds conciliatory light on the historic testimonies, which are not challenged fundamentally for their ethical, rhetorical or aesthetic positions.

Discussion of the travel accounts' value as historical sources is also almost non-existent in the exhibitions – perhaps because the museums' function is founded on and legitimised by the credibility of their sources. In relation to the Congo, travel accounts are not presented as illustrations of subjective interpretations of history, but rather as kaleidoscopic history writing retold in an accumulative collage of citations. Attention is thus diverted from what has been described above as the inherent repression of Congolese history – something that applies to the rhetorical design of most twentieth-century travel accounts. And while the museums' pioneer work of obtaining and organising the abundant material is a splendid feat, the texts' rhetorical forms are being overlooked – resulting in what we might phrase *a repression of repression*. Exhibitions and their catalogues often ask the question *why* Scandinavians' contribution to colonialism in the Congo has been forgotten until recently, and the implied answer is a guilty postcolonial conscience or a lack of desire to take responsibility.

The present book's readings of exemplary travel accounts, however, provide a different answer. Across differences in time and genre, these texts were actively contributing to a large-scale, profound forgetfulness even while they were being produced, which not only reduced and repressed Congolese history and autobiographical testimonies about Scandinavian collaboration – it also created a template for textual oblivion. When Freiesleben writes without any shame about his theft of a village's fetish, ending the anecdote by admitting that he has unlawfully stolen the life force from the place and can expect the gods' wrath, we are obviously dealing with a mock confession. The aim of the anecdote is to consolidate the notion that the Congo is in a state of emergency, where normal legal and ethical rules are suspended and where natives and their gods are powerless against the powerful stranger. Nevertheless, the text

is in some sense stricken by the wrath of the gods, since the fetishisation of the fetish – the reification and aestheticisastion Freiesleben performs – does not bring life but death to the text, which comes across as self-obsessed, fake, underhand and cliché-ridden. Similarly, when Jungsbøll tells the story of his use of the chicote despite writing that it is one he would rather forget, he does so with so many reversals of right and wrong, and so many conditions applying to the validity of the testimonies, that not only the unlawful violation but also the account have *already* been blotted out. For the same reason, the people the texts try to present as wonders – black women, Pygmies and leopard men – are completely devoid of wonder; they are mere imitations, and therefore do not function as phenomenological rifts in time.

Martini and Schønberg's travel account and several of the other accounts, letters and diaries from the pioneer era of the Free State mentioned in Jenssen-Tusch's monumental work are characterised by an astonishing – and today disturbing – naivety, which allows them to describe the events as entertaining scenes without losing their credibility, among other reasons because the writers never question their right to be there. The texts are neither apologetic nor critically humanistic in relation to colonialism, but their unique combination of naivety and credibility makes them appear objective, despite their obvious shortcomings. They paint a stark but lively picture of history as random, meaningless violence and death. After the Reform Association's campaign, the pattern changed: travel accounts often chose either the apologetic or critical position, regardless of the fact that these attitudes built their historical narratives on repressed material, which was strongly influenced by events in each writer's own time such as the rise of fascism or the cold war.

Without the Reform Association's documentary style of displaying atrocities and testimonies, the critical tradition adopted elements from the abolitionists' rhetoric, where indignation and appeals to the reader's conscience were balanced by melodramatic sentimentality and aesthetic romanticism – but as a kind of Biedermeier kitsch, in which neither the writer's sense of art nor his sense of self is challenged, as was the case in nineteenth-century orientalism travel literature. The apologetic position, on the other hand, constructed its exotic and exclusive account on the basis of a state of emergency that included historical, legal and rhetorical matters, and within which the Reform Association's critical objections can only be traced in an indirect, masked defence of the necessity of unlawful exercise of power.

Among the Danish accounts, it is only Knud Jespersen's *A Danish officer's Congo journey* (1930) that seems able to avoid this pattern of either sentimental criticism or fake admiration: Jespersen stays loyal towards the colonial project and stands by his own contribution, whilst his criticism of brutality and misuse of power is merciless. He writes about the state of affairs in the district under the aforementioned Jürgen Jürgensen, who he describes as "hyper-nervous", plagued by paranoia and trying desperately to escape an area that has for a long time been at the mercy of his subordinates' meaningless violence. Although Jespersen has been assigned to assist Jürgensen, the latter flees in the belief that the "law" is after him. This account adds a biographical dimension to Jürgensen's stories about the outpost, while self-critically drawing attention to the many aspects of what in his novels he calls the "espionage system". Jespersen's report "was surely a mosaic work, consisting of true accounts, cover ups, explanations, selections, suggestions, etc. – all with intention" (Jespersen, p. 51). It is therefore perceived to be a highly credible source, for instance by Samuel Nelson in his *Colonialism in the Congo Basin 1880-1940*.

However, this is the exception from the rule that says the colony is in a state of emergency and a number of discourses are therefore exempt from their normal obligations. Even the two anniversary texts – from before and after the Congo's independence – perpetuate this figure, though they pretend to be sober, objective and committed to history. The reporter's critical, inquisitive model in Edvard Andersen's text is a cloak for the cold war defence of all the barbaric necessities of the 'atomic age', and Arne Falk-Rønne's attempt to reconstruct Stanley's journeys through an unbiased account of the current political situation in Central Africa disintegrates in a manner that exemplifies the general collapse of the writing of both historical and travel accounts – in both cases literally selling out as regards credibility. From the perspective of the present book, the collapse of the travel account as reportage is not limited to these two particular examples, but applies to the genre at a whole. Crucially, the apocalyptic vision of such texts is not linked to experiences made on the journey; it is already installed as the point of departure and effectively determines the plot.

Åke Sparring's *With Søren and Anne to Congo* (1963) is an example of the new attitude to teaching in the sixties, when social studies, geography and natural history were blended in a cross-disciplinary approach. This includes a critical attitude towards the colonial past and a positive attitude towards collaboration with the new independent state. Søren and Anne travel with their parents, who have jobs in the mining city of Elisabethville. When their grandmother pays them a surprise visit, they show her around the big country. The father's instructive monologues provide an overview of the country's geography and societal structure, including a brief but candid account of the terrors of King Léopold's 'red rubber', highlighting, with indignation, the extraordinary 700 % returns that he made on the investment. Subsequently, the history is presented in a more didactic form through dialogues between the parents and the grandmother.

ÅKE SPARRING
MED
SØREN OG ANNE
TIL
Kongo
BRANNER OG KORCH

Jørgen Clevin's drawings illustrate the chapter "Blood Rubber", which begins with the following words: "–You are probably already aware how it happened when white people conquered Africa? began Dad, when he was about to talk about rubber after dinner. – Well, yes, that was not at all pleasant, said Søren". The father sums up his history lesson with the comment, "– Nowadays they don't do it like that in the Congo". However, he is contradicted by the grandmother who believes that the conditions could be better. In the pedagogical style of the era, pros and cons are carefully balanced, while colonial history is out of sight.

The father, and especially the mother, resist the grandmother's accusations and appeal to her for patience by referring to the country's huge challenges: "– Forward, forward, snorted granny. Of course, things are moving forward. You wouldn't want them to move backwards, would you? But the question is how quickly things should go forward. – There, there, said mum. Things are not that bad. Granny looked at her. – Let me tell you one thing, my little girl. The white people who live down here are suddenly becoming completely blunted" (p. 45). The grandmother occupies the same role as Per Just or Edvard Andersen's naïve "guest", immediately reacting to the situation on the basis of European standards, but she is lectured about the unique case of the country by the parents, who occupy the role of the reporter.

V. M. Aubert's *Letters from the Congo and Elsewhere* (1908) is a collection of letters written under the pen name Bille to Norwegian newspapers in 1905 and 1906, during which time he was a judge in Stanleyville. The first letter states the aim of entertaining "the large bloc of consumers of newspapers, whose knowledge of the Congo probably dissolves in lots of more or less empty words such as: Livingstone, Stanley and Emin Pasha, – King Léopold, – very big country, – damned climate, caoutchouc, ivory and abuse of the natives; however, through this one has already displayed general education and compassion with the wretched blacks!" (p. 4). The style of these letters can be seen either as condescending towards the readers, or as part of a concerted effort to address the educated reader who despises the rabble's superficial knowledge, which is based on newspapers and bestsellers. The collection also contains letters from boat journeys along the Norwegian coast and skiing trips in the mountains. Unlike the Congo letters, these appear to be addressed to a select circle of

friends, illustrating the gap between the vast mob of newspaper readers and the intimate circle of "doctors, lawyers, engineers and officers" who, in the preface, are mentioned as "Bille's many friends". The irony is thus an early example of the pattern in which the text operates between two reader positions, which are put into dialectical interplay in order to legitimise and sanction the state of emergency for which the text pleads. The implication is that compassion for the natives on the basis of assumed abuse is a reaction of the rabble, clearly in conflict with knowledge and education. Bille is obviously referring to Morel's reform campaign, and his letters are a comprehensive, lengthy defence of King Léopold's colonial rule in the Congo. Rhetorically, they appeal to a traditional solidarity among the class of educated government officers, who – according to his logic – must be sceptical of Morel's mass propaganda, later to be classed as rumours associated with the rabble: "they are screaming so loudly about it in England" (p. 11).

Bille's letters will not be studied in detail here. They are displays of all the worst prejudices about Africans imaginable, continuing the manipulation with the double reader position launched in the first letter. However, given that Bille's hidden agenda is to refute the Reform Association's accusations, he also invokes his legal authority as a judge, and his formulation of the state of emergency thus becomes conspicuous and precarious, establishing a pattern that is distinguishable in subsequent travel accounts. In the letter "Justice among Negroes", this duality is expressed though a series of changing positions: an accusation – for example about the use of the chicote – is initially refuted only to be answered more moderately later on, in a peculiar process that simultaneously accepts and belittles the accusation. Accusations are typically refuted with reference to the colony's laws and decrees, which do not allow physical punishment, and in that respect are far more protective of workers against "bodily offense" – even to the point of mentioning the possible punishment of those who unlawfully use the chicote; everybody is equal before the law. The moderated answer admits that the chicote is used for physical punishment, but only towards soldiers and state workers, and always "very moderately". Moreover, it is understood that flogging is the only thing that works with Negroes, given that imprisonment only encourages the culprits to cultivate their inherent laziness. State workers have signed written contracts in which they give their consent to physical punishment, and since the Congolese appear to enjoy the method, "the general argument against flogging" does not apply to a "Congo Negro" – "that it degrades the individual, blunts his self-esteem, depraves his mind, lowers his human worth and makes him unfit for civil society" (p. 56). Also, the Negroes' skin is tanned by the sun and wind, and "therefore it probably does not induce excessive pain when the leather strap hits their leather backs" (p. 57).

The question of whether the situation constituted slavery or alternatively an "obligation to work" as a fair reciprocation of Léopold's philanthropic investment in the country's future, as well as other items on the Reform Association's agenda, are treated in a similar manner. In the same passage, the Norwegian judge in Stanleyville manages to assert the letter of the law and plead for the necessity of allowing for exemptions when the law is enforced in practice. The legal aspect of the argument is pure syllogism and precludes anyone from questioning, for instance, the natives' right to disagree with the stipulations in their contract with the state, while the practical side of the argumentation states examples – like the cases of Jungsbøll and Freiesleben – for the fact that there is tacit agreement on, and acceptance of, breaches of the law. This is an aporia; it is also a logical contradiction that would not obviously stand legal examination. The use of letter form, which traditionally feigns intimacy and confidentiality between sender and receiver, and the legal discourse, which speaks in favour of a state of emergency, reveals a template for twentieth-century travel accounts, which – regardless of individual writers' potentially good intentions – achieves nothing but oblivion.

As mentioned by Sven Lindqvist and Adam Hochschild, the Musée Royal de l'Afrique Centrale in Tervuren has been a telling example of the Belgians' historical repression of the colonial era, especially the atrocities during Léopold's rule. Before the 2005 exhibition *La mémoire du Congo. Le temps colonial*, the museum's vast exhibition space did not contain a single critical remark about the exhibited objects; rather, they were presented from within a nationalistic, paternalistic discourse. With the 2005 exhibition, the new director Guido Gryseels wanted to allow for what was billed as an objective, balanced story, which would simply present the facts to the audience, and thus invite critical considerations. *La mémoire du Congo. Le temps colonial* can be viewed as an attempt to accommodate the call for soul-searching that Lindqvist and Hochschild had launched ten years earlier, garnering much international attention. This claim, however, is repudiated by the museum and prominent historians, who regard Hochschild's and Lindqvist's books as insubstantial pamphlets of grand stories about the struggle between good and evil that only contribute to further mythologisation and repression. Hochschild, on his part, refused to accept that the exhibition was a genuine attempt to create an unbiased narrative about Belgium as a colonial power.[162] He is of the opinion that too little attention was paid to atrocities, which were overwhelmed by the amount of space given to neutral topics of a geographical and ethnographic nature. First and foremost, however, Hochschild's objection is that curators, historians and politicians have not officially acknowledged – in text or speech – that what took place in the Red Rubber era was genocide, although Hochschild himself expressed reservations about the use of the term in the first edition of his book in 1998.

Poster celebrating the 50th anniversary of the Congo as a Belgian state colony, on which occasion a spectacular exposition was held, *L'Expo 58*. Among other things, the display 'Congorama' showed a multimedia presentation of the progresses of the colony in science, health, and mineralogy, and the group for 'Belgian-Congolese nuclear energy' presented the miracles that could be performed with uranium mined by Belgian companies in the Congo. The narrative was characterised by a childish naivety on par with the travel accounts *Per Just on Congo Adventures* and *With Søren and Anne in the Congo*.

The details of this controversy are beyond the scope of this book, but the fundamental issues can throw light on the interpretation of twentieth-century travel literature as lost in oblivion. Both Sven Lindqvist's and Adam Hochschild's books emphasise their documentary characteristics by means of numerous rhetorical effects. Aside from the meticulous referencing, many expressions are used to conjure up the image of a tireless researcher retrieving a repressed truth from a vast archive. However, historians are capable of proving Hochshild's biased use of the sources, which he selects and combines in a way that contravenes the rules of source criticism to impose on the reader the pathetic story of "Greed, Terror, and Heroism". The chapter "A Reckoning", for instance, claims to be a statistically credible presentation of the probable number of victims of the Red Rubber era, but Belgian historians refute it as guesswork founded on isolated testimonies by more or less peripheral observers, including Edmund Morel.[163] As is the case with Lindqvist, this method reproduces the Reform Association's form of argumentation, in which isolated accounts of atrocities are sanctioned as testimonies with much appeal to pathos, but little to logos. The books are thus endowed with authenticity on the basis of their indignation and sensitivity, which ultimately simulates an attitude to events in the past similar to that of a shocked witness – a role assigned to both author and reader. The estimated extent of the atrocities and the unquestionably moral cause excuse this biased appraisal of the sources, and criticism is replaced by simplified generalisations

The Brussels International Exposition 1897 was one in a series of colonialist expositions in Belgium featuring the possessions in the Congo. For the 1894 exposition in Anvers/Antwerp, Danish Lieutenant Schou helped bring a large group of natives, which were described as curious wonders outside of their natural context. The 1897 exposition multiplied the format and scale of earlier expositions, with several Congolese villages placed along the shore of the lake in front of the palace in Tervuren and spectacular naval battles modelled after Stanley's descriptions. Up to 40,000 visitors arrived every day to marvel at the 267 Congolese who had been brought there. Today, the palace in Tervuren also houses a museum of Central African culture and ethnography, and Stanley's diaries are kept in one wing, protected by strict security measures. The exhibition aesthetics of the museum have not changed significantly since 1897: touching slavery scenes and displays of leopard men are still part of the art nouveau decor of the pompous building. The visitor is struck by such a strong sense of anachronism that the focus turns to *how* efforts were made around the turn of the century to shape the European perception of Africa. In Belgium, discussions therefore address whether this speaks for maintaining the exhibition as it is – a museum of a museum – or whether it should be modernised and the display cases filled with educational, colonial-critical information texts.

of Conrad, Morel and Casement as incorruptible human rights fighters, while Léopold, Stanley and a number of other Europeans are demonised as sadistic criminals. Projections such as this lose sight of causes and preconditions, and, ultimately, historicity.

There is good reason for having reservations towards *all* historical narratives, including those of the exhibition "La mémoire du Congo". Among other factors, these critiques mention that the way the exhibition carefully confines the descriptions of terror to the Red Rubber era in reality facilitates a problematic acquittal and active repression of the forced labour, floggings and forced relocations that continued throughout the entire colonial period.[164] Contrary to their declared intentions, Lindqvist and Hochschild contribute to this repression of history in their reciprocal hypostatisations of testimony and genocide respectively, which are allowed to supplant history. This tendency in twentieth-century narratives about the Congo can be viewed in relation to the phenomena Andreas Huyssen has described generally as a "globalization of traumatic memory discourses in which the tropes and rhetoric of the Holocaust play an increasingly prominent role in different national and political contexts"[165]. By pretending to

View of one of the Congolese villages that were built by the shore of the lake in Tervuren.

"In the waterfalls at Uelle", one of 16 friezes in the colonial palace and exhibition building of Tervuren.

present hitherto unheard testimonies in order to discover repressed historical truths, these narratives want to appear as correctives to the dominant, totalising histories; however, at the same time they refrain from critically questioning the individual testimonies and their contexts. Confronted with this discourse, which – as mentioned above – enters into reciprocal action with influential human rights campaigns, it is impossible for historians to respond critically to the testimonies without being accused of holocaust denial by default. Furthermore, recommendations to study a number of contemporary, alternative sources, or base conclusions on broader knowledge of the albeit less fascinating topics of politics and economics are easily brushed aside as attempts to disregard a hidden, xenophobic atrocity.[166]

We are dealing with a problematic drift between testimony narratives and the writing of history that began with the Reform Association's early criticism of the Free State. However, the controversy about Belgium's collective memory loss has also spurred internal disputes among the historians involved. Jean-Luc Vellut phrased the issue in a fundamental, historiographic form in an interview with the most prominent historian of the Congo before colonial times, Jan Vansina. While Vellut agrees with Vansina's criticism of Belgian historians' silence about the use of violence in the colony, which – with a few notable exceptions – dominated positivistic history until the mid-sixties, he has serious reservations about the revisionism Vansina represents. According to Vellut, the Congo and the museum in Tervuren have become battlefields for history. He refers to the French subtitle of Hochschild's book, "l'holocauste oublié", warning against

the holocaust paradigm becoming a new revisionist standard for twentieth-century history, in which the Congo and other cases – with support from Hannah Arendt's essay about totalitarianism – are read as pro-Nazi experiments, and Joseph Conrad "is shamelessly recycled to serve as an incriminating witness".[167] In the scope of the present book, it is interesting that Vellut considers revisionism to be a return to a former discourse on Africa:

> "We are once again entering a melancholy cycle (…): nostalgia and eulogy are succeeded (or preceded) by "black books", and so the process unfolds. Now the mood is to renew with the abolitionist tradition, to denounce the evil, to bring the liberating word and paternally to put Africa in the debt of the liberal west" (p. 4).

While the revisionist discourse, which is also a characteristic of branches of postcolonial criticism, fundamentally writes colonial history by means of simplified juxtapositions – Belgium and the Congo, for example, become directly opposing cultures – the alternative according to Vellut is history describes the relationship from a transnational perspective as a dynamic, complex interaction. He mentions Pierre Halen, who also appears in this book, and highlights new deconstructive curating strategies – like those of the Tervuren exhibition *ExitCongoMuseum* (2000-2001), sometimes referred to as "Ex Shit Congo" – which aimed to free history of the old antagonisms: "The aim is to dispose of the liberal discourse on Africa, to break into smithereens the colonial/anti-colonial nexus and indeed any trace of a coherent ethical image of the colonial past" (p. 5).[168]

One of the problems with Lindqvist's and Hochschild's revisionist model is the continuation of the abolitionist movement's rhetoric and myths, the consequences of which will be investigated in the following. Another problem is that we are dealing with poor readings of the archival texts. Apart from the fact that they are historically problematic, Casement, Morel and Stanley are being read without any understanding of their form or communicative contexts. The prose perspective, on the other hand, insists on this complexity as an important term in appraising the texts – as literature, historical documents and testimonies. This analysis has avoided making "Greulgeschichte" out of the twentieth-century

From *L'Expo 58*, the anniversary exposition immediately before the colony broke away from Belgium. A group of invited diamond workers from the Kasai province are looking at Paul Wissaert's sculpture *Les Aniota* (1913).

travel accounts, instead locating the fundamental mechanisms, including a consistent rhetoric of exclusion, which facilitate disregarding the actual content of a testimony even while it is being presented or interpreted.

The totalising and encyclopaedic endeavour of Jenssen-Tusch's *Scandinavians in Congo* was made possible by the author's distant position and his strange collages of extracts from the letters and travel accounts of the diseased or dying – testimonies from a world that had already become a motionless, unreal mirage. The book was planned to portray a vision of Africa as full of opportunity; however, it was completed as a book of the dead. The encyclopaedia is lifeless; wonder has been degraded to sensational entertainment and farce, and what should have been a celebration of the progress of history and civilisation turns into fatality statistics. *Scandinavians in Congo* comes across as a dismal *fin de siècle* text, in which the end of the century is not only perceived as the end of history, but also as a closing of the atlas as an album of opportunities to discover new worlds.

Arne-Falk Rønne's authorship, like with many others in the twentieth century, can be viewed as a stubborn denial of the fact that there was nothing new to report on the old national and colonial terms. His style is an attempt to

rediscover the authenticity of the travel genre by searching for the truly foreign and going to great lengths – running personal risk – to build credibility, but his travel account collapses under the weight of fabricated testimonies and personal bewilderment. Several times, Falk-Rønne reminds the reader that after Stanley 'opened' the continent, Scandinavia has forgotten it: "Today, we are forgetting Africa again. By all means, we hear many political reports about the conditions, one president's attack on another, but is it not often the case that the individual person, the average African, appears rather blurry before our eyes?" (Falk-Rønne, p. 175). In a time "when still more fast-flying jet machines spin their webs above our heads and eliminate time differences", we ought to prepare ourselves for being "part of it all" (p. 176). Arne Falk-Rønne acknowledges the globalised conditions and the challenges they present, dutifully mentioning them several times in the book, but his failed book also illustrates that, in relation to Africa, the travel description in its classical form has exhausted its potential as an authentic genre, and authors' desperate attempts to find solutions that will enable them to continue the tradition of explorations on global terms are bound to fail.

2 The Congo in Novels: Graham Greene, V.S. Naipaul and Urs Widmer

Conrad's *Heart of Darkness* is beyond any doubt the best known high literature text about the Congo. It is positioned at the centre of a pivotal field of transformation, from which it exercises significant influence on subsequent literature about the Congo -though it is debateable how much it actually has to do with the country or its history. Graham Greene and V.S. Naipaul both regard Conrad's text as an exclusive authority to which they must respond in their own travel diaries from the Congo and their subsequent novels. The metaphorical intensification around the title's heart of darkness presents a challenge to both authors - defining their travel routes and constituting the textual form of their works.

In a sense, twentieth-century authors do in fact use the traditional pattern for travel accounts from Africa, which must establish the image of what is African by journeying inland - both in a concrete and a metaphorical, epistemological manner - as is clear in the metaphor and the cluster of associations linked to the figure of 'heart of darkness', which also predates Conrad's text. If Greene and Naipaul, as neo-realistic, politically engaged authors, had wanted to gather new knowledge about the Congo, they could have drawn on abundant archives of travel accounts and descriptions of the country's history; however, they chose to engage with Conrad, because he holds a privileged position in the literary canon. They must both respond to Conrad in their struggles to achieve high positions in the rankings of world literature, because he consolidates the myth that reinterpreted the experience of impenetrability as a universal enigma. In this sense, Conrad serves to highlight the poetological conflicts in both authorships.

Graham Greene, *A Burnt-out Case*

Graham Greene's *A Burnt-out Case* (1961) came before Naipaul's novel about the Congo, and it is arguably somewhat removed from the literary lead this chapter aims to discover. The travel book *In Search of a Character. Two African Journals* (1961) and the journey that gave rise to it are the declared sources of the novel, and they contain numerous reminders that the Congo was chosen merely as a particular *setting* for the novel's investigation of the main character's moral,

religious and artistic issues, which are treated as universally applicable psychological and philosophical human concerns. Africa and the Congo were selected as the background because Greene believed that they would help reduce the noise that a more recognisable social and historical context would have produced, obscuring the moral-religious conflict. Through his choice, Greene also emphasises – as a 'case' – important characteristics of the "gaze drift"/"dérive du regard", which is also present in Naipaul's text.

The title of *A Burnt-out Case* refers to the cases of leprosy that have been cured when the sufferers have only lost their fingers and toes. The main character, Querry, is a spiritual leper when he arrives at a colony for lepers that is located some distance inland in the Congo. It is a coincidence that he gets off at that particular station, and we soon understand that the journey in every respect has been without a goal. Querry simply wished to escape everything he was, but now he has lost hope in starting over or finding a new home. Among the lepers and the catholic missionaries who manage the colony, Querry finds a place to hide, where he can be left in peace and find some pleasure in helping Doctor Colin, who in return makes time for philosophical conversations with the rather self-centred Querry.

The first parts of the novel consist of gradual revelations of Querry's true identity, and the disease from which he suffers. He has been a world famous architect, particularly successful in designing Catholic churches, and also successful with women. He has perceived his Catholic faith, artistic talent and love affairs as genuine, fundamental traits of his nature; however, at some point he realised that his success eroded his faith, talent and passion. Querry begins to look at his former life as if it belonged to someone else, and his present life as devoid of all human emotion and passion. Like the lepers, his nerves cannot register pain or deprivation.

The last parts of the novel recount Querry's recovery, during which he – with some irony – finds himself to be so comfortable among the lepers that he once again becomes capable of feeling pain and deprivation. Soon, however, all kinds of disasters hit the colony, disturbing his sanctuary. His past catches up with him in the form of a journalist from an international magazine, who represents the mass audience's expectations of the template truths that destroyed his ability to create anything new, and which he believed he had escaped. When he finally starts *reacting* instead of merely *philosophising* about his meaningless existence and lost faith, it is too late – naturally, according to Greene's logic: everything that Querry does to avoid the masses worshipping him as a saint, fetish and myth is misinterpreted and ends up amplifying the false perception of his self-sacrifice on the altar of faith. The only exception from this cult occurs when a young, naïve woman trapped in a horrible marriage involves Querry in the most intimate entanglements of her life: perhaps she is genuinely in love with Querry, or perhaps she just uses him as a means to escape by inventing a story about him being the father of her child. Instantly, this lie causes all his admirers to see him as a seducer – a truth which, in his self-loathing, he has tried to make everybody believe but no longer believes himself. Towards the end, when Querry is actually able to act like a human being with moral responsibility, he is killed by the young woman's husband. Her childish, innocent lie, while it led to his death, can be interpreted as the original, creative act that brought Querry back to life.

In his travel book, Graham Greene is aware that the plot is at risk of taking over; he is about "to succumb to that abiding temptation to tell a good story" (*In Search of A Character*, p. 57). However, he contains the risk with the almost mathematical stringency imposed on the text. Other factors also indicate that *A Burnt-out Case* is not the careless comedy Greene has sometimes suggested it is, but rather a novel that, in a paradoxical, twisted and limited manner, solves the problems of his poetics. The travel book's excerpt from a diary written during a stay in the Congo between 31 January and 8 March 1959 will help illuminate some of these basic layers in the novel, as well as clearly exemplifying the withdrawal from social reality that is an important tendency in the history of travel literature in the twentieth century.

The peculiarities of both travel and travel account are indicated in the title "In Search of a Character". Graham Greene writes, by means of introduction, that he has a completely rudimentary idea for a main character: one day, X arrives at a colony for lepers in Africa. He himself suffers from a spiritual version of leprosy, which – on par with the physical version – causes self-loathing and personality changes. The real journey follows the lead of the fictitious X, and the novel is the answer to the questions that Greene asks the enigmatic person, who is, in a sense, given a role that is more real than that of the novel's Querry. Much effort is put into underlining the inner necessity of the character and plot, including numerous interpolations, footnotes and stage directions, which categorically – and a little self-indulgently – reject various possible directions for the novel with reference to the fact that not only would they be unlikely, they would counteract the character's *true* nature. The travel book is a report on the author's detective work of reconstructing logical incentives in a hypnotic-but-real course of events, expressed artistically in *A Burnt-out Case*. "The novel is an unknown man and I have to find him: a situation that I cannot yet even vaguely imagine: a background as strange to me as it was to him at his first entrance" (p. 13).

This peculiar reversal is emblematic of Greene's originality. The artist has created X, yet the reversal enhances the novel's authenticity from a rhetori-

To Graham Greene, the Congo was "a region of the mind", but also a Quixotic landscape where boundaries between text and reality were dissolved. The journey to the leprosy hospital in the Congo, his background research for the novel *A Burnt-Out Case* (1961), is described in *In Search of a Character* (1961). The main character in the novel has, like the author himself - and Joseph Conrad - had his photograph on the cover of *Time Magazine*. The plot and travel descriptions of the novel, with reference to the legacy from Conrad, are attempts to place the author in a position that avoids ideological dogma on the one hand and popular fiction on the other. It was with Congo as a backdrop that Greene managed to establish his authorship in the good company of world literature authors like Cervantes and Conrad.

cal point of view - because the claim is that X is not fictitious and invented: despite his many unique qualities, he is found and real. Even during the first days of the journey, however, author and main character start to merge. Like X, Greene is exposed to malicious pests who want to hang on to their fixed image of him as a great Catholic author, and like X, Greene escapes his admirers and the success that is killing his ability to create anything new and original. An additional twist is added to the connections between journey, travel book and novel, when it is more than hinted that X is not a different person but in fact Graham Greene himself, fleeing from his role as an author, loathing his mass audience, irritable, burnt-out, still alive but maimed and devoid of emotion and creative ability.

The search for a character is therefore also a description of the writer's escape from his role as author, and as the main character is pieced together through observations of the lepers in the colony and the novel assumes its form, the author re-emerges, cleansed and purified, as he who can sign a new masterly tale. This game of logic is even designed to be an effective antidote against interpretations of the main character's and the novel's dealing with Catholic themes as a direct expression of the author's Catholicism.

In relation to the descriptions in the travel book, these twists and turns make the foreign appear as a mere backdrop for the main character's and author's antics. After a few days, it is impossible to recreate "the familiar in the very heart of the strange" (p. 27) – something that is emphasised by a ritualised description of every day according to the same predictable pattern: reading, drinking whisky, writing letters, etc. As for the setting of the novel and X's motives, Greene's investigation is – apart from one dilettantish trip – limited to the immediate environment of the colony, the patients, the doctor, the priests and a few visits to Belgian "colons".

It is an explicit point that the great world is absent. The radio newscast about turmoil in Brazzaville, and the feeling "that European Africa is rapidly disintegrating", is perceived as "one of the science-fiction stories of Ray Bradbury" (pp. 65-66). Colonialism is described as a play – a poor staging of *The Merchant of Venice* – while Greene passes time reading books by Julian Green, who he does not like, and other authors who have nothing to do with the matter. These imaginary outings offer an alternative whereabouts to his current location in the Congo, which more than anything annoys him, and is perhaps not even satisfactory as a setting for the troublesome novel. Several times Greene considers using a "mis-en-scene" from Sierra Leone or French Guiana, and he makes comparisons with his novels from Indochina, as if the world outside Europe were the same everywhere and the unfamiliarity is merely waiting for the same familiarity to be installed. Compelled by the inner artistic necessity of the concept and the metaphysics on which it is based, Greene rejects many possibilities for X or Querry, but ends up using all the 'local' clues in the travel book regarding the girls' breasts, the lepers' deformations, the colour of the river, a few native proverbs and anecdotes, etc.

Greene's travel library also includes *Heart of Darkness*, which is mentioned several times, not as a diversion from time and place, but as a challenge related to the journey and the novel. Greene writes that for a long time he has pro-

hibited himself from reading Conrad, because the influence was too extensive and destructive: "The heavy hypnotic style falls around me again, and I am aware of the poverty of my own. Perhaps now I have lived long enough with my poverty to be safe from corruption" (p. 48). However, Greene also has an eye for Conrad's shortcomings:

> "Conrad's *Heart of Darkness* is still a fine story, but its faults show now. The language is too inflated for the situation. Kurtz never comes really alive. It is as if Conrad had taken an episode in his own life and tried to lend it, for the sake of 'literature', a greater significance than it will hold. And how often he compares something concrete to something abstract. Is it a trick that I have caught?" (p. 51).

Graham Greene often made reference to Conrad as a problematic father figure – along with Rider Haggard – and the references to *Heart of Darkness* and *In Search of a Character* makes the link between the two novels obvious. In the same way that Naipaul's *A Bend in the River* is not only a novel with its own ends, but also an original, albeit failed, attempt to correct Conrad's, *A Burnt-out Case* is caught up in a problematic rivalry with the great predecessor. Greene and Naipaul both criticise the novel's lack of inner necessity, and it is tempting to interpret Greene's affectedly pedantic emphasis on metaphysical laws in plot and character as a correction of the predecessor's elaboration on a random autobiographical event with the aim of creating literature. Furthermore, there are noticeable, albeit superficial, parallels between Kurtz and Querry – the latter in several respects constituting a satirical comment on the former. Like Naipaul's novel and travel book, Greene's criticism applies just as much to the weak points in his own position.

Graham Greene introduces *A Burnt-out Case* with two texts: a dedication in the form of a letter to Michel Lechat, who was the colony hospital manager during Greene's stay in the Congo and subsequently became an internationally known expert in leprosy (he lectured at the annual Graham Greene Festival in 2006), and an "Introduction" in which the author tries to determine the novel's position in his oeuvre. In the dedication, Greene explains that he has only used superficial elements from the colony in the Congo; the novel is not "a *roman à clef*", and "This Congo is a region of the mind". The novel is an attempt to give "dramatic expression to various types of belief, half-belief and non-belief, in the kind of setting, removed from world-politics and household-preoccupations, where such differences are felt acutely and find expression" (*A Burnt-out Case*, p. vii).

Critics have often identified what has come to be known as "Greeneland" with political hot spots on the world map – Indochina, Cuba and Africa – while

Greene in contrast emphasises that the exotic settings in this instance rather aim to scour the stories of "world-politics" and "household-preoccupations". In the "Introduction", this point of view is underpinned by the lengthy argument for the Congo novel's position in his oeuvre. It is an attempt to drag the author out of the suffocating template that since *The Heart of the Matter* both Marxists and Catholics have put him in, using him as an example of a non-believer or a believer respectively. Both Marxism and catholic theology have a propensity to rely on speculative evidence, which leads to a far too abstract and dogmatic understanding of the issues, while *A Burnt-out Case* lets the question of faith unfold in "that tragi-comic region of La Mancha", where the author "expect[s] to stay" (p. xvii).

To Graham Greene, the Congo is thus both "a region of the mind" and the landscape where Don Quixote tried to conquer the world but failed, because he was unable to distinguish between text and reality. In his "Introduction", Graham Greene wants *A Burnt-out Case* to be appreciated as a master move in the Jesuit game of faith, metaphysics and art, but the reference to Cervantes also identifies the novel as a parody. It is tragicomic that Querry struggles just as much to convince the believers about his non-belief as believers struggle to convince non-believers about God's existence, and the end game's syllogistic reversals of guilt and punishment are both a satire of Jesuit scholasticism and a caricature of the novel and the author. That the game comes out perfectly in what the novel calls a surprising "happy ending" for everyone, including the spiritual leper Querry, is a caricature of Greene's famous flair for accomplished plots and necessary characters. In view of this, the novel should not only be read as a rebellion against a specific ideological straitjacket, but also as Greene's attempt to write his way out of an unbearable aesthetic-literary expectation of always writing "great novels".

Viewed from this self-critical perspective, which is obviously significant if we include the merging of X and the author in *In Search of a Character*, *A Burnt-out Case* is also an ambiguous reappraisal of Graham Greene's own division of his oeuvre into "entertainments" and "novels" – his thrillers and spy stories belonging in the former category, and his religious novels in the latter. The composition, characters and plot of the novel are parodies of the theological idle talk that characterises the religious novels and particularly their reception; and like Cervantes' great novel, it is an entertaining and sneering exposure of all dogma, including clear divisions between genres. At the same time, Greene's own statements counteract the novel's more entertaining than instructive point: with an affected reference to the authorship's world-wide success, Greene mentions that "success is more dangerous than failure", and he calls *The Heart of the Matter* "a success in the great vulgar sense of that

term", further associating its success with a corrupt and problematic appeal "to weak elements in its readers".

The portrait of the character Querry is far removed from any success that is based on a false, fetishised admiration for the artist as saint and role model, and in Greene's explicit comments on the novel, we find the same reservations about success that is based on erroneous identification of the author as political or religious witness or prophet. This regards the artist's originality and the author's subjectivity in favour of the dogma of ideology – whether it is Catholicism or Marxism; in the shadow of myths, the author is made non-human, reduced to a mechanical replica. When Querry's all-pervading self-knowledge, which is part of his illness, is ultimately taken unawares by the lie of an innocent woman, he can only laugh at himself – while her mediocre husband shoots and kills Querry in a tragicomical turn of events, because he thinks the laugh is on him. Due to the merging of author and main character, which is made clear in the travel diary, the ending is also a suicidal break with the authorial role that prevents Greene from creating something original, while at the same time he expresses his artistic originality performatively by staging his own disappearance from and then reappearance on the scene of world literature – no longer in the intolerable role of "Catholic author in England, Europe and America", but as Cervantes' heir.

In response to the idea of the novels as either entertainment or pre-packaged Catholic ideology, *A Burnt-out Case* is Greene's attempt to occupy a third space, "that tragi-comic region of La Mancha", where entertainment and classic art are unified without contradiction.[169] The novel is a shrewd contribution to Greene's renewed position in world literature. It averted the increasing criticism of his being far too popular, ideological and predictable. It is brilliantly done, and as a reader it is difficult not to perceive the design of this game – including the clearly edited documents from the journey, the introductions, the novel and the letter that both refute and confirm the reader's assumptions that the main character and the author overlap – as a sign that Greene learnt a few tricks when he worked for British intelligence, where one of his colleagues was the famous Philby. The novel, however, is also a risky business, and according to the biographies, Greene was not only burnt out like Querry; he was in love with his illness – what in the novel's term is called leprophilia, love of leprosy – which both kept him alive and maintained his self-loathing.[170] While the first part of the novel parodies through Querry's cynical criticism all philosophical, religious and literary dogmas as either sentimental escapism or masks for the selfish, violent abuse of power, the fabricated, fake and ironic "happy endings" also parody the cynicism of the beginning.

This is how the way was paved for Greene's reappearance on the stage of world literature, but the new beginning apparently came at great cost: the image of literature that the novel leaves, in dialogue with the travel book, is not a postmodern poetics but an outline of a *suicidal literature*, which has realised that it has nothing to tell the world but is willing to go far in order not to be forgotten. The Congo, and Graham Greene's journey to the country, first and foremost provides an opportunity to expose the author's conflicting feelings when faced with the threatening mechanisms of the world literature canon. Greene's journey and novel are evidently inspired by Conrad's journey and novel and Conrad's similar trouble with discarding the popular and ideological in order to win a position in "the great tradition". However, by making this link, it is as if Greene illuminates why *Heart of Darkness* also appealed to "weak elements in its readers" instead of outright defeating his literary predecessor, thus gaining a place among the immortals. In a rephrasing of the aforementioned criticism of Conrad, it appears that Greene has taken an episode from Conrad's work and – for the sake of 'literature' – given it a greater significance than it will hold.

Complicated mechanisms in Graham Greene's management of the relationship between travel book and novel, presented above, bear witness to fundamental formal problems in the authorship, especially in relation to the strategies he used when faced with dilemmas about his own canonisation in the culture of high literature, his success on the literary world market and his role as a celebrity, featured – like Querry – on the cover of *Life Magazine*. These strategies also exemplify the general structures of the twentieth-century representations of the Congo relevant to the present study.

The novel's camouflage technique, which masks psychoanalytical and biographical interpretations without weakening the author's authority, can be understood as an early example of a general characteristic of postmodern literature. In this light, the journey to the Congo, the diary and the novel are all aspects of the same game of hide-and-seek with the critics and readers, and the location is insignificant. However, this appears inconsistent with the pedantic care with which Greene considered his settings – something that was also the case in *A Burnt-out case*, as we have seen. In the introduction to *Graham Greene's Narrative Strategies*, Murray Roston mentions a possible reason for Greene's great popularity, which can also help explain the apparent contradiction between thorough research, which aims at creating the right atmosphere in the novel, and the description of the landscape as empty or purely mental geography.[171] While many of Greene's fellow British authors from the thirties experienced a drastic drop in popularity, to the extent that most of them were completely forgotten by the 1950s and 1960s, Greene's success among readers continued to grow into the 1980s. Roston finds the explanation for this in Graham Greene's

background as a journalist and intelligence agent, paired with his special ability to sense changes in the themes that interested readers, as well as in global politics, before they became known to the general public. Before the Americans even intervened in Vietnam, Greene formulated a critical platform in *The Quiet American*, which earned the novel huge popularity when Lyndon Johnson's policy later came under attack from the mass media. According to Roston, the leper colony in *A Burnt-out Case* was Greene's way of exploiting the media hype around the Nobel Prize winner Albert Schweitzer, and according to the hypothesis about Greene's instinct for high political conflict zones, the Congo was a choice setting for the novel.

Although – or perhaps because – the novel does not relate explicitly to the wars of independence in the region, which in the following years would come into the spotlight of the global mass media, Greene's readers could relate to the place both as "a region of the mind" and a location where the cold war's battle for world dominion took place for a while. Greene did not travel to search for existential experiences to provide material for his novels, and he was definitely not interested in describing places on the terms of their own histories; he travelled to place his stories in "localities he believed to be potentially topical" (p. 5). In his novel, Graham Greene creates a malicious portrait of the gossip journalist Parkinson, who contacts Querry in the Congolese jungle in order to get an interview with the great artist. Querry mocks Parkinson for not knowing where he is and for having incorrectly located Stanley's expedition route on the map. However, Querry has no idea where he is either, and to Graham Greene consideration for one's readers is as important as it is to Parkinson: the world is thus depicted as a dramatic stage or a department store, full of entertainment and opportunity, where the author can hide and transform humankind's universal questions into philosophical games.

A Burnt-out Case uncovers this relationship between world stage and location, which is not unique to Greene, but common to the twentieth-century western literary search for themes and motives that can be staged at distant locations on the planet. Greene's remark that he by chance heard news while he was in the Congo that made him aware "that European Africa is rapidly disintegrating" – which is perceived as being like "the science-fiction stories of Ray Bradbury" – is a precise description, not of the main character he was searching for, but of the reader who the author could neither stand nor do without.

V.S. Naipaul, *A Bend in the River*

The main part of Naipaul's *A Bend in the River* (1979) is set in Kisangani, the former Stanleyville, by the great waterfalls at the middle of the big bend in the

Congo River, halfway between the Atlantic and the Indian Ocean. The first person narrator, Salim, grew up in East Africa in an Arab-Persian-Indian-Portuguese enclave influenced by Christian Europeans, Islamic Africans – including some descendants of slaves from the inland and Arab slave traders – and Indian Hindus, who migrated there generations ago. Nazruddin, a friend of Salim's family with good business sense and timing, has sold a small grocery shop in Kisangani to Salim because of the exposed and vulnerable position of the place in the turmoil that followed independence. Nazruddin moves his business to Uganda until rebellion and turmoil begin to be a threat there too, after which he ends up in London among those who managed to escape before the uncontrollable African conflict destroyed their lives and property. Salim's childhood friend, Indar, completes a university education in England, which is intended to qualify him to return to Africa as an advisor, lecturer or expert, but instead makes him feel rootless – always on his way somewhere else, fleeing from reality. The novel begins with Salim's arrival at this godforsaken place in the centre of Africa, and ends with his departure to London – escaping a new, unpredictable political conflict that threatens to destroy Kisangani and the hope of progress once more.

Salim is a self-aware spectator of life and history. As a child, he gets into the habit of experiencing objects and situations as if they were played out on a stage. His observation of images of the Arab *dhow* on local postal stamps, for instance, leads to a situation in which he sees the real boats on the ocean as illogical, foreign bodies that do not belong in time or space. Salim's narrative position is extremely distanced and distancing. He is a spectator of his own spectatorship; however, this also helps him – in Naipaul's characteristic, coolly revelatory realistic style – to see through what is coincidental, random and illusory, for example in the political changes of the time. This is due to the fact that the spectator position is linked to an omniscient perspective, which, in the design of the novel, must be attributed to the knowledge Salim acquires in London after the end of the novel. There are many references to the books he will come to read, while in the plot he is still a simple merchant with good observational skills. Nevertheless, Naipaul cannot prevent the reader from sensing a conflict in the relationship between Salim's level of insight into the narration and his insight as the narrator.

However, the effect of this perspective and the cyclic, open composition, in which the narrator finishes with the same feeling of rootlessness he had when he began, is a negation of the significance of spatial and temporal coordinates. Everything is seen from a galactic perspective, as local clashes and conflicts are mere ripples compared to the surge of man's and the Earths' history. That an ethnic group such as the Indians would fall from grace and be forced to flee

from East Africa is merely an effect of the same historical tides that made them settle there in the first place. And the cultural forms that we normally perceive as identities are – in the novel's perspective – nothing more than temporal habits, which can be swept away at any time. Salim's – and Naipaul's – position is thus sceptical of any idealism based in concepts of cultural or ethnic essence and origin. On the other hand, Salim is not nihilistic, merely pragmatic, as his motto shows: "The world is what it is" (*A Bend,* p. 21).

One simply occupies a place in the world for a certain amount of time, living life in pragmatic balance with others. This pragmatism includes a constant process of risk assessment, which might lead to a decision to move somewhere else. It is a fleeting, moving world – or, in Naipaul's words, "a world in flux". Towards the end of the novel, the narrator acknowledges that his previous combination of scepticism and the unity of experience – his dream of being able to travel somewhere else and start from scratch – is nothing more than comforting self-deception; it is a variation of his family's old way of life, which contains more profound meaninglessness: "We had become what the world outside had made us; we had to live in the world as it existed. (...) Use the aeroplane; trample on the past, as Indar had said he had trampled on the past. Get rid of the idea of the past; make the dreamlike scenes of loss ordinary" (p. 252).

In the novel, the history of Kisangani and the Congo is part of an overarching framework of understanding, in which the significance Salim and others ascribe to time and place is increasingly exposed as unfounded illusion. When Salim arrives at his store, the grandiose colonial structures have become ruins, absorbed by the jungle. When the city apparently comes to life under the relative stability of Mobutuism, European architecture once again becomes a part of it – now in the form of European restaurants and night clubs – and when Salim leaves his store and all his friends in the city, the forest once again closes in on it. The story is narrated as a tidal wave, which alternately conceals and reveals fragile manifestations of human civilisation. Another distancing and ironic dimension is added to this perception of history: Father Huisman, the Belgian headmaster of the city's upper secondary school, shows Salim an engraving on a monument that was erected to celebrate the 60th anniversary of the steam ship's connection with the capital. It reads "Miscerique probat populos et foedera jungi" (p. 110); 'He approves of the mingling of the peoples and their bonds of union'. The Father explains that the inscription is a garbled quotation from a poem about the foundation of ancient Rome. The original formulation in Virgil, however, relates how a Roman god warned against settling in Africa, against peoples mingling and against treaties between Africans and Romans. Nevertheless, to the Father the words are not empty; they give some meaning to his own presence as a European. Salim, on the other hand, is shocked at the mockery of history represented by the moss-covered, ruined monument and its absurdly garbled message. To him, the original poem is more apt than the inscription, but he refrains from correcting Huisman's belief in the Europeans' role, quickly withdrawing into his distanced spectator role.

Father Huisman's other motto is met with a similar mix of empathy, solidarity and irony – Naipaul's trademark. The headteacher refers to the school motto, "Semper aliquid novi", explaining that Pliny wrote that from Africa there came "always something new". To Huisman, the motto is particularly significant in relation to the masks and wood carvings he keenly collects. Avoiding all copies, he is only interested in unique pieces produced for specific religious uses. "He looked in masks and carvings for a religious quality; without that quality the things were dead and without quality" (p. 67). Salim is jealous of Huisman's interest in religion and fetishes, and his equally distinct lack of interest in the state of the country. To Salim, these objects are goods; to Huisman they are full of imagination and meaning – "His Africa was a wonderful place, full of new things" (p. 67).

Salim thinks of Huisman as the last witness of a world that is disappearing, and when Huisman himself disappears – killed on a collection trip, decapitated and displayed as one of the first forewarnings of a new rebellion in the province – his little school museum dies with him. The masks decay, the objects lose their meaning, and an American steals the remnants and takes them to the USA. As Salim concludes elsewhere, it is because of the Europeans that the Congolese have a history, but as Huisman's fate shows, it is only a museum history, built on fetishised worship of the beauty of dead objects.

To Salim's penetrating gaze, the African intellectuals and European advisor who are coming to Kisangani as part of Mobuto's authenticity project are also contributors to the falsification of history, especially the key figure Raymond, who used to be personal advisor to the president. In the beginning, Salim is drawn to the educated façade of the circle around Raymond, to whom he is introduced by his childhood friend Indar, who arrives in the city in his capacity of advisor to the new African state. Before long Salim starts to perceive the fabricated originality of the project as abuse of power, deceit and vanity, which – in conjunction with a failed relationship – ultimately leads to his leaving Africa.

At his first party in Raymond's home, Salim falls completely for Raymond's wife, Yvette. The fancy party, Yvette's chic European appearance and, most of all, her Margit Brandt blouse – which was purchased in Copenhagen and presents her bosom to alluring effect – arouses Salim while at the same time making him feel strangely safe. It seems to him that this magic circle offers an

opportunity for sexual emancipation that is very different from his habitual visits to the brothel, and that these people have grasped the right principles for the restoration of Africa and the future, while still protected themselves from the harsh reality. Joan Baez's voice, the nicely decorated flat, the Margit Brandt blouse and the party guests – who alternate between dancing and discussing politics, declaring that Africa should not be built on imported principles but on "real ideas", and expressing thoughts on Africa's "sad destiny" – lend a tinge of melancholy aestheticism to his spectator role. The relationship with Yvette, which after the party turns into an intimate affair, is described as one of depraved lust, albeit lust that is watched from the outside. It is intensified when Salim surprises Yvette in the daytime, her "housewifely ordinariness" revealed behind the cosmopolitan stylishness, and the record player "with its smoked perspex cover showing dust in the bright light" (p. 177).

The affair with Yvette replaces "the African situation" in Salim's field of vision; he is now a voyeur of his own lust, finding perverse pleasure in watching his and Yvette's depravation, which is consciously choreographed as an anti-romantic and violent affirmation of the existence of the body, even when reality disappears out of sight. During the affair, Salim's usual talent for risk assessment – an important aspect of his inherited business acumen – is replaced by an aesthetic and voyeuristic self-forgetfulness in which he believes he has discovered himself. Eventually, he acknowledges that this is also self-delusion, and he returns to his original pragmatism, now even more disillusioned. His pain and melancholy at the world's disappearance is also a comforting sanctuary; one must live with the fact that such losses are absolute.

Naipaul describes all the attempts to found a political future for the Congo on notions of origin and ideas of ethnic identity as distorted, fatal illusions. However, he also distances himself from this distance, when it indulges in melancholy, aestheticism and a refusal to see "the world as it is". In this sense, the novel is a cool exposure of the many-layered illusions about Africa, with particular emphasis on the rootless traveller's flickering perspective, which – through the novel's overarching framework – is ultimately not specific to the Congo or Africa, but applies to the global "flux" of people and goods.

Nevertheless, this extremely distancing construction and the total perspective come to limit the novel's insight. The themes are identical with the theatricality of Mobutuism, in its propaganda and parades. The dominant aspects of Congolese life in the 1960s are beyond the scope of the novel, which is implied by the character Zabeth. Zabeth is a "marchande" from one of the villages, who buys a few select things from Salim's store – toothbrushes, razor blades, pencils, notepads and aluminium frying pans – which she can sell in the villages. She sails on the river which all the goods have travelled at some point, but her own world remains secret to Salim and the reader. She always disappears in one of the small tributaries known only to a select few.

Everything outside the city's ruinous mix of colonial estates, sheet metal shacks and new burger bars is unknown, and the villages are described as "hidden". Everyone in the city (in accordance with Salim's and Naipaul's perspective) is terrified at the idea of sudden, unpredictable reactions from this hidden, *other* world, which – according to the novel's logic – is only held at bay by the city's civilisation. The portrait of Zabeth never becomes more than a tentative sketch of a demonised, barbarian other world, where primitive fetish worship and inherent violence are far from being under Mobuto's control – even if it is increasingly linked to the circulation of goods on the river and all over the world via Zabeth's narrow passage.

The style of the novel changes along the way: Salim's initial losing himself in Yvette and Raymond's designer reality is exposed as an escape into a state of self-forgetfulness that indicates the suppression of their reality. The light of day that reveals the dust on the record player's perspex cover also exposes the fetishistic nature of the worship of the Margit Brandt blouse and the voyeuristic and melancholy fascination with things disappearing. Traditional African fetishism, on the other hand, is perceived either as a thing of the past, which is revived in a carnevalesque manner in Mobuto's propaganda, or as something visible but dead and powerless in the objects in Huisman's museum; they belong to a sphere of hermetic mystery, to which the novel's otherwise penetrating gaze does not try to gain access. However, objects in the novel also appear in the form of the goods that are traded and exchanged without fetishistic worship; Nazruddin, Salim and Zabeth are business people who facilitate the movement of goods without fetishising them. They are thus the carriers of the novel's ethos, which can be condensed to the fact that it is the movement of goods, not people, that controls development and the future.

Naipaul's *A Congo Diary* (1980) consists of notes from a journey to the Congo in 1975 – partly on the occasion of his invitation to a UN conference, and partly because he wanted to travel into the country to Kisangani, former Stanleyville. The journey can be seen as part of the author's research into "the African problem", which had already taken him to other destinations on the continent. In his diary, Naipaul notes down anything and everything: his annoyance with the poor food, extortionate exchange rates, leaking cisterns and bad taste, and his excitement when he encounters unexpected elegance, working air conditioning and bartenders who know what they are doing. These observations are loosely connected to brief, unfinished reflections on the country's political situation under Mobuto and the 1974 decree on nationalisation. They follow a summary of a conversation with a schoolteacher, or help pass the time in an airport. At

the same time, the text contains quite a few descriptions of objects and everyday situations that are neither directly relevant to the political considerations or consistent with Naipaul's snobbish idiosyncrasy. This idiosyncrasy makes him intensely observant, but it also brings him to rash conclusions about various correlations. The descriptions are often listed under a heading, which are used in a more or less unchanged form in the novel:

"Other impressions: the livid grey sky at Mbandaka, dark and livid to one side, bright to the other side; beyond the airport garden with the MPR flag fluttering on its spear-tipped flagpole, the runway and the low level line of forest. The man who wanted beer: he said that the plane was about to arrive, to encourage people to abandon their beer, and then hung around and asked for the Air Zaire bottle of Primus beer. The man in ragged clothes who turned up, surprising in a glass-visored fireman's helmet: an African dancing mask, it seemed at first, an eccentric's disguise. He too wanted beer and took a half-full bottle. Later we were to see him standing, with a colleague, similarly helmeted, beside the aeroplane. So he was a fireman after all. The old negro in an embroidered black cap; the woman with the baby offering living grubs in plastic bags; the Belgian woman reading Peyton Place: the other old negro who turned up, during the storm, in a pale-blue towelling bathrobe and a grey felt hat" (*A Congo Diary*, p. 21).

Notes like these are obviously checklists for the novel, to which the diary refers several times – the novel correspondingly being characterised by the profusion of detail, as well as by a realism that has a tendency to become caricature. And as the extract illustrates, Naipaul's notes seem to pave the way for the extremely distanced style of his novel's descriptive passages. These particularities, which aim at rooting the plot in a Congolese reality, often spring from the diary's random, often rather curious observations from the trip to Kisangani, which had to be cut short. First, the plane had to return to the place of departure, and when Naipaul finally arrives in Kisangani, all the hotels are fully booked because of the president's imminent visit. Naipaul had to leave after only one night, taking the river steamer under circumstances that resemble Salim's escape at the end of *A Bend in the River*.

The surprising outcome of a comparison between diary and novel is not that elements of the former are included in the latter, but that the entire framework of the novel and many of its details are already present in the diary, before being used to their full potential in the novel's realistic fiction. This applies to the overall political plot, the future consequences of Mobutuism that in the diary are formulated as an open hypothesis, which is tested with a negative result in the novel's laboratory. It also applies to the various elements of nationalisation and the concept of originality with "le petit peuple" at the centre. These concepts are present as fragments in Naipaul's chance conversations on the steamer or at the embassy. The diary also contains keywords for the novel's fundamental dynamics between city and forest, ruins and Roman inscriptions, as well as Salim's position as a wandering outsider, Yvette's elegant, alluring designer reality and the promiscuity of African women, the hidden villages, whose existence one only glimpses in the small canoes that transport goods in the Congo River, the idea of the disappearance of things – in the diary discussed as "The Empire of Things" – etc.

This link between diary and novel is very telling of Naipaul's observational skills and his standing as an author; however, it also indicates the limited scope of the knowledge on which the novel is based. In the diary, Naipaul does not doubt for a second that he immediately understands everything he sees – that his isolated observations allow him to draw extensive conclusions – and he is convinced that his journey on the river enables him to understand the country, even though he, like Salim, has never really been there. What he does *not* see is contained in broad categories such as "complexity" or "life". This is particularly evident in the following two passages, the first from the beginning of the river journey and the second from the diary descriptions:

"The accommodation on the steamer is so arranged that the passengers who were waiting outside the Onatra office were hidden from view. To look down on them one has to peer through the dining-room windows; and then a great covered area – a kind of travelling market, as it turned out, with WCs – blocks the further view, so one is hidden from *them*. But it is there that the life lies" (p. 29).

"The size of the country remains something hard to grasp. We have travelled perhaps 400 miles through unchanging scenery. I tell myself it is a privilege to be doing this, winding through a complex primitive world, witnessing, noting. The life is complex; the goods are complex (they have taken only those Belgian products that they need). The complexity of life is surprising. And this morning, going out briefly to the bows – briefly because of the heat which quickly makes one sicken and feel faint – I saw many young people reading magazines. Another dimension." (p. 33).

The diary bears witness to Naipaul's grasp of the complexity of the theme. The dynamics behind the circulation of goods on the river and the Congolese attitude to using and consuming, as well as the overall vision of history's great surges and "the flux of the world", for instance, are substantiated in the novel's characters and plot.

This juxtaposition between omniscient vision and limited knowledge about

the world described, most striking in Naipaul's Africa novel, is often a point of criticism. Writing in the *Times Literary Supplement* in 1980, Chinua Achebe launches an attack on *A Bend in the River* for its caricatured, stereotypical portraits of Africans, and for the use of Africa as the antithesis to European rationality.[172] In "Out of Darkness. Conrad and Other Third World Writers", Peter Nazareth points out Naipaul's fatal lack of knowledge about the international power struggle in relation to the Congo's natural resources, which to a large degree defined the terms for Mobuto and the self-government.[173] The juxtaposition between omniscient vision and limited concrete knowledge, however, becomes clearer in the light of Naipaul's criticism of Conrad.[174]

In the article "Conrad's Darkness" (1974), Naipaul directs his criticism at Conrad's whole oeuvre, though it is clear, as indicated in the title, that *Heart of Darkness* is the most direct challenge. Compared with Naipaul's usually fluent prose, the argumentation here is incoherent, the form loose and taciturn. One minute he attacks one text, the next moment another, and the essay clearly struggles to find footing and reach a conclusion. Throughout, more and more disconnected appraisals are made of the predecessor's style, ideals and morality, providing a picture of how Naipaul interprets *Heart of Darkness* and other works. It appears from the essay's impatient and intense approach that much is at stake for Naipaul, but that he is unable to define or express the conflict.

Naipaul senses a common destiny between himself and Conrad, both writing from and about mixed cultures and "half-made societies". Naipaul writes that he used to feel that Conrad, at a very concrete level, described the fluid world which was Naipaul's childhood and youth in Trinidad. One particular scene from *Heart of Darkness* made a powerful impression – the one in which Marlow finds the handbook *An Inquiry into Some Points of Seamanship,* because the book with its "honest concern for the right way of going to work" pointed to a secure place in the middle of the nightmare that resembled Naipaul's need for security in a time of "political panic".

Apart from this superficial recognition, however, Conrad is given rough treatment in the essay, the disorganised arguments of which often hit home, but also inadvertently reveal the critic's own position. To Naipaul, the peculiar and mysterious are central concepts in Conrad. As textual strategies they aim to set up an encounter between the works' romanticism and the reader's imagination; however, this ambition is hindered by Conrad's counteractive desire to stay "true to facts" – "Fidelity required him to be explicit" (p. 56). The main problem is that Conrad's "truths" are often complex and difficult, subject to many layers of illusion and cultural ambiguity, and therefore he feels compelled to explain his "wonders" by commenting on the story, instead of allowing the story to tell itself. It only makes the situation worse that in some of the stories, including

Heart of Darkness, Conrad has decided the text's truth in advance, which results in the meaning appearing applied and allegorical. Naipaul writes about Conrad's portrait of Kurtz: "Beguiling words, but they are abstract: and the idea, deliberately worked out, remains an applied idea" (p. 62).

We find many versions of this brutal criticism in the essay. Conrad's style is too "wordy", his novels are like simple films in which characters and settings are clear, while the realism is built on trivial dialogue and events, and the ever-melodramatic endings amplify the impression of the "slowness and bad proportions of what has gone before" and "the fact that the characters were actors" (p. 56). Wishing to explicate the mystery in order to stay true to facts, Conrad betrays the "wonder" that is central to his romanticism, causing the texts to become mysterious in a negative sense – i.e. unintelligible to the reader, which is a betrayal of realism. In Naipaul's opinion, Conrad is both too romantic and too realistic in his ambitions, and therefore he fails in executing both ideals. "In fiction he did not seek to discover; he sought only to explain" (p. 62). This relates to another key point in the criticism: because Conrad lacks "a vision", he does not have the courage to trust the story to discover its own meaning while it is being written; instead, the stories are forced explanations of predefined concepts.

Returning to *A Bend in the River* and *A Congo Diary*, the essay about Conrad is informative in several respects. Firstly, it makes sense to perceive Naipaul's interest in the Congo as a continuation of Conrad's interest in "half-made societies". Unlike the great novelists of the nineteenth century, who – as Naipaul mentions in the essay – wrote about highly organised societies, the two authors create worlds that are barely societies, not to mention nations. Given that the essay about Conrad was written around the same time that Naipaul went to the Congo, it makes sense to see the two texts as interrelated. In the essay, Naipaul comments that his interest in *Heart of Darkness* is particularly linked to the novel's background – "'the demoralized land' of plunder and licensed cruelty": "The background now seems to me to be the most effective part of the book" ("Conrad's Darkness", p. 58). In continuation of his constant regret that "History has vanished here" (*A Congo Diary*, p. 9), Naipaul observes that "no one, African, Asian, European, has heard of Conrad or *Heart of Darkness*" (p. 13). In this sense, Naipaul's journey can be seen as a repetition of Conrad's, and *A Bend in the River* as *Heart of Darkness* revisited, while critics have focused on more or less invented intertextual references.[175]

The essay and the travel book together provide an explanation of the novel's inherent juxtaposition of the omniscient total perspective and the limited, concrete knowledge shown about the African state in question. Naipaul uncritically adopts Conrad's handling of the story's background, which – as we have

seen – completely lacks concrete content, present only in allusions to a mysterious, impenetrable darkness. In the essay, Naipaul describes this as a specific, preconceived position that enables him to assume the text's background of violence and savagery. It is exactly this precondition that is continued in the travel book's guesswork regarding the Congo's social and political reality, based on the limited, superficial perspective from the airport or the river journey and the dualistic construction of a difference between the light and civilisation of the city and the darkness and barbarism of the forest.

A Bend in the River is an attempt to correct wanting romanticism and failed realism in Conrad's writing; however, in some respects it actually amplifies the problem, which is analysed in detail in the discussion of the reception of *Heart of Darkness*. Naipaul's novel wants to weed out Conrad's romanticism by removing all layers of illusion from its characters' understanding of the world, in the same way that it wants to correct his realism by submitting to a vision. Regarding the novel's tangible realism, the travel book's curiosities and Conrad's notion of chaos updated to "complexity" are deemed sufficient, resulting in Naipaul maintaining a preconceived image of the Congo as an example of "half-made societies that seemed doomed to remain half-made" ("Conrad's Darkness", p. 59). When that which Naipaul sees in the novel is described as mere set piece, and that which he does not see is demonised as "darkness", his narrative becomes an illustration of an overall vision – an allegory of the rootless narrator who has already seen everything and whose greatest challenge is to forget all he has seen. Naipaul's precise criticism of Conrad thus rebounds on himself. *A Bend in the River* does not manage to break free either from romanticism – which unfolds unimpeded through the narrator's painful experience of loss – or from illustrative realism. Having read the novel, one is left with an even fainter and more unreal image of the Congo. Reading in solidarity with Salim's and Indar's – and Naipaul's – wandering perspective, it is about experiencing the disappearance of the world, the past and individual place. As such, it is a novel that thematises its own limitations.

Urs Widmer, *Im Kongo*

The novel *Im Kongo* (1996) earned Urs Widmer a "definitive position as a Swiss world author on a par with Frisch and Dürrenmatt", according to the review in *Die Welt*.[176] In Britain, his book *Der Geliebte meiner Mutter* (2000) was published under the title *My Mother's Lover* (2011), and was also received very positively. As an advocate for German literature after the fall of the Berlin Wall, Urs Widmer is becoming a well-known representative of a new wave in German-language literature called "the liberated narrative", which some critics define as "postmodern"; other readers point out the kinship with Robert Walser, thus putting less emphasis on narrative symmetries and built-in boxes at the expense of other noticeable characteristics of Widmer's style of prose.[177]

Widmer is also a world author in the sense that his authorship explores the Swiss 'heimat' through literary journeys to distant destinations, such as Africa and Australia. This provides opportunities for reflections on Switzerland's neutrality in the middle of a European borderland marked by conflict, and on the country's position in the Alps in relation to political and geographical antipodes such as the Australian desert or the African jungle. Christophe Bourquin claims in his book *Schreiben über Reisen. Zur ars itineraria von Urs Widmer im Kontext der europäischen Reiseliteratur* (2006) that the travel motif is consistent and fundamental throughout the oeuvre, though it is often used in an experimental and fabulating form that seems far removed from traditional travel accounts.[178]

Urs Widmer's *Die Forschungsreise. Ein Abenteuerroman* (1976), for instance, is a description of an exploration that begins in the narrator's room, including the generic inventory - sextant, binoculars, anemometer, water bottles, etc. Soon, however the book gets lost in everyday phenomena, which the adventurous traveller ought to leave behind, and in a passionate reading of the great predecessors such as Livingstone, Stanley and Hilary.[179] In this sense, *Die Forschungsreise* is an overly loyal continuation of the basic characteristics of the genre - it features fascination and recognition of its predecessors - while at the same time turning on its head the traditional hierarchies of exploration and the safe distribution of domestic and foreign, near and far. The novel does not reject the basic driving forces behind exploration, and while it is very witty - for example in a telephone conversation with the pope - it is not condescending or satirical. Widmer expresses solidarity with the longing for knowledge of the world that propels all real explorations, even when they appear pretentious, end in comical wild goose chases or get lost in the hidden pitfalls and time warps of home - or, like the narrator, in the incessant regress of the footnotes.

The novel *Im Kongo* is a continuation of this early use of the travel motif as myth, reality, profound metaphysics and light entertainment. It is also a combination of the longing for a mother that was the theme of the autobiographical *Der Geliebte meiner Mutter* and the author's lifelong fascination with Joseph Conrad, whose *Heart of Darkness* Widmer translated in 1992 as *Herz der Finsternis* and provided with an epilogue.[180] In the novel's design, autobiographical, concrete and intimate anecdotal elements swap places with the distant 'unheimliche' - which results in an extraordinary happy ending for both 'ends'. *Im Congo* furthermore includes a historical axis, around which doubt is raised about Switzerland's declared neutrality and innocence during

Greene's, Naipaul's, and Widmer's Congo novels all enter into dialogue with Conrad's *Heart of Darkness*. Greene and Naipaul try to overcome the great predecessor by criticising what they see as shortcomings, while Widmer uses exaggerations and jokes to exorcise the grave legacy of the image of the Dark Continent. 'The heart of darkness' by Kisangani is the location of Widmer's brewery, because if there is anything Africa needs, it is beer. However, Widmer's prose also manages to juxtapose Switzerland and the Congo as real and contemporary places in the same world. The hint of farce that is also present in Conrad's narrative, often overlooked by criticism, is picked up by Widmer, at the same time as the myth is deflated.

the era of National Socialism. Through one of Widmer's symmetries, this is mirrored in Mobuto's infamous regime in the Congo, resulting in a subtle processing of colonial and postcolonial stereotypes, which stirs up Europe's and Switzerland's position on the political world map. As world literature, the novel is first and foremost an encouragement to look at the world in a different light – a literary utopia in which places can be described anew, and thus be reborn.

The main character is a young man, Kuno, who works as a care home assistant somewhere in Zürich. According to one of the residents, he is nice and helpful, but thick as two short planks. In fact, Kuno is ignorant and naïve, rather than stupid; he does not have much knowledge about his own or his country's history, and his relation to both the small world (e.g. his ideas about women) and the big world (e.g. Africa) is determined by a superficial reading of a strange mix of newspapers, myths and adventures. His scope is therefore extremely limited, as if since his mother's death he has been unable to let go of the manageable topography of his childhood home in a village on the edge of the Alps and the great forests. When we first meet Kuno, he is removing a piece of chewing gum from one of the rooms in the care home, where his father is about to move in. The gentleman in the neighbouring room, old Herr Berger, is entertaining him with fantasies about Sister Anne, who is drop-dead gorgeous, and to whom Kuno has proposed, only to receive the answer that she will marry him the day he is as black as a Negro.

Whilst removing the gum, Kuno complains to Herr Berger about the fact the he – like his father – has no destiny. While everybody else in the century has a destiny, Kuno and his father have played no part worth mentioning. Parallel to this, he is telling the reader about the day during the war when he found his mother and the gardener in the tomato bed, shot through their heads. To Kuno, his father is a "langweiler", a killjoy, who has only become even duller through a lifetime of work for the town's electricity plant, while Kuno's best friend Willy is full of destiny: "He consisted of destiny alone!" When Kuno hesitates to seize the destiny that his childhood sweetheart, Sophie, is ready to give him, Willy without hesitation takes her with him to the Congo, where one of the town's wealthy people, Anselm Schmirhahn – a former neighbour of Willy's and Kuno's childhood homes – has appointed Willy to manage a brewery in Kisangani. Kuno's account is anecdotal and straightforward, as if he has told it many times before and is simply using it to reaffirm his own conviction that his life is eventless – a mere continuation of his and Willy's former pastime, peeping through the windows when the Schmirhahn family hosted lavish parties. Herr Berger struggles to concentrate on commonplace events, but he comes to life when Kuno's father, with much ado, arrives at the care home, and the two aging gentlemen recognise each other, after forty years' separation, as old friends from the army.

It turns out that Kuno's father is far from the "langweiler" Kuno thought he was. He used to be head of the intelligence agency, where he worked with Herr Berger, who – as a producer and seller of advanced optical equipment – came in close contact with the SS, and even had an audience with Hitler, from which he passed on crucial intelligence to the circle of secret agents called Wiking. To Kuno's surprise, the two old men have experienced numerous fateful hours, which they relate as if they were adventures or scenes from spy films. The annoyed Kuno demands that they tell the war stories with the seriousness and pathos their heroic, life-saving and potentially fatal efforts deserve – "As if the war has been an adventure! You have fought for your lives! And for the lives of your children. For everybody's lives!" This is

followed by Kuno – as if to remind them of the history they have forgotten and suppressed – frenetically conjuring up all the terrors of the war, albeit in a version which also appears like a catalogue or a series of film clips, which provide his only way of accessing the war:

"I was not done yet. 'And those starving'. I was not done at all. 'Frozen to death in the ice, without shoes, for weeks. Those who clung on to the landing gear of the last plane – in which were those who had driven them to their deaths – and they plunged when their hands could no longer hold on to the cold metal. Those who stepped on mines. Those who ran around as human torches. Others, who pressed the barrel of a gun against their temple and pulled the trigger. When the low-flying planes arrived, and people – to the pilots' amusement – ran zigzag'" (p. 71).

The list of terrors is long, and when Kuno finally ceases, the two old men shamefully admit that the excitement of seeing each other again got the better of them. Later that day, Herr Bergen tells, objectively and in detail, about the exchange of secret intelligence, including his meeting with Hitler. This scene is both terrifying and very funny slapstick, which is in stark contrast to the serious risk run by all parties involved, and to the circumstances surrounding the mother's murder, which is an inviolable, vivid memory in Kuno's story. At one point, he is given a photograph showing himself, the mother and the gardener – both of whom were Wiking agents. The photograph has been in the Gestapo's possession and probably served as identification for the sniper who shot them.

Kuno wants to arrange an interview with the two heroes – "a 'Spiegel' interview" – but his father is annoyed with his tabloid-inspired, unbiased, heroic idea of the resistance and warns him that if he is expected to make a public appearance, he will also tell about the quislings and collaborationists in the resistance's own ranks. These people profited from the war, like Herr Berger, who produced efficient sights for fighters and cannons. The perspective, and the way in which the war is presented, changes during the nightly conversations; on the same page the style can change from light satire to crude slapstick, objective description, sensationalism or heroic adventure, and the voice similarly can be aggressive, compassionate, pathetic, forgiving, guilty and so on.

When the question of war profiteering is raised, it is not with reference to Herr Berger, who nevertheless pleads guilty, and when Kuno – piece by piece – gathers knowledge about his own, his father's and the country's past, it is figured as a loss of innocence. In his first story, the focus of the Schmirhahn parties he used to spy on was the erotic entanglements and operetta-like events as seen from the outside, his nose against the window. The additional information from the two former Wiking agents, however, results in the same parties being described from the inside, the guests with well-defined functions as SS people and collaborationists – with the mother's killer probably among them.

What unfolded in the two neighbouring houses on the edge of the forest and the Alps, on the outskirts of Zürich, was anything but a neutral, unfated event. The nightly stories not only expose Switzerland as an active player in the war, on both the Nazi and the resistance sides; it also encompasses the post-war generation's self-induced innocence and ignorance, represented by Kuno. His declaration that he is without destiny and his emotional outbursts about the terrors of war in a style that resembles pages in a screenplay are presented in the novel's design as repetitions without any sense of memory or history – a kind of kitsch. While the two old men apparently reconcile themselves with their war experiences by retelling them in light genres such as adventure or comedy, they do not deny the reality of the terrors and they are prepared to view history and their own participation in it from changing, critical perspectives – if it were not for Sister Anne, with whom they are all completely in love, and who wants them to get their rest.

It seems like a logical consequence of Kuno's newfound knowledge, which eliminates his former neutrality and innocence, when Anselm Schmirhahn, now an ancient man, turns up at the care home. He wants to send Kuno to Kisangani to bring Willy home, so he can report back about the failing earnings of *Brasserie Anselme du Congo*. Before this happens, Anne and Kuno find the dead body of the home's Tamil cook, who has committed suicide in order to avoid being sent back to Sri Lanka, where not only he but his entire family would be punished as traitors. This brings the global wave of communal violence inside the protective walls of the care home. When Kuno arrives in Kinshasa, his connecting flight has been cancelled due to the chaotic conditions under Mobuto, the descriptions of which have a striking resemblance to those in Naipaul's book. Instead, Kuno boards the river steamer *Perle des Afriques* to Kisangani, which provides the narrator with an opportunity to paraphrase Conrad's *Heart of Darkness*, which the author had translated briefly before. The description of Kisangani at Stanley Falls is also quite similar to Naipaul's in *A Bend in the River*, while Kuno's project is identical to Marlow's – to bring back Kurtz, whose decadence at this the last post of civilisation has transgressed any sense of reason.

In the same way that Kuno was marked in the conversations at the care home by his generation's blindness towards fascism, mistakenly identifying it as something that only existed outside the idyll of the mountainous nation, his journey to Africa is characterised by stereotypical expectations of endless forests, "unspeakable rites", animalistic violence, monsters and promiscuity. When he eventually arrives in the heart of darkness, discovering to his astonishment that Willy and Sophie have transformed completely into black Negroes with frizzy hair and thick lips, he maintains for a long time that it is all a deceit and that his old friend and his former fiancée have become victims of a cannibalistic atrocity – though Willy and Sophie assure him at the dinner table that the transformation has taken place completely undramatically.

The contrast between, on the one hand, Kuno's European terror and warped interpretation of the foreign as demonic, and, on the other, Willy's purely pragmatic way of handling things, is manifest in one of the novel's spectacularly comical scenes. Like Kurtz, Willy has become a kind of chieftain, because he has money and power. His grand vizier has died from one of the usual illnesses – malaria or whatever – and Kuno must therefore take over his position. Very soon there is to be a meeting somewhere in the jungle, at which the area's chieftains ceremonially test each other's fetishes and magical powers. During the ceremony, a scene that could have been written by Burroughs, Kuno is terrified, lost in *Heart of Darkness* fantasies, while Willy and the other chieftains soon take off their masks and launch into prosaic negotiations about deliveries of beer and exchange of prostitutes, who are from Brussels, and not jungle Amazons like in Conrad's book. The day after, when they leave the party with enormous hangovers, they do not leave in the canoes in which they arrived, but in buses and jeeps that have been waiting some way from the scene of the ceremony.

Willy persuades Kuno to travel back to Zürich to get Schmirhahn to sign a will saying that he will hand over the position as manager of the brewery in Kisangani to Kuno. In the plane on the way home, Kuno discovers that he has also been transformed into a black person, thus meeting Sister Anne's impossible terms, giving in to her passionate yearning for everything Africa: her room at the care home is full of fetishes. The two ends of the novel are thus tied together in a utopian conclusion, in which Kuno and Anne – who has also become a true Congolese (it turns out it is the beer that has the effect) – become the managers of the *Brasserie Anselme du Congo* and take on Willy's obligations, including the chieftain ceremonies in the jungle. Kuno's mother's death remains unsolved, but it becomes clear that it was not Willy, as Kuno's memory wanted it to be, who gave the identifying photograph to Anselm that was passed on to the Gestapo; it was Kuno himself. Willy is no fascist or criminal, as the story has suggested so far, but unlike Kuno he is a practical man who has no illusions; he is prepared to create his own happiness by seizing the opportunity when it arises.

The novel begins with Kuno, who is the narrator, describing the forests around his childhood home of Witikon – a village that has now merged with

Zürich. In a glade that was only known to him, there were dwarves and gnomes who gave him a magical potion that enabled him to transform into a giant, taller than the tallest trees in the forest. The dwarves sang such terrifying songs that anyone who heard them was bound to shudder, except Kuno the giant, who had made them up. At the end of the novel, Kuno is back in a forest, in a shelter in the top of a tree near Stanley Falls, writing the story on his laptop. He has decided to do it in seventy-two hours, and will reward himself with two beers when the work is done. The manuscript he will print and send to Willy in Zürich – or perhaps he will scatter the pages as water lilies on the river, or put the hard drive in the freezer and let future generations decide what to do with it. From his observation post he watches the sun rise over the boundless jungle, but he can also see where the horizon merges with the sky; "Timbuktu's gold-gleaming pinnacles, or the Tuareg tents in the Sahara. Tiny little triangles. Alexandria, its columns. The Mediterranean. And, hard to believe, sometimes the white tops of the Alps" (p. 215). When he finishes writing, he has caught up with sixty-five years of his life, "Now! Now I am writing and existing at the same time. Naturally, I let out a scream of joy, and while I am screaming, I am writing that I am doing it. Ahh!" After this, he wants to climb down from the tree in the first light of the sun, leave the forest and run up the stairs in his house to find Anne lying in bed with her black feet sticking out from under the mosquito net.

The text on his laptop becomes the ultimate magical object, generating a series of events that are contrary to nature, for example the fact that he can sometimes glimpse the Swiss Alps from his tree at Stanley Falls, or that Swiss people, pale as Emmental cheeses, transform into frizzy-haired Congolese after having drunk a few beers from the brewery in Kisangani. The dwarf in his childhood glade granted him the ability to narrate and change the world and its proportions, and when his story ends, the monsters in the forest, far from being exorcised, count among reality's pragmatic hierarchies of phenomena against which one must take precaution, although one cannot completely expel their magic.

In this manner, the introduction and the conclusion bring the two forests in two different continents together, helping to settle the novel's many scores. Kuno's expectation that he will find the origin of all evil in the Congo is expressed through the journey's imitation of Naipaul and – especially – Conrad; however, it is established at the text's beginning, where the narrator inserts passages in italics that, in a hypnotising style, repeat the myths about inner Africa as hell on earth. In the novel's design, these passages can be attributed to Kuno's nightly writing sessions on his laptop, when he must tie himself to the tree in order not to be torn away by the sounds of the night. Instead, he

gives in to all the sentimental fantasies of childhood, which he finally manages to rein in during the daytime.

The novel is built up around numerous symmetries, parallel drifts and mirror effects, which might qualify it as postmodern literature. Echoing the novel's idea of writing as an act of magic, Urs Widmer said in an interview about the novel that "Writing has something to do with magic" – indicating that the grand design is ultimately some magic of fiction, a spectacular joke.[181] What is unique about Widmer's novels is, on the contrary, his insistence that realism and adventure are not mutually exclusive but complementary. For example, Herr Berger and Kuno's father's stories about the war take off in a fabulating, adventurous form that does not seal off access to history, rather the opposite, stimulating dialogue and ultimately facilitating completely new insights for Kuno. And though the projections from one axis, such as the repressions of neutral Switzerland, onto the other axis, such as European stereotypes about Africa, make use of effects from comical genres including mix-ups and exaggerations, there is still an element of seriousness, bearing the mark either of sadness, as in the mother's death, or of criticism, as in the themes of fascism and misuse of power in both Europe and Africa.

In a similar manner, the novel's attitude to the Congo is both realistic – based on a lifelong interest in the region and in Conrad's novel – and a utopian transgression of the paradigms that have characterised the literary tradition after Conrad, as well as the reports and travel descriptions that have aimed to convey the truth about this African hotspot. In the epilogue for *Herz der Finsternis*, Urs Widmer claims that Conrad, despite all his text's ambiguities, critiques colonialism – a common claim that has been nuanced in the present study. While in the epilogue, and in interviews, Widmer talks respectfully about his great predecessor – and demonstrates a thorough knowledge of the history of the Congo – the novel *Im Congo* remains a correction of Conrad's key metaphor of the heart of darkness, and turns the central 'relief' story on its head. 'Blackness' is a thoroughly positive metaphor in the novel, and when Anne and Kuno settle down in Kisangani, which – according to Marlow and countless of his historical and fictitious successors – is a purely dystopic place, they are perfectly happy, both having fulfilled a dream and overcome the loss of a mother. Violence and chaos are not denied, but they have nothing to do with inherent evil. It is possible to speak with the demons, as well as to love, eat and drink beer that is just as refreshing as that in Switzerland, where there is just as much evil behind the neighbour's window, if one takes a proper look – and where it is only too easy, as Kuno's mistaken impression of Willy as a pro-fascist shows, to fall for the temptation to demonise that which is mere personal drive.

The novel's utopian transgression of Joseph Conrad's condensed myth about the Dark Continent, and subsequent continuations of the drift gaze, is simultaneously a transgression of Stanley's panoramic vista in which Africa was conquered in one single, supreme rhetorical gesture. Kuno's view in the novel's conclusion pans across continents and deconstructs the usual hierarchies and cartographic forms of representation, comparing the Tuareg tents with the Alps and with great African cities of the past like Alexandria and Timbuktu. Both colonial supremacy and postcolonial criticism's widening of the gap between 'them' and 'us' through duality principles and cultural relativism are, in Widmer's universe, subject to a strategy of reversal and exaggeration, which exposes the inertia of opposition as needless and false. The brewery in Kisangani "is, in itself, nothing bad", said Widmer to the interviewer, who insisted on perceiving the book as anti-colonialist criticism. And when during the ceremony in the forest the chieftains have a break to go for a wee, they remove their masks and talk about this and that. In the novel's utopian geography, the forest in the Congo where Kuno finally finds his home can be the same as the one in which he grew up, as well as the point where both places are reborn through the novel's adventure: Switzerland and the Congo – more specifically the two places' boundaries between town or city and forest – become parts of a topography that is emancipated from contrived concepts of the past, in the form of white, neutral innocence and black, demonic evil.

Several distinctive characteristics of *Im Congo* earn it a unique place in literature about the Congo, and in world literature. Firstly, the effect of the utopian element – which more than anything is expressed in the unnatural yet logical transformation of whites to blacks – is *not* that the novel's locations appear as unreal or philosophical constructions. The two elements of the etymological sense of the word – which is from both Greek *outopia*, 'non-place', and *eutopia*, 'a good or happy place' – are found, respectively, in the novel's deconstruction of cartographic representation that facilitates a juxtaposition of the Alps' and Central Africa's forests, and in its representation of both the Congo and Switzerland as happy places to live. At the same time, the places are completely realistic: the brewery in Kisangani and the care home in Zürich are described in a classic realistic form, and both narratives are influenced by the seriousness linked to the missed mother and, more generally, the wish to find a new home and start over. If we consider the parodic aspects of the novel, particularly Kuno's prejudices as imitations of all Conrad's stereotypes about impenetrable darkness and omnipresent terror that are soon exposed as childish and comical misinterpretations, it makes sense to perceive the style as satire and meta-fiction. However, the imitation of Conrad is not scornfully retrospective; rather, it is elegantly forward-looking, as if to demonstrate how

easy it is for literature to expel terror and show the way forward. Finally, this conjunction of gravity and lightness, comic and tragic, is – according to Erich Auerbach's classical definition in *Mimesis* (1946) – what characterises the great works of realism in world literature.

3 The Congo in Popular Literature: Bizarre Truths in Bizarre Stories

It was not just Stanley's travel books that were pivotal in the development of nineteenth-century travel literature, but also his journeys and biography. Livingstone's travel descriptions became part of the abolitionist movement's campaigns, constituting one of the main reasons for Europe's presence in Africa and the 'opening' of the continent. The books' contents and form were designed to sell a product to a mass audience, while the earnings from the same books also funded follow-up expeditions and, in that sense, had an influence on their extent, equipment and routes as well as their chances of success or failure. Livingstone's branding as icon and pilgrim was, as described by Clare Pettitt, a precursor of the celebrity culture that gained impetus via the merging of the British and American newspaper readers – among other factors as a consequence of the copper cable across the Atlantic Ocean. Livingstone's and Stanley's meeting became a celebration of the first event in media globalisation as well as a symbolic representation of the new Anglo-American alliances. The view of the world as a stage for entertainment and symbolic shadow plays of roles and identities, used in a refined version in Graham Greene's novel, was obviously known from Shakespeare and renaissance culture, but its modern, globalised point of departure is in media events such as the iconic meeting between Stanley and Livingstone.

Both Stanley's and Conrad's texts about the Congo formed part of – and were dependent on – popular cultural market mechanisms and appeal – albeit with very different outcomes in relation to their forms of modernism. Nevertheless, both Stanley's use of New Journalism's visual method and fascinating 'graphic scraps', and Conrad's simultaneously nostalgic and sceptical use of the adventure genre, gothic romance and popular travel literature, contributed to the concept of the Congo as a stage that was accessible to an unlimited number of uncensored productions of grandiose, engrossing pulp fictions. The many travel accounts by European employees stationed in the colony supported the myth about a place in the back of beyond, while high literary fictions such as Conrad's amplified the ongoing creation of the myth of the Dark Continent – i.e. a location on the world map where the usual boundaries between reality and fantasy were suspended.

For these reasons, in twentieth-century popular culture the Congo has been

"Photographing gorillas", from Paul du Chaillu's *The Country of the Dwarfs* (1901). Du Chaillu boasted of having taken the first photograph of a living gorilla. But it was only possible with his heavy equipment because the young gorilla's mother was dead and it was clinging to her breast for milk and comfort. "Her death was painfully like that of a human being", adds Chaillu to the description of "the wonderful creature which God has made almost in the image of man". The photograph was lost, but du Chaillu was able to tell and illustrate the story in the book and repeat it in his talks to the *National Geographic Society* back home in America. Subsequently, during the Dian Fossey affair, photographs in *National Geographic* would become crucial to raising money for the endangered species.

a preferred territory for melodramatic stagings of apocalyptic visions of terror within a broad, mixed field of genres, including crypto-zoology, horror movies, hard core natural science, tragic tourism and internet blogs. Needless to say, this is a large quantity of material to process, but given that it all forms part of the transformation of the comprehensive field of travel literature representations of the Congo, some key currents will be presented below.

The National Museum of Denmark has recently established a website containing databases, archival material and articles about the artistic, literary and anthropological objects from the Congo exhibition, and Bornholm Museum in Denmark has hosted an extensive exhibition focusing on travellers from Bornholm to the Congo as well as publishing the book *Bornholm, Congo, return*. This book looks at the Congo from almost every angle imaginable, from the missionary societies to the region's anthropology, freshwater fish, the okapi – the forest giraffe that became one of the wonders of the twentieth-century – and the collections of art objects that Danes brought home with them as private trophies or commodities. These exhibitions, websites and catalogues are indications of the tension between testimony and wonder which permeates all textual representations of the Congo. They are attempts to establish scientific explanatory frameworks to organise texts and objects so that they provide testimonies to the truth as well to right and wrong. However, this re-contextualisation is the consequence of a previous de-contextualisation, which edited and exhibited the phenomena as wonders; wonder as a discourse is still present as an element in the contemporary researchers' "style of inquiry", which displays both hesitation and fascination towards objects and tropes that stand out as impenetrable and out of proportion.

In this respect, the new museum exhibitions adhere to a fundamental fascination with the Congo as exclusive and unique that was initiated in the first travel accounts, in which Upper Congo especially was described as an inexhaustible reservoir of wonders – a notion that subsequently took hold in the public imagination, especially in popular fiction.

Apes

The 1995 film *Congo*, directed by Frank Marshall and based on a novel from 1980 with the same title by the author of *Jurassic Park*, Michael Crichton, makes use of a series of the most trite wonders of the Congo (to use a deliberate oxymoron), in addition to repeating several key political motifs from the existing catalogue. The film is about a series of failed expeditions to an area of the Ituri forest close to the great volcanoes of East Congo. On the pretext of scientific research – like countless real expeditions in the 1880s – an expedition is launched to reintroduce the gorilla Amy, who has learned to speak by means of a special robotic glove, to the jungle. Amy leads the expedition into King Solomon's secret city, where the diamonds are guarded by a hitherto unknown species of gorillas, who Solomon's soldiers in times of yore trained to kill all intruders. At the last moment, the heroes are saved from the trained killer gorillas by the trained speaking gorilla, and despite her difficulties communicating with the real mountain gorillas, who do not understand English, Amy is eventually rehomed in her jungle habitat in a carefully executed, ecologically sound ending.

Legends about Christian kingdoms in the area around the great lakes have played a role since the renaissance, both for those who heard and delivered rumours from journeys up the Nile, and for those who actually tried to penetrate the area. The first travellers noticed the area's well-organised kingdoms and the fertile, wholesome landscape, perceiving the natives to be more talented

and noble than in other parts of Central Africa. Among other things, this resulted in the region – contradicting the general notion about African culture as timeless – being attributed with a historical dimension, which from a wider perspective prepared the ground for ideas about old, forgotten civilisations, especially in the great Ituri Forests. Victorianism and Conrad's image of the continental inland as a realm of dark and timeless nature thus competed with Stanley's travel accounts, as we have seen, with later popular fiction and with alternative concepts of the area as a place with privileged access to enlightenment and renaissance.

One of the characters in *Congo* points out this strange situation: "Clichés contain elements of truth. Many bizarre stories contain many bizarre truths". The film is first and foremost a display and exploration of dominant commonplaces that fascinate us though we cannot understand them. Furthermore, the human/gorilla/robot theme unfolds colonial motifs from the Congo's history of plundering of natural resources into politically correct, postcolonial, ecological models of reconciliation. However, the distinction between good and evil gorillas – in which the latter are monsters that obey neither beast nor man, and only calm down when an ape gives them commands in human language, while the former affectionately accept teaching from humans – also makes the film a grotesque parallel to and repetition of the white Europeans' deeply rooted concepts of educating 'the Negro'. The theme has many ramifications, and the relationship between ape and man was obviously something that fascinated the very first explorers. Stanley, for instance, considered the possible kinship between chimpanzees, gorillas and Pygmies, and questioned whether the infamous skulls on the palisades around the villages came from apes or humans. An obvious inspiration for Crichton's novel is the zoologist Dian Fossey's account *Gorillas in the Mist* (1981), which follows a mission to save threatened mountain gorillas in the border region between the Congo and Rwanda, sponsored by *National Geographic*, and which contained and reversed a number of the earliest motifs about apes.

The story about Dian Fossey, both as she herself describes it and as it has been pieced together in biographies that attempt to explain her extraordinary life and – in particular – her mysterious death, is a 'go native' story that has much in common with Conrad's story about Kurtz. In order to protect the animals, which she thinks about more than she does people, she is prepared to transgress the norms of civilisation, and organises a scare campaign with the usual repertoire of punitive measures. In order to control the natives who are living on the reservation, she acts as a magician whose fetishes enable her to cast horrible spells, and she burns down villages, kidnaps children and lynches people. Inside the boundaries of the reservation, Fossey thereby establishes colonial rule based on

"Giant gorilla". From Jenssen-Tusch's *Scandinavians in the Congo*. Images of killed gorillas, held up on display by natives, are part of the standard repertoire in travel books from the turn of the century.

a mix of totalitarianism and witchcraft, in clear opposition both to the natives who lived in the area before it became a reservation and to the local authorities, who see her wilful methods as a major problem in relation to the earnings from tourism that are crucial to the impoverished district. Fossey's fundraising to preserve the reservation uses a rhetoric that is similar to the abolitionist movement's – including photographic campaigns which, via *National Geographic*, are distributed to the waiting rooms of the medical clinics, presenting the gorillas' habitat as an original Arcadian idyll while telling about violations and mutilations. Another parallel to the abolitionist movement is that the campaign results in an increased demand for gorillas from the world's zoos, meaning that Dian Fossey inadvertently paved the way for illegal poaching activities in the reservation. With the big male gorilla, named Digit, in an important role, the film *Gorillas in the Mist: the Story of Dian Fossey* starring Sigourney Weaver wallows in gory images of mutilated apes, whose hands and feet have been severed – which refers back to the Congo Reform Association's display of atrocities. The fundraising that initially took place through organisations such as the Dian Fossey Gorilla Fund International and The Digit Fund in the UK was later carried on in campaigns that continued to exploit Fossey's global brand, despite the fact that the same organisations had turned their backs on her in her last years, until she was killed under violent and unsolved circumstances.

Fossey's own story, and the earliest campaigns, films and biographies, such as Harold Hayes' *The Dark Romance of Dian Fossey* (1990), all contribute to a myth that takes its central motifs and rhetoric from early travel accounts and human rights campaigns. *National Geographic* and the website for The Dian Fossey Gorilla Fund International continue this process in their current initiatives in connection with the civil war and the threat it poses to the area's mountain gorillas.[182] One of the effects of the rhetoric used – which is eagerly disseminated in the global news media – is that the animals appear more human than the humans who inhabit the area, and excite more humanitarian sympathy and support, while the victims of the civil war fade into the background.

The story of Dian Fossey raises a number of questions that all deserve detailed analysis, but are beyond the scope of the present study. Many factors indicate that in her initial campaigns Fossey *staged* the traditional rhetorical figures of disgust and compassion that have stuck to the place since Conrad. Later, however, she became caught up in her own fiction or "dark romance", just like Kurtz. Naturally, the story's fascination is enhanced by the riddle of who killed her – a fascination that has been rewoken by testimonies given in connection with The International War Crimes Tribunal after the genocide in Rwanda. However, the fascination with Fossey also thrives on the search for the unlikely answers to what can cause this kind of transformation in a person's life. Are we primarily dealing with the power of rhetoric in conjunction with the global magic of media? Or are there really dark forces at play, which – like fetishes – created a dramatic persona of someone who initially thought that she was merely staging a play in order to fool everybody else?

Conrad's descriptions of Kurtz's post at Stanley Falls, his private army of silent, native warriors that protect the enormous ivory heaps, the savage and noble Amazon, Marlow's contemplations on his and Kurtz's teaching of cannibals and so on are all elements that find echoes in the parallel patterns that characterise film's and Conrad's own dependency on "bizarre truths" in "bizarre stories". On Edgar Rice Burroughs' map of Africa, Lord Greystoke's farm is situated in Kenya; however, when the farmer is short of money, he journeys into East Congo in the guise of Tarzan, and it is here the adventure of *Tarzan and the Jewels of Opar* (1918) unfolds. It features the entire catalogue of Congo clichés, including hidden kingdoms – Opar is the sunken Atlantis with tremendous treasures, guarded by savage warriors – and the conflict between Belgian colonisers, who are bureaucratic and cruel, Arab slave traders and Englishmen, who seek to promote free trade, morality and justice. Tarzan is both someone who drains the country of treasures as he pleases, and – like Amy the chimpanzee – acts as an intermediary between the separate districts and zones of the Congo, and between humans and animals. Burroughs' portraits of Tarzan and Opar are

E. R. Burroughs' map of Tarzan's Africa, from Borberg et al.'s *The Tarzan Myth* (1980).

not very different from Conrad's descriptions of Kurtz and the post at Stanley Falls, which shows the persistent effect of these wonders across genres and time.

The same wonders feature in different genres and historical contexts, albeit with noticeable changes in their functions. In Conrad's novel, the wonder discourse is used as a literary effect, which in the second part of the novel increasingly contaminates the text and delocalises the plot. This gives it a universal, aestheticised quality, while at the same time eroding the concrete. This is an early repetition of the renaissance wonder discourse, which lends some authority to the representation, additionally by drawing in recognisable elements from the explorers' prominent, prestigious discourse. On the other hand, the wonder is trivialised by being reduced to literary effect. In the renaissance and until the middle of the eighteenth century, wonder was a well-defined category of pleasure and thinking, which belonged in the field of the real at the same time as being a source of scientific observation and philosophical speculation; Conrad, however, does not employ the discourse as a way of understanding the world, but as a trick that paves the way for shaping the travel material in a literary form and blurring the sense of place, giving the *fin de siècle* and decadence motifs free rein. His own travel account was noticeable because of its complete lack of wonder,

and the addition of wonder to *Heart of Darkness* is, in that respect, merely a repetition of stereotypical figures for the primitive, barbaric and uncanny. The proud Amazon, the skulls on the palisades and the sound of drums in the night are automated figures from a staple repertoire – the most dominant of which provides the book with its title. The novel's strengths are to be found elsewhere, although we might be able to detect traits of a continuation of the renaissance discourse of wonder.

As mentioned in the introduction, Lord Kames and other eighteenth-century writers felt that curiosity and wonder were in danger of ceasing to be a basic source of knowledge and philosophical thought, instead toppling into an infantile, vain or narcissistic desire to possess, stimulated by the new position of wonders as attractive commodities. Critics of popular culture, including the World's Fairs and the colonial exhibitions that still had vast audiences even in the 1960s, have focused on the latter aspect. What follows, in contrast, will focus on the former: from the prose perspective, popular fiction's use of wonder is not necessarily more objectionable than its use in novels or travel accounts, although it *can* be, as briefly demonstrated in the case of Dian Fossey. Popular fiction's representation of places, whether topological, topographical or in the form of singular, wondrous and yet well-known locations, can – when appraised as reality work – have both an opening and a closing effect in relation to understanding and dialogue. The modern multimedia configurations of early tropes replicating the Reform Association campaigns, especially from the Red Rubber era, exemplified in Dian Fossey's gorilla campaign in biographies, photo-series, on film and the Internet, are often presented without the modesty traditionally found in travel accounts and novels. From a performative prose perspective, they also convey, as we are about to see, a powerful *media critical* potential, which is directed at the technological conditions of the prose itself.

Leopard Men, Tintin, Tarzan and Trader Horn

In Edgar Rice Burroughs' novels about Tarzan, and in Hergé's second album about the renowned Belgian reporter, *Tintin au Congo*, wonder is also represented in the form of props that are taken from a depot of well-known images, in order to rouse the reader's interest by evoking images of the foreign and unintelligible that are never so shocking, however, that readers cannot find their way home again. Nevertheless, popular culture's use of wonders is closer to the original discourse than Conrad's. Both *Tarzan and the Leopard Men* (printed as a serial in 1931, the book published in 1935) and *Tintin au Congo* (1931) include accounts of leopard men and Anioto sects, not as stereotypical figures for something distant and indefinable taken from a lost past, but as fascinating references to the

Paul Wissaert's sculpture *Les Aniota* (1913), which is exhibited at the MRAC exposition in Tervuren, where Hergé used it as a model for the leopard men who play an important part in *Tintin au Congo* (1931). The Anioto motif was popular in Belgian colonial literature and was also central in Jungsbøll's *Black Man's Land*. This secret sect or terror organisation, which, on the basis of a mix of religious and political motivations, spread terror by killing selected natives, dressed in specially designed leopard costumes. It remains unclear how much truth there was in the widespread rumours, partly because the eyewitness accounts of Anioto murders are often hallucinatory or manipulated. This not only makes the motif exotic; it makes it a strange element within exoticism.

actual testimonies of the time. The uncertainty as to what the phenomenon is, and to what degree it is political, religious, natural or supernatural, is obviously used to its full literary potential, but the effect is very much a result of the fact that this wonder cannot be rejected as mere imagination; it exists somewhere out there. While the curious in renaissance culture was open to description, even if it could not be integrated into traditional knowledge frameworks - descriptions would employ different viewing angles expressed through changing points of view in the essays - wonders such as leopard men are not accessible via realistic description and precise observation. They are secret and invisible, and on a general level they do not appeal to philosophical wonder, but rather to hermeneutic paranoia. One important quality in popular culture's use and redefined function of the renaissance fascination with curiosities is that they are either recognisable imitations of the iconography of the foreign, or they remain within the sphere of the secret and occult. Burroughs' and Hergé's stories draw on this predictable catalogue, using the expected drifts between the well-known and the secret, but they also make a number of additions that show an awareness of their own historical contexts and inherited topographies of the Congo in a manner that is far from trivial. In the terms of the market and globalisation, these fictions thus maintain curiosity towards the phenomenological wonder, which, as was the case in the renaissance mix of knowledge

and entertainment culture, allows for the participation of both scholars and the uneducated. A search on the relatively new media that is the Internet will, unsurprisingly, result in countless hits about leopard men, most of which approach the phenomenon as something paranormal. It is a consistent feature that the leopard men's place of origin is located in Liberia, Sierra Leone and Upper Congo, and that the first cases are dated around 1900 with several booms in activity in the 1930s and the period that led up to the Congo's independence. Furthermore, the phenomenon is loosely linked to assumptions about certain initiation rites, which, however – like the phenomenon at large – remain secret. This sanctions an endless web of diverse and often conflicting hypotheses about the leopard men's secret societies.

In his thesis "*Le petit Belge avait vu grand*". *Une littérature coloniale* (1993), Pierre Halen documents the vast dissemination of the Anioto motif in Belgian colonial literature; however, Halen readily admits that it is difficult to approach the topic analytically and frame it in an ethnographic or literary context. The phenomenon is one massive rumour that can neither be disproved nor confirmed, and in colonial literature it is more than mere exoticism; it is a foreign element within exoticism, which apparently causes scientific, legal and religious discourses to collapse and deviate from traditional procedures concerning the presentation of evidence, even today. One article by Veronica Bellers in the web archive British Empire Articles stands out by going to the sources of extremely dubious court cases in Nigeria in the 1940s, when 95 native men were hanged for so-called "leopard murders". Several government officers tried in vain to question the sentenced men's guilt in the murders, which – to all appearances – were caused by real leopards that had begun attacking humans in certain areas for completely natural reasons. Belief, however, outweighed fact, and due to inventions rooted in common hysteria, as well as some people's scapegoating of their enemies, a group of suspects were identified, some of whom even gave false evidence by admitting to their part in the alleged crimes. According to Bellers, the whole affair started because of a combination of two cases. One was the finding of a victim of a leopard attack, whose cause of death could not be established because of the body's state of decomposition. The other was about a woman who initially claimed that her child had been taken by a leopard, but subsequently altered her explanation, claiming instead that the child had been attacked by a man wearing a leopard hood. Eventually, she identified the man as Billy Eshiet, though she had explained earlier that she could not see the man's face. Over the course of a few years, a consensus was formed that the inexplicable murders were related to secret Anioto sects. In the British press in Nigeria, the paranoia escalated to a point at which any native person was seen as a potential leopard man, while the native population contributed to the paranoia by reporting an increasing number of leopard killers, partly fuelled by their religiously determined fear of people who could change into animals, and partly as a pragmatic means in power struggles between rivalling parties. The article exposes how the leopard men, as a modern, fabricated wonder suspended the established legal system, launched a series of violent acts that were rooted in fear and revenge and were adopted in literature and politics – as we saw in Viggo Jungsbøll's, Edvard Andersen's and Arne Falk-Rønne's texts.

Most of the websites that address the topic do not doubt the leopard men's horrible deeds, but rather contribute to the spreading terror by expanding the field of uncertainty regarding the phenomenon. They do so by filling the gaps in existing knowledge with fantastical conspiracy theories, which never go beyond hints and guesswork, or by ascribing it to a paranormal register – perceiving the leopard men as real transformations of men, like werewolves. It is a staple element in both varieties that a reoccurrence of leopard men is a possibility; perhaps, like other terror organisations, they have gone underground and are only waiting for some secret sign to tell them to return and wreak more havoc.

On a Danish website there is an article titled "A Dane's struggle against the horrifying Aniotos", signed Leif Birger Holmstedt, author and curator, specialist in African masks. The article is an almost word-by-word retelling of Viggo Jungsbøll's account of how he eventually managed to acquire the irrefutable proof for the sect's existence, which led to the hanging of 14 men. Contrary to the present study, which – parallel with Veronica Bellers – interprets the story as either fiction or miscarriage of justice, and probably a mix of both, Holmstedt views Jungsbøll's story as completely true. Another, more cryptic website, signed Gueux des Flandres, contains a number of "messages" about "les Aniotos", which – despite the factographic style – bears witness to an uncritical fascination with the phenomenon that borders on obsession.[183] Information is presented as scientific fact, but it lacks sources – with two exceptions, which indicate the speed at which a curiosity on the Internet can transgress usual discursive limits. First, Gueux de Flandres refers to the Musée Royal de l'Afrique Centrale and an exhibited sculpture that depicts a leopard man, dressed in leopard costume and metal claws, dramatically looming over his victim like an illustration from a Tarzan novel. Second, the writer refers to Hergé's *Tintin au Congo*, in which one of the intrigues thought up to sideline Tintin is a cunning and dramatic use of the Anioto people, who are, at this point, known to the reader. The connection between the two references is created by the hypothesis that Hergé probably did his research for the album on visits to the Musée Royal de l'Afrique Centrale, where he saw the sculpture that – apparently – depicts an actual anthropological phenomenon. However, all signs indicate that the exhibition of leopard men at the museum is based on costumes and claws that were acquired through the

widespread trade in fake ethnographica, in which natives produced and sold various artefacts because there was a demand among colonial collectors and not because they were used in original, ritual practices.[184]

Tintin au Congo

Tintin au Congo was published in 1930 as a series of black-and-white comic strips in the newspaper *Le Petit Vingtième*. The following year, it was published as an album, and in 1946 Hergé and his publishers chose to release an edited version of the story as a colour album, which has attracted attention for toning down the original's most direct and paternalistic references to the colonial question. The edited version, however, was still impossible to stomach in the political climate of the 1970s, when a combination of left-wing child pedagogy and political correctness led to accusations of racism. We will return to this matter shortly.

Tintin has much in common with Stanley: he is a fearless and dynamic reporter; newspapers around the globe are fighting to get exclusive rights to his stories; and his fame is highlighted by the many different currencies in which the newspaper editors try to outbid each other. A sequence in which Tintin derails a locomotive, and as a consequence has to put the lazy, obstinate natives to work, is a paraphrase of Stanley's road construction work and transportation of river steamers. Tintin's use of modern media, such as film and sound tapes, to expose plans of a coup d'état while holding the natives in a magical grip is a parallel to Stanley's use of "tara-tara" – the notebook as fetish. Tintin's role as peacemaker also imitates Stanley's account. However, this modelling of Tintin in Stanley's image is also influenced by events in the colony after Stanley, and by the Reform Association's campaign. The natives are crude caricatures, both in the way they are drawn and in their simplified Negro French. At the same time, they are remarkably critical towards Tintin – "Li missié blanc, très malin!" (*Tintin au Congo*, 1946, p. 20) – until they realise that he liberates them from superstition and oppression. The comedy often occurs because it is clear to the reader that the natives are most openly critical in situations when Tintin is actively trying to help them. The Reform Association's campaign, however, is a more central theme in the plot: American criminals, in conspiracy with a native medicine man, try by any means to put a stop to Tintin's journey and reportage – the explanation for which, in the end, turns out to be because they are in cahoots with Al Capone. The infamous gangster is trying to organise a mafia in the Congo to control the diamond mines. At the end, Tintin can comfortably read the news about his deeds in the Congo on the front pages of all the world's newspapers – heroic deeds that prevented foreign powers from taking over the country's di-

In recent years, *Tintin au Congo* has been brought to trial on the grounds of assumed racism or violations of animal welfare. Soon after publication, the successful reporter faced harsh criticism, and Hergé changed the style in subsequent albums to fit in with the cultural relativism of the time; he also revised the first albums to mitigate their prejudices. However, comparing the original black-and-white version with the subsequent versions, the former is far more critical towards the colonial rule, which is described with the metaphor of an all-devouring leopard, while the paternalistic lesson is exposed as parody. In fact, the original version of *Tintin au Congo* is unique in literature of the era in that it relatively explicitly criticises the colonisation.

amond mines. At the same time, the world has been warned that in the future gangsters will try to spread terror in the country in order to seize control of its resources. The headline in *l'Africain*, for instance, reads: "Le Congo va-t-il devenir la colonie de Chicago?" (1931 version, p. 275); "L'Afrique va-t-elle devenir la ... de Chicago?" (1946 version, p. 53).[185]

The stage on which the Belgian reporter operates is clearly that of the twentieth-century global media. Like Stanley's, his travel account uses "graphic scraps" to address the literary world market, which is also staged with real-world welcome processions in Brussels to celebrate Tintin's returns from the Soviet Union and the Congo. His disclosure of financial crime in the Congo is also addressed to the scandal-starved world press. However, it is described with a characteristic openness that makes it possible to read the Reform Association's Edmund Morel into Tintin's role as relentless reporter on the world's injustice, while at the same time sensing an echo of the propaganda King Léopold used to defend himself against Morel's campaign: that all accusations of violations in the colony were, in fact, attempts to establish a basis for British expansion in Central Africa. The Belgian presence in the country, then and now, basically aimed at protecting the natural resources against all-devouring empires.[186]

The intrigue is built around the legendary leopard men – the sect Hergé calls "les Aniotas" – who once had the gangsters' ally, the medicine man Muganda, among their members. When Tintin announces that he wants to go leopard hunting – he does in fact kill many wild animals on his journey – Muganda conjures up a wily plan, according to which he will kill the officious reporter while wearing a leopard costume. Muganda explains:

> "I am telling you there is a secret society, called "Aniota". They organised to stop civilisation by white men! ... Aniota kill black chiefs who support white men. Aniota wear special costume, looking like leopard skin. On their fingers they wear steel claws, like those of leopard. What is more, they carry stick, with end carved like leopard's claw" (1931 version, p. 236).[187]

To Muganda's regret, his disguise is revealed, and Tintin gets the upper hand, ultimately exposing Al Capone and making the front pages. Thus, it appears that Hergé supports the theory of the leopard men as a kind of freedom fighter, who did not kill randomly but targeted collaborators and covered up their crimes by making them look like leopard attacks. The medicine man, however, is neither leopard nor leopard man; he is merely a ridiculous Negro dressed up as Anioto, and Tintin's cool gaze soon sees through any mystery in the case.

Hergé's first albums have subsequently been perceived as crude, extremely offensive racism, which led to the publishers Casterman removing the album from their catalogue in the years 1966-1970, after which it was rehabilitated and published again, partly on the request of the government of the Congo, where the album was hugely popular, and actually a source of inspiration for Congolese comics.[188] Hergé was known for the thorough research carried out for the "Aventures de Tintin", but according to critics, the first two albums were to a large degree subject to prejudice and myths about the exotic destinations, and were less based on anthropological knowledge than the later

albums, beginning with *Le Lotus bleu* (1934).[189] This distinction only makes sense from a superficial perspective, given that although the later albums appear more politically correct and free from explicit racism, they are more subtly but also massively problematic in relation to the cultural relativism they borrow from modern anthropology. The earlier albums are far more open towards the potential conflicts in the material: though *Tintin au Congo* clearly expresses solidarity with Belgian colonial politics, the sequences contain so many transformations, disguises and rewritings of the material that prejudices are also exposed and processed. Furthermore, the colony's prehistory is not concealed or forgotten, unlike in most travel accounts; quite extraordinarily for literature about the Congo, it is brought to light and made *visible* in the sequences inspired by silent cinema.

One example is when Tintin shoots an ape in order to use its skin to disguise himself – albeit still wearing his indispensable pith helmet – and in an encounter with another ape ends up in an argument about his pith helmet and gun, which – contrary to the dialogue with the native Congolese – is conveyed in equally correct French. Here, the disguises transcend the established antitheses that characterise typical colonial prejudice. Prejudices are set in motion and exaggerated by ascribing more developed linguistic competences to the ape than to Tintin's guide, Coco, highlighting the fact that the differences are constructed, not essential: the European's symbols of civilisation and superiority, the pith helmet and gun, are merely part of a costume or attire. Another example is the medicine man Muganda, who stages an accusation against Tintin for stealing the village fetish. The plan backfires, because Tintin's far stronger medicine – sound and film recordings – prove that Muganda, like Mobuto would later, uses the fetish to keep the village in ignorance and fear. On the one hand, the sequence leaves an impression of the Congolese as blind, ignorant victims of superstition; on the other, it does tell the story about the colonisers stealing fetishes and directs attention to the fact that modern mass media are the Europeans' magical, and potentially dangerous, fetishes. Similarly, the Anioto sequence is a continuation and repetition of the myth that is expressed in the sculpture at the Musée Royal de l'Afrique Centrale, but Hergé makes it mundane by revealing it as a cover for political infiltration, and he demythologises the game of disguises by turning it into a joke. The concluding drawing consists of a comical and very exaggerated mix of stereotypes, pertaining both to the Congo and to Europe. A Congolese throws himself in admiration at the feet of two sculptures depicting Tintin and Snowy, while two other Congolese in a café are expressing prejudices and stereotypes about Europe: "Them say, in Belgium, all whites are like Tintin"

(1946 version, p. 62). A sequence in which a missionary gives Tintin an assignment as a substitute teacher in a school is often identified by both critics and fans as an example in the discussion about racism. In the first version, Tintin teaches about "our distant Belgium", while in the second version the lesson is in maths. Defenders of Hergé use this example to substantiate the standard claim – that Hergé did not know any better in 1930; he was influenced

by the widespread perceptions of his conservative background, "conservative prejudice", and furthermore, he had been asked by his publisher to write about the Congo, because the colony was in need of workers and needed advertisement. The 1946 edition, and Hergé's subsequent apologies for the album's offensive descriptions of the Congolese, supports an acquittal of Hergé and suggests that the album should be perceived as an interesting expression of a historical era that has come to an end – a stance that is represented in prefaces to the reissues, which, however, also warn the reader about attitudes that may come across as offensive. This, however, was not enough for critics who, in July 2007 in the USA and England, and in August in Belgium and Sweden, started a dispute about the album that led to appeals to the courts to have the album banned with reference to its racist, xenophobic contents. In India, an organisation for animal welfare has demanded that the album be banned, because the album is "replete with instances that send a message to young minds that it is acceptable to be cruel to animals", as Anuradha Sawhney from People for the Ethical Treatment of Animals has said. Sawhney refers to studies that prove that children who are cruel to animals also show tendencies to be cruel to humans when they grow up. As mentioned, Tintin skins an ape, in addition to making a snake swallow itself by feeding it its own tail and blowing up a rhinoceros with dynamite.

However, a close reading of the sequence will reveal that both critics and defenders of Hergé have misinterpreted it. Initially, Tintin wants to teach the native children about the colony's distant motherland, but he is interrupted before he gets going; first by a leopard, which Tintin resolutely gets to swallow a blackboard eraser and drink a bucketful of water. The leopard's stomach swells up and Tintin can kick it out of the classroom. However, before he can manage to finish his first sentence, he is interrupted again, this time by the director of an American circus, Jimmy Mac Duff, who claims that the leopard is tame and accuses Tintin of animal abuse. Mac Duff is astonished by Tintin's surprising answer: that the leopard must swallow a blackboard, which will occupy the eraser and in time heal the patient. The third time Tintin stands up in front of the blackboard with his pointer, repeating the sentence "Belgium is ...", he is interrupted by the missionary, who has returned to thank the reporter for "giving our little ones such a good idea of our far-away country".

What this sequence contains is not fascism or colonial ideology; it is a sophisticated deconstruction of a series of colonial stereotypes, begun with the first interruption. "Belgium is what is called --- a leopard!" The lesson, which the missionary believes to have given a "good idea of our far-away country", is actually about Belgium as a greedy leopard that turns out to belong to an American circus. The question of whether the leopard is tame or wild, influenced

by American interests, imitates the intrigue in the previous sequence about the leopard men, as well as the main plot about the gangsters' attempt to seize control of the Congo's diamonds. A one-sided tutoring in colonial values is thus caricatured and turned on its head, and the leopard/King Léopold/Belgium is ordered onto a surreal diet that recommends that they swallow their own paternalistic attributes.

In the 1946 version, the surreal lesson has become a lesson in maths, the leopard's meal has been edited out and the sequence's ominous reversals have transformed into harmless slapstick. Tintin experts have complained that, in the 1931 version, Tintin does not appear very thrilled about the exotic environment, and that Hergé does very little to add atmosphere to the place, instead describing it coolly and distantly. The colour version from 1946 did not manage to allay these objections entirely, but the exotic environment was accentuated and the references to colonial relations erased. Instead of the Congo and Belgium, references are made to the vaguer "Afrique". The focus of criticism among fans and critics, especially in relation to the 1931 version, is what Pierre Halen calls the tintinologists' embarrassment towards Hergé's and Tintin's noticeably disinterested, impartial attitude – which Halen interprets as an attempt to keep a distance from "colonial value systems" – a very different role for a European traveller than the one that is dominant in most other narratives, including Joseph Conrad's exoticism. *Tintin au Congo* does not establish a discourse in which the other is unintelligible, mysterious and inaccessible, but rather relies on a notion that "the world is comprehensible".[190] Attempts to sustain a postcolonial criticism of the album therefore stall in fundamental doubt, with the observation that *Tintin au Congo* does not represent "a Manichean vision of Africa", but contains a disturbing number of "false notes" that do not allow for it to be put in a critical straitjacket.[191] If we also take into account the album's surrealist elements, it makes more sense to view *Tintin au Congo* as a precise and challenging travel description that transcends norms in several of its aspects. The album creates an "imaginary museum" where objects and phenomena on the one hand belong in a recognisable, everyday, fully understandable world, and, on the other, are shifted in the montage, resulting in uncertainty regarding their near or distant place in time and space.[192] In this sense, *Tintin au Congo* manages to express that which is usually unsaid or repressed – for instance that the Congo's past and future fate is determined by foreign powers' endeavours to steal the country's natural resources – while at the same time thematising the globalised and media-related terms under which the themes are expressed. This manoeuvre also appears in older narratives about the Congo, such as the disputes between the Reform Association's campaigns and King Léopold's media apparatus.

The Tintin album's global penetration resulted in a huge influence on world literature, even in comparison with *Heart of Darkness*. It has had a global impact on our understanding of the world and of the Congo, and it is therefore unsurprising that *Tintin au Congo* caused furious reactions and many have wanted it banned. These reactions are misconceived; they have little to do with the text, but rather thrive on a tradition for viewing other places in the world with a sentimental attitude that pretends to be intimate and intense, but is – in reality – light years away from historical realities. Both defenders of Hergé who refer to the prejudices in his historical background, and critics who want to silence him with censorship, participate in the repression of history, with immense consequences. And as one person in a French chat forum for young people wrote in reply to the question "what do you think about *Tintin au Congo*?": Albert Camus' novel *L'Etranger* is xenophobic and colonialist – although in a completely different context – but who would seriously consider banning it?

Tarzan and the Leopard Men

Edgar Rice Burroughs' *Tarzan and the Leopard Men* was written at a staggering pace between July and September 1931, then published in a serialised form between 1932 and 1933 and as a book in 1935. As the title indicates, the leopard men are also at the narrative centre of this book, which both thematises and contributes to a complex field of media criticism, literature and politics. Like *Tintin au Congo*, *Tarzan and the Leopard Men* has a marginal and vulnerable position in the canon. It is more complex and ambiguous than Rice Burroughs' other books, and according to its critics also more racist, because it associates the murderous cult with African natives. As is the case for Tintin, however, critics have also directed attention to elements in the text that transcend the trivial. The Tarzan enthusiast and prominent member of the bibliophile Tarzan society, R. E. Prindle, for example, states in the web article "Tarzan and the Leopard Men" that the Anioto sect is not a prejudice but a historical fact like the mafia.[193]

The canonised Tarzan books cannot be accused of unambiguously cementing stereotypical formulae for hierarchies between whites and blacks, or between animals and humans, though the ideology criticism of the 1970s warned children and teachers that it did. On the contrary, *Tarzan and the Leopard Men* subverts the simplified literary and anthropological models employed by critics as a result of the widespread notion that popular novels are by default trivial and reactionary.

In the novels' geography, the Congo is a central location, though several of the them suggest Lord Greystoke's fashionably cosmopolitan role by having the plot take place in New York, Paris or London. The historical context is characterised by explicit and harsh attacks on the "arch-hypocrite" Léopold and criticism of the Free State's slavery. Tarzan's parents, John and Alice Clayton – Lady Alice, presumably named after the steel boat Stanley took with him and named after his girlfriend – are dispatched by the British colonial ministry to investigate and report violations against natives in Congo. In that sense, they

are inspired by Casement's diplomatic mission, which – as mentioned before – led to the foundation of the first human rights movement. There are direct references to the Red Rubber affair:

"From the records of the Colonial Office and from the dead man's diary we learn that a certain young English nobleman, whom we shall call John Clayton, Lord Greystoke, was commissioned to make a peculiarly delicate investigation of conditions in a British West Coast African Colony from whose simple native inhabitants another European power was known to be recruiting soldiers for its native army, which it used solely for the forcible collection of rubber and ivory from the savage tribes along the Congo and the Aruwimi. The natives of the British Colony complained that many of their young men were enticed away through the medium of fair and glowing promises, but that few if any ever returned to their families" (*Tarzan. King of the Apes*, p. 1).[194]

On the first page of the first novel in the series, *Tarzan. King of the Apes* (1912), this inscription in history is found alongside discussions of the credibility of the account – an echo of Defoe's presentation of *Robinson Crusoe* – making the novel part of the debate in which the entire Casement affair was a key factor: conflicts, doubt and authority were all elements of the complex interrelationship between eyewitness accounts, travel diaries and the report of a ministerial investigation.

"When my convivial host discovered that he had told me so much, and that I was prone to doubtfulness, his foolish pride assumed the task the old vintage had commenced, and so he unearthed written evidence in the form of musty manuscripts, and dry official records of the British Colonial Office to support many of the salient features of his remarkable narrative. I do not say the story is true, for I did not witness the happenings which it portrays, but the fact that in the telling of it to you I have taken fictitious names for the principal characters quite sufficiently evidences the sincerity of my own belief that it *may* be true" (*Tarzan. King of the Apes*, p. 1).

The narrator presents the novel as the retelling of a story he heard at a dinner party, where the host – under the influence of vintage wines – broke his promise never to tell anyone about Tarzan. When the narrator reacts rather sceptically to the peculiar tale, the host breaks another promise, substantiating his story with confidential, secret written evidence, diaries and ministerial reports. The narrator emphasises that he has not witnessed the events, but he cannot reject the story; the fact that he uses fictitious names is used to support the claim that the story *may* be true. Regardless of whether the reader finds the story about Tarzan believable or not, he will no doubt agree with the narrator that it is "unique, remarkable, and interesting" (p. 1).

While the following story is in many respects based on the adventure genre, it is worth noticing the novel's obvious roots in the crucial issue of testimonies in literature about the Congo. Like Jules Verne, Edgar Rice Burroughs thought it important that extraordinary journeys did not venture into the field of the irrational or fantastic, but rather remained within imaginable and possible reconfigurations of known, verifiable knowledge. Burroughs distanced himself from fantastic literature, which to him was treason against the real in the same way as any kind of religion; at the same time, he was sceptical of dogmatic science, such as Darwinism. Burroughs' novels can be seen as experiments that test and challenge Darwinism by inventing and rendering probable anthropological intermediates, missing links and go-betweens. The story is simultaneously extraordinary and probable, literary and historical, and a critique of both science and religion. It pretends to be part of a testimony that can be confirmed with historical documents while clearly being a second-hand account based on disclosed confidential documents, which not only links it thematically to Morel's pamphlets and the Congo Reform Association, but also shows a rhetorical connection.

In the first, most canonised of the Tarzan novels, the heroic narrative includes criticism of Darwinism, the concept of progress and the moral decadence of industrial society, though a critical distance is kept from the technocratic disciplining of body and nature. This primitivist perspective is, naturally, unfolded with a focus on the Tarzan/Clayton figure's formative trajectory and the alternate portrayals of European/American high culture and the Congolese wilderness. In *Tarzan and the Leopard Men*, the most sombre book in the series, one of many noticeable differences is that Tarzan is far from playing a heroic key role – even though, obviously, he saves many critical situations – and the formative development that is a staple part of the rest of the series has in a sense collapsed.

In the main part of the novel, Tarzan suffers from memory loss. He is wandering aimlessly around in the Ituri Forest, believing that he is a "muzimo", a magical being that is both a spiritual guide for a native person and an emanation of the forest. Because of this, Tarzan does not develop or take part in the intrigue; he acts as a sleepwalker, mechanically carrying out the dirty work on request. The description is therefore not heroic, but critical and paranoid, and the former hero comes across as depraved, masked and completely engulfed by the forest. The other Europeans may be fully conscious; however, they have all lost their way in life as well as in the forests, which threaten to swallow and dissolve them. Old Timer and The Kid are poachers on the hunt for ivory, who are portrayed as raw frontier characters on the verge of a breakdown. They have both turned their backs on civilisation because of unhappy love affairs. An important element in the intrigue is that the partners – as their names sug-

gest – have chosen to give up their former identities, not even knowing each other's until the end. The same applies to The Girl, who is the first character to whom we are introduced in the initial scene of a terrible storm in the jungle, during which she is seconds away from being raped by her native carriers. The reader does not know who she is, or why she is drifting around on an extremely daunting expedition in the land of the Pygmies.

All the answers come at the end. The Girl finds what she is looking for – her brother, who turns out to be The Kid, and whose name she can clear of the scandal that led him to run away. In Old Timer she finds the lover she has been missing all along, though throughout the book she has seen him as a rude, self-obsessed cowboy. What is special in the novel's composition, however, is that all the sub-plots are unusually unwilling to give away information about the master plot until the entire riddle is solved. There are hardly any hints that make sense in retrospect, which normally defines a meaningful narrative. The composition instead consists of numerous sequences that are cross-edited in a cinematic, dramatic narrative form, as one sequence is interrupted at a hair-raising cliff-hanger in order for another parallel narrative to be recommenced. All this, however, is played out without any basic design or plot, which is normally compulsory in an epic narrative. The majority of the sequences contain similar thematic and rhetorical structures, built around three or four main elements: an unsuccessful rape of the girl, who all men regardless of race and position desire to a degree that they are willing to break laws and rules to gain exclusive rights over her body; a kidnapping of one of the main characters, which includes the natives, who are implicated in the fight over the girl; and a surveillance situation in which secret knowledge is unwillingly conveyed to a spying third party – in most cases Tarzan.

Due to the impenetrability of the forest, which only allows for transportation on the rivers, the novel's sub-plots can avoid meeting before the end and all the main players are unaware of vital parts of the complete course of events, of which only the reader is gradually able to form an idea. As mentioned, Tarzan does not perform any autonomous activities, because his memory loss causes the delusion that he is a "muzimo". Tarzan is not at the centre of the narrative; he is reduced to being a spy and messenger between the separate spheres of the novel. His ability to hide and move quickly through the tree tops is crucial, but his usual heroism is gone. The absence of an active hero, and the extreme narrative delay of meaning, causes the space of the novel to become ghostly and paranoid in a way that is very similar to Stanley's descriptions of the same geographical location in *In Darkest Africa* – especially the forest chapter, in which the explorer is also reduced to a "muzimo", a spirit being that hovers in the indefinable zone between forest and man.

Drawing by J. Allen St. John for the cover of *Tarzan and the Leopard Men* (1935). Burroughs was closely involved with the film industry, and Hollywood plays a part in the story about secret sects and conspiracies in the Congo. The novel's inspiration came from two fronts: the fear of communist infiltration of the film industry and subsequent mind control, and the rivalry with the novel and film *Trader Horn*, which threatened to outmatch *Tarzan* and steal the monopoly Burroughs believed to have on Africa.

The paranoid environment is obviously also created by the secret society of the leopard men. Several of the key native characters have double identities as inhabitants in the village of the good Utengas – for whom the sleepwalking Tarzan believes himself to be a protective fetish – and as bloodthirsty, fanatical religious avengers when they transform into leopard men. However, it is noticeable that the paranoia in the novel is not limited to the terror of the Anioto sect; it includes all the characters in the intrigue, who understand nothing, conceal everything and must rely on incomplete, random fragments of knowledge that

leave them, literally, in a state of nameless terror. And because Tarzan does not act heroically but merely delivers his secret messages in a detached, zombie-like manner, he contributes nothing to the illumination of the novel's paranoid geography – quite the contrary.

In the articles "Tarzan and the Leopard Men" and "Debunking The Debunkers", E. R. Prindle points out several reasons why the novel stands out from the other books in the series. Firstly, it can be read as a thematic rendering of the Jewish-communist 'infiltration' of Hollywood, which Burroughs feared in an era when Chaplin, H. G. Wells and many other 'reds' in the industry were believed to be under the direct influence of Stalin. The leopard men, in this interpretation, are disguised communists that infiltrate the Utengas' peaceful Hollywood in order to gain control of the media's manipulation of the susceptible masses. Secondly, Burroughs' paranoia is linked to the increasing competition to which the Tarzan books and films were exposed in the period around 1930. In particular, it was frustrating for Burroughs that another Africa story took over Tarzan's position at the top of the bestseller list, also triumphing as the most spectacular adventure film ever.

Trader Horn: A Young Man's Astounding Adventures in 19th Century Equatorial Africa was first published in 1927 as a non-fiction travel book about the adventurer Trader Horn's experiences in Africa. For five years after the publication it remained one of the bestselling books in the USA.[195] The story is told to the South African author Ethelreda Lewis, and in addition to probable diary-inspired descriptions of Horn's journeys, it also contains accounts of improbable and fictitious events, including a spectacular rescue of a white goddess. The film *Trader Horn* was nominated for an Academy Award for best film in 1931 and became an immense success, not least because the story, now entirely fiction, featured the first shoots on location in Africa, where the actress Edwina Booth, playing the white goddess, became ill and brought the first charges of their kind against MGM. It only added to the sensation that Harry Carey, who played Horn, almost had his leg bitten off by real crocodiles in a river over which he was swinging. When Burroughs saw the film in 1931, he stopped his work on *Tarzan Triumphant* in order to write *Tarzan and the Leopard Men*, finishing it in only two months and including a number of parallels to Horn's story and the film version.[196] Burroughs' novel can therefore be viewed as an attempt to enter the territory of the successful rival and prevent a hostile takeover of his own territory.

The book deals with the fear of hostile communist infiltration of Hollywood, which Burroughs saw as a threat to his own position, but it is also a complex symptom of another type of fear, the fear of the influence of a competing story about Africa – another trade mark – whose success was, to a large degree, based on the use of effective elements copied from early Tarzan books; *Trader Horn* is clearly inspired by Burroughs's fictions and Du Chaillu's travel books. Consequently, when Burroughs stopped his work in the canonised Tarzan tradition in order to write a book that imitated *Trader Horn*, it was an imitation of his own work, which would come to have a great impact on his subsequent authorship. The unusually gloomy and paranoid novel, which questions all information and identities and describes all its characters as potential victims of hostile invasion and mind control, was written against the background of this double fear of influence in relation to literary genre and form, as well as in relation to power struggles in and between media.

Tarzan and the Leopard Men thus marks a break with the Homeric style that had dominated the canonised Tarzan books. E. B. Holtsmark's *Tarzan and Tradition. Classical Myth in Popular Literature* (1981) argues for a strong influence from role models such as Homer and Virgil, who were part of the author's educational background (though he was reluctant). This influence made Tarzan a prototype of the Homeric hero and structured the style, for instance in the descriptions of landscape and the consistent use of classical rhetorical figures such as antithesis, chiasmus and repetition. In Holtsmark's opinion, this continuation of the inheritance from antiquity saves Burroughs from the 1970s' critical attacks against sexism, racism and right wing extremism. The main part of Holtsmark's study, however, is not based on textual analysis or literary history; it is a catalogue of archaic tropes and figures in the five or six Tarzan novels that are the most noticeable examples of neoclassicism – those that most clearly continue the myth of the quick-footed Achilles in the guise of the ape man. From a different perspective from Holtsmark's, we may claim that Burroughs' impact is a result of his ability to combine the classical material with modern "heroic fantasy", the anachronism of which also implies *transcendence* of the ancient sources of inspiration, challenging political, scientific and religious dogmas. In *Tarzan and the Leopard Men*, this transcendence is so striking that the Homeric characteristics have vanished completely to the benefit of gothic, decadent twilight fiction. The hero's vision and independent will is gone, and the ideal of transparency and illumination has been replaced by the impenetrable forest, the night and the gloaming, which results in a blurring of the classic antitheses of light and darkness, culture and nature, and so on. All that is left is a ghostly limbo in which the hypnotised Tarzan is difficult to discern.

This emphasises the parallel between Burroughs' novels and Stanley's travel books. In both cases we are dealing with a topographical distribution of light and darkness on the basis of anthropological, geographical and stylistic roots in antiquity's ideals. The region around Lake Victoria and Uganda's highlands, where native warriors are portrayed as Hector's and Achilles' kinsmen, is per-

ceived as enlightened and attributed with a prehistory of civilisation based in loose hypotheses about King Solomon's mines and immigration of ancient apostolic Christians. The Ituri Forest, on the other hand, in both authors' works stands for a collapse in the classical rhetoric of Homeric epic, including the fundamental anthropological juxtapositions of civilisation and barbarianism, human being and animal, space and history and body and mind. Furthermore, both *Tarzan and the Leopard Men* and *In Darkest Africa* were deeply involved in debates about rights that pertained to human rights, copyrights and literary ownership of the Congo. This applies in particular to the Ituri Forest, which stands out as an extremely fertile wonderland that in the histories of science and literature have led to remarkable findings, for instance the okapis (which are among Tarzan's prey), countless variations of species and missing links between primates and humans, for instance the beings called "hairy men". Both authors not only demonstrate the question of rights and as a matter pertaining to the distribution of the books; they also make it an element of their texts' rhetoric, form and materiality. Copyrights and trademarks were crucial in relation to their identity and authority, as well as to their texts' positions in the literary world market.

The scenes in E.R. Burroughs' book that are viewed from a hiding place also repeat the combination of superiority and paranoia that is characteristic of Stanley's descriptions of the Ituri Forest's native villages. Here, however, the paranoia is radicalised, partly due to the fiction's often completely anonymous observer position - simply indicated in expressions such as "other eyes watching" - and partly due to the extreme theatricalisation of those watched. They are like actors on a stage that the narrator clears in the dense forest. The acting is also marked with irony, for instance in a comment about Gato Mgungu, the leopard men's chieftain, who has not known the advantages of civilisation because he has "never been to Hollywood" (*Tarzan and the Leopard Men*, p. 74).[197] The atrocious rituals are, on the one hand, "acting" with no real religious piety; on the other hand, they are without "self-control" - indulging in "religious and alcoholic drunkenness" (p. 70). Hollywood teaches all its actors to perform the same atrocious rituals, linked to similar secret societies that fanatically worship false religious or political gods, but they do it with an exercise of self-control that makes it impossible to distinguish between evil leopard men, Jews and communists on the one hand and good Utengas and patriotic Americans on the other. Tarzan instinctively senses who are double agents and cannot be trusted. However, he is himself a victim of memory loss, which makes his intelligence work for the Utengas pure reflex, carried out blindly as an automated consequence of his role as village "muzimo". This is equivalent to Burroughs' perception of his own role in the village of Hollywood: a zombie in an environment that was infiltrated by disguised Jewish and Stalinist agents, ready to create a society based on religious or political dogma.

There are several arguments for reading *Tarzan and the Leopard Men* as a complex literary happening. In relation to Burroughs' oeuvre, the Homeric tradition in which he had written until then was reinterpreted, and Odysseus was forced to go undercover in a situation where the trademark Tarzan and the world's most fertile location for wonder were threatened by hostile invasion. From a broader perspective, the novel is part of the travel literature about the Congo, repeating and radicalising central elements of the gothic decadence of Stanley's *In Darkest Africa* and exaggerating a number of paranoid characteristics in the leopard men's topology. The novel, expectedly, ends with Tarzan becoming himself again, rebuilding law and order and leaving the formalities to the colonial administration's soldiers before returning to his own jungle district. Nevertheless, Burroughs is miles away from establishing a stereotypical, safe model in which evil must simply be identified and exorcised by good, for instance by establishing problematic special laws like the ones that were justified in Jungsbøll's and Freiesleben's travel books.

On the contrary, the uncertainty about identity is fundamental throughout the book, affecting natives, Europeans, narrator and author. Viewed in the context of Burroughs' criticism of politics and media, the topography of the Ituri Forest provides an opportunity to fight the political infiltration of Hollywood and reclaim some of the lost territory in the world market. The risk, however, is that the use of a different form of literature results in a subversion of his identity as an author – a conflict that is mirrored in Tarzan's role as "muzimo", which when amplified by the hypnosis almost makes him identical to the terrorist leopard men. The novel is a unique, radical and precise representation of the African material, which – rather than cementing a stereotypical understanding of Africa as distant and exotic – sets the traditional figures in motion. The topography surrounding the heart of darkness thus displays striking, consistent characteristics, as well as an ability to drift into completely different geographical and mental landscapes, like Hollywood, and shuffle the world literary market's usual distribution of near and far.

By the beginning of the 1950s, Edgar Rice Burroughs had sold around 50 million books featuring Tarzan as the all-important hero. The golden age of Tarzan fiction was in the 1930s, when a vast number of films, cartoons and radio shows (around 1000, typically 15 minutes each) accompanied the novels – all of which were distributed all over the world. All these products secured steady profits for Burroughs Inc., supplemented with earnings from sales of the rights to the Tarzan brand as early as 1913, as well as Tarzan chewing gum, bread, coffee, swimming suits, petrol etc. Tarzan became a worldwide brand – according to

researchers by far the world's best-known literary character of the time: nobody in the entire world, these researchers claim, had not heard of Tarzan, who ensured transparency and justice in colour strips in the newspapers of more or less chaotic parts of the world, across borders between north and south, and ideologies and markets that confined the dissemination of competing literary rivals. In the 1950s, however, Tarzan lost ground – tired and exhausted, like the author who had brought the legendary hero into the world in 1912 as his final resort to survive under capitalism's law of the jungle, having failed in attempted careers as a magazine vendor, photography developer, miner and pencil sharpener salesman. In 1961, a teacher in California removed two Tarzan books from a school library, after a parent complained that the jungle hero and Jane lived together without being married, which made the child they had together illegitimate. Tarzan fans protested, pointing out that Tarzan and Jane were married in *The Return of Tarzan* in 1915, and the controversy spurred so much renewed interest in the novels that the bookshops could not meet the demand. The six million unauthorised publications that followed violated the copyrights; Burroughs Inc. brought charges and won several hundred court cases all around the world, once again creating massive media attention – from Finland to Kenya – which resulted in a veritable Tarzan boom, resulting in authorised republications of the novels and luxury editions of the albums.

Tarzan's parents, John and Alice Clayton, were dispatched on a secret mission by the British foreign ministry to investigate reports on violations against natives in the Congo Free State. Imitating Roger Casement's real investigative expedition in 1903, *Tarzan. King of the Apes* was created in 1912 as the result of a controversy about human rights. The novel was also inspired by Rice Burroughs having read Buel's *Heroes of the Dark Continent* from 1890, which was an unauthorised publication that included parts of Stanley's travel accounts about early Christian immigrants to Uganda – the land of milk and honey and the place where Tarzan relaxes on his ranch – as well as the Emin Pasha relief and British officers' involvement in cannibalistic orgies in the Ituri Forests by the Aruwimi River in north-eastern Congo. It is in this area that Tarzan's adventures among the Pygmies and "hairy men" take place, and where immense resources can be found: hidden and forgotten civilisations from the time of the pharaohs and a multitude of crypto-zoological life forms and missing links. As a parallel to Rice Burroughs' lifelong fight for the copyrights to Tarzan and the story about Africa, Tarzan is involved in political conflicts in relation to the enforcement of international law, human rights, property rights and territories. But contrary to Clayton/Casement, Tarzan is sceptical of universal human rights; as we all know, he prefers the law of the jungle and critically observes the hypocritical and vain civilisation of man from an animal's perspective.

Stanley's *In Darkest Africa* was one of Burroughs' inspirations for the description of the Ituri Forest's mental geography, and – as mentioned in the beginning of this section – the series of novels is rooted in narratives about the atrocities of the Red Rubber era.[198] Tarzan's upbringing among apes, and his role as a go-between, is caused by and linked to his parents' mission, which imitates Roger Casement's investigative expedition in 1903. The novel series was from the very beginning conceived as a contribution to the dispute between competing, incredible testimonies, and to a large degree it draws its themes from travel accounts and reports about the Congo. Examples include the identity conflicts of *fin de siècle* novels, in which civilisation and nature swap places, and doubt about the credibility of the accounts is linked to the narrators' and Tarzan's authority as witnesses, which – in turn – is linked to the narrators' and the audience's positions, class and national backgrounds. In *Tarzan and the Leopard Men*, this interplay gains an extra dimension when we see the novel as a reaction to the author's alarm at the influence of *Trader Horn*, which – both in the book and in the film version – was a success on a scale so huge that a serialised production was under consideration, posing a threat to Burroughs' position in the world market.

Trader Horn

Trader Horn is undoubtedly a qualified opponent for *Tarzan*. The narrative construction and style is unique, and the story synthesises more or less all the central topics from novels and travel accounts about Africa, including, as mentioned, elements from *Tarzan. King of the Apes*. The title alone indicates the classic travel genre trick, which Defoe cultivated with much sophistication: "Trader Horn. The Ivory Coast in the Earlies. Written at the age of seventy-three, with such of the author's Philosophy as is the gift of Age and Experience, taken down and here edited by Ethelreda Lewis". The author Ethelreda Lewis is, according to the introduction, a kind of editor of Alfred Aloysius Horn's oral account, and the subtitle's claim that the story was "written" by Aloysius Horn is therefore questionable. The reference to the author's lifetime of experiences feigns authenticity, which supposedly is the result of the narrator's tough existence as a gold digger in the area around the Congo River. According to Lewis, the narrator thus filters centuries of Victorian and Scottish culture; for instance, in a casual remark he will ponder on whether Bacon wrote Shakespeare's immortal works or not. The excess layer of education has been peeled off Horn's "Philosophy", but his "Age" also results in random rambling, repetitions and a very liberal use of historical data. Therefore, the account has not only been "taken down" but also "edited" by Lewis, whose

unusual comments make it hard to believe the claim that Horn is in fact the author of the written text.

A preface by John Galsworthy makes the prediction that the book will become a goldmine, and that it will have "countless readers". The style of the subtitle is continued with the remark that "in these days of fakes" – perhaps a reference to Burroughs – readers might be tempted to think that the story is "all too good to be true". Nevertheless, Galsworthy assures the reader that he has met "the 'Old Visiter' and his editress" in Johannesburg and seen with his own eyes that the book's "character" is on a par with reality. All of this is guaranteed by Galsworthy's authority as a well-known author and signed via facsimile. The first line of Ethelreda Lewis' introduction continues to claim that "This is a true story of a real man. So real that I have thought it necessary to alter names here and there, including his own surname" (*Trader Horn*, p. 9). These measures are more than play to the gallery, because the account is a mix of anything and everything from Horn's life, some elements of which come across as more or less realistic, while others are highly improbable – notably the tale about the mysterious jungle princess Lola D., "the white goddess", daughter of a "noble English family".

In the introduction, Lewis also explains the book's unique construction. In the beginning, she had imagined that based on interviews and notes, she would know so much about the story that she would be able to write it. However, the old man's account goes in circles around a staple inventory of "four or five things branded on his brain, as a youth: Egbo, Lola D., the wicked French, gorillas, his shortened thumb" (p. 19), so instead she chooses a different method aiming at evoking more detailed memories in Horn: every week he writes a chapter which Lewis discusses with him while taking notes. After that, they plan the design and plot for the following chapter. The notes are integrated into Horn's text, while each chapter is supplied with the so-called "conversations" during which Lewis inquires into and tests the narrative's key points. Lewis emphasises how Horn in this way is born as the "author" of an autobiography, increasing his consciousness of style – though it remains a "Victorian style"; "an old-fashioned idea that the written word must be elegant rather than colloquial" (p. 22). Luckily, the supplementary conversations, which reproduce the liveliness that is a consequence of "the proximity of a listener", according to Lewis make up for Horn's slightly rigid and too elegant style. The sceptical reader might get the idea that this discussion of style aims at diverting attention from the fact that the story is not written by a restless adventurer but an established author. In "Conversations", the focus seems to be more on style than content:

> "If it's facts you're wanting I can give facts and novelties too. They are the basis of solid interest. The English set a great deal of store by facts, but if a book's to be sold in America you must keep an eye on the novelties. I know America. Best not throw too high a light on some of my experiences on the Coast. It never does to give good folk a shock. Aye. Talk of dreadful scenes … A young lad brought up never to think of evil nor read it in a book – and he gets to the Coast at eighteen … Seventeen it might 'a' been … He feels Revolt, Ma'am. The shock of it's like to make him sick. He'll shy at everything, like a colt first driven through the streets that's known nothing but the fields. Aye." (p. 60).

In a later conversation after a chapter that includes, among other phenomena, gorillas and Pygmies – "dwarves" – Horn exclaims, according to Lewis' notes:

> "Aye the dwarf will provide the novelty. I sure thought he'd come in well in this chapter. His strange antics provide a little relief. (…) Aye, the Americans must have novelties, whether in search of these breakfast foods or in literary matters. I'm not saying it's good for them. Bacon for breakfast and Shakespeare for reading've been good enough for Lancashire and England, generally speaking, for a number of generations" (p. 106).

Similar discussions of style and the market appears in many passages in the text, and Horn's – or perhaps rather Ethelreda Lewis' – stylistic considerations are to a striking degree based on the different tastes of different nations' audiences. "The wicked French" are a linguistic and cultural error; they are not to be trusted and cannot be understood; "French is a language writ in water on the earth's surface. Water and scent". The Germans will love his book, Horn believes; the English appreciate facts without "novelties", while the Americans want both. Furthermore, it is hinted that the Americans' taste for "facts" is a symptom of a preference for everything that can be weighed and measured, while the English wish to achieve more profound knowledge, i.e. "truths". Aloysius Horn has grave financial problems, which is why he has contacted the author Lewis. He wants to adapt the account to appeal to both the British and the American markets, and he is prepared to tone down the Shakespearian elements in favour of "breakfast foods". This explains the stylistic balancing act between realism and "novelty". The strategic considerations of how much or how little can be told about the Red Rubber atrocities without deterring the reader is a rare, explicit example of the self-censorship that characterises the rhetoric of travel accounts from the time after the Congo Reform Association's campaign. In *Trader Horn* it is also suggested that the narrator has been implicated in horrible actions, for instance as a rubber collector by the Congo River, but the horror is presented in a dual rhetoric – time after time sketched out as a fascinating background with aposiopeses and dashes, or projected onto the native ceremonies, which are considered more fit for description. One of the novelties of which Aloysius Horn speaks attracts special attention because it refers back to classical travel texts as well as forward towards the media context and popular culture to which the account tries to appeal. In the introduction, Lewis tells that only on her third visit did Horn remember the story about the compass and music box of the famous French explorer, Paul Du Chaillu, which Horn claims to have found in the central country in the district of "the white goddess":

"There was still a bit of a tinkle in it when I saw it. *Trovatore* or something. Picture of a lady in one of these chignons. There's a weakness, Ma'am, in all dago music, and never more so than when heard in a cannibal's hut (facsimile of the notes for Da Da da da de da Da – de da –). 'Tis notably thin stuff. But, as magic, a notable addition to voodoo in that part of the world. That and the compass he left. Aye, they feared that little trembling finger more than the sounds in the musical box. Too quiet to be very reassuring.... The mariner's compass. One of Nature's discoveries that'll never be commonised by the sons of men. Aye, something above the edicts of the mechanical" (p. 20).

When Lewis finds it necessary to include the notes for the insignificant melody – "notably thin stuff" – it can only be as a reference to a famous case in which the French explorer Jean de Léry, on hearing the Tupinamba Indians' strange singing, felt compelled to print the notes for the melody in his account in order to give the reader an impression of the simultaneously hideous and wondrous experience he had then and each time he tried to remember the song afterwards.[199] In Horn, it is the French explorer, whose writing is like scented water, who brings a popular melody with him into the jungle in order to present the natives with a wonder. But the natives prefer the compass, because as a fetish it contains invisible magic that surpasses the mechanical reproduction of the music box.

This anecdote supports other accounts that portray the French as amateurs – both as explorers and colonists – and since the caricature of Du Chaillu also becomes a caricature of Léry, the satire is expanded to encompass the efforts of the French from their explorations in South America in the renaissance to the current colonisation of Africa. Furthermore, wonder is presented as a devalued, no longer primary source of knowledge; in accordance with the criticism of the discourse of wonder towards the end of the eighteenth century, it is deemed bad taste, vanity and cheap entertainment. However, in this sense, the story about Du Chaillu's music box also characterises *Trader Horn*: as we have seen in the book's "conversations", it is very much preoccupied with selling the sights as "novelties" to the American market, where the novel is first and foremost a commodity on a par with cornflakes and other cereals. After several successful chapters, Aloysius Horn, according to Lewis, begins a conversation as follows: "It'll be a ponderous work, it sure will. But it's weaving out very nicely. Aye. Facts are what they want. Facts; with a little bit of Old Times for sentiment. Looked at from a distance the Past is often as good as fiction. The Past is what the Americans amuse themselves with" (p. 77). What we cannot know for certain is whether Du Chaillu's music box belongs in the category of facts, or has been included to satisfy the Americans' need for "sentiments". For the same reason, we do not know whether the assertion of the Americans' tendency to perceive the past as fiction also works in reverse, so that a fiction, when pretending to deal with events that are far back in time, can pass as an account of real events. In this sense, it is not just the compass but also the music box – the account as both fiction and testimony – that possesses magical properties when it comes to selling the product to the wide world. The many literary techniques and thematic drifts in Burroughs' *Tarzan and the Leopard Men* imply the powerful opponent Tarzan is facing in Trader Horn. *Trader Horn* reuses all the best elements from earlier travel accounts from Africa within a framework that – by means of subtle effects that create authenticity – refutes that it is imitating its predecessors, while at the same time openly admitting its view on the literary market. This provocative candour and exclusion of the French from the literary world market – as well as excluding them as colonisers – reveals *Trader Horn* as an attempt to relaunch the travel account's classical wonder in a new form. This form takes into account the economical leisure market conditions in which the novel is both "novelty" and commodity without exposing itself to traditional criticism's discrediting of 'scented' reality.

Tintin au Congo, Tarzan and the Leopard Men and *Trader Horn* all include subtle paraphrases of their own media and genre bases. Contrary to the travel accounts from the Congo that conceal, repress and actively forget their own history, and novels that veil their conditions in order to appear as autonomous works, these popular cultural texts reflect and expose the prosaic medial and historical terms on which they exist. While representing colonial violence, they are also performative narrations about media critical history on global market terms. However, they also reflect basic conditions for prose, which strengthens rather than weakens their critical scope – although academic criticism, with a few exceptions, has claimed the opposite. The performative and media-critical interpretation suggested in the present study, however, provides a better explanation of why, for example, *Tintin au Congo* continues to enjoy great success in the Congo.

4 *The Congo, I Presume:* Anthropoetic Narrative

As explained in the introduction, the prose perspective entails a way of reading that emphasises the texts' reality work and performativity – i.e. the broad field of processes which the work creates and in which it partakes – at the expense of the characteristics that are normally analysed in the formalistic tradition of literary studies. It has functioned as an important assumption that we are currently witnessing a prosaic turn in literature, which can be viewed as an acute challenge to the usual divides between fiction and documentary, and between genres, types and circulations. It also results in a transformed view of literature, of which the present book provides an example. In Wlad Godzich's terminology, prose such as W. G. Sebald's is *emergent literature*. Not only does it call for a revision of foundational literary-historical narratives; it transforms the entire field, not just moving the 'pieces' into new positions, but requiring the rules of the game to be redefined entirely.

As in Arne Melberg's essays about the role of travel literature in such a process, the assumption about a prosaic turn can only be that: an assumption or prophecy. The prose perspective has resulted in altered definitions and attention being paid to relations other than those represented in traditional literary history or genre-based presentations of, for example, the history of travel literature. The perspective also results in alternative appraisals from those determined by the dominant postcolonial tradition. The present book has placed more focus on the material investigated than on methodological and theoretical subjects. Peter Tygesen's *The Congo – I Presume* will be the final stop in its long series of readings. In other words, we will end up in the middle of the material and the narrative, where it all began. Focusing on the discussion of witnessing and testimony, the next part of this book, "The Congo in Prose", will summarise some of the literary-historical currents and patterns that have been detected in and across the prose narratives.

Peter Tygesen's *The Congo – I Presume. Narratives from Dreamland* (2001) follows, as suggested in the title, in the wake of the doubt about the true state of the Congo, which is part of all literature about the country, regardless of whether it is fiction or journalistic reportage. Tygesen's book was broadly recognised for its insights, its stylistic combination of objective, narrative and analytic perspectives and its close understanding of everyday life in the Congo. The book was also praised for drawing attention to an apparently forgotten chapter in the history of the world, and for highlighting international society's – not least Denmark's and Scandinavia's – active part in the history of the Congo, and thus its responsibility for the current, disastrous state in which the country finds itself.

The chapters in the book, which are organised under headings like "Conquest", "Moral", "Danish work", "Happiness", "Love" and "Power and means", contain accounts of the Congo's political history from King Afonso's conflict with the Portuguese to the permanent, chaotic power struggles throughout more than fifty years' of independence. These chapters are all collected under the heading "List of kings" – an ironic reminder that the country's political government has always been, and is still, at the mercy of rulers whose own prosperity has been their main goal, and whose regimes have never been more than vague illusions. Today, the Congo is divided into districts and zones that are controlled by local warlords, who are financed and controlled by the neighbouring states, which, in return, have access to gold, oil or coltan. The civil war that has ravaged the Congo in recent years, costing millions of human lives, is – according to Tygesen's analysis – related to natural resources. It is exploitation on an historically unparalleled scale, even compared to the colonial exploitation of the Congo at the end of the nineteenth century. It is a continual process: while the country, against all odds, saw a democratic election in 2006, it is still war-torn, particularly the regions bordering on Uganda and Rwanda, partly as a consequence of the influx of refugees after the Tutsi genocide in Rwanda but also because of the immense natural resources in these areas.

In addition to the "list of kings", the chapters contain interviews and portraits – including of an aspiring singer and a failed lawyer – which link the documentary report with staged narrative. The portraits disclose harsh facts, for instance about a completely inexpedient system for the exchange of labour and products, while at the same time manifesting the dreams that individual citizens, in spite of everything, have of a better life and a transformed country.

When Tygesen in the title calls the Congo a "Dreamland", it is with reference to two juxtaposed factors in the book. The Europeans' dreams about the Congo have, from the very first encounter, staged and disseminated an unreal simulacrum that reduced and adjusted the country to fit in with the colonial cause, while also encompassing anxiety and fantasies related to impenetrability and darkness, which would subsequently come to justify a labelling of the region as unintelligible – fascinatingly out of rationalism's reach, and conveniently beyond the responsibility of western powers. The second meaning of the word refers to the Congolese's own dreams: "When we hear about the Congolese's reality, we are stricken by how different it is from our own. But when we hear about their dreams, we recognise them. The story of how they pursue their dreams is a key to understanding the Congo and the Congolese" (p. 8).

In *The Congo – I Presume* we encounter a strategy unique in travel literature, in which testimony, critical journalism and the wondrous converge in one critical, analytical gesture. In the case of the Congo, where the real – for both Congolese and Europeans – often only appears as unintelligible nightmares and simulacra, the country's history and the sketch of its future is kept solely in the individual's private and very mundane life dreams, which cannot be expropriated. In Tygesen's communication of these dream testimonies, he manages to re-contextualise and humanise the wonders which, since Conrad, have stood in the way of understanding and responsibility. At the same time, giving testimony becomes something universally human – part of everybody's responsibility. In Tygesen's narrative, wonder has once again returned to mundane everyday phenomena that incite curiosity and facilitate knowledge. Similarly, testimony is rooted in a concrete historical and political reality, instead of a universal, compassionate discourse or transcendental ideals for human rights.

Whereas the metaphor of the "heart of darkness" has dominated the description of the areas around the Congo River and contributed to the country's status as one of the world's most impenetrable wonders, Tygesen's metaphor is the diamond on the book's front cover. The diamond obviously represents the natural resources which ought to provide the Congolese with brilliant opportunities to prosper, but have instead resulted in exploitation for five hundred consecutive years. At the same time, the diamond, with its polished facets, indicates that the Congo is by no means unintelligible; it just requires a particular reflective strategy and writing style. In this sense, the diamond represents Tygesen's analytical, multi-perspectival presentation, which does not aim to understand the country in one universal concept, but in a gradual exposure of layers and facets.

Tygesen's method and style of writing differs from that of most writing about the Congo, and is most similar to Carsten Niebuhr's balanced, open and rational anthropology and prose. From the perspective of the present book, it is therefore a contribution to travel literature that makes important progress compared with the tendencies that for so long have dominated both literary, fictitious travel descriptions and journalistic reportage – and in that respect it points forward towards a possible renaissance for the genre. The potentials of such a renaissance are, as Tygesen's political analyses exemplify, not only of interest to literary historians or researchers of genre; they are fundamental to the media-constructed understandings of the world in accordance with which we all act.

Every chapter ends with a section of the "list of kings", which gives a chronological exposition of eras. In these sections, the style is broadly descriptive, objective and analytical – almost traditional history, albeit with few generic sources. The reader is guided from the country's earliest history to the present day, which ties things together from beginning to end. The immediate impression is of the traditional patterns for general travel descriptions and literature about the Congo. The accounts given, of the first Portuguese explorers through to Stanley, Conrad, the missionaries and the many Danish employees in the Free State – and later in the Belgian colony – create an impression of consistent authenticity and archival meticulousness, while at the same time recounting history in an indirect, shifted form, through the works of others. However, contrary to tradition, Tygesen does not employ the accounts of others to elevate his own account to an omniscient, transcendent and supreme perspective.

There are expressions from the past as well as from the present of the comprehensive experience that has shaped the country for good or bad. It is a central point in the book's view of history that the long series of setbacks in the basic societal structures of the Congo is not seen in a moralising or aesthetic light. Though the book does not refrain from defining King Léopold's, and especially Stanley's, personal attributes as contributing factors to the colonisation, the foundational mechanisms are consistently seen as economic. *The Congo – I Presume* avoids the widespread tendency to sensationalise colonial history, seen in Adam Hochschild's perception of events as a conflict between the greedy imperialism of evil white men and the conscientious demands for human rights posed by the Reform Association. Rather, Tygesen describes the colonisation process as a consequence of three major waves in the history of globalisation: the trans-continental slave trade in the seventeenth and eighteenth centuries; industrialism's demand for raw materials and the expansion of the market at the end of the twentieth century; and, finally, the cold war in the 1950s and 1960s, when the Congo's opportunity to achieve independence and democracy was crushed by the superpowers' struggle for world political influence. Regional conflicts and development delays are not mystified; the critical perspective remains transnational from beginning to end – something that is most clear in the final chapter on the list of kings, which deals with Joseph Kabila. In this chapter, the Congo's devastating wars in recent years are compared with the Thirty Years' War in Europe, and the mercenaries who fought bloody battles that would come to define the borders between Europe's modern nation states.

Each chapter, however, begins in a completely different genre. "Happiness" begins with a story about the girl Chantal, who is pushing her way through the crowds of Kinshasa, aiming for the fashion shop Boutique de Luxe, where she wants to buy a wig. She is stopped on the way by the African superstar Tabu Ley, who calls her from a car to offer her a job as a mannequin and dancer. He has noticed her walk, of which she has not been aware, and suddenly a dream

of a different life has come alive. Unlike most girls, Chantal has been studying, but when her father, who had a good job, was murdered by envious colleagues, she could not continue. Chantal is tempted by the offer, but just as she is about to ask her aunt's permission, they receive a message that changes the situation: a boy who is under her aunt's guardianship has been hit and killed by a lorry. Instead of a conversation about Chantal's future, the scene becomes a chaotic dispute between the boy's and the aunt's families – a conflict that includes death threats and the use of harmful fetishes, indicating a hopeless dependency on ancient traditions, which appear as absurd antipoles to the introductory sketch of lightness and idyll. Nevertheless, Chantal manages to open the door to a world that provides her with a chance to start over. In several passages we see her practising her dancing, and we see her gradually settling into her new role. The second from last section is about her appearance in a show in Kinshasa for the city's prominent citizens, also referring to Tabu Ley's role in various presidential campaigns. Furthermore, brief sections, which are disconnected from the story about Chantal, describe the Congo's economy as seen from the perspective of ordinary people. "Elegy to a destroyed economy", for example, is seen through the eyes of a passer-by who notices a long list of products in the shops – bags of flour, spare car parts – and first and foremost that almost nothing is happening. Also disconnected from the other components of the chapter is a reproduction of an article from *La Gazette de l'Orient*, about a new version of the national anthem "Debout Congolais" – "Arise Congolese". Meanwhile, the list of kings has arrived at "Prime Minister Lumumba of Dreamland".

In Chantal's intimate story, the third-person narrator reveals an insight into the girl's secret thoughts and dramatises dialogues he could not possibly have overheard. The contrast between the sudden appearance of a life-changing opportunity and the fateful inertia of tradition is also a striking, dramatic orchestration of the conflict between individual-oriented modernity and family-based tradition. These characteristics indicate that we are dealing with a novel. However, the interruptions, despite the fact that they are inspired by established fiction genres, tell a different story in which Chantal's happiness is shown as an exception, while the focus is on the economical and anthropological background for understanding why the Congolese are tempted to leave things up to fate or indulge in the dream of sudden luck.The chapter also links Chantal and Tabu Ley's show to political manipulation of the media, thus addressing a number of facets of the term "happiness", all of which are isolated instances: Chantal's happiness is undoubtedly positive to her – an opportunity few people get – as is the music and professionalism of Tabu Ley's show. However, from another perspective, exposed through genres other than romance, the music is not only self-forgetfulness and compensation for the individual; it is part of a large-scale mechanism of forgetfulness that keeps people in ignorance, thus in reality contributing to the economic ruin for which it compensates. Ultimately, the show is an important element of the simulacrum of oppression.

There are montage-like insertions, such as the article about the national anthem, but continuity is maintained through subtle overlaps. For example, "Elegy to a destroyed economy" takes place in the same street in which we have just left Chantal, while the article about the national anthem, which appears as a surrealistic joke, continues the theme of music and art's role in the national representation of the Congo – as well as foreshadowing the section about Lumumba as a leader who, in many respects, was full of good intentions, but also a unrealistic, dreaming, anachronistic leader.

In "Happiness", the preconditions for Chantal's story are not given, but we must assume that they are similar to those presented in the book's introductory chapter, "Conquest". This chapter makes use of the same dramatised close-ups in the present tense of the mercenary Rambo, but also includes sections in which the narrator is located in the text as an 'I' whose narrative terms are at the mercy of coincidences and the Congolese reality. The narrator's main source of inspiration is his fear of being discovered, and the meetings between interviewer and witness are therefore characterised by stress and ongoing negotiations of fees and advances, which might be fair, or they might be parts of an obscure power struggle. Obviously, this also raises questions about the credibility of the witness. Rambo's story, as it is recounted by the narrator, is not necessarily true from beginning to end: rather, it is a hypothetical version of the truth, based on the meeting with the mercenary and the narrator's own knowledge about the political, military and economical background of his current, precarious situation – factors that are unknown to Rambo.

In the last three chapters of the book, "Power and means", "The tumult of war" and "The Republic of Banalia", the tension between fictionalisation, testimony and report is intensified. The scene changes from Kinshasa to Kisangani, and from there farther out into the lawless war zone. The writer's access to accounts is now not only filtered through anxious or tiresome mediators; both his legal presence and, ultimately, his life are in danger. Simultaneously, the gap is widened between the fictionalised aspects and the presentation of solid facts – as if the diamonds that are the consistent motif in all three chapters play a double role, both as wonders that awaken feeble dreams and as mineralogical facts with far-reaching political consequences.

The first section in this part of the book is called "The amazing story about Ngoyi Kassanji's diamond and what happened later", clearly establishing a narrative kinship with the fable. However, the chapters include many other genres, where numerous changes of perspective and tense cut through the nar-

rative, creating visible traces of both the reporter's and narrator's increasing stress and facets of what we might call the political history of the diamond. A strictly objective and clear account explains the Kabila era's political and economic history as shifting layers in the extremely complex network of interests, alliances, conflicts and betrayal, which together – with the diamond at the centre – resulted in the civil war. Objectivity, however, is interrupted by effects from thrillers and burlesque novels. These effects expose the narrator's increasing desperation until, in the last pages of the book, he succumbs to a combination of real danger and paranoia.

The narrator's own experience of gradually losing his sense of reality is thus part of the narrative, while montage is used to insert a corrective, rational analysis. The convergence of the two directions – the narrator who can organise his impressions sitting at his desk at home withthe help of other sources, and the traveller whose experiences are dependent on senses that are influenced and exasperated by his surroundings – results in a massive reduction of the pathos that is usually linked to eyewitness accounts and to the journalistic report's objectivity becoming relative. The total effect of these strategies, far from all of which have been described, is a design and narrative technique that stands out in the genre in general, and in travel literature about the Congo in particular. It is tempting to categorise *The Congo – I Presume* as New Journalism, because the book uses a number of conventions of that genre: scenic presentation rather than historical narrative; dramatised dialogue rather than quotation; changing perspectives, including internalised vision and speech; descriptions of objects and interiors inspired by the realistic novel; and so on. Nevertheless, the label would be misleading. Peter Tygesen's stories are both more subtle and more radical, and there is clearly something different at stake than in Tom Wolfe's or Hunter S. Thompson's writing, in which the writer's personal style is very much part of the message.

It is equally tempting to perceive the marked presence of the travelling subject in the text as a sign that the narrative is written in the tradition of sentimental travel accounts from the eighteenth century. However, while the report of sentimentality places the individual at the centre of all observations, and the journey seems merely to facilitate the traveller's exploration of self, *The Congo – I Presume* is completely free of this introverted, aestheticised tendency. The narrator only occasionally makes himself heard in the montage form's mix of staged testimonies and objective reports, and the individual's voice is therefore on a par with the other voices in the text, rather than enjoying a privileged positions. This is in fact a rare rhetorical structure in which it is possible to express consideration and solidarity with characters, like the dancer Chantal, without becoming empathetic or condescending. The montage form neutralises sentimentality's tendency to confuse empathy with solidarity – which usually makes empathy merely a variety of the dominant narcissistic mode. The staging of Chantal paradoxically allows her to hold on to the story as her own, and the narrative technique as a whole contributes to a perspective on the historical processes that is both human and objective. Furthermore, the perception of the world through the aesthetics of the sublime, which is widespread in sentimental accounts, is completely absent in Tygesen's style. Faced with the country's anarchy and apparently meaningless mechanisms, the violence and the power of nature, the text patiently looks for explanations in societal structures, economical conditions and geology. It does not deny that the dissolution of societal institutions results in collapsing norms and changing behaviour, but these observations are never referred to the domain of irrationality or demonised in the manner of which we have seen many examples. That which is not immediately understandable is not indescribable, and it does not facilitate indulgence in the narrator's fear or ecstasy, which – in sublime aesthetics – replace understanding. Wonder is not absent from the account, but it belongs to this world. Everyday wonders include a barber's chair in the evening sun, a serendipitous encounter between a girl with a swaying gait and a superstar – and the finding of a 265-carat diamond.

A brief comparison with two relevant examples will serve to highlight some exemplary characteristics of *The Congo – I Presume*. Ryszard Kapuscinski's famous travel reports, some of which are about the Congo – including the turmoil in connection with the murder of Patrice Lumumba in 1961 – have been praised for the invention of a specific kind of literary travel account, termed by the author himself "New Text". However, Kapuscinski's strategy is also highly problematic – a fact that a number of recent biographies and criticisms have pointed out.[200] On many occasions, the author has spoken for the important role of the reporter as an eyewitness who observes crisis points at which history is shaped, and he has emphasised the reporter's great responsibility as a creator of the reader's images of locations in the world. However, Kapuscinski's own standards according to this ideal have been harshly criticised: the literary form of his reports is, in many cases, used to mask sources and testimonies, which subsequently proved to be false. His meetings with Che Guevara and Lumumba never took place; much of what he wrote was based on reports from informants that did not exist, and Africa experts have accused him of "Gonzo orientalism", because he – a bit like Naipaul – creates a melancholy, generalised image of a timeless continent with no scientific tradition. On the other hand, *The Congo – I Presume* can also be compared with David Reybrouck's *Congo. A History* (2010), which has achieved international popularity and recognition, as well as receiving several literary prizes. The book has been praised for its engaging dissemination

of history, providing a complex, balanced understanding of the Congo's history from Stanley's explorations to the arrival of the Chinese today. Furthermore, it is described as a unique combination of narrative testimony and source-based history – something that is often attributed to Reybrouck's dual profession as a literary author and archaeologist. In spite of these qualities, *Congo. A History* carries with it a fundamental, unsolvable problem, which pertains to the emphatic authenticity with which its testimonies are presented: the book is composed as a fugue of Congolese voices, arranged by a classical, omniscient narrator. With rhetorical meticulousness, Reybrouck substantiates the credibility of his witnesses, so that each and every one appears as an incorruptible witness to the truth of the presentation's unambiguous history. The eyewitness account becomes a master narrative in its own right, appearing as a template version and linked to both pathos of memory and repression. *The Congo – I Presume*, in contrast, exposes its own editing processes and uncomfortable imperfections, but without resorting to 'literary' – in the sense of fictionalised – representation.

The stories in *The Congo – I Presume* are fuelled by a strong involvement in the region's development, and from an overall perspective can be read as an appeal to the reader's contribution to changing Europe's Africa policies, especially the relationship with the Congo. However, this consistent ethical appeal in the text is not based on compassion, bad conscience or pathos – which are the dominant rhetorical appeals in literature about the Congo, postcolonial criticism and human rights campaigns. Instead, its basis is rationalism, and we find no traces of the abolitionist movement's aestheticised idyll or the Reform Association's display of atrocities, both of which called for the reader's compassion at the expense of rationality – which had a number of demonising, infantilising, and de-humanising consequences. Tygesen's combination of narrative techniques, which avoid the discourses of the sentimental and the sublime, and his pragmatism, result in a reality work – a "prosaic approach" – that once again positions the Congo on the world map and in the reader's presence. In this sense, *The Congo – I Presume* is far removed from the tradition, which in Bernard Piniau's term has been described as "gaze drift" – "la dérive du regard". Tygesen's book is about the Congo and nothing else, and it is the first time in the Danish public sphere since Jürgensen's novels and Knud Jespersen's travel account that the Congo has been described not as a fantasy, but as a location in the world with which we can and ought to negotiate.

The Congo – I Presume is a model example and a realisation of exemplary characteristics in Stanley's *Through the Dark Continent* and *In Darkest Africa*. Stanley's travel books, as mentioned, hesitate to open the last closed door to the journey, and therefore remain marked by the myth of the Dark Continent – despite their intention. Tygesen creates a hope that travel accounts about Africa may finally

From Herbert Ward: *Five Years with Congo Cannibals* (1890).

overcome "the rule of darkness", which – according to Patrick Brantlinger – has existed since the abolitionist movement was dominant in the nineteenth century, and – according to the argument in the current study – has also dominated the twentieth century. It is fair to call *The Congo – I Presume* a unique event in the history of travel accounts and prose, however it is an event that entails the question asked in the introduction and treated in the last section: is this book, possibly together with a select few other examples, really 'unique', or are we dealing with a breakthrough of a new form of prose with a very long prehistory?

V

The book conveys a largely marginal and forgotten literary history, which is not clearly linked either to the centre or the periphery but played out in the space between them. Modern experiences of transnational identity and globalised conditions for place and space become visible in the ruptures between institutions, markets and prose forms.

The Congo in Prose

The many pages of this book began as a single chapter on the history of travel literature. This chapter was merely something that I had to complete before more inviting material could be investigated, for instance about journeys to Tahiti. However, the theme became engrossing. Joseph Conrad's *Heart of Darkness* was, at this point, already a central and much-discussed text in the critical literature, whereas Stanley's hugely influential travel books remained largely untouched. They therefore became my point of departure, and proved to be far more conflicting and rich in perspective than any of the explorer's biographers had suggested. In this capacity, they also came to define access points to a broad field of other, very different narratives about the Congo: well-known novels by V. S. Naipaul and Graham Greene, forgotten Danish Congo novels and travel accounts, which I chose to read in conjunction with popular culture's images of the Congo, from *Tintin au Congo* to Dian Fossey's *Gorillas in the Mist.* In addition, Peter Tygesen's *The Congo – I Presume* (2001), and David Reybrouck's *Congo. A history* (2010) pointed to a history that was unknown, but vital for our understanding of and responsibility to Africa – including from a Danish perspective. Finally, I made acquaintances among some Congolese refugees on the Danish island of Samsø, who told me fragments of the history of violations and chaos from which they had fled.

While Peter Tygesen and David Reybrouck write history to attempt to bring the reader closer to daily life and dreams in the Congo, I undertook the task of writing about the *literary* history that underlies our repression of this history. Let me begin this conclusion with an event that both expresses the book's central focus on prose as a dynamic approach for understanding the multitude of texts linked to the place, and illustrates a number of the

patterns in the narratives about the Congo that reveal the framework for our approach to Africa today. I am referring to the 1996 film *When We Were Kings*, which describes what has been called 'the rumble in the jungle': the heavyweight world championship boxing match between George Foreman and the title challenger Muhammad Ali, who had lost his title when he refused to enlist for service in Vietnam, referring to the fact that no Vietcong had ever called him "nigger". The match took place in 1974 in Kinshasa, the capital of the Congo – or Zaire, as it was called then. Mobuto, the country's dictator, provided the arena and money needed, in return for the attention of the entire world for as long as the match lasted.

The film is an example not of what the place *is* but rather how it is *created* by narrative effects. The narrative is located in more than one place; it contains and addresses several places and situations at the same time – the boxing ring, the river, the arena, the cold war and the civil rights movement in the USA – all of which are staged as an encounter between two black pilgrims in the centre of Africa. It also evokes the primitive and noble associations of the encounter between Marlow and Kurtz in Conrad's novel, and like the encounter between Stanley and Livingstone a hundred years before, the boxing match is hyped by the media as an event of worldwide interest. The film invites us to feel close to the place by means of peculiar or artificially peculiar phenomena, while at other moments preventing us from identifying where we are.

Against all odds, the artistic but lazy Muhammad Ali defeated the fearsome Foreman in a knockout in the eighth round. There were two, perhaps three, main reasons for his victory. First was the special technique Ali later termed "rope-a-dope": leaning against the ropes, letting Foreman using all his energy on punching his stomach while the ropes absorbed the power of the punches, eventually allowing Ali to floor his exhausted opponent. Second, his rhetorical talents helped focus the media and the Congolese public: "Ali – Bomaye! Ali – Bomaye! – Ali – kill him!" the Congolese were taught to sing. Foreman, on the other hand, lost all support because he brought with him a German shepherd, which was a hated symbol of the Belgian colonial power. Third – as the adventure author George Plimpton suggests in the film – perhaps Ali had magic on his side. Mobuto's *feticheur* magically helped Ali on his way to victory, an idea underlined in the film's editing and the music by B. B. King, James Brown and Miriam Makeba, who were among the musicians who played at a warm-up music festival prior to the match. It was also taken up by the boxing experts Plimpton and Norman Mailer.

The foreign greets us in recognisable forms in the film. In regard to the Congo, these forms – partly because of the country's inaccessibility – were created in the latter part of the nineteenth century and perpetuated in travel accounts, which typically incorporated their predecessors, and in testimonies, which adhered to their recipients' expectation of recognisability.

Norman Mailer wrote *The Fight* in 1975, which follows the match closely.[201] The book has a rather special way of referring to itself and its author: the *author* Mailer distances himself from the *reporter* Mailer, whose literary vanity he mocks in a relatively affected manner. In the chapter "The Millionaire", he writes this about the book's intended anonymity:

"Now, our man of wisdom had a vice. He wrote about himself. Not only would he describe the events he saw, but his own small effects on events. This irritates critics. They spoke of ego trips and the unattractive dimensions of his narcissism. (...) If he was wondering about what name he ought to use for his piece about the fight, it was out of no excess of literary ego. More, indeed, from concern for the reader's attention. It would be hardly congenial to follow a long piece of prose if the narrator appeared only as an abstraction: The Writer, The Traveler, The Interviewer. That is unhappy in much the same way one would not wish to live with a woman for years and think of her as the Wife. Nonetheless, Norman was certainly feeling modest on his return to New York and thought he might as well use his first name - everybody in the fight game did. Indeed, his head was so determinedly empty that the alternative was to write a piece without a name. Never had his wisdom appeared more invisible to him and that is a fair condition for acquiring an anonymous voice" (pp. 31-32).

Having considered the different options, Mailer opts for referring to himself as Norman, albeit not consistently, as he also uses the name No'min Million, which the Congolese gave him after it got out that he received a million dollars from the publishers for the essay novel *The Fight* (he desperately needed the money to provide for his five ex-wives). Mailer calls himself "the literary champ", an heir of Hemingway, envied among colleagues and critics for his position in the heavyweight class of world literature. As a parallel to the different roles that together establish the text's combination of intimacy, intensity and anonymity, the narrative makes use of a series of scenes.

At the centre - or at least that is what we think - is the boxing arena; it is the quintessence of the philosophy of the fight, which Mailer places in a racial, political and national context with reference to American history, including himself as a "White Negro". Outside the boxing ring, we see how authors and journalists compete to convey the match in the most hard-hitting and effective prose - New Journalism - in a struggle for rank, glory and, not least, money. The renowned Hunter S. Thompson was also present, but he did not make it to the match because he was dissolving in a bathtub with a bottle of gin. The floor of the boxing arena was splashed with blood, as Mailer says in the film; the

basement under the boxing arena was a prison in which several hundred people were killed in the weeks that led up to the event. The Congo is mentioned in brief, rambling passages that refer, for example, to Conrad's *Heart of Darkness*; it is an "out-of-place" spot in Africa, caught – for a moment – in the spotlight of the global media. The whole design of the event excludes everything else and leaves the country in the oblivion that has shrouded it since around 1900, when the Congo Free State, due to disputes about human rights, was the subject of the same type of media interest as Afghanistan is today. This oblivion lasted throughout the twentieth century, with the exception of the chaotic time around independence in 1960, when western media dispatched foreign correspondents to this sudden hotspot in the cold war media battle.

During training, Foreman gets a cut near his eye, so the match has to be postponed; this gives Mailer an opportunity to take a quick trip to New York, where he acquires some books about the Congolese Bantu philosophy, which, he writes, is very similar to his own. In Bantu philosophy, humans are not "beings" but "forces". Mailer writes:

"A man was not only what he contained, not only his desires, his memory, and his personality, but also the forces that came to inhabit him at any moment from all things living and dead. (...) In the presence of a woman who is finely dressed, an African might do more than salute the increase of power that accrues to the woman with her elaborate gown. To his eye, she would also have taken on the force that lives in the gown itself, the *kuntu* of the gown. That has its own existence. It, too, is a force in the universe of forces. (...) And the word is water and heat. The force that carries the word comes out of the mouth in a water vapor which is both water and word. Nommo is at once the name of the word and the spirit of water. So Nommo lives everywhere: in the vapor of the air and the pores of the earth. Since the word is equal to water, all things are affected by Nommo, the word" (pp. 39-40).

"What exhilaration!", is Norman's conclusion of this brief lecture – and it becomes clearer what Mailer's nonfiction novel *The Fight* is about. The author initially sees the Congolese and the black American's "ego capital", their power, as a deficiency in himself, but the concepts of *kuntu* and *nommo* provide him with a way to transform his own deficiency into a surplus: his hallmark as an author is prose that is fuelled by an *anonymous* power. This power is not primarily rooted in beings, but emanates from and permeates all things living and dead. As Mailer stresses in the film, "We're going to dance, said Ali, We're going to da-ance, and da-ance". Mailer does the same. The feat of the book and the narrative's "deep play" – to use a term from Clifford Geertz's famous analysis of Balinese cockfights – is not the boxing match but Norman

Mailer's dance in a forcefield in which the power of words is channelled out as magical prose.

The Fight may be problematic in its representation of the Congo as a place, but it is a formidable study of the conditions for writing about it, in the sense of creating a simulacrum. In this sense, the book (novel?) resembles the novels of Graham Greene, V. S. Naipaul and Urs Widmer investigated earlier in this book: the Congo is an almost absolute necessity, while at the same time only superficially significant as a concrete historical and geographical location. This conflict is challenged within a forcefield of prose that both causes anonymity – for example in the author's position – and invites the reader to try a plethora of critical positions, which according to Wlad Godzich is an early constitutive characteristic in the history of prose. The narrative is not a finished construction with an individual nature, but a field of forces that work for good and evil in the world – and this is just as much the case outside 'high' literature. With the Congo as a topic, the competing forces that crisscross these literary fields, for instance between court room and marketplace, as well as their historical conditions, are of specific interest to me, and this book is my attempt to write literary history about them.

In this light, it is important to emphasise that New Journalism was originally a term for a new style of writing around the end of the nineteenth century, of which Stanley – the main character in the present book – was the most prominent representative. Stanley's sense of the power and magic of prose is rediscovered in Mailer's writing; it includes the perspective both of the native population and of the European and American readers and the market, where Stanley's books were magical objects with a powerful effect both in Africa and in western culture.

In the narratives about the Congo, Stanley's tomes *Through the Dark Continent* and *In Darkest Africa* hold a special position. They founded his reputation as "Africa's greatest explorer", but also substantiated his subsequent role as scapegoat – the one person who best incarnates the notion of imperial cruelty. This image, however, is based on an allusion to Joseph Conrad's *Heart of Darkness*, as well as a disregard of the narratives' power as prose. The present study is the first actually to *read* Stanley's travel books, as well as studying and extracting the dynamic pragmatism of his and his fellow travellers' field notes and diaries in the Stanley Archive in Tervuren. This forms the basis for reintroducing the texts at the centre of literary colonial narratives about the Congo, as well as model examples of prose that keeps our ideas of distant places open and changeable. Stanley's New Journalism continued exemplary characteristics of the eighteenth-century travel account in a new form of prose that operated in historical and technological terms.

Conrad's *Heart of Darkness* was the starting point for the present book's chapter on tales of terror from the Red Rubber era, named after the brutal methods with which crude rubber was collected in the 1890s, partly due to the increasing demand for car tyres. Conrad's text was not subjected to close reading, but rather an example of what Franco Moretti has termed "distant reading". I chose to read the text within a broad spectrum of other prose texts about Red Rubber, emphasising – in contrast to the traditions of both literary studies and popular history – that Conrad's novel does *not* stand alone. Through the prose perspective, the book is nuanced and contested by other testimonies that convey other stories and often more complex experiences. This emphasis on other testimonies and criticism of the use of Conrad's text as crown witness to atrocities in the Free State takes into consideration Paul Ricœur's simple demand of history: that it should be based on testimonies as well as the criticism of testimonies. In addition, it has been highlighted that the novel itself points to the problem of conveying a message the audience does not want to hear – a factor that indicates a different, and more powerful, critical potential than the dominant tradition has extracted.

Pierre Halen and Bernard Piniau perceive the Conrad discourse as more dominant than the Stanley discourse in the twentieth century in novels, travel accounts and media reports on the Congo – something that only contributes to keeping the Congo at bay as a place beyond our reach and responsibility. The reception of Conrad's novel, and its massive influence, also contributes to a perception of the place as an "espace fermé", while Stanley's discourse, on the other hand – for instance in relation to the free trade doctrine – contains alternative ideas of the place as open, and "espace ouvert" that is part of 'our' world and 'our' presence.[202] I argue for the importance of seeing this symmetry in the more nuanced light of broad and varied text material, thus anticipating the objection that this could be perceived as revisionist history that aims simply to reverse the roles of heroes and villains. Nevertheless, my literary history relies on the conviction that the purpose of reading and disseminating the stories of the past is basically to extract model examples from which we can learn, in relation to the understanding of both places and narratives. This encompasses a dimension of critical discernment – that is, recognising that some texts are more exemplary than others.

This book is built on the assumption that a prosaic turn is taking place in current literature – a turn that fundamentally shifts dogma and genres, fiction and documentary, high and popular literature, narrator and author, work and event. With reference to Wlad Godzich, I suggest that it will prove fruitful to view this turn not only as affecting a variety of known forms, which can be assimilated and described as a new genre, but also as a kind of literature that changes the very field, thus calling for a new method of criticism. Attentive reading – listening, as Arne Melberg calls it – must be at the forefront of such a method. The prose perspective leads to a largely forgotten and also a different history of literature, which attempts to make good a history of repression.

The ongoing disputes about *Heart of Darkness* – about whether it is racist or critical of imperialism, whether it should be read as universal or in its historical context and so on – has secured the text a position in the world literary canon, where it has influenced works by authors such as Graham Greene, V. S. Naipaul and Urs Widmer, who in trying to avoid its influence inherited it instead. The novel's status in anthologies, typically accompanied by its own criticism and testimonies about violations and "atrocities" in the Congo in the period 1885-1904, has furthermore resulted in classrooms all over the world using it as a testimony to colonial terror in Africa. Influential books, such as Adam Hochschild's bestseller *King Leopold's Ghost*, employ *Heart of Darkness* as a shocking testimony to a forgotten holocaust, while Conrad himself is represented as a brave front-runner for human rights movements – the same movements that did not hesitate to adopt him as their historic role model.

This, however, is a fallacy, which has had far-reaching consequences for the writing of both history and literature, exposing some problems related to these disciplines' methods. A brief summary of the central arguments against the tendency to read Conrad in a genocide/holocaust perspective is necessary here. First, his diary from his unsuccessful journey on the Congo River, in the capacity of skipper in Léopold's service, is completely devoid of moral scruples. Conrad is merely disappointed that the journey does not live up to his romantic and literary expectations, and appears to be oblivious of the world in which he is travelling. Conrad is sick and isolated, and he has to be carried out of the country in a hammock after only a few months. Contrary to the popular notion, Conrad did not write his novel on the basis of first-hand knowledge about "atrocities". It is noteworthy – compared with contemporary prose narratives and travel accounts from the same area, including some written by Danes – that Conrad does not even mention the Arab slave traders' destruction of villages, the concentration camps and so on. A synchronous look at the novel from the broad prose perspective will therefore result in a reappraisal of the text's status as testimony.

Secondly, Conrad's relationship with the Congo Reform Association was a complex affair. In 1903 the association launched a campaign against King Léopold's regime in the Congo. The media campaign was rhetorically organised in a manner that became a model for subsequent human rights movements. In London, a series of campaign 'kits' were produced, which contained slides depicting alleged atrocities and mutilations, as well as 'manuals' for arranging

so-called "atrocity meetings" in Europe and the USA. During these meetings in blacked-out meeting houses, shocking images were shown by means of a new, almost hallucinatory technique, so-called Congo psalms were sung and testimonies given. It was a highly effective campaign, albeit one that was founded on hypnosis and repression: it demanded acute amnesia, not historical understanding and remembrance.

Even then, Conrad's novel was associated with the campaign and used as evidence of King Léopold's Red Rubber terror, despite the fact that the Red Rubber era came after Conrad's stay in the Congo and the novel does not mention it. Conrad willingly let the association use him as an eyewitness. In a letter he wrote that he was "keeping my ears and eyes open", and that "my informants were of all sorts"; soon *Heart of Darkness* almost achieved the status of a report. In conclusion, the novel's status as eyewitness account was a subsequent construction of the Reform Association's propaganda, which had far-reaching consequences for the way in which the Congo was perceived throughout the twentieth century and even today. This is evident in *The River*, Edward Hooper's 900-page book about the origin of AIDS, which is localised in "the heart of darkness"; it includes experiments on apes carried out in an 'inner station' managed by an equivalent to Kurtz, Human Rights Watch campaigns and blogs written by voluntary development aid workers, such as Sahara Sarah's "Breaking Hearts in the Heart of Darkness", and most notably coverage of the bloody events that surrounded independence in 1960 and the 15 years of civil war - the so-called "forgotten war".

If we compare *Heart of Darkness* with the era's complicated network of competing works and texts, for instance Octave Mirbeau's far more sophisticated criticism in his automobile novel from 1907, or Conrad's probable inspiration, Cutcliffe Hyne's 1897 story "The Transfer", it becomes clear that the novel is not a piece of evidence for violations and genocide, but a critique of the conditions for giving such evidence.

Via several references to his pledge not to reveal business secrets, Marlow provides a precise and concrete explanation of the novel's secrecy. The meaning is not to be found in "the heart of darkness", but outside the story; the darkness is not some mystical property of the place, but rather a discursive precondition for narrating about it. Marlow lies, but he lets us know that he does it, thus pointing to the factors - like the stance of *Blackwood's Magazine*, in which the text was first published - that prevent the text from writing its testimony. In other words, it is a narrative about the difficulties of telling a story that readers do not want to hear.

When I write about reading from a prose perspective, simply put, I mean reading critically and with a focus on detail (something that historians quite often struggle to do) – while at the same time comparing several competing testimonies (which literary historians often refrain from doing). The most important job for literary historians is giving a qualified critique of testimonies. Contrary to the media's culture of remembrance, it is our task to seek out the testimonies that lost status in posterity, and to read and try to understand their historical and textual preconditions.

Instead of concentrating on the mystifying discourse about the Congo, which is based on faulty readings that have had a powerful effect on literary history and reception, I chose to focus on Stanley's prose as providing an alternative view that is practical and pragmatic. Stanley addresses the emergence of a new world and rebels against conservative and national institutions, as well as literary forms. His early travel accounts in particular deserve the role of exemplary models, in which free trade and rhetorical movement and transparency are two sides of the same coin. The first, uncensored publication of *Tintin au Congo* and Peter Tygesen's *The Congo – I Presume* can be seen as Stanley's inheritors: they are attempts to define the Congo as a real place in the world, within a shared European, American and African sphere that is characterised by rational negotiation and a considered critical perspective.

In Darkest Africa is Stanley's account of the expedition to find Emin Pasha, who served as a sort of governor in Equatoria – a loosely defined province in southern Sudan, bordering on the Congo's vast Ituri Forests. The text is very gloomy, compared with earlier, utopian accounts about the land of milk and honey. Everything goes wrong, and at the centre of the book – and all Stanley's officers' diaries, as well as the British and American newspapers – is the scandal that the public refused to believe, though testimony followed testimony.

James Jameson, the expedition's natural historian, was left in the rear column, while Stanley continued though the forests towards Emin. The rear column's camp sunk into decadence, and Jameson in particular stood out for his unnatural interest in severed heads and hands, which he sketched with the same care and attention as his preserved birds. This practice of "skinning" and "sketching" converged and culminated in the so-called "cannibal story", according to which Jameson paid six handkerchiefs to have a twelve-year-old girl killed, so he could draw how she was dismembered and eaten.

Jameson died of a fever, but his diary, in which the story is described in detail with no sign of moral regret, was published by his family – partly with the intention of demonstrating what a respectable person Jameson was, and thus repudiating the rumours of perverted corruption in the rear column that had reached London before Stanley arrived with his version.

At the time, Stanley was working on *In Darkest Africa* in Cairo – a very troublesome project that was interrupted by the arrivals of telegrams that an-

nounced court cases in the wake of the scandals, and others that wanted to appoint him as an honorary doctor or discuss the possibilities of publishing the account in America. Stanley's version of events was deemed trustworthy, in particular because of his formidable ability to address the new, differentiated and globalised prose market. However, his huge contemporary success – his brand appearing in jigsaw puzzles, tea advertisements, musicals and so on. – also became the reason he was forgotten by history: the books were published in several unauthorised, abridged versions that focus on particularly dramatic and bloody events, which sealed his fate as either a forgotten writer or a scapegoat for postcolonial criticism.

A focus on this context, however, also entails that reading *In Darkest Africa* requires more than just an eye to the way in which the Congo is represented as a place; it demands that we read and consider how the place is *created* as an effect of the interplay between many, often incongruent, places at the same time – something that the descriptions of Stanley's treks through the Ituri Forest clearly demonstrates.

The scandal resulted in a dispute over credibility, which involved conflicting testimonies and challenged established legal and scientific authorities. However, even before the expedition set out, the scandal was anticipated in a number of contractual terms pertaining to copyrights and other factors, which affected the journey and the travel account's form and material. Furthermore, the media storm that followed the cannibal story involved numerous competing scenes, court rooms, institutions and marketplaces, all of which the texts incorporate as internalised, conflicting spaces. It was not simply a case of the public assimilating the book; the book assimilated the public as well.

The field of meaning – with Jameson's scandal at centre stage – is vast and filled to bursting with narrative and vibrant stories of race, nation and identity. These stories are lacking in definitive narrative structure, because typically they are without beginning and end, and do not have a fictional narrator who can announce how everyone fared ever after. Nevertheless, we are dealing with themes of profound and decisive cultural characteristics with consequences we can still witness today. The writing of literary history does not, therefore, accord the work the central position – particularly not the work of art and its meaning – but instead looks to the cultural function and social significance of the text or book in a given situation. This means, for instance, that it does not make sense to analyse the American Dave Eggers' *What is the What* (2008), an account given to Eggers by a Sudanese refugee, in isolation from the networks and platforms that make up its paratext. On the contrary, it is more productive to analyse the text as a social act – investigating what it *does* within a broad field of external and internal relations and specifically within the network of endless narratives the impenetrability and crises of which we are trying to understand.

The discursive shifts and collapses we can witness in Jameson's text, and their challenge to our usual concepts of textual and cultural wholes, also apply to the role of the expedition and travel literature in the *fin de siècle* value crisis.

The events of the expedition, and the rhetorical preconditions for *In Darkest Africa* and the diaries, were affected by a pre-structured discourse that saw testimonies and credibility in relation to the literary market, legal-moral discourse and legitimisation difficulties in the public political sphere. Narratives about England's worldwide prestige, and the relief committee's attempt to establish a contractual monopoly, affected the expedition's testimonies as they were given and as the stories were told. However, the reception of the testimonies was also subject to a number of discursive terms for what *could* be said – regardless of whether it was true or not. Focus was thus redirected to the aspects of the rhetoric, for instance, that related to decorum – that is, how the material was delivered with regard to what was considered appropriate behaviour in the situation, including ethical, aesthetic and rhetorical rules of "appropriateness", "bienséance" and decency.

In an overall appraisal, the diaries – especially Jameson's – point to one of the most fundamental reasons behind colonial violence and subsequent oppression in the twentieth century: masked as aesthetic sensibility, a scene is created in which repression of the reality of the place is combined with a perverted pleasure in watching the suffering of others. The sentimental style and aesthetic sensibility, combined with the world's lack of recognition, had fatal consequences for the reality that was ejected in the aestheticised act. In Jameson's case, we are dealing with a scandalous transgression of what normally remains within the confines of voyeuristic fascination. This transgression – its formal characteristics of payment, narrative and sketches and the exhilarated, uncertain reception resembling that of horror fiction – indicates a deep structure in sentimental, affect-seeking narratives about far-away places in the world.

1 Congo Literature: A Cross-sectional View

One of the most noticeable consequences of reading from the prose perspective is, naturally, the absence of limitation that was emphasised in the introduction. How is it even possible to operate within a field where the usual priorities and categories, provided in part by the genre system, no longer have the same level of authority, and where the number of potentially relevant texts grows exponentially, thus challenging the current core criterion for literary history: relevance? The answer consists of two parts.

First, we are dealing with an appraisal of importance and relevance that is based on revised classical criteria such as the text's influence and impact at the time of publication as well as on posterity. While this argument strives to avoid canonised material, it still results in what we might term sub-canons each with their respective rivalries for position and rank. Tintin, Dian Fossey and Tarzan, for instance, are undoubtedly key figures in the canon of popular literature; however, their positions have not been uncontested - either in their own time, as we saw in the case of Trader Horn's threat to Tarzan's territory, or in the present day, for example in human and animal rights organisations' proceedings against *Tintin au Congo*. Greene's, Naipaul's and Widmer's novels have similarly prominent positions in the canon of world literature; however they also express (especially in Greene's case) the schism between success and recognition, when the success is achieved under globalised market conditions. In the canon of explorers, Stanley is undoubtedly a key figure, but his texts' canonical status has been a topic of much debate, partly because of their prominent part in the formation of the market conditions. As for Conrad's *Heart of Darkness*, this book has illuminated the text through its links to a number of prose narratives which either support or weaken its canonical status - some even placing it in different, competing canons, such as the canon of modernist literature or of holocaust testimonies. In this sense, the prose perspective does not necessarily entail abandoning the idea of key works, but it does require that they be selected from a broader field and grouped in different constellations. Even within the 'forgotten' travel literature, there are some prominent authors, including Jenssen-Tusch and Jürgen Jürgensen, who in this book are compared to lesser known - or entirely unknown - texts.

Second, the material is organised in a way that - put briefly - has two significant consequences. The first is that the individual text is read as an example or model; its reality work is, as exemplified in Bougainville and Diderot, *instructive*, particularly regarding the role of literature in the creation of images of places in the world. Highly diverse texts like Stanley's, Jürgensen's, Hergé's, Mirbeau's and Tygesen's are excellent models; the same applies to Greene's, Naipaul's and Widmer's novels, when read from this perspective, although my reservations here, especially about the reception of Greene's, are greater. The second consequence of the perspectival method is that the individual text is viewed within changing constellations with other texts, which explicitly or implicitly unfold or display some of the primary text's specific characteristics, and thus in some sense 'read' it. Octave Mirbeau's discourse critical travel novel helps expose discourse critical characteristics in Conrad's novel, while at the same time exposing its limitations. In the most detailed example of this book, Stanley's travel books are shown in textual constellations that illuminate different non-congruent spaces in the primary material. The importance and relevance of the perspectival method depends on whether argument can be made for a meaningful and exemplary selection of comparative texts.

I have chosen to leave out canonical texts, such as André Gide's *Voyage au Congo* (1927) and Redmond O'Hanlon's *Congo Journey* (1996), as well as interesting, albeit curious, publications, such as *Che in Africa. Che Guevara's Congo Diary* (1999) and Madeleine Kalb's *The Congo Cables. The Cold War in Africa – From Eisenhower to Kennedy* (1982).[203] Gide's journey is mainly concerned with the French Congo and the furore that followed his reports on forced labour in the colony. Bernard Piniau refers to Gide as an example of Conrad's all-pervading influence on subsequent travellers, mentioning, among other factors, the disappointment Gide felt when the landscape did not live up to his expectations formed on *Heart of Darkness*, and how he was relieved when finally he found a real 'Conrad forest', where he could localise the coveted "Mystères ténébreux". Che Guevara's Congo diary and Kalb's book illuminate, each from their side of the frontier, how the cold war rhetoric and the established tropes of the Congo's internal chaos merged into the image of a politically uncontrollable zone. *The Congo Cables* presents hitherto confidential documents from American intelligence and telegrams from the American embassy about the USA's active involvement in the Congo's civil wars after independence, in view of the threatening Soviet infiltration of the Congolese army. The book would provide a useful basis for an investigation of how issues pertaining to Roger Casement's and the Reform Association's various forms of policy and rhetoric were carried on in the 1960s' tactical deliberations and rhetoric of ideological discourses on free trade, freedom and atrocities. Che Guevara's diary, on the other hand, first and foremost provides a portrait of the experienced guerrilla soldier who lost his patience with the Congolese rebels, with whom it was impossible to enter into binding, unifying military agreements because of conflicts among rival tribes. Gide's

book is not about the Belgian but the French Congo, and its attitude to Africa and concept of art are closely related to Greene's and Naipaul's; O'Hanlon's travel book is beyond my geographical scope, though its mix of sentimental, bitter, witty and ironic style alone deserves attention as a rare parody of what I have termed 'tragic tourism'.

A writer who might have assumed a key position alongside Stanley, Conrad and Mirbeau in the history of prose narratives about the Congo, is Roger Casement, who wrote a report in relation to a journey to the 'heart of darkness' in 1903 that was the decisive factor in Léopold's handing over the Free State to Belgium. Casement's work constituted an important link between the Congo and Europe, and was a catalyst for the foundation of Morel's reform campaign, which subsequently influenced human rights campaigns and, consequentially, the canonisation of Conrad as a holocaust witness. During Casement's collaboration and later encounter with Stanley in the Congo, the men expressed mutual sympathy. Casement was British consul in the Free State between 1901 and 1904, during which time he became engaged in the criticism of forced labour and of Léopold's violations of the original free trade agreements. He also served as consul in Brazil between 1906 and 1911, where he tried to bring attention to the native population's rights on the basis of testimonies about forced labour in rubber plantations under conditions that were far worse than those of the Red Rubber regime.[204] Subsequent dramatic events led to Casement being exposed as a traitor and homosexual; these include his attempt to launch an armed rebellion in Ireland in 1916 with German support. He was hanged by the British and subsequently became a national hero in Ireland. During the court case against him, British intelligence leaked Casement's secret "Black Diary", which contained detailed descriptions of his homosexual activities. Even today, the diary causes disputes between those who believe that it was a forgery created by the intelligence service, and those who consider it to be real: the opinion is divided between Irish nationalists, who do not want their national symbol put in the stock for being gay, and the gays, who need a gay national hero. This in turn indicates diverging appraisals of Casement as an advocate of human rights.

Roger Casement's case is thus relevant for this book's investigation of anthropoetic narratives that operate within a strategic field between diary confessions; diplomatic reports; human rights campaigns; anthropological descriptions of natives in the Congo, Brazil and Ireland; court case trials of testimonies and credibility;, and questions of nationality, race and gender.[205] Like Mirbeau, Casement redefined the map of Europe and the map of genres, and his report on the Congo can be read as a projection of secret political leanings and sexual preferences as a prosecuted revolutionary, Irish nationalist and homosexual. Read from the prose perspective, Casement's friendship with Stanley and Conrad also defines a common ground for all three, which is a noticeable and overlooked element in their history. The three main characters' presence in the Congo and their meetings took place as results of their employment in the Free State. They were all supporters of the free trade concept and increasingly critical of the Belgian administration; their criticism of the colony was based on a comparison with British efficiency. Furthermore, they were all outsiders with unresolved or split national identities. Casement, and to a lesser degree Conrad, took part in the critical activity against Léopold, while Stanley in his private letters expressed increasing mistrust, but still clung to his hopes of progress and naïve conception of the Free State as a free trade zone. Stanley's naivety was ironically based on the colonial powers' entering into the Treaty of Berlin, which was only signed by France and Portugal on the condition that Léopold dissolved his contract with Stanley, who was de Brazza's rival. From 1885, this condition forced Stanley out of the Congo; Casement and Conrad, on the other hand, were involved in the colony in the 1890s. The relationship between the three key players bears witness to the development from criticism of the colonial management of agreements on free trade to criticism of atrocities. A point of departure in Roger Casement's narratives therefore serves to illuminate one of the underlying threads in this book, to which I will return shortly. However, rather than being a *different* story, it can largely be defined as *another* story.

The history of travel literature in the twentieth century is characterised by collapse – both in communicating genuine wonder, which might spark phenomenological and philosophical curiosity in the reader about the world we inhabit, and in the authority that traditionally supported the credibility of the genre as testimony to places, customs and historical events beyond the reader's horizon. The devaluation of both witnessing and wonder was a process that happened in fits and starts at the end of the nineteenth century, and saw a continuation in twentieth-century travel literature. Only a few texts, like Knud Jespersen's *A Danish officer's Congo journey*, manage to bring wonder and knowledge together in narratives of both authority and quality. The modern travel account's most common form is a combination of journalistic report and exploration – a form that most directly addresses the issue of the heritage of the genre as testimony to the world. In opposition to the one-dimensional day-to-day images of the news media, the ambition is often to delve deeper into the real stories of the world, and thus reawaken the idea that it is still waiting to be discovered – and full of unpredictable events that will shock and revitalise the sleepwalking westerner. In contrast, Edvard Andersen's and Arne Falk-Rønne's reports from the Congo, written on either side of independence, are both narratives about the credibility crisis and collapse of the genre. Their testimonies are borrowed or bought, and

their dystopic stories focus more on justifying the cold war design of the world than on providing meaningful images of the Congo. These are the misanthropic characteristics of the history of travel literature in the twentieth century that have been emphasised in both literary and anthropological studies respectively by Patrick Holland and Graham Huggan in *Tourists with Typewriters* (1998) and Claude Lévi-Strauss in *Tristes Tropiques* (1955). These characteristics, however, assumed a radical expression in relation to the Congo.

In the twentieth century, the travel report appears to have been unable to communicate its own doubt as part of the narrative - instead projecting it in misanthropic descriptions of the world as meaningless. Popular fictional works such as *Tarzan and the Leopard Men* and *Trader Horn*, on the other hand, are far more preoccupied with questions of authenticity, genre and copyrights, which are foregrounded in the texts, while the adventurous plot is a mere backdrop. In this respect, *Tarzan* and *Trader Horn* are not only sophisticated uses of the exotic material provided by travel accounts; they are also commentaries on - and critical readings of - the collapse and decline of travel literature (cf. Du Chaillu's music box in *Trader Horn*). This means that the contributions of popular literature about the Congo contain far more critical potential than twentieth-century travel reports, as well as Graham Greene's and V. S. Naipaul's novels, which - according to Bernard Piniau - are far removed from the world. They basically deal with the authors' own feelings of wandering loneliness, though - when read from the prose perspective - they also display transcending and exemplary characteristics.

In this context, Allen Carey-Webb has identified something of crucial importance in his article "Heart of Darkness, Tarzan, and the 'Third World': Canons and Encounters in World Literature, English 109" (1993).[206] On a par with the earlier mentioned reservations about *Heart of Darkness* and its status as compulsory reading in the English-language literature curriculum, Carey-Webb writes about his insurmountable difficulties getting students to read and understand Conrad's classic. Carey-Webb mentions a teaching experiment in which *Heart of Darkness* was read in conjunction with *Tarzan*, without any previous definition of the texts within a high literature/colonialist/anti-colonialist and a trivial literature tradition respectively. The experiment is interesting in relation to the transcendence of the distinction between popular and high literature, "the Great Divide", which was a decisive factor in Conrad's canonisation. The students noted that there were many parallels between the two texts, but that Burroughs' "colonialist and racist images" are more striking, while Conrad's "literariness" masks these images. We may add that Burroughs is also far clearer in his criticism of both Darwinism and Belgian colonialism. However, the students also found *Tarzan* to be a better and more relevant text than Conrad's - an opinion they based on the developed plot and direct language, which facilitated both entertainment and their readerly response to the text. Conrad's impressionism, on the other hand, caused a diffuse and disengaged reading experience that required extensive knowledge of secondary material - which has been mentioned with regards to the anthologisation of the novel. The experiment raised doubts about the use of the traditional juxtaposition of high and popular culture - the fact that while "we are supposed to criticize "popular" fiction, in "great art" we willingly suspend disbelief" (p. 130). The world literary framework of the course thus paved the way for reflection on assumptions about literary and modern cultural qualities that form the basis of our institutionalised approaches to reading, showing that these approaches are historical rather than 'natural'; nevertheless, they constitute the most basic mechanisms in literary history's canonisation processes. The comparison of the two texts made the students ask questions that cannot be easily answered within the established confines of literary studies. For example, why is the plot complexity of popular literature less valuable than the "complexity of symbolism"? And what criteria exclude *Tarzan and the Leopard Men* from the canon of world literature, while including Joseph Conrad's *Heart of Darkness*?

Cutcliffe Hyne's "The Transfer" is a marginal text in an extensive, albeit forgotten, oeuvre - and the likely inspiration of Conrad's famous novel. "The Transfer" expresses that which *Heart of Darkness* conceals, and the title anticipates a vast number of texts, both popular and 'high' literature, and both fictitious and documentary, that continued its contraband and falsely valued cargo. One recent example is John le Carré's *The Mission Song* (2006), which employs motifs from "The Transfer" to represent the tense situation that led up to the election in 2006. Le Carré's novel puts strong emphasis on the problematic field of international law and the plans to provoke a state of emergency in the Kivu Province of eastern Congo, as well as continuing the focus on the narrator as a filter through whom the history of the Congo is translated.[207] The plot includes all the elements of Hyne's text, and is equally precise and objective in its uncovering of complicated political and economic interests that underlie the plot about a seemingly altruistic intervention by the British intelligence agency. The perspective, however, is turned on its head: the main character is a Congolese who is living in England, where he works as an interpreter of Central African languages for MI5. His fiancée is not oblivious to the old empire's amateurish plans of a coup; she is a fellow Congolese who is actively involved in sabotaging MI5's attempts to prevent the first democratic election. The main part of the story does not take place on the deck of a ship, but on some small Norwegian or Danish island, where the interpreter is interviewing Congolese citizens who have been invited as prospective main players in the coup. As

in "The Transfer" and *Heart of Darkness*, the interpreter – who has until then acted as a neutral go-between – intercepts a piece of information that was not meant for his eyes and ears; however, unlike Marlow and Gering, he chooses to do the right thing instead of sticking to the lie. *The Mission Song* thus confirms the impression of consistent and constant thematic and formal structures, but also of popular fiction's ability to avoid the discourse of distance, to address significant political issues through the motifs we have traced in both topology and literary topography and to treat them critically. Compared with the typical travel report, which pretends that translation is an innocent and neutral activity, le Carré's novel reveals a number of the points that are emphasised by translation theorists, including Susan Bassnett: that since translation is always already *in* media it is limited, garbled, conveyed and edited under the influence of rhetorical and cultural filters, and constituted by local as well as global conditions, including historical concepts of the place. And as is the case in conflict zones, the translator plays the composite role of communicator, negotiator, traitor, victim and scapegoat.[208]

In "The Transfer", this transference and traffic from text to text, and from genre to genre, is indicated in a curious detail about how Caissier's farcical enforcement of "International Law" is carried out while he is sitting on an ammunition box, while the proceedings are recorded in "the margins of a novel". It is possible that this detail is echoed in the anecdote about Marlow's finding of *An Inquiry into some Points of Seamanship* and what he believes to be encrypted comments in the book's margin. However, it is also an indication of the textual strategy described in relation to Diderot's supplements to Bougainville's description of his experiences on his journey to Tahiti. In Diderot's hypothetical dialogue between A and B, the initial travel account is read with added comments in the margin, which – rather than overwhelming it – carries on the prose that does not entirely pertain to the travel account, essay or novel, and therefore, in a moveable and inclusive manner, includes the juxtaposed perspectives of Europe and Tahiti, near and far.

In relation to the question of the field, the prosaic turn in current culture provides a perspective on eighteenth-century travel literature that facilitates a reading of Diderot's additions as exemplary, leading to similar strategies and connections in both synchronous and diachronous literary-historical developments. Tarzan and Tintin are, like Greene's, Naipaul's and Widmer's novels, supplements and readings of an early group of European texts, with Stanley's travel books, Conrad's *Heart of Darkness* and "The Transfer" at the centre; moreover, they have been read as a consequence of the prosaic turn, which changes their position in the literary field. Similarly, in this type of reading, Casement's report does not alter, but fundamentally reaffirm, basic characteristics of the field. As mentioned earlier, the assumption of a prosaic turn in current literature is a hypothesis that may be proven or rejected by future literary studies. In any case, the current study has been able to provide a meaningful description of the topic, in relation to Wlad Godzich's terms, by assuming the prosaic turn to be a transformation of the crucial characteristics of the field due to an emergent form of literature. The prose perspective has not only resulted in the literary-historical repositioning of individual works; it has changed the very 'map' on which literary history is written. On the one hand, my readings of Stanley, Conrad, Mirbeau and Hergé would not have been possible without an alternative map that kept them connected. On the other, it has organised the readings in a comprehensive, literary-historical narrative that tells a different story from the one we know from postcolonial criticism – a story based on different textual approaches from the ones we know from the formalist tradition of literary studies.

2 Place

Another parameter for the selection and limitation of the field has been topographic. More attention has been given to 'reality work' – perceived as the texts' use of the idea of the Congo – than to representation of the place, although the two aspects in practice are inseparable. This focus is related to a current academic interest in the "functional performativity" of texts. Regarding the texts' use of European ideas about the Congo, this entails that the focus on 'place' is projected through a number of relations that are both internal and external to the texts, including their materiality and medial transformations. As for the performativity perspective, Wolfgang Behschnitt writes that it is not "possible to talk about the text's performativity without considering its concrete materiality, mediality and basis in a specific situation".[209] This understanding of the reality work as dealing with place is most developed in my reading of Stanley, but it also justifies the inclusion of Dian Fossey, Tintin, Tarzan and the book about AIDS, all of which can be seen as medial transformations of central topographies.

I will not summarise the examples here, but only repeat, as mentioned in the introduction, that there is a basis for demonstrating the significant long-term effect – or constant influence – of the earliest texts on the subsequent ones, which may be related to the geo-physical characteristics of the place and country, as well as to the influences from the earliest history of the colony.

The topographical representation of the Congo basically uses a number of geo-physical obstacles as discursive barriers that must be passed before the traveller can journey inland. However, the topography of the Congo also forms part of another, more expansive topographic distribution, which is the position of the place on the world map. Descriptions of the journey from Europe to the Congo – or in Naipaul's case from East to West Africa – are usually accounts of sweeping transformations of the traveller's identity and sensory apparatus. These transformations take place in the traveller's description of self *before* arrival, thus influencing what they experience once they reach their goal, and how they describe it. Jungsbøll, Freiesleben, Roos and Conrad all carefully describe the journey as a transformation that not only expands their moral and aesthetic perceptive scope and prepares the reader for unexpected and irregular events, but also serves to initiate the traveller into becoming an author. Joseph Conrad's letters to his aunt, who helped him when he wanted to go – like Marlow – and when he wanted to return, also function as preliminary practice for his literary travel novel and his poetics. During the outbound journey, however, these transformations also express a different, fundamental topographical problem: the question of the description's *distance* from that which it aims to describe.

If we use this parameter as a critical approach to the material, a different pattern appears from when the texts are approached on the basis of formal-aesthetic or postcolonial theory. Following Bernard Piniau's term "tradition conradienne", which is characterised by "dérive du regard" or 'gaze drift', Naipaul's and Greene's novels, as well as the texts I mentioned under the label of 'tragic tourism', are defined by an enormous distance from the Congo as a place. However, the prose perspective also facilitates a correction of crucial points in Bernard Piniau's and Pierre Halen's criticism, which will be briefly outlined below.

Some of the earliest travel accounts, including Martini and Schønberg's jolly confessions and Casement's report, are *not* subjected to the rhetoric of exoticism, and they do not attempt to sell the coveted commodity to readers. The same applies to *Tintin au Congo*, which is often criticised as racist propaganda, but is actually strikingly objective and precise in its dealings with fundamental themes in the history of the colony, which is not embellished, veiled or silenced, but explicitly revealed in surrealist strips. Just as the narrative core in "The Transfer" exposes the most important issue of the relationship between Europe and Africa then and now – namely the clashes between international law and regional states of emergency – *Tintin au Congo* explicitly exposes the infiltration of globalised crime in Congolese economy and politics. In both cases, as Pierre Halen has pointed out, the Congolese reality is represented as entirely intelligible. In Halen's terms, the style of both Stanley's travel books and Hergé's album is not exoticism but anti-exoticism – a de-mystifying, positivistic endeavour that resists both Congolese and European demonisation.[210]

From the prose perspective, the cartoon can be described as a differentiation of prose, adapted to new technologies and new discursive conditions and opportunities in national as well as global markets. In his double role as "petit Belge" and global reporter, Tintin is this principle incarnate. The success of the cartoon medium in Belgium, where it enjoys a privileged position in national literature, can be explained through the fact that this visual form of communication transcends the language conflicts that continue to threaten the country's unity as state and nation. The cartoon medium's transnational potential has secured it a central role in Belgium's "nation building", while at the same time resulting in global distribution, especially for the Tintin series. All over the world, including in the Congo, readers can observe "la Belgité" from their own perspective, and marvel at the small country's painful experiences with fragile European borders and its exposed position during the cold war.

In *Tintin au Congo*, colonial history is told in a globalised perspective, reflected in the prose narrative about the manipulation of media and testimonies, and in the strips of the prose form, which enable the reader to observe ruptures, seams and editing in history's drift within and between media. Tintin displays the critical potentials that were explored later in so-called "graphic novels", for instance Art Spiegelman's *Maus. A Survivor's Tale* (1991), in which issues pertaining to trauma and witness literature are communicated via forms that elastically combine epic narrative, visualised drawing, documentary, pop art, autobiography, comic strips and holocaust memory. And, like *Tintin au Congo*, this form of work links questions about the limits of humanity with questions about the limits of what can be expressed – and in which media.

In Bernard Piniau's and Pierre Halen's opinion, the anti-exotic tradition is subdued by an exotic tradition, the starting point of which they define as *Heart of Darkness*. Regardless of the novel's attitude towards colonialism and aesthetic power, even today this exoticism dictates a problematic distance in the perception of Africa, as well as a notion of the place as exclusive and asynchronous. Contrary to Stanley's strategy, which aimed at demystifying the Congo and include it as part of the global market as an equal, synchronous space in the world, the Conrad tradition's discourse isolates the place, resulting in an obstruction of rational criticism and dialogue. Piniau and Halen agree that this rhetorical isolation, which has been maintained in the media coverage of its independence and subsequent civil wars, has had a direct geo-political impact on the country. The Congo, according to the international community, is still an exception from "International Law", as is the case in "The Transfer", and even emergency aid workers like Sahara Sarah who are working to change the state of emergency contribute to perpetuating the myth when they use terms such as "Breaking Hearts in the Heart of Darkness".

The prose perspective of this book has put emphasis on the texts' reality work, focusing on their effects on the European reader's images of Africa. In this context, I very much concur with Piniau's and Halen's criticism. Their categorisation allows for other comparisons and tendencies, such as my reading of Stanley as a model example – an approach that nuances the widespread and dominant model of 'otherness' in postcolonial criticism. However, at the same time it is a problem that Piniau's and Halen's distinction between two alternative, fundamental and antagonistic discourses in practice continues the simplifying symmetrical mindset of postcolonial criticism. Pierre Halen emphasises this as an advantage, and as a significant factor in Piniau's arrival at his original thesis that he is not literary and not committed to a predisposed veneration for the canonical works. However, this point of departure is also a limitation. In this book, I have instead tried to be very inclusive in the selec-

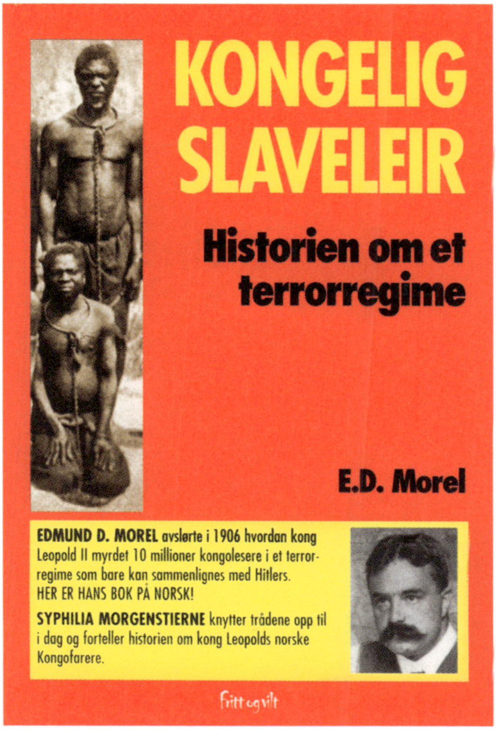

Royal Slave Camp. The Story of a Terror Regime (2002) is a Norwegian translation of Morel's *Red Rubber* (1906). The publication is illustrated with the usual atrocity photographs from Morel's book, supplemented with photographs from Stanley's accounts, which indicates a direct link between the explorations and the rubber terror. The publishing company, Fritt og vilt, know how they want to present the story: the book shows "how King Léopold II murdered 10 million Congolese in a terror regime that can only be compared to Hitler's". The cover can be ordered as a poster on the company homepage for the book, which contains more atrocity photographs. Both book and advertisement are examples of a tendency to simplify and distort the early history of the Congo with biased definitions of heroes and villains, and to fit the events into a subsequently constructed mould that equates the oppression of the Red Rubber era with the holocaust. The agitation represses more nuanced historical prose and results in another layer being added to the twentieth-century oblivion regarding the Congo.

tion of material, while at the same time reading the individual texts in a fairly detailed way. The individual texts are thus not read as opposites, but illuminated in changing clusters of prose narratives whose total body draws lines and patterns that are *asymmetrical*.

Twentieth-century travel descriptions of the Congo, which quantitatively make up the largest group of texts by far, are neither part of a Conrad tradition – with the exception of the texts I read under the title "tragic tourism" – or a Stanley tradition. Jungsbøll, Freiesleben, Edvard Andersen and Falk-Rønne do not write in the style that Piniau and Halen describe as exoticising. Their style is not mystifying and indirect, and they do not convey a perception of the place as indescribable; on the contrary, their descriptions are transparent. They represent a matter-of-fact positioning of the Congo on the world map that reflects a colonial division of the world – a division that between 1900 and 1960 was based on colonial exhibitions and textbooks. The texts do not

explicitly operate to the exclusion of the topography, but they do make use of a number of other techniques of exclusion, the comprehensive effect of which is forgetfulness and repression of the history of the place. While the place is actually expropriated, it is erased from memory in a process by which both the topic of the narrative and the narrative as event are forgotten and repressed. On the other hand, the criticism of this effort to forget is largely linked to revisionist history, which is based on a holocaust paradigm that carries on the initial forgetfulness as a renewed repression of anything that contradicts the narrative about atrocities. This includes the garbled positioning of Conrad as witness. In both cases, neither of which clearly fit into one or the other of Halen's "Alternative Discourses", the texts' reality work in relation to the place are processes of erasure and repression.

Twentieth-century Congo novels have been described by Bernard Piniau as influential works that consolidate and enhance Conrad's exoticism – a viewpoint I have supported throughout this book. Seen from the perspective of place, there is no doubt that Greene's, Naipaul's and Widmer's knowledge is extremely limited, which manifests itself in problematic topographies. However, Piniau's criticism is actually based on a narrow and literary reading of the texts as representations, though Halen has claimed the opposite. From the prose perspective, their criticism therefore needs correction, partly with regards to the different places and spaces that influence the texts simultaneously. Especially in Stanley's travel books, I wanted to investigate and demonstrate that it is not only the Congo, but also the texts' European spaces and conditions that are being addressed. And the novels belong to similar performative creations of spaces in which experiences can be expressed and communicated.

Seen from Piniau's perspective, *Heart of Darkness* contributes to the exoticist gaze drift, while from the prose perspective it is also a critical exposure of the discursive terms for the colony's 'espionage system' and for narrating about it – though I have argued against the widespread interpretation of the text as a testimony to atrocities. The novel attempts to clear a way for itself through dealing with several incongruent places and spaces simultaneously: the colony, the ship's deck, *Blackwood's Magazine*, Stevenson, Cook and Flaubert. Greene's, Naipaul's and Widmer's novels are, in much the same way, more than topographies of the Congo; they are critical investigations of the conditions, including the market conditions, for writing about a world in which they can move freely, but which they cannot grasp in its entirety. Greene's "a region in the mind", Naipaul's distanced gaze and its limits in Zabeth's world and Widmer's utopian transcendence are supplements to Conrad's novel that propagate not only its exoticism but also its modern reflection of located placelessness as an aesthetic experience of limits to knowledge and participation.

The novels about the Congo, including *Tarzan and the Leopard Men* and *Trader Horn*, are written on global terms, but they are still linked to locations in Switzerland, London, South Africa and Hollywood. The texts accordingly address their own perspectives and performative dimensions; Urs Widmer's laptop in the tree tops, or E. R. Burroughs in cinemas. And although none of the texts can be said to represent the Congo in a manner that is in any way comprehensive – something that is practically impossible – they compel European and American readers to reflect on their own location as a starting point for understanding the world. Some authors only paid brief visits to the Congo and others, like Mirbeau, Hergé, Burroughs and Widmer, had never been there, but they were nevertheless able to carry out reality work that facilitates a better understanding of place than many testimonies, which tend to elevate the value of the account's "I was there, I saw it".

It has often been emphasised that the authenticity of witness literature is more concerned with the reader's reception than with the reference to the actual, witnessed event. Diderot was not present on Tahiti, but his additions position the place more accessibly on the world map than any other text. Furthermore, they reveal basic characteristics of the anthropoetic narrative, which – from the prose perspective – can be identified in travel accounts such as Mirbeau's, and in novels such as Greene's, Naipaul's and Widmer's, which deal with places, borders, nationalities and identities in a mix of fiction, autobiography and history that investigates what it is to be human.

3 Testimony

An understanding of history on global terms is also made on prose's terms, meaning that history is perceived through anthropoetic narratives that are not fictions, eyewitness accounts or documentary reports, which is one of several reasons for writing it from a prose perspective. An eyewitness account of a historical event is not necessarily closer to the truth than other competing accounts, and it does not stand alone, but is part of a contested network, which the historian, in the role of literary historian, must try to read.

The testimony is communicated through text and is thus part of textual and institutional relations. This may appear obvious, but it is often overlooked in the expanding research field that focuses on testimonies and witness literature.[211] In literary studies, there is a tendency to continue traditional methods of reading in this new field, and treat the question of the authenticity of testimonies as an ethical and aesthetic one that can be appraised on the isolated text's autonomous terms. A prosaic approach to testimonies, on the other hand, emphasises the context in which the testimony is performed, on the basis of pragmatic ethics that take into account the everyday space of which the text is part. This approach is exemplified in Gary Morson's use of the terms "prosaic wisdom" and "prosaics" (the opposite of "poetics") in his reading of Bakhtin.[212] The element of ethics in relation to Bakhtin is not a question of rules or abstract philosophical problems; rather, it is located in particular, everyday networks of social relations and events, the 'thickness' and polycentric structure of which are expressed very well in novels.

In their article "Trust in Testimony: The Institutional Embeddedness of Holocaust Survivor Narratives", Aaron Beim and Gary Alan Fine reach the same conclusion regarding testimony's prosaic ethic, albeit from a different perspective.[213] Beim and Fine's topic is the relationship of testimony and remembrance at American holocaust museums, but their basic points are coherent with the perspective I have employed in my readings of literature about the Congo. First, the eyewitness account is no guarantee of truth – it is a fragmented and rhetorical construct, as Ricœur argued. Second, any testimony ought to be perceived, not as a descriptive statement, but as a performative linguistic act that processes a vast number of social contexts, partly with the intention of creating or recreating the witness' identity. Third, the credibility of the testimony is not a question of a precise representation of the event, but a rhetorical construction based on the testimony's narrative and style, as well as various rhetorical conditions defined by the context – for example whether the witness is being paid – and also the institutional framework and rituals for the presentation and reception of the testimony. The rhetorical conditions translate expectations into conviction through the performer's and recipient's subconscious imitations of structures pertaining to credible accounts. In other words, a testimony can create credibility by *imitating* an established narrative and institutional procedure for credibility.

The present book has focused a great deal on the performative and conceptual aspects of testimony. The truth about the events in the Yambuya camp and Jameson's cannibal story has not been sought in one ultimate, convincing testimony, but in descriptions of the reception of conflicting testimonies, as well as the rituals and rhetoric – including what I termed decorum – of the institutions that were in a position to verify or reject a testimony, and of market mechanisms such as copyrights. As mentioned in the introduction, the travel account's epistemological play on fact and fiction has therefore been of only minor importance.

The travel account, in my reading, has no privileged position in literary history, because it can in a sense be seen as an eyewitness account. My reservations towards some critics' tendency to misrepresent Conrad's journey to the Congo, and consequently portray the novel as a testimony in the narrow sense, should be viewed in light of this. In its capacity of anthropoetic narrative, the travel account, and the network of narratives of which it is part, is on the contrary an important source – or testimony – for understanding the mechanisms that produce credibility and expectations of recognisability. Both Stanley's and Octave Mirbeau's travel accounts are good examples of this, and though the latter is not a testimony about atrocities in the Congo, it is a prodigious exposure of the conditions for testimonies. This constitutes a prosaic challenge to the reader's ethics with far more scope than an eyewitness account, for instance, which – setting aside motivations and justifications – would be yet another witness account that is based on, and reaffirms, a recognisable narrative structure that was conceived by the abolitionist movement, refined by the Congo Reform Association and continued by twentieth-century human rights organisations.

If we turn our attention to the institutional frameworks for testimonies, and the narrative design that complies with the mechanisms of acceptance and credibility highlighted by Beim and Fine, we will discover one of several explanations for the striking *constancy* in the main material: the heart of darkness as a term is, in this light, an institutionalised rhetorical mechanism – a topos in rhetoric, rather than in the world –that paradoxically legitimises and sanctions the credibility of testimonies about the Congo. This happens without any representation or recognition of the place; instead, the narrative makes itself

recognisable as testimony. Peter Bates' television film *White King, Red Rubber, Black Death* (2003; German and French versions in 2004)[214] demonstrates these deeply rooted mechanisms in an exemplary form. The film's central narrative device is a fictionalised staging of the international tribunal through which Morel wanted to prosecute King Léopold – at a time when such a process had no institutional basis. In the film, Léopold is put in the dock, where he silently listens to a series of testimonies to atrocities from missionaries, soldiers and officers in the Free State, as well as from the victims. The editing includes other noticeable narratives, one being a number of interviews with experts, who present contemporary historical-scientific appraisals of the terror regime and its subsequent repression, the other being clips from a kind of report on the Congo, where a Congolese historian employed by the École des Hautes Études en Sciences Sociales in Paris is travelling through the country while telling its history to both viewers and natives, most of whom have unresolved relationships with the colonial period. There are also some fragments of *Heart of Darkness*, which – in isolation – can be perceived as an expression of indignation. Furthermore, there are some sequences that reconstruct forced labour, the burning of villages and punishments.

It is clearly the film's intention to make up for the repression of history and, by reopening the archives and showing the imagined court case, to contribute to providing delayed redress for the oppressed. It is extremely suggestive, almost hypnotic, with its sequences of stark depictions of violence and mutilation. At the same time, viewers are denied any opportunity to make their own critical appraisal, though they act as judges to whom the evidence is presented. The ceremonial, narrative recognisability of the court room is so compelling that it is impossible to question the fact that the case – and the film – does not allow for any defence. The officers and soldiers presented on the witness stand are all part of the prosecution, and Léopold is not allowed to answer; he is merely represented as an inhumane monument of evil – an effect that is achieved via frequent superimpositions of the actor playing Léopold as a living, silent man and Léopold as the dead marble of one of his statues. The effect can be seen in relation to another striking technique: the Reform Association's display of photographs and slides depicting mutilation is part of the film's montage. The original photograph of the missionary couple Harris' group of children dressed in white, all missing a hand or a foot, for instance, is shown and superimposed with fictionalised filmic sequences in which the children are moving with the white clothing draped and swirling around their black bodies. In this sense, Peter Bates updates the Reform Association's rhetoric with the possibilities that film offers, but he stays within the confines of early agitation. Montage is also mainly used to create a hypnotic rhetoric of affect, which rather than allowing for historical understanding establishes renewed bias, bringing some testimonies to life, while others are silenced. The simulated court case does not contribute to illuminating history, but leaves fragmented and mystifying impressions – like Peter Bates' other television productions about Nazi secrets and lost expeditions.

This is very similar to the main tendency in the twentieth century that I have described as a rhetoric of repression: the striking homogeneity in design and preferred figures of many colonial travel accounts indicate the texts' adaptation to institutionalised patterns of recognition, which guarantee that the reader will accept the narratives, despite the fact that they may be highly unlikely. While the underlying basis of the discourse of testimony aims to establish a form of collective memory, as is the case in holocaust museums, human rights narratives or exhibitions on colonialism, it is also extremely dependent on the testimony's recognisability and repeatability – mechanisms that are closely related to those of the myth. Lindqvist's and Hochschild's histories are particularly conspicuous examples of mythologised testimonies and collective memory, whereas Stanley, Mirbeau and Hergé – in very different ways – *break* with the institutionalised rules and rituals of representing and receiving testimonies, thus keeping the door ajar for historical memories of the place.

The former secretary of the Nobel Prize Committee of the Swedish Academy, Horace Engdahl, has established a formula for the prevalent literary approach to testimonies in recent years: one which in my view is arguable. Engdahl writes that the credibility of a testimony depends on the community's recognition, but given that the experience expressed in testimonies often conflicts with common sense, both for the witness and the listeners, a bond must be established between victim and community in recognition of this unintelligibility. According to Engdahl, the testimony's enemy is therefore not silence, but rather historiography and "ready-made explanations".[215] From this perspective, witness literature should maintain the witnessed event as "enigma" and "scandal", while I, on the other hand, have argued for the urgent need to look for accounts that counteract the idea of the place or event as an enigmatic and unintelligible scandal. Scandal is one of the reasons why terror never seems to stop in this part of the world. The German historian Martin Sabrow has pointed out that while the eyewitness account promised a much-needed revision of history writing's totalitarian narratives in the 1960s, today it has itself become totalitarian so that it represses the writing of critical history, which was obliged to compare and test different sources and testimonies.[216] The problem is that an eyewitness' authenticity is produced on the media's terms, confirming the individual witness' credibility by referring to other anonymous testimonies within a genre contract that obstructs critical inquiry into the witness' context (cf. the Congo

reform campaign). Rhetorical claims about the testimonies' authenticity are no guarantee of truth, as we have seen in the cases of Hochschild and Lindqvist. Historians and literary historians are obliged to investigate the forces that are not represented by individuals, and to review collections of different testimonies. This obligation is echoed in the French historian François Hartoq's demand that historians always search for other voices in the archive.[217]

4 Atrocity Accounts and Human Rights

The aforementioned issue also concerns what we might call the pattern of patterns in European prose narratives about the Congo. A connection has been drawn several times between the Congo Reform Association and present-day human rights campaigns, which perpetuate basic characteristics of Morel's atrocity campaign. Sharon Sliwinski and John Peffer have investigated this connection. Sliwinski researches visual culture, and in "The Childhood of Human Rights: The Kodak on the Congo", she provides a detailed analysis of the Reform Association's use of slideshows featuring "atrocity" photographs.[218] The use of the new medium, the so-called "laterna magica", very much refuelled the campaign, which – after Morel's first book – had lost impetus with the public. The shows were organised as more or less identical, stringently structured events, in which recorded accounts of atrocities and around sixty slides, together with psalms and sermons, aimed to create a strong emotional response.

In addition to the self-evident problems related to the testimony status of these accounts and images, some of which I have mentioned, Sliwinski notices three issues: that individual accounts and images were anonymous and mass-produced without any time and place being established; that the shows defined a pattern for reproduction of the narrative structure and presentation of testimonies; and, most importantly, that perception took place in a communicative situation that was fundamentally phantasmagorical and hallucinatory – feverish. The particular characteristics of individual cases were erased to produce a standardised and recognisable version, built on the powerful images of severed hands, which lead the spectator to draw universal conclusions about the rights of others. The biggest problem is thus that the sensory raw material for the formation of modern international models for responsibility and rights was defined through this 'dreamwork'. John Peffer similarly argues for a highly problematic connection between the Congo Reform Association and subsequent human rights campaigners. The slideshows provoked powerful emotional responses, but in a hypnotised context the effect of which relied on repression of the terrifying images' context, including omission of the missionaries' active participation in colonial exploitation and staging and re-enactment of floggings, for instance, which were part of the photographs' reality. Referring to Susan Sontag's essay "Regarding the Pain of Others" (2003), Peffer writes that "sentimentality is entirely compatible with a taste for brutality or worse", and that every repetition of the misdeed, both in the

Søren Assenholt: "Locked-out from the Inside" (2008). On the DVD cover of Peter Bates's *The Congo – White King, Red Rubber, Black Death* (2003), the film is described as "a journey into the original heart of darkness". The director interprets Conrad's tale as a testimony to genocide and Morel's campaign as a human rights movement. The red thread through the film is a staging of the court of human rights Léopold never faced. Here, shocking testimonies are presented, with the film viewer as judge, while an unaffected Léopold acknowledges the accusations in silence. The hallucinatory style of the *laterna magica* displays of the reform association is continued in the imagery of the film. The aim is to appeal to compassion; however, in reality the rhetoric holds the viewer in a firm grip of helplessness. One reviewer wrote that the superimpositions of present and past help us to "humanize" events that are distant in time and place; another compared the film to *Hotel Rwanda*, the Hollywood film from 2004 about the genocide in Rwanda - although the form of presentation is problematic, without these films we would know nothing about genocides in Africa. In Belgium, the film was initially subject to censorship, until a political compromise made it possible to show it on TV, albeit with commentary by specialists from the museum in Tervuren to counteract the bias of the film. British newspapers made fun of the controversy, thus replaying the British anti-Belgian campaign from the beginning of the twentieth century. They claimed that the Belgians' sensitivity - which made it necessary for the government to get involved - was due to the fact that Belgium has never been a nation state and that the monarchy is the only thing that brings the population together. The artist Søren Assenholt included a collection of documentary images called "Locked-out from the Inside" in his installation series *Planners & searchers* (2008), which, among other things, show a key to a locker in the museum in Tervuren, where Assenholt has put a DVD of Bates's film. The series also contains an imaginary restoration of Stanley's boat, Lady Alice, altered drawings of Conrad's and the artist's 'cards of memories', and a parcel of books for a student of architecture in Kinshasa who is hoping to become president one day. The parcel represents the western debate about how to develop the third world most effectively. See www.assenholt.dk.

missionary photographer's arrangement of it and the subsequent display in Europe, was a violent deed.[219]

From a performative perspective, the Reform Association's campaign established the notion that spectators, through visual confrontation with atrocities, could erase the effect of violent deeds from a distance by passively experiencing compassion for the victim. When this notion is simultaneously linked to universal and transcendental ideals of humanity, dignity and obligation, it results, according to Sliwinski, in a complete loss of clear ideas of the reality for those involved, which is mirrored as a problem in modern human rights movements

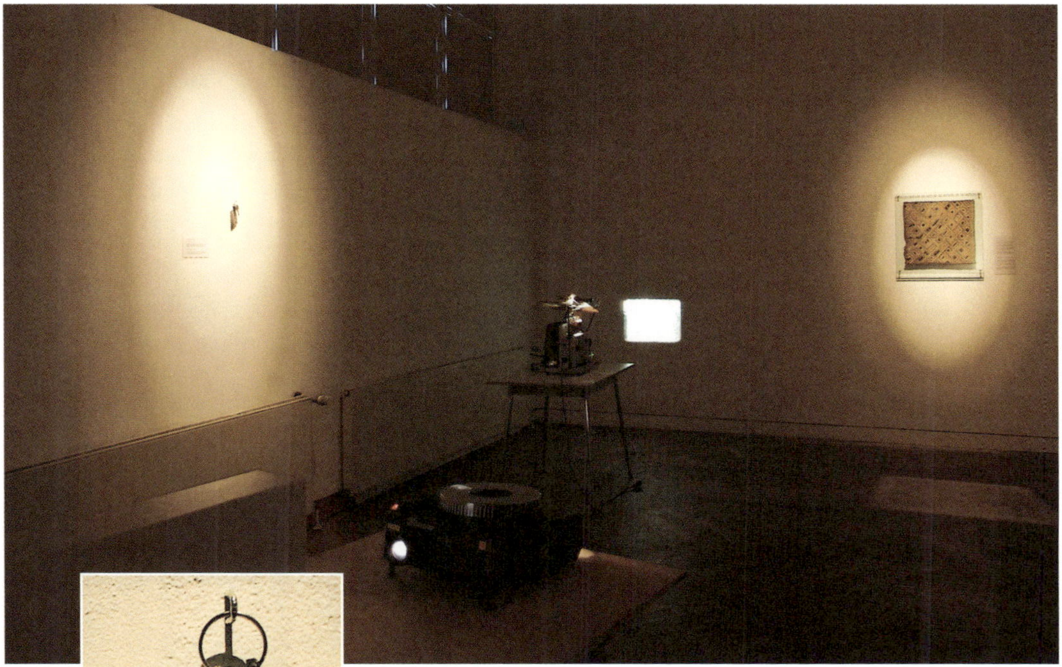

and the form of "liberal humanitarian discourse" represented by Peter Bates' film. *White King, Red Rubber, Black Death* is an example of precisely this kind of rhetorical montage of dreamwork, wishful thinking, hypnosis and history-repressing laterna magica and court room. In the campaign, the atrocity images were initially used as propaganda; however, the audience response to the shows was wishful thinking about the images' magical ability to undo the wrong – even though in reality they maintained the spectator's helplessness. One counter example, mentioned earlier, is W. G. Sebald's use of photographs in a way that accentuates their materiality, and their unfinished and incomplete representation of the place, thus resisting melodramatic interpretations.[220]

One among many examples of the contemporary continuation of the rhetoric and media forms of the Congo Reform Association can be found on Human Rights Watch's website for a campaign against atrocities in the Katanga Province during the ongoing civil war.[221] "Triangle of Death. A Place of Horrors in Katanga Province" is a site where the same discourses meet and are mixed in a multi-media staging of 'horror', in a manner that is similar to the anti-terror

campaigns' laterna magica shows. The 'dreamwork' on the Internet permits the user to switch between and superimpose a "slide show" of the photographer Marcus Bleasdale's black-and-white photographs of atrocities, "audio commentary", which presents a series of accusations to hypnotising effect, and the so-called "victim stories" and "legal analysis", both of which have the same basic characteristics as Morel's pamphlets. The dissemination of atrocity accounts no longer needs shows in local halls and meeting houses around the world; it takes place constantly on the global Internet, which – on the one hand – supports the universal appeal of the rhetoric, while – on the other hand – it highlights the viewer's distance from the origin of the accounts. According to Sliwinski's analysis, this does not encourage active participation, but rather sentimental compassion that only grows more distanced and passive due to the website's linking of atrocity accounts, "legal analysis" and the appeal "take action", because all these elements – including letters to the president or minister of justice of the Congo – are mere empty statements, which we know only too well do not lead to any changes in the situation described.

The crisis of the rhetorical basis for human rights and aid campaigns has been exposed in two provocative art documentary films: Dane Mads Brügger's *The Ambassador* (2011) and Dutchman Renzo Marten's *Episode III: Enjoy Poverty* (2008). Both films use baroque and burlesque exaggerations to turn the tales of compassion and terror that drive the international emergency aid industry in Africa inside out. The films show that it is doubtful whether aid organisations are in fact easing the suffering that motivates their presence, and – more fundamentally – that the representation of the suffering of the Congolese in western media, for instance, ultimately contributes to maintaining, or even amplifying, the unequal power balance. Martens said in an interview: "The real question is how we, the audiences, feel. That will decide who gets aid and who will be bombed. So I try to infiltrate, and adopt, on the spot, the most important role in contemporary war: that of its audiences. The film is not about the Congo at all, but about the power relations between those watching and those being watched."[222] The strategy of both films is to cynically expose the exploitation of native populations that is part of the humanitarian campaigns' sentimentality. Martens, for instance, says to an inhabitant in a village whom he has encouraged to photograph his own misery and to sell to western media, that he is definitely not going to help him any further when he returns to Europe: "Experiencing your suffering makes me a better person. You really help me. Thank you".

The underlying structure that this book has exposed in Morel's tales of terror has a long prehistory in the missionary accounts, as Patrick Brantlinger has demonstrated; however, it has also had a sweeping after-effect that reaches beyond present-day atrocity accounts in the media and human rights campaigns. In *Tarzan and the Leopard Men* and *Tintin au Congo* we encounter clear traces of the early campaign, in the choice of material, plot and rhetoric; however, the analyses in this book argue for the fact that these works were not blind to the problems linked to the rhetoric. More surprisingly, in Dian Fossey's gorilla stories, as well as her mysterious biography, we also encounter noticeable rhetorical techniques and motifs from the Congo Reform Association. This perpetuated use has given the human rights rhetoric its institutional power throughout the twentieth century, while at the same time exposing its weaknesses. The compassion the gorilla campaigns aimed to awaken in recipients and contributors was based on the same terror pathos as that used by the Reform Association, including a similarly basic and primitive identification of family feelings for endangered children. Through physical contact, naming and the attribution of nuclear family identities, the gorillas in the reflection and inversion of the narratives became more human than the inhumane humans, while – on the other hand – the human rights appeal to human nature often represents the victim as atavistic, instinctive and primitive – a child or animal. In relation to this, Conrad's criticism of Kurtz – who also saw himself as a bearer of light and his project as humanitarian – is also a criticism of humanitarian storytelling and its tendency to repress the reality it speaks for. Gillian Whitlock has pointed out a similar connection between the Dian Fossey story and its numerous recreations in various media on the one hand, and so-called "rape warfare" in the ongoing conflict in the Kivu Province of East Congo.[223]

As mentioned, the missionary accounts played a similar role, in addition to contributing to the repression on a basic and destructive level; the Swedish Elin Börrison was mentioned above as an example. The missionaries and their accounts were key players in the colonisation of the Congo, and in the long run they bear the main responsibility for the chaos that followed in the wake of independence and still rules today. The Swedish missionary E. V. Sjöblom's testimony to violations, presented at a talk in London, was a decisive factor in the formation of the Congo Reform Association. However, the majority of missionaries supported King Léopold, and the protests, especially from protestant movements, usually related their discontent to the fact that the Free State favoured catholic movements.[224] According to Morel's own appraisal, as well as Mary Kingsley's, missionary evidence around 1900 became increasingly unreliable due to the standardised narrative model of evangelical light versus darkness. Morel's campaign can therefore be perceived as an attempt to mix missionary testimonies in a new form and in new media, scoured of evangelical rhetoric in order to reappear as legally and statistically valid evidence about human rights. Indirectly, this exposed a crisis of legitimacy in the missionary

work's moral and educational project, which later gave rise to novels and travel accounts such as John Le Carré's *The Missionary Song*, Barbara Kingsolver's *The Poisonwood Bible* (1998) and Liéve Jori's *Retour au Congo* (1987).[225] Sjöblom's travel account *In the Shade of Palms* (1907) contains testimonies to atrocities while at the same time being an extremely complex text, which indicates that his accusations are far more ambiguous than the Reform Association made them out to be when they institutionalised his testimony as a "report". Sjöblom's criticism mainly pertained to the fact that the authorities would not help him convert the stubborn natives, and during his second stay in the Congo between 1901-1903, he collaborated with the state against the natives and saw forced labour as a necessary step in their education. David Lagergren has proved that the Swedish missionary movements actively supported Léopold's tax reforms in return for military protection and driving away the Arabs. However, at a more fundamental level, it was the missionaries' very rough introduction of written culture that resulted in the long-term effect of repression. While the missionaries saw writing as a means to spread light – albeit more in the spirit of evangelism than enlightenment – the project in practice focused on destroying the powerful oral tradition and the collective historical consciousness that was its effect. Writing was very much a *different* culture: the texts were Belgian, and in the time around independence in 1960 there was thus a feeling of a historical void. While illiteracy rates were the lowest in Africa, the level of education was also very low.

My critique of the development in the literature of humanitarian campaigns from the abolitionist movements to the present time has emphasised what I view as problematic rhetorical or performative consequences for describing and understanding the Congo as a place. The critique is rooted in a literary-historical exposition, rather than a philosophical or legal one, although it does refer to increasing signs of crisis in the justification discourse of human rights organisations. As Kenneth Cmiel points out in an account of the recent history of the discourse, there is a big leap between the activists' often naïve self-image and the campaigns' actual, often negative consequences, which become particularly clear in the cases when criticism of breaches of human rights have led to military intervention.[226] From the cool perspective of history, Cmiel questions whether human rights campaigns have had any preventative effect whatsoever for the people they aimed to protect. He claims that the majority of recent research in the history of human rights is carried out by researchers who look at organisations from within, and he requests other, more critical accounts from different perspectives. I hope the present book will be one such alternative account.

Although philosophical criticism of human rights is not the focus of this book, it is necessary to make my position clear. In brief, there are two dominant critical approaches, both of which – predictably – address the claim that human rights are universal. Relativists object that there are no universally valid moral truths. On the contrary, morality is a social and historical phenomenon – a claim for which anthropology is constantly offering new evidence. The other dominant approach is the assumption that there is a rational or objective argument for human rights – that morality is based in subjective, individual sympathies. In the article "Human rights, rationality, and sentimentality" Richard Rorty describes human rights as a "sentimental vision of humanity", that cannot be substantiated rationally.[227] Nevertheless, Rorty himself – ironically – perceives human rights as a good that has no philosophical justification and is therefore better off being promoted through the kind of emotional appeal which I have criticised. As I have argued by means of this book's most striking example – Jameson's cannibal story – sentimentality is no guarantee for solidarity. It can, however, lead to a different kind of pleasure – the pleasure of watching the events happen – which is both intimate and contemptuous.

As mentioned early in this book, it is possible to imagine alternative models that maintain the possibility of critical dialogue without relying on universal values, confining relativism or emotional sympathies. Diderot's supplement to Bougainville was mentioned as a prosaic model example that read the original text without subsuming it, and questioned customs and morals on the basis of rationality not emotion, both in Paris and on Tahiti, without resorting to universalism or relativism. As a generalised model, I described this form of criticism with Wlad Godzich's term 'anthropoetic narrative', which should be understood as neither universal nor relativistic: anthropoetic narratives *reflect* the global conditions for the formation of notions of morality, humanity, race, law and history, at the same time as *situating* the narratives in the places' different concrete realities. Rather than claiming human rights are universal and presenting horror stories, anthropoetic narratives display a consciousness of boundaries or place. The globalised market does not entail that values and living spaces are or have become uniform; on the contrary, the anthropoetic narrative shows that places retain something that we can and ought to relate to as real, historical and social. In the context of the conflicts in the Kivu Province, which – despite the presence of UN forces and temporary truces – continue to terrorise the area's native population, the human rights campaign's universal appeal actually diverts attention from obvious concrete answers and options. Though there has been some consolation, such as the disarmament in 2013 of the M23 militia, who were responsible for the worst violence, an actual solution to the conflict would require the involvement of a multitude of military factions through a far more committed engagement from the international

community. Most importantly, the EU must take responsibility for the former colony, as was promised by several countries, including Denmark, at the Berlin Conference. Confrontations must be stopped in order to create the terms for the necessary redistributions of land and property.

Sliwinski emphasises that Morel's criticism of Léopold's regime was not made on the basis of human rights principles, but on international law, specifically breaches of the Berlin Treaty. Morel's main concern from the beginning was Léopold's breach of the free trade agreements, and the atrocity campaign was, in that respect, more a means than an end – though it soon came to dominate the media with the consequences highlighted by Sliwinski. The difference between, on the one hand, criticism of breaches of international law and free trade agreements, and, on the other, criticism of breaches of human rights on the basis of transcendental ideals of dignity, is crucial in what I have called the "pattern of patterns" in the narratives about the Congo.

For Morel and Casement, as for Adam Smith, the instigator of the doctrine, free trade was the core of human freedom – including property rights and ownership of one's own labour. The Berlin Treaty between the colonial powers was based on these principles, but they were subverted by Léopold, resulting in the immense gap between political ideals and political reality that still mars the country. This was also the foundation of Conrad's criticism of the colony – a fact that is completely overlooked by those critics who present *Heart of Darkness* as evidence in the history of human rights. Conrad's criticism of the colony's "masquerade" was directed against inefficient administration, the espionage system and the discrepancy between the declared free trade zone and the reality of the monopoly – and not against atrocities. Stanley also hailed the idea of free trade as an ideological foundation, something that shines through in the texts' open, transparent spaces. While the discourse of human rights tends to describe the places where violations happened in an excluding rhetoric, as inhumane non-places, the discourse of free trade operates inclusively, treating the Congo as a synchronous, real place in the world where trade can be done and agreements can be made. Naipaul uses this notion in his travel diary, in the hypothesis about "The Empire of Things", and it reappears in his novel *A Bend in the River*, with its focus on the merchant Zabeth and the traffic of wares. Widmer's transcendence of the excluding rhetoric about the heart of darkness in *Im Kongo* follows a similar pattern, which is firmly established when the author maintains in an interview that there is nothing evil about a brewery in Kisangani. It is a parallel to Roger Casement's report on the big cargo canoes' disappearance from the river, which expressed hope that the marketplace in inner Congo that he had experienced in the initial years of the colonisation might be re-established.

5 Oblivion and Historical Narrative

The critical horizon of the present book's analyses of travel accounts and literature about the Congo has been the conspicuous and problematic oblivion that permeate the country and place, to which the texts – with a few noticeable exceptions – actively contribute. The Congo Free State, Belgian Congo, Zaire and DR Congo have played an important political and economic role in the world because of the region's immense natural resources and its position as an ideological battlefield during the cold war; the downside has been that its resources ended up being supplied to the West as the raw materials demanded by each technological leap. First it exported slaves and ivory, then later crude rubber for the car industry, copper and tin for the weapons industries during the world wars, uranium for the nuclear industry and coltan for the communications industry. The result has been that since Stanley's explorations foreign interests have split the country up into so-called "zones of interest", destroying the necessary conditions for state and civil society to function. The armed conflict in East Congo, Africa's world war has been called "The forgotten War", though it is the most violent, and has cost the most lives, since the Second World War. A consistent ambition of the present book has been to trace the literary-historical preconditions for this repression with regards to the place and country, which is so striking when we consider the de facto involvement of the world's superpowers and all European countries.

A central explanation for the repression, which both Peter Tygesen and David Reybrouck point out, is undoubtedly the embarrassment that comes with admitting one's co-responsibility and thus inheriting the obligation to solve the present, complicated conflict. The argument of this book, however, is that the bulk of the narratives contribute to forgetting the very place to which they devote themselves. This is a basic rhetorical mechanism that is oppressive in a different manner from, for instance, the use of imperialist and racist stereotypes, which have been the focus of postcolonial criticism. It has become clear that both Stanley and Conrad each in their own way respond to institutional conditions for communicating testimonies to a public that cannot – or will not – listen. Their subsequent reception has disregarded this potential for criticism of the discourse of testimony, while the colonial era's mainly apologetic narratives have far more firmly installed oblivion as part of the narrator's contract with the reader: let us forget together what I am telling you.

In that respect, we are not dealing with a situation in which the individual

text simply contributes either to forgetting or experiencing the place, but rather with what the anthropologist Johannes Fabian has described as a dynamic relation: "Forgetting is not: memory = remembering vs. forgetting = not-remembering. But memory requiring memory work carried out as remembering and forgetting". Or: "there is no narration as remembering that is not also narration as forgetting".[228] Primarily by comparing one text's testimony with other, competing, testimonies, this book has attempted to uncover such complex patterns of forgetting and remembering. Jenssen-Tusch's monumental *Scandinavians in Congo*, for example, was interpreted as an Orphean book of the dead, which – contrary to its intention – exposed the Free State's all-pervading meaninglessness. Octave Mirbeau's book, on the other hand, was interpreted as a discourse critical exposure of the typical narratives about the Congo of the time.

The selection of narratives in this book has been made with the aim of investigating why the international community, especially Europe, has forgotten and repressed its contribution to the Congo's history. In other words, it has not investigated the Congolese reality – for instance by reading anthropological texts or field studies – or how Congolese narratives have contributed to, or attempted to oppose, the dominant discourse which has been mapped in this study. Such a project would have confronted serious challenges, both theoretical and practical: in 1975, Naipaul published his essay "A New King for Africa", featuring the provocative claim that Zaire had no literature, and that Mobuto by decree had therefore ordered authors to create national literature. This is not entirely true, and the picture has changed since then; however, it is true that we are dealing with a special case, compared with other former colonies. There are very few examples of "the Empire Writes Back" in Congo-Kinshasa, while the former French colony of Congo-Brazzaville on the other side of the river has seen a far more significant literary production, both in terms of volume and quality. Adam Hochschild apologises that – despite an ardent effort – he has not been able to find any Congolese anti-narratives in his archival studies; David Reybrouck's otherwise extensive research produced only a few written Congolese sources, which is why he relies almost exclusively on oral testimonies. Johannes Fabian's *Remembering the Past* (1996) is based on Thismumba's historic paintings and oral narratives, which were developed in collaboration with the author. Kasongo Kapanga has proved that the few Congolese texts from colonial times were, in fact, often written by Belgian missionaries as part of the propaganda about the colony's progress and the Europeans as models for a newly literate and Christian native population. Noticeable prose has only begun to emerge from the Congo in recent times, for instance Valentin Mudimbe's *Les corps glorieux* (1994) and Thomas Mpoyi-Buatu's *La Ré-production* (1984). These works, however, define intermediate points – on the one hand rebelling against the missionary schools' values, on the other leaning on European texts and philosophy from a postcolonial position in Paris or the USA.[229]

The statement that Belgian Congo – and later DR Congo – has no national literature makes sense in the context of several factors rooted in Léopold's use of the Free State as a purely financial tool, without any developed political organisation. As a Belgian colony after Léopold, the state had a tripartite structure in which most administration was carried out by Belgium, education was assigned to the missionaries and infrastructure, work and health were the responsibility of private associations. The missionary schools worked against illiteracy, but on the basis of a written culture and a curriculum that was not relevant to Congolese history, which until then had been disseminated via a powerful oral narrative tradition. The tripartition ensured that the Congolese population remained at a basic level of education, despite their advanced reading and writing skills, which was the main cause of chaos after independence, because no Congolese had access to leadership positions. It also explains the lack of a national literature and a collective historical consciousness. On the other hand, dance, painting and especially music have played crucial roles since independence. Attempts to write a national history of literature are fragmented, often building on the contradictory fact that the majority of the corpus comes from Congo-Brazzaville, rather than Congo-Kinshasa.

Despite its vast area and significance in world history, DR Congo is not a nation – it exists in the "night watchman" state described by Naipaul. The country cannot claim the minimum requirements Anthony Smith has listed as defining a nation: "fixed homeland", "high autonomy" and institutionalised forms of "historical records and historical thinking". Furthermore, the possibility of an "imagined community" as a basis for national identity was complicated by the Belgian colonial administration's anthropological and administrative partition of the native population into ethnographic systems and tribes, which were subsequently affirmed and made absolute as strategic pieces in political games after independence.

Referring to the fact that the era of the Congo Free State was, in principle, an international issue, and that the region's subsequent history has been dominated by European narratives, the present book's readings have not been rooted in national literary history, but in a comparative, transnational perspective. The idea has been that Danish or Swedish travel accounts from the Red Rubber era, or the didactic youth literature from the Belgian colony, are not significantly different from, for instance, British or Belgian accounts.

That said, I will admit that the issues of this book implicate Belgium more than any other country. The museum in Tervuren has an extensive collection of travel accounts from the Congo, which has yet to be studied systematically,

while the high literature tradition of writing about the Congo has been studied by Pierre Halen and Pierre-Philippe Fraiture, among others.[230] However, as numerous recent discussions have pointed out, Belgian contributions to remembering Congo's colonial history have encountered much opposition. One general reason for this, presented in the editorial preface to a themed issue of *Yale French Studies* about "Belgian Memories: Taboo and Trauma in Belgian Memory", is that it does not fit in with the country's self-image to have been a brutal colonial power – on the contrary, a key part of the nation's understanding of itself is founded on its having been invaded by large neighbouring nations.[231]

More specifically, the disputes about language and constitution between Belgium's Walloon and Flemish populations have complicated the issue of the historic responsibility for the colonisation of the Congo. Both Walloons and Flemings were implicated, though in different areas: the Flemings were missionaries and workers, while the Walloons were mainly officials, officers or plantation and factory owners. According to Antoon van den Braembussche, the federalisation of Belgium entails federalised memory, in which the two population groups' struggle to gain influence in the school curriculum, for instance, has resulted in fragmentation of the collective memory – especially regarding traumatic events during the First and Second World Wars, and the question of the Congo and literature about the Congo.[232] Valerie Rosoux and Laurence van Ypersele mention that critical statements by Foreign Minister Karel De Gucht as late as 2008 caused controversy about how the colonial past ought to be described. In the same vein, Flemish nationalists' criticism of colonial practices is used to attack the monarchy and the French elite.[233] While the winds have changed, among other things allowing for the Lumumba commission to be set up and for the state to admit co-responsibility for the murder of the Congo's first president, the public sphere is still marked by silence. It is as if the attempts to reach parliamentary agreement across the separatist boundaries are taking place under a tacit agreement not to make the question of Congolese history the focus of national self-understanding.

6 World Literature and Globalisation

In this book, European literature about the Congo has been read from a prose perspective, the framework of which was outlined in the introduction. With reference to Stephen Greenblatt and James Clifford, I established that literary history and anthropology are determined not only by their material, but also by the position from which they are written. The same applies to the travel accounts, as well as to the research: the material is seen from a perspective and defines a position. Diderot's, Stanley's and my own accounts all take a stand on their material; however, as I have argued, the relations are far from static. Below, I will briefly outline the present study's position within the field of research, criticism and debate pertaining to Africa.

The research focus on the consequences of globalisation for culture and literature has had a vital influence on the present book's horizon. Travel literature and travel accounts have been foregrounded, because they tell us about the formation of identities and nationalities in relation to places and borders, while also contemplating, challenging and sometimes transcending them in the trans-cultural movement of the journey. I have avoided a genre-based approach, finding instead that the field is best covered from the broad prose perspective, which provides greater opportunities to use contrasting examples. The postcolonial perspective has not been adopted in these readings, which have attempted rather to point to a different tendency in travel literature research by following Tim Youngs' suggestion to give up postcolonial criticism's focus on "images of the other" and look for a less ideological, more pragmatic understanding of the texts' performative creation of meaning.[234] My readings of Stanley, Conrad and others have been discussed in relation to the term 'world literature', which is often presented as literary studies' answer to globalisation. However, I prefer the term 'globalised conditions', because it emphasises an important premise of the argument: that literature is always locally rooted in language and body, while the text's whole sum of meaning is defined by newly global terms for identity, nationality, communication and understanding of place. Literature is an excellent tool with which to reflect on and communicate concrete experiences of the consequences of globalisation, since it can both confront the complexity of such experiences and present them through, for example, polycentric structures that can contain complexity without simplifying it. The point is not that a select group of literary works are particularly apt expressions of globalisation: this condition applies to all texts. Likewise, this is

not a specific, current phenomenon; it applies equally to older texts, which are now being rediscovered and put into perspective as the prehistory of present-day globalisation. It is also the case – as I have shown, first and foremost with regards to Stanley – that literary texts not only challenge the forms of knowledge and communication of their time: they can be used to reflect on present-day models for understanding place, movement and space. When we read the history of literature from a globalised or prose perspective, it becomes possible to extract complex globalised conditions for identity, nationality, testimony and the media, which cannot be illuminated to the same degree by investigating present-day phenomena on the Internet.

In the introductory chapter to *Comparative Literature in an Age of Globalization*, Haun Saussy traces the origin of the discipline of comparative literature to the internationalisation of a vast number of organisations that took place between 1850 and 1900, which have been mentioned in relation to Stanley.[235] The worlds' fairs, international congresses for linguists and philologists, the Red Cross, international postal unions, Socialist International and so on, as well as the Berlin Conference on the partition of Africa, are given as examples. The theme and comparative method of Saussy's book, according to which patterns in literary history are defined through comparisons of different prose narratives, can thereby be said to return to the beginning, albeit with the conditions of globalisation as baggage. The book's transformation field is limited to the period 1870-1910 – often referred to as *fin de siècle* – although it contains other loci and literary forms of dissemination than those that have typically been the focus of comparative studies of relations between European national literatures in particular. This also applies to comparative studies in travel literature in Greece, Portugal, Spain, Italy and France. Saussy's aim, however, is not to present yet another discussion about the possibilities and impossibilities of writing literary history; it is actually an attempt to do so on globalisation and prose's conditions.

In response to Saussy's ACLA report, Jonathan Culler indicates a similar overcoming of the conflict between the subject area's two dominant wings: formalistic/deconstructive readings of individual works and "cultural studies", which was the paramount theme of Charles Bernheimer's report from 1993. "Comparative literature involves reading texts of diverse sorts but 'reading literarily'", writes Culler. In the phrase "diverse sorts" he hints at the expansion of the field of comparative literature that is the result of the recent orientation towards global and world literary processes, as well as the expansion of the canon, genres, issues and media.[236] In the context of the present study, it can be expressed both as a transformation of the understanding of the limitations for what constitutes literature – a consequence of globalisation and the prosaic

Søren Assenholt: *Planners & Searchers*: "Lady Alice" (2008). Caption: "...As the driver argued why he would not take me to the Ethnographic Museum, I imagined the current condition of the boat and where it might be in need of attention ..."

"The original boat, which the explorer Henry Morton Stanley in 1874 used to explore the Congo River, today rests in the courtyard of the Ethnographic Museum in Kinshasa, DR Congo. As shown by Stanley's own illustrations and notes, the boat could be broken down into five parts and thus carried over land by just twenty men.

Today 'Lady Alice' is reportedly in a severe state of decay. The museum is located on a hill above the Congo River. The site is currently inaccessible to the public due to its strategic military significance". Photography: Honza Hoeck.

turn – and as a continuation of the high literary reading method in an expanded field that might include, for instance, Stanley and E. R. Burrough.

Andreas Huyssen also points out the consequence of a global perspective on literature and culture studies in his article "Geographies of modernism in a globalizing world".[237] Modernity and modernism on the one hand, and globalisation on the other, have until recently been described as processes in European and American culture, while the rest of the world has been perceived as either uninvolved or blindly reproducing western culture. Huyssen suggests the terms "alternative modernities" and "modernism at large" to allow for a less reductive and more dynamic understanding of these processes in the last 150 years. Modernist art in the European metropolises developed in interaction with colonial experiences, while places such as Shanghai and Rio de Janeiro display examples of modernity and modernism that are not mere reflections or varieties of European forms, but transformations of locally anchored value systems, including different media hierarchies and concepts of literature.

The prose perspective is my means of avoiding the dichotomies of postcolonial criticism, the 'us' and 'them'. It is related to Huyssen's so-called "transnational suggestions", of rewriting colonialism's and modernism's history from the beginning without pre-organising the texts in staple value hierarchies that favour high literature and marginalise all other media. Modern experiences of transnational identity and globalised conditions for place and space become visible in the ruptures between institutions, markets and prose forms we find in Stanley's writing, while an approach that disqualifies his travel books on the grounds of their obvious contribution to market mechanisms prevents itself from understanding crucial conditions for – and mechanisms of – modernity and modernism.

Mary Louise Pratt's "Modernity and Periphery. Toward a Global and Relational Analysis" is on a par with Huyssen in suggesting a rethinking of modernity as a global and relational narrative that basically challenges temporal explanatory models, including those of Jürgen Habermas.[238] Pratt points out that a number of narratives about – and definitions of – modernity, which were developed in European and American metropolises, are constructed via spatial juxtapositions with pre-modern cultures. For example, the centres' positive concepts of change, progress, individuality and science are rooted in assumptions about stability, myth and a cyclic perception of time as basic elements in non-western cultures. The problem is the same one that Pratt, elsewhere, has investigated in relation to postcolonial criticism of travel literature: the dichotomy obstructs the interaction between centre and periphery, inevitably limiting our understanding of modernity's cultural processes. The prose narratives about the Congo, not least in this book's central examples of Stanley and Conrad, can – in Bruno Latour's words – be understood as information dense mobiles which challenge rather than confirm modernity's simplified juxtapositions of civilised and dynamic places with places that are perceived as primitive and static.

The combination of perspective, prose and topic – the relationship between the Congo and Europe – defines the framework for the present book's literary history. It is largely a marginal and forgotten history, linked unambiguously neither to the centre nor the periphery, but told in the space in between. It is not a postcolonial account of the colonies' own literature in the tradition of "the empire strikes back"; neither is it a history of European literature in Europe.[239] The perspective and the topic make the book highly relevant in relation to current discussions about the world literature concept; however, I have distanced myself from the use of world literature as a canonisation tool, which dogmatically excludes Stanley and includes Conrad. My opinion of world literature is on par with Franco Moretti's well-known definition: it is not an object but a field of discussion; not a quality but a function. Like Huyssen and Pratt, we may choose to describe world literature as an analytical reaction that addresses the literary traffic between centre and periphery, investigating different narratives about modernity and globalisation from the ones that are narrated from one pole or the other. In this light, the present book deals with stories that tell a forgotten and repressed history and question established models within the European and the postcolonial narrative. Read as literature, the texts furthermore tell stories about their own acts of repression, as I have tried to demonstrate in relation to the colonial travel account and the criticism of "Greulgeschichte".

In a review, Torsten Petterson locates the Norwegian *World literature. The Western tradition* (2007) somewhere on the threshold of a paradigm shift in literary history.[240] The title and the genre perspective point away from traditional literary history's national literatures and author biographies; however, the ambition is only half-heartedly and problematically fulfilled. The title alone indicates an internal conflict, and in practice the topic is not really world literature of the kind defined by Franco Moretti, but rather the same Western European material found in earlier histories of literature.[241] Another problematic issue highlighted by Petterson is an inconsequential, albeit widespread, definition of the term 'literature', and hence the genre history associated with it. The authors of *World Literature* acknowledge that the term 'literature' was far more inclusive before 1800 than after; yet they have difficulties deciding whether to select their material according to the definition of the studied periods or the present day. In practice, the authors write literary history about older material according to the expanded definition of literature, while literary history from the eighteenth century until today has been written in accordance with the narrow definition,

limiting itself to prose fiction and excluding, for instance, the eighteenth century's flourishing essay tradition and the nineteenth century's philosophical literature. In this sense, *World Literature* is far from realising the expansion of the literary field in which Saussy, Culler and Huyssen include popular literature and the book as medium. The latter in particular emphasises that the narrow definition of literature is a historically and geographically limited construction and, we might add, never completely dominant – which the history of travel literature in the nineteenth century illustrates.

H. R. Jauss formulated the issue programmatically in the 1987 article 1967 "Literary History as a Challenge to Literary Theory": it should be our goal at any given time to consider the basis of literary history writing with a point of departure in the challenges to present culture.[242] As opposed to the hermeneutics of literary history, which are based on an assumption about the relative autonomy of literature – for which Jauss argued at the time – basis and method need to be different today, because the literary situation has changed completely.

While research in, and dissemination and teaching of, literary history since Jauss and the aesthetic turn in the 1980s has been based on analyses of autonomous individual works, in spite of the inconsistent perspectives, the starting point for this work has been that a renaissance of the subject area can only take place via a return to the foundation of the comparative tradition on 'post-literary' conditions. By 'post-literary' I allude to the far-reaching contemporary transformation of the literary system: the development of new media and the globalisation of the literary market not only entail new literary platforms and functions; they alter the entire literary field. Textual forms, author roles and reading patterns today are closer to the eighteenth-century heterogeneous literary culture than the relative autonomy which for a long time has been perceived as marking the eternally dominant institutionalisation of literature. The market, media and globalisation have caused the elimination of autonomy that the avant-garde and neo-avant-garde dreamed of. Performativity studies, fictionality theory and new narratology, correspondingly, question the neo-classical perception of the individual work as the focal point of the subject field – a perception which, in practice, has defined literary studies and history since New Criticism – as well as questioning divides between and conditions for formalistic and hermeneutic methods.

Prose studies in both contemporary literary culture and older literature challenge divides between 'non-literary prose' and 'literary prose', and between high and popular culture, while the globalised perspective emphasises that the definition of literature on which literary canonisation is based is historically brief and geographically limited. The writing of literary history on the basis of testimonies, which has gained a footing over recent years, has furthermore proved to be problematic when it elevates eyewitness accounts and favours the individual text's authenticity. The writing of history has an obligation to seek out and compare *other* testimonies – the texts in the archives that the subsequent memory culture has *not* favoured.

Research in the field of comparative literature is looking for explanatory connections in literary history across national literatures and isolated, individual works. The transnational approach indicates a convergence of traditions within the field of world literature, which is enjoying much success in the USA as a university discipline, but should first and foremost be perceived as an ambitious attempt to manage the canon and canon criticism rather than a method of actual literary history. The attention to isolated, individual works, in contrast, defines a common interest in a number of extremely different traditions in the twentieth century, from Russian formalism to structuralism and discourse analysis, including these fields' emphasis on the fact that it is the cross-disciplinary models and patterns that appear from comparisons which are the objects of the field – *not* the individual works. Moretti's suggestion that looking for cross-patterns in world literature – such as 'the tree' or 'the wave' – must always happen through so-called "distant reading" can consequentially be interpreted as a consistent attempt to update the comparative method while uniting two major tendencies in the history of literary critique. However, Moretti's theses have only had limited practical impact – probably because of his sacrifice of 'close reading' – and it was a long time ago that the comparative method appeared as a strong recipe for writing literary history.

The ACLA report of 1993, "Comparative Literature in the Age of Multiculturalism", described the crisis in the field as a conflict between those who expanded it to encompass so-called "global cultural studies", according to which literature is only one of many discourses – philosophical, psychological, medical, legal, as well as the discourses of film, popular culture and so on – and those who wanted to preserve the individual literary text as the primary topic. In the ACLA report of 2006, the conflict between cultural studies and studies of literary works is replaced by a discussion of how comparative literature should relate to the field of world literature, which, at the time, was spreading rapidly in American universities. Because world literature apparently both contains global cultural studies and maintains a focus on individual literary works, the discipline has been able to reconcile its earlier conflict. However, as Nathalie Melas, Jonathan Culler and others have pointed out, the resolution has had its costs: the compared works are, in practicee, ascribed to the canon or the hyper-canon, which is the hidden standard on which the comparison is established. Furthermore, in my opinion, it is too easy to lose sight of the cross-disciplinary and cross-discursive effort to read literature in 'the expanded

field' for which fleeting promises were made in Edward Said's *Orientalism* and Stephen Greenblatt's *Marvelous Possessions*. Comparative literature carried out as world literature ironically leads to provincial literary history, which is out of step with literary – or rather *post*-literary – cultures of both the West, Asia and Africa.

Haun Saussy and Culler have both suggested that the challenge instead be formulated as an effort to read "literarily" – that is, with all the understanding of texts' rhetorical complexity cultivated in "close reading" – but in a subject field determined by a broad array of discourses, genres and media.[243] In relation to the objection about the topic's fundamental boundlessness, Culler refers to Erich Auerbach's term "Ansatzpunkt", which is a pragmatic definition and explication of the method that allows comparisons to be made in a heterogeneous and broadly construed cultural field.[244] Auerbach writes that a good "Ansatzpunkt" is characterised by the concrete and concise, while at the same time having the potential for centrifugal, "radiating" expansion. This is a method, not a theory, the scope of which Auerbach demonstrated in his literary-historiographic masterpiece *Mimesis* (1946), which – across divides between genres and discourses – extracts basic literary-historical patterns of development through close readings and comparisons of selected passages instead of individual works. It makes sense to call this kind of comparison true structuralism, because as Michel Serres and others have pointed out it does not search for structures *in* a work – a formula that does not make sense – but investigates structure in the form of repetitions of "isomorphic" patterns between and across texts, fables and discourses.[245] The aim of the analysis is not the individual text, but the structure that is maintained in the comparison.

An updated version of comparative literature, built on present-day performative, medialised and globalised culture does not have to choose between, on the one hand, close reading and literature, and, on the other, distant reading and cultural studies; it can do both, conducting close reading and comparisons of literature 'in the expanded field'. Literature in the expanded field is not the total of individual works, but a network of narratives, narrativity and events without definitive narrative structure, the impenetrabilities and critical points of which it aims to describe and understand. In the introduction to the anthology *Global French* (2010), Susan Rubin Suleiman and Christie McDonald write that global comparisons must leave behind the exclusive focus on individual literary works, the canon and criticism of the canon that the discipline of world literature entails, instead developing other terms and categories than those instigated by postcolonial tradition's dichotomies between centre and periphery, nation and colony and so on. The focal point is the spatial and temporal dynamics of globalisation and the changeable physical, geographical and geopolitical spaces that create and determine literature in the expanded field.[246] Comparative literature on globalised conditions means readings that acknowledge the "perplexity" that occurs when we look at texts and places from several moveable perspectives at the same time. The effort of the current book can, in this connection, be seen – most obviously in the investigation of the significance of the Congo River in the narratives – as an attempt to carry out what Bertrand Westphal has termed "geocriticism". This term characterises an analysis of how a place is created via a complementary dynamic between its physical properties and the associations linked to it – resulting in ideas between "stone and paper".[247]

Overall, however, the present book is motivated less by theoretical speculation than by the wish to investigate specific material and appraise the consequences and results of the process. My work has been guided by the model examples of criticism mentioned in the introduction, but also by model literary examples. Diderot and Niebuhr, for instance, provide models for writing about and interpreting cultural encounters, as well as for reading texts. The model example as a reading principle has been applied to texts by Stanley, Mirbeau and Hergé, from whom many critics have distanced themselves. I have similarly attempted to extract exemplary characteristics from Conrad, Greene, Naipaul and Widmer. This obviously does not mean that the critical work in relation to other research and to the literary texts has been suspended. I have used the term "reality work" to emphasise that it is more a case of appraising the texts' effect on the perception of the place than their representations of it. The readings in this book should be understood as examples of this type of criticism – and thus as a contribution to a qualified debate about the reception of current literature, which is often positioned in the same grey areas as the book's prose narratives.

In addition to research and criticism, this book thus contributes to what we may call the discourse on Africa, which is on the agenda of the news media and international politics: civil wars, climate disasters, human rights and trade agreements are centres of attention that reflect the global nature of these issues. I have aimed to present historical examples that advocate caution towards the continued use of the abolitionist movement's combination of idyllic and demonising rhetoric – a combination that was also emphasised as a characteristic of the collapse of the travel account in Stanley's use of "misery" and "mystery" narratives to describe the corruption of the Emin Pasha Relief Expedition. Stanley, and to a lesser degree Casement and Morel, was, on the other hand, an advocate for free trade as the basis of equal interaction between Europe and Africa – an idea that seems more relevant today than ever before.

It is beyond the scope of this book to enter into a detailed discussion of Africa according to the West. However, my readings identify a division between pathetically compassionate, exclusionary rhetoric – the geopolitical expression of which has been termed "Africa pessimism" – and pragmatic and inclusive

Søren Assenholt: *Blank Spaces (A to C)* (2008). Caption: "Originally from Joseph Conrad's and my own childhood fantasy".

rhetoric that encourages -for instance in relation to the EU's Lisbon Conference - the West to perceive Africa as a marketplace with equal opportunities for the exchange of products. This approach is also the horizon of both Naipaul's and Widmer's novels. The division, in other words, is not a literary or literary studies issue; it draws up the battle lines in hard political assessments of the effects of adjustments on trade restrictions, and on development and disaster aid. In the concluding chapter of the previous section, I wrote about Sliwinski's criticism of the linkage between horror campaigns and human rights from a media theoretical approach. Economists and anthropologists express similar reservations about the effects of a "liberal, humanitarian discourse" in relation to third world countries. Liisa Malkki's article on such rhetoric in relation to international emergency aid to Hutu refugees in Tanzania after the genocide in Rwanda highlights the need to remain critical towards the twentieth-century discourse on international crises. Malkki argues that, contrary to the campaign's intention, the performative effect of the discourse on humanitarian intervention was de-historicising and de-politicising. The effect was a repression of the complicated conflicts, which are transnational and therefore cannot be formulated within the nation-based internationalism of the humanitarian discourse.[248] This objection was also voiced at an international conference in London in 2001, where two journalists from the world press and a number of specialists discussed how Africa is covered in the media. In step with Bernard Piniau's opinion, to which I have referred several times, it was a point of criticism that reports about the continent are continuously "mediated through a 'heart of darkness'-lens", thus inadvertently contributing to a perception of the violence as atavistic, senseless and anarchistic, making it pointless to intervene.[249] This criticism has been followed by burgeoning soul-searching in the human rights movements, for example in a report on the media and human rights from The International Council on Human Rights Policy, which warns that the long-term effects of the reductionism, sensationalism and negativity in the continued use of atrocity tales about Africa's endless wars result in blindness towards the local and regional historical and economic background of the problems, and thus in political indifference.[250]

The climate and food crises enhance the dilemma: on the one hand, there is an acknowledgement of a continued need for development aid, though the effect is far from the goals; on the other, experts point out that the only long-term solution to the problems is to lift the numerous trade barriers that are impeding Africa's access to the world market and contributing to the downward spiral because of insufficient production and import of food. Stanley's hyperbolic space, in which he predicts that philanthropic capitalists will invest in Central Africa's fertile lake highlands and create a thriving trade between mutually hostile tribes, leading to peace and civilisation, was ruthlessly disregarded by Léopold and subsequently by Belgium, various despots and international consortiums' de facto expropriations of the country's labour force and resources. The history of the Congo in the era covered in this book is largely determined by the fact that the colony was launched as an example of a free trade zone – and realised as the opposite. Nevertheless, it is possible that a solution lies herein to the hardship of the population of the Congo. This argument is put forward by Congolese and European, including Belgian, politicians, as well as being the attitude among the refugees from the war-ridden Kivu Province to whom I have been able to talk, because they have settled in Denmark. If only

Rwanda, Uganda, Angola, China and the USA and their puppets in the Congo could be stopped from stealing the country's immense riches, which it is hoped will happen after the next election, the focus will shift from "authenticity" and independence - which both Mobuto and Kabila emphasised, while in reality compromising on everything - to welcoming the Europeans, including the Belgians, back to do business.

Notes

1 Karl Schlögel: *Im Raume lesen wir die Zeit*, 2006.

2 Some of these differences are discussed in Susanne Gehrmann: *Kongo-Greul: zur literarischen Konfiguration eines kolonialkritischen Diskurses (1890-1910)*, 2003. Regarding Belgian travel accounts and Belgian nationality, see Pierre Halen's thesis *'Le petit Belge avait vu grand'. Une littérature coloniale*, 1993.

3 Interestingly, Jakob Wassermann's *Bula Matari; Stanley, Conqueror of a Continent* (1933) opens with a fictitious dialogue between friends who are trying to make the author shelve the biography because Stanley has been forgotten and banished to the dustiest corners of our memories. The author admits that Stanley's historical significance is minimal, but he turns this fact to his advantage: Stanley's importance as a role model lies in his superhuman strength and anachronistic nature. Byron Farwell's *The Man Who Presumed* (1957) is different from most biographies because of its critical attempt to sort the often conflicting tales that are used in most biographies as a means of structuring and presenting Stanley's life story as a fairytale. This method characterises Symons's *H.M. Stanley* (1950), as well as more recent biographies, including Martin Dugard's *Into Africa: The Dramatic Retelling of the Stanley-Livingstone Story* (2003).

4 Positive reviews include Tom Adair in *The Scotsman*: *Mister Stanley, I presume* (2 March 2007); John Carey in *The Sunday Times*: *A good man in Africa?* (18.03.2007); and Tim Gardam in *The Observer*: *Livingstone was just the beginning* (1 April 2007). Other positive reviews maintain reservations towards the book's revisionist tendency, including Nick Smith's *Reappraising an impossible life* in *The Geographical* (04.2007). There are few outright critical reviews: Bernard Porter's *Did he puff up his crimes to please a bloodthirsty readership?* in *London Review of Books* (5 April 2007) is one of them. Another one is, unsurprisingly, Frank McLynn's *Stanley* in *History Today* (No. 4, 2007), which instigated a quarrel between the two rival biographers.

5 The discussion is found in many biographies from 1980 onwards; however, it was already used as a theme in Ian Anstruther's *I Presume: Stanley's Triumph & Disaster* (1956).

6 E.g. Karin Hansson (ed.): *Journeys, Myths and the Age of Travel: Joseph Conrad's Era*, 1998; Laura E. Franey: *Victorian Travel Writing and Imperial Violence: British Writing on Africa, 1855-1902*, 2003; Barbara Korte: *English Travel Writing from Pilgrimages to Postcolonial Explorations*, 2000.

7 The most noteworthy exception is Clare Pettitt's *Dr. Livingstone, I Presume? Missionaries, Journalists, Explorers, and Empire* (2007). Pettitt's main focus is on Livingstone, but a summary about Stanley and his legacy – inspired by Tim Jeal and others – claims that we have not even begun to understand the enormous influence Stanley's travel accounts had on culture and politics around the turn of the century, including the development of global media.

8 Apart from the aforementioned Tim Jeal, this tendency includes John Bierman: *Dark Safari*, 1992 and Frank McLynn: *Stanley. The Making of an African Explorer*, 1990.

9 Norman R. Bennett (ed.): *Stanley's Despatches to the New York Herald 1871-1872, 1874-1877*, 1970.

10 Emile van Balberghe: "*Cinq années au Congo* de Henry M. Stanley. Une étude bibliophilique" in *Annales Aequatoria*, No. 24, 2003.

11 Stanley, Henry M. (ed. Dorothy Stanley): *The Autobiography of Henry M. Stanley*, New York, 1909, p. 384.

12 According to Tim Jeal (and Frank McLynn before him), the phrase is Stanley's fictitious addition, added to the telegram to the *New York Herald*, which since then – to his regret – stuck to his name and gave it a comical tinge.

Clare Pettitt's *Dr. Livingstone, I Presume?* investigates the meeting's iconographic afterlife in popular culture up to recent days, supplemented with an analysis of the constituting and scenic elements of the earliest illustrations.

13 Kate Campbell: "Journalistic Discourse and Constructions of Modern Knowledge" in Laurel Brake, Bill Belle and David Finkelstein (ed.): *Nineteenth-Century Media and the Construction of Identities*, 2000.

14 Stanley can also be said therefore to take a central position in the historical transformation from hero to celebrity. Cf. Daniel Boorstein: "From Hero to Celebrity" in P. David Marshall: *The Celebrity Culture Reader*, 2006.

15 Frank McLynn: *The Making of an African Explorer*, 1990, p. 93.

16 Wlad Godzich and Jeffrey Kittay: *The Emergence of Prose. An essay in prosaics*, 1987, p. xvii.

17 Lars Nylander: *Prosadikt och Modernitet*, 1990, p. 41.

18 Jill Marie Bradbury: "New Science and the 'New Species of Writing': Eighteenth-Century Prose Genres" in *Eighteenth-Century Life*, Vol. 27, No. 1, 2003.

19 J. Paul Hunter: *Before Novels. The Cultural Contexts of Eighteenth Century English Fiction*, 1990, p. 176.

20 Arne Melberg: "Bortom fiktionen. Sebald, Solstad med flera resenärer i landet prosa" in *Norsk Litteraturvitenskapelig Tidsskrift*, Vol. 7, No. 2, 2004.

21 Thoroughly described in Neil Rennie: *Far-Fetched Facts. The Literature of Travel and the Idea of the South Seas*, 1995.

22 John Hawkesworth: *An Account of the Voyages undertaken by the order of his present Majesty for making Discoveries in the Southern Hemisphere, And successively performed by Commodore Byron, Captain Wallis, Captain Carteret, and Captain Cook, in the Dolphin, the Swallow, and the*

Endeavour: drawn up from the Journals kept by the several Commanders, and from the Papers of Joseph Banks, Esq., 1773.

23 Louis Antoine de Bougainville: *Voyage de la frégate la Boudeuse et de la flute l'Étoile autour du monde*, 1980 (1771).

24 Denis Diderot: "Supplément au voyage de Bougainville" in Paul Vernière (ed.): *Œuvres philosophiques*, 1964, p. 489.

25 Paul Gauguin: *NoaNoa*, 1954.

26 Peter Brooks: "Gauguin's Tahitian Body" in *Body Work*, 1993.

27 Charles Forsdick: *Victor Segalen and The Aesthetics of Diversity: Journeys between Cultures*, 2000.

28 John Sturrock: "Victor Segalen Abroad" in Christopher Prendergast (ed.): *Debating World Literature*, 2003.

29 Wlad Godzich: "Space and Temporality in Thinking: Globalization at the Turn of the Millennium", lecture at the conference *Space and Temporality in Fin de Siècle Culture*, Aarhus 22 September, 2000.

30 Frits Andersen: "Eighteenth Century Travelogues as Models for 'Rethinking Europe'" in *European Review*, Vol. 15, No. 1, 2007.

31 James Clifford's recommendations following his criticism of Edward Said's static model in *Orientalism* (1978): "On Orientalism" in *The Predicament of Culture*, 1988.

32 Franco Moretti: "Conjectures on World Literature" in *New Left Review*, No. 1, 2000.

33 Tzvetan Todorov: *La Littérature en péril*, 2007.

34 A challenge which is also reflected in recent attempts, hitherto fruitless, to delimit a field of "Travel Studies", which are growing increasingly stronger in international research as centres and disciplines are devoted to the study of this fragile area. Examples that confront the issue are: James Buzard: "What Isn't Travel?" in Hagen Schulz-Forberg (ed.): *Unravelling Civilisation: European Travel and Travel Writing*, 2005; Jan Borm: "Defining Travel: On the Travel Book, Travel Writing and Terminology" in Glenn Hooper, Tim Youngs (ed.): *Perspectives on Travel Writing*, 2004. Several German theses attempt meticulously to define the genre and use it as the starting point for establishing a method – though without much success. See e.g. Peter J. Brenner: *Der Reisebericht in der deutchen Literatur: ein Forschungsüberblick als Vorstudie zu einer Gattungsgeschichte*, 1990.

35 Timothy Reiss: *The Discourse of Modernism*, 1982.

36 Martin Gossman: "Marco Polo's Voyages: The Conflict between Confirmation and Observation" in Zweder von Martel (ed.): *Travel Fact and Travel Fiction*, 1994.

37 Valerie Flint: "Travel Fact and Travel Fiction in the Voyages of Columbus" in op.cit.

38 Michel Foucault: "Des Espace Autres" in *Architecture /Mouvement/ Continuité*,1984.

39 Neil Rennie: *Far-Fetched Facts*, 1995.

40 Mary Louise Pratt: *Imperial Eyes*, 1992, pp. 87-90.

41 Edward Said: *Orientalism*, 1979.

42 Gustave Flaubert: Pierre-Marc de Biasi (ed.): *Voyage en Égypte*, 1991.

43 James Clifford: "On Orientalism" in *The Predicament of Culture*, 1988.

44 See also Frits Andersen: "Felix Arabia", *Kritik*, No. 162-63, 2003.

45 Michael Harbsmeier "Indledning" in Carsten Niebuhr *Rejsebeskrivelse fra Arabien og andre omkringliggende lande*, 2003, p. 27.

46 Katie Whitaker: "The culture of curiosity" in *Cultures of natural history*, op.cit. A comprehensive historical outline can be found in Lorraine Daston, Katherine Park: *Wonder and the Order of Nature, 1150-1750*, 1998.

47 Barbara M. Stafford: *Voyage into Substance. Art, Science, and the Illustrated Travel Account*, 1984.

48 Lord Kames: *Elements of Criticism*, 1970 (1762), pp. 319-20.

49 Robert Darnton: *The Forbidden Best-Sellers of Prerevolutionary France*, 1996; *The Corpus of Clandestine Literature in France, 1769-1789*, 1995.

50 Bakhtin: "From the Prehistory of Novelistic Discourse" in *The Dialogical Imagination*, 1986.

51 Nicholas Thomas: *Entangled Objects: Exchange, Material Culture, and Colonialism in the Pacific*, 1991.

52 Felix Driver and Luciana Martins (ed.): *Tropical Visions in an Age of Empire*, 2005.

53 Tim Jeal's *Livingstone* (1973) was the first biography to question the canonised perception of Livingstone as a saint in Africa. Felix Driver followed up on the criticism in the chapter "Missionary of Science: David Livingstone and the Exploration of Africa" in *Geography Militant* (2001).

54 Bertrand Westphal: *Geocriticm. Real and Fictional Spaces,* 2011

55 Wlad Godzich: "Emergent Literature and the Field of Comparative Literature" in *The Culture of Literacy*, 1994.

56 Claude Lévi-Strauss: *The Savage Mind* 1972, p. 261

57 Paul Ricœur: "Humanities between Science and Art", http://www.hum.au.dk/ckulturf/pages/publications/pr/hbsa.pdf (accessed 22 February 2008), p. 15.

58 In relation to the former, Tim Youngs' introduction to the Africa volume of the anthology *Nineteenth-Century Travels, Explorations and Empires* (2004) perceives the explorations as more vulnerable but also more dynamic.

59 Pratt's *Imperial Eyes* has achieved almost canonic status in postcolonial and travel literature studies. The few critics of the panoptic fallacy include: Nigel Leask: *Curiosity and the Aesthetics of Travel Writing 1770-1840* (2004) and Greg Garrett: "Relocating Burton: Public and Private Writings on Africa" in *The Journal of African Travel-Writing*, No. 2, 1997.

60 The Stanley Archives at the Musée Royal de l'Afrique Centrale contain thousands of texts. In relation to his expeditions, distinctions will be made between "Notebooks", "Field Notebooks", which are notes written on marches, and "Journals", which are expanded transcripts of the Notebooks. See: http:/www.Africamuseum.be/

61 Stanley Archives No. 15, *Field Notebook* (15.08.1875-01.03.1876), No. 16. *Journal* (01.01.1873; 12.11.1874-11.09.1876). The diary mentions Safeni's initial conversation with the island's natives as "friendly speeches", which in *TDC* is developed into a complex, antique figure

relating the classical orator; meanwhile, the casualties change from "Killing one of the foremost and wounded another" to nine dead in *TDC*.

62 Tim Jeal: "The Island of Death" in *Stanley. The Impossible Life of Africa's Greatest Explorer,* 2007 p. 182-83.

63 Laura E. Franey: *Victorian Travel Writing and Imperial Violence: British Writing on Africa, 1855-1902*, 2003. Franey's very harsh postcolonial criticism is mainly aimed at Rider Haggard and Conrad; in regard to Stanley, it is linked especially to the Emin Pasha Relief Expedition, the admittedly abundant macabre details of which are all read as examples of the imperialistic glorification of violence.

64 In *The River Congo* (1978), Peter Forbath relates the story of Prester John with a specific focus on the myth's link to the earliest discovery of Congo. In *Antropologi i middelalderen og renæssancen* (2006), Ole Høiris presents a thorough historic exposition of the localisation of Prester John in East Africa (Ethiopia, to be more precise) in the mid-fourteenth century. In the fifteenth, the myth underwent yet another geographic shift; now Prester John's Christian kingdom was to be found in Central Africa, where the myth was linked to others - which later proved to be more accurate - about two great inland lakes which were the sources of the Congo and Nile rivers. Høiris, pp. 352-68.

65 François Hartog: *Le Miroir d'Hérodote. Essai sur la représentation de l'autre*, 1989.

66 Stephen Greenblatt: *Marvelous Possessions. The Wonder of the New World*, 1988, pp. 10-14.

67 George W. Stocking, Jr.: "Ethnology on the Eve of Evolution (1830-1858)" in *Victorian Anthropology*, 1987.

68 James L. Newman: *Imperial Footprints: Henry Morton Stanley's African Journeys*, 2004.

69 Iain Smith: *The Emin Pasha Relief Expedition 1886-1890*, 1972.

70 Dorothy Middleton (ed.): "Editors Introduction" in *The Diary of A.J. Mounteney Jephson*, 1969.

71 The note also thanks the printing works and bindery for their extraordinarily quick production: "Bearing in mind that the first line of this work was written in the Hotel Villa Victoria, Cairo, on the 25th day of this year (1890); that the Author worked continuously for fifty days, averaging over twenty pages a day; that the first portion of manuscript was placed in the printer's hands on the 12th of March, and the last proof-sheet returned for press on the 3rd of June - Messrs. Clowes, whose names we mention last, are far from being the least entitled to gratitude." *In Darkest Africa*, p. iii.

72 Daniel Liebowitz and Charles Pearson's *The Last Expedition. Stanley's Mad Journey through the Congo* (2005) is another dramatic account with an even greater amount of terrifying detail, particularly about the expedition's illnesses.

73 In the chapter "Consuming Stanley", Tim Youngs investigates the newspapers' reception of the expedition. Tim Youngs: *Travellers in Africa. British Travelogues, 1850-1900*, 1994.

74 Tim Youngs op. cit., p. 15.

75 A.J. Mounteney Jephson: Dorothy Middleton (ed.): *The Diary of A. J. Mounteney Jephson*, 1969, p. 256

76 James Jameson: Ethel Jameson (ed.): *Story of the Rear Column of the Emin Pasha Relief Expedition by the late James S. Jameson, Naturalist to the expedition*, 1890, p. xx.

77 Emma Spary: "Codes of Passion: Natural History Specimens as Polite Language in Late 18th-Century France" in Hans Erich Bödeker (ed.): *Wissenschaft als kulturelle Praxis 1750-1900*, 1999.

78 Ruth Rempel: "Not a 'Cloth Giver': Entitlement, Hunger and Illicit Transfers on The Emin Pasha Relief Expedition, 1886-1890" in *International Journal of African Historical Studies*, Vol. 39, No. 1, 2006.

79 Timothy Reiss: *The Discourse of Modernism*, 1982.

80 Jan B. Gordon: "'Decadent Spaces': Notes for a Phenomenology of the Fin de Siècle" in Ian Fletcher (ed.): *Decadence and the 1880s*, 1979.

81 Richard Hall: *Stanley. An Adventurer Explored*, 1974, p. 309.

82 "New Publications. Jameson's own story" in *New York Times*, 23 March 1891.

83 The chapter "Centres of Calculation" in Bruno Latour: *Science In Action: How to Follow Scientists and Engineers Through Society*, 1987.

84 Mathilde Leduc-Grimaldi: "De l'atlas au roman. L'Album bleu de Henry M. Stanley" in *Études photographiques*, No. 14, 2004.

85 Paul K. Saint-Amour: "Modernist Reconnaissance" in *Modernism/modernity*, Vol. 10, No. 2, 2003.

86 David Finkelstein: "The Globalization of the Book 1800-1970 in Simon Eliot, Jonathan Rose (ed.): *A Companion to the History of the Book*, 2007.

87 Felix Driver has written a chapter on the collapse in legitimacy that characterised the *Royal Geographical Society* in the latter half of the nineteenth century: "The Royal Geographical Society and the Empire of Science" in *Geography Militant*, 2001.

88 Thomas Richards: *The Commodity Culture of Victorian England. Advertising and Spectacle 1851-1914*, 1990. In addition to the chapter on the world's fair and the Crystal Palace there is another with the title "Selling Darkest Africa". Here, Richards mentions several examples of advertisements, shows etc., that came in the wake of Stanley's *In Darkest Africa*; unfortunately it is more a catalogue than an analysis, marked by Marxist critique and its narrow definition of "commodities".

89 Barbara Maria Stafford: *Voyage into Substance*, 1984; Barbara Maria Stafford, Frances Terpak and Isotta Poggi: *Devices of Wonder: From the World in a Box to Images on a Screen*, 2001.

90 "Stanley Strikes Back" in *New York Times*, 17 November 1890.

91 "In Darkest Africa; or, the Quest, Rescue, and retreat of Emin, Governor of Equatoria. By Henry M. Stanley, M.R.G.S. Two volumes, London 1890" in *Edinburgh Review*, 1890.

92 Robert Kimbrough (ed.): *Joseph Conrad Heart of Darkness. An Authoritative Text. Background and Sources. Criticism*, 1988.

93 Peter Nazareth: "Out of Darkness: Conrad and the Third World Writers" in *Conradiana*, Vol. 14, No. 3, 1982.

94 Franco Moretti: "Conjectures on World Literature" in *New Left Review*, No. 1, 2003.

95 More or less every mention and review of the book highlighted a link between the Congo Reform Association and the human rights campaigns of the present day, mentioning Hochschild's book as a justification of the latter's glorious basis in the former, including Jeremy Harding "Into Africa" in *The New York Times* (20.09.1998). "A New Era for Congo" by "senior DRC Researcher" Anneke Van Woudenberg, is another pertinent example; it was printed before the election in *London Review of Books* (19.10.2006) and also appeared on the *Human Rights Watch* homepage. The article shows how rhetorical shifts and exaggerations in Hochschild's presentation have been continued into usually sober historical accounts when tempted by demagogic simplifications of human rights issues. For instance, the campaign leader Edmund Morel is mentioned as "witnessing the happenings, committing it to paper and bringing it to the attention of the world". Morel was a propagandist, *not* a witness.

96 Albert Guerard in Robert Kimbrough (ed.): *Joseph Conrad Heart of Darkness. An Authoritative Text. Background and Sources. Criticism*, 1988, p. 193.

97 Tim Jeal: "Stanley, Léopold and the Atrocities" in *Stanley. The Impossible Life of Africa's Greatest Explorer*, 2007. Helen Carr: "Roger Casement in the Amazon, the Congo, and Ireland" in Peter Hulme (ed.): *Writing, Travel, and Empire. In the Margins of Anthropology*, 2007.

98 Joseph Conrad: *An Outcast of the Islands*, 1896.

99 Joseph Conrad: *A Personal Record*, 1912, p. 13.

100 The significance of this 'fact' is contested. Richard Curle notes in *The Last Twelve Years of Joseph Conrad* (1928) that Mrs Conrad did not ascribe any importance to the diary in relation to the novel. (Kimbrough, p. 197.)

101 Jakob Lothe: "Conrad and Travel Literature: From Conrad's 'Up-river Book' and 'Congo Diary' (1890) via *Heart of Darkness* (1899) to Redmond O'Hanlon's *Congo Journey* (1996)" in Karin Hansson (ed.): *Journeys, Myths and the Age of Travel: Joseph Conrad's Era*, 1998.

102 Syed Islam: *The Ethics of Travel*, 1996.

103 David Finkelstein: *An index to Blackwood's Magazine 1901-1980*, 1995, p. xiv.

104 John Masefield writes in a review of the book edition in 1903: "he (Conrad) has set down page after page of stately and brilliant prose, which is fine writing, good literature, and so forth, but most unconvincing narrative. His narrative is not vigorous, direct, effective, like that of Mr. Kipling. It is not clear and fresh like that of Stevenson, nor simple, delicate, and beautiful like that of Mr Yeats. It reminds one rather of a cobweb abounding in gold threads. It gives one a curious impression of remoteness and aloofness from its subject. Often it smells very palpable of the lamp, losing all spontaneity and becoming somewhat rhetorical." Quoted from Norman Sherry: *Conrad. The Critical Heritage*, 1973, p. 142.

105 James Stewart: *Dawn in the Dark Continent*, 1903.

106 Felix Driver analyses a spectacular example, William Booth's *In Darkest England, and the Way Out* from 1890, in which the event related to Stanley's *In Darkest Africa* was quickly reused in a pamphlet for the Salvation Army, transferring the source's topographical figures to the English landscape. The chapter "Exploring 'Darkest England': Mapping the Heart of Empire" in F. Driver: *Geography Militant*, 2001.

107 Brantlinger refers to Fredric Jameson's analysis in *The Political Unconscious: Narrative as a Socially Symbolic Act*, 1981.

108 Homi K. Bhabha: *The Location of Culture*, 1994.

109 Tzvetan Todorov: "Knowledge in the Void: Heart of Darkness" in *Conradiana*, Vol. 21, No. 3, 1989.

110 Hunt Hawkins: "Conrad and Congolese Exploitation" in *Conradiana*, Vol. 13, No. 2, 1981.

111 Ray Stevens: "Three Voices of Conrad's Narrative Journey" in Attie de Lange (ed.): *Conrad in Africa: New Essays on 'Heart of Darkness'*, 2002.

112 Allan Simmons: "The Language of Atrocity: Representing the Congo of Conrad and Casement" in Attie de Lange (ed.): *Conrad in Africa*, 2002.

113 Richard Kuppel: "*Heart of Darkness* and the Popular Exotic Stories of the 1890s" in *Conradiana*, Vol. 21, No. 1, 1989.

114 Ermien van Pletzen: "Mine is the Speech that cannot be Silenced": Confession and Testimony in "Heart of Darkness" in Attie de Lange (ed.): *Conrad in Africa*, 2002.

115 Tim Jeal: *Stanley. The Impossible Life of Africa's Greatest Explorer*, 2007, pp. 443-52. Helen Carr: "Roger Casement in the Amazon, the Congo, and Ireland" in Peter Hulme and Russell McDougall: *Writing, Travel, and Empire*, 2007, pp. 172-73.

116 This question is contentious; we will return to the discussion in the next section. In this context, see: "La violence dans l'histoire de l'Afrique" and Philippe Marechal: "La controverse sur Léopold II et le Congo dans la littérature et les médias. Réflexions critiques" in Jean-Luc Vellut (ed.): *La mémoire du Congo. Le temps colonial*, 2005.

117 Elikia M'Bokolo in Marc Ferro (ed.): *Le livre noir du colonialisme*, 2003.

118 Susanne Gehrmann: *Kongo-Greul. Zur literarischen Konfiguration eines Kolonialkritischen Diskurses (1890-1910)*, 2003.

119 George Washington Williams: "A Report upon the Congo-State and the Country to the President of The Republic of the United States of America" in Robert Kimbrough: op.cit.

120 E. D. Morel: *History of the Congo Reform Movement*, 1914, quoted from Barbara Harlow (ed.): *The Scramble for Africa, Archives of Empire*, No. 2, 2003, p. 764.

121 E. D. Morel: *Red Rubber. The Story of the Rubber Slave Trade Flourishing on the Congo in the Year of Grace 1906*, 1906.

122 Kevin Grant: *A Civilised Savagery. Britain and the New Slaveries in Africa, 1884-1926*, 2005, pp. 40-63.

123 Roger Casement: "The main report" in Séamas Ó Síochaín and Michael O'Sullivan (ed.): *The Eyes of Another Race: Roger Casement's Congo report and 1903 diary*, 2004, p. 49.

124 Samuel Nelson: *Colonialism in the Congo Basin 1880-1940*, 1994.

125 Mark Twain: "King Léopold's Soliloquy", 1905, quoted from *The Scramble for Africa, Archives* op.cit.

126 E. D. Morel: *King Leopold's Rule in Africa*, 1904, p. 117.

127 Frederick Karl and Laurence Davies (ed.): *The Collected Letters of Joseph Conrad, Vol. 3 1903-1907*, 1988, p. 96.

128 Joseph Conrad: "Correspondence", 22 July 1896, cited from Kimbrough: op.cit.

129 Pierre Halen: "Stanley et Conrad, paradigmes de deux traditions discursive sur l'Afrique centrale" in Jean-Claude Kangomba (ed.): *L'Œil de l'autre*, 2000. An abbreviated English version can be found in Elisabeth Mudimbe-Boyi (ed.): *Remembering Africa*, 2002.

130 Olof Lagercrantz: *A Journey with the Heart of Darkness*, 1989.

131 Richard Ruppel: "Heart of Darkness and the popular exotic stories of the 1890's" in *Conradiana*, Vol. 21, No. 1, 1989.

132 The short story was published in the collection *The Derelict* (1901).

133 Jürgen Jürgensen: *The big and the small river*, 1913. The last pages of the book are dedicated to a number of longish quotations from newspaper reviews of the earlier publications referred to here.

134 Jürgen Jürgensen: *Christian Svarre's Journey to the Congo*, p. 128.

135 Jürgen Jürgensen: *Fever*, p. 5.

136 Hannah Arendt: *The Origins of Totalitarianism*, 1985.

137 Bert Blom: *Navigator in The Heart of Darkness*, 1999, p. 36.

138 Christian Martini and Christian Schønberg: *Two Danish Travellers to Congo. Memoirs from our first stay in the Congo State*, 1890, p. 5.

139 The edition referred to here is Octave Mirbeau: *La 628-E8*, 1910. There also exists a luxury edition with illustrations by Pierre Bonnard and Octave Mirbeau: *La 628-E8. Édition de luxe*, 1908. In the first editions, a controversial section was edited out in which Mirbeau claimed that Mme Hanska was unfaithful to Balzac while he lay dying in the room next door. It is included in *La 628-E8, Soixantième Mille. Comprenant en annexe. Le chapitre intégral "Balzac" supprimé lors de l'apparition en 1907*, 1939. For bibliophiles, a small printing of the 1907 edition exists from which the infamous section had not yet been deleted.

140 James Clifford: "On Etnographic Surrealism" in *The Predicament of Culture*, 1988.

141 Recent years have seen a renewed interest in Mirbeau's path-breaking role, thanks to his biographer and editor Pierre Michel, who in numerous publications and on the internet advocates for Mirbeau's unique position in politics and literature. See the homepage for La Société Octave Mirbeau for a large database with references. There are also two recent publications in English, Reg Carr: *Anarchism in France: the Case of Octave Mirbeau* (1977) and Christopher Lloyd: *Mirbeau's Fictions* (1996).

142 E.g. René Cornelis: *Anvers et l'exposition universelle de 1885*, Bruxelles 1885. M. Bernardin: *Les richesses naturelle du globe et l'Exposition universelle d'Anvers*, Anvers, 1885. See also Jean-Luc Vellut (ed.): *La mémoire du Congo. Le temps colonial*, 2005.

143 André Breton: *Les vases communicant*, 1932.

144 For Mirbeau's art criticism, including his work on Monet, see Octave Mirbeau: *Combats esthétiques*, 1993.

145 Here, an "explorer", characteristically an Englishman, is the subject of sharp satire, while the colonial understanding of self – "the western snobbery" – is criticised in the narrator's strange mix of prosaic precision and ecstatic pleasure in the decadently sadistic tableaux. The following remark is attributed to the English explorer: "Negroes? (...) They are gentle and gay ... they are like children ... have you ever seen rabbits playing in the meadow in the evening, at the edge of the woods? (...) They make pretty, frolicsome movements; they shine their fur with their paws and bound about and roll in the mint-leaves. Well, negroes are like young rabbits ... it's very charming!". *Le jardin des supplices*, 1988 (1899), p. 305.

146 Émile Van Balberghe has reprinted the chapter and added much bibliographical information. Balberghe does not analyse the text, but he points to a vast number of documents from the time which Mirbeau probably incorporated and turned inside-out, including very rare and anonymous satires of Léopold's exploitation of the so-called Free State. Émile Van Balberghe (ed.): Octave Mirbeau: *Le caoutchouc rouge. Suivi de Un Sadisme colonial par Émile Van Balberghe*, 1994.

147 Bernard Piniau: *Congo-Zaïre 1874-1981. La perception du lointain*, 1992.

148 Edward Said: *Culture and imperialism*, 1993.

149 E.g. Hunt Hawkins, Brian Shaffer (ed.): *Approaches to Teaching Conrad's 'Heart of Darkness' and 'The Secret Sharer'*, 2002.

150 Lennard J. Davis: "The Value of Teaching From a Racist Classic" in *Chronicle of Higher Education*, Vol. 52, No. 37, 2006.

151 E.g. Michael Lackey: "The Moral Conditions for Genocide in Joseph Conrad's Heart of Darkness" in *College Literature*, Vol. 32, No. 1, 2005, and Henry Laskowsky: "Heart of Darkness": A Primer for the Holocaust" in *Virginia Quarterly Review*, Vol. 58, No. 1, 1982.

152 Fredric Jameson: *The Political Unconscious*, 1981.

153 William Atkinson: "Bound in Blackwood's: The imperialism of "The Heart of Darkness" in Its Immediate Context" in *Twentieth Century Literature*, Vol. 50, No. 4, 2004.

154 F.R. Leavis: *The Great Tradition*, 1948.

155 Terry Collits: *Postcolonial Conrad*, 2005.

156 Norman Sherry (ed.): *Conrad. The Critical Heritage*, 1973.

157 For an introduction to "commodity reading" see Simon Frost: *The Business of the novel – Economics, Aesthetics and the Case of Middlemarch*, 2012.

158 B. Malinovski: *Argonauts of the Western Pacific*, 1922. Claude Lévi-Strauss: *Tristes tropiques*, 1955. See also Mary Louise Pratt: "Fieldwork in Common Places" in James Clifford and George Marcus (eds.): *Writing Culture. The Poetics and Politics of Ethnography*, 1986.

159 David Punter: *Gothic Pathologies: The Text, The Body and The Law*, 1998.

160 An editorial article in *Nature* by Robin A. Weiss refers to Hooper's resistance to data as follows: "The new data may not convince the hardened conspiracy theorist who thinks

that contamination of OPV by chimpanzee virus was subsequently and deliberately covered up. But those of us who were formerly willing to give some credence to the OPV hypothesis will now consider that the matter has been laid to rest. (...) When the preliminary results of the investigations were announced at the Royal Society in London last September, Hooper nonetheless dismissed them as "irrelevant to the OPV hypothesis". But that simply isn't so – on the contrary, some beautiful facts have destroyed an ugly theory." *Nature* 26 April 2001.

161 Ann Vibeke Knudsen (ed.): *Bornholm, Congo, tur/retur. Fortællinger om bornholmere, andre danskere og congolesere samt lidt om Congos historie fra 1870erne til nu*, 2003. Peter Tygesen and Esben Wæhle (eds.): *Congospor. Norden i Congo – Congo i Norden*, 2006.

162 Adam Hochschild: "In the Heart of Darkness" *The New York Review of Books*, 6 October 2005.

163 A series of articles in Jean-Luc Vellut's *La mémoire du Congo. Le temps colonial* (2005) critically examines Hochschild's claims.

164 "Un autre regard sur Tervuren – Guide alternatif de l'exposition. 26 mai 2005". http://www.intal.be/fr. 26 April 2008. See also Jan-Bart Gewald: "More than Red Rubber and figures alone: A critical appraisal of the memory of the Congo Exhibition at the Royal Museum for Central Africa, Tervuren, Belgium" *The International Journal of African Historical Studies*, Vol 36, 2006 and Marouf Hasian: "Colonial Amnesias, Photographic Memories, and Demographic Biopolitics at the Royal Museum for Central Africa (RMCA)" *Third World Quarterly*, Vol. 33, 2012.

165 Andreas Huyssen: "Diaspora and Nation: Migration into Other Pasts" in Murtie-Aude Baronian (ed.): *Diaspora and Memory: Figures of Displacement in Contemporary Literature*, 2007.

166 A similar critical discussion can be found in Sarah De Mul: "The Holocaust as Paradigm for the Congo Atrocities: Adam Hochschild's *King Leopold's Ghost*" *Criticism*, Vol. 53, 2011.

167 Jean-Luc Vellut: "Jan Vansina and The Belgian Historiography of Africa: Around the Agenda of the Bombing Raid. A Reply to 'History Facing the Present: An Interview with Jan Vansina'" http://www.h-net.msu.edu/-africa/africaforum/Vellut.htm. 24 April 2008.

168 See e.g. http://cas1.elis.rug.ac.be/avrug/exshit.htm 22 November 2008.

169 The critical reception of *A Burnt-out Case* was therefore extremely divided. Most critics read the novel as an expansion on Greene's religious themes, in which Catholicism plays an even more profound and philosophical part compared with previous novels, while at the same time expressing their reservations towards the literary technique – ironically based on its lack of inner necessity and the many overlaps between Querry and Greene, who is criticised for his lack of inventiveness. A recent criticism deems *A Burnt-out Case* the least accomplished work in the oeuvre, referring to the fact that it does not clearly choose sides in its attitude towards Catholicism, and therefore fails as a serious novel. Bernard Bergonzi: *A Study in Greene: Graham Greene and the Art of the Novel*, 2006.

170 A profusion of biographies have been written about the popular author with his controversial political and religious ideas and his cosmopolitan travels to exotic destinations all over the world. He was part of everything that goes with being a celebrity - scandals, a life led in luxury on the French Riviera and a past career as an intelligence agent. The Conrad expert Norman Sherry was appointed by Greene to write the ultimate biography, for which the author would harness his declared practice of sending journalists and critics on wild goose chases when they asked about his private life. On Greene's journey to the Congo and *A Burnt-out Case*, see Norman Sherry's *The Life of Graham Greene: volume three (1955-1991)* (2004). For a precise and critical appraisal of Sherry's infatuation with the object of the biography, see George Walden: "A Burnt-out Case. The story of a vain sexual adventurer told by an assassin of language - George Walden on why Graham Greene got the biographer he deserved", in *New Statesman*, 25 October 2004.

171 Murray Roston: *Graham Greene's Narrative Strategies. A Study of the Major Novels*, 2006.

172 Chinua Achebe: "Viewpoint", *Times Literary Supplement*, 1980.

173 Peter Nazareth: "Out of Darkness. Conrad and the Third World Writers" *Conradiana*, Vol 14, issue 3, 1982.

174 V. S. Naipaul: "Conrad's Darkness" in *New York Review of Books*, 1974. Printed in Robert D. Hamner (ed.): *Critical Perspectives on V.S. Naipaul*, 1979, which is the version cited here.

175 Olav Lausund: "Revisiting the "Heart of Darkness": V.S. Naipaul's *A Bend in the River*" in Jakob Lothe, Anne Rønning (ed.): *Identities and Masks: Colonial and Postcolonial Studies*, 2001.

176 Urs Widmer: *Im Kongo*, 1998.

177 Hans Carl Finsen "Den befriede fortælling - Urs Widmer, Christoph Rasmayr, Robert Schneider", in Henning Goldbæk (ed.): *Tysk litteratur efter murens fald*, 2006.

178 Christophe Bourquin: *Schreiben über Reisen. Zur ars itineraria von Urs Widmer im Kontext der europäischen Reiseliteratur*, 2006.

179 Urs Widmer: *Die Forschungsreise. Ein Abenteuerroman*, 1976.

180 "Nachwort von Urs Widmer" in Joseph Conrad: *Herz der* Finsternis, 1998.

181 Ingmar Weber, Jürgen Sander: "Schreiben hat etwas mit Zauberei zu tun! Ein Interview mit Urs Widmer über seinen Roman *Im Kongo*, die Schicksalslosigkeit der Schweizer und den Schwarzen in ihm". http://www.buechergilde.de.archiv/exclusivinterviews/widmer.shtml. Accessed 3 December 2007.

182 One example from a relatively calm period is Paul F. Salopek's "The Mountain Gorillas of Africa. A Fragile Home Threatened by War" in *National Geographic* (1995).

183 http://www.caroloscrabble.be/article.php3?id_article=118. Accessed 23 November 07.

184 Vicky van Bockhaven: "Leopard Men of the Congo in literature and popular imagination" *Tydskrif vir letterkunde*, Vol. 46, 2009

185 Hergé: *Tintin au Congo* in *Archives Hergé. Versions originales des album Tintin au Pays des Soviets (1929), au Congo (1930), en Amerique (1931)*, 1973 and Hergé: *Tintin au Congo. Les aventures de Tintin*, 1974 (1946).

186 Hergé would have preferred to send Tintin to America after the journey to the Soviet Union, but his publisher decided that the Belgian colony needed the publicity. Michael Farr: *Tintin. The Complete Companion*, 2001.

187 In the 1946 version, Muganda is speaking primitive French: "Toi y en a connaître les Aniotas? Non? ... Ca y en a société secrète pour lutter contre Blancs. Quand un Aniota reçevoir ordre exécuter chef noir favorable aux Blancs, li mettre costume et masque de léopard. A ses doigts, li fixer griffes de fer aussi comme léopard, et porter bâton avec bout sculpté comme pattes de léopard. Alors, Aniota li va tuer li Noir et laisser partout empreintes avec son bâton. Et tout li monde li croire li vrai léopard être coupable" (op. cit., p. 30).

188 Nancy Rose Hunt: "Tintin and the Interruptions of Congolese Comics" in Paul S. Landau and Deborah D. Kaspin (eds.): *Images and Empires. Visuality in Colonial and Postcolonial Africa*, 2002.

189 This opinion is shared by fans and critics. Michael Farr: *Tintin. The Complete Companion*, 2001. Numa Sadoul (ed.): *50 år med Tintin. Hergés oplevelser*, 1979.

190 Pierre Halen: "Tintin, paradigme du héros colonial belge?" in Anna Soncini Fratta (ed.): *Tintin, Hergé et la "Belgité"*, 1994, pp. 44-46.

191 Marie Rose Maurin Abomo: "Tintin au Congo, ou la stratégie d'une démarche coloniale" in Anna Soncini Fratta (ed.): *Tintin, Hergé et la "Belgité"*, 1994, p. 69.

192 At a concrete level, the anthropological museums played an important role in Hergé's research. Michel Baudson: *Le Musée imaginaire de Tintin*, 1980.

193 www.erbzine.com/mag16/1662.html. Accessed 23 November 2007.

194 http://burroughs.thefreelibrary.com/Tarzan-of-the-Apes/1-1 Accessed 23 November 2007.

195 Ethelreda Lewis (ed.): *Alfred Aloysius Horn Trader Horn. The Ivory Coast in the Earlies*, 1927.

196 About the film, see Jon Tuska: "*Trader Horn*: A Cinematograph" in Jon Tuska: *A Variable Harvest. Essays and Reviews of Film and Literature*, 1990. Tuska mentions that Van Dyke has written a book about the filming in Africa: *Horning into Africa*, 1931.

197 http://gutenberg.net.au/ebooks05/0500201h.html. Accessed 23 November 2007.

198 Georges Dodds mentions J. W. Buel: *Heroes of the Dark Continent*, 1890 as one of Burroughs' main sources of inspiration for Tarzan. Buel's book is illustrated, dramatising summaries of travel books, especially Stanley's, including conflicting accounts of the Emin Pasha Relief Expedition. It was one of the popular unauthorised versions on the American market, which Stanley's publisher, Marston, warned about in *How Stanley Wrote In Darkest Africa.* http://www.erbzine.com/mag18/buel.htm Accessed 20 January 2009.

199 In Du Chaillu's own account, he loses his entire equipment of scientific instruments, and no less than "five Geneva musical boxes", the purpose of which is not explained. Paul Du Chaillu: *The Country of Dwarfs*, 1901. Jean de Léry: *History of a Voyage to The Land of Brazil otherwise called America*, 1990 (1577).

200 Robert Mackey: "Fact, Fiction and Kapuscinski" *New York Times* 8 March 2010. John Ryle: "A play in the bush of ghosts. Tropical baroque, African reality and the work of Ryszard Kapuscinski" *Times Literary Supplement* 27 July 2001. Artur Domoslawski: *Kapuscinski Non-fiction*, 2010.

201 Norman Mailer: *The Fight*, 1975

202 Pierre Halen: "L'ouvert et le fermé: Une typologie de l'espace centre-africain dans toutes sortes d'histoires européennes" in Ernst Leonardy and Hubert Roland (eds.): *Descriptions et créations d'espaces dans la literature*, 1995.

203 André Gide: *Voyage au Congo. Suivie de Le retour du Tchad. Carnets de route*, 1981 (1923). Redmond O'Hanlon: *Congo Journey*, 1997. William Gálvez: *Che in Africa. Che Guevara's Congo Diary*, 1999. Madeleine Kalb: *the Congo Cables. The Cold War in Africa – From Eisenhower to Kennedy*, 1982.

204 Helen Carr: "Roger Casement in the Amazon, the Congo, and Ireland" in *Writing, Travel, and Empire. In the Margins of Anthropology*, op. cit. Michael Taussig: "Culture of Terror – Space of Death: Roger Casement's Putumayo Report and the Explanation of Torture" in Alexander L. Hinton (ed.): *Genocide. An anthropological reader*, 2002. See also Roger Burroughs: *Travel Writing and Atrocities: Eyewitness Accounts of Colonialism in the Congo, Angola, and the Putumayo*, 2010.

205 Jeffrey Dudgeon: *Roger Casement. The Black Diaries – with a study of his background, sexuality, and Irish political life*, 2002. Roger Casement: *The Crime against Europe*, 1915.

206 Allen Carey-Webb: "Heart of Darkness, Tarzan, and the 'Third World': Canons and Encounters in World Literature, English 109" in *College Literature*, 1993.

207 John le Carré: *The Mission Song*, 2006. In a travel essay that provides a very precise and far from exoticising portrait of the Kivu Province, John le Carré concludes with characteristic self-irony by denying that the novel is about the Congo: "But then I wasn't really writing about Congo, was I? It was all those other things. Congo was just backcloth". John le Carré: "Congo Journey" *The Nation* 2 October 2006. *Weekendavisen*, 15 September 2006.

208 Susan Bassnett: "Writing Time, Writing Space" in Karen-Margrethe Simonsen (ed.): *World Literature. World Culture*, 2008.

209 Wolfgang Behschnitt: "Text, teater, handling. Om performativitet som litteraturvetenskapeligt forskningsperspektiv", op. cit., p. 42.

210 Pierre Halen: "Stanley and Conrad: Founders of Alternative Discourses about Central Africa" in Elisabeth Mudimbe-Buyi (ed.): *Remembering Africa*, 2002.

211 Horace Engdahl: *Witness Literature*, 2001.

212 "Global concepts: Prosaics, Unfinalizability, Dialogue" in Gary S. Morson: *Mikhail Bakhtin. Creation of a Prosaics*, 1990.

213 Aaron Beim and Gary Alan Fine: "Trust in Testimony: The Institutional Embeddedness of Holocaust Survivor Narratives" in *European Journal of Sociology*, 2007.

214 http://www.dailymotion.com/video/xhfvy_genocidecongo_news. Accessed 15 October 2008.

215 Horace Engdahl: "Philomena's tongue" in H. Engdahl (ed.): *Witness Literature*, 2002.

216 Martin Sabrow, Konrad Hugo Jarausch: *Verletztes Gedächtnis: Erinnerungskultur und Zeitgeschichte im Konflikt*, 2002.

217 François Hartoq: *Évidence de l'histoire: Ce que voient les historiens*, 2008.

218 Sharon Sliwinski: "The Childhood of Human Rights: The Kodak on the Congo" in *Journal of Visual Culture*, 2006.

219 John Peffer: "Snap of the Whip/Crossroads of Shame. Flogging, Photography, and the Representation of Atrocity in the Congo Reform Campaign" *Visual Anthropology Review*, Vol 24, 2008.

220 Arne Melberg: "Sebald's photographic prose" in *Aesthetics of prose*, 2008.

221 http://humanrightswatch.net/campaigns/drc/2006/katanga/legal.htm Accessed 20 November 2008.

222 Martin Herbert: "Renzo Martens by Martin Herbert", *ArtReview*, 2009.

223 Gillian Whitlock: "Remediating Gorilla Girl: Rape Warfare and the Limits of Humanitarian Storytelling" in *Biography*, Vol. 33, 2010.

224 David Lagergren: *Konflikt i Kongo. Mission och stat under gummikrisen*, 1971. Ruth Slade: *English-Speaking Missions in the Congo Independent State, 1878-1908*, 1959.

225 Henriette Roos: "The sins of the fathers: The missionary in some modern English novels about the Congo" *Tydskrif vir letterkunde*, Vol. 46, 2009.

226 Kenneth Cmiel: "The Recent History of Human Rights" in *The American Historical Review*, No. 129, 1, 2007.

227 Richard Rorty: "Human rights, rationality, and sentimentality" in S. Shute and S. Hurley (eds.): *On Human Rights: the Oxford Amnesty Lectures 1993*, 1993.

228 Johannes Fabian: "Forgetful Remembering: A Colonial Life in the Congo" in *Africa*, Vol. 73, 2003.

229 Susanne Gehrmann: "Remembering colonial violence: Inter/textual strategies of Congolese authors" and Kasongo Kapanga: "Legitimizing the invented Congolese space: The Gaze from within in early Congolese fiction", in *Tydskrif vir Letterkunde*, Vol. 46, 2009.

230 Pierre Halen *Quand le petit belge a vu grand*, 1993. Pierre-Philippe Fraiture: *Le Congo Belge et son récit francophone à la veille des indépendances*, 2003. See also Luc Renders: "In black and white: a bird's eye overview of Flemish prose on the Congo" in *Tydskrif vir Letterkunde*, Vol. 46, 2009. Pierre-Philippe Fraiture: "Modernity and the Belgian Congo" in *Tydskrif vir Letterkunde*, Vol. 46, 2009.

231 See also Antoine Tshitungu Kongolo: "Colonial Memories in Belgian and Congolese Literature" *Yale French Studies*, No. 102, 2002.

232 Antoon van den Braembussche: "The Silence of Belgium: Taboo and Trauma in Belgian Memory" *Yale French Studies*, No. 102, 2002.

233 Valerie Rosoux and Laurence van Ypersele: "The Belgian national past: Between commemoration and silence" *Memory Studies*, Vol. 45, 2012.

234 Glenn Hooper and Tim Youngs: "Defining travel: On the travel book, travel writing and terminology" in Glenn Hooper and Tim Youngs (eds.): *Perspectives on Travel Writing*, 2004.

235 Haun Saussy: "Exquisite Cadavers Stitched from Fresh Nightmares" in Saussy (ed.): *Comparative Literature in an Age of Globalization*, 2006.

236 Jonathan Culler: "Comparative Literature, at Last", op. cit., p. 241.

237 Andreas Huyssen: "Geographies of modernism in a globalizing world" in Peter Brooker and Andrew Thacker (eds.): *Geographies of Modernism: Literatures, Cultures, Spaces*, 2005.

238 Mary Louise Pratt: "Modernity and Periphery. Toward a Global and Relational Analysis" in Elisabeth Mudimbe-Boyi (ed.): *Beyond Dichotomies. Histories, Identities, Cultures, and the Challenge of Globalization*, 2002.

239 P. Halen and J. Riesz (eds.): *Littératures du Congo-Zaïre. Actes du colloque*, 1995.

240 Jon Haarberg, Tone Selboe and Hans Erik Aarset: *Verdenslitteratur. Den vestlige tradisjonen*, 2007. Torsten Petterson: "Litteraturhistoria i paradigmskiftets tid", in *Norsk Litteraturvitenskapelig Tidsskrift*, Vol 10, No. 2, 2007.

241 Christopher Prendergast (ed.): *Debating World Literature*, 2004.

242 H. R. Jauss: "Literary History as a Challenge to Literary Theory" *New Literary History*, Vol. 2, 1970.

243 Jonathan Culler: "Whither Comparative Literature" *Comparative Critical Studies*, Vol. 3, 2006. Haun Saussy: "Exquisite Cadavers Stitched from Fresh Nightmares" *Comparative Literature in an Age of Globalization*, 2006.

244 Erich Auerbach: "Philology and Weltliteratur" *The Centennial Review* Vol. 13, 1969.

245 Michel Serres: *La communication*, 1968.

246 Christie McDonald and Susan R. Suleiman (eds.): *Global French. A New Approach to Literary History*, 2010.

247 Bertrand Westphal: *La géocritique. Réel, fiction, espace*, 2007.

248 Liisa H. Malkki: "Speechless Emissaries: Refugees, Humanitarianism, and Dehistorization" in *Genocide. An anthropological reader*, op. cit.

249 Robert Burroughs: "In Conrad's Footsteps: Critical Approaches to Africanist Travel Writing" in *Literature Compass*, No. 3-4, 2006.

250 Roger Kaplan: *Journalism, media and the challenge of human rights reporting*, 2002, p. 91.

Bibliography

Andersen, Edvard: *Eventyrlige Congo*. Copenhagen: Fremad 1957.

Andreopoulos, George J.: *Genocide: conceptual and historic dimensions*. Philadelphia: University of Pennsylvania Press 1994.

Anstruther, Ian: *I presume: Stanley's triumph and disaster*. London: Bles 1956.

Arendt, Hannah: *The origins of totalitarianism*. New York: Harcourt 1951.

Aubert, V.M.: *Breve fra Kongo og andetstedsfra*. Kristiania: Aschehoug 1908.

Bachtin, Michail & Michael Holquist: *The dialogic imagination: four essays*. Austin: University of Texas Press 2000.

Baggesgaard, Mads & Lotte Philipsen (eds.): *Hvad er verdenskunst?* Aarhus: Klim 2009.

Baker, William, Nicholas Thomas, Tim Youngs, Neil L. Whitehead & Peter J. Kitson: *Nineteenth-century travels, explorations and empires: writings from the era of imperial consolidation, 1835-1910*. London: Pickering & Chatto 2004.

Balberghe, van Émile: *Octave Mirbeau: La Caoutchouc Rouge suivi de Un sadisme colonial par Émile van Balberghe*. Bruxelles: Les libraires momentanément réunis 1994.

Barker, Francis, Peter Hulme & Margaret Iversen: *Cannibalism and the colonial world*. Cambridge: Cambridge University Press 1998.

Barker, Francis, Peter Hulme & Margaret Iversen: *Colonial discourse, postcolonial theory*. Manchester: Manchester University Press 1996.

Barttelot, Walter George: *The life of Edmund Musgrave Barttelot: Captain and Brevet-Major Royal Fusiliers, Commander of the Rear Column of the Emin Pasha relief Expedition: Being an account of his services for the relief of Kandahar, of Gordon, and of Emin: From his letters and diary*. London: R. Bentley & Son 1890.

Baudson, Michel: *Le Musée imaginaire de Tintin*. Bruxelles: Casterman 1980.

Baudson, Michel, Hergé & Palais des Beaux-arts (Bruxelles): *Tintins museum*. Copenhagen: Carlsen 1982.

Beaufils, Thomas & Marc Ferro (eds.): *Kolonialismens sorte bog: 500 års forbrydelser*. Copenhagen: Høst 2005.

Bergonzi, Bernard: *A study in Greene. Graham Greene and the art of the novel*. Oxford: Oxford University Press 2006.

Bessière, Jean & Jean-Marc Moura: *Littératures postcoloniales et francophonie. Conférences du séminaire de Littérature comparée de l'Université de la Sorbonne Nouvelle*. Paris: Champion 2001.

Betts, Raymond F.: *The scramble for Africa. Causes and dimensions of empire*. Lexington, Mass.: Heath 1972.

Bhabha, Homi K.: *The location of culture*. London: Routledge 1994.

Bierman, John: *Dark Safari. Life Behind the Legend of Henry Morton Stanley*. London: Sceptre 1992.

Birklund Andersen, Ole, Per Dahl & Frits Andersen: *1700-tallets litterære kultur*. Aarhus: Aarhus University Press 1999.

Bivona, Daniel: *British imperial literature, 1870-1940. Writing and the administration of empire*. Cambridge: Cambridge University Press 1998.

Blom, Bert: *Dagbøger og breve fra mørkets hjerte: mareridt & inferno*. Copenhagen: Thorup 2006.

Blom, Bert, Handels- og Søfartsmuseet på Kronborg & Selskabet Handels- og Søfartsmuseets Venner: *Navigatør i mørkets hjerte*. Helsingør: Handels- og Søfartsmuseet på Kronborg 1999.

Bocquet, José-Louis, Jean-Luc Fromental & Stanilas Barthélemy: *Hergés oplevelser*. Copenhagen: Fahrenheit 2005.

Booth, William: *In darkest England and the way out*. London: International Headquarters of the Salvation Army 1890.

Borberg, Christian, Ulrich Breuning & Torben Weinreich: *Tarzanmyten: romanerne, filmene, tegneserierne*. Copenhagen: Borgen 1980.

Bougainville, Louis Antoine de: *Voyage autour du monde, par la frégate du roi 'la Boudeuse', et la flûte 'l'Étoile': en 1766, 1766, 1768 et 1769*. Paris: Saillant et Nyon 1771.

Boulger, Demetrius C.: *The Congo state is not a slave state*. Liverpool: J. Richardson & Sons 1903.

Bourquin, Christophe: *Schreiben über Reisen. Zur ars itineraria von Urs Widmer im Kontext der europäischen Reiseliteratur*. Würzburg: Königshausen und Neumann 2006.

Brake, Laurel, Bill Bell & David Finkelstein: *Nineteenth-century media and the construction of identities*. Basingstoke: Palgrave 2000.

Brantlinger, Patrick: *Rule of darkness: British literature and imperialism, 1830-1914*. Ithaca: Cornell University Press 1990.

Brenna, Brita Astrid Staxrud: "Disiplinerte drømmer. Verdensutstillinger i London og Paris 1851-1867" in *TMV skriftserie*, No. 14, 1996.

Brenner, Peter J.: *Der Reisebericht in der deutschen Literatur. Ein Forschungsüberblick als Vorstudie zu einer Gattungsgeschichte*. Tübingen: Max Niemeyer 1990.

Brenner, Peter J.: *Der Reisebericht. Die Entwicklung einer Gattung in der deutschen Literatur*. Frankfurt am Main: Suhrkamp 1989.

Brooker, Peter & Andrew Thacker: *Geographies of modernism: literatures, cultures, spaces*. London: Routledge 2005.

Brooks, Peter: *Body Work: Objects of Desire in Modern Narrative*. Cambridge, M.A.: Harvard University Press 1993.

Brooks, Peter: *The novel of worldliness: Crébillon: Marivaux, Laclos: Stendhal*. Princeton, N.J.: Princeton University Press 1969.

Browne, Ray B.: *Objects of special devotion: Fetishism in popular culture*. Bowling Green, O.H.: Bowling Green University Popular Press 1982.

Browne, Ray B.: *Rituals and ceremonies in popular culture*. Bowling Green, O.H.: Bowling Green University Popular Press 1980.

Buel, J. W.: *Heroes of the Dark Continent. A complete History of all the great Explorations and Discoveries in Africa, from the earliest Ages to the present Time. Reprinted [1889]*. New York: Books for Libraries Press 1971.

Burnett, Patrick & Firoze Manji: *From the slave trade to 'free' trade. How trade undermines democracy and justice in Africa*. Nairobi: Fahamu 2007.

Burroughs, Edgar Rice: *Tarzan og leopardmændene*. Frederiksberg: Williams Forlag 1973.

Burroughs, Edgar Rice & Inc NetLibrary: *Tarzan and the jewels of opar*. Raleigh, N.C.: Alex Catalogue 199-?.

Burroughs, Edgar Rice & Inc NetLibrary: *Tarzan of the apes*. Raleigh, N.C.: Alex Catalogue 199-?.

Burroughs, Roger: *Travel Writing and Atrocities: Eyewitness Accounts of Colonialism in the Congo, Angola, and the Putumayo*. London: Taylor & Francis 2010.

Burrows, Guy: *The land of the pigmies: With introduction by H.M. Stanley*. London: C. Arthur Pearson 1898.

Butcher, Tim: *Blood river: a journey to Africa's broken heart*. London: Chatto & Windus 2007.

Bödeker, Hans E. & Peter H. Reill (red.): *Wissenschaft als kulturelle Praxis 1750-1900*. Göttingen: Vandenhoeck & Ruprecht 1999.

Börrisson, Elin: *I de svartas land*. Stockholm: Svenska missionsförbundets förlag 1922.

Cameron, Ian: *To the farthest ends of the earth: the history of The Royal Geographic Society 1830-1980*. London: Macdonald 1981.

Caminero-Santangelo, Byron: *African fiction and Joseph Conrad. Reading postcolonial intertextuality*. Albany, N.Y.: State University of New York Press 2005.

Carr, Reg: *Anarchism in France: The case of Octave Mirbeau*. Montreal: McGill-Queen's University Press 1977.

Casati, Gaetano: *Ten years in Equatoria and the return with Emin Pasha*. London: F. Warne 1891.

Casement, Roger: *The crime against Europe: The causes of the war and the foundations of Peace: Re-issue*. Berlin: The Continental Times 1915.

Chamberlain, M. E.: *The scramble for Africa*. London: Longman 1999.

Cheyfitz, Eric: *The poetics of imperialism. Translation and colonization from The Tempest to Tarzan*. Philadelphia: University of Pennsylvania Press 1997.

Clark, Steve: *Travel writing and empire: postcolonial theory in transit*. London: Zed Books 1999.

Clifford, James: *The predicament of culture: twentieth-century ethnography, literature, and art*. Cambridge, Mass.: Harvard University Press 2002.

Clifford, James: *On the edges of anthropology: (interviews)*. Chicago, I.L.: Prickly Paradigm 2003.

Clifford, James: *Routes: travel and translation in the late twentieth century*. Cambridge, M.A.: Harvard University Press 1997.

Clifford, James & George E. Marcus: *Writing culture: the poetics and politics of ethnography*. Berkeley: University of California Press 1986.

Collits, Terry: *Postcolonial Conrad. Paradoxes of empire*. London: Routledge 2005.

Conrad, Joseph: *Lord Jim*. Ware: Wordsworth 1993.

Conrad, Joseph: *Mørkets hjerte*. Copenhagen: Fremad 1986.

Conrad, Joseph: *An outcast of the islands: Cop. ed. 2 vol.* Leipzig: Tauchnitz 1896.

Conrad, Joseph: *A personal record*. London, Toronto, Paris: J. M. Dent 1919.

Conrad, Joseph, Frederick R. Karl & Laurence Davies: *The collected letters of Joseph Conrad*. Cambridge: Cambridge University Press 1983-2008.

Conrad, Joseph & Robert Kimbrough: *Heart of darkness: an authoritative text, backgrounds and sources criticism*. New York: Norton 1971.

Conrad, Joseph & Zdzislaw Najder: *Congo diary and other uncollected pieces*. New York: Doubleday 1978.

Cookey, S. J. S.: *Britain and the Congo question 1885-1913*. London: Longmans 1968.

Coombes, Annie E.: *Reinventing Africa: museums, material culture and popular imagination in Late Victorian and Edwardian England*. New Haven: Yale University Press 1994.

Darnton, Robert: *The forbidden best-sellers of pre-revolutionary France*. New York: W.W. Norton 1996.

Darnton, Robert: *The corpus of clandestine literature in France, 1769-1789*. New York: W.W. Norton & Company 1995.

De Lange, Attie, Gail Fincham & Wiesław Krajka: *Conrad in Africa: new essays on 'Heart of Darkness'*. Boulder, C.O.: East European Monographs 2002.

Diderot, Denis & Herbert Dieckmann: *Supplément au Voyage de Bougainville*. Genève, Lille: Droz 1955

Diedrich, Maria, Henry Louis Gates & Carl Pedersen: *Black imagination and the middle passage*. New York: Oxford University Press 1999.

Driver, Felix: *Geography militant. Cultures of exploration and empire*. Oxford: Blackwell 2001.

Driver, Felix & Luciana Martins: *Tropical visions in an age of empire*. Chicago: University of Chicago Press 2005.

Du Chaillu, Paul: *The country of the dwarfs*. New York and London: Harper & Brothers 1901.

Dudgeon, Jeffrey & Roger Casement: *Roger Casement: the black diaries: with a study of his background, sexuality and Irish political life*. Belfast, Northern Ireland: Belfast Press 2002.

Dugard, Martin: *Into Africa: the dramatic retelling of the Stanley-Livingstone story*. London: Bantam 2003.

Edwards, Elizabeth: *Raw histories: photographs, anthropology and museums*. Oxford: Berg 2001.

Edwards, Elizabeth, Chris Gosden & Ruth B. Phillips: *Sensible objects. Colonialism, museums, and material culture*. Oxford: Berg 2006.

Eliot, Simon & Jonathan Rose: *A companion to the history of the book*. Malden, M.A.: Blackwell Pub. 2007.

Emin-Pascha & Georg Schweinfurth: *Emin-Pascha: Mit… Lebensskizze…* Leipzig: Brockhaus 1888.

Engdahl, Horace: *Witness literature: proceedings of the Nobel Centennial Symposium*. Singapore: World Scientific Publishing Co Pte Ltd 2002.

Ette, Ottmar: *Literature on the Move*. Amsterdam: Rodopi 2003.

Falk-Rønne, Arne: *I Stanleys fodspor gennem Afrika: 100 år efter mødet med Livingstone*. Fredericia: Lohses Forlag 1972.

Farr, Michael: *Tintin: the complete companion*. London: John Murray 2001.

Farwell, Byron: *The man who presumed*. London: Henry Holt & Company 1957.

Ferro, Marc (ed.): *Le livre noir du colonialisme*. Paris: Robert Laffont 2003.

Finkelstein, David: *Print culture and the Blackwood tradition, 1805-1930*. Toronto: University of Toronto Press 2006.

Finkelstein, David & Alistair McCleery: *The book history reader*. London: Routledge 2006.

Firchow, Peter Edgerly: *Envisioning Africa. Racism and imperialism in Conrad's 'Heart of darkness'*. Lexington: University Press of Kentucky 2000.

Flaubert, Gustave & Pierre-Marc de Biasi: *Voyage en Égypte*. Paris: Grasset 1991.

Fletcher, Ian: *Decadence and the 1890's*. London: Edward Arnold 1979.

Forbath, Peter: *The river Congo: the discovery, exploration and exploitation of the world's most dramatic river*. London: Secker & Warburg 1978.

Forsdick, Charles: *Travel in twentieth-century French and Francophone cultures: the persistence of diversity*. Oxford: Oxford University Press 2005.

Forsdick, Charles: *Victor Segalen and the aesthetics of diversity: journeys between cultures*. Oxford: Oxford University Press 2000.

Fossey, Dian: *Gorillas in the mist*. London: Phoenix 1981.

Fowler, Elisabeth & Roland Greene (eds.): *The Project of Prose in Early Modern Europe and the New World*. Cambridge: Cambridge University Press 1997.

Franey, Laura E.: *Victorian travel writing and imperial violence. British writing on Africa, 1855-1902*. Basingstoke: Palgrave Macmillan 2003.

Freiesleben, Victor: *Kongo kalder*. Copenhagen: Carl Allers Bogforlag 1944.

Frost, Simon: *The Business of the Novel – Economics, Aesthetics and the Case of Middlemarch*. London: Pickering & Chatto 2012.

Fuglede, Niels: *Hvide og sorte: Oplevelser i Congo*. Copenhagen, Kristiania: E. Jespersen 1919.

Gallop, Alan: *Mr Stanley, I presume?: the life and explorations of Henri Morton Stanley*. Stroud: Sutton 2004.

Gálvez, William: *Che in Africa: Che Guevara's Congo diary*. Melbourne: Ocean Press 1999.

Gauguin, Paul & Victor Segalen: *Noa-Noa. Séjour à Tahiti*. Paris: Editions Complexe 1989.

Gehrmann, Susanne: *Kongo-Greuel. Zur literarischen Konfiguration eines kolonialkritischen Diskurses (1890-1910)*. Hildesheim: Georg Olms Verlag 2003.

Gehrmann, Susanne & János Riesz: *Le blanc du noir. Représentations de l'Europe et des Européens dans les littératures africaines*. Münster: Lit 2004.

Gide, André: *Voyage au Congo: Carnets de route*. Paris: Gallimard 1927.

Gilbert, Helen & Anna Johnston: *In transit. Travel, text, empire*. New York: Peter Lang 2002.

Godzich, Wlad & Jeffrey Kittay: *The Emergence of Prose*. Minneapolis: University of Minnesota Press 1987.

Godzich, Wlad: *The culture of literacy*. Cambridge, M.A.: Harvard University Press 1994.

GoGwilt, Christopher: *The invention of the West: Joseph Conrad and the double-mapping of Europe and empire*. Stanford, C.A.: Stanford University Press 1995.

Goldbæk, Henning & Steen Klitgård Povlsen (eds.): *Tysk litteratur efter murens fald: ni essays*. Odense: Syddansk Universitetsforlag 2006.

Grant, Kevin: *A Civilised Savagery. Britain and the New Slaveries in Africa, 1884-1926*. New York and London: Routledge 2005.

Greenblatt, Stephen J.: *Marvelous possessions: the wonder of the New World: The Clarendon Lectures and the Carpenter Lectures 1988*. Oxford: Clarendon Press 1992.

Greenblatt, Stephen J.: *Learning to curse: essays in early modern culture*. New York: Routledge 1992.

Greene, Graham: *På jagt efter en hovedperson: to afrikanske dagbøger*. Copenhagen: Hasselbalch 1962.

Greene, Graham: *Rejse uden kort*. Copenhagen: Westermann 1952.

Greene, Graham: *A burnt-out case*. London, Melbourne, Toronto: William Heinemann 1961.

Greene, Graham: *In search of a character: Two African journals*. London: The Bodley Head 1961.

Greene, Graham: *Journey without maps: A travel book*. Melbourne, Toronto: William Heinemann 1950.

Gualtieri, Claudia: *Representations of West Africa as exotic in British colonial travel writing*. Lewiston, N.Y.: Edwin Mellen Press 2002.

Haarberg, Jon, Tone Selboe & Hans Erik Aarset: *Verdenslitteratur: den vestlige tradisjonen*. Oslo: Universitetsforlaget 2007.

Haggard, H. Rider: *King Solomon's mines*. London: Penguin 1994.

Haggard, H. Rider & Stephen Coan: *Diary of an African journey (1914)*. London: Hurst 2001.

Halen, Pierre: *'Le petit Belge avait vu grand'. Une littérature coloniale*. Bruxelles: Éditions Labor 1993.

Halen, Pierre & Riesz: *Littératures du Congo-Zaïre. Actes du colloque*. Amsterdam: Rodopi 1995.

Hall, Richard: *Stanley – an adventurer explored*. London: Collins 1974.

Hamner, Robert D.: *Critical perspectives on V. S. Naipaul*. London: William Heinemann 1979.

Hanbury-Tenison, Robin (ed.): *De store rejser*. Copenhagen: Gyldendal 2006.

Hansson, Karin (ed.): *Conrad and the Age of Travel*. Karlskrona: Karlskrona Universitet 1998.

Harlow, Barbara & Mia Carter: *Archives of Empire*. Durham: Duke University Press 2003.

Harms, Robert W.: *River of wealth, river of sorrow: the central Zaïre basin in the era of the slave and ivory trade, 1500-1891*. New Haven: Yale 1981.

Hartog, François: *Évidence de l'histoire: Ce que voient les historiens*. Paris: Éditions de l'École des hautes études en sciences sociales 2005.

Hartog, François: *Mémoire d'Ulysse. Récits sur la frontière en Grèce ancienne*. Paris: Gallimard 1996.

Hartog, François: *Le miroir d'Hérodote. Essai sur la représentation de l'autre*. Paris: Gallimard 1991.

Hawkesworth, John: *An account of the voyages undertaken by the order of His Present Majesty for making discoveries in the southern hemisphere and successively performed by Commodore Byron, Captain Wallis, Captain Carteret and Captain Cook*. London: W. Strahan and T. Cadell 1773.

Hawkins, Hunt & Brian W. Shaffer (eds.): *Approaches to teaching Conrad's 'Heart of Darkness' and 'The Secret Sharer'*. New York: MLA 2002.

Hayes, Harold: *The dark romance of Dian Fossey*. New York: Simon and Schuster 1990.

Hemmungs Wirtén, Eva: *No trespassing: authorship, intellectual property rights, and the boundaries of globalization*. Toronto: University of Toronto Press 2004.

Henson, Louise: *Culture and science in the nineteenth-century media*. Aldershot: Ashgate 2004.

Hergé: *Archives Hergé. Totor, C.P. des Hannetons et les versions originales des albums Tintin au pays des Soviets (1929) au Congo (1930) en Amérique (1931)*. Paris: Casterman 1973.

Hibbert, Christopher: *Africa explored: Europeans in the dark continent, 1769-1889*. London: Allen Lane 1982.

Hilton-Simpson, Melville William: *Land and peoples of the Kasai. Being a narrative of a two years' journey among the cannibals of the equatorial forest and other savage tribes of the southwestern Congo*. London: Constable 1911.

Hinton, Alexander Laban (ed.): *Genocide: an anthropological reader*. Malden, M.: Blackwell 2002.

Hochschild, Adam: *Kong Leopolds arv: en fortælling om grådighed, terror og heroisme i kolonitidens Afrika*. Copenhagen: Lindhardt og Ringhof 2001.

Hochschild, Adam: *King Leopold's ghost: a story of greed, terror, and heroism in colonial Africa*. Boston: Mariner Books 1999.

Hoecke, Sony Van & Jean-Pierre Jacquemin: *Africa Museum Tervuren 1898-1998*. Tervuren: Musée royal de l'Afrique centrale 1998.

Holland, Patrick & Graham Huggan: *Tourists with typewriters. Critical reflections on contemporary travel writing*. Ann Arbor, M.I.: University of Michigan Press 1998.

Holm, Erik: *Dansk kriger i Congo: en dokumentarisk fortælling*. Egå: Illerup 1987.

Holtsmark, Erling B.: *Tarzan and tradition: classical myth in popular literature*. Westport, C.T.: Greenwood Press 1981.

Hooper, Edward: *The river. A journey back to the source of HIV and AIDS*. London: Allen Lane 1999.

Hooper, Glenn: *Landscape and empire, 1720-2000*. Aldershot: Ashgate 2005.

Hooper, Glenn & Tim Youngs: *Perspectives on travel writing*. Aldershot: Ashgate 2004.

Horn, Alfred Aloysius & Ethelreda Lewis: *Trader Horn. The Ivory Coast in the earlies*. London: Cape 1931.

Hughes, W.: *Dark Africa and the way out or a scheme for civilizing and evangelizing the dark continent*. London: Sampson Low, Marston & Co. 1892.

Hulme, Peter & Russell McDougall: *Writing, travel and empire: in the margins of anthropology*. London: I. B. Tauris 2007.

Hulme, Peter & Tim Youngs: *The Cambridge companion to travel writing*. Cambridge: Cambridge University Press 2002.

Hunter, J. Paul: *Before novels: the cultural contexts of eighteenth-century English fiction*. New York: Norton 1990.

Lindqvist, Sven: *Utrota varenda jävel*. Stockholm: Albert Bonniers 1992.

Livingstone, David: *Missionary travels and researches in South Africa: including a sketch of sixteen years' residence in the interior of Africa, and a journey from the Cape of Good Hope to Loanda on the west coast; thence across the continent, down the river Zambesi, to the Eastern Ocean*. London: John Murray 1857.

Livingstone, David & Charles Livingstone: *Narrative of an expedition to the Zambesi and its tributaries: and of the discovery of the lakes Shirwa and Nyassa: 1858-1864*. London: John Murray 1865.

Lloyd, Christopher: *Mirbeau's fictions*. Durham: University of Durhaam 1996.

Lomas, Robert: *The invisible college. The Royal Society, freemasonry and the birth of modern science*. London: Headline 2002.

Lothe, Jakob: *Joseph Conrad*. Oslo: Gyldendal 2002.

Lothe, Jakob, Anne Holden Rønning & Peter Young: *Identities and masks: colonial and postcolonial studies*. Kristiansand: Høyskoleforlaget 2001.

MacGaffey, Wyatt: *Kongo political culture: the conceptual challenge of the particular*. Bloomington: Indiana University Press 2000.

Marshall, P. David: *The celebrity culture reader*. London: Routledge 2006.

Marston, E.: *How Stanley wrote 'In darkest Africa'. A trip to Cairo and back*. London: Sampson, Low, Marston, Searle & Rivington 1890.

Martels, Zweder R. W. M. von: *Travel fact and travel fiction: studies on fiction, literary tradition, scholarly discovery and observation in travel writing*. Leiden: Brill 1994.

Martini, Christian & Christian Schønberg: *To danske Kongofarere: Erindringer fra vort første Ophold i Kongostaten*. Copenhagen: V. Pontoppidans Forlag 1890.

McCullum, Hugh: *Africa's broken heart: Congo, the land the world forgot*. Geneva: WCC Publications 2006.

McLynn, Frank: *Stanley: the making of an African explorer*. London: Scarborough House 1990.

Melberg, Arne: *Aesthetics of prose*. Oslo: UniPub 2008.

Melberg, Arne: *Å reise og skrive: et essay om moderne reiselitteratur*. Oslo: Spartacus 2005.

Melberg, Arne: *Mitt i litteraturen: självkritiska minnen från Akademia med sex återbesök samt ett försök att tänka nytt*. Eslöv: B. Östlings bokförlag Symposion 2002.

Miller, Andrew H.: *Novels behind glass. Commodity culture and Victorian narrative*. Cambridge: Cambridge University Press 2008.

Mirbeau, Octave: *Le Jardin des supplices*. Paris: Librairie théâtrale 1929.

Mirbeau, Octave: *La 628-E8*. Paris: Bibliothèque-Charpentier 1910.

Mirbeau, Octave, Jean-François Nivet & Pierre Michel: *La Mort de Balzac*. Tusson: Lérot 1989.

Møller, Peter, Georg Pagels & Edde Gleerup: *Tre år i Kongo. Skildringar*. Stockholm: P. A. Norstedt & Söner 1887.

Montefiore, Arthur & Birger Hall: *Stanleys Liv og Virksomhed*. Kristiania: Malling 1890.

Morel, E. D.: *Red rubber: The story of the rubber slave trade flourishing on the Congo in the year of grace 1906*. London: T. Fisher Unwin 1906.

Morel, E. D.: *King Leopold's rule in Africa*. London: William Heinemann 1904.

Morel, E. D.: *Affairs of West Africa: With illustrations and maps*. London: William Heinemann 1902.

Moretti, Franco: *Atlas of the European novel, 1800-1900*. London: Verso 1999.

Morson, Gary Saul & Caryl Emerson: *Mikhail Bakhtin: creation of a prosaics*. Stanford, C.A.: Stanford University Press 1990.

Mounteney-Jephson, A. J.: *Emin Pascha and the rebellion at the Equator. A story of nine month's experiences in the last of the Soudan provinces*. London: Sampson Low, Marston, Searle & Rivington 1890.

Moura, Jean-Marc: *Littératures francophones et théorie postcoloniale*. Paris: Presses universitaires de France 2007.

Moura, Jean-Marc: *Lire l'exotisme*. Paris: Dunod 1992.

Mowat, Farley: *Dian Fossey og bjerggorillaerne i Afrika*. Copenhagen: Samleren 1988.

Mudimbe-Boyi, Elisabeth (ed.): *Beyond Dichotomies: Histories, Identities, Culture and the Challenge of Globalization*. Albany: State University of New York Press 2002.

Mudimbe-Boyi, Elisabeth: *Essais sur les cultures en contact. Afrique, Amériques, Europe*. Paris: Karthala 2006.

Mudimbe-Boyi, Elisabeth: *Remembering Africa*. Portsmouth, N.H.: William Heinemann 2002.

Naipaul, V. S.: *Ved en krumning på floden*. Copenhagen: Gyldendal 1980.

Naipaul, V. S.: *A bend in the river*. London: Deutsch 1979.

Naipaul. V. S.: *A Congo diary*. Los Angeles: Sylvester & Orphanos 1980.

Nelson, Samuel H.: *Colonialism in the Congo Basin, 1880-1940*. Athens: Ohio University Press 1994.

Newman, James L.: *Imperial footprints*. New York: Potomac Books Inc. 2004.

Niebuhr, Carsten: *Carsten Niebuhrs Rejsebeskrivelse fra Arabien og andre omkringliggende lande*. Copenhagen: Vandkunsten 2003-2005.

Nylander, Lars: *Prosadikt och modernitet: prosadikt som gränsföreteelse i europeisk litteratur med särskild inriktning på Skandinavien 1880-1910*. Stockholm: Symposion 1990.

O'Hanlon, Redmond: *Congo journey*. London: Penguin 1997.

Pakenham, Thomas: *The scramble for Africa. 1876-1912*. London: Weidenfeld and Nicolson 1991.

Park, Mungo (ed.): *Rejser i det indre af Afrika udført under direktion og protektion af The African Association i årene 1795, 1796 og 1797 & Dagbog fra en ekspedition til det indre af Afrika i året 1805 tilligemed øvrige dokumenter og breve vedrørende samme ekspedition*. Copenhagen: Vandkunsten 2006.

Parke, Thomas Heazle: *My personal experiences in Equatorial Africa. As medical officer of the Emin Pasha Relief Expedition*. London: Sampson Low, Marston & Company 1891.

Pascha, Emin, Franz Stuhlmann & Hermann Schubotz: *Die Tagebücher*. Hamburg: Westermann 1927.

Peters, Carl & Otto Wilhelm Ålund: *Nytt ljus öfver det mörkaste Afrika: Redogörelse för den tyska Emin-Pascha-expeditionen, dess vandringar och äfventyr bland östra Ekvatorialafrikas vilda folkstammar*. Stockholm: Albert Bonniers Förlag 1891.

Pettitt, Clare: *Patent inventions. Intellectual property and the Victorian novel*. Oxford: Oxford University Press 2004.

Pettitt, Clare: *Dr. Livingstone, I presume?: missionaries, journalists, explorers, and empire*. Cambridge, M.A.: Harvard University Press 2007.

Piniau, Bernard: *Congo-Zaïre 1874-1981. La perception du lointain*. Paris: L'Harmattan 1992.

Porter, Dennis: *Haunted journeys. Desire and transgression in European travel writing*. Princeton, N.J.: Princeton University Press 1991.

Pratt, Mary Louise: *Imperial eyes: travel writing and transculturation*. London: Routledge 1992.

Prendergast, Christopher & Benedict R. Anderson: *Debating world literature*. London: Verso 2004.

Punter, David: *Gothic pathologies. The text, the body, and the law*. Basingstoke: Palgrave 1998.

Punter, David & Glennis Byron: *The Gothic*. Oxford: Blackwell Publishing 2004.

Reinius, Lotten Gustafsson: *Förfärliga och begärliga föremål. Om tingens roller på Stockholmsutställningen 1867 och Etnofrafiska missionsutställningen 1907*. Stockholm: Etnografiska museet 2005.

Reiss, Timothy J.: *The discourse of modernism*. Ithaca: Cornell University Press 1982.

Rennie, Neil: *Far-fetched facts: the literature of travel and the idea of the South Seas*. Oxford: Clarendon Press 1995.

Reybrouck, David: *Congo. Une histoire*. Paris: Actes Sud Editions 2012.

Richards, Thomas: *The imperial archive. Knowledge and the fantasy of empire*. London: Verso 1993.

Richards, Thomas: *The commodity culture of Victorian England. Advertising and spectacle, 1851-1914*. London: Verso 1990.

Ries, Olaf: *Congos erobring: fra Congo til Zaïre*. Copenhagen: Aschehoug 1988.

Roos, Saga: *Bröllopsresa i Belgiska Kongo*. Stockholm: C. E. Fritzes bokförlag 1950.

Rosendahl, Mads (ed.): *Verdenslitterær kritik og teori*. Aarhus: Aarhus University Press 2008.

Roston, Murray: *Graham Greene's narrative strategies: a study of the major novels*. Houndmills, Basingstoke, Hampshire: Palgrave 2006.

Sadoul, Numa: *50 år med Tintin: Hergés oplevelser*. Bagsværd: Runepress 1979.

Said, Edward W.: *Culture and imperialism*. New York: Alfred A. Knopf 1993.

Said, Edward W.: *Orientalism*. New York: Vintage Books 1979.

Saussy, Haun & American Comparative Literature Association: *Comparative literature in an age of globalization*. Baltimore, M.D.: Johns Hopkins University Press 2006.

Schechner, Richard: *Performance studies: an introduction*. London: Routledge 2002.

Schildkrout, Enid & Curtis A. Keim: *The scramble for art in Central Africa*. Cambridge: Cambridge University Press 1998.

Schlögel, Karl: *Im Raume lesen wir die Zeit*. Frankfurt am Main: Fischer-Taschenbuch-Verlag 2006.

Schulz-Forberg, Hagen: *London-Berlin. Authenticity, modernity, and the metropolis in urban travel writing from 1851 to 1939*. Bruxelles: P.I.E.-Peter Lang 2006.

Schulz-Forberg, Hagen: *Unravelling civilisation. European travel and travel writing*. Bruxelles: P.I.E.-Peter Lang 2005.

Schweizer, Bernard: *Radicals on the road. The politics of English travel writing in the 1930s*. Charlottesville: University Press of Virginia 2001.

Sebald, W. G.: *Die Ringe des Saturn: eine englische Wallfahrt*. Frankfurt am Main: Eichborn 1995.

Segalen, Victor: *Gauguin dans son dernier décor et autres textes de Tahiti*. Fontfroide: Bibliothèque artistique et littéraire 1986.

Segalen, Victor: *Les Immémoriaux*. Paris: Plon 1982.

Segalen, Victor: *Gauguin dans son dernier décor et autres textes de Tahiti*. Montpellier: Fata Morgana 1975.

Segalen, Victor: *Les immémoriaux: Avec 25 illustrations hors texte: La plupart tirées de l'oeuvre de Paul Gauguin*. Paris: Plon 1956.

Segalen, Victor & Yaël Rachel Schlick: *Essay on exoticism: an aesthetics of diversity*. Durham: Duke University Press 2002.

Segalen, Victor & Henry Bouillier: *Œuvres complètes*. Paris: Laffont 1995.

Segalen, Victor-Ambroise-Désiré & Annie Joly-Segalen: *Essai sur l'exotisme. Une esthétique du divers (notes)*. Paris: Fata Morgana 1978.

Seierstad, Åsne: *Boghandleren i Kabul: et familiedrama*. Copenhagen: Gyldendal 2003.

Sell, Jonathan P. A.: *Rhetoric and wonder in English travel writing, 1560-1613*. Aldershot: Ashgate 2006.

Sherry, Norman: *The life of Graham Greene*. London: Cape 1989-2004.

Sherry, Norman: *Conrad. The critical heritage*. London: Routledge & Kegan Paul 1973.

Sherry, Norman: *Conrad's Western world*. Cambridge: Cambridge University Press 1971.

Shute, Stephen & Susan Hurley: *On human rights*. New York, N.Y.: BasicBooks 1993.

Siegel, Kristi: *Issues in travel writing. Empire, spectacle, and displacement*. New York: Peter Lang 2002.

Simmons, Allan: *Conrad's Heart of darkness: a reader's guide*. London: Continuum 2007.

Simonsen, Karen-Margrethe & Jakob Stougaard-Nielsen (eds.): *World literature. World culture*. Aarhus: Aarhus University Press 2008.

Síochaín, Séamas Ó & Michael O'Sullivan (eds.): *The Eyes of Another Race*. Dublin: University College Dublin Press 2004.

Slade, Ruth: *King Leopold's Congo: Aspects of the development of race relations in the Congo Independent State*. London, New York, Accra: Oxford University Press 1962.

Smith, Andrew, William Hughes 1964- & Inc ebrary: *Empire and the Gothic: the politics of genre*. Houndmills, Basingstoke, Hampshire: Palgrave Macmillan 2003.

Smith, Iain R.: *The Emin Pasha relief expedition 1886-1890*. Oxford: Clarendon 1972.

Smith, Vanessa: *Literary culture and the Pacific: nineteenth-century textual encounters*. Cambridge: Cambridge University Press 1998.

Soncini Fratta, Anna (ed.): *Tintin. Hergé et la belgité*. Bologna: CLUEB 1994.

Sparring, Åke & Gunnar Nyborg-Jensen: *Med Søren og Anne til Kongo*. Copenhagen: Branner og Korch 1963.

Spurr, David: *The rhetoric of empire: Colonial discourse in journalism, travel writing, and imperial administration*. Durham: Duke University Press 1994.

Stafford, Barbara Maria: *Artful science. Enlightenment entertainment and the eclipse of visual education*. London: MIT Press 1999.

Stafford, Barbara Maria: *Body criticism. Imaging the unseen in Enlightenment art and medicine*. Cambridge, M.A.: MIT Press 1997.

Stafford, Barbara Maria: *Voyage into substance. Art, science, nature and the illustrated travel account, 1760-1840*. Cambridge, M.A.: MIT Press 1984.

Stafford, Barbara Maria & Frances Terpak: *Devices of wonder. from the world in a box to images on a screen*. Los Angeles: Getty Research Institute 2001.

Stanley, Henry M., Denzil M. Stanley & Albert Maurice: *Unpublished letters*. London, Edinburgh: Chambers 1957.

Stanley, Henry M.: *How I found Livingstone: Travels, adventures, and discoveries in Central Africa: including four months residence with Dr. Livingstone*. London: Sampson Low and Marston, Low and Searle 1872.

Stanley, Henry M.: *Stanley's despatches to the New York Herald, 1871-1872, 1874-1877*. Boston: Boston University Press 1970.

Stanley, Henry M.: *Kalulu, Kongesøn og Slave: Fortælling fra Afrika*. Copenhagen: Erichsen 1925.

Stanley, Henry M.: *I det mørkeste Afrika eller Opsøgelsen og befrielsen af samt tilbagetoget med Emin Pascha, guvernør i Ækvatoria*. Christiania: Malling 1890.

Stanley, Henry M.: *In darkest Afrika or The quest, rescue, and retreat of Emin Governor of Equatoria*. New York: Scribner 1890.

Stanley, Henry M.: *My Early Travels and Adventures in America and Asia*. London: Sampson and Low 1895.

Stanley, Henry M.: *Congofloden og Grundlæggelsen af den frie Congostat: en Beretning om Arbeide, Forskning og Opdagelse*. Copenhagen: Forlagsbureauet 1885.

Stanley, Henry M.: *Gjennem det mørke Fastland eller: Nilens Kilder, rundt om Æqvatorial-Afrikas store Indsøer, nedad Livingstone-Floden til Atlanterhavet*. Kristiania: Malling 1882.

Stanley, Henry M.: *Through the Dark Continent or The sources of the Nile, around the great lakes of equatorial Africa, and down the Livingstone River to the Atlantic Ocean*. Hamburg: Grädener 1878.

Stanley, Henry M. & Dorothy Stanley: *The autobiography of Henry Morton Stanley*. London: Sampson, Low, Marston and Co. 1909.

Stengers, Jean: *Congo. Mythes et réalités. 100 ans d'histoire*. Paris: Duculot 1989.

Stewart, James: *Dawn in the dark continent: Or Africa and its missions: The Duff missionary lectures for 1902*. Edinburgh and London: Oliphant, Henderson & Ferrier 1903.

Stjerneklar, Jørn & Peter Tygesen: *Det danske Congo-Æventyr*. Copenhagen: Det Danske Filminstitut 2006.

Stocking, George W.: *Victorian anthropology*. New York: The Free Press 1987.

Strang, Herbert: *Tom i Kongo*. Copenhagen: Jespersen 1920.

Symons, A. J. A.: *H. M. Stanley*. London: Falcon Press 1950.

Sørensen, Hans Meinert: *Tekst, fortolkning og historicitet*. Aarhus: Modtryk 1998.

Tayler, Jeffrey: *Facing the Congo*. St. Paul, M.N.: Ruminator Books 2000.

Teilmann, Katja (ed.): *Genrer på kryds og tværs: antologi*. Odense: Syddansk Universitetsforlag 2004.

Thomas, Nicholas: *Entangled objects: exchange, material culture, and colonialism in the Pacific*. Cambridge: Harvard University Press 1991.

Thomsen, Mads Rosendahl: *Mapping world literature. International canonization and transnational literatures*. London: Continuum 2008.

Todorov, Tzvetan: *La littérature en péril*. Paris: Flammarion 2007.

Todorov, Tzvetan: *Poétique de la prose*. Paris: Editions du Seuil 1971.

Turner, Victor: *The anthropology of performance*. New York: PAJ 1988.

Tuska, Jon: *A variable harvest. Essays and reviews of film and literature*. Jefferson, N.C.: McFarland 1990.

Tygesen, Peter: *Congo – formoder jeg: fortælllinger fra drømmeland*. Copenhagen: Lindhardt og Ringhof 2001.

Tygesen, Peter & Esben Wæhle: *Congospor*. Copenhagen: Nationalmuseet 2006.

Vellut, Jean-Luc (ed.): *La mémoire du Congo. Le temps colonial*. Gent: Snoeck 2005.

Ward, Herbert: *Chez les cannibales de l'Afrique centrale 1884-1889*. Paris: Plon-Nourrit et Cie 1910.

Ward, Herbert: *My Life with Stanley's Rear Guard*. London: Chatto & Windus 1891.

Wassermann, Jakob: *Bula Matari: das Leben Stanleys*. Berlin: Fischer 1932.

Weedon, Alexis: *Victorian publishing. The economics of book production for a mass market, 1836-1916*. Aldershot: Ashgate 2003.

Westphal, Bertrand: *La Géocritique. Réel, fiction, espace*. Paris: Éditions de Minuit 2007.

White, Andrea: *Joseph Conrad and the adventure tradition. Constructing and deconstructing the imperial subject*. Cambridge: Cambridge University Press 1993.

Widmer, Urs: *Im Kongo. Roman*. Zürich: Diogenes 1998.

Widmer, Urs: *Die Forschungsreise: ein Abenteuerroman*. Zürich: Diogenes 1976.

Wilde, Johannes: *Michelangelo: six lectures*. Oxford: Clarendon Press 1978.

Winternitz, Helen: *East along the equator. a Congo journey*. London: Bodley Head 1987.

Wirtén, Eva Hemmungs: *No Trespassing. Authorship, Intellectual Property Rights, and the Boundaries of Globalization*. Toronto: University of Toronto Press Inc 2004.

Wrong, Michela: *In the footsteps of Mr. Kurtz. Living on the brink of disaster in the Congo*. London: Fourth Estate 2001.

Youngs, Tim: *Travellers in Africa. British travelogues, 1850-1900*. Manchester: Manchester University Press 1994.

Index

Rights

p. 2: Photo of African tribal leader. © HP.1956.15.10298, collection RMCA Tervuren; photo C. Lamote (Inforcongo), RMCA Tervuren.

p. 4: Drawing from *Tarzan and the Leopard Men*. © Edgar Rice Burroughs, Inc.

p. 18: Front page of the *National Geographic* 1995. © Michael Nichols/National Geographic Creative.

p. 21: Drawing from *Tarzan and the Leopard Men*. © Edgar Rice Burroughs, Inc.

p. 51: Photo of Stanley dressed as a Bedouin. © SA.5153-7, collection King Baudouin Foundation, on deposit at the RMCA Tervuren.

p. 120: Cover of Jeffrey Tayler: *Facing the Congo*. © Ruminator Books.

p. 159: Excerpts from Stanley's field notebook. © SA.18, collection King Baudouin Foundation, on deposit at the RMCA Tervuren.

p. 140: From Carsten Niebuhr: *Rejsebeskrivelse fra Arabien og andre omkringliggende lande*. © Forlaget Vandkunsten.

p. 217: Letter to Barttelot. © SA.56, collection King Baudouin Foundation, on deposit at the RMCA Tervuren.

p. 256: Sketch of Joseph Bell. © Stanley Archives.

p. 324: Photo of Stanley with gun and servant. © SA.5153-12, collection King Baudouin Foundation, on deposit at the RMCA Tervuren.

p. 326: Photo of Stanley's grandson at a Stanley memorial. © HP.1955.17.288, collection RMCA Tervuren; photo C. Lamote (Inforcongo), 1954, RMCA Tervuren. In: VELLUT, J.-L. (ed.). 2005. *La mémoire du Congo. Le temps colonial*. Tervuren: RMCA, Gent: Snoeck, p. 28.

p. 331: Illustration from Marcus Bleasdale: *100 Years of Darkness*. © MB VII.

p. 373: Photo of chieftan captured by 'La force publique'. © PhotoCollection Knud Jespersen, Bornholm Museum, Denmark. In: VELLUT, J.-L. (ed.). 2005. *La mémoire du Congo. Le temps colonial*. Tervuren: RMCA, Gent: Snoeck, p. 219.

p. 376: Portrait of King Léopold. © HO.1986.63.1, collection RMCA Tervuren. In: WYNANTS, M. 1997. *Des Ducs de Brabant aux villages congolais*. Tervuren: RMCA, p. 93.

p. 460: Exhibition of Congolese village. © Collection FelixArchief Antwerpen; photo Ch. Bernhoeft, 1894. In: WYNANTS, M. 1997. *Des Ducs de Brabant aux villages congolais*. Tervuren: RMCA, p. 55.

p. 482: 1920's advertisement for luxurious trips to the Congo. © HO.1981.1.152, collection RMCA Tervuren. In: VELLUT, J.-L. (ed.). 2005. *La mémoire du Congo. Le temps colonial*. Tervuren: RMCA, Gent: Snoeck, p. 95.

p. 491: Cover of Arne Falk-Rønne: *I Stanleys fodspor*. © Lohses Forlag/Arne Falk-Rønne.

p. 494: Photos from Arne Falk-Rønne: *I Stanleys fodspor*. © Arne Falk-Rønne.

p. 496: Photo from Arne Falk-Rønne: *I Stanleys fodspor*. © Arne Falk-Rønne.

p. 499: Cover of Paul Hyland: *The Black Heart*. © Victor Gollancz

p. 513: Drawing from Åke Sparring: *Med Søren og Anne til Kongo*. © Jørgen Clevin/billedkunst.dk.

p. 516: Poster celebrating the 50th anniversary of the Congo as a Belgium state colony. © HO.2004.2.1, collection RMCA Tervuren. In: VELLUT, J.-L. (ed.). 2005. *La mémoire du Congo. Le temps colonial*. Tervuren: RMCA, Gent: Snoeck, p. 167.

p. 517: Poster for the International Exposition in Brussels 1897. © HO.1965.29.1, collection RMCA Tervuren. In: WYNANTS, M. 1997. *Des Ducs de Brabant aux villages congolais*. Tervuren: RMCA, p. 48.

p. 518: Photo of the view of a Congolese village. © Collection Etienne Libert. In: WYNANTS, M. 1997. *Des Ducs de Brabant aux villages congolais*. Tervuren: RMCA, p. 122.

p. 519: A frieze from the colonial palace and exhibition building of Tervuren. © HO.0.1.3883, collection RMCA Tervuren. In: WYNANTS, M. 1997. *Des Ducs de Brabant aux villages congolais*. Tervuren: RMCA, p. 111.

p. 520: Poster for the International Exposition in Brussels 1910. © HO.1986.2.2, collection RMCA Tervuren. In: WYNANTS, M. 1997. *Des Ducs de Brabant aux villages congolais*. Tervuren: RMCA, p. 163.

p. 521: Photo of diamond workers viewing the sculpture *Les Aniota* by Paul Wissaert. © HP.1970.45.5-91, collection RMCA Tervuren; photo B. Noppe, 1958. In: VELLUT, J.-L. (ed.). 2005. *La mémoire du Congo. Le temps colonial*. Tervuren: RMCA, Gent: Snoeck, p. 169.

p. 526: Cover of Time Magazine, October 29 1951. © Time/Ernest Hamlin Baker.

p. 561: Photo of the sculpture *Les Aniota* by Paul Wissaert. © HO.0.1.371, collection RMCA Tervuren.

p. 565: Cartoons from Hergé: *Tintin au Congo*. © Hergé/Moulinsart 2015.

p. 567: Cartoons from Hergé: *Tintin au Congo*. © Hergé/Moulinsart 2015.

p. 569: Cartoons from Hergé: *Tintin au Congo*. © Hergé/Moulinsart 2015.

p. 571: Cartoons from Hergé: *Tintin au Congo*. © Hergé/Moulinsart 2015.

p. 577: Cover of Edgar Rice Burroughs: *Tarzan and the Leopard Men*. © Edgar Rice Burroughs, Inc.

p. 631: Photos of "Locked-out from the Inside" by Søren Assenholt. © Søren Assenholt.

p. 643: Photos of "Lady Alice" by Søren Assenholt. © Søren Assenholt.

p. 650: Photos from Søren Assenholt's series *Blank Spaces*. © Søren Assenholt.

The Dark Continent?

Translation by William Frost and Martin Skovhus
Original layout and cover design by Jørgen Sparre
Image from H.M. Stanley *Through the Dark Continent* and V. Jungsbøll *Zanga*
Typeset and printed by Narayana Press, Gylling on 130 g Munken Lynx
Denmark, 2016
ISBN 978 87 7124 853 1

Aarhus University Press
Langelandsgade 177
8200 Aarhus N
Denmark
www.unipress.dk

International distributors:

Gazelle Book Services Ltd.
White Cross Mills
Hightown, Lancaster, LA1 4XS
United Kingdom
www.gazellebookservices.co.uk

ISD
70 Enterprise Drive, Suite 2
Bristol, CT 06010
USA
www.isdistribution.com

Published with the financial support of Aarhus University Research Foundation

The book is a revised version of the Danish dissertation *Det mørke kontinent?* which was accepted for defence for the higher doctoral degree in philosophy and subsequently approved by the Faculty of Arts, Aarhus University.